Public Finance
and the
Price System

FOURTH EDITION

FOURTH EDITION

Public Finance
and the
Price System

Edgar K. Browning
Texas A&M University
Jacquelene M. Browning

MACMILLAN PUBLISHING COMPANY
New York

MAXWELL MACMILLAN CANADA
Toronto

MAXWELL MACMILLAN INTERNATIONAL
New York   Oxford   Singapore   Sydney

Editor: Jill Lectka
Production Supervisor: Helen Wallace
Text Designer: Angela Foote
Cover Designer: Cathleen Norz
Cover illustration: Greg Couch

This book was set in ITC Garamond Light by Compset, Inc. and printed and bound by
R.R. Donnelley, Crawfordsville. The cover was printed by LeHigh.

Macmillan Publishing Company
866 Third Avenue, New York, New York 10022

Macmillan Publishing Company is part
of the Maxwell Communication Group of Companies.

Maxwell Macmillan Canada, Inc.
1200 Eglinton Avenue East
Suite 200
Don Mills, Ontario M3C 3N1

Library of Congress Cataloging in Publication Data

Browning, Edgar K.
Public finance and the price system / Edgar K. Browning,
Jacquelene M. Browning.—4th ed.
p.   cm.
Includes bibliographical references and index.
ISBN 0-02-315671-6
1. Expenditures, Public.   2. Public goods.   3. Finance, Public—
United States.   I. Browning, Jacquelene M.   II. Title.
HJ7461.B75   1994
336.73—dc20   93-34339
                                                                    CIP

Printing: 1 2 3 4 5 6 7 8   Year: 4 5 6 7 8 9 0 1 2 3

To Deborah

IN ITS FOURTH EDITION, *Public Finance and the Price System* continues to provide a thorough and up-to-date treatment of major topics relating to government expenditure and tax policies. Its broad purpose is to help students learn how to apply economic principles in an analysis of the effects of government policies, especially tax and expenditure policies. The emphasis is analytical, with factual and institutional material introduced only when it is relevant to an understanding of the important consequences of policies. It is not worthwhile, in my opinion, to burden students with an encyclopedic description of the activities of governments; such material becomes dated quickly and is of little lasting value. Instead, the text reflects my view that it is better to analyze carefully and systematically major topics to illustrate principal concepts and techniques which are of general applicability.

A distinguishing feature of the book continues to be its balanced approach to the treatment of tax and expenditure policies. Most public finance texts describe in great detail the major taxes and analyze their economic effects, but they do not apply the same approach to the expenditure side of public budgets. I devote five chapters each to expenditure analysis (Chapters 4 to 7 and 9) and tax analysis (Chapters 10 to 13 and 15), showing how the same theoretical principles can be used to identify and evaluate the major consequences of both expenditure and tax programs. The enthusiastic response to this approach, by both instructors and students, encouraged me to continue to give equal emphasis to both sides of public budgets.

While the general approach to the subject remains the same as in previous editions, the fourth edition represents the most thorough revision yet. About

40 percent of the material in this edition is either new or totally rewritten. Among the major changes are the following:

- A new chapter devoted entirely to the analysis of budget deficits, with a concluding section emphasizing the hidden debt in social security that is several times larger than the overt national debt. (Chapter 14)
- The chapter on health care totally rewritten to emphasize the causes and consequences of rising costs and growth in the uninsured population, phenomena which have motivated proposals for major reform. (Chapter 6)
- A new section on the application of externality theory to environmental issues and an analysis of environmental policies. (Chapter 2)
- An expanded treatment of the future crisis in social security financing and the role of the surplus accumulating in the trust fund. (Chapter 7)
- A detailed analysis of the earned income tax credit, which has recently become a major player among our welfare programs. (Chapter 9)
- A discussion of lotteries as a source of revenue for state governments. (Chapter 16)
- A new section examining the growth in income inequality and its relevance for the welfare system. (Chapter 8)
- Greater emphasis on the marginal welfare cost of taxation, its determinants, and its relevance for the analysis of expenditure policies. (Chapters 4, 10, and 15)
- A new section examining the political and economic factors responsible for the expansion in the role of government in the U.S. economy (and all other industrial economies) in the twentieth century. (Chapter 3)

These are but a few of the more important changes in this edition. In fact, every chapter contains significant new material. All of the graphs have been redrawn in a new two-color format to make it easier for students to follow the analysis. The number of end-of-chapter questions has been substantially increased. In addition, the Instructor's Manual by Joseph Sulock of the University of North Carolina at Asheville contains additional problems and discussion questions and a test bank of multiple-choice questions.

Although most readers of this text will be economics majors who have completed a course in intermediate microeconomic theory, it has become increasingly common for students with a more limited background in economics to take courses in public finance. To make the text accessible for these students, I have included an appendix at the end of the book that explains the rudiments of consumer choice theory. This is the only analytical technique used in this book that may not be adequately covered in principles of economics courses. For those unfamiliar with consumer choice theory (or needing a quick review), the appendix should be read early in the course. With that preparation, readers with a limited background in economic theory should have no difficulty with the material.

I would like to extend my appreciation to a number of people who have helped in the preparation of the fourth edition. Several economists provided detailed comments and suggestions on the third edition that aided me in revising. They are David M. Betson, University of Notre Dame; Gary M. Galles, Pepperdine University; Donald Haurin, The Ohio State University; William J. Hunter, Marquette University; Charles R. Knoeber, North Carolina State University; Wallace E. Oates, University of Maryland; Steven F. Rushen, Pennsylvania State University; Joseph Sulock, University of North Carolina; and Philip Trostel, North Carolina State University. In addition, I would like to thank my editor at Macmillan, Jill Lectka, for her encouragement and advice, and I am also grateful to Douglas Wills for his research assistance.

Edgar K. Browning

CONTENTS

CHAPTER 1
Introduction   1

CHAPTER 2
Market Failure: Public Goods and Externalities   26

CHAPTER 3
Public Choice   64

CHAPTER 9

Analyzing Income Transfer Programs   272

CHAPTER 12

The Corporation Income Tax   383

CHAPTER 15
The Tax System   456

CHAPTER 16
Federalism   494

Introduction

*P*UBLIC FINANCE IS THE FIELD OF ECONOMICS devoted to the study of how government policy, especially tax and expenditure policy, affects the economy and the welfare of its citizens. Despite its name, public finance does not concentrate on the financial arrangements of government but on the consequences of public policy on resource allocation and income distribution. No one familiar with American society can doubt that these consequences are substantial, but determining their exact nature requires the careful application of economic analysis. This book develops the tools that are most useful for the economic analysis of government policies, and it illustrates their application to a variety of the most important tax and expenditure programs.

In the United States, tax and expenditure policies are carried out by federal, state, and local governments. These policies are designed to deal with some of the most pressing social issues of the day, and public finance provides a useful framework for the examination of how well these policies function. Among the issues and policies that come within the purview of public finance are medical care financing, welfare reform, the federal deficit, social security, income tax reform, and environmental policies. All of these issues, and many others, will be considered in later chapters. In this chapter we will first give a brief overview of the U.S. fiscal structure and then describe some features of economic theory that are relevant to the analysis of tax and expenditure policies.

Overview of Public Sector Fiscal Operations

Government Expenditures and Their Growth

Government expenditures and taxes are today an important part of our everyday lives. The total volume of government spending provides an indication of the involvement of government in national economic affairs. As Table 1–1 shows, the combined expenditures of federal, state, and local governments were $1,836.7 billion ($1.8 trillion) in 1990. This is more than $7000 for every person in the United States! The federal government is responsible for more than two thirds of this total, a reversal from earlier years in this century when state and local governments spent substantially more than the federal government.

In examining Table 1–1, note the immense growth in government spending over the twentieth century. Total expenditures were more than a thousand times larger in 1990 than in 1902. Much of this growth is accounted for by inflation—a dollar is worth a lot less in 1990 than it was in 1902. In addition, the population has more than tripled, and per capita real incomes have risen greatly. For these reasons, we can get a more accurate view of how important government spending is in the economy by comparing that spending to the size of the economy. That is done in the last column of Table 1–1, which gives total government expenditures as a percentage of net national product (NNP).

Government budgets have clearly been growing relative to national income throughout the twentieth century. In 1902, total government expen-

Table 1–1   _Government Expenditures, Selected Years (in $ billions)_

Year	Federal Government Expenditures	State and Local Government Expenditures	Total Government Expenditures	Expenditures as Percent of NNP
1902	$ 0.6	$ 1.1	$ 1.7	8.7%
1929	2.6	7.8	10.3	11.0
1950	40.8	22.5	61.0	23.3
1960	93.1	49.5	136.4	29.8
1970	204.3	133.5	313.4	34.6
1980	613.1	361.4	861.0	35.4
1985	969.9	472.6	1,342.2	37.3
1990	1,270.1	698.8	1,836.7	37.3

Note: Federal grants-in-aid to state and local governments are included in both federal and state and local expenditure figures. Total expenditures are adjusted to avoid this duplication.

Source: _Economic Report of the President,_ 1991, Tables B-77 and B-20.

ditures were only 8.7 percent of NNP, but that figure had reached 37.3 percent by 1990. Government now spends nearly $2 of every $5 generated as income in the American economy. Note, however, that the growth in the relative size of government spending has slowed in recent years. Between 1950 and 1970, the government share of total spending rose by nearly one half (from 23.3 to 34.6 percent), but the years since 1970 have added only 2.7 percentage points to the government share.

The United States is not the only country to see its government spending increase dramatically in the twentieth century. Indeed, this has happened in most industrialized countries, and many have gone further down this road than the United States. (Government spending in Sweden, for example, exceeded 60 percent of its NNP in the 1980s.) The growth in the role of government in economies worldwide highlights the importance of analyzing the consequences of government expenditures.

Composition of Government Expenditures

What do governments spend nearly $2 trillion on? It is impossible to describe succinctly and accurately the variety of policies involved; there are just too many. (A listing and a brief description of federal spending programs required over 800 pages in the federal budget for fiscal year 1992.) Nonetheless, by combining programs that serve the same general function into categories, it is possible to present a rough overview of the major general areas where spending takes place. Following this approach, Table 1–2 provides a breakdown of government expenditures by functional categories for fiscal year 1990.[1]

Considering combined expenditures by all levels of government, Table 1–2 shows that spending exceeded $100 billion in five areas: social security, defense, education, interest on debt, and public welfare. Social security is the largest single category of all, followed closely by national defense. Prior to 1990, defense expenditures always exceeded spending on social security, but with the demise of the Soviet Union, defense spending has declined. Social security (which includes spending on Medicare) has been expanding rapidly over the past 40 years. The third major category is education, which includes spending on primary, secondary, and higher education. Most spending here is carried out by state and local governments, while defense and social security are funded exclusively by the federal government. Interest on the debt—the interest payments required to finance previous deficits—is now a major expenditure category following the federal budget deficits of the 1980s. Public welfare rounds out the top five expenditure categories and consists of a large number of programs designed to assist low-income households.

---

[1]Do not be concerned that the figures in Table 1–2 do not correspond exactly to those in Table 1–1. This is partly because Table 1–1 is on a calendar year basis and Table 1–2 is on a fiscal year basis (October 1 to September 30) and partly because of differences in accounting procedures.

Table 1–2   *Government Expenditures by Function for all Levels of Government 1989–90 (in $ billions)*

Function	Total Spending	Federal Spending	State and Local Spending	Intergovernmental Grants
Defense	$ 344.1	$ 344.1		
Social security	350.4	350.4		
Education	310.0	17.8	$292.2	$ 22.8
Interest on debt	237.7	188.0	49.7	
Public welfare	140.7	33.4	110.5	60.5
Health and hospitals	92.5	17.9	74.6	6.8
Natural resources	80.9	70.3	12.3	2.3
Highways	61.9	0.9	61.1	14.2
Postal services	39.1	39.1		
Police	35.9	5.3	30.6	
Other	525.5	179.0	341.6	40.5
Total	$2,218.8	$1,246.1	$972.7	$147.0

Source: U.S. Department of Commerce, Bureau of the Census, *Government Finances: 1989–90* (December 1991), Tables 1, 2, and 3.

These functional categories give only a rough view of what governments spend on. For example, medical care is more important than indicated by the "health and hospitals" category because that category does not include spending on Medicare and Medicaid. In addition, it should be emphasized that the effect of government need not be proportionate to the size of expenditures. This is true in the case of policies dealing with the environment. Spending by the Environmental Protection Agency is only a small part of the "natural resources" area in Table 1–2, but the impact on the economy is better indicated by the approximately $120 billion annual cost borne by the private sector to comply with environmental regulations.

A more detailed analysis of many individual expenditure programs, and the political decision-making process that produces them, is provided in Chapters 2 through 9. For example, we shall consider how social security affects the incentives to work, retire, and save; how subsidies to higher education influence a student's choice of what university or college to attend; how insurance and government subsidies affect the market for medical care; and how welfare programs affect the work incentives of low-income persons and why poverty has proven so difficult to eliminate.

Sources of Government Revenue

In contrast to the bewildering variety of expenditure policies, there are a relatively small number of tax policies in use. Table 1–3 indicates the major taxes and the revenue they generated in 1990. Individual income and payroll

Table 1–3   *Government Revenue by Source and Level of Government, 1989–1990 (in $ billions)*

Source	Total	Federal Revenues	State and Local Revenues
Individual income	$ 572.5	$ 466.9	$105.6
Payroll*	495.2	371.2	124.0
Corporation income	117.1	93.5	23.6
Property	155.6		155.6
Selective excises	93.8	37.2	56.6
General sales	121.3		121.3
Death and gift	15.4	11.5	3.9
Customs duties	16.8	16.8	
Motor vehicles	19.6		19.6
Other	80.5	6.4	74.1
Charges and miscellaneous general revenues†	359.3	148.2	211.1
Total	$2,047.0	$1,151.7	$895.3

*Includes all insurance trust revenues (including contributions to social security and unemployment compensation).

†Includes miscellaneous charges, assessments, interest earnings, and revenues or public enterprises (e.g. school lunches, postal fees, fees for parks and recreation, net revenues from utilities, liquor stores).

Source: U.S. Department of Commerce, Bureau of the Census, *Government Finances: 1989–90* (December 1991), Table 4.

taxes top the list, and these two taxes generated almost $1,100 billion in revenue. This is more than half of the total revenue from all sources. These two taxes are used by both the federal and state-local governments but are relatively more important at the federal level, where they provide nearly three fourths of federal tax revenue.

Other important taxes include the corporation income tax, property taxes, selective excise taxes, and general sales taxes. The importance of these taxes also varies from the federal to the state and local levels. The federal corporation income tax is the third largest federal tax, although it is a distant third behind income and payroll taxes. Property taxes (levied mainly by local governments) and general sales taxes (levied mainly by state governments) have historically been the largest sources of revenues at the state-local level, but income and payroll taxes are of comparable importance today.

One important source of revenue that is not included in Table 1–3 is deficit finance. Governments can finance expenditures in excess of the tax revenues they collect by borrowing from the public, that is, by engaging in deficit finance. This is a particularly important financing method for the federal government (many states have constitutions prohibiting or limiting deficit finance), with the federal deficit exceeding $200 billion a year several times in recent years. This makes borrowing the third most important revenue source for the federal government, behind income and payroll taxes.

How these taxes (and the deficit) actually affect the economy is examined in Chapters 10 through 15. For example, we shall try to determine who really bears the burden of each tax—often quite different from who pays the taxes to the government—and how tax burdens are distributed among the population. In addition, we shall see that these taxes frequently have significant impacts beyond providing the funds that finance government expenditures.

The facts in Tables 1–1, 1–2, and 1–3 indicate much about the size, growth, and composition of government budgets, but they do not tell us a great deal about the consequences of these governmental activities. The rest of this chapter is devoted to setting forth the broad framework of analysis that economists use to study tax and expenditure programs, and much of the remainder of the text shows how this framework can be applied to help us understand how these policies actually affect us all.

The Nature of the Economic Effects of Policies

To begin our discussion, it will be helpful to explain three different ways that government tax and expenditure (or other) policies may affect the operation of the economy.[2]

Allocation

Almost all government policies have an effect on the allocation of resources. In other words, the mix of goods and services produced by the economy is altered as a result of government policy. If the government spends money to build missiles, it bids resources—personnel and capital—away from the production of other goods and services. As a result, economic resources are reallocated so that *more* missiles are produced and *fewer* other goods and services are provided. Economic resources are scarce, and using these resources to produce one type of good necessarily implies sacrificed production of other goods.

One of the most important issues in public finance is the determination of exactly how each of the vast array of government tax and expenditure policies affects the allocation of resources. What goods and services do we

---

[2]Richard A. Musgrave developed the following useful classification in his *The Theory of Public Finance* (New York: McGraw-Hill, 1959), Chapter 1.

get more of, and at what cost in terms of smaller quantities of other goods and services? In some cases, the impact on resource allocation is fairly obvious, but in others it is not. As we will see, some government subsidies have little or no effect on resource allocation; for example, if the government provides free food to people, the recipients may simply curtail their private purchases of food, leaving total food consumption unchanged. Other policies have seemingly counterintuitive effects, such as when public housing leads to lower housing consumption for some recipients.

To understand the allocative effects of government policies, we must know how the policy operates and how the economic behavior of people is influenced by the policy. Does a welfare program undermine incentives to work? If so, the earnings of the poor will fall when they are provided assistance. Does the provision of social security pensions lead people to save less privately for retirement? If so, the economy's rate of growth will be affected. Economic analysis does not provide unambiguous answers to all such questions concerning the allocative effects of policies, but it provides some, and it represents a general framework that is helpful in evaluating these effects.

Distribution

Over any period of time, the economic system produces a certain mix of goods and services that is consumed by its citizens. Not only is the total output of goods and services of interest, but also the manner in which it is distributed among the public. Government policies often affect both the mix of goods and services and their distribution, that is, the distribution of real income. Knowing that a particular medical policy increases the total amount of medical care consumed and reduces the total amount of other things consumed does not imply that each person, or income class, ends up with more medical care and less of other goods. Some may have more of both and others less of both than before. If this is so, the policy will also alter the distribution of real income by benefiting one group at the expense of the other.

When trying to determine the distributional impact of any policy, we are attempting to answer this fundamental question: *Who is benefited and who is harmed by the policy?* Popular discussion often obscures this issue. Advocates of any policy generally stress that the "nation" will be benefited, whereas opponents argue that the policy is "not in the public interest." Such language is misleading. As far as we know, there has never been any policy that benefits everyone or one that harms everyone. Most policies benefit certain persons and groups at the expense of others. In some cases, this may be intentional (e.g., redistributional welfare programs), and in other cases it may be unintended (a defense program harming "doves"). In any event, the extent to which income is redistributed, and the direction of that redistribution (whether in favor of the poor, the elderly, homeowners, etc.), are important effects of government policies.

Economic analysis is often essential in determining how government policies affect the distribution of real income. In some cases the effects are more obvious than in others. It is fairly clear, for example, that several of the programs comprising our welfare system redistribute income in favor of certain low-income groups. But who is benefited and who is harmed by social security or unemployment insurance? Who bears the true burden of the corporate income tax? What is the overall effect of all taxes and expenditures on the distribution of income? Questions such as these pertaining to the distributional effects of policies are not easy to answer, but they are clearly important issues and will be considered in later chapters.

Stabilization

The overall level of expenditures and taxes, in conjunction with monetary policy, can have important effects on the aggregate level of employment, output, and prices. Indeed, most people first study taxes and expenditures in terms of their impact on aggregate demand. Stabilizing the economy at high (and perhaps growing) levels of output and employment is today considered a major responsibility of the federal government.

In this textbook, the macroeconomic effects of the fiscal operations of government will be largely ignored. Our neglect of this set of important issues stems from the fact that most students will take a separate course in macroeconomic analysis, and any treatment given in a chapter or two would necessarily be repetitive and probably inferior to the more detailed discussion in other courses. There is, however, a more substantive reason for giving little attention to macroeconomic effects: They are of little importance in the analysis and evaluation of individual tax and expenditure programs. Only when all taxes and expenditures are considered in the aggregate do these effects become significant. This point will be elaborated further when the effects of expenditure policies are studied in more detail in later chapters.

Positive Analysis and Value Judgments

Most people study economics, we suspect, with the intention of learning what types of economic policies are desirable and what types are undesirable. Because most of public finance deals with public policies, it is important to understand what economic analysis can contribute to determining what is a good policy.

Logically, to decide whether a policy is good or bad involves two steps: positive analysis and a value judgment. First, it is necessary to determine what the consequences of the policy will be, that is, its effects on resource allocation and income distribution. This is the realm of *positive economic analysis* dealing with the measurable or observable outcomes of policy. We might consider, for example, how minimum wage law affects unemployment, or whether a particular tax loophole works to the advantage of the wealthy, or how capital taxation affects interest rates. Positive analysis of policies therefore consists of propositions about the effects of policies. The distinguishing feature of positive analysis is that it deals with propositions that can be tested with respect to both their underlying logic and empirical evidence. Positive analysis is scientific, since it draws on accepted standards of logic and evidence that are potentially capable of being used to ascertain the truth or falsity of statements.

Economic analysis therefore can assist in determining what is desirable government policy by providing a framework for positive analysis that generally yields correct propositions about the consequences of policy. Identifying the consequences of a policy, however, is not sufficient to determine that it is desirable. A second step is necessary: We must decide whether the consequences themselves are desirable. To make this evaluation, it is necessary for each person to make a subjective assessment, a *value judgment,* to determine if the consequences of a policy are desirable. By its nature, such a judgment is nonscientific since it cannot be proven right or wrong by facts or evidence. For instance, believing that a more equal distribution of income is desirable is an example of a value judgment. People may agree that a particular government policy produces greater equality, but some may hold that this outcome is desirable and others that it is undesirable. Their value judgments differ.

Although the distinction between positive analysis and value judgments, and the role each plays in the evaluation of policies, may seem abstruse, they are nonetheless essential to clear thinking. *Economic analysis cannot demonstrate that any policy is desirable* (and neither, for that matter, can any other scientific branch of knowledge). Holding that something is desirable requires a nonscientific judgment of what constitutes desirability that cannot be supplied by a technique of analysis; only individuals can make this type of judgment. Nonetheless, economics can assist in making that judgment by helping us determine the likely consequences of policies, which is an important contribution. Many people disagree about the desirability of policies not because of differences in their values but because they have different conceptions about their effects.

Criteria for Policy Evaluation

In a general sense, we have seen that the evaluation of a public policy must be based on a value judgment about its consequences. Some types of value judgments are widely shared and frequently used in evaluations of public policies, and further discussion of these may be helpful. Although the following criteria for the evaluation of policy do embody explicit value judgments and therefore cannot be demonstrated to be desirable, they are widely (and often unthinkingly) used, so it is important to understand the strengths and weaknesses of each.

Equity

Perhaps the most widely used criterion in the discussion of policy is that of equity, or fairness. Generally, it is felt that government policies should be equitable in their effects on people. This criterion has the advantage of being accepted by virtually everyone; no one thinks unfairness in a policy is desirable. Yet the superficial consensus in favor of equitable treatment obscures the real difficulty of defining exactly what equity means. Although everyone approves of equity, few interpret the term in the same way.

A few examples will illustrate the difficulty of making a judgment about equity. Is minimum wage law equitable? The minimum wage results in higher wage rates for some people, unemployment for others, and higher costs for the consuming public. Are its effects on all groups fair? What about public schools? Is it equitable for families without children to pay taxes to finance public schools? Is it equitable to require people to provide for their retirement through social security rather than in other ways they might prefer? If questions like these are considered seriously, as they should be, some of the difficulties in making an equity judgment will become apparent.

Consider the following statement: "The tax-exempt status of the interest income from state and local government bonds enables the wealthy to avoid their fair share of the tax burden by receiving tax-free interest income." Is the tax exemption granted these bonds fair? Judging from the frequency of such statements, this preferential treatment is generally considered unfair. Yet the statement misconstrues the effects of this tax exemption. People who hold tax-free bonds are not the major beneficiaries of this policy. Instead, state and local governments can sell bonds bearing a lower interest rate than other borrowers can and are the major beneficiaries. For example, a tax-free bond might require an interest rate of 6 percent to compete with a 9 percent (taxable) corporate bond. Eliminating this tax exemption would mean that state and local governments would have to pay 9 percent to compete with the other bonds. Wealthy taxpayers would then pay taxes on higher interest income, but it is not clear whether their net after-tax incomes would be any lower.

Tax-exempt state and local bonds are a good example of the importance of positive analysis in making equity judgments. Most people are prone to make judgments without a careful consideration of the actual effects of economic policies. Yet the equity issue is concerned with the actual consequences of policies, and positive analysis is necessary to determine these consequences.

Probably few people have a clearly defined idea of what equity really means, and even if they do, individual interpretations will differ. Consequently, equity is a difficult criterion to use in practice, but this does not imply that it is unimportant. Although the concept of equity may be difficult to pin down precisely, there may still be wide agreement at a fairly general level. For example, few people would argue that a policy that taxes poor people to subsidize the yachting activities of wealthy individuals is equitable. Unfortunately, most real-world issues are not so clear-cut.

Among economists, the question of equity often takes on a very narrow meaning, referring to the distributional effects of a policy. If a policy results in any redistribution, the major emphasis is on whether the people benefited are poorer (or more deserving in some sense) than the people harmed. Economics is well designed to explore how policies affect the distribution of income, but that is probably only one dimension of the equity issue. Although economics can help to identify the consequences of policies—notably the distributional effects—each person must ultimately decide whether these consequences are equitable.

Economic Efficiency

Economic efficiency, or as it is sometimes called, *Pareto optimality,* is a criterion widely used by economists in policy evaluation. Although efficiency is highly regarded by economists, it is not so widely used by noneconomists and is, in fact, often disparaged as dealing with such materialistic issues as cost minimizing, profit maximizing, and so on. In part this rejection of efficiency as a criterion reflects a misunderstanding of its meaning as used by economists. Far from being materialistically oriented, *efficiency is defined in terms of the well-being of people.* Roughly speaking, an efficient economic system is one that makes people as well off as possible, taking into account *all* the ways the economy influences their well-being. Interpreted in this way, economic efficiency is a criterion that would probably command wide acceptance.

A more careful definition of efficiency can be stated: *An efficient allocation of resources is one in which it is impossible, through any change in resource allocation, to make some person or persons better off without making someone else worse off.* In short, when the economy is operating efficiently, there is no scope for further improvements in anyone's well-being unless someone is harmed. A corollary to this definition is that an inefficient allocation of resources is one in which it is possible, through a change in resource allocation, to make some person or persons better off without making anyone else worse off. Inefficiency implies waste in the sense that the economy is not catering to the wants of people as well as it could.

These definitions can be clarified with the aid of a diagram. To make matters simple, assume that society consists of only two people, Samantha and Oscar, although the discussion can be generalized for any number of people. In Figure 1–1, the level of Samantha's well-being, or welfare, is measured horizontally and Oscar's welfare is measured vertically. The farther to the right we go in the diagram, the better off Samantha is (the higher indifference curve attained), whereas the farther up in the diagram we go, the better off Oscar is.[3] Any allocation of resources corresponds to a certain level of welfare for each person and can thus be plotted in the diagram.

---

[3]In effect, the diagram tells us only how each person ranks alternative resource allocations. It does not tell us by how much better or worse Samantha or Oscar believes one allocation to be in comparison to another.

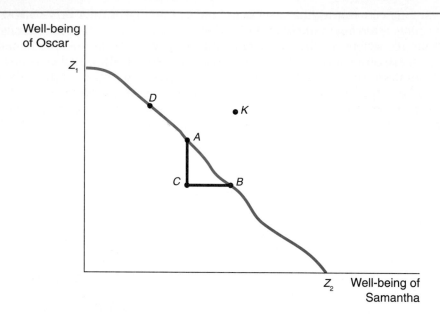

Figure 1–1   *Welfare frontier*

Because of limitations in the amount of resources available to produce goods and services, there are limits to how well off Samantha and Oscar can be. These limits are shown by the *welfare frontier* (or *utility frontier*) $Z_1 Z_2$. Any point that lies outside this frontier is unattainable. The society, for example, cannot produce a mix of goods and services that would make Samantha and Oscar as well off as indicated by point K. By contrast, any point lying on or inside the frontier is attainable. That is, it is physically possible to allocate existing resources in a way to achieve any combination of welfare for Samantha and Oscar that lies inside or on the $Z_1 Z_2$ frontier.[4]

Using this construction, we can see that *any allocation of resources that implies a point lying on the $Z_1 Z_2$ frontier is efficient.* For example, point A represents an efficient allocation of resources because it is not possible to make Samantha better off without making Oscar worse off—because it is impossible to move outside the frontier. Note, however, that this is also true of point B; any possible move from point B makes at least one of the two worse off. Indeed, *every* point *on* the frontier satisfies the definition of efficiency, so there are really innumerable efficient allocations. The efficiency criterion does not allow us to claim that there is only one best state of affairs.

The different efficient points on the welfare frontier represent different distributions of welfare, or real income, between Samantha and Oscar. Thus,

[4]For a discussion that demonstrates how this utility frontier can be derived, see Edgar K. Browning and Jacquelene M. Browning, *Microeconomic Theory and Applications,* 4th ed. (New York: HarperCollins, 1992), Chapter 19.

efficiency does not resolve the question of how real income should be distributed among people. Suppose that there is only one good produced, food, and an efficient use of resources yields 100 units of food. Point A could represent the situation when Oscar has 60 units and Samantha 40 units, whereas at point B, Oscar has 40 units and Samantha 60 units. Both ways of dividing the food are efficient because there is no way to make one person better off except by giving him or her more food, and that requires taking food from the other person. The efficiency criterion provides no way of comparing points like A and B because both are efficient. Instead, an explicit value judgment is required to compare different distributions of real income.

Now consider point C. This is an inefficient point, perhaps where the economy is producing only 80 units of food. (Even in our simple one-good world, this need not imply unemployment of resources; instead, resources may be used unwisely and produce less output than is possible.) Point C is inefficient because it is possible to change things and benefit one person without harming the other. By moving from C to A, Oscar is made better off without harming Samantha; alternatively, moving from C to B would benefit Samantha without harming Oscar. Indeed, moves within the CAB area benefit both Samantha and Oscar. Thus, inefficiency implies that there are changes in resource allocation possible that will mutually benefit all people. Since most people would make the value judgment that changes making everyone better off are desirable, economists tend to think that efficiency is a good thing.

It should not be inferred, however, that *all* efficient points are better than *all* inefficient points. Consider a move from point D, an efficient point, to point C, an inefficient point. (For example, Samantha may get 20 more units of food, but Oscar loses 40 units of food.) Admittedly, this is a change from an efficient to an inefficient allocation of resources, but the change benefits Samantha at Oscar's expense. Only if we are unconcerned about the distribution of real income, however, would we unequivocally say that point D is better than point C. Perhaps Samantha is poor and Oscar wealthy, so the move from point D to point C is a redistribution in favor of the poor person. A person who makes the value judgment that greater equality is highly desirable might prefer point C to point D despite the fact that it is inefficient. Economists, however, would generally argue that if we intend to redistribute from Oscar to Samantha (starting at point D), it would be better to do so in a way that ended up on Z_1Z_2 in the AB range rather than at point C. A redistribution from point D to point A, for example, would benefit Samantha as much as a move from D to C would, and it would leave Oscar better off. In this way, efficiency considerations are relevant in situations involving redistribution. There are efficient and inefficient ways to redistribute income.

Clearly the efficiency criterion does not resolve all questions of economic policy. In particular, it is neutral with respect to distributional questions, which still require nonobjective value judgments. Furthermore, there are some practical questions about applying the criterion. For example, in the complex real world, determining exactly what policies will be most efficient is difficult because a great deal of information (that we often do not have) is required to make that judgment. In addition, we may sometimes object to a criterion based on the assumption that the welfare of all individuals *as they themselves evaluate their well-being* is what counts. Do we want to cater to the wants of children or criminals?

Despite these obvious drawbacks, the efficiency criterion is widely used. If, in your view, a good policy is one that promotes the welfare of people as they themselves judge their welfare, then you will be led to give some weight to efficiency in evaluating policies.

Paternalism

Government policy may, in some cases, be intentionally designed to provide services that would not be selected by people if they had a choice. Instead of catering to the wants of people, the government overrides, or disregards, their wants. A policy of this type could be described as paternalistic and is ultimately based on the premise that some individuals in certain situations may not be able to make wise choices.

A few examples illustrate this criterion. A justification sometimes given for social security is that people would not independently save enough for their old age. If we assert, however, that the level of savings that some people would choose to make is too small, then we are ignoring their expressed wants and substituting someone else's conception of the proper level of saving. Similarly, many welfare programs do not permit the poor to spend the government assistance as they wish but require that it be spent on food, housing, medical care, and so on. Children are required to attend schools until a specified age, regardless of their (or their parents') desires. And the fact that 13 percent of the public has no form of health insurance is sometimes cited as an argument for mandatory health insurance (national health insurance) for everyone. (We don't mean to imply that these policies can be supported only by paternalistic arguments, but merely to suggest how paternalistic considerations can play a role in the evaluation of policies.)

Many people support some government policies not because they think these policies give the public what it wants but because they think the government knows better what is good for the public than the public itself does. This does not imply that paternalism is in any sense bad (a value judgment)—we all approve of paternalistic policies in some cases. For example, most people agree that small children should not be permitted to purchase liquor or drugs or guns even if (and perhaps especially if) they want to. The government may be in a better position to evaluate highly specialized knowledge, such as in the area of consumer safety, and in some cases make "better" (in some sense) choices than people could on their own.

Paternalism does not, however, supply any clear basis for the evaluation of policies. Because there is no absolute standard by which people's choices can be judged, there is no limit to what could be justified on this basis. Moreover, paternalism as a criterion contains a definite antidemocratic element. If individuals are not thought competent to make decisions that mainly affect themselves (like saving for retirement), then, taking this a step further, they must be even less competent to make decisions that affect everyone in society through the voting process.

Individual Freedom

Many people place a high value on individual freedom and wish to see government restrict that freedom as little as possible. Actually, the concept of freedom is difficult to pin down precisely. Individual freedom is generally taken to mean, at least in the economic sphere, that economic arrangements are voluntary. The multitude of exchanges that characterize economic organization take place through a series of mutual agreements between buyers and sellers, with the terms of trade (prices) agreed to by both parties.

Although a case can clearly be made for individual freedom, it is not clear that this criterion provides much guidance for policy issues that are dealt with in the field of public finance.[5] Whenever the government taxes people to finance public expenditures, it deprives them of the freedom to spend part of their incomes as they would have individually chosen. With subtle interpretation, however, it may be possible to argue that in certain cases some taxes or expenditures are more consistent with freedom than others are. On the expenditure side, for example, it might be argued that a welfare program of cash transfers that permits recipients to spend cash assistance as they wish is more consistent with the notion of individual freedom than is a program in which the assistance is restricted to food or housing. Even so, in the bulk of cases, it is difficult to hold that one tax is a greater infringement on freedom than another. This is not to say that individual freedom is unimportant, but only that it may not offer much specific guidance for choices among alternative tax and expenditure policies.

Trade-offs Among the Criteria

The four criteria discussed so far do not exhaust all the ways in which economic policies may be evaluated, but they do provide some idea of the range of effects that may be considered. Forming an overall evaluation of a policy is clearly a difficult task. Not only is it necessary to determine how well the policy satisfies each of the criteria deemed relevant, but a decision of how much weight to give each separate criterion is also necessary. Generally it will be impossible to satisfy all criteria simultaneously. For example, a policy that is considered equitable may be quite inefficient, or a policy to achieve greater efficiency may necessitate a loss of equity. Some of the criteria, in fact, are inherently contradictory. This is true of paternalism and efficiency

---

[5]For contemporary arguments emphasizing the importance of individual freedom, see Friedrich Hayek, *The Constitution of Liberty* (Chicago: University of Chicago Press, 1960), and Milton Friedman and Rose Friedman, *Free to Choose* (New York: Harcourt Brace Jovanovich, 1980).

because efficiency involves catering to the wants of people as they themselves define those wants, whereas paternalism substitutes another judgment of what people should have. In short, a policy evaluation must reflect not only how it performs according to the separate criteria but also how the relative importance of each criterion is judged.

Economists typically emphasize two of these criteria, efficiency and equity, more than any others. In part, this simply reflects the fact that economic analysis is better suited to identifying how efficient policies are likely to be and how they affect the distribution of real income (generally felt to be relevant to making equity judgments). This emphasis also reflects the value judgment that these two broad criteria emphasize worthwhile goals. In the final analysis, however, each person must decide what criteria are important. As pointed out previously, economic analysis cannot demonstrate that policies are good or bad, but as we show in the remainder of this book, it can help in making that judgment by clarifying many of the consequences of tax and expenditure policies.

The Price System

Much economic activity is organized through private markets in which competitive forces determine prices. These market-determined prices are signals that guide resource allocation, and a system that relies on prices determined in open markets to coordinate economic activities is often referred to as a *price system,* or *market system.* In studying public finance, an understanding of how the price system functions is important for two somewhat different reasons. First, relying on the price system is the major alternative to the use of government tax or expenditure policies as a means of resolving economic problems. For example, the price system offers ways for individuals to insure against medical risks and to provide for their retirement; these methods are alternatives to using government policies such as national health insurance and social security to perform these functions. Thus, in evaluating how well social security operates, it should be compared with the way the price system would perform the same function.

Second, the way in which tax and expenditure policies interact with and influence the price system has important implications for the effects of these policies. Often government policies create incentives that change the functioning of private markets. When state and local government bonds are made tax exempt, for example, the price system responds by generating a lower interest rate on these securities, which will induce heavier borrowing by state and local governments. Similarly, the provision of social security benefits may lead to less private saving for retirement, and national health insurance may result in higher prices for medical care. Therefore, to understand the full effects of tax or expenditure policies, it is important to analyze how the price system will respond to them.

This is not the place to explain in detail how a price system functions since it is assumed that the reader already has a basic understanding of microeconomic, or price, theory. It may be helpful, however, to consider briefly how a price system performs in terms of the criteria just discussed.

Economic Efficiency in a Price System

One of the major conclusions of modern economics is that a competitive price system tends, under certain conditions, to produce an efficient allocation of resources. Business firms in competition with one another for the patronage of consumers have incentives to provide goods in the quantities and qualities that are most preferred by consumers. The incentives provided by prices encourage resource owners to employ their resources in ways that are valued most highly by consumers. If the output of one good, beer, for example, is too high, and the output of clothing is too low, the price of beer will be too low to cover costs, and beer producers will suffer losses. Clothing producers will be making profits, and the lure of higher profits in clothing production will encourage resources to move from the beer industry to the clothing industry. In the end, the mix of clothing and beer output will reflect consumer preferences as indicated by market demands for the goods.

The way that efficient levels of output are determined in competitive markets can be explained in greater detail by examining a specific market. In Figure 1–2, the competitive demand and supply curves for beer are shown. For

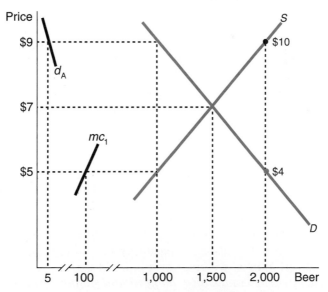

Figure 1–2   *Efficient output in a competitive market*

well-known reasons, the competitive equilibrium rate of output is 1,500 units at a price of $7 per unit where the quantity supplied and the quantity demanded are equal. Our question is whether this equilibrium level of output is also the most efficient level. To explore this question, suppose instead that output is only 1,000 units. Now we wish to know if the additional, or marginal, benefits of a larger output are greater than the marginal costs of producing it. If so, the net benefits—the excess of benefits over costs—received by the public can be increased by producing more beer.

At an output of 1,000 units, the *marginal benefit,* or marginal value, of output is equal to $9 per unit. Nine dollars is a measure of how much consumers are willing to pay to get an additional unit (the 1,001st unit) of beer. This is approximately equal to the price that will prevail if 1,000 units are placed on the market, as given by the height to the market demand curve at 1,000 units of output. Note that each consumer will be willing to pay $9 (more precisely, infinitesimally less than $9) for another unit of beer; that is why we can say that *the* marginal value of beer is $9 because it is the same for all beer consumers. This can be seen by noting that each consumer will consume beer up to the point where the marginal unit is worth $9. (Individual A, for example, with demand curve d_A, will purchase five units, at which point A's marginal valuation of beer is $9.) Equivalently, recall that each consumer is in equilibrium when the marginal rate of substitution between money spent on other goods and beer is $9. The marginal rate of substitution between money and beer is a measure of the marginal benefit of more beer, that is, how much another unit is worth to the consumer.

The height to the market demand curve is thus a measure of the good's marginal importance to consumers. Although this marginal benefit is commonly measured in dollars, this is just a means of registering the importance of beer in comparison with other goods. Saying that the marginal benefit is $9 means that consumers are willing to give up $9 worth of other goods to get another unit of beer.

Now let's consider the cost of producing more beer. The height to the competitive supply curve measures the marginal cost of beer production. At an output level of 1,000 units, the marginal cost is $5. (The marginal cost is also $5 for each firm producing beer, just as firm 1 would be operating on its marginal cost curve, mc_1, at an output rate at which marginal cost is $5.) This $5 measures the cost of the resources needed to produce one more unit of beer. To produce more beer, $5 worth of resources must be withdrawn from the production of other goods. If other markets are competitive, when $5 worth of resources is diverted to beer production, the output of other goods will fall by exactly $5. In other words, when the marginal cost of beer production is $5, this is a measure of the value of other goods that must be sacrificed to produce one more unit of beer.

Recognizing that *the competitive demand and supply curves can be interpreted as measures of marginal benefits and costs* makes it easy to determine the efficient rate of output. At 1,000 units of output, consumers are willing to give up $9 in other goods to get one more unit of beer; but it is only necessary to sacrifice $5 worth to produce one more unit. Additional beer production is worth more than it costs, so 1,000 is an inefficient (too low) rate of output because more beer and less of other things are preferred by consumers.

The efficient rate of output is where marginal benefit and marginal cost are equal. This occurs where output has expanded to 1,500 units, when marginal benefit and cost are equal at $7. By analogous reasoning, we can see that any output in excess of 1,500 units will be too great. At an output of 2,000, for example, the marginal cost of beer production is greater than its marginal benefit, and consumers will be better off with less beer and more of other things. Thus, because 1,500 units is the competitive equilibrium output, the competitive output with its careful balancing of benefits and costs is also the most efficient rate of output. (Note that 1,500 is the efficient output even if the beer market is not competitive; the relevant comparison is between the real schedule of marginal benefits and costs, and these remain unchanged, regardless of the market structure.)

Let's relate this analysis to our earlier discussion of efficiency using a welfare frontier (Figure 1–1). The important point is that a competitive price system yields an efficient resource allocation, and that means the economy is operating at one point on the welfare frontier. Consequently, there is then no way to change a competitively determined resource allocation without harming someone. Although our discussion has emphasized only one aspect of the efficiency issue—the rate of output of a good—the results hold generally when the framework is broadened.

A competitive price system generally gets high marks with respect to the criterion of economic efficiency. Nonetheless, the price system may not always function as smoothly as the preceding analysis suggests. In particular, under certain conditions a private market, even a competitive one, will not function efficiently. These conditions, which involve the presence of public goods and externalities, are considered in Chapter 2.

Equity in a Price System

As previously suggested, the criterion of equity must reflect subjective and individual standards of fairness. As such, it is not possible to prove that the price system is equitable or inequitable in the same way that efficiency can be appraised. Nonetheless, a few observations should be made.

One frequent objection to the contention that a price system is efficient runs like this: How can we say that markets cater effectively to genuine needs when the children of the poor go without toys or milk, and yet the pets of the wealthy wear diamond collars? This raises a valid objection to total reliance on the price system, but it is important to see that the issue is really one of equity, not efficiency. Those with larger incomes influence resource allocation to a greater degree than those with smaller incomes. This outcome is not perverse; the market is merely responding to people's desires and other relevant circumstances, including the distribution of income.

Given the distribution of income, a competitive price system efficiently caters to individual needs as backed up by money. One may object to the fact that some people end up with more goods and services than others do, but this is not inefficient—it simply reflects the fact that some have more income than others do. (Put somewhat differently, expressed in terms of Figure 1–1, the objection is that we are at one efficient point, D, but another one, B, would be better.)

Substantial inequality in the distribution of income can be, and frequently is, objected to on equity grounds. In general, a person's income in a competitive price system depends on how well he or she can meet the demands of consumers by supplying labor and other productive resources. Because incomes typically reflect productivities, those who are, for whatever reason, less productive will have lower incomes, and their needs will be less fully catered to by the market. Our view of what income people ethically deserve may differ from what they receive when paid on the basis of their productivity; the distribution of income generated by the price system may not necessarily conform to one's notion of equity.

Despite the evident importance of income distribution from an equity standpoint, it would probably be a mistake to view equity solely in terms of how the system distributes incomes. The process by which incomes are determined (as distinct from the end result) is also important. Is the price system a "fair game" in which people have reasonably fair opportunities to influence the size of their incomes? It is sometimes pointed out that a person's income is, after all, voluntarily given to the individual by the purchasers of the person's productive services, and everyone is free to compete in trying to offer more valuable services. To a large extent, the price system rewards traits such as ambition, foresight, and hard work, and that seems equitable to many people. Nonetheless, some persons are not fortunate enough to own productive resources that are highly valued by markets and will end up with low incomes in a price system. For them, the fact that the process is believed by many to be fair will be little consolation for their lack of income. Both the nature of the process and the results are relevant in making an equity judgment.

Paternalism and Individual Freedom in a Price System

Paternalism and individual freedom can be dealt with briefly. From a paternalistic perspective, a price system may not function well. It gives people what they want and not what someone else thinks they should want. Some people may deplore the fact that the "system" allocates resources to the production of professional wrestling matches, motorcycles, cigarettes, carnival side shows, fattening foods, and video games, but these goods are produced only because some people are willing to pay for them. A person who dislikes the preferences of other people has only one avenue of influence: to try to persuade others that there are better ways to spend their money. The slow and gradual process of persuasion is a frustrating one for those who think they know (and perhaps some do) what is good for the rest of us. A paternalist will probably not consider a price system to be the best way of allocating resources in all cases.

On the other hand, a price system receives high marks for preserving individual freedom. People can choose what jobs to perform and how to dispose of their incomes, subject only to the constraint that they cannot force other people into involuntary exchanges.

The Welfare Cost of Inefficient Output

One of the most important uses of economic analysis is to help us identify when an allocation of resources is efficient or inefficient. We have seen, for example, that a competitive market tends to organize resources efficiently; by contrast, you probably know that monopoly results in an inefficient output. In this book, we will identify many other instances where markets and policies are inefficient. In addition to being able to determine when resources are inefficiently allocated, it is often important to have some quantitative measure of the magnitude of the inefficiency. An inefficient allocation implies that people are not as well off as they could be, and the *welfare cost* due to the inefficiency is a dollar measure of the loss in well-being compared to an efficient allocation. Let us look at a simple example to see how the welfare cost can be measured.

Consider the market for pizza in a college community. It is assumed that the market is initially competitive, and furthermore, for simplicity, that the supply curve is horizontal. (This case, involving a constant-cost industry, implies that suppliers are not harmed or benefited by variations in output, so we can concentrate on consumers.[6]) The supply and demand curves are shown by S and D in Figure 1–3. At the market equilibrium, 1,200 pizzas per month are purchased at a price of $9 per pizza. (We will also assume that the consumers are 1,000 identical students, each of whom consumes 12 pizzas per month.) As we explained previously, this is an efficient output.

Now suppose that an overzealous college nutritionist somehow succeeds in restricting consumption to 8 pizzas per month for each student, or 800 altogether. (Assume that this policy can be enforced in some way.) Students are now purchasing 800 pizzas, still at a price of $9 per pizza, as indicated at point F in Figure 1–3. This output is, of course, inefficient, because the marginal benefit of another pizza is $12 (the height to the demand curve at

---

[6]A constant-cost industry arises when input prices (e.g., wage rates) are not affected by expansion or contraction of industry output. In other words, if output falls, the workers who lose their jobs can find jobs in other markets at the same wage rates, so their well-being is not (in the long run, at least) affected by the reduction in output.

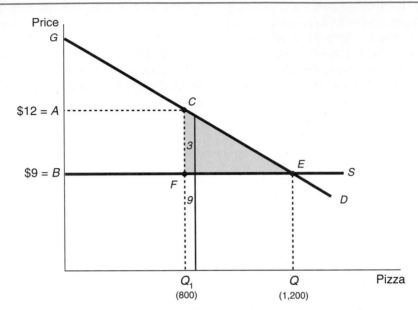

Figure 1–3 *Welfare cost of inefficient output*

consumption of 800), whereas it only costs $9 to produce another pizza. Put differently, students are worse off than they were before. Each student is consuming 8 pizzas, but he or she would be better off consuming 12 pizzas. The question we wish to answer is: How much harm is done to students by this restrictive policy? In other words, how large is the welfare cost due to the inefficient output?

Actually, with the information in the graph, it is possible to place a dollar measure on the harm to students. First, however, note that the harm is not measured by the reduction in spending on pizzas. Students are spending $36 less on pizza than they desire ($3,600 total, or area $FEQQ_1$), but that does not mean they are $36 worse off because they can now spend that amount on something else (say, hamburgers). The harm is due to the fact that they are worse off spending the $36 on hamburgers than they would be if that much extra were spent on pizzas.

The welfare cost, or net loss, of having output reduced from 1,200 to 800 is also the net gain from expanding output from 800 back to 1,200, and it is perhaps easier to explain that way. Starting at an output of 800, therefore, consider what an additional pizza (the 801st) is worth to students. This is shown in the graph by the height to the demand curve, or by the narrow rectangle with a width of one pizza indicated in the graph. (This is a trapezoid as drawn, but the width is greatly exaggerated, and it would approximate a rectangle if drawn to scale.) This shows that the 801st pizza has a marginal benefit of $12 to students. The marginal cost of providing that pizza, however, is only $9—shown by the area of the rectangle below the supply curve. The excess of marginal benefit over marginal cost, or $3, is the net gain possible from increasing output by one unit. This $3 measures the welfare cost of not providing the 801st unit of output.

Now consider the 802nd unit. This will have a marginal benefit of just below $12 (because the demand curve slopes downward), but still a marginal cost of $9, so there is a welfare cost of just under $3 associated with not producing that unit. We can proceed in this way for all the units from 800 to 1,200: Each successive unit is worth more to students than it costs to produce, and the excess of marginal benefit over marginal cost is shown by the difference between the height to the demand curve and the height to the supply curve. Therefore, if we sum up the welfare costs associated with all the units from 800 to 1,200, we would arrive at the shaded triangular area in the graph. *This triangular area, area CEF, is our measure of the total welfare cost of producing 800 units rather than 1,200 units.* Put differently, the area $CEQQ_1$ is the combined value to students from consuming 1,200 rather than 800 pizzas, and the area $FEQQ_1$ is the combined cost of producing the additional units; the difference in these areas (area CEF again) is the net gain from having 1,200 rather than 800, or the net loss (welfare cost) from having 800 rather than 1,200.[7]

So how large is the welfare cost of the inefficient output in this example? It is equal to the area of triangle CEF, and a triangle's area equals one half the base times the height. Thus, the welfare cost here is equal to 1/2 times distance CF (the base of the triangle) times distance FE (the height of the triangle), or 1/2 ($3)(400), or $600 per month. Note that in order to actually calculate the welfare cost, we must know the relevant portions of the demand and supply curves.

In this simple example, the welfare cost is the net loss to students since no one else's well-being is affected (if we ignore the nutritionist's). In many actual applications that we will see later in the book, parties in addition to consumers may be affected, and we will need to incorporate the effects on them in our evaluation of the welfare cost. The concept of welfare cost is intended to represent the combined net loss to everyone who is affected, and that is sometimes more difficult to evaluate than in the case examined here. Nonetheless, the result is often shown as a triangular area between curves representing marginal benefits and marginal costs, just as it is here.

---

[7]For those familiar with the concept of consumer surplus, this welfare cost can be arrived at in a different way. Note that consumer surplus at the competitive equilibrium is shown by area *GEB,* but this is reduced to area *GCFB* by the restrictive policy. The reduction in consumer surplus, area *CEF,* is in this example the welfare cost, or net loss.

Review Questions and Problems

1. Which measure of government expenditures provides the most information about the size of government: nominal dollars, constant dollars, constant dollars per capita, or fraction of GNP?

2. Choose a public policy about which you have particularly strong feelings. Sketch out your argument for or against this policy. Which parts of your argument are positive propositions and which are value judgments? Explain how a person could disagree with your conclusion but accept your value judgments.

3. Define efficiency. Explain how it differs from equity as a criterion for evaluating public policies.

4. Competitive markets are generally efficient. What would be wrong, if anything, with permitting competitive markets to develop with respect to babies (that is, allowing childless couples to purchase unwanted babies rather than going through adoption procedures)?

5. If $5 billion in benefits from a program intended to help the poor goes to middle-class families, is this inefficient (as that term is used by economists)?

6. This chapter discusses four criteria that are commonly used to evaluate public policies. What are they? For each criterion, give examples of public policies that do well and poorly in terms of that criterion.

7. Consider a public program that collects taxes from wealthy persons and gives the funds to destitute persons. Can you give any reasons for favoring this redistribution of income, other than your belief that it is fair? (You may want to review your answer after reading Chapter 8.)

8. Explain why the output of a competitive industry is efficient. Does this mean that no one would benefit if the government subsidized production so that consumers could purchase the good at a lower price? If not, what exactly does it mean?

9. Efficiency and equity are the criteria that economists usually emphasize in their analyses of public policies. Can you think of any policies in which other criteria are more important to consider than these two? Are there other criteria, in addition to the four discussed in this chapter, that you think are important to consider?

10. What is a welfare frontier? With it in mind, what does it mean to say that some policy is in the public interest?

11. Is it possible for a policy to affect the allocation of resources without changing the distribution of income? If so, give an example of such a policy; if not, explain why not.

12. What is a welfare cost, and how does it relate to the concept of inefficiency?

13. Assume that an overzealous college nutritionist believes that eating pizzas was good for students (increased their intelligence) and somehow succeeds in increasing consumption to 14 pizzas per month per student. Would there still be a welfare cost? Explain.

Supplementary Readings

BAUMOL, WILLIAM J. *Welfare Economics and the Theory of the State*. Cambridge, Mass.: Harvard University Press, 1965.

FRIEDMAN, MILTON, and ROSE FRIEDMAN. *Free to Choose*. New York: Harcourt Brace Jovanovich, 1980.

HAYEK, FRIEDRICH A. *The Constitution of Liberty*. Chicago: University of Chicago Press, 1960.

HEAD, JOHN G. *Public Goods and Public Welfare*. Durham, N.C.: Duke University Press, 1974, Chapter 10.

JUST, RICHARD E., DARRELL L. HUETH, and ANDREW SCHMITZ. *Applied Welfare Economics and Public Policy*. Englewood Cliffs, N.J.: Prentice-Hall, 1982.

MURRAY, CHARLES. *In Pursuit of Happiness and Good Government*. New York: Simon and Schuster, 1988.

MUSGRAVE, RICHARD. *The Theory of Public Finance*. New York: McGraw-Hill, 1959, Chapter 1.

Market Failure: Public Goods and Externalities

*I*N CHAPTER 1 WE EXPLAINED HOW A COMPETITIVE price system tends to produce an efficient allocation of resources. The demonstration of efficiency was incomplete, however, because it depended on the implicit assumption that there were no public goods or externalities. Public goods have peculiar characteristics that make it unlikely that private markets will provide the efficient quantity. When this happens, *market failure* is said to occur. The modern economic rationale for many types of government intervention is based on the inability of the price system to function efficiently in such situations. To appreciate how government intervention may improve on the workings of the price system, we must understand what public goods and externalities are and how they affect the allocation of resources.

The Nature of Public Goods

The term *public good* does not necessarily refer to a good that is provided by the government. Instead, it refers to a good (or service) that has two characteristics, regardless of whether or not the government provides it. These two characteristics are *nonrival consumption* and *nonexclusion*.

Nonrival Consumption

A good is nonrival in consumption when, with a given level of production, consumption by one person need not diminish the quantity consumed by anyone else. In other words, a number of people may simultaneously consume the same good.[1] Some examples will clarify this concept. Consider an antimissile system that reduces the likelihood of foreign attack. Note that the protection of your property and person does not reduce the protection received by others; even if you did not exist, the level of protection available to others would be unaffected. Thus an antimissile system simultaneously protects a large number of people.

National defense—of which an antimissile system is a component—is generally considered to be one of the most clear-cut examples of a good that is nonrival in consumption. This characteristic, however, does not mean that people are necessarily benefited to the same degree. A given defense effort could afford greater protection to some geographic areas than others. Possibly, if you live near a missile base, you might actually feel that your life and property are in greater danger because a foreign attack might concentrate on wiping out our missile systems. Similarly, if you are a pacifist, you might secure negative benefits from the defense effort. Nonetheless, an antimissile system is still a good that is nonrival in consumption because it simultaneously affects (to different degrees) a large number of people.

Once the nature of nonrival consumption is understood, it is easy to find more examples. A flood control project, for instance, is nonrival in consumption for people living in the region where the probability of flooding is reduced. The project would not benefit people living in other regions, but it is still nonrival for residents of the protected area. (As we shall see later, the geographic extent of the nonrivalry is important in considering what level of government is best equipped to deal with the good.) Weather forecasting, pollution abatement, and some public health measures that reduce the spread of disease are other examples of goods or services that are nonrival in consumption.

By contrast, most goods and services that we deal with in economics are rival in consumption. For a given level of production of hamburgers (or watches, shoes, houses, or cars), the more you consume, the less will be available for others. In these cases, consumption is rival because there is a problem in deciding how to ration output among the competing (rival) consumers. The price system resolves this problem by allocating a larger quantity to individuals who place a higher value on the good (i.e., people who are willing to pay more for it). With a good that is nonrival in consumption, there is no rationing problem. Once the good is produced, it can be made available to all consumers without reducing any individual's level of consumption.

Nonexclusion

The second characteristic of a public good is nonexclusion. *Nonexclusion means that it is impossible, or prohibitively costly, to confine the benefits of the good (once produced) to selected persons.* A person will benefit from the

---

[1]Nonrival consumption is sometimes referred to as *collective consumption* or *indivisibility of benefits.*

production of the good, regardless of whether or not he or she pays for it. Although nonrivalry and nonexclusion often occur simultaneously, there is a distinction between the two concepts. Our definition of nonrivalry said that consumption by one person *need not* (not *does not*) interfere with consumption by others; this means that although all *could* consume simultaneously, it may still be possible for one person to consume the good and for others not to. There are cases in which we have potential nonrival consumption but in which it is possible to prohibit consumption by some people at a moderate cost. In these cases the goods in question are not public goods.

Television broadcasting can make the distinction between nonrivalry and nonexclusion clear. When a television program is broadcast, any number of people (in the relevant area) can receive the signal and watch it without interfering with the reception of others. Thus, a broadcast has the nonrival characteristic of a public good. It is, however, possible to exclude selected people from viewing the program. People without television sets, for example, will be unable to watch, or programs could be scrambled so that viewers could watch a program only after paying for a decoder. A television broadcast is, therefore, nonrival in consumption, but exclusion is possible at a moderate cost; such a good then does not have both necessary characteristics of a public good.

In many situations, nonrivalry and nonexclusion go together; then we have a public good. National defense is a good example. How could we protect you and not your neighbor? Your neighbor might be deported and thereby excluded from securing any benefits from the defense effort. Similarly, the same means could be used to exclude potential beneficiaries of the flood control project. In both cases exclusion is possible, but it involves high costs. Whether a good is nonexclusive is ultimately a matter of degree because in some cases the cost of exclusion is higher than in others. The relevant question is whether the cost is low enough to make exclusion feasible. In the case of national defense, most people would agree that exclusion is too costly. Thus, national defense fits our definition of a public good. In contrast, most people would probably agree that exclusion is feasible with television broadcasting, so it is not a public good.

The existence of public goods creates problems for a price system. Once a public good is produced, a number of people will automatically benefit, regardless of whether or not they pay for it (because they cannot be excluded), so it is difficult for private producers to provide the good. Unless producers can collect money for supplying the good, they will be unable to cover their costs. On the other hand, with private goods—where consumption is rival and nonpayers can be excluded—private producers have an incentive to provide the goods because they can extract payment from consumers. With private goods the price system can function effectively, but with public goods voluntary cooperation encounters a serious hindrance: the free rider problem.

Public Goods and the Free Rider Problem

A crucial question is whether voluntary cooperation through the price system will provide the appropriate quantity of a public good. To understand why voluntary cooperation often will not work, consider a community of ten people thinking of financing the construction of a dam to lessen the probability of flooding. The dam is a public good for residents of the community. Assume that the dam provides flood protection valued at $1,000 by each person and that the total cost of the dam is $5,000. If the dam is built, the benefit to each of the ten people is $1,000, so the total benefit is $10,000. Because the benefit exceeds the cost, it is in the community's interest to build the dam. Note in particular that the dam could be built if each person contributed $500, and then *everyone* would be better off (i.e., each would receive a benefit of $1,000, at a cost of $500).

Will voluntary agreement among the ten persons lead to the dam's being built? Actually it is not possible to give an unequivocal answer, but we can see the problem that could arise. Suppose one of the ten people believes that the other nine will finance the good whether or not he or she contributes anything toward the dam's construction. Due to the high cost of exclusion, if the dam is built, each resident will receive protection, regardless of whether he or she participates in its funding. But the possibility of being able to benefit from the dam without bearing any of its cost gives each resident an incentive to withhold any voluntary contribution. Each behaves as a *free rider,* attempting to avoid bearing any cost in the financing of a public good.

In this particular example it is possible that the dam would still be financed despite the free rider problem, with the remaining members of the community bearing somewhat higher costs. Whether this occurs depends on how prevalent free rider behavior is within the group. If, however, enough people in the community behaved as free riders, the dam would not be built. Although the outcome of this example is indeterminate, we can explain under what conditions the free rider problem would be most likely to create a serious misallocation of resources. Basically, it is a matter of the size of the group over which benefits are nonrival.

The larger the group, the more severe is the potential free rider problem, and hence the more likely it is that a public good could not be financed by voluntary contributions. Consider a small group of two neighbors for whom the public good is the removal of a dead tree lying precisely on the property line separating their properties. Only two people need agree on financing the tree removal, and each will recognize that without his or her participation the tree may not be removed. It is probable that both will contribute and that the tree will be removed. (There is an element of indeterminacy concerning exactly how the cost will be shared, but as long as the combined benefit of the neighbors exceeds the cost, it is likely that they will bargain until agreement on financing is reached.)

The dam and tree examples differ in a significant way. With the dam, the residents in the flood-controlled area will realize that each contribution will have only a small effect on whether or not the dam is built. Even if one person contributes nothing toward the project, other people may finance the dam, so he or she will receive the benefit at no cost. The problem is that if enough people reasoned this way and withheld their contributions, the project would not be undertaken. On the other hand, in the tree case, each neighbor will realize that each contribution will have a significant impact on the outcome. Unless both contribute, the tree will probably not be removed, so it is more likely that both will contribute.

As the group size increases, it is more likely that everyone will behave as a free rider, and the public good will not be provided. If we change the dam example slightly and assume that the dam benefits 1,000 people, each by $10 (so the total benefit is the same as before), it is less likely that the good will be financed than in the previous examples. In the large-group case, each person's contribution will have virtually no effect on the ultimate result. Put differently, the outcome depends mainly on what the other 999 people do and whether any one person contributes will not affect what the others do. *Choosing not to contribute in this case is the most rational behavior.*[2] Because this is true for every person, few, if any, people will contribute, and the good will not be provided.

Therefore, when the benefits of the public good are nonrival over a large group, it is unlikely that the good will be provided (or, if provided through the contributions of a few individuals, it will not be provided in sufficient quantity). This is true even though it is in the people's interest to have the good provided, that is, even though the benefits exceed the costs. The failure of the price system—based as it is on voluntary cooperation—to function efficiently in providing public goods is a major economic justification for government intervention. In the last example, the government could levy a tax of $5 on each person and use the $5,000 in tax revenue to finance the dam, and each person would be better off. Each resident of the flood-controlled area would receive services from the dam worth $10 at a cost of $5 in taxes. The government expenditure of $5,000 on the dam thus would lead to a more efficient allocation of resources than would the price system.

Exactly how large the group must be before the free rider problem becomes serious is unclear because it depends on the bargaining and negotiating costs, the strategies adopted by people in these negotiations, and so on. There is little doubt that, generally, a group of 1,000 people would encounter great difficulties in reaching voluntary agreement on the financing of a public good. (Consider, however, that many small communities—but

---

[2]A formal analysis of the relationship between group size and the free rider problem can be found in James M. Buchanan, *The Demand and Supply of Public Goods* (Skokie, Ill.: Rand McNally, 1968), Chapter 5.

notably not large ones—manage to provide fire protection through *volunteer* fire companies.) It is in the large-group setting, such as national defense, that the strongest case for government action can be found.

There are many real-world examples that provide empirical support for the importance of free rider behavior. A particularly good example occurred in 1970, when General Motors tried to market pollution control devices for automobiles at $20 (installed) that could reduce the pollution emitted by 30 to 50 percent. Pollution abatement is a public good, at least for certain geographic areas. We may suppose that the benefits of a 30 to 50 percent reduction in pollution far outweighed the cost of $20 per car. (If this assumption is not valid, the government has made a sizable mistake, because it now requires pollution control devices on all new cars that reduce pollution by about 95 percent, at a cost of approximately $1,500 per car.) Yet GM withdrew the device from the market because of low sales. This was simply the large-group free rider problem at work. Everyone might have been better off if all drivers used the device, but it was not in the interest of any single individual to purchase it because the overall level of air quality would not be noticeably improved as a result of that solitary action.

The free rider phenomenon is not necessarily a bad thing, however. In some cases it serves a useful function. For example, the free rider problem may inhibit the formation of collusive agreements among businesses to restrict output and raise prices. The free rider problem also makes it more difficult to finance lobbies that try to persuade Congress to adopt (or reject) certain policies.[3]

Our examples of free rider behavior have dealt primarily with public goods—goods with nonrival consumption and infeasible exclusion. When a good has both characteristics in a large-group setting, the market will fail to provide the good or to provide it in sufficient quantity. If, however, a good is nonrival in consumption but exclusion is feasible, markets can provide the good, and there are many examples of this type of good. Movie theaters, for instance, provide a good with nonrival benefits, at least up to a group size equal to the capacity of the theater. Exclusion, however, is possible because only those who pay the cost of admission are permitted to see the movie. Thus, theaters can collect money from consumers, and this provides an inducement to incur the costs necessary to produce the good. Concerts, circuses, and sporting events, as well as schooling, are quite similar to movies in this regard. Pay television, such as HBO, for which viewers must pay for the programs they view, is also possible because the necessary metering devices are not overly costly.

We have seen that the price system will not provide public goods efficiently in the large-group case. The following section shows how, in

---

[3]A reader who wonders how some groups containing hundreds of thousands of people have been able partially to overcome the free rider problem and finance lobbies (such as union members, doctors, and farmers) should consult Mancur Olson, Jr., *The Logic of Collective Action* (New York: Schocken Books, 1968).

principle, the efficient level of output can be determined, as well as the difficulties encountered in attempting to put this theory into practice.

The Efficient Output of a Public Good

As with most other economic decisions, determination of the efficient output of a public good involves a comparison between the marginal benefits and marginal costs associated with different levels of output. The marginal cost of a public good reflects the cost of resources used to produce the good, just as with a private good. However, the marginal benefit of a public good differs from that of a private good because of the nonrival nature of public goods. With a private good like hamburgers, the marginal benefit of producing an additional unit is simply the value of the hamburger to the single person who consumes it. With a public good like defense, the marginal benefit of producing an additional unit is not the value that any individual alone places on it because a large number of other people also benefit simultaneously from the same unit. Instead, we must add the marginal benefit of every person who values the additional unit of defense, and the resulting sum indicates the combined willingness of the public to pay for more defense, that is, its marginal benefit.

The way in which we derive the social marginal benefit of a public good— in this example, a dam designed to control flooding—is illustrated in Figure 2–1, where units of the public good are measured in terms of the height of the dam. For simplicity, assume that only two people, A and B, benefit from the dam, although the analysis can be generalized for any number of people. The demand curves of the two consumers are shown as D_A and D_B. Recall that the demand price on a consumer's demand curve at any rate of output (i.e., the height to the demand curve) measures the marginal benefit for that consumer. *To determine the marginal benefit to society, we must add the demand prices of all consumers. Geometrically, this involves a vertical summation of the consumers' demand curves.* For example, in Figure 2–1 we add the marginal benefit to A for the first unit ($100) to the marginal benefit of B for the first unit ($180) and arrive at the social marginal benefit of $280 for the first unit. Proceeding in this way, we can derive the social demand or *marginal social benefit* curve, *MSB,* from the sum of D_A and D_B.[4]

At any output where *MSB* lies above the marginal cost curve, *MC*—drawn here as horizontal at $200 for simplicity—people are willing to pay more for additional units of output than their marginal cost; thus efficiency requires an expansion of output. In Figure 2–1, at any level of output below 10, in-

---

[4]Use of terms like *social* benefits and *social* costs should not be interpreted as meaning that the benefits and costs fall on some entity called *society* or that everyone is benefited or harmed. Instead, the terms simply refer to the combined benefits or costs to the individuals affected, however many that may be.

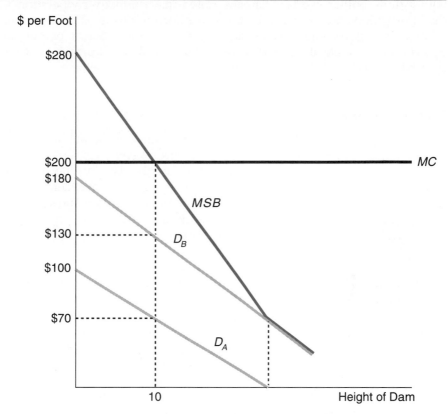

Figure 2–1   *Efficient output of a public good*

dividuals *A* and *B* together are willing to pay more for another unit of output than the marginal cost of $200 (because *MSB* lies above *MC*). Thus, an increase in output can be financed by individuals *A* and *B* in a way that will benefit both (with each paying somewhat less than the maximum amount he or she is willing to pay). At any output greater than 10, on the other hand, too much of the public good is being produced. That is, when the cost of the additional output is greater than the combined benefit to individuals *A* and *B,* a reduction in output can benefit both of them. Therefore, the most efficient rate of output is 10, where *A*'s marginal benefit of $70 plus *B*'s marginal benefit of $130 just equals the marginal cost.

The efficient output of a public good is that level of output at which MSB, obtained by vertically summing the demand curves of all consumers, equals the marginal cost of production. This is the level of output at which the relevant marginal benefit and marginal cost are equal. Our discussion has been in terms of finding the efficient level of output, a 10-foot dam in this example. There is no presumption that this output will be the actual, or equilibrium, output. We have already noted that voluntary cooperation in the large-group case would *not* lead to production of the efficient output. Whether the government would actually finance the efficient output depends on how political forces determine public policies, a matter to be examined in Chapter 3. Here we have simply identified the efficient level of output.

Who Should Pay?

In our example, a 10-foot dam is the efficient output of the public good. If this output is financed by government, however, taxes must be collected from the citizens to provide the funds. Financing the dam by a tax leads us naturally to the question of how to divide the tax burden between individuals A and B to collect the $2,000 necessary to build the dam. The key point here is that efficiency considerations alone do not permit us to say how the $2,000 tax burden should be divided; equity considerations are also involved in this choice.

To illustrate what is involved, let's consider alternative ways of financing the dam. One possibility would be to charge each taxpayer an amount per unit equal to the marginal benefit the taxpayer receives from the provision of the public good. At the efficient output, A's marginal benefit is $70, and so that person's total tax liability would be $700 ($70 per unit times ten units), whereas B, whose marginal benefit is greater, would pay $1,300 in taxes. This division of the cost has the advantage of ensuring that both persons are made better off from the tax and expenditure policy. (Each person pays what the marginal, or tenth, unit is worth, but previous units are worth more than this sum.)

The way in which this specific tax combined with the provision of the dam affects the well-being of both persons is illustrated with the welfare frontier in Figure 2–2. Before the dam is provided, individuals A and B are located at the inefficient point E inside the welfare frontier. After the dam is built *and* the taxes are paid, both persons are at point F, better off than before the project was undertaken. An efficient outcome, one lying on the frontier, has been achieved.

Dividing taxes according to the marginal benefits that taxpayers receive from government services accords with the *benefit theory of taxation*. This is not a theory as much as a proposition that holds that taxes should (a value judgment) be allocated among people in this way.[5] If you believe that the beneficiaries of government expenditures should pay taxes in proportion to the benefits they receive, then this arrangement will represent an appealing solution to the question of who should pay. On the other hand, we must emphasize that economic efficiency does not require taxes to be apportioned in this manner.

---

[5]Chapter 10 contains a further discussion of the benefit theory of taxation.

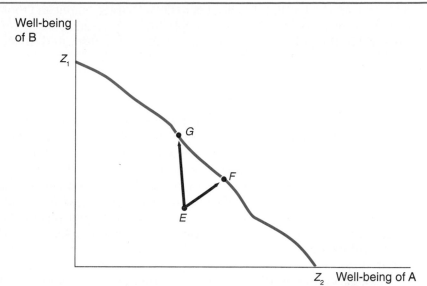

Figure 2–2   *Alternative ways to finance the public good*

Suppose instead that the $2,000 cost of the dam is financed by both individuals paying a tax of $1,000, or $100 per unit (foot) of the public good. Financing the dam in this way will make individual A worse off than if the dam were not provided at all: To individual A, the first unit is worth $100, but each additional unit is worth less. Nonetheless, the final outcome is an efficient one unless distributing the tax burden in this way changes the individuals' demands for the public good.[6] What would happen in this case is illustrated in Figure 2–2 by the move from point E to point G. Individual B is better off and individual A is worse off than under the alternative method of finance (point F), but we still end up on the welfare frontier. Efficiency, that is, getting to the frontier, requires that the 10-foot dam be built, but it does not resolve the question of exactly where on the frontier we should be located.

Thus, our analysis shows how to determine the efficient output for a given pattern of consumer demands; it does not, however, indicate that any particular distribution of the tax burden is preferred. This is not to say that the tax distribution is solely a question of distributional equity; there are relevant efficiency aspects to this question, but they are simply not incorporated in this analysis. For example, if individual A is heavily taxed, A might emigrate from the taxing jurisdiction. Furthermore, taxation unrelated to benefits

---

[6]The efficient output is unchanged if the income effects on A's and B's demand curves are negligible *or* if B's increase in demand (because B has $300 more income) is exactly offset by A's decrease in demand.

would lead those who pay little (or no) tax to favor a larger output and those who pay heavy taxes to favor a smaller output, thereby creating conflicting pressures within the political process. These matters are discussed in later chapters.

Further Considerations Relating to Efficiency

Government financing of a public good with taxes overcomes one aspect of the free rider problem, the tendency of people to withhold payment. It circumvents this problem by forcibly collecting the money. There is, however, another aspect of free rider behavior that government financing does not overcome: People have no incentive to reveal their demands accurately for the public good. To determine the efficient output of a public good, we must know every person's demand curve (so that we can add them vertically to obtain *MSB*). How can we find out how much a public good, like defense, is worth to millions of people? This is probably the most difficult practical problem in implementing the analysis.

The (marginal) value of private goods to consumers is revealed in their purchasing decisions, so market-determined prices reflect the relative values of private goods. If the government finances a public good, however, the political process does not reveal the value of that good to the taxpayer-voter with any degree of accuracy. When a person votes for candidate *A* rather than for candidate *B,* that vote reveals very little about how much incremental amounts of defense, education, or welfare are worth to that person. Nevertheless, it is conceivable that despite this problem, there is an "invisible hand" in the political process that works to promote efficiency. We will examine this question in Chapter 3.

One other matter deserves some attention. The use of vertically added demand curves to determine efficient output is a consequence of the nonrival characteristic of a public good and is not related to whether exclusion is feasible. When exclusion is feasible, private producers face demand curves that reflect some form of vertically added individual demand curves. For example, the marginal cost of showing movies in theaters is covered by the *sum* of the admission prices paid by the viewers. (In contrast, the marginal cost of a Big Mac is covered by the price that the individual consumer pays.) When exclusion is possible, the price system can provide goods with nonrival benefits. However, is the result of private provision of such goods an efficient allocation, that is, should potential customers be excluded when it is possible?

A case can be made that consumers should not be excluded from a good with nonrival benefits even if it is possible. Once a good with nonrival benefits has been produced, an additional person can consume the good and not interfere with the consumption of others. Since excluding a person from consuming the good will harm that person without benefiting anyone else, it is often argued that such exclusion is inefficient. This has led some economists to maintain that the nonrival characteristic of certain goods alone will lead to market failure because the use of prices by private firms will exclude some consumers.

On the other hand, the charging of prices by movie theaters, for example, does not necessarily exclude anyone. People who are willing to pay the price do consume the good. Only those who are unwilling to pay the price of admission will be excluded, and even this problem is often mitigated by using lower prices for some groups, such as children and senior citizens. There may be some inefficiency, but it must be weighed against the advantage of having production linked closely (if not perfectly) to consumer demands and having market-determined prices as a guide (possibly incomplete) to the value of the good. In any event, the degree of inefficiency in market provision will be far less for a nonrival good when exclusion is possible than when it is not. Hence, the more serious problems occur for goods with both characteristics, that is, public goods.

Externalities

Sometimes in the processes of production, distribution, or consumption of certain goods, there are harmful or beneficial side effects called *externalities* that are borne by people who are not directly involved in the market exchanges. These side effects of ordinary economic activities are called *external benefits* when the effects are beneficial and *external costs* when they are harmful. The term *externality* stems from the fact that these effects are outside, or external to, the price system, so their impact is not determined through mutual agreement among all those affected. A few examples will make the nature of these effects clear.

Immunization against a contagious disease is an example of a consumption activity involving external benefits. When a person is inoculated, that individual benefits directly because his or her chance of contracting the disease is reduced (this benefit is *not* the external benefit). The decision to be inoculated also confers benefits indirectly on others because they are less likely to catch the disease from the inoculated person; this is the external benefit. The fact that other people benefit from the individual's actions, however, will not influence that person's decision as to whether being immunized is worth the cost. What the person is concerned with is the effect on his or her own health. Thus, the benefit the inoculation generates for others is external to the person's decision.

Maintenance of a person's lawn or home may also produce external benefits for neighbors. If the neighbors' well-being is improved by living in a more attractive neighborhood, then there is an external benefit associated with home lawn maintenance. On a somewhat grander scale, education is often alleged to involve external benefits such as a reduction in juvenile delinquency, an improvement in the functioning of the political process, or greater social stability.

External costs are also quite common, and the best examples can be found in the area of pollution. Driving an automobile or operating a factory with a smoking chimney pollutes the atmosphere that other people breathe; thus the operation of a car or factory imposes costs on people not directly involved in the activity. Similarly, operating a motorcycle produces a level of noise that is often irritating to those nearby, just as the noise level of a supersonic (or subsonic) airplane may be annoying to people living near airports. Congestion is also an external cost. When a person drives during rush hour, the road becomes more congested not only for the driver, but for other commuters as well.

At a formal level, externalities and public goods are very similar. If a person is inoculated for a contagious disease, there are nonrival benefits; both that person and others benefit from the inoculation. In addition, it would be very difficult to exclude other people from benefiting from this person's inoculation. The same is true of pollution, but in this case there are nonrival costs. A large number of people are simultaneously harmed if the atmosphere is polluted, and it would be difficult to have the atmosphere (in a particular area) polluted for some and not for others.

If there is any difference between externalities and public goods, it may be the fact that external effects are the unintended side effects of activities undertaken for other purposes. For example, people do not pollute because they enjoy breathing a polluted atmosphere; they simply want to transport themselves conveniently in a car from one place to another. In addition, the distribution of the benefit, for example, from consuming a good with external benefits, is usually very skewed. Each of us may receive some benefit from an individual's becoming better educated, but clearly the benefit that individual receives is many times greater. In contrast, public goods tend to benefit people more evenly. These distinctions, however, are matters of degree, so a basic similarity between the concepts remains.[7]

Recognizing the similarity between externalities and public goods greatly facilitates appreciation of the significance of externalities. *Externalities generally lead to an inefficient allocation of resources, or market failure, just as public goods do.* Market demands and supplies will reflect only the benefits and costs of the participants in the market; the benefits and costs that fall on others will not be taken into account in determining production. For example, a person may decide against being immunized because the improvement in his or her health is not worth the cost involved. If, however, the benefits of improved health for others are added to the person's benefit, the combined benefit could exceed the cost. In this case, the person's decision not to be immunized would represent an inefficient use of resources.

---

[7]For attempts at making a rigorous analytical distinction between externalities and public goods, see S. E. Holtermann, "Externalities and Public Goods," *Economica*, 39:78 (Feb. 1972); and Ezra J. Mishan, "The Relationship Between Joint Products, Collective Goods, and External Effects," *Journal of Political Economy*, 72:329 (May 1969).

External Benefits

To examine the implications of externalities more fully, assume that the consumption of some product generates external benefits. The competitive supply and demand curves are shown in Figure 2–3 as S (drawn horizontally, implying a constant-cost industry) and D_P. The demand curve, however, reflects only the private demands of individuals who actually purchase and consume the product. Given these relationships, the market equilibrium occurs with an output of Q_1 and a price of $5. External benefits can be represented by the *marginal external benefit* curve, *MEB,* which reflects the marginal benefit to people other than the direct consumers. At each quantity, the height to the *MEB* curve measures how much an additional unit of consumption is worth to the externally affected parties. For example, at Q_1, the externally affected parties would receive a marginal benefit of FQ_1, or $3, from an additional unit of consumption. Since there may be more than one externally affected party, the *MEB* curve is really the vertically summed demands of all those affected. Vertical summation is used because the external benefits are nonrival for those who are externally affected.

The competitively determined output in this market, Q_1, is inefficient. At Q_1, the benefit to consumers of another unit is $5 (the height to D_P). If another unit is consumed, however, people other than the direct consumer

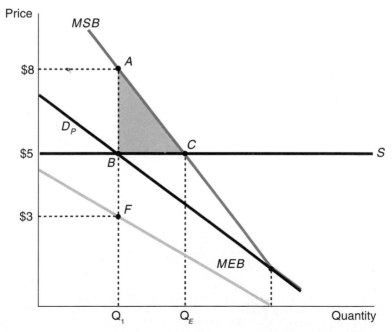

Figure 2–3   *External benefits in a competitive market*

of the product will receive a benefit valued at \$3 (the height to *MEB*). Thus, the combined marginal benefit—the marginal social benefit—of another unit of output is \$8, and this exceeds the \$5 cost of producing the good. The marginal social benefits are shown by the *MSB* curve, which is derived by vertically adding (again, because the benefits are nonrival) *MEB* and D_P. By comparing *MSB* and S at Q_1, we can see that the competitive output is too low because the relevant marginal benefits of the greater output exceed the marginal costs. Yet there is no tendency for competitive pressures to produce a larger output because the additional benefits to the direct consumers are less than the \$5 price per unit they must pay.

Figure 2–3 illustrates the general tendency for an activity to be underproduced when external benefits are involved and when production is determined in competitive markets. The competitive output is Q_1, but the efficient output is Q_E—where *MSB* intersects S.[8] At Q_E, marginal social benefit equals marginal cost. Note that attaining the efficient output does not require expanding output until marginal external benefits are zero. Even though externally affected parties would receive additional benefits from consumption in excess of Q_E, it is inefficient to expand output beyond that point because the marginal costs of doing so would exceed the marginal social benefits.

When external benefits result in the output in a competitive market being at an inefficient level, there is a welfare cost involved. The welfare cost is shown in Figure 2–3 by the triangular area *ABC*. This welfare cost is simply the amount by which the combined benefits to consumers and externally affected parties of expanding output from Q_1 to Q_E (area ACQ_EQ_1) exceeds the cost of expanding output (area BCQ_EQ_1). It also measures the maximum potential net gain possible from using some government policy to expand output, a possibility we will examine later.[9]

External Costs

The analysis of external costs is symmetrical to that of external benefits. Suppose that firms in a constant-cost competitive industry produce wastes as a by-product of their production and dispose of the effluents by dumping

---

[8]This analysis is based on the assumption that external benefits are related to total consumption of the good, irrespective of who consumes the output. In some cases, external benefits will depend on the level of individual consumption, and then efficiency may require only that consumption of some of the consumers be increased. For an analysis of this type of situation as applied to external costs, see T. F. Pogue and L. G. Sgontz, "Taxing to Control Social Costs: The Case of Alcohol," *American Economic Review,* 79:235 (Mar. 1989).

[9]There is an important case in which the existence of external benefits does not mean that the market is inefficient. Suppose that marginal external benefits are smaller, such that the *MEB* curve in Figure 2–3 lies farther to the left and touches the horizontal axis at an output lower than Q_1. Then the marginal external benefit is zero at the competitive output, and the competitive output is the efficient output. There is still an externality, however, but it is an *inframarginal* (inside the margin) *externality.* To imply inefficiency, the marginal external benefit must be positive at the competitive output.

them into a nearby river. For a variety of reasons, these wastes irritate (i.e., harm) people living downstream, so the production of the industry's product involves external costs. In this case, the competitive output will be too large because the external costs are not taken into account in the firms' production decisions.

Consider Figure 2–4. The competitive demand and supply curves are shown as D and S_P, and the equilibrium output is Q_1, with a price of $6 per unit. The marginal damage suffered by people downstream is shown by the *marginal external cost,* or *MEC,* curve. The *MEC* curve is drawn upward sloping to reflect the assumption that additional amounts of pollution inflict increasing costs on people living downstream as the water becomes more polluted. (Nothing important would be changed if the marginal external costs were constant, however.) At Q_1, the marginal external cost is $3 (the height to *MEC* at Q_1, or FQ_1), implying that people downstream would be $3 better off if one unit less of the product (and the waste) were produced. (Since there are many people downstream, the *MEC* curve is obtained by vertically adding the marginal costs borne by each person; the external costs are nonrival.)

With external costs the competitive output is too large. Firms expand output as long as consumers will pay a price that covers *their* (the firms') costs, but the resulting price will not cover *all* costs of production; it ignores the damage done by pollutants to people living downstream. At Q_1, firms incur

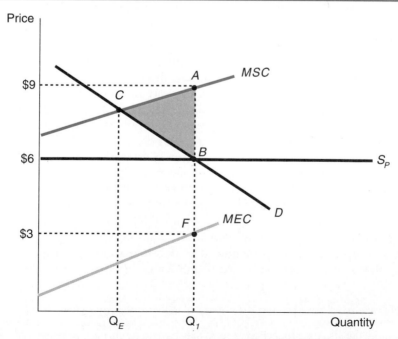

Figure 2–4 *External costs in a competitive market*

a cost of $6 per unit, which is just covered by the price paid by consumers, but there is still a cost of $3 borne by people downstream. At the competitive level of output, the *marginal social cost* of production (the sum of the marginal private cost given by S_P and the marginal external cost) is $9, but the marginal benefit to consumers is only $6. The marginal social costs of production are shown by the curve *MSC,* obtained by vertically adding *MEC* to the private supply curve, S_P.

Because the marginal social cost is larger than the marginal benefit of the product at the competitive output, that output is too large. The efficient level of output occurs where marginal social cost equals the marginal benefit to consumers, and that is shown by the intersection of the *MSC* and *D* curves at an output of Q_E. Output must be reduced from the competitive level until consumers are willing to pay a price that covers *all* of the marginal costs resulting from production of the product. Note that efficiency does not require that output be reduced until there are no external costs. (That would result in output being reduced to zero in this example.)[10]

There is a welfare cost from having too large an output due to external costs, just as there is a welfare cost from having too small an output when there are external benefits. The welfare cost in Figure 2–4 is shown by the triangular area *ABC.* This area measures the excess of the cost saving from reducing output over the benefits given up. Costs go down by the area CAQ_1Q_E when output is reduced to the efficient level, but consumers lose a smaller amount, area CBQ_1Q_E. Note that the area of welfare cost is also the maximum potential net gain from using some government policy to reduce output.

Corrective Policy and Externalities

The central implication of externality theory is that private competitive markets will generally function inefficiently in the presence of externalities. At the same time, the analysis helps us understand the nature of the inefficiency, and that provides insight into how policies might be designed to overcome the problem. Let us consider how government policies could lead to more efficient results in the examples of external benefits and costs that we have just discussed.

Figure 2–5 shows the same market situation as Figure 2–3, where external benefits are associated with consumption of the product. (The marginal external benefit curve is not drawn in explicitly here, but it is implicitly given since marginal external benefits are equal to the vertical distance between the *MSB* and D_P curves.) Recall that the market equilibrium is Q_1 and the efficient output is Q_E. In principle, it is possible to design a government policy that will increase output to the efficient level. For example, in this

---

[10]This analysis is based on the assumptions that the waste bears a fixed relationship to output and that it can be disposed of only in the river. In more realistic situations, not only output but also the production process may have to be changed to achieve efficiency. This point is discussed more fully later.

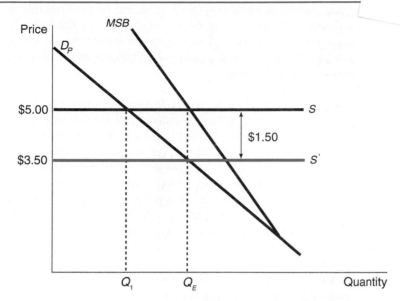

**Figure 2–5   *Efficient output achieved with an
excise subsidy***

case an excise subsidy of $1.50 per unit of output paid to firms will do the job. That subsidy causes the supply curve confronting consumers to shift downward by $1.50 to S'. Although the cost of production for firms is still $5 per unit, the government is in effect bearing $1.50 of this cost, so consumers need pay only the net price of $3.50. At a price of $3.50, consumers would choose to purchase Q_E units, as shown by the intersection of their demand curve D_P and S', and that is the efficient level of consumption.[11]

Note that the subsidy has lowered the price to consumers by $1.50, and that is exactly the amount of the marginal external benefit at the efficient level of output (as shown here by the distance between *MSB* and D_P at Q_E). The subsidy should not be equal to the marginal external benefit at the competitive output, which is $3 per unit. A subsidy of $3 per unit would lead to output that was larger than Q_E, and the result would be inefficiency due to too large an output. This indicates one of the difficulties in designing government policy to achieve efficiency: We need to know the magnitude of marginal external benefits not only at the competitive output but also over

---

[11]This analysis assumes that there are no costs associated with the government's raising tax revenue (like administrative costs), the only costs to taxpayers being the direct costs of providing the funds spent on the subsidy. We will drop this assumption when we consider analysis of expenditure programs in more detail in Chapter 4.

a range of output. Information about the magnitude of externalities is not easy to obtain. Moreover, an error in choosing the size of the subsidy can be costly. Overshooting the mark and subsidizing too heavily, so that output is inefficiently large, can be worse than not subsidizing at all. (You may want to show this situation in the graph.)

Economists frequently advocate the use of subsidies to deal with external benefits. In many cases, a properly designed subsidy of the correct size can achieve an efficient resource allocation. It should not be thought, however, that everyone necessarily benefits when we achieve efficiency in this way. In our example, consumers of the product and those externally benefited would benefit from the subsidy, but the taxpayers who finance the subsidy (unless they belong to the former two groups) would be worse off. What the inefficiency due to the external benefit means is that it would be possible, given enough information and ignoring administrative costs, to divide the costs of the subsidy between the consumers and those externally affected so that all affected parties benefit. That would rarely, if ever, happen in practice.

Finally, it should be emphasized that policies other than a subsidy are capable of achieving efficient output, although often with different distributional effects (different groups benefited and harmed). For example, the government might simply require consumers to purchase Q_E units at their own expense (much as people are required to purchase automobile liability insurance). This would make the consumers worse off since it is in their interest to purchase only Q_1 units. However, this policy would result in an efficient outcome since the benefits to the externally affected parties would be greater than the costs to consumers. Choosing among different potential policies to deal with externalities, as these examples suggest, often involves how much information is needed to design the policies, the administrative costs and difficulties of administering the policies, and so on. We will not go into these issues here, but it is important to understand that externality theory doesn't demonstrate what type of policy is best.

Turning to the external costs case, Figure 2–6 again shows the market with external costs associated with output. (The MEC curve is not shown separately, but it can be derived from the MSC and S_P curves.) With external costs, the corrective policy most often advocated by economists is a tax. For example, an excise tax of $2 per unit of output levied on the firms would shift the supply curve upward by $2 to S_P'. This leads to an increase in the price from $6 to $8, and consumers respond by reducing their purchases from Q_1 to the efficient quantity, Q_E. In effect, this tax changes the market price confronting consumers, so that the new price is equal to the marginal social cost of producing the product at output Q_E. Note that for the tax to result in the efficient output, it must equal the marginal external cost measured at the efficient output, $2 per unit (the vertical distance between MSC and S_P at Q_E). A tax equal to the marginal external cost at the competitive output, $3 per unit, would reduce output too much. Once again, it is clear

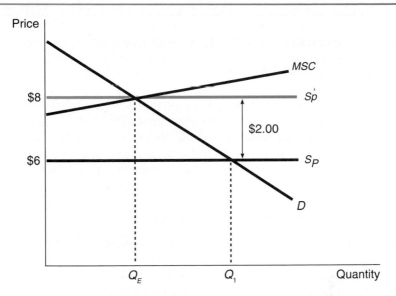

Figure 2–6   *Efficient output achieved with an excise tax*

that the information requirements in designing an efficient policy are substantial.

The purpose of the tax in this case is not to raise revenue for the government but to create incentives to change the allocation of resources. Of course, the fact that tax revenue is raised by the policy that reduces pollution to the efficient level may be an added plus, for it makes it possible to reduce other taxes that have harmful effects. For instance, since this policy clearly harms consumers of the product, it can be argued that the revenue should be used to reduce other taxes these consumers bear. Even so, it is likely that consumers will be harmed by this policy, while the primary beneficiaries are the externally affected parties who get a reduction in pollution at no cost to themselves (unless they are also consumers).

Just as with external benefits, it is possible to conceive of other policies that could promote greater efficiency when there are external costs. In fact, in cases of environmental pollution, taxes are rarely used, even though economists often advocate them. Instead, the government generally relies on regulatory policy. For example, there are strict limits on the amounts of allowable automobile emissions, which requires firms to produce different types of automobiles (often more expensive) than consumers would choose in the absence of the regulations. We will discuss some issues related to environmental economics later in this chapter.

Applying Externality and Public Good Analysis

Understanding how public goods and externalities lead to market failure provides important insight into the possible use of government intervention to promote greater efficiency. In such cases, there are potential mutual benefits from government action, so economists understandably attach much significance to these phenomena in their discussions of public policy. Our brief introduction to public goods and externalities, however, has ignored some relevant issues, so now let's consider some common objections, misunderstandings, and problems in applying the analysis.

Voluntary Bargaining in the Small Group

In an important theoretical paper, Ronald Coase showed that voluntary bargaining can lead to efficient outcomes even when externalities exist.[12] Coase illustrated his analysis by considering a rancher and a farmer with adjoining properties. The rancher's cattle would occasionally stray onto the farmer's property and destroy some of his crops: an external cost associated with cattle raising. Our earlier analysis would suggest that there would be too much crop damage, but Coase argued that this might not be correct. If the rancher were legally liable for damage caused by his cattle, he would bear a cost as a result of straying cattle. In this case, the damage caused by his cattle would not then be an external cost, but a direct cost borne by the rancher (and therefore taken into consideration in his decision making), because the rancher would have to compensate the farmer for crop damage.

Coase went further and argued that even if the rancher were not liable, an efficient solution could emerge without government action. This would happen because the farmer has an incentive to offer to pay the rancher to reduce the number of cattle that stray because a reduction in crop damage will increase the farmer's profits. An agreement could therefore be struck that would reduce cattle straying to the efficient level.

Coase's ingenious analysis not only shows that voluntary bargaining can lead to efficient outcomes but also illustrates the intimate connection between external effects and property rights. As long as property rights are clearly defined and enforced, bargaining between the parties involved resolves the problem. It is irrelevant how property rights are assigned. Whether or not the rancher is liable for damage, cattle straying will be reduced. The *distributional* effects, however, depend on the exact definition of property rights. When the rancher is liable, he will compensate the farmer; alternatively, when the rancher is not liable, the farmer will pay the rancher to reduce cattle straying. In both cases, cattle straying and crop damage are reduced to the efficient level, but different people bear the cost.

---

[12]Ronald H. Coase, "The Problem of Social Cost," *Journal of Law and Economics,* 3:1 (Oct. 1960).

Coase's analysis is applicable in many cases far removed from his agrarian example. Consider the case of legislation to ban smoking in public facilities and private businesses. The proponents of such legislation often argue that it is needed to protect nonsmokers from the health hazards of cigarette smoke. If cigarette smoke does harm nonsmokers, this would appear to be an instance of external costs in which excessive smoking would take place in the absence of remedial action.

This example invites two comments. First, an outright ban on cigarette smoking would probably be inefficient, possibly more inefficient than permitting unrestricted smoking is. Efficiency requires that we take into account the preferences of *both* smokers and nonsmokers, not just the wishes of nonsmokers. An intermediate solution, perhaps one that permits smoking at certain times or in certain places, would probably be more efficient than would an outright ban.

Second, Coase's analysis suggests that we consider a more basic question: Is government legislation required to achieve an efficient solution? The answer, perhaps surprisingly, is no—at least with respect to private businesses. Private businesses already have incentives to take the preferences of their smoking and nonsmoking customers into account. If a business has trouble recruiting workers or loses customers when smoking is permitted, it has an incentive to consider alternatives that restrict smoking. Many businesses already do this. Some restaurants, for example, do not permit smoking or permit it only in certain areas. Thus, no government action is required in the case of private businesses, at least if the goal is to promote efficiency. (It should be noted, however, that some states have passed laws restricting smoking. Nonsmokers are understandably not interested in efficiency; some will support restrictions on smoking since it benefits them, regardless of the harm done to smokers.)

Is there then *ever* a need to rely on government in these situations? We have already provided the answer in our discussion of the free rider problem. Private bargaining can work efficiently when small numbers are involved, as in the Coase example in which only one farmer is harmed by the straying cattle. When a factory pollutes the atmosphere breathed by thousands of people, however, private bargaining cannot be expected to lead to an efficient outcome. *Our earlier conclusion of market failure is still correct, therefore, in the large-group case.* Many issues of great importance, such as defense, pollution, and police protection, are large-group externalities or public goods, and the price system cannot be expected to function effectively in these areas. Coase's analysis should caution us, however, against concluding that every phenomenon that appears to be an externality requires government intervention.

Identifying the Externality or Public Good

A first step in correctly applying externality (or public good) theory is to identify exactly what constitutes the external effect. With air pollutants emitted by automobiles, the production or use of automobiles is not an externality; it is the emission itself. Externality theory predicts that there will be too much pollution, not necessarily that there will be too many cars. An efficient policy must be designed to reduce pollution directly, not indirectly, for example, by reducing the number of automobiles or by making it harder to get a driver's license. A tax on automobiles would be inappropriate because a tax would do nothing to induce auto manufacturers to produce cars that pollute less. An automobile tax would reduce the output of all cars by increasing their cost to drivers—irrespective of whether, or how much, they pollute. If a tax is to be used, it should be levied on pollution itself. (The tax rate should vary with the amount of damage done by pollution; for example, the pollution damage in large metropolitan areas—because there are more people to pollute and to be polluted—would be greater than the damage done in rural areas. As a consequence, the pollution tax should be higher in the larger, more densely populated areas.) Such a tax would give producers and consumers the proper incentive to reduce pollution in any way that costs less than the taxes levied.

The importance of determining exactly what constitutes the externality is frequently overlooked in policy analysis. Consider the frequent assertion that education produces external benefits—possibly in the form of a more stable society. Exactly what type of education produces these effects? Is instruction in dance, music, home economics, and physical education beneficial to anyone other than those who receive it? Yet if only certain types of education generate external benefits, then only these types should be subsidized. A policy that induces students to acquire skills they are unwilling to pay for—if these skills fail to generate external benefits—is inefficient.

Or consider the claim that education generates external benefits because it enables students to earn higher incomes and hence makes it less likely that they will become criminals. Note that it is criminal activity that is the harmful effect. A subsidy to education would be inefficient because it would encourage overconsumption of education by pupils who would never become criminals. An efficient policy would be one that penalized, and thus deterred, criminal activity per se. To see the problem intuitively with this argument, note that it really claims that raising the incomes of potential criminals will reduce crime. This relationship may be correct, but it does not mean that raising the incomes of criminals is the least costly way of reducing crime. Generally, it will not be.

As a final example, consider a proposal to stop economic growth, citing such undesirable consequences as pollution and congestion. But the growth in pollution and congestion, or even their absolute levels, may be reduced without directly reducing the growth in other goods and services. A corrective policy would be more effective if designed to deal with pollution and congestion explicitly and not with economic growth.

In general, it should be emphasized that taxing or subsidizing *output* will often be inappropriate.

Pecuniary Externalities

Suppose that the demand for housing by college students increases and drives up the price of housing for nonstudents in a college community. Although the demand for housing by nonstudents has not increased, they will be paying a higher price and consequently are made worse off. The increase in demand by students harms nonstudents. Is this an external cost we need to worry about? The answer is no. This damage to nonstudents is transmitted through the price system (in the form of higher prices), not outside it. It is not external to the price system. Unfortunately, this type of effect has been given the name *pecuniary externality,* meaning that it is monetary rather than real. All the externalities we have discussed so far are real, or as they are sometimes called, *technological externalities.*

Pecuniary externalities are intrinsic to the workings of a price system. Every time a price, wage rate, or interest rate changes, as thousands do every day, some people are harmed and others are benefited. There is no inefficiency produced by these effects; the markets are simply adjusting efficiently to changes in the underlying demand or supply conditions. The reason there is no inefficiency involved is that the harm done to nonstudents, for example, when housing prices rise is not a *net* cost to society. Instead it is simply a *transfer* of purchasing power from renters to owners of rental housing. A higher price harms the buyer but benefits the seller to the same degree, so there is no net loss. The situation is quite different with pollution, where the harm done to the pollutee is not offset by a gain to the polluter. Technological externalities, or just *externalities,* as we refer to them, reflect net costs or benefits not taken into account by the market system. For this reason, technological externalities are a source of inefficiency, whereas pecuniary externalities are not.

Pecuniary externalities can easily be confused with the real thing. Sometimes it is argued, for example, that the vocational education of welfare recipients is a (technological) external benefit for taxpayers: Vocational education may increase the earning capacity of welfare recipients, resulting in a reduction in welfare payments (and a reduction in tax liabilities for taxpayers). This effect on taxpayers is a pecuniary externality, not a technological one, although in this case it is transmitted through a government policy rather than through the price system. The reduction in welfare payments and tax liabilities is a transfer from welfare recipients to taxpayers, with the loss to transfer recipients equal to the gain to taxpayers. Vocational education for recipients does not, of itself, lower taxes. Instead, it is the decision to reduce welfare payments that lowers taxes, and this has a purely redistributive effect.

From now on when we refer to *externalities,* we will mean the technological variety that can cause resource misallocation, not the pecuniary variety that indicates only transfers of income.

When Is Government Intervention Worthwhile?

Once you become attuned to the concept of externalities, it is easy to spot many of them in the world around you. For example, crying babies in supermarkets, people who don't use deodorants, and barking dogs are sources of external costs. Does this mean that government intervention is justified in these and innumerable similar cases? Or is there a way in which these examples differ from the external costs imposed by the buildup of "greenhouse gases" (possibly leading to global warming)?

There is a *quantitative* difference among externalities that makes corrective policies more important for some than for others. In a sense, this is obvious: Some external effects are big and some are small, and it is more important to deal with the big ones. But the exact way in which the size of the external effect is relevant is far from obvious, yet it has important implications for the way we view the justification for corrective policies.

Let us consider a case where there are external benefits associated with consumption, and we are considering a subsidy to expand output. In Figure 2–7, the competitive supply and demand curves are S and D_P, so the market equilibrium is at an output of Q_1 (1,000) with a price of \$1.00. One assumption we will make here is that the demand and marginal social benefit curves

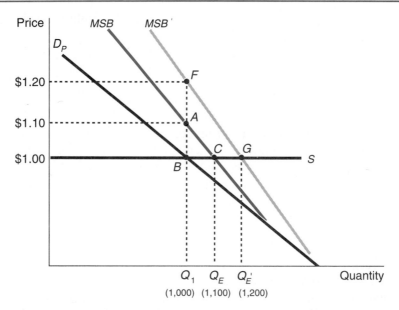

Figure 2–7   ***Welfare cost depends on the size of the marginal externality***

are of unit elasticity over the relevant ranges.[13] (This is a reasonable inter-mediate assumption to make in a hypothetical example since empirically estimated elasticities differ among products, with many exceeding 1 and many others being below 1.) The elasticity of the relationships also affects how important it is to correct for the externality, but we leave that issue for a later chapter and concentrate on the size of the external effect here.

Suppose that the marginal external benefit is 10 percent as large as the market price at the competitive equilibrium. Then the marginal social benefit curve will be *MSB* in the graph. Note that this implies (along with our elasticity assumption) that the efficient output is also 10 percent greater than the competitive output.[14] The welfare cost in this case is shown by area *ABC*. Recall that the welfare cost is also a measure of the maximum potential net gain from corrective policy to deal with the externality: In this sense, it measures how important it is to attempt to improve the situation since the welfare cost is the potential payoff. How large is it here? It is 1/2 ($0.10)(100), or $5. To put this in perspective, note that it is one half of 1 percent (0.5 percent) as large as consumer outlays on the product ($1,000) at the competitive equilibrium.

A potential gain equal to one-half of 1 percent of the size of the market does not sound like much of a reason to have government intervene. That, in fact, is the point: *It may be better to do nothing about small externalities.* But we should consider a little further the reason intervention may be unwise. Suppose that an excise subsidy is used to expand output to 1,100. This requires a subsidy per unit of approximately $0.09 since at a price of $0.91 consumers would purchase about 1,100 units. A subsidy of $0.09 applied to 1,100 units means that total outlays for the subsidy would be approximately $100. Thus, the government would have to spend $100 in order to realize a gain of $5. Why not do this, even though the gain is small? There are several reasons. One is that the gain materializes only if the government designs exactly the right subsidy, and this would be difficult to do even with the best intentions. Another reason is that administrative and compliance costs (and other costs we will discuss in later chapters) of both the tax and the subsidy must be subtracted from this potential gain. For example, if the administrative cost of collecting the required revenue is 5 percent of the revenue, or $5, there would be a zero net gain from the subsidy. It is easy to see that the likelihood of an actual gain in this case is probably slight.

Now consider another case: Suppose that the marginal external benefit is twice as large at the competitive equilibrium. The marginal social benefit

---

[13]We are speaking of *arc elasticity* here since curves with constant point elasticities of unity are shaped like rectangular hyperbolas.

[14]Recall that unit elasticities imply that the product of price (or marginal value) and output along the curve is a constant. For example, the product of marginal social benefit and output at the competitive level is ($1.10)(1,000), or $1,100. Unit elasticity implies that at an output of 1,100, marginal social benefit must be $1.00 to keep the product unchanged.

curve is then *MSB'*, and the marginal external benefit at 1,000 units of output is $0.20. At first, you might think that doubling the externality would double the welfare cost, but it does not. It quadruples the welfare cost! Now the welfare cost is shown by area *FBG,* and both the base and the height of the triangle are doubled. The welfare cost is equal to 1/2 ($0.20)(200), or $20, four times as large as when the marginal external benefit was half as large.

In this case, a subsidy of about $0.17 per unit would be required to expand output to the efficient level of 1,200, and the total government outlay would be about $200. If the administrative cost of raising the revenue is 5 percent of the revenue (and that is the only hidden cost), as we assumed earlier, a net gain would be realized since the potential gain of $20 is only offset by a cost of $10. Clearly, the case for government intervention is stronger the larger the size of the marginal externality.

The general point is that the welfare cost rises more than proportionately to the size of the externality, and this suggests that intervention is more likely to produce net gains when dealing with large externalities rather than with small externalities. Exactly how large is large enough cannot be specified without considering the other factors (like administrative costs) that interact to determine the net impact of policies. Much of the material covered in the remainder of this text is relevant to evaluating this issue.

It is, of course, difficult to determine the magnitude of external effects. One recent study of spending on public education suggests that external effects, at least in that important case, may be relatively small. Wyckoff used survey data and voting choices in an ingenious attempt to estimate private and external benefits in a Michigan community.[15] His estimates implied that marginal external benefits were about 10 percent as large as marginal private benefits. There is bound to be a large margin of error associated with such estimates, but if Wyckoff's estimate is approximately correct, in light of the previous discussion it suggests that the efficiency case for government subsidization of education is not very strong. (There may be reasons other than just external benefits for subsidizing education, however.)

Environmental Policy: An Application

A recent survey of the literature on environmental economics noted: "The source of the basic economic principles of environmental policy is to be found in the theory of externalities."[16] Externality theory can make significant contributions to the design of policies to protect the environment. Let

[15]J. Wyckoff, "The Nonexcludable Publicness of Primary and Secondary Public Education," *Journal of Public Economics,* 24:331 (Mar. 1984).

[16]Maureen L. Cropper and Wallace E. Oates, "Environmental Economics: A Survey," *Journal of Economic Literature,* 30:678 (June 1992).

us consider a simple example and then relate our findings to U.S. environmental policies.

Suppose that there are two firms, A and B, that emit a pollutant into the atmosphere as a by-product of their production. Polluting the atmosphere constitutes an external cost for people in the surrounding area. How can we design an efficient policy to protect the environment? There are, in fact, two components of overall efficiency in this case. Up to now, we have considered efficiency only as it relates to the total output of some good or service. *Output efficiency* is also relevant here since we are concerned with the efficient output of pollution. There is, however, a second type of efficiency: how to allocate the responsibility for reducing pollution between the two firms. If pollution is to be reduced by 200 units, for example, each firm could be required to reduce its pollution by 100 units, or firm A could be required to cut back by 150 and firm B by 50, or any other combination that yields a total of 200 units. The cost of reducing pollution by 200 units can depend greatly on how we divide the cutbacks between the two firms. *Production efficiency* involves achieving whatever level of output (here, reduction in pollution) is produced at the lowest possible (social) cost.

To investigate this issue further, assume that both firms produce 200 units of pollution (400 total) in the absence of any environmental policy. There are costs involved if pollution is to be reduced from the initial level, and these costs can be shown with curves identifying the marginal costs of *pollution abatement*. This is illustrated in Figure 2–8. Note that in the diagram we are measuring the amount of pollution emitted by each firm from *right to left*. Measuring pollution from right to left means that we are measuring pollution abatement—the number of units by which pollution is reduced from its initial level— from left to right. The reason for adopting these units of measurement on the horizontal axis is that each firm incurs costs from reducing (abating) pollution, and this procedure yields marginal cost curves with the familiar (upward-sloping from left to right) shape.

In the absence of any environmental policy, no firm will voluntarily incur costs to avoid polluting (since the firm receives no benefits from cutting pollution), so both firms will be located at point P in the graph. The marginal costs of pollution abatement are shown by MC_A and MC_B. (We have drawn the graph to show different marginal cost curves for the two firms because evidence indicates wide variations in the costs of reducing pollution for different firms.) Now suppose that it is decided that total pollution should be reduced from 400 to 200 units. We would like this to be done in the least costly fashion, but what does it entail? Suppose that we simply require each firm to reduce its pollution by 100 units. Then each firm will be required to produce PX units of pollution abatement; firm A will be at point G on its marginal cost curve and firm B at point F on its marginal cost curve.

That this policy does not achieve the 200-unit reduction in pollution at the lowest possible cost is easily seen. Compare the marginal costs at which the firms are now operating. The marginal cost for firm A is $90 per unit of pollution abatement, while it is $20 for firm B. If firm B were to cut back

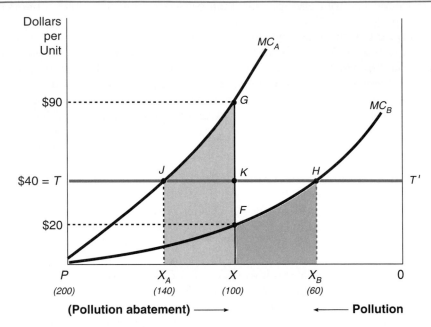

Figure 2–8   *Production efficiency with external costs*

pollution by one more unit, it would add only $20 to its costs. If firm A increased pollution by one unit (produced one unit less of pollution abatement), it would reduce its costs by $90. Having firm A pollute one unit more and firm B one unit less leaves total pollution unchanged, but it reduces the firms' combined costs by $70. As long as the marginal costs of pollution abatement differ, we cannot have achieved production efficiency. A difference in marginal costs makes it possible to reduce the total cost of pollution abatement by increasing pollution abatement where its marginal cost is lower and reducing it where marginal cost is greater.

Achieving production efficiency requires operating at output levels where the firms' marginal costs are equal. In Figure 2–8, shifting the production of pollution abatement from firm A to firm B should continue until B's marginal cost has just risen to equal A's since each unit step of this process reduces their combined costs. In the graph, production efficiency is achieved when firm A is operating at point J on its marginal cost curve (producing PX_A units of pollution abatement) and firm B is operating at point H on its marginal cost curve (producing PX_B units of pollution abatement). Total pollution is unchanged, but it is now achieved at a lower total cost. Compared to the situation where both firms were required to cut back to 100 units of pollution, firm A's total cost has fallen by area $JGXX_A$, while firm B's total cost has risen by area FHX_BX. The cost savings of firm A exceed the cost increase of firm B by the sum of the areas JGK and KHF; this is the net gain from using an efficient method to reduce pollution by 200 units.

This analysis has important implications for the evaluation of U.S. environmental policy. Most U.S. environmental policies are what are called *command-and-control* regulatory programs under which the government uses direct controls to limit pollution. In some instances this involves imposing a maximum upper limit to the pollution allowed from each source (e.g., a factory or an automobile), and in other cases it even prescribes the technology that must be used. The result is invariably that marginal costs of pollution abatement differ widely among sources, just as in our preceding example, where both firms are required to limit their pollution to 100 units. This implies that it would be possible to achieve the same level of pollution reduction at a lower cost to society.

There is an extensive body of empirical studies that find pollution control costs to be substantially higher than necessary under existing programs. The results of 17 of these studies are summarized in a book by Thomas Tietenberg.[17] In 10 of the 11 studies dealing with different air pollution policies, it was found that the costs would be 42 to 93 percent lower if production efficiency were achieved. In the six studies dealing with water pollution, the range of potential cost savings was 11 percent to 68 percent. This means that the American people are bearing much higher costs than are necessary to get the environmental protection achieved by current policies.

The costs involved are not negligible. The Environmental Protection Agency estimated that expenditures to reduce pollution were at least $115 billion in 1990, or about 2 percent of GNP (expected to rise to 2.6 percent by 2000).[18] These costs are borne by the population in the form of reduced wages, reduced profits, or higher prices for products; they are much like a hidden tax we all pay to finance our environmental policies. (As a tax, the magnitude is comparable to the revenues from all sales taxes in the United States; see Table 1–3.) Although it is impossible to ascertain exactly how much of this $115 billion is wasted through unnecessarily high costs, it seems likely that at least half is. In other words, the welfare cost due to production inefficiency in environmental policies may be on the order of $60 billion per year, or about 1 percent of GNP.

Taxation to Control Environmental Externalities

In order to achieve production efficiency in reducing pollution, it is necessary to have all sources of (the same type of) pollution operate where the marginal costs are equal. It might seem that this arrangement places an impossible burden on regulatory authorities: How can they possibly know or find out the marginal cost curves of thousands (sometimes millions) of

[17]See Thomas H. Tietenberg, *Emissions Trading: An Exercise in Reforming Pollution Policy* (Washington, D.C.: Resources for the Future, 1985), Chapter 3.

[18]*Economic Reports of the President* (Washington, D.C.: U.S. Government Printing Office, 1992), p. 183.

polluters? Surprisingly, there is a policy that can achieve production efficiency without requiring the authorities to know individual polluters' marginal costs, and we have already discussed that policy in general terms. It is a tax on pollution.

Let us consider how a tax of $40 per unit of pollution would affect the firms in Figure 2–8. If each firm continued to pollute 200 units, it would have to pay $8,000 in taxes. However, the tax creates an incentive for the firm to curtail its pollution, since for each unit of pollution it abates, it saves $40 in taxes. If, for example, it costs less than $40 for the firm to reduce pollution by one unit, it is in the interest of the firm to incur the cost and save $40 in taxes. *The primary purpose of the pollution tax is to create this strong market incentive for the polluters themselves to reduce pollution.*

The tax is shown in Figure 2–8 by the horizontal line *TT'*. Looked at from left to right, *TT'* is much like a demand curve confronting each firm for its production of pollution abatement: It shows a gain in net revenue (the tax savings) of $40 for each unit of pollution abatement produced. To maximize profits in the presence of the pollution tax, each firm should reduce pollution to the point where the marginal cost of pollution abatement is $40. Thus, firm *A* will reduce pollution to 140 units and pay a total tax of $5,600 instead of the $8,000 it would have paid if it had continued generating 200 units of pollution. The same analysis is relevant for firm *B,* but because *B* has lower costs of reducing pollution, it has an incentive to cut back more. Firm *B* will maximize profits by cutting pollution to 60 units.

Note what this means: Both firms are operating at a level of pollution where the marginal cost equals $40. Their marginal costs are the same, which implies that the 200-unit reduction in total pollution has been achieved in the least costly way. And this outcome has occurred without requiring the government to know either firm's marginal cost curve. The total amount of pollution can be regulated by changing the tax per unit. If the tax is increased to $50 per unit of pollution, both firms will cut back further, and the reduction in pollution that results will be achieved at the minimum possible cost.

There are three important advantages of using taxes to control environmental externalities rather than the command-and-control approach. First, taxes automatically achieve production efficiency, as we have just seen. Second, there is a greater incentive for firms to find new ways of reducing pollution further. Under the tax, a firm that finds a way of reducing its marginal cost curve for pollution abatement will realize increased profits, hence the incentive. By contrast, once a firm has met the current standard under the command-and-control approach (e.g., pollute no more than 100 units), it has little incentive to reduce pollution below 100 units and may even run the risk of being slapped with a tougher standard if it invents a new technology. Third, the tax provides direct information regarding the marginal social cost of reducing pollution further. With the $40 tax, for example, the marginal cost of reducing pollution is $40 for both firms, and that is the marginal social cost. That is a very valuable piece of information, for we need to know the marginal social cost (along with marginal social benefit) to determine whether it is desirable to reduce pollution further.

Economists overwhelmingly believe that taxation is a better way to control pollution than the command-and-control approach now in use. Why does the government use the command-and-control approach? One reason is suggested by Alan Blinder: "An interview survey of sixty-three environmentalists, congressional staffers, and industry lobbyists—all of whom were intimately involved in environmental policy—found that not one could explain why economists claim that pollution can be reduced at lower cost by emissions fees [i.e., a tax on pollution] than by direct controls. Not one! This lack of knowledge, however, was not inhibiting; many of those surveyed opposed the idea anyway."[19] Other reasons may be suggested by the analysis in the next chapter.

Efficient Level of Pollution

We have not yet completed our analysis of environmental policy. We have shown how to achieve *any* given level of pollution abatement at the lowest possible cost (production efficiency), but we must now consider how to identify the efficient level of pollution abatement. That task is undertaken with the aid of Figure 2–9. Pollution is measured from right to left, as before, but now it is the total amount of pollution from all sources (rather than the pollution per firm, as in Figure 2–8). The marginal social cost of pollution abatement is shown by the *MSC* curve. Ideally, this curve will represent the lowest-cost method of reducing pollution. If so, it is derived by horizontally summing the marginal cost of pollution abatement of all the sources of the type of pollution in question (e.g., the two firms in Figure 2–8). (The *MSC* curve is, in fact, derived from the sources' marginal cost curves in the same way a competitive industry supply curve is derived from individual firms' marginal cost curves.) We have drawn the curve fairly flat for low levels of pollution reduction but rising sharply as we approach zero pollution. This is in accord with the empirical evidence that suggests that pollution abatement becomes very expensive at low levels of pollution.

The marginal social benefit curve, *MSB,* identifies the marginal benefit to the population from reducing pollution. (Looked at from right to left, it measures the marginal social damage from increasing pollution.) This curve will be the vertically summed marginal benefit curves of all the people affected by the pollution since pollution abatement has nonrival effects on many people. The particular nature of the benefits, whether improved health, lower dry cleaning costs, or just aesthetic pleasure from a cleaner environment, depends on the type of pollution being examined, but whatever the nature of the benefits, the *MSB* curve quantifies the monetary value to the public from achieving different levels of pollution abatement.

[19]Alan S. Blinder, *Hard Heads, Soft Hearts* (Reading, Mass.: Addison-Wesley Publishing Company, Inc., 1987), p. 137.

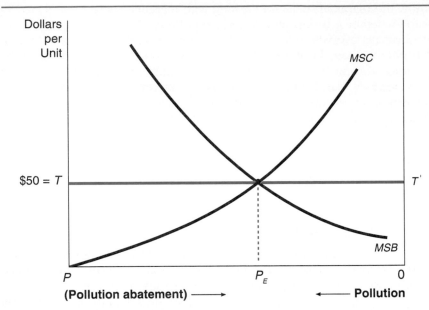

Figure 2–9 *Achieving the efficient level of pollution*

Given both the *MSC* and *MSB* curves, identifying the efficient level of pollution is straightforward. It occurs at the point of intersection, where marginal social benefit and cost are equal, at OP_E units of pollution in the diagram. Note that this level of pollution could be achieved with a tax of $50 per unit of pollution. In principle, there are other policies that could achieve this efficient outcome. However, if policies that imply production ineffi-ciency, as existing policies do, are used, they cannot be fully efficient. With such policies, we would be incurring costs greater than those shown by the *MSC* curve, and at these higher costs we should reduce pollution less. The net gain from the policy would be correspondingly smaller.

Of course, a great difficulty in achieving an efficient level of pollution is that we do not know the marginal social benefits of pollution abatement, nor is there any feasible way to measure them accurately. Economists have developed estimates of some of these benefits using some ingenious tech-niques,[20] but there are large margins of error with all such estimates. Paul Portney, for example, estimates that the most likely value for the benefits of the additional improvement in air quality resulting from the Clean Air Act of 1990 is $14 billion a year, and he cites another estimate of $16 billion.[21] Since

---

[20]See Cropper and Oates, "Environmental Economics," for a discussion of the ways economists have approached the estimation of benefits.

[21]Paul R. Portney, "Economics and the Clean Air Act," *Journal of Economic Perspec-tives,* 4:173 (Fall 1990).

the costs of complying with the provisions of this legislation are estimated to be $29–$36 billion per year, these estimates suggest that we have exceeded the efficient level of pollution abatement in this area. (In terms of Figure 2–9, the output of pollution abatement would be greater than PP_E.)

Global Warming and International Externalities

Environmental externalities need not be limited in their effects to residents of countries generating the externalities. Some external effects may affect literally everyone on the planet. One such possibility that has attracted much scientific and popular attention recently is the way some human activities produce effects that may alter the climate worldwide. Specifically, it has been argued that the burning of fossil fuels (and some other activities) release gases into the atmosphere that intensify the normal greenhouse effect of the earth's atmosphere and that this will lead to global warming.

Like some other externalities (such as the effects of air pollution on human health), a primary issue is scientific. How do human activities interact with other factors to determine the world's climate? Like economics, climatology is not an exact science, and much remains unknown. What does appear to be fairly well established is that there has been a buildup of "greenhouse gases" (principally carbon dioxide, but also methane, hydrocarbons, and other trace gases) in the atmosphere over the past 100 years, and that this buildup is due largely to the burning of fossil fuels (e.g., oil and coal), but also to some other factors like deforestation. Measuring the greenhouse gases in terms of their carbon dioxide (CO_2) equivalents, the increase in the atmosphere has been from about 310 parts per million (ppm) in 1900 to 430 ppm in 1990. Given current trends, it is estimated that the level will reach 600 ppm by the middle of the next century, a doubling from the level in the late nineteenth century.

That much is widely agreed, but what this means for the world's climate is much less clear. Several computer models designed to predict worldwide climate patterns have been developed, and these have generated predictions ranging from a 1.5°C increase in global temperature from a doubling of equivalent CO_2 to an increase of 5.0°C. The predictions from these models have received a lot of publicity, for there is no doubt that temperature increases at the upper end of this range would change the world as we know it.

Happily, but unfortunately not so well known, there is a lot of scientific evidence that casts doubt on the likelihood of any apocalyptic climate events.[22] For example, since there has already been a 40 percent increase in equivalent CO_2, we can compare the historical record with the predictions of the models. Some of the predictions of the models accord well with the

---

[22]For a balanced survey of the scientific evidence, see Robert C. Balling, Jr., *The Heated Debate* (San Francisco: Pacific Research Institute for Public Policy, 1992). A briefer treatment of the scientific issues is contained in Dixie Lee Ray, *Trashing the Planet* (Washington, D.C.: Regnery Gateway, 1990), Chapter 4.

evidence, but on the crucial question of global temperature there is great discrepancy. For instance, the models would predict at least a 1.0°C increase in global temperature from the atmospheric increase in CO_2 over the last century, but the actual increase has been 0.45°C. Some of that increase is known to be due to factors other than greenhouse gases (such as the urban heat island effect), so the increase due to the greenhouse gases appears to be even less. Thus, the models predicting doomsday scenarios in the future do not explain the past very well. There is, in fact, an even greater discrepancy: Most of the global temperature rise occurred before 1940, but most of the greenhouse gas increase has occurred since 1940. The timing of the global temperature change also does not fit the predictions of the models.

There is also the question of whether global warming, to the extent that it does occur, will be on balance a net cost or a net benefit. Most popular discussions, pointing to melting icecaps and rising sea levels, see only disaster. However, for many countries, such as Canada and the former Soviet Union, warming would probably be beneficial. In fact, there is some evidence that agricultural productivity would improve: Plants thrive in CO_2-rich environments, and greater precipitation is predicted by the climate models.[23] Given the importance of agriculture in the world economy, this could offset many of the negative consequences of a warmer environment. Finally, warming might forestall another ice age. One of the best-documented characteristics of worldwide climate is that there have been a series of about 17 ice ages over the last 2 million years (no one knows why), each lasting for about 100,000 years. Between the ice ages are warmer periods called *interglacials,* which have typically lasted for about 10,000 years. We are now living in an interglacial period that has lasted for about 10,800 years, so it appears that another ice age could begin at any time. If global warming keeps this from happening, we should be thankful.

There is no scientific consensus concerning the consequences of the buildup in greenhouse gases in the atmosphere, but the evidence certainly casts doubt on doomsday scenarios. Nonetheless, it is interesting to speculate on how we might deal with the situation if we knew that there would be major harmful consequences from the greenhouse gases that human activity injects into the atmosphere. Economists have suggested a simple solution, which will come as no surprise: Levy a "carbon tax," which would be based on the extent to which various fuels and activities lead to CO_2 emissions. That would lead to higher prices of gasoline, oil, and electricity generated by coal burning. There would then be fewer emissions, and the higher prices would lead to greater use of energy sources that do not produce greenhouse gases, such as nuclear energy.

The one problem with this scenario is that the carbon tax would have to be levied worldwide to be effective. The United States produces only about 20 percent of worldwide CO_2 emissions, and acting alone, it could not affect

---

[23]See Sylvan H. Wittwer, "Rising Carbon Dioxide Is Great for Plants," *Consumers' Research,* 75:25 (Dec. 1992).

the global climate to any appreciable degree; other countries account for even smaller amounts of greenhouse gases. Thus, there would be a free rider problem, as each country would like to get the benefits from having other countries reduce their greenhouse gas emissions without bearing the cost of reducing their own. This problem is intensified because some countries would view global warming as good for them. How fiercely independent national governments could be induced to cooperate to reduce greenhouse emissions is an interesting problem.

We are not, of course, advocating a worldwide carbon tax since we don't believe that the present evidence warrants such action. However, it is certainly worthwhile to continue investigating the scientific issues and to be ready with policy options in case they prove needed. In this connection, it is worth pointing out that research that produces new scientific knowledge has the characteristics of a public good. The federal government now spends more than $1 billion annually supporting global climate change research.

Review Questions and Problems

1. Suppose that there are three people in society, two "hawks" and one "dove." The dove is a pacifist and receives negative benefits from national defense; the hawks positively value national defense. Show graphically how an efficient output of defense would be determined in this case. Is there any way that the government could finance this efficient quantity that would benefit all three people?

2. A competitive market is in equilibrium. At the equilibrium output, there is a marginal external benefit of $1 per unit of output. If the government subsidizes production with a subsidy of $1 per unit, will this achieve an efficient output? Support your answer with a graph.

3. In Figure 2–4, which depicts the pollution externality of an industry, would the externality still exist if no one lived downstream? How would your solution to the externality problem be different depending on whether the industry or the people living downstream were there first?

4. What is the marginal social benefit curve for a product the consumption of which generates external benefits? How is it related to the market demand curve and the marginal external benefit curve? How is it related to the efficient output of the good?

5. "External costs result in a welfare cost, but external benefits result in a welfare gain." Do you agree? Explain.

6. Are there any external benefits associated with students' receiving a college education? Put differently, in what way does your receiving a college education benefit other people? What type of subsidy, if any, would be appropriate for dealing with the externalities you mention? (You may want to review your answer to this question after reading Chapter 5.)

7. What are pecuniary externalities and inframarginal externalities? Give an example of each. Do they lead to inefficient allocations?

8. What is the condition for efficiency in the output of a public good? How is an efficient output identified graphically? How should the efficient output be paid for?

9. "Individuals have more of an incentive to reveal their true preferences about ice cream than about national defense." True or false? Explain.

10. What are the characteristics of a public good, and why do they imply that voluntary arrangements cannot ensure the efficient output of such a good?

11. In evaluating government activity in some area, why is it important to consider whether public goods or externalities are involved? Can you give examples of government expenditures on goods that do not involve public goods or externalities? If so, explain why you favor or oppose these expenditures.

12. Does the free rider problem arise in connection with externalities? Explain.

13. Is the noise from crying babies an externality? How, if at all, does it differ from pollution emissions? Is it consistent to argue that the government should deal with pollution but should not regulate the noise from crying babies? Explain.

14. In what way is the size of an externality related to the importance of undertaking corrective public policy?

15. Instead of allowing each firm to produce 100 units of pollution, suppose that each firm was given the right to pollute 100 units and that these rights were tradable on a unit basis. Would the allocation of pollution be different from the tax example on pages 55 to 57? Would the total amount of pollution or the total cost be different?

16. Distinguish between production efficiency and output efficiency. How would each apply to an analysis of public schools?

17. How would you respond to an argument that the tax pollution plan is antienvironment because it allows the worst polluters (older equipment) to pollute the most?

Supplementary Readings

BUCHANAN, JAMES M. *The Demand and Supply of Public Goods.* Skokie, Ill.: Rand McNally, 1968.

COASE, RONALD. "The Problem of Social Cost." *Journal of Law and Economics,* 3:1–44 (Oct. 1960).

CORNES, RICHARD, and TODD SANDLER. *The Theory of Externalities, Public Goods, and Club Goods.* New York: Cambridge University Press, 1986.

CROPPER, MAUREEN L., and WALLACE E. OATES. "Environmental Economics: A Survey." *Journal of Economic Literature,* 30:675–740 (June 1992).

DEMSETZ, HAROLD. "The Private Production of Public Goods." *Journal of Law and Economics,* 13(2):30–43 (Oct. 1970).

DORNBUSCH, RUDIGER, and JAMES M. POTERBA, eds. *Global Warming: Economic Policy Responses.* Cambridge, Mass.: MIT Press, 1991

HEAD, JOHN G. *Public Goods and Public Welfare.* Durham, N.C.: Duke University Press, 1974.

LEE, DWIGHT R. "Environmental Economics and the Social Cost of Smoking." *Contemporary Policy Issues,* 9:83–92 (Jan. 1991).

MISHAN, E. J. "The Postwar Literature on Externalities: An Interpretive Essay." *Journal of Economic Literature,* 9:1–28 (Mar. 1971).

OAKLAND, WILLIAM H. "Theory of Public Goods." In *Handbook of Public Economics,* Vol. 2. Edited by A. J. Auerbach and Martin Feldstein. Amsterdam, The Netherlands: Elsevier Science Publishers, 1987.

POGUE, THOMAS F., and LARRY G. SGONTZ. "Taxing to Control Social Costs: The Case of Alcohol." *American Economic Review,* 79:235–243 (Mar. 1989).

Public Choice

*I*N THE LAST CHAPTER WE SAW THAT EXTERNALITIES and public goods generally lead the price system to produce inefficient results. If the welfare cost due to market failure is large enough, this means that it is *possible* for government to intervene with a policy that will lead to a more efficient allocation of resources. The existence of market failure, however, does not mean that any government intervention will always improve the situation. To determine whether government will enact and implement policies that promote efficiency or equity, we require a theory of how government functions, and this is what the theory of public choice is designed to supply.

The theory of public choice is the study of how governmental decisions are made and implemented; as such, it essentially involves an analysis of the political process. Public choice theory tries to explain what government *actually does* (or *will do* under different circumstances), as distinct from an attempt to prescribe what government *should do*. This approach is based on the premise that individuals attempt to further their own interests in their political activities, just as in their economic activities. The view that people are schizophrenic—behaving in a greedy and materialistic way in their market transactions but in a public-spirited and altruistic way in the voting booth—is explicitly rejected. The same people who are our consumers and workers in economic models are also our voters and politicians when we study the political process. According to the public choice approach, the difference between political and economic behavior lies not in the differences in human motives but in the rules and institutions governing human interaction in the two spheres.

Basing the analysis of the political process on the assumption that *individual* actions are based on the attempt to achieve personally desired goals does not prejudge the collective results in the form of *governmental* actions. Competitive markets often yield socially efficient outcomes when firms, consumers, and workers try to achieve the greatest gain for themselves. Similarly, some sort of "invisible hand" may also be at work in the political realm. Indeed, it is, at least in part, the purpose of public choice theory to determine whether this is so.

One disclaimer is in order at the outset. Since public choice theory has been seriously studied only for the past three decades or so, we do not have as complete an understanding of political processes as we do of market processes. Therefore, this chapter provides no pat answers and no general model that can easily be applied in all situations. Instead, we only introduce certain topics that recent research suggests have significant implications for the functioning of the political process.

Voting and Resource Allocation

Direct Majority Voting

Many political decisions emerge from a process of majority voting. We begin by analyzing majority voting directly by citizens as a method of determining the total outlay to be made for the production of a public good. In reality, citizens seldom have the opportunity to determine the output of a public good directly by their votes, but it is still interesting to consider how such a process would work. Although our assumptions are unrealistic, the results of the analysis may be applicable to more realistic settings. In other words, the outcomes of citizens' first electing representatives who then vote on policies may be quite similar to the outcomes of citizens' voting directly on the policies themselves. We will consider whether this relationship holds later.

Assume for simplicity that we have a three-person community composed of individuals *A, B,* and *C.* By majority voting, these individuals must determine how much output of a public good to finance through taxes. Suppose that the citizens have decided to divide the total cost of the public good equally among themselves. If the marginal cost for each unit of the good is $30, then each citizen will pay $10 per unit of the good produced. The number of units of output to be produced (and hence each citizen's total tax liability) will be determined by majority voting.

Figure 3–1 can be used to illustrate the voting process. The demand curves of the three voters are shown as d_A, d_B, and d_C; these curves indicate the marginal benefits to each voter from different levels of output. In deciding how to vote, each voter compares the benefits he or she would receive from a change in output with the associated change in tax costs that must be borne. The tax costs are summarized in the line TP_i, indicating the *tax price* per unit of the public good for each voter. Because we are assuming that the public good costs $30 per unit and the voters will share the costs equally,

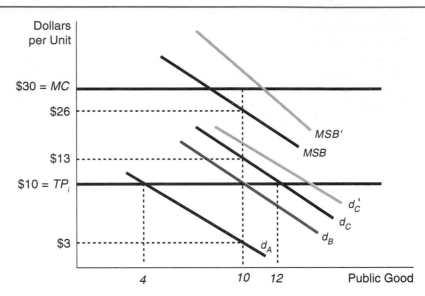

Figure 3–1 *Majority voting process*

the tax price per unit of output for each taxpayer is $10.[1] Total tax liability will depend on the number of units produced. As shown in the diagram, *A* prefers 4 units of output, *B* prefers 10 units, and *C* prefers 12 units. Majority voting will be used to determine a unique level of output.

The process of majority voting can be thought of as proceeding in this way. Beginning at a zero level of output, suppose that a proposal is made to provide publicly two units, for example, with the costs divided as explained. Each voter compares the benefits with the tax costs. If the voter is better off with two units of the public good provided *and* paying taxes of $20, compared with no tax and none of the public good, the voter will support the proposal. If a majority of the citizens vote in favor of the proposal, it will pass. Even if a proposal for two units passes, however, this may not be the *equilibrium* level of output under the voting process. Other proposals to increase or reduce output can be made and voted on. *An equilibrium occurs at the level of output where any proposal either to increase or reduce output would be opposed by a majority.*

Figure 3–1 allows us to identify the equilibrium in the simple setting depicted there. If output is initially zero, all three voters will support a proposal

---

[1]Under all real-world tax institutions, the same tax price does not confront all voters. For example, under a proportional income tax, a voter with twice the income of another would pay twice as much in taxes and hence face a tax price per unit of government output that is twice as high. Although the diagrammatic analysis becomes more complicated, the general conclusions derived in the text remain valid.

to increase output to two units, because the marginal benefits of the first two units exceed marginal costs (the tax price) for all three voters. Similarly, a proposal to expand output to four units will pass unanimously. At four units, however, a proposal to increase output to five units will be favored by B and C but opposed by A. Because a majority prefers five to four, output will be increased. The process does not stop here, however, because both B and C will vote in favor of increasing output to 10 units. Ten units of output is the equilibrium level of output, characterized by the fact that a majority of voters will oppose any change from that level. Note that a majority of voters (A and B) will oppose any increase beyond 10 units and that a different majority (B and C) will oppose any reduction below 10 units. Hence, a proposal to provide 10 units can defeat any other proposal; this is another way to describe the equilibrium under majority voting. Ten units of output will thus be provided, and each voter will be assigned a $100 total tax liability to cover the $300 cost of providing the good.

A basic implication of this analysis is that the *median* quantity preferred by voters will be selected by majority voting. Of the three preferred quantities (4, 10, and 12), 10 is the median preferred quantity, with the same number of voters favoring a larger and a smaller output. Thus, the quantity favored by the *median voter,* here voter B, becomes the collective choice, and for that reason this model is sometimes referred to as the *median voter model.*

Although this model is quite simple, it helps us understand a number of important characteristics of political decision making by majority vote. First, note that the median voter is the only voter fully satisfied with the politically determined level of output; everyone else prefers either more or less output. (Of course, in the unlikely case in which everyone had the same demand for the public good, all voters would unanimously agree.) It is *not* accurate to say that majority voting "gives the majority what it wants," because "the" majority that supports any given proposal will seldom agree among themselves.

Second, it is possible to see why so many people feel that government is not responsive to *individual* wants. By its very nature, the political process responds to an individual's wants only when they are in agreement with those of a substantial number of fellow voters; voters with preferences that are quite different from those of the bulk of voters are likely to remain dissatisfied.

Third, majority voting is likely to be unresponsive to *changes* in individual wants. Suppose that individual C's demand curve shifts to d'_C. Despite the fact that individual C wants a larger quantity of output, the equilibrium level of output remains unchanged. This characteristic is sometimes described by saying that majority voting ignores the *intensity of preferences.* All a person can do is vote yes or no, and an impassioned yes carries no more weight than a weak yes. Only if the median preferred quantity changes is the actual outcome likely to vary.

Finally, there is no inherent tendency for majority voting to produce efficient policies. Recall from Chapter 2 that the efficient level of output is the point at which the vertically summed marginal benefits equal the marginal cost. In Figure 3–1, the individual marginal benefits for taxpayers A, B, and C at 10 units of output are $3, $10, and $13, so the combined marginal benefit is $26. (MSB is the vertical summation of the three individual demand curves.) Because the marginal cost is $30, the tenth unit of output is worth less than its cost. Nonetheless, an output of 10 units is the equilibrium under majority voting. In this case, majority voting produces too large an output. The opposite is also possible. If individual C's demand were d'_c instead of d_c, the summed marginal benefits would be given by MSB', and the equilibrium level of output (still 10) would be lower than the efficient level.

Thus, there is no inherent tendency for efficient outcomes to be produced through majority voting because voting cannot reflect how strongly people feel about the various outcomes. This may not, however, be a devastating criticism of majority voting. What is relevant is a comparison of majority voting with other alternatives. Majority voting may produce an outcome closer to the efficient one than, for example, the outcome produced by reliance on private markets. This is certainly likely to be the case for provision of a public good like national defense when the welfare cost of relying on private markets would be huge. However, when the inefficiency of relying on a private market is only slight, as in the case of minor externalities or monopolistic elements, the chance that majority voting would produce a greater welfare cost than leaving matters alone is also a possibility.

Logrolling

Even when majority voting is the decision rule for determining policies, under certain circumstances it is possible for policies to be adopted that are actually opposed by a majority of voters. One way this can occur is through *logrolling*. Logrolling is a process of trading votes to achieve the majority necessary for approval. A simple example will indicate why it occurs and the types of results it may produce.

Suppose that we have three voters, Sarah, Walt, and Doug. Three spending proposals are being considered: to subsidize college students, hospital construction, and recruitment of more police personnel. Sarah is the only voter who favors the college program (the other two oppose it), Walt is the only voter who favors the hospital program, and Doug is the only voter who favors the police program. At first glance, it would appear that the proposals for all three subsidies would have to fail because each one is opposed by a majority of the voters. This, however, may not be the outcome. Sarah could go to Walt and say that she will vote for his favored policy (hospital spending) if he will vote for the policy she favors in return (college spending). This *vote trading* may be to their mutual advantage, and if so, we would expect the deal to go through. Then both proposals will get the needed majority, even though each subsidy is really opposed by two of the three voters.

Table 3–1 allows us to examine this situation in greater detail. In Case I, we also give the net gain or loss for the voters if each spending proposal is adopted. For the hospital subsidy, for example, Sarah's net gain is $100, while Walt and Doug suffer net losses of $50 and $100 (perhaps because they pay the taxes). Each proposal is opposed by a majority, but the two persons constituting the majority differ in each case. Note that as we have constructed Case I, all three spending programs are inefficient—the losses to the voters who are harmed are larger than the gain to the voter who benefits. This is shown in the last row, which gives the combined net loss or gain for the three voters together.

If each proposal is voted on separately, with each voter registering his or her true interest, all three proposals will fail to secure majority approval, and this result will be efficient in this case. Logrolling is likely to change the outcome. Note that Sarah is better off if both the hospital and college programs are enacted (100 − 75); Walt is also better off if these two programs both pass (125 − 50). Thus, it is in their interests to support each other's favored program and in that way put together a majority vote for the hospital and college programs. Both are enacted, even though they are inefficient.

This is not the only possible outcome. Walt and Doug might trade votes to secure passage of the college and police programs, or Sarah and Doug might trade votes and get the hospital and police programs enacted. Which outcome would actually occur is unclear, but in all these cases an inefficient outcome results.

It is possible, however, that logrolling can lead to the adoption of efficient policies that would not be enacted in its absence. This is illustrated in Case II in Table 3–1. Here, we have only changed the magnitudes of the gains and

Table 3–1	*Logrolling*		
Voters	**Hospital**	**College**	**Police**
	Case I		
Sarah	$ 100	$ − 75	$ − 80
Walt	− 50	125	− 100
Doug	− 100	− 125	150
Total net effect	$ − 50	$ − 75	$ − 30
	Case II		
Sarah	$ 100	$ − 50	$ − 60
Walt	− 50	125	− 40
Doug	− 20	− 50	150
Total net effect	$ 30	$ 25	$ 50

losses in comparison with our previous example. Now there is a combined net gain from each of the three programs. There is a larger benefit to Sarah from the hospital subsidy, for instance, than the costs that fall on Walt and Doug. All three programs are efficient, but if voted on separately, a majority will oppose each program. In this case, vote trading can work to secure the passage of efficient programs that would otherwise be rejected under majority voting. For example, Sarah and Walt may trade votes to secure the passage of the hospital and college subsidies.

Our examples suggest that logrolling can lead to the passage of both efficient and inefficient policies that would not otherwise be enacted. Which of these outcomes is more likely? Unfortunately, it does not seem possible to rule out either possibility. It may be that logrolling sometimes operates to promote efficiency and in other cases to thwart it. Certainly an examination of actual policies often yields the impression that some policies benefiting only a small minority of the population are inefficient and some are efficient. Until we know more, we may have to be content with the conclusion that sometimes logrolling produces desirable outcomes and sometimes it does not. In any event, logrolling does offer an explanation for the existence of policies that operate to the detriment of a majority of the population.

The process of logrolling is often defended as a means of protecting minority interests. On a particular issue, a minority of voters may passionately favor a particular policy, but under majority voting without logrolling their interests will be ignored, implying a "tyranny of the majority." Logrolling, however, provides a method by which minorities can secure favorable legislation by agreeing to support other policies. Although logrolling can in this way protect minority interests, there is also the possibility that it leads to overrepresentation of minority interests.

A final point should be made. Logrolling among individual voters is not likely to occur when there are large numbers of voters (or when there is a secret ballot). In national elections, for example, there is little incentive for individual voters to exchange votes for senators and congressional representatives because it would have no perceptible impact on the final outcome. Logrolling is most likely to occur when a vote trade will have a significant impact on the outcomes of the votes, and that will generally be true only when a relatively small number of votes is required to achieve a majority. Decision making by representatives within legislative bodies apparently involves a small enough number of voters for logrolling to be effective because it is quite common in such settings.

Electing Representatives

In the United States, candidates of the two major political parties run against one another for political office, and majority voting generally determines which candidate will serve.[2] Our general approach can be used to shed some

---

[2] When more than two candidates are running, the one with the most votes (not necessarily a majority) wins. This is called *plurality voting*.

light on the likely outcomes of such elections. Begin by assuming that candidates are distinguishable only in terms of a liberal–conservative spectrum. In other words, candidates will be classified according to how far left or right their policy positions are. Further assume that the voters will support the candidate whose position is closest to their own. Thus, the voter's choice is narrowed to a single issue. Although this is perhaps an oversimplified example, it serves to make some simple but important points.

The distribution of voters according to political ideology is shown by the bell-shaped curve in Figure 3–2. The line drawn at point M separates the total electorate in half; half the voters have positions to the right of this middle-of-the-road position, and the other half have positions to the left. Now consider an election between two candidates, a Republican and a Democrat. If the candidates take positions shown by R and D, who will win the election? Clearly, the Democrat will win because a majority of the voters have political beliefs closer to the Democratic candidate's than to the Republican's. A dashed line can be drawn halfway between R and D, and we will assume that all voters with beliefs to the left of the dashed line will vote for the Democrat and those to the right will vote for the Republican. Voters will then be supporting the candidate whose views are *closer* to their own position.

Faced with this likely outcome, the Republican candidate's chances of winning the election would be strengthened by shifting his or her position to the left. By doing this, the Republican candidate can attract some votes near the middle without losing any support to the right. For example, by taking the position at R', where M is halfway between D and R', the Republican will get exactly half the votes. By staking out a position a little to the left of R', the Republican will get a majority. Of course, the Democrat can change positions too. In the limit, both candidates have an incentive to move

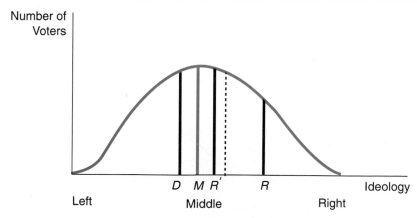

Figure 3–2 *Middle-of-the-road politics*

to the middle-of-the-road position at *M*. The voters will be divided between the candidates, and the likely outcome will be a tie vote.

Of course, candidates do not take identical positions, and elections rarely end in ties. The analysis indicates, however, the tendency for politicians to adopt middle-of-the-road positions as they seek voter support. Because they do not have complete and accurate information about voters' preferences, this is only a general tendency, but one that accords well with political realities. (As casual evidence to indicate the importance politicians place on discerning voters' preferences, recall the extensive use of polls in recent national primaries and elections.) When a politician has the courage (?) to stake out a position far from *M*, he or she is usually defeated. This happened in the presidential election in 1964 when Senator Barry Goldwater took a position like that at *R*, offering voters "a choice, not an echo," and was soundly defeated. It happened again in 1972 when Senator George Mc-Govern took a position well to the left of *M* and suffered a similar fate. Such occurrences are relatively rare because politicians are astute enough and sufficiently interested in winning to stay fairly close to the middle.

This is simply another example of the importance of the median position in majority voting because *M* is the median. It does, however, serve to indicate why it is generally correct for voters to feel that they are not offered much choice at election time. Insofar as the lack of real choice is a result of politicians' successfully locating the median preference, this outcome is not necessarily bad. In any event, it is what should be expected from competition among politicians for votes.

In many respects, this model is an oversimplified representation of reality. When there are hundreds of policies on which politicians must take positions, it is not possible to compress all of the choices into a single left-to-right continuum. As we shall see, politicians do not always have an incentive to take the median position on every issue (even if they can locate the median).

The Cyclical Majority Phenomenon

There are some situations in which there is no equilibrium under majority voting. No matter what policy is chosen, there is another policy that is favored by a majority. Sound impossible? Consider the situation described in Table 3–2. There are three voters, *A*, *B*, and *C*, and there are three possible policies: a small budget (*S*), a medium budget (*M*), and a large budget (*L*). The ranking of these alternative policies for each voter is given. For example, *A*'s first choice is the medium budget, followed by the small budget and lastly the large budget. Confronted with two alternatives, each voter will vote for the higher-ranked alternative.

If majority voting is used to select among the three alternatives, the choices must be considered on a pairwise basis. *M* can be pitted against *S*, and the winner of that vote can be pitted against *L*. In a selection between *M* and *S*, *M* will win because voters *A* and *B* prefer *M* to *S*. When *M* is run against *L*, *L* will prevail because *B* and *C* prefer *L* to *M*. It appears that *L* is

Table 3–2	*Cyclical Majority Phenomenon*		
Voters	*A*	*B*	*C*
Ranking	M	L	S
	S	M	L
	L	S	M

the winner until we notice that if *L* is run against *S* (which was defeated by *M* in the first vote), then *S* will win because *A* and *C* prefer *S* to *L*. To summarize the outcomes: *S* can defeat *L*, *L* can defeat *M*, and *M* can defeat *S*. There is no equilibrium because every policy can be defeated by one of the others. No matter what is chosen, something else is preferred by a majority. This is called the *cyclical majority phenomenon* because policy choices can cycle from *M* to *L* to *S* to *M* and so on indefinitely.

Understanding how this phenomenon can occur is simple, but appreciating its general significance is more difficult. To some, it has shaken their faith in democracy and majority rule; to others, it is only a theoretical curiosity of little practical relevance. What is really at issue is how often the phenomenon actually occurs in political decision making.

Clearly, there are some situations in which the cyclical majority phenomenon would not occur. In Table 3–2, if *C*'s ranking were *SML* instead of *SLM*, then *M* could defeat both *L* and *S* and represent a stable equilibrium. The cyclical majority phenomenon occurs only when the rankings of voters bear a certain relationship to one another. How likely is it that voters' rankings of alternatives will produce no stable equilibrium? If we assume that all possible combinations of rankings are equally likely, then the cyclical majority phenomenon would occur in about 11 percent of the cases. Some scholars, however, have argued that this overstates the probability of its occurrence, because the rankings that produce the cyclical outcomes are inherently unlikely. As an example, consider *C*'s ranking in Table 3–2: *SLM*. *C* prefers both extremes—the large and the small budgets—to the intermediate position—the medium budget. Although this is conceivable, it is odd because generally the intermediate position would be preferred to at least one of the extremes. This, for example, is true of the situation shown in Figure 3–1. For any three levels of output that are specified, no voter will prefer both the largest and the smallest output to the one in between. The rankings of voters implied by Figure 3–1 will produce a stable equilibrium: 10 units of output.

This argument implies that when voters are determining how much to spend on one particular project and when the costs are prorated in advance, a stable equilibrium is likely to result. Many political decisions, however, do not fit this description, and it is our view that the cyclical majority phenomenon is quite common in more realistic settings. Let us begin by using an example to illustrate how it might occur. Suppose that the government is going to divide $1,000 among 100 voters and initially proposes to give each voter $10. Then someone proposes that the entire amount be divided among 51 voters. The second proposal would defeat the first because 51 voters, a majority, would prefer it. Next a third proposal is introduced: Give a still larger amount to two members of the original 51-member majority (to induce them to change sides) and divide the remainder among the 49 who would receive nothing under the second proposal. The third proposal would defeat the second one. In short, no matter how the $1,000 is divided among the voters, it is always possible to design another proposal that would give less to a minority and more to a majority, and that proposal would be favored by a majority. In this situation, there is no proposal that could consistently defeat all others under majority voting. This example is characteristic of real-world situations when voters select among politicians who take stands on a variety of issues. The reason is that alternative combinations of policy issues have different effects on the distribution of income (i.e., on who benefits and who loses) just as in the preceding example.

For example, a politician might favor higher social security benefits, higher tariffs, and higher price supports for agricultural products. The combined impact of these three policies might redistribute income in favor of a majority, so the politician could secure majority approval. A second politician, however, might propose a policy package composed of higher food stamp subsidies, higher subsidies to college students, and even higher (than that proposed by the first politician) tariffs. The combined impact of these three policies might benefit a majority when compared with the proposals of the first politician, so the second politician could defeat the first. No matter what combination of policies is proposed, it is always possible to design another combination that would benefit a majority because it is always possible to use government policies to redistribute income in favor of a majority. When all government policies are considered as a package—which is what happens when we choose among political candidates—there is no combination of policies that represents a stable equilibrium under majority voting.

The nonexistence of a stable equilibrium does not mean that we would expect to see constant cycling among alternatives, with no decision ever being reached. Decisions are made simply because when a vote is taken on one issue, or in one election, one of the two alternatives being voted on will necessarily win (barring ties). What the absence of an equilibrium means is that the political decisions actually reached are not favored by a majority over all other alternatives.

Another possibility raised by the cyclical majority phenomenon is that a policy can be selected that will make everyone worse off. This is illustrated in Table 3–3, in which the value of each of four policies for the three voters is given. Two of the three voters (A and B) prefer policy II to policy I, two of three voters (B and C) prefer policy III to policy II, and two of the three voters (A and C) prefer policy IV to policy III. It is therefore possible that a series of majority votes will lead to the selection of policy IV, in which all three voters are worse off than with policy I.

Table 3–3 **A Voting Sequence That Leaves All Voters Worse Off**

Policy	Value of Policy to Each Voter		
	Voter A	Voter B	Voter C
I	$1,000	$1,000	$1,000
II	1,200	1,200	400
III	600	1,300	600
IV	800	800	800

At least two important insights can be obtained from an understanding of the cyclical majority phenomenon. First, underlying inconsistencies in government policies should be expected. Minimum wage laws that create unemployment coexist with job training to put the unemployed to work. Farm price supports raise the cost of food to the poor, but food stamps lower the cost. Some subsidies (such as aid to colleges) tend to benefit the relatively affluent, others benefit the poor, and still others benefit middle-income families. It is not possible to examine actual policies and infer a consistent set of "social priorities" because choices through the political process should be expected to be inconsistent. The group of voters who form an effective coalition favoring farm price supports is different from the group favoring food stamps. Because the preferences or priorities of the different groups and individuals differ, there is no reason to expect political choices to be consistent. Some political choices reflect the dominance of the views of one group, and others reflect the dominance of a different set of values.

Second, an underlying instability in government should be expected. No matter what the government does, an astute politician can always find a new policy package that will secure majority approval. This suggests that government may provide no stable framework of laws, taxes, and expenditures within which individuals can confidently plan their lives. Frequent change can be predicted. Of course, if voters believe a stable framework is important, they may place limits on the types of policies governments can enact. Presumably, this feeling underlies the views of those who favor constitutional limitations on the power of government.

We must be cautious of attaching too much importance to the cyclical majority phenomenon. Perhaps voters' underlying preferences effectively limit the range of issues over which cycling can theoretically occur, or actual political institutions may operate to make the phenomenon occur more rarely than theoretical considerations would suggest. At this stage in the development of public choice theory, the significance of the problem is unknown.

Participants in the Political Process

Many different groups of people influence government decisions: voters, politicians, government employees, lobbies, judges, the media, intellectuals, and so on. Examining the incentives confronting some of these participants and their likely behavior can contribute to a broader understanding of the political process.

Voters

It is appropriate to begin by considering citizens in their role as voters. The voting public elects many government officials and thereby empowers them to make and enforce government policy. The voting decisions of the public therefore determine who will run the government and indirectly influence the policies enacted. Given the importance of the role played by voters, it is instructive to examine their behavior to ascertain if they have incentives to seek out and support political candidates who favor efficient and equitable government policies.

Many factors influence a person's vote: a candidate's personality; spouse; wit; honesty; and ethnic, religious, and regional background. Naturally the candidate's position on policy is also likely to be important. Other things being equal, voters will favor the candidate whose policies they believe will yield them the greatest net benefits (or smallest net costs). Voters will cast votes in an attempt to further their self-interest. This is not necessarily bad; recall that the pursuit of self-interest in a competitive price system generally tends to produce socially desirable outcomes. It is, in fact, this characteristic of voters that gives political candidates an incentive to formulate policies that benefit the public.

The basic question is whether voters will tend to favor policies that are efficient, that is, policies that have total benefits in excess of costs. In answering this question, it is helpful to distinguish between two different cases in which a policy will benefit a specific voter. In one case, a policy benefits voter A *and* involves total benefits in excess of total costs when the effects on all persons are considered. In this situation, the policy is an efficient one, and the voter will support it (and the candidate who favors it, other things being equal). In the second case, a policy benefits voter A *and* involves total costs greater than total benefits. This policy is inefficient; yet voter A will still support it because it benefits him or her.

There is no inherent tendency for voters to support efficient government policies. Even the most inefficient policies generally benefit some groups of voters (although at greater costs to the rest of the public), and those who benefit will support them. Thus, we can expect producers to support higher tariffs on competing imported products, dairy farmers to support higher milk price supports, nonsmokers to support limitations on smoking in public, the elderly to support greater social security benefits, and college students (and professors) to support higher subsidies to colleges. We do not mean to prejudge all of those policies as necessarily inefficient or inequitable, but only to suggest the importance of the pursuit of personal gain in motivating voters. People are not narrowly *self*-interested in their market behavior and then *public*-interested in the voting booth. Instead, they strive to obtain whatever goals they have through both processes. In short, voters are more interested in whether policies benefit *them* than in whether policies are efficient or equitable in some broader context.

Actually, voters are seldom given the opportunity to express a preference on a single policy. Instead, they must choose among candidates offering different bundles of policies. In this setting, voters can easily justify supporting a candidate who favors a policy greatly in their interest. A college student is likely to support a candidate who will halve college tuition. Although this clearly augments the student's wealth at the expense of the general taxpayers, the candidate also favors a multitude of other policies that benefit other groups. The student, in rationalizing his or her vote, can claim that the candidate has "something for everyone" and that the tuition subsidy indicates that the candidate has a deep concern for college students as well as other groups. Most voters no doubt believe they act "in the public interest," but people have an amazing capacity to believe (like General Motors) that what benefits them is good for the country. Sometimes it may be true, but not always.

The behavior of voters is strongly conditioned by another influence: the tendency of voters to be rationally ignorant of the consequences of their political choices. *Rational voter ignorance* is one of the most important forces operating in the political process, and it has far-reaching effects. Rational voter ignorance can best be understood as the hypothesis that voters will be relatively less informed about their political decisions than about comparable private market decisions. It does not mean that people have perfect information in the marketplace and zero information about activities in the public sector. Because acquiring information involves costs, people will seldom be perfectly informed about any choices they make.

To see why voters are rationally ignorant, let us compare the amount of information collected (and the relative costs) by a person considering the purchase of private health insurance in contrast to a voter's decision on whether or not to support a national health insurance policy. To make a wise choice about private health insurance, a person would like to have a great deal of information: the types of illnesses covered by the policy, the costs of different parts of the policy, the probabilities of contracting the illnesses covered, the costs of being treated for all these illnesses, and so on. Clearly, few people will acquire all the needed information, and this behavior is rational, given the cost of acquiring information.

To evaluate national health insurance proposals, however, much more information is required. To make an informed decision, a person would need to know not only all of the previously mentioned facts about alternative proposals but also how much of a tax burden the voter would bear (not an easy matter to determine), the likely impact of alternative national health insurance schemes on medical care and other prices, how the cost controls in the plan will actually affect the voter, and so on. In short, the voter needs a great deal more information to make a wise decision about the government policy, and the additional information is of a different nature because it is more like knowledge that requires scientific research to substantiate.

The higher information cost is one reason to expect voters to be relatively uninformed in their political decision making. In addition, there is a second reason that is perhaps of even greater importance. *The gain that a person can realize from acquiring political information is much less than the gain from acquiring information about goods purchased privately.* Suppose that a person spends several months researching national health insurance; what are the benefits? The voter can patriotically cast a better-informed vote, but it is only one vote among millions, and it will have no perceptible effect on the outcome. The same national policy is almost certain to be enacted, regardless of whether any single person is well informed. Consequently, people have little incentive to obtain information about the operation of the government, the actions of politicians, or the effects of government policies. In contrast, the purchase of private goods is different. If a person becomes better informed about alternative private health policies, the person will receive the benefits of choosing the one better suited to his or her needs. The consumer's private choice is decisive in influencing the outcome, which contrasts sharply with his or her voting decision. In the marketplace, the benefits associated with becoming better informed are greater, the costs of information are lower, and the consumer will acquire more information.

We should stress that *voter ignorance is rational.* Observers often bemoan the lack of knowledge and interest on the part of voters, but no amount of cajoling is likely to effect a change. It is far more important for most people to obtain information of use in their daily lives than to engage in scientific research on social problems.

The existence of rationally ignorant voters has important repercussions for the workings of the political process because the political process caters to voters as they actually are, not as they would be if they were fully informed. For example, rational voter ignorance accounts for the generally low level of political discourse. Political speeches (as well as newspaper editorials) often rely on slogans, oversimplifications, inadequate theories, and misleading facts. Appearances and plausibility count for more than truth. Voters lack the necessary information to evaluate the assertions made by politicians, which in turn gives politicians little incentive to achieve accuracy and balance in their views.

Although voters will generally be rationally ignorant about most government policies, some voters will be relatively more informed on certain issues. Dairy farmers are likely to know more about how milk price supports affect them than is the remainder of the public. When the consequences of a policy for some voters are desirable or disastrous and involve large benefits or costs, the affected voters are more likely to realize whether or not they will benefit. In these cases, the benefits of acquiring more information exceed the costs, and the affected groups will be better informed. Often voters will base their voting decisions on a small subset of policies that affect them strongly. It may be rational for college students to favor the candidate who wants higher tuition subsidies. The students know they will benefit directly from that policy but find it difficult to determine what the net effect of all the other policies favored by their candidate would be for their welfare. This type of reasoning often leads voters to evaluate political candidates almost wholly on the basis of a few issues that affect them directly. As we shall see, this is one reason for the prevalence of special interest legislation.

As another example, voter ignorance is the explanation for the frequently noted tendency of politicians to emphasize the obvious and short-term effects of policies while ignoring the hidden, long-term consequences. It is well known that an incumbent president is extremely concerned with the state of the economy just before the election. Reducing the unemployment rate by November may be a good strategy even if the cost is a higher rate of inflation several months later. Voters may not be aware of the long-run costs of reducing unemployment quickly, nor will they make the connection later.

An additional issue concerning voters is the decision to vote itself. Only 40 to 60 percent of potential voters actually cast ballots in national elections. In fact, it is easier to explain why people do not vote than why they do. Each individual's vote will have no perceptible effect on the outcome of an election, so little benefit can be expected from influencing actual policy. In addition, perhaps some potential voters may feel as a bumper sticker during one election cynically noted: "Don't Vote: You'll Only Encourage Them!"

Politicians

Those who seek office and those who hold elected offices play a role in politics similar to the role of businesspersons in private markets. Businesspersons are the moving force in markets: They make the actual decisions concerning what to produce and in what quantities. Similarly, politicians— at least successful ones—determine what government does; their voting and logrolling activities determine the broad outlines of government policy. To stay in business, businesspersons are led to take account of consumers' interests by having to produce a product that consumers want. Likewise, politicians are led to take voters' interests into account by having to offer a policy package that attracts enough voters to stay in office. In both the political and the market spheres, the process used to make decisions gives us some reason to believe that the public's interest will be served.

The analogy between political and business entrepreneurs cannot be pressed too far because there are important differences. A businessperson does not require approval of a majority of the public to operate a business; yet a politician frequently does. A businessperson cannot force any consumer to purchase a product, but a politician's programs are financed by taxes levied on many who opposed the programs. A businessperson offers wares for sale, one at a time, day after day, in competition with numerous other competitors, but a politician sells a package of hundreds of policies once every several years, and generally in competition with only one other candidate. These differences are not intended to imply that one process is any better than the other, but only that the market and political processes differ in many ways.

In trying to understand the behavior of politicians, public choice specialists have found it useful to assume that politicians behave in a way that they believe will maximize the votes they receive at the next election.[3] This is not a cynical assumption but a realistic one. Elected officials will remain in office only if they continue to attract enough voter support. Political survival requires that politicians pay attention to the vote-gaining and vote-losing effects of their actions, just as business survival demands attention to the profit picture. Successful politicians—the ones who actually make government decisions—will be the ones who are best at attracting votes. Politicians may believe they are acting "in the public interest" (and indeed may be, according to their own conception of the public interest), but they would not be successful unless their actions *also* attracted votes.

The important question is: What types of government policies will result from an attempt by politicians to maximize votes? This is a complex question and one to which public choice theory as yet provides no complete or simple answer. In trying to determine an answer, two points should be recalled. First, politicians are elected on the basis of their positions on many issues; the overall "package" offered in comparison with that of competing politicians is what counts. Politicians thus need not please the majority on each separate issue. Second, the voters are rationally ignorant of much of what politicians stand for, their past actions, and the likely consequences of their proposed policies.

The importance of these points can be illustrated by looking at some examples. Consider a politician who must take a position on the three policies listed in Table 3–4. Each program benefits only 20 percent of the voting public. Yet a politician who opposes all three policies might be defeated by another who favors them. The reason is that each group benefits from one of the policies and may secure benefits in excess of the harm done to it by the other two policies. Farmers, for example, may believe that the higher taxes they would pay to finance the college and welfare subsidies will be less than the gain they would receive from higher price supports; in their view, all three policies are better than none. If all three groups feel this way, they will vote for a politician favoring all three policies when the alternative is a politician opposing all three.

This example illustrates how *special interest legislation* may be passed, even though a large percentage of the public is harmed. Special interest

---

[3]Alternatively, it might be assumed that they will just attempt to achieve a majority of the votes cast. In most cases, it would make little difference which assumption is made.

Table 3–4   *Implicit Logrolling*

Policy	Favored by	Opposed by
Farm price supports	20%	80%
Welfare assistance	20%	80%
College tuition subsidy	20%	80%

legislation can be thought of as policies that yield large individual benefits to a small proportion of the public, coupled with small individual costs falling on a large proportion of the public. For example, a policy may grant benefits of $1,000 a year to 2 percent of the voters, at a cost of $25 a year to the remaining 98 percent. A politician may win votes by favoring this policy. The candidate is almost certain to gain the votes of the 2 percent who are benefited, regardless of the politician's position on other issues (at least, in comparison to an opponent who opposes this policy). Moreover, the candidate may not lose much support among the remaining 98 percent, even though this policy harms them, because the damage done is small and may be offset by benefits under other policies he or she supports.

In effect, special interest legislation that enables a politician to put together an overall majority by combining numerous programs that benefit separate minorities is an example of *implicit logrolling*. As noted earlier, logrolling makes voters consider different policies simultaneously, and that is exactly what must be done when voters choose among candidates offering different policy packages. In this way, voters are led to support a politician who favors some policies they do not want to obtain the one program they do want.

Rational voter ignorance often increases the incentive of politicians to favor special interest legislation. The harm done to each member of the majority by one policy is quite small and in many cases difficult to estimate. (What annual cost do you bear from milk price supports or subsidies to airports?) Voters are often rational in not making an attempt to estimate the damage done from hundreds of policies that affect them only slightly and often indirectly. Instead, they concentrate on policies that have large and obvious effects on their own well-being, that is, on special interest legislation that benefits or harms them.

Rational voter ignorance has still other effects on the behavior of vote-maximizing politicians. Any policy has both costs and benefits, but the visibility of these effects (that is, how obvious they are to voters) varies widely from policy to policy. Some consequences of policies are more hidden and difficult than others are for the average person to perceive. For example, a policy with hidden benefits but apparent costs is unlikely to be favored by politicians because voters underestimate the true benefits. The political process is consequently biased against policies with hidden benefits and visible costs. Conversely, it is biased toward policies with highly visible benefits and hidden costs.

Consider a policy of subsidizing medical research out of general income taxes. The benefit is an increased probability of finding a cure for some disease, but many voters who might benefit in the future if a cure is found are likely to be unaware of this benefit (some would not even be born). The tax costs, on the other hand, are quite obvious. If voters sufficiently underestimate the benefits, politicians may be led to oppose the policy even if it is efficient.

In fact, politicians may have incentives to design policies in ways that make benefits clear to those who benefit and costs difficult to perceive for those who are harmed, if it is possible. The most obvious costs are generally taxes, but even these can often be levied in a way to obscure their burden. Taxes that are nominally paid by businesses often are actually borne by consumers or workers, but the people who bear the final burden may be unaware of it. Corporate income taxes, excise taxes, customs duties, the employer portion of social security taxes, and deficit finance are all methods of financing expenditures that depress the disposable incomes of people who may be unaware of it. It is probably no accident that nearly 50 percent of all federal expenditures are financed by these methods.

Elected representatives may also find that the information and arguments they are exposed to are not exactly balanced. James Payne examined the testimony at 14 House and Senate committees dealing with spending programs and tabulated the orientations of the more than 1,000 witnesses who testified: "The results were dramatic. One thousand and fourteen witnesses appeared in favor of the spending; only seven could be counted as opponents. . . . In other words, pro-spending witnesses outnumbered anti-spending witnesses 145 to one!"[4] What effect this barrage of pro-spending arguments has on congresspersons is not clear, but Payne believes it makes them more likely to accept uncritically the view that government spending is more beneficial than private spending. On the other hand, politicians must know that they will also be held responsible for the taxes that finance these programs, and this should act as a check on any tendency to overspend.

Although it is impossible to be precise in this matter, it seems clear that vote-maximizing politicians are sometimes led to favor genuinely efficient policies and sometimes to favor highly inefficient policies. *All other things being the same,* the greater the total benefits received by the voting public relative to the total costs of some policy, the more votes a politician can gain by supporting it. This is the positive aspect of the incentives political institutions give politicians. Other things, however, are not always the same, and politicians can sometimes gain votes by favoring policies that benefit some voters but impose greater (possibly hidden) costs on others.

[4]James L. Payne, "The Congressional Brainwashing Machine," *The Public Interest,* 100:4 (Summer 1990).

Bureaus and Bureaucrats

Congressional actions can be thought of as expressing a collective *demand* for public services, but there is also a need for an institution to design and implement policies. Government agencies or bureaus are generally empowered to carry out the policies enacted by Congress. Recent research has suggested that bureaus do not simply respond passively to the dictates of Congress but instead take an active role in the decision-making process and exercise some degree of power in determining policy.

The term *bureaucracy* is often used to refer to any large organization, but it is necessary to recognize important differences between public and private bureaus. Private bureaus are usually part of a business organization that is operated for a profit, so the activities of private bureaus are subject to a market test: They must produce something that people are willing to purchase. Government bureaus are nonprofit organizations that do not sell their services directly to the public. In a sense, they sell their services to Congress, but they do not set a price per unit and allow Congress to determine the quantity. Instead, they obtain an annual lump-sum appropriation to cover the total costs of all the services provided. In addition, public bureaus, as distinct from private bureaus, are generally monopolies. The Department of Health and Human Services, for instance, is responsible for almost all policies dealing with medical care; there are no other bureaus competing with it to obtain funds from Congress in this area.

Given these differences between public and private bureaus, we should expect that the bureaucratic supply of public services would produce different results than the private supply. To see how the results are likely to differ, let us begin by considering what goals might motivate the top-level bureaucrats. Bureaus are not allowed to operate at a profit, so we cannot assume that they try to maximize profits. Alternatively, however, bureaucrats can attempt to maximize the total size of their budgets.[5] A larger budget will generally mean higher salaries, more power, and more prestige for top-level bureaucrats. In addition, the internal advancement of personnel virtually ensures that those who reach the top will consider the activities of the bureaus highly beneficial and worthy of enlargement.

Assuming that bureaucrats attempt to maximize their budgets is not equivalent to assuming that they will be successful. (Recall that competitive firms are assumed to maximize profits; yet they end up with zero economic profits.) Congress, after all, must approve budget requests. Bureaus, however, may be in a favorable bargaining position to realize their goals. From observing congressional action over a period of years, bureaus have a fairly good idea of the maximum budgets Congress will approve. By proposing a budget of this size on a take-it-or-leave-it basis, the bureau may secure approval of a budget larger than Congress would actually prefer.

[5]William A. Niskanen, Jr. *Bureaucracy and Representative Government* (Chicago: Aldine-Atherton, 1971).

If the proposed budget is larger than Congress desires, why doesn't Congress just appropriate a smaller amount of money? The answer is that the entire legislative body does not know the actual costs associated with various programs overseen by the bureau. Legislators have to oversee thousands of different programs, and lack the time or the incentive (because their constituents are rationally ignorant) to become informed about the program costs and options in each area. Members of Congress must rely heavily on what the experts (frequently from the bureaus!) tell them about costs and benefits. In this setting, the typical congressional representative has little option but either to approve or to disapprove the bureau's proposed budget. A representative may vote to approve a budget that is larger than the one he or she would support if aware of the relevant alternatives. The all-or-nothing nature of the choice confronting members of Congress, together with lack of information, makes it possible for bureaus to secure overlarge budgets.

This analysis suggests that the interaction between Congress and government bureaus has a tendency to produce budgets that are too large. There are factors, however, that may limit this tendency. For example, Congress may take a more active and informed role in determining bureau policy, perhaps by employing its own experts (e.g., the Congressional Budget Office) to help formulate policy alternatives. In addition, the tendency toward overexpansion probably does not operate with equal force for all bureaus. If the policies being administered are sufficiently simple and easy to understand, Congress will not have to rely so much on the bureau for advice and can more effectively monitor the bureau's activities. Simplicity, then, from the bureau's point of view, may have its drawbacks; bureaus may be led to make the policies so complicated that they can be understood only by the bureau's own experts.

Bureaus may also have an incentive to produce a different type of service than would be provided by competitive firms under identical cost and demand conditions. C. M. Lindsay observed that the "product" of a bureau is usually a complex good with many characteristics that can be produced in different proportions.[6] For example, hospital care can be provided in lavish rooms with little attention from doctors or with much attention from doctors in sparsely furnished rooms. Lindsay argued that some characteristics are more visible and easily monitored than others are. Just as voter ignorance may lead politicians to neglect policies with hidden benefits, ignorance on the part of politicians may lead bureaus to provide highly visible and easily measured services at the expense of other, possibly more important, services. As evidence supporting this hypothesis, Lindsay examined the operation of Veterans Administration hospitals and found that they provide small quantities of "invisible" services (e.g., good-quality service) but relatively large quantities of highly "visible" services (e.g., long average lengths of stay for patients in hospitals).

---

[6]Cotton M. Lindsay, "A Theory of Government Enterprise," *Journal of Political Economy,* 84:1061 (Oct. 1976).

To see how this concept of relative visibility may sometimes give bureaucrats perverse incentives, consider the Food and Drug Administration (FDA). Amendments in 1962 gave the FDA the authority to withhold drugs from the market until they were proven safe. A bureaucrat administering this program can impose costs on the public in two different ways. First, genuinely effective drugs can be withheld too long, causing suffering and death because of the unavailability of the drugs. Alternatively, dangerous drugs can be approved for sale, causing suffering and death from their use. These two errors differ greatly in their visibility. Those who become ill or die because drugs are not marketed are unlikely to know enough to blame the FDA for the delayed introduction of the drug. If, alternatively, the FDA mistakenly approves a dangerous drug such as thalidomide, the subsequent suffering will be readily connected with its cause. Faced with these alternatives, which type of mistake would you expect the FDA to make more often? It seems likely that the FDA would be overly cautious and delay the introduction of drugs for longer periods of time than the public's interest requires so as to avoid the possibility of the highly visible disastrous effects of approving a dangerous drug. Empirical evidence suggests that this has, in fact, been true.[7] For example, approval of beta blockers (drugs that can reduce heart attacks) was delayed by the FDA for 10 years, and during that time an estimated 10,000 people died from ailments that the drug could have prevented.[8]

Pressure Groups and Lobbies

Perhaps the most maligned groups in politics are the organized lobbies, which actively attempt to influence legislators' votes on pending legislation, as well as the content of bills brought to a vote. The American Medical Association, agricultural interests, the National Rifle Association, labor unions, the Sierra Club, Common Cause, and many more groups finance lobbies that attempt to influence legislation. To many people, the successes of these organizations exemplify what is wrong with the political process.

Before considering the impact such organizations have on policy determination, we should begin by asking why lobbies exist in the first place. Groups of people often have a common interest in influencing legislation of a certain type, but that does not explain how such lobbies can be financed. A lobby that pushes for a certain type of legislation simultaneously helps all those who will benefit from the legislation; in effect, it provides a *public good* for those who favor the legislation (and a *public bad* for those who oppose it). Thus, the free rider problem will hinder the voluntary formation of lobbies. After all, each one of us has an interest in promoting (or opposing) hundreds of different policies, but we rarely donate money to support lobbies in these areas.

[7]Sam Peltzman, *Regulation of Pharmaceutical Innovation* (Washington, D.C.: American Enterprise Institute, 1974).

[8]William H. Wardell, "A Close Inspection of the 'Calm Look'," *Journal of the American Medical Association,* 239:2010. (May 12, 1978).

Compared to the hundreds of thousands of "special interests" affected by government policy, the few hundred active lobbies are more noticeable for their relative scarcity than anything else. The free rider problem explains why there are not more lobbies, but how can we explain the ones that do exist? One explanation is that lobbies arise when there are relatively few parties greatly affected by a particular type of policy. When small numbers are involved, the free rider problem can be overcome; this probably accounts for the way businesses in a concentrated industry are able to lobby for policies like tariffs. Alternatively, Mancur Olson developed a theory to explain the existence of lobbies in a large number of settings.[9] Often a lobby results as a by-product of an organization that is formed to further some nonpublic good type of interest. Workers often pay dues to labor unions, for example, not to obtain favorable labor legislation from lobbying efforts but rather in order to obtain employment (a private good). Unions can use part of the dues to finance the public good, lobbying, for its members; thus, lobbying activities are actually a by-product of union membership. Olson shows how this "by-product theory" can explain the way many important lobbies representing the interests of thousands of people obtain financial support. Nonetheless, the difficulties of overcoming the free rider problem are apparently severe enough that there are relatively few powerful lobbies.

Given the existence of lobbies, are they able to secure favorable legislation? Actually, how lobbies will be able to influence legislation is not at all obvious. Politicians are interested in the vote-getting potential of their actions, and the members of unorganized groups (with no lobbies) can vote just as easily as the members of organized groups.[10] To mention an obvious example, Congress passed dozens of pieces of legislation in the 1960s benefiting the poor and elderly, but these groups were not represented by professional lobbies. This legislation was passed because members of these groups represented large voting blocs. Members of groups with lobbies also vote, but they can cast no more votes by virtue of having a lobby than they could without one. How, then, do they represent a stronger political force than an unorganized group does?

Once the prevalence of rational ignorance on the part of voters and politicians is recalled, it is possible to understand how a lobby can have an impact greater than an unorganized group of the same size. Politicians do not have full knowledge of the interests of their constituents: A lobby can inform a politician that there are x thousands of voters with a deep interest in a particular issue. Voters often do not know what politician is most likely to further their interests, but their lobby can inform them, and once informed, they are more likely to vote. In a world of rational ignorance, lobbies can probably mobilize more voters and bring these votes to the

---

[9]Mancur Olson, Jr., *The Logic of Collective Action* (New York: Schocken Books, 1968).

[10]Richard E. Wagner makes this point in his review of Olson's book "Pressure Groups and Political Entrepreneurs: A Review Article," *Papers on Non-Market Decision Making* (Charlottesville, Va.: Thomas Jefferson Center for Political Ecoomy, 1966), pp. 161–170.

attention of the relevant politicians more readily than if the group were unorganized. So lobbies may exercise some independent influence on legislative decisions.

Although lobbies can have a differential impact for these reasons, their power is probably much less than is popularly supposed. We have already explained why the political process can produce special interest legislation even without lobbies. Lobbies perhaps accentuate the tendency for special interest legislation, but most of the pressure would exist even in their absence.

Public Choice Analysis: Two Examples

At present public choice theory does not provide a formal framework that can be easily applied to the analysis of concrete problems. Rather, it emphasizes a way of looking at the incentives confronting participants in the political process that can give us valuable insights into how government works. The following two examples illustrate attempts to apply this approach.

Governmental Provision of Goods and Services

In some cases, governmental units provide goods or services that can also be provided by private firms. This makes it possible to evaluate the performances of these alternative methods of production. Consider the results of several studies that have attempted to make this comparison.

Richard Muth estimated that public housing projects cost about 20 percent more to produce than comparable housing built privately.[11]

In a study of garbage collection in 260 cities, E. S. Savas found that the cost of garbage collection provided directly by municipal governments was about 50 percent greater than when the same service was provided by private firms contracting with cities.[12]

Roger Ahlbrandt found that the cost of providing fire-protection services in Scottsdale, Arizona, where they are provided by a private firm under contract to the community, was 47 percent less than the cost in comparable communities where the services are provided directly by the government.[13]

Commenting on a survey of some 50 studies comparing public and private provision, Dennis Mueller comments: "In only 2 ... were public firms found to be more efficient than their private counterparts. ... The evidence

[11]Richard Muth, *Public Housing* (Washington, D.C.: American Enterprise Institute), 1973.

[12]E. S. Savas, *The Organization and Efficiency of Solid Waste Collection* (Lexington, Mass.: D. C. Heath, 1977).

[13]Roger Ahlbrandt, "Efficiency in the Provision of Fire Services," *Public Choice,* 16:1 (Fall 1973).

that public provision of a service reduces the efficiency of its provision seems overwhelming."[14]

These studies suggest that there may be a general tendency for governmental provision to involve higher costs to provide a given level of service. From a public choice perspective, the basic questions are why this might be the case and whether anything can be done about it.

To understand why government provision of certain goods or services may involve higher than necessary costs, public choice theory suggests that we should consider the incentives confronting the people involved. Do providers have an incentive to produce the service at the lowest possible cost? In a private firm, if costs can be cut without sacrificing quantity or quality, profits will rise, and the prospect of higher profits gives private firms the incentive to hold costs down. In addition, if costs get out of hand, a private firm may be driven out of business by competition.

A government agency, however, is a nonprofit organization. An administrator of a government agency may not gain by reducing costs. There is no single individual (manager or owner) who receives the "profit" from a successful cost-cutting activity; instead the gain from any cost-cutting endeavor is spread widely among the general (and rationally ignorant) public. In fact, government administrators may actually suffer personal losses from improving efficiency. As a businessman who was asked to manage the postal service in 1972 noted: "Postmasters were actually paid [based] on how many employees they had, how many branch offices they had, on how many trucks. . . . Can you imagine a greater disincentive?"[15]

In a government organization, it is difficult to give managers or employees a strong incentive to control costs since the profit motive is absent. Some incentives, however, may be provided by Congress or whatever legislative body oversees the organization. But at this level, too, we must consider whether members of Congress have much incentive to perform their constitutionally mandated oversight function well. Congress passes more than a thousand pieces of new legislation each year, and the number of existing agencies, laws, and regulations that Congress is supposed to oversee must run into the tens of thousands. Knowing how well existing legislation is enforced is not a prerequisite for election to Congress (with a rationally ignorant voting public). Members of Congress may be better able to enhance their prospects for reelection by proposing new legislation, giving speeches, writing to constituents, and so on, than by carefully supervising the myriad programs already in existence.[16]

---

[14]Dennis C. Mueller, *Public Choice II* (Cambridge: Cambridge University Press, 1989), pp. 261, 266.

[15]Quoted in Charles Wolfe, Jr., "A Theory of Nonmarket Failure: Framework for Implementation Analysis," *Journal of Law and Economics,* 22(1):107 (Apr. 1979).

[16]Some casual evidence that Congress is very lax in performing its oversight function is given by Donald Lambro, "Congressional Oversights," *Policy Review,* 16:115 (Spring 1981).

When looked at from a public choice perspective, it is thus not surprising that governmental services may sometimes be provided at unnecessarily high costs. Whether there is any way to alleviate this problem is not clear. When the good or service can be provided by private firms and sold to the government, we can make use of market incentives to contain costs by having government purchase from the private sector rather than provide the good itself. When the good or service must be provided directly by government, however, there is no such easy solution.

Will Government Policies Benefit the Poor?

It is often taken for granted that government policies benefit the poor. Certainly there is a large number of programs designed to provide assistance to poor persons, as we will see in later chapters. There is also a large number of programs that benefit high-income persons (e.g., agricultural subsidies) and middle-income persons (e.g., social security). Taking all government policies together, it may not be so obvious that the poor come out ahead. There are difficult factual and analytical issues involved in determining the overall distributional effect of government, and we will also examine them in later chapters. Here we wish to consider a related theoretical issue: whether the political process can be expected to redistribute income to lower-income persons on balance.

In a provocative analysis, two scholars well versed in public choice theory, Dwight Lee and Richard McKenzie, have argued that government policies on balance probably hurt the poor! In their words: "There is no *a priori* reason ... for believing the distributional outcome of political activity will differ much, if any, from that of market activity. ... [E]xpanding government for the stated purpose of improving the relative position of the poor will almost surely fail to do so."[17]

The Lee-McKenzie argument can be summarized as follows. They suggest that we conceive of the political process as a competitive arena where people interact as they attempt to secure benefits for themselves by getting particular policies enacted. The poor compete in the political process, but so do other nonpoor persons. Because the institutions, or rules of the game, differ between the private market and the political process, we would not necessarily expect the same people to be equally successful in both settings. However, "Whether under market or political competition, the more aggressive, ambitious, articulate, hardworking and persistent individuals are, the more likely they are to be successful. Thus, people who are poor because they lack the skills to succeed in the marketplace are unlikely to compete successfully for resources in the public sector."[18]

[17]Dwight R. Lee and Richard B. McKenzie, "Helping the Poor Through Governmental Poverty Programs: The Triumph of Rhetoric Over Reality," in *Public Choice and Constitutional Economics,* edited by J. Gwartney and R. Wagner (Greenwich, Conn.: JAI Press, 1988), pp. 387, 390.

[18]Ibid., p. 390.

In short, Lee and McKenzie argue that the same lack of skills and abilities that result in people's having low market incomes will place them at a competitive disadvantage as they try to get enacted public policies that benefit them. This argument, if correct, undermines a major rationale for many government policies, since achieving a more equal distribution of income by raising the incomes of those at the bottom is the express justification for much government activity.

Are Lee and McKenzie correct? As we mentioned at the outset of this chapter, there is no well-established and accepted body of public choice theory that we can call on to answer this question. Nonetheless, there are at least two characteristics of the political process that would appear to work in a direction opposite to the one they emphasize.

First, the ability to influence public policy may be more equally distributed than the ability to generate market incomes. Lee and McKenzie point out that the poor may not be able to articulate and promote their cause as effectively as other groups, but they are just as able to cast votes. Even though a wealthy person may have 10 or 100 times the resources of a poor person, both still have just one vote each. That gives the poor person a *relative* advantage in the political process as compared with the market process. Votes are much more equally distributed than market incomes, and as a first approximation we would expect this arrangement to be reflected in more egalitarian political outcomes than market outcomes. For a politician, the prospect of benefiting (and getting the votes of) 10 million low-income persons with, say, a food stamp program that can be financed with taxes on 1 million high-income persons (possibly losing their votes) must look like an attractive proposition.

Of course, it should also be pointed out that a smaller proportion of the poor vote than do the nonpoor, which weakens this argument. Still, it is true that actual votes are much more equally distributed than market incomes.

A second factor, however, also suggests that policies will be enacted that redistribute income downward. That is the altruism of many nonpoor persons toward the poor. The poor do not have to depend only on their own political skills to get policies to help themselves. Numerous opinion surveys show that many middle- and upper-income Americans favor programs that help the poor and are willing to pay taxes to finance them. Even if the poor did not vote at all, we suspect there would still be welfare programs for their assistance (though perhaps not as generous as when the poor also vote for them).

It is worth pointing out that when some or all of the nonpoor care about the well-being of the poor, policies that transfer income to the poor provide a public good. Many nonpoor persons simultaneously secure benefits when actions are taken that help the poor; the benefits are nonrival. Thus, there will be votes to be gained from among the nonpoor by politicians who favor redistributive policies.

For these two reasons, we suspect the political process has a tendency to redistribute income downward. The evidence, cited in Chapter 8, we think supports this proposition. Nevertheless, the argument of Lee and McKenzie should not be totally discounted, for it reminds us that the political process is subject to many competing forces, and their interaction is not well understood. Certainly many of the policies that emerge from this process help the nonpoor at the expense of the poor (e.g., agricultural policies that raise the price of food), and that does raise questions about how well the political process really works.

The Growth of Government

As pointed out in Chapter 1, government spending has grown relative to the size of the economy throughout this century. A central question for public choice theory is: Why has this growth occurred?[19] At one level, the growth has occurred because U.S. citizens have elected representatives who have voted to increase spending, but that reason does not really clarify the underlying factors. If voters are just now getting the amount of government they want, why is that so much greater than in 1900? Furthermore, whatever the underlying cause or causes, it must be worldwide in scope, for governments have grown in importance over this century throughout the world, as indicated for a few industrial societies in Table 3–5. This suggests that the forces enlarging government are not peculiar to any specific society, so we should not suppose, for example, that Franklin Delano Roosevelt's presidency was a major cause.

Among the many possible causes of government growth, we will examine four of the more prominent ones emphasized in the literature on this subject.

Government Growth from Changes in the Economic Environment

This argument basically assumes that the government is providing what the public wants, and it holds that factors have changed so that the public wants to spend a larger proportion of its income on government-provided services. To evaluate this argument, think of the government as passively providing as much of some set of public goods or publicly provided services as demanded. What determines the quantity demanded? In economics, we would emphasize income, prices, and tastes as primary determinants of demand. So we can begin by considering whether changes in these factors over time would lead to greater government spending being chosen by a representative taxpayer (the median voter).

---

[19]Two helpful surveys of the literature dealing with this subject are Mueller, *Public Choice II,* Chapter 17, and Thomas E. Borcherding, "The Causes of Government Expenditure Growth: A Survey of the U.S. Evidence," *Journal of Public Economics,* 28:361 (Dec. 1985).

Table 3–5   Growth of Government Expenditures (percentage of GDP)

Year	Sweden	Japan	Canada	U.S.	U.K.	Germany
1900	6.5%		4.9%	2.8%	15.6%	
1910	7.0		5.7	2.1	13.2	
1920	7.5		9.5	7.2	29.1	
1930	8.1	11.2%	7.7	12.2	27.1	
1940	10.7	14.9	28.5	20.3	31.8	37.9%
1950	16.8	16.0	22.0	24.4	39.2	28.6
1960	26.8	13.0	25.1	26.6	29.5	28.1
1970	35.9	13.9	28.5	31.3	33.5	34.0
1980	56.9	25.0	37.5	32.6	41.5	43.1
1990	59.1	26.2	44.0	34.6	38.1	42.6

Sources: 1. *1960–1990 Historical Statistics OECD Economic Outlook,* Table 6.4; 2. Thelma Liesner, "1900–1950: One Hundred Years of Economic Statistics," *The Economist* (1989).

Real per capita incomes have grown throughout this century. At higher incomes, people demand larger quantities of all (normal) goods. But when will they choose to spend a larger *percentage* of income on goods when income rises? The answer depends on the income elasticity of demand, which relates percentage changes in quantity demanded to percentage changes in income. When income elasticity is unity, this means that a 10 percent increase in income leads to an equal 10 percent increase in quantity demanded, and thus no change in the percentage of income spent on the good. An income elasticity of demand greater than 1 for government-provided goods would lead, other things being equal, to a growing share of income spent on government when incomes grow. A number of studies have attempted to estimate the income elasticities of demand for a variety of government-provided goods,, and in some cases the estimates imply an income elasticity exceeding 1 (but not by much), but in more cases the estimates are below 1. It appears that growth in per capita real incomes by itself cannot account for the growth of government.

A second economic factor is price, the cost per unit of government-provided goods. Recall that if the price rises and the price elasticity of demand is below 1 (in absolute value: an inelastic demand), desired expenditures on the good rise. There is some evidence that unit costs of government-provided goods have risen faster than those of privately provided goods, so the relevant relative price of government-provided goods has risen over time. (This is thought to be due to the fact that many government-provided goods are services, such as education, where productivity gains are slow.) In addition, most estimates suggest that price elasticity of demand is lower than 1 for many government services. However, empirical examinations suggest that this factor can explain only a small fraction of the growth in spending.[20] It cannot explain very much because a lot of government spending is not on goods and services but instead involves transfers of income.

That leaves us with tastes as a determinant of demand. Economists are reluctant to use a change in tastes as an explanation since that often is just an ad hoc explanation that can be used to explain anything. Can we believe that people today just have more intense desires for the things government does than they did 100 years ago (and that this has happened in all countries)? That offers an explanation, but not a very satisfying one and one that is very difficult to evaluate against the evidence. Another taste change, in a broader sense, would be a change in political ideology. Socialism did emerge in the late nineteenth century and became popular in this century. But it is hard to believe that pro-government ideologies have driven all Western governments to gradually become larger throughout the century.

Expansion from Redistributional Forces

This explanation holds that political forces lead to increased redistribution of income over time in democratic societies. It is true that much of the growth of government in all countries has been in redistributive activities, broadly conceived (to include not only rich-to-poor transfers but also redistribution between other groups, such as from the young to the elderly, as with social security). So if we are to explain the growth of government, we need to explain why government plays a much more active redistributional role now than in the past.

But why is there more redistribution now? It might be thought that as people become wealthier, they would want to give more to the poor. That is probably true, but to account for growth in the share of income redistributed, the income elasticity of demand would have to exceed 1. At least as inferred from charitable contributions, that is not true: Wealthier people do not tend to give a larger share of their income to charities.[21]

There have been some formal voting models that attempt to explain redistribution as resulting from the voting behavior of those who gain from it. In one such model, people with incomes below the median level vote to transfer income to themselves from those with higher incomes.[22] But why would redistribution rise over time? One answer is that the expansion of voting rights to people who have lower incomes (women, minorities) might cause this result. However, working in the other direction is the fact that incomes have generally become more equally distributed over this century,

---

[20]See Mueller, *Public Choice II,* pp. 325–26, for a discussion and citations to the literature.

[21]Charles T. Clotfelter, *Federal Tax Policy and Charitable Giving* (Chicago: University of Chicago Press, 1985), Chapter 2.

[22]Allan H. Meltzer and S. F. Richard, "A Rational Theory of the Size of Government," *Journal of Political Economy,* 89:914 (Oct. 1981).

and this voting model would predict that change would lead to less redistribution. In addition, this model explains only the rich-to-poor redistribution, not the large social welfare spending that shifts income around between middle-income groups.

Although public choice models can explain why redistribution occurs, it is more difficult to explain why this activity of government has grown so much over time.

The Declining Cost of Collecting Taxes

In the nineteenth century, it would have been technologically and administratively very difficult to collect taxes representing a large share of national income. The United States was predominantly an agricultural economy, with much income produced and consumed on the farm. Systematic records were not kept; accounting procedures were undeveloped. The most important taxes were customs duties (tariffs) that could be collected at a few major ports and a few excise taxes. Income and payroll taxes did not exist, and even if they did, they would have been difficult to administer given the nature of the economy.

Today, of course, things are quite different. Records are kept of most economic transactions, and it is feasible for the government to tax just about anything. In short, the technology of tax collection has changed, making it feasible for government to spend and tax large shares of national income.

There is much truth to this argument, but it does not provide the explanation we seek. Even if fully correct, it seems to imply that the democratic pressures toward big government always existed but were thwarted by the practical difficulties of collecting taxes. The argument does not tell us what these pressures are. In addition, the fact that governments have continued to grow since 1950, when all major taxes were in place, suggests that something else must be involved. Finally, the argument does not explain why some national governments spend so much more than others.

The Role of Pressure Groups and Government Bureaucrats

Almost every study of the growth of government mentions pressure groups as a possible cause. We have argued that it is possible for pressure groups to have an impact on government policy, and it is certainly true that the number of organized lobbies has grown tremendously. However, the exact process that leads to a growing role for government policy is unclear. One study has found that the number of organized interest groups in a country is positively related to the relative size of the public sector.[23] But it could be that bigger government leads to more organized pressure groups rather than the reverse. The American Association of Retired Persons (AARP) became a potent political force many years after social security was enacted.

---

[23]Dennis C. Mueller and P. Murrell, "Interest Groups and the Size of Government," *Public Choice,* 48(2), 1986, pp. 125–45.

Government agencies and bureaucrats may also play a role in expanding government. Generally, bureaucrats wish to see their programs expanded beyond the level desired by the public. The institutional environment may make it possible for bureaucrats to succeed in getting legislatures to fund larger budgets. However, most models of bureaucracy only explain why government programs may be bigger than the public wants, not why they grow over time.

Despite these difficulties, the activities of pressure groups and government bureaucracies, and possible interactions between them, are high on most lists of possible causes of government growth. It should be noted that this explanation differs in a very important respect from the first three that we examined. The first three explanations essentially have government size respond to the demands of the citizens, but this last argument suggests that government growth may be contrary to the wishes of the public.

It is clear that we do not have a satisfactory explanation of why governments have grown. Although bits and pieces of the puzzle have perhaps been identified, the whole picture remains tantalizingly elusive. This is a reflection of our earlier caveat that there is no fully developed, adequate theory of public choice. But the issue of what determines the size of government indicates the importance of continued work in this area.

Significance of "Government Failure"

For many years economists have studied the functioning of private markets. Circumstances under which markets function well and under which they function poorly are fairly well understood. When markets produce inefficient results, *market failure* is said to occur. Monopolies, externalities, and public goods are now familiar examples of market failure.

Only in relatively recent years have economists (and other social scientists) begun to study how the political process *actually* functions (as distinct from how it would function in some nonexistent utopia). The result of this inquiry is the emerging theory of public choice. It has become clear that there is such a thing as "government failure," that is, government's enacting policies that produce inefficient and/or inequitable results as a result of the rational behavior of participants in the political process.

The public choice approach to the analysis of political decision making should lead to a major alteration in the way government is viewed. Thirty years ago, it was not uncommon for economists, observing that Congress had passed a housing subsidy, to make a statement like "We, the people, through our elected representatives, have decided that housing should be subsidized." As a *partial* description of the forces that shape actual government decisions, which emphasizes the positive aspects of democratic processes, this statement may be adequate. It is, however, incomplete and naive. Just as we should not think that private markets always function efficiently, it is equally incorrect to picture government as always operating to reflect accurately the public's interests.

Public choice theory, with its implication of occasional government failure, is significant for two somewhat different reasons. First, we must keep the possibility of government failure in mind when we evaluate the market and find it not functioning too well in some area. Although one frequently hears the argument "The market has failed; therefore, the government *should* intervene," this is a logical non sequitur. Both the market and the political system are processes for allocating resources and distributing incomes, and each has defects. The fact that the market is inefficient does *not* imply that government will do any better. It is always possible that government intervention will make a bad situation worse. The converse of this non sequitur is also logically invalid. In situations in which the government has performed poorly, it does not follow that the market will necessarily function better. Consider this argument: "The influence of the military-industrial complex has led to great waste in the defense budget; therefore, we should rely on the market to provide national defense." The fallacy is clear. Both arguments are still far too common.

In deciding whether the market or the government will produce better results, we must choose between two imperfect mechanisms. The forces that shape both market and government outcomes must be understood in order to make wise decisions. Unfortunately, public choice theory is not sufficiently developed to identify the areas in which government is likely to be relatively inefficient, but it does raise the proper questions, and future research may provide the answers.

There is a second reason why the public choice approach is important. Public choice theory emphasizes how governmental decisions depend on procedures and institutions in the political process and on the incentives created for participants in the process. These institutions and procedures are not sacrosanct; they can be changed. Reform of the governmental decision-making process may lead to the selection of better government policies. Although our emphasis in this chapter has been on the way current political institutions function, public choice theory can also be used to compare alternative methods of making and enforcing government policy.

In recent years, there have been several highly publicized reforms in the political process: Lowering of the legal voting age, easier voter registration requirements, and limits on campaign contributions are examples. As should be clear from the analysis in this chapter, these reforms are unlikely to have any significant impact on actual policymaking. They do not in any way modify the important factors we have identified in the political process. They are largely window dressing, exactly the types of reforms we would expect to emerge from current political processes and institutions.

What would a reform that would have major repercussions look like? Consider, for example, the following:

1. Members of Congress shall be determined by a process of random selection from among the general public.
2. Some types of legislation shall require a three-fourths majority, rather than a simple majority, to pass.
3. Decisions on major policy proposals shall be made by direct majority voting by the general public rather than by Congress.
4. Every expenditure proposal shall be linked to a (visible) tax increase so that individual voters can easily determine their share of the cost.

Clearly, these reforms would have far-reaching effects. We do not mean to imply that we think these reforms would necessarily improve the public choice process, but they illustrate substantive proposals for meaningful reform. (The reader will find it an instructive exercise to apply the approach of this chapter to determine the advantages and disadvantages of these proposals.) Even if we can identify desirable reforms, the sticky question remains: Should we expect the imperfect political process to adopt these reforms?

Review Questions and Problems

1. In a majority voting model like that illustrated in Figure 3–1, what will be the effect on the equilibrium output if a proportional tax on income is used instead of the equal-per-person tax shown in the diagram?

2. What is rational voter ignorance? Does it lead voters to prefer larger or smaller government budgets than they would if they understood completely the effects of government policies?

3. How would political outcomes differ if majority voting were used to determine the spending on each policy separately instead of having voters elect representatives who then make these decisions.?

4. If majority voting is used to determine the output of a public good, will all voters be satisfied with the output selected? Will the output be efficient?

5. You are the chairperson of a three-person committee that is going to use majority voting to decide on which of three dates a test will be given. A vote will be taken on two dates, and the winner of that vote will vie with the third date to determine the final choice. If you know the preferences of the other committee members, can you influence the outcome by deciding the order of the votes? Give an example to support your answer. (*Hint:* Consider the cyclical majority phenomenon.)

6. What effect would a presidential line item veto have on logrolling in Congress?

7. Provide an explanation of why House and Senate committees dealing with spending programs hear more pro-spending witnesses.

8. Discuss possible reasons why a government continues to provide a service even though it could be provided by private firms at a lower cost.

9. How does the material in this chapter help you evaluate the following statement: "Private firms pollute too much because they ignore the external costs, so government must intervene to stop them."

10. How can we explain the existence of government policies that are opposed by a majority of voters?

11. "An alternative to majority voting is to require unanimous consent before a program is enacted. This would guarantee that fewer people would be harmed by the policy, whereas some people are always harmed when majority voting is used. Therefore, unanimity is a better voting rule than majority voting is." True or false? Explain.

12. "Democracy gives the majority what it wants." Discuss.

13. That government spending grew from 8.7 percent of net national product in 1902 to more than 37 percent today shows that *either* government spending was too small in 1902 *or* that it is too large today. True or false? Discuss.

14. Are there reasons to expect the political process to redistribute income in favor of low-income persons? How do you explain the existence of programs that tend to favor middle-income persons?

15. What are the four reasons discussed in the text for the growth of government? Can you think of other reasons why governments have grown?

Supplementary Readings

BORCHERDING, THOMAS E. *Budgets and Bureaucrats: The Sources of Government Growth.* Durham, N.C.: Duke University Press, 1977.

BUCHANAN, JAMES M. *Public Finance in Democratic Process.* Chapel Hill: University of North Carolina Press, 1967.

BUCHANAN, JAMES M., and ROBERT D. TOLLISON, eds. *The Theory of Public Choice—II.* Ann Arbor: University of Michigan Press, 1984.

BUCHANAN, JAMES M., and GORDON TULLOCK. *The Calculus of Consent.* Ann Arbor: University of Michigan Press, 1962.

DOWNS, ANTHONY. *An Economic Theory of Democracy.* New York: Harper & Row, 1957.

———. "Why the Government Budget Is Too Small in a Democracy." In Edmund S. Phelps, ed., *Private Wants and Public Needs,* rev. ed. New York: W. W. Norton, 1965.

GWARTNEY, JAMES D., and RICHARD E. WAGNER, eds. *Public Choice and Constitutional Economics.* Greenwich, Conn.: JAI Press, 1988.

INMAN, ROBERT P. "Markets, Governments, and the 'New' Political Economy." In Alan J. Auerbach and Martin Feldstein, eds. *Handbook of Public Economics.* Amsterdam, The Netherlands: Elsevier Science Publishers, 1987, pp. 647–777.

MUELLER, DENNIS C. *Public Choice II.* Cambridge, England: Cambridge University Press, 1989.

SCHULTZE, CHARLES L. "Is There a Bias Toward Excess in U.S. Government Budgets or Deficits?" *Journal of Economic Perspectives* 6(2):25–43 (Spring 1992).

WYCKOFF, P. G. "The Simple Analytics of Slack-maximizing Bureaucracy." *Public Choice* 67(1):35–47 (October 1990).

NISKANEN, WILLIAM A., JR. *Bureaucracy and Representative Government.* Chicago: Aldine, 1971.

Principles of Expenditure Analysis

*E*XPENDITURE ANALYSIS INVOLVES USING ECONOMIC THEORY to determine the consequences of government expenditure programs. Unfortunately, there is no general analysis that is applicable to all expenditure programs because these programs take many different forms. The consequences vary greatly, depending on exactly how the government spends the funds. Consequently, it is necessary to proceed case by case, although some types of programs are clearly more important than others. In this chapter we will examine some of the more significant economic effects of fairly common types of expenditure programs. In later chapters, we will consider specific programs in more detail.

The economic effects of expenditure programs fall primarily into two categories: allocative and distributive. *Allocative* effects refer to the way an expenditure program affects the pattern of goods and services produced by the economy. For example, does a particular subsidy lead to an increase in the output and consumption of the subsidized good? Although common folklore assumes that a subsidy increases output, some important real-world subsidies have had the opposite effect, at least for some of the people being subsidized. As we will see, subsidies to housing and education can have this effect.

The *distributive* effects of government expenditures refer to their impact on the distribution of real income or well-being. Put most briefly, who benefits and who loses from the programs? Many government expenditures benefit some groups at the expense of others and consequently redistribute income. Such effects are obviously important but frequently are not self-evident. For example, unemployment insurance, subsidies to higher education, and agricultural subsidies have benefited middle- and upper-income families far more than low-income groups.

In this chapter we analyze some of the important effects of three basic types of expenditure programs: expenditures on nonmarketed goods, fixed-quantity subsidies, and excise subsidies. In each case, our concern will be with the allocative and distributive effects of these expenditures. In the Appendix to this chapter, we describe benefit-cost analysis, a technique for systematically appraising the efficiency of government projects.

Expenditures on Nonmarketed Goods

Governments spend substantial sums of money to stimulate the production of goods and services that would not be provided by private markets (or, if provided, would be provided in negligible amounts). We call such goods *nonmarketed* goods. Examples include defense programs, foreign aid, and space exploration. Economic analysis of these expenditure programs is somewhat limited, in part because the goods often have the characteristics of a public good, so there is no readily available measure of the value of the good to the public. Nonetheless, a few basic points can be made.

Allocative Effects

There are two ways the government can spend to stimulate output of some good that is not provided by private markets. One approach is to pay private firms to produce the good. In this case the government expenditure represents a market demand for the good that gives private firms the incentive to produce it. Another way is for the government to hire the resources (labor, capital goods, etc.) itself and oversee the production directly. There are numerous examples of both types of programs. For instance, the government purchases airplanes and rifles from private firms for use in defense activities; in providing postal services, however, the government employs resources and oversees production directly.

Whichever method is used, the allocative effect is to increase the output of the desired good. Moreover, in both cases, resources that would have been used to produce other goods in the private sector are used instead to produce goods in the public sector. Thus, we get more of one good and less of others. This trade-off is illustrated in Figure 4–1, in which the output in the government sector is measured horizontally and the output in the private sector is measured vertically. ZZ is the production possibility frontier that shows all combinations of these goods that can be produced with available resources. Initially, suppose that we are at point C, with the economy producing $0G_1$ in the public sector and $0P_1$ in the private sector. Then the government increases its production so that government sector output increases to $0G_2$, or by G_1G_2. The result is a move to point B. Note that as a consequence, the private sector output falls from $0P_1$ to $0P_2$, or by P_1P_2. The opportunity cost associated with the increase in government output, G_1G_2, is a loss of other goods and services equal to P_1P_2. This loss reflects the fact

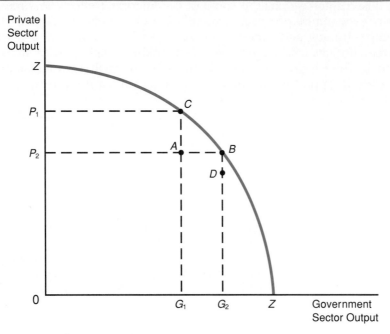

Figure 4–1   *Allocative effects of government provision*
of goods and services

that the resources used in the government project must be drawn from the private sector, where they would have been used to produce other goods and services.

Government expenditures that stimulate the output of some nonmarketed good therefore have an *opportunity cost* that takes the form of a reduction in other goods and services in the private sector. This is an extremely simple point but one that is frequently overlooked. Government-provided goods and services, even though they are not sold directly to the public, are not free. Yet this does not mean that they may not be worthwhile. Quite possibly the benefits accruing from the G_1G_2 increase in government sector output are greater than the costs associated with the P_1P_2 sacrifice of other goods. In Chapter 2, for example, we saw that there are cases in which private markets would not provide some goods, even though the benefits exceeded the costs. Here we are only pointing out the nature of the cost involved when the government undertakes to provide some good.

Distributive Effects

When the government stimulates the production of nonmarketed goods, the distribution of benefits to different individuals or groups is generally difficult to determine, just as the overall benefit to the public is difficult to ascertain. This is because there are no market prices to register values that people either individually or collectively place on this type of good. Clearly, however, different people may benefit to very different degrees, just as hawks may benefit more than doves do from defense spending. Similarly, outdoor enthusiasts probably benefit more from national parks than other groups do. Without considerable information about people's preferences and the specific government-produced good in question, little can be ascertained about the distributional impact of providing the good.

Production Inefficiency

Recall that the opportunity cost of increasing government output by G_1G_2 is shown as P_1P_2 in Figure 4–1. Actually, this is the *minimum* possible opportunity cost associated with the production of the government good. Only if the government output is produced in the least costly way will P_1P_2 reflect the actual cost. There are many ways to combine resources to produce the additional G_1G_2 units of product, and some of them will involve a larger sacrifice than P_1P_2. In other words, if government production is inefficient, we could end up at point D in Figure 4–1 when $0G_2$ is produced. This involves a cost (sacrifice of other goods) of DB greater than is necessary to produce $0G_2$. Although D is inside the production frontier, this does not necessarily mean that resources are unemployed. If, for example, resources are misallocated so that labor resources that would be relatively more productive in producing private goods are used in the government sector, then the economy will be operating inside the frontier.

Governmental sector output is sometimes produced inefficiently, with results like those depicted in Figure 4–1. In the last chapter, we cited several studies that provided evidence of this situation in specific cases. As we explained, the reasons that such an outcome may occur are found in the incentives confronting decision makers in the political process. Designing government expenditure programs so that the relevant decision makers have an incentive to provide services in the least costly way is not an easy task. In some cases, it may be feasible to have the government purchase the good from private firms. Because firms are profit oriented, they have an incentive to produce in the least costly way. Even here, though, some forms of government procurement, such as sealed bid contracting and cost-plus contracts, have led to inefficiency.

It is not known exactly how important such inefficiency generally is, and further research in this area is needed. However, the fundamental point is that expanding government sector output involves opportunity costs in sacrificed private sector output, and sometimes this sacrifice is larger than necessary.

The Role of Taxes

Considering the opportunity cost of government expenditure programs naturally brings taxes to mind. Because we have discussed the opportunity cost without any reference to taxation, a logical next question might be what role taxes play in the analysis of government expenditures. Actually, *expenditures have an opportunity cost irrespective of how they are financed.* In terms of Figure 4–1, private sector output must fall by at least P_1P_2 when the government project is undertaken. This result holds regardless of whether the government taxes, borrows, or simply prints money to finance the spending. Nonetheless, taxes are most often the tangible embodiment of this cost, and it is convenient to think of the opportunity cost of government spending as reflected in the taxes needed to fund the program.

The exact role of taxes in financing government expenditures is twofold. First, the tax (or other method of finance) determines the composition of the sacrificed output in the private sector. As mentioned earlier, P_1P_2 measures the aggregate reduction in private sector output, but whether this reduction is mainly composed of fewer cars, less food, smaller homes, or less of some other goods depends on the exact method of funding. A tax on cars, for example, would obviously concentrate the reduction in output more on cars than a tax on food would. However, the overall reduction in output, P_1P_2 (considered as an index of all private sector output), would be the same.[1]

Second, the tax would also determine exactly who will bear the opportunity cost, P_1P_2. Although the opportunity cost for the community is P_1P_2, different taxes will distribute this burden differently among the public. For example, a progressive income tax would place a larger share of the cost on high-income families than would a tax on food.

Clearly, then, the precise method of finance used has allocative effects (what goods are sacrificed) and distributive effects (who sacrifices these goods) of its own, in addition to the allocative and distributive effects of the government expenditure. In a complete analysis of government policies, both tax and expenditure policies must be considered simultaneously. As a practical matter, however, this is seldom feasible because expenditure programs are not linked to specific taxes. Consequently, expenditure programs are usually analyzed separately, without regard to the precise method of finance. In doing this, however, it must be remembered that the expenditures do have opportunity costs and that these costs normally take the form of a tax that someone must pay.

A more detailed consideration of alternative taxes is postponed to later chapters, but further discussion of the role of taxes in the analysis of expenditure programs is provided at the end of this chapter.

Macroeconomic Effects

So far our emphasis has been on the opportunity cost associated with a government project. The conclusion that the private sector output must fall is based on the assumption that the economy is initially operating on its

---

[1]We are ignoring here the fact that some taxes may have a larger real burden than others raising the same revenue because of the welfare costs of taxes. This point will be developed when we consider tax analysis in Chapter 10.

production possibility frontier. In cases of involuntary unemployment of resources, the economy will be operating inside its frontier, as at point A in Figure 4–1. Starting at point A, a government expenditure program could conceivably result in a move to point B, employing previously unemployed resources to produce the G_1G_2 increase in public sector output. Note that the incremental government output does not result in a reduction in output from the private sector.

At first glance, the opportunity cost of government spending might appear to be zero when there is substantial unemployment. This is wrong, but because in one form or another it is a common error, let us consider it in some detail. The error lies in failing to understand that the notion of opportunity cost relates to alternative uses of resources. In Figure 4–1, the alternative to using the unemployed resources in the public sector is to employ them in the private sector. In other words, we could move from point A to point C. (This could perhaps be accomplished by a tax reduction, an increase in the money supply, or an increase in cash transfers by government to stimulate employment in the private sector.) Point C is an alternative to point B, so the opportunity cost of using previously unemployed resources in the government sector is that they cannot be used in the private sector to increase output from $0P_2$ to $0P_1$. *The opportunity cost of increasing government output from $0G_1$ to $0G_2$ is thus correctly viewed as P_1P_2 even if resources are initially unemployed.*

A similar error occurs in the frequent discussions of government spending programs that allegedly create jobs. Government employment of workers in public works or other programs does not create jobs; instead it simply induces people to work for the government rather than in the private sector. Government spending diverts workers (and other productive resources) to the government sector. Just as in the preceding case, this is true even when the workers are initially unemployed. The important question is whether the workers' services are more valuable in the government sector or elsewhere, and the concept of opportunity cost forces us to face that question.

The possible impacts of government expenditures on the overall price level (inflation) have frequently been cited by presidents as a reason to oppose or veto a particular expenditure bill. This is also a source of confusion. An expenditure program is not intrinsically inflationary if taxes are used to finance the program. If taxes are not used and the government prints money to finance the program, inflation can result, but even this is not an obvious reason to oppose the program. Inflation can be thought of as a type of tax that reduces the value of cash balances. An objection that an expenditure program is inflationary can then be seen as an objection to the particular type of tax used to finance it. Although it may be true that inflation is more harmful than other taxes are as a method of financing an expenditure program, it must be recognized that the possible inflationary impact of an expenditure program is not a valid objection to the program itself. The same program could be financed by other, noninflationary, means.

Therefore, the potential impact of government expenditures on the over-all level of employment, output, or prices is largely irrelevant in an analysis of specific expenditure programs. Where these effects are important is in an examination of the combined impact of monetary policy and all taxes and expenditures on macroeconomic variables. Entire courses on these matters are taught, and our neglect of these issues does not imply that we think them unimportant. As long as there are many policy combinations compatible with full employment, however, macroeconomic considerations provide no method of analyzing and comparing the allocative and distributive conse-quences of different points on the production possibility frontier (i.e., of different positions of full employment). The assumption of full employment, which we will rely on throughout most of this text, is simply a convenient way to stress the relevant alternatives.

Fixed-Quantity Subsidy for Marketed Goods

Much of the growth in government spending over the past several decades has taken the form of subsidies for goods that are, or could be, provided through the market mechanism. Subsidies for education, food, child care, housing, job training, old-age pensions, energy, and medical care (among others) involve subsidizing goods and services that people would have pur-chased anyway (but perhaps not in the same quantity). To understand the consequences of such subsidies, we must determine how people—both consumers and producers—respond to the subsidy, and this depends in part on what type of subsidy is used.

A common form of subsidy is one through which the government makes a certain quantity of a good available to a consumer at no cost or at a cost below the market price. The essential characteristic of this particular type of subsidy is that the quantity of the good being subsidized is beyond the con-trol of the consumer. We call this a *fixed-quantity subsidy* to emphasize that the quantity being subsidized is beyond the control of the recipient; the government determines what quantity of the good is made available at the zero or subsidized price. (This is a form of *in-kind* subsidy, so called be-cause the subsidy is linked to the consumption of a particular good.) For example, the government may provide food stamps that a consumer can use to purchase $1,500 worth of food, but if more than $1,500 worth of food is desired, the consumer must pay for the additional amount at the full market price. Here the subsidy applies only to a given quantity, $1,500 worth of food.

Similarly, public schools make available a certain quantity or quality of schooling, and if more is desired, it must be paid for by the consumer. That is, if parents are not satisfied with the education provided by public schools, they can send their children to private schools at their own expense, or if parents wish to supplement their children's education (with tutoring or spe-cial classes), they may, but again they must bear the full cost. In both of these examples, as well as many others that could be mentioned, the subsidy applies to a fixed quantity of the good being subsidized, and if recipients of the subsidy want a larger quantity, their only option is to purchase additional units at the full market price. Fixed-quantity subsidies can have various effects on the consumption and well-being of recipients, depending on the size of the subsidy, the good being subsidized, and who pays for the subsidy. These possibilities are examined next.

Reduced Private Purchases

One major impact of a fixed-quantity subsidy is that it causes a reduction in out-of-pocket expenditures on the subsidized good. Such a reaction on the part of consumers is intuitively obvious because if the government provides a good, consumers will need to purchase less on their own. There are also situations in which the consumers reduce their out-of-pocket expenditures by an amount equal to the quantity provided by the government, so that their total consumption does not increase.

To illustrate the consequences of this type of subsidy more clearly, consider a consumer whose presubsidy budget line relating the subsidized good to other goods is shown by MN in Figure 4–2. The budget line reflects the consumer's income of $1,000 (equal to $0M$) and the market price of food,

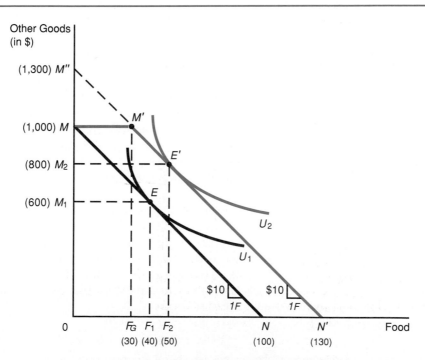

Figure 4–2 *Fixed-quantity subsidy: reduction in private purchases*

$10 per unit (the slope of *MN*). Prior to receiving any subsidy, Percy, our consumer, is in equilibrium at point *E*, consuming 40 units of food and $600 worth of other goods and services.

Now suppose that the government gives Percy 30 units of food for free.[2] This means that Percy could consume at point *M'*—accepting the 30 units of food and spending his income of $1,000 on other goods and services. If he wants, however, Percy may also use some of his own income to purchase additional units of food at a price of $10 per unit. His entire budget line is therefore *MM'N'*. The *M'N'* segment has the same slope as the original budget line because Percy must pay the unchanged market price for each unit beyond 30. Note that if the government had given Percy a cash transfer of $300—the cost to the government of the food subsidy—Percy's budget line would have been *M"N'*. (*M"M* is the dollar cost of the subsidy.) *The effect of this fixed-quantity subsidy on consumption opportunities is the same as a cash transfer, except that the dotted portion of the budget line, M'M", is not available to the consumer.* (Actually, if Percy is able to sell some of the food provided by the government at $10 per unit, he could move along the *M'M"* part of the budget line. It is assumed, however, that resale is not allowed.)

Percy's exact response depends on how the budget line is affected, which we have just determined, and on his preferences concerning food and other goods, which we will now consider. If we assume that food and other goods are normal goods, then we know that after receiving the subsidy Percy will choose a point along *M'N'* involving more consumption of both. This is illustrated by the postsubsidy equilibrium at *E'* on *M'N'*, with Percy consuming 50 units of food and $800 worth of other goods. Recall that at the original equilibrium, *E*, Percy purchased 40 units of food; after the subsidy, his consumption of food has increased by only 10 units, even though the government provides 30 units of food. Percy's *private* food purchases have fallen from 40 ($0F_1$) to 20 (F_GF_2) in response to the subsidy, but *total* consumption has risen to 50. Note also that the subsidy has allowed the consumption of other goods to increase. Before the subsidy, Percy spent $400 on food and $600 on other things; after the subsidy Percy spends $200 of his own income on food (and receives a $300 subsidy) and has $800 left for other goods and services.

A reduction in private purchases should be expected with a fixed-quantity subsidy. In addition, as long as the quantity provided by government (30) is less than the consumer would purchase if given the subsidy in the form of cash (50 units would be consumed with an unrestricted cash transfer), this type of subsidy is equivalent in its effects to a cash transfer. Thus, consumption of the subsidized good increases only to the extent that the consumer would choose if given money instead of food.

---

[2]It makes no difference to the analysis whether the government provides the consumer with funds that must be spent on food. This is essentially what the food stamp program does, a policy we shall examine in the next chapter.

Unchanged Total Consumption

So far our analysis of the consumer's response to a fixed-quantity subsidy has neglected the taxes required to finance the subsidy. There are two polar possibilities to consider. First, someone other than the subsidy recipient may pay the required taxes. In that case, our previous analysis is complete, at least insofar as the effect on the recipient is concerned. Second, the recipient of the subsidy may also pay taxes to finance the subsidy, just as many families pay taxes to finance the schools their children attend. In this case, it is worthwhile to consider the combined effects of the tax and subsidy on the consumer's choice and well-being.

Figure 4–2 can be reinterpreted to handle the case in which Percy pays a tax as well as receives the subsidy, at least when it is assumed that the tax is equal to the $300 subsidy received. Although this would not normally be true for all consumers, *on average the tax paid must equal the subsidy* (if a tax is used to finance the program), so this is a convenient starting point. Suppose, then, that Percy's before-tax-and-subsidy budget line is $M''N'$, his income is $1,300, and he is in equilibrium at point E'. A tax of $300 would shift his budget line to MN. When the government returns the tax to the consumer in the form of 30 units of food, Percy's post-tax-and-subsidy budget line becomes $MM'N'$. Thus, *the combined tax-expenditure policy leaves Percy's budget line completely unchanged, except for making it impossible to consume along the original $M'M''$ portion.* If Percy had not chosen a point in this region anyway, as is true for the indifference curves shown, he would have ended up purchasing the same quantities of food and other goods after the tax plus subsidy as he did before.

These conclusions suggest that many government expenditure programs may have little or no effect on the allocation of resources. To the extent that taxpayers receive benefits they pay for in taxes, government spending may simply replace private spending. However, our analysis depended on a number of assumptions concerning the nature of the subsidy. In some cases these assumptions are not appropriate, and by modifying the analysis we can determine when and how this type of subsidy can affect resource allocation.

Overconsumption

When the consumer receives the subsidy but pays no taxes, Figure 4–2 shows how this fixed quantity subsidy can have exactly the same effects as a cash transfer of equal cost. There are times, however, when a fixed-quantity subsidy will increase consumption by more than a cash transfer. This happens when the quantity provided by the government is greater than the consumer would purchase if he or she had cash rather than the in-kind subsidy. Consider Figure 4–3. MN is the presubsidy budget line with a consumer, Sybil, purchasing F_1 units of food. If the government provides F_G units of food at no cost, the budget line will shift to $MM'N'$. Given the consumer's preferences as shown by her indifference curves, her new equilibrium is at point M'. If Sybil had been given cash equal to the cost of the subsidy (MM''),

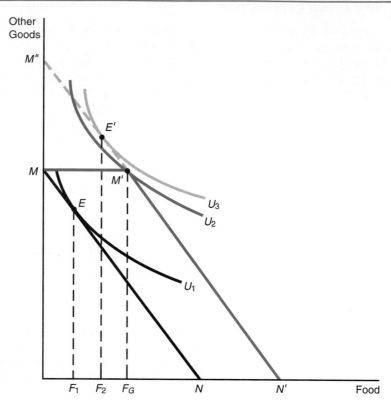

Figure 4–3   *Fixed-quantity subsidy: overconsumption*

her budget line would have been $M''N'$, and she would have consumed less food, F_2, at E'. *In this case, the fixed-quantity subsidy has increased consumption more than a cash transfer of equal cost would have.* One implication of this greater consumption with the fixed-quantity subsidy, however, should be emphasized: It means that Sybil would be better off if given cash instead of the fixed-quantity subsidy. Note in Figure 4–3 that Sybil would have a consumption bundle that places her on the indifference curve U_3 with the cash transfer, but she attains only the lower indifference curve U_2 with the fixed-quantity subsidy. Thus, the increase in consumption in comparison to the cash transfer, F_2F_G, is really *overconsumption* of the subsidized good.

We have just compared the effect on the consumption and well-being of the fixed-quantity subsidy with that of an equal-cost cash transfer. It is also possible to use the same graph to analyze the effect of the fixed-quantity subsidy when it is financed by a tax on Sybil herself. In this case, $M''N'$ is the initial before-tax-and-subsidy budget line, MN is the after-tax budget line, and $MM'N'$ is the after-tax-and-subsidy budget line. Thus, the subsidy and tax together have the effect of changing Sybil's consumption point from E' to M'—increasing her consumption of food but making her worse off. Basically, this is because subsidies that taxpayers pay for themselves (and on average, they must pay for them) do not increase consumption possibilities—the final equilibrium must lie on the initial $M''N'$ budget line—but just induces the recipient to choose a different point, here M' rather than E'.

Because the recipient of the subsidy is worse off with the fixed-quantity subsidy than with the equal-cost cash transfer (and she is worse off with both the tax and the subsidy if she pays the tax), what is the justification for this type of subsidy? This is a good question. It should be emphasized that we are only examining the effects on the direct consumer here. If there are external benefits associated with consumption, then it is possible that point M' in Figure 4–3 represents a more efficient consumption pattern than point E'. Even though the immediate consumer would prefer to consume less food than at point M', other people (those who receive external benefits from her food consumption) are better off when she consumes at M' rather than at E'. That is why economists look for possible external benefits when evaluating subsidies. In the absence of such external benefits, however, a fixed-quantity subsidy that leads to overconsumption is unequivocally inefficient.

Underconsumption

It is often taken for granted that a fixed-quantity subsidy will increase consumption, but we have seen that in some cases it may lead to the same level of consumption as a cash transfer does. In addition, there are other situations in which this type of subsidy will actually reduce consumption! *This paradoxical outcome can occur when it is very costly, or impossible, for the consumer to supplement the quantity of the good provided by government.* Earlier we assumed that the consumer could purchase additional units of food at the market price and thereby supplement the subsidized quantity provided. For some types of goods and some types of subsidies, it is very costly to consume more than the quantity provided by the government.

An example will make this clear. Suppose that the subsidized good is housing, and the government offers a family a two-bedroom apartment at no cost. The family may prefer a three-bedroom apartment and might be willing to pay the difference in cost between a two-bedroom and a three-bedroom apartment to obtain a larger apartment. The way the program is administered, however, this option is not available. The family cannot accept the government two-bedroom apartment and, by paying the cost of an extra bedroom, convert it into a three-bedroom apartment. Instead they must either accept the two-bedroom apartment or forgo the subsidy altogether and pay the entire cost of housing themselves. In this setting, it is quite possible that the family will choose the two-bedroom apartment when the government foots the bill rather than the three-bedroom apartment they would have chosen in the absence of the subsidy.

Note how the housing subsidy differs from the food subsidy considered earlier. With the food subsidy, the consumer could supplement the subsidized quantity by purchasing additional units of food at the market price. With the housing subsidy, the nature of the good provided by government makes supplementing it costly, if not impossible. Housing is typical of a good that is not highly divisible into small units; it is "lumpy," and to increase the quantity consumed usually requires moving into a larger or better housing unit. A subsidy such as that described earlier provides a housing unit of a given size and is therefore difficult to supplement.

Let us see how this looks in the framework we have been using. In Figure 4–4, the presubsidy budget line relating housing and other goods is MN. (Even though housing is "lumpy," the budget line showing market options is smooth, because the family can choose more or less housing when selecting a particular housing unit to rent.) In the absence of any subsidy, H_1 units of housing are consumed. Now assume that the government offers the family a smaller (or lower-quality) housing unit of H_2 units at no cost. *The budget line becomes MM'RN.* Note the difference between this and the food subsidy. With the food subsidy the budget line would be $MM'N'$ because the consumer could consume more of the subsidized good (to the right of M') by paying only the cost of additional units. But to consume more housing

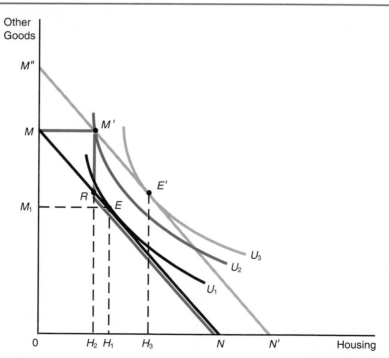

Figure 4–4   *Fixed-quantity subsidy: underconsumption*

than H_2, the consumer must forgo the subsidized housing unit and bear the entire cost of the housing units along the RN portion of the original budget line.

Confronted with the $MM'RN$ budget line, the family would choose to accept the subsidized housing and consume at M', even though this involves less housing than they consumed without the subsidy. Although the family sacrifices H_1H_2 units of housing, they gain M_1M units of other goods, and the net result is that they are better off at M' than at E.

Actually, the more relevant comparison is between the consumption pattern with the subsidy (at M') and with an equal-size cash subsidy that the family can spend as they wish. Because MM'' is the cost of the housing subsidy, a cash transfer of this sum would yield the $M''N'$ budget line, and the family would choose point E', with H_3 units of housing. The family would also be better off at E', on indifference curve U_3, because the extra H_2H_3 units of housing are worth more than their cost. H_2H_3 is a measure of the underconsumption produced by the housing subsidy.[3]

It is important to recognize that this type of subsidy can lead to underconsumption for some consumers, overconsumption for other consumers, and the appropriate level of consumption for still others. The exact outcome depends on the size of the subsidy in relation to the preferences and incomes of the recipients of the subsidy. In general, the subsidy is most likely to restrict consumption when the quantity being subsidized is small, when the consumer's income is high, or when the unsubsidized quantity chosen by the consumer is large. The opposite combination of circumstances is likely to lead to overconsumption.

There are a number of real-world subsidies of this sort that can lead to underconsumption. Subsidies for public schools and institutions of higher education are probably the most important examples because schooling is a lumpy good, just as housing is. Similarly, public housing, medical services provided by public health clinics, and Medicaid are other obvious examples. It is theoretically possible for these subsidies to lead to underconsumption, but whether they actually do is an empirical question.

Two empirical studies have investigated this question and concluded that some subsidies of this type have, in fact, operated to restrict consumption, at least for some recipients. John Kraft and Edgar Olsen studied a sample of public housing tenants and estimated that 49 percent of the families were consuming less housing than if they had been given the subsidy as cash.[4] In

---

[3]Note that the same diagram can be used to analyze the effects of a nonredistributive housing subsidy in which the consumer pays a tax equal to the subsidy received. In this case, $M''N'$ is the before-tax budget line, and the consumer is initially at point E'. The tax shifts the line to MN, and the subsidy then produces the $MM'RN$ budget line. The net effect of the tax-plus-subsidy reduces housing consumption and makes the consumer worse off.

[4]John Kraft and Edgar Olsen, "The Distribution of Benefits from Public Housing," in *The Distribution of Economic Well-Being,* Vol. 1, *Studies in Income and Wealth,* edited by F. Thomas Juster (Cambridge, Mass.: Ballinger, 1977), pp. 51–64.

another study, Sam Peltzman studied the effects of state-supported colleges and universities on the consumption of higher education.[5] He found that the expenditures per student would be higher in the absence of subsidies to higher education, which supports our contention that some fixed quantity subsidies result in underconsumption. Peltzman also found that more students attended college as a result of the subsidies. Thus, some students consume less schooling and others (those who would not have attended college without the subsidy) consume more as a result of state support of institutions of higher education.[6] These studies, therefore, provide some empirical support for our analysis.

Redistribution of Income

We have seen that the fixed-quantity type of subsidy can increase, reduce, or have no effect on the consumption of the subsidized good. The exact outcome probably varies widely from one subsidy to another and from one consumer to another. Although it is difficult to generalize, the quantitative impact of such subsidies on the allocation of resources is probably much smaller than is widely believed: This type of subsidy is not very effective if its goal is to increase consumption.

Before concluding that fixed-quantity subsidies have only minor consequences, however, it should be pointed out that they often serve to redistribute income to certain groups. For example, food stamps, housing subsidies, and Medicaid subsidies are concentrated exclusively on low-income households and therefore act to increase their real incomes. In addition, even though public schools and social security (subsidized retirement pensions) are more widely distributed, when account is taken of the taxes that finance them, we find that many families gain on balance, while other families lose; income is effectively redistributed. In general, it is plausible to suppose that the way such subsidies serve to redistribute income may be more important in an overall evaluation than their possibly minor impacts on consumption patterns.

Excise Subsidy

A fundamentally different form of subsidy is one in which the government pays part of the per unit price of a good but allows the quantity of the good to be determined by consumer purchases. For example, suppose that the

---

[5]Sam Peltzman, "The Effect of Government Subsidies-in-Kind on Private Expenditures: The Case of Higher Education," *Journal of Political Economy,* 81:1 (Jan./Feb. 1973).

[6]At the risk of pointing out the obvious, it should be noted that we are discussing estimates and not facts. Effects of this type cannot be directly observed, of course, so we must rely on empirical estimates.

government decided to pay the consumer $5 for each unit of housing consumed. The quantity and, hence, the cost to the government depend on the level of consumer purchases and so are not fixed by the nature of the policy. Such a subsidy is called an *excise subsidy*—just the opposite of the more familiar excise tax.

Examples of excise subsidies are less common than examples of fixed-quantity subsidies. Unemployment insurance is a type of excise subsidy, but with some significant differences from the "pure" type considered here. Some welfare programs operate much like excise subsidies. (These programs will be discussed in greater detail in later chapters.) But perhaps the most common examples are found in special provisions of the tax laws. These "tax subsidies" or "tax loopholes" will also be examined in later chapters. Here we will simply consider how such subsidies affect output and consumption levels.

There are two types of excise subsidies, *ad valorem excise subsidies* and *per unit excise subsidies*. With an ad valorem excise subsidy the government pays a certain percentage of the per unit cost of some good or, what amounts to the same thing, a specific percentage of the consumer's total expenditures on the good. In contrast, with a per unit excise subsidy the government pays a certain amount for each unit of the good consumed, as in the housing subsidy mentioned earlier. In this chapter, we will concentrate on per unit excise subsidies, although the allocative and distributive effects of both types of excise subsidies are nearly identical. In Chapter 11, when we analyze tax loopholes, we will consider ad valorem excise subsidies in greater depth.

Allocative Effects: Market Perspective

To examine the consequences of an excise subsidy, let us begin by assuming that the food industry is to be subsidized and that the industry is a constant-cost competitive industry. In Figure 4–5, the initial price and quantity are $10 and Q_1. Now suppose that an excise subsidy of $4 per unit of food is to be extended to the industry. This subsidy could be paid either to the firms or to the consumers; we will initially assume that it is paid to the firms.

When firms receive a subsidy of $4 per unit of output, this has the effect of reducing their net per unit production costs by $4. Thus, the effect can be shown as a downward shift in the supply curve to S', where S' is obtained by subtracting the subsidy per unit, R, from the original supply curve. As a result of the lower net cost of production, the industry has an incentive to expand output, and that leads to a lower price for consumers. The new equilibrium is established at the intersection of S' and D. Total government spending on the subsidy is equal to $PAKP'$, or the per unit subsidy times the quantity produced.

Note that the ultimate effect of this subsidy, even though it is paid to the firms, is to reduce the price to consumers by $4, the amount of the per unit subsidy. (As we will see later, when the industry is an increasing cost industry, the price to consumers will not fall by exactly the amount of the subsidy.)

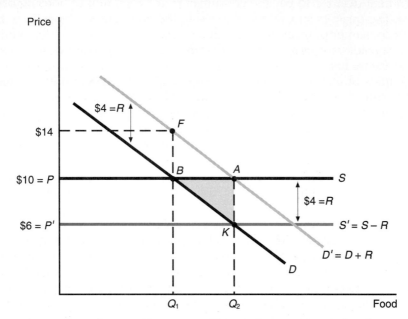

Figure 4–5   Allocative effects of an excise subsidy

As a result, consumers are confronted with a $6 price, and at the lower price, consumption increases to Q_2. *With an excise subsidy, consumption and output unequivocally increase.*

Some care is necessary in interpreting the results of the subsidy. Although we have analyzed the subsidy by shifting the supply curve, it is clear that the subsidy does not reduce the true cost of production. It will still cost $10 worth of resources to produce a unit of food; the S' curve just shows the part of the cost that consumers will have to cover when the government is effectively paying $4 of the cost per unit. Subsidies do not reduce the marginal social cost of production—still shown by the original supply curve; they just reduce the net costs to participants in the subsidized market by having someone else (the taxpayers) bear part of those costs. At the final equilibrium, the subsidy per unit enters as a wedge (AK) separating the price received by producers (still $10, $6 from consumers and $4 from government) from the price paid by consumers.

An excise subsidy can also be granted directly to consumers rather than to firms. That, in fact, is the way various tax subsidies operate, as we will see in later chapters. To see what difference this makes, suppose that consumers receive $4 from the government for each unit they purchase; the firms are not subsidized. The subsidy then increases the per unit price that consumers are willing to pay to firms. At Q_1, for instance, consumers are willing to pay a maximum of BQ_1 (the height to the demand curve), or $10 per unit, out of their own pockets. However, because the government will give them $4 per unit, their demand price *including the subsidy* will be $14 (at Q_1). In other words, the subsidy per unit can be added to the original demand curve to yield D', the new demand curve confronting sellers of the product. With D' and the unchanged supply curve S, equilibrium occurs at point A, with output Q_2. At Q_2, producers are receiving $10 per unit—just as they did when the subsidy was paid to them. Also consumers are now paying a net price of only $6, or KQ_2; the remaining $4, AK, reflects the government subsidy.

Thus, we reach the surprising conclusion that an excise subsidy has the same effect, regardless of whether consumers or producers are subsidized. In each case, the final equilibrium is at Q_2, with a price of $10 received by producers and a price of $6 paid by consumers. The consequences are the same, regardless of which side of the market is subsidized. One implication of this finding is that we can analyze the subsidy either as an upward shift in the demand curve or as a downward shift in the supply curve.

Turning to an evaluation of the consequences, note that the expansion in output from Q_1 to Q_2 represents overconsumption by the consumers. The benefit of the additional Q_1Q_2 units to consumers is less than the cost of producing the additional output; the only reason consumers purchase the additional output is that someone else is bearing part of the cost. In Figure 4–5, the benefit of increasing output from Q_1 to Q_2 is equal to BKQ_2Q_1 because the height to the original market demand curve gives the marginal value of each successive unit. The cost to the economy of producing the additional output is BAQ_2Q_1, or $10 per unit times the Q_1Q_2 increase in output. (Recall that the original supply curve continues to show the marginal social cost of production.) The cost of expanding output exceeds the benefit by area BAK, the welfare cost of the subsidy. (Of course, if there are external benefits associated with production or consumption, there might be a welfare gain from the subsidy.)

What this welfare cost means is that consumers would prefer that the resources used to produce the Q_1Q_2 increase in output be used elsewhere to produce other goods and services. In other words, the subsidy artificially stimulates the output by drawing resources from other uses where they are more valuable to consumers. The subsidy results in an output level where the marginal benefit (KQ_2) to consumers is less than the marginal social cost of production (AQ_2).

Allocative Effects: Individual Perspective

Greater insight into the nature of the allocative effects of an excise subsidy can be gained by examining the impact on an individual consumer. In Figure 4–6, the presubsidy budget line is MN, and the consumer is in equilibrium at point E. The excise subsidy lowers the price of food, so the budget line rotates and becomes flatter, as shown by MN'. Faced with the lower price, the individual's new equilibrium is at E', involving a larger consumption of food, q_2. The total cost of the subsidy is equal to $E'T$. This can best be seen

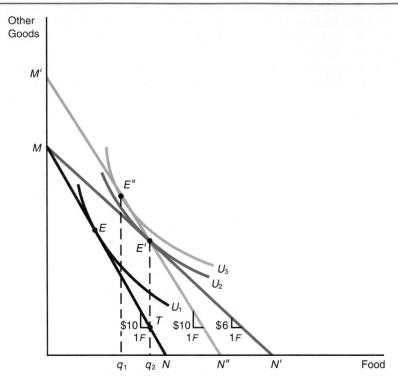

Figure 4–6   *Allocative effects of an excise subsidy: individual consumer*

by recognizing that if the consumer purchased q_2 units without the subsidy, he or she would have had only Tq_2 dollars left to spend on other goods. With the subsidy, the consumer purchases q_2 units and has $E'q_2$ dollars left to spend on other goods. So in purchasing q_2, the consumer saves the difference, $E'T$; this is the portion of the total cost of q_2 that is borne by the government.

The postsubsidy equilibrium at E' represents overconsumption: The artificially low price encourages consumers to purchase more food and less of other goods, and this outcome is inefficient. This inefficiency can be demonstrated by assuming that the consumer is given the subsidy in cash rather than as a subsidy that lowers the price of food. Because the cost of the excise subsidy is $E'T$, the government can give, at no additional cost, cash equal to MM' (equal to $E'T$). This cash transfer produces a parallel movement of the budget line from MN to $M'N''$ passing through point E'. This means that the consumer could still choose the consumption mix at point E' if given the subsidy in the form of cash. Given the preferences shown, however, the recipient would prefer point E'', purchasing less food and more of other goods. The consumer would therefore be better off with an unrestricted cash transfer. Compared with the cash transfer of equal cost, the excise subsidy produces a welfare cost: The consumer is on U_2 with the excise subsidy but can reach U_3 by consuming a different combination of goods of the same total cost with a cash transfer.

We have assumed that people other than the recipient of the subsidy pay the taxes to finance the subsidy. The same diagram, slightly reinterpreted, applies when the consumers must pay the taxes themselves. In Figure 4–6, we can interpret $M'N''$ as the before-tax-and-subsidy budget line, MN as the after-tax budget line, and MN' as the budget line showing the combined effect of the tax and subsidy. In this case, the net result is to increase food consumption from q_1 to q_2 and to make the consumer-taxpayer worse off. Overconsumption of food and a loss in welfare are, once again, the outcome. Thus, the excise subsidy produces a welfare cost by artificially stimulating food consumption in both cases. The only difference is that the welfare cost associated with the subsidy when others pay the taxes reflects the fact that the consumers would be better off consuming less food with a cash transfer. (Recall that the recipient is on a higher indifference curve with a cash transfer.) When the consumers pay the taxes themselves, the welfare cost reflects the fact that consumers would be better off consuming less food without any tax or subsidy. The nature of the welfare cost is the same; an artificially lower price stimulates too much consumption.

Figure 4–5 and Figure 4–6 both illustrate the welfare cost of an excise subsidy, but from different perspectives. In Figure 4–5, total overconsumption (or, equivalently, overproduction, because what is produced is consumed) equals Q_1Q_2, and area BAK is a measure of the total welfare cost. In Figure 4–6, overconsumption by an individual consumer is shown as q_1q_2, and the welfare cost is represented by the difference in well-being associated with consuming at E' rather than E''[7].

Distributive Effects

Who benefits and who loses from a subsidy depend on the exact type and size of subsidy (as well as on the distribution of the tax burden). Now let us consider another dimension to the problem of determining the distributional impact: the relationship between the market structure and the incidence of the subsidy.

Economists use the term *incidence* to refer to the distributional effect of a tax, subsidy, or other policy. In the last section, the incidence of the excise subsidy fell on consumers because the price paid by consumers decreased by the full amount of the per unit subsidy. Thus, consumers benefited and sellers did not. Sometimes, however, the benefits do not accrue entirely to consumers.

---

[7]In advanced courses in economic theory, the conditions under which these two approaches are exactly equivalent are discussed in detail.

Figure 4–7 illustrates the effect of an excise subsidy for a good produced by an *increasing cost* competitive industry. The only difference between Figure 4–7 and Figure 4–5 is that in Figure 4–7 the supply curve is assumed to be upward sloping, implying that per unit production costs rise as the total industry output expands. The subsidy is $4 per unit and is shown by the upward shift in demand from D to D'. The final equilibrium occurs at K, where D' and S intersect. In this case, however, the net price to consumers is $7, only $3 below the unsubsidized price. Part of the subsidy is received by sellers who now are paid $11 per unit, $1 more than before. The incidence, or benefit, of the subsidy falls on both buyers and sellers.

The extent to which buyers and sellers benefit from an excise subsidy depends on the relative elasticities of the supply and demand curves. With a perfectly elastic supply curve (shown as S_1), the benefit accrues entirely to consumers. The more inelastic the supply curve is, the smaller the price reduction for consumers and the larger the price increase for sellers will be. In fact, with a perfectly inelastic (vertical) supply curve the consumers receive no benefit because the selling price rises by the full amount of the subsidy. The reader should also be able to work out how the incidence varies with the elasticity of demand for any given supply curve.

We have been referring to "sellers" benefiting from the subsidy, and this requires some further explanation. Recall that in equilibrium competitive

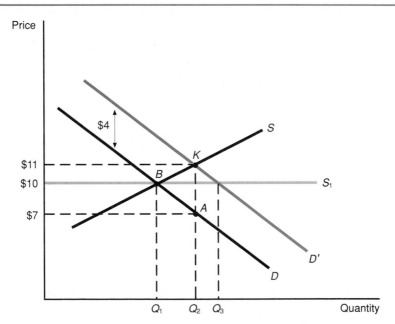

Figure 4–7   *Incidence of an excise subsidy for an increasing cost industry*

firms make zero economic profits (i.e., they earn a normal return on investment but no "abnormal" profits). Businesses per se probably do not benefit from an increase in the product price induced by the subsidy because their costs of production eventually rise. As industry output expands, its demands for productive factors—labor, raw materials, and so on—increase, bidding up wage rates, prices of raw materials, and so on. Higher wage rates represent higher production costs to firms and account for the upward slope in the supply curve. These "sellers" who benefit from the higher selling price are typically owners of factors of production whose prices are bid up as total industry output expands. Thus, the benefit of the subsidy on the supply side will probably be dispersed among a number of economic groups, making it unlikely that business profits will receive more than a temporary boost.

Where the benefits from a particular subsidy accrue depends on the structure and the reaction of the market affected by the subsidy. Our discussion of incidence has been in the context of an excise subsidy, but the incidence of other subsidies (and taxes) can also be ascertained only by analyzing the reaction of the relevant market. For example, some of the benefits of fixed-quantity subsidies can accrue to sellers of the subsidized product. If the fixed-quantity subsidy does, on balance, increase consumption, this reflects an effective increase in demand. Coupled with an upward-sloping supply curve, a fixed-quantity subsidy that increases demand will increase price, just like the excise subsidy in Figure 4–7. This relationship may explain some of the support by educators (such as teachers' unions and colleges and universities) for subsidies to education or by construction unions for housing subsidies.

With a constant-cost industry, the incidence of an excise subsidy is entirely on consumers, and sellers derive no long-run benefit. Assuming a horizontal supply curve simplifies the analysis because we need not worry about possible changes in wages and other input prices. Fortunately, research in industrial organization suggests that constant costs over the relevant range of output are quite common, so the assumption of a horizontal supply curve may be a reasonably close approximation in many cases.

Note that the welfare cost due to the excise subsidy in Figure 4–7 is shown by area BAK. The welfare cost due to overconsumption of Q_1Q_2 is measured by the difference in the cost associated with producing the additional output (given by the upward-sloping supply curve) and the benefits to consumers (given by the demand curve). If the supply curve were vertical, there would be no overconsumption and no welfare cost. (Verify this.)

Subsidies to a Subset of Consumers

So far, our formal analysis of excise subsidies has considered subsidies that apply to all consumers of some product. Actually, many subsidies are given to only some of the consumers of a particular product. This is true, for example, of food stamps, Medicaid, housing subsidies, Medicare, job training programs, and others. Our analysis can be modified to cover instances in which only a subset of all consumers is subsidized.

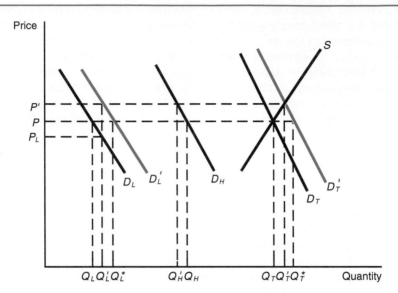

Figure 4–8   *Excise subsidy for low-income households*

Suppose that only low-income consumers of food are subsidized. In Figure 4–8 we can disaggregate the total market demand, D_T, into the separate demands of low-income consumers, D_L, and high-income consumers, D_H. Given the supply and demand relationships, the initial equilibrium price and quantity are P and Q_T. At a price of P, low-income consumers purchase Q_L units and high-income consumers purchase Q_H units. Note that $Q_L + Q_H = Q_T$.

An excise subsidy given only to low-income consumers increases their demand to D_L'. (A fixed quantity subsidy *could* increase demand in this way as well.) At the initial price, P, the recipients would prefer to consume Q_L^*, or $Q_L Q_L^*$ more than before. Although the demand of unsubsidized consumers is not affected,[8] total demand has increased. The new total demand curve is D_T', obtained by summing D_L' and D_H (so $Q_L Q_L^* = Q_T Q_T^*$). Since the total market demand for the product in relation to supply is what determines the market price and total output, the market price rises to P' and the quantity to Q_T'.

Higher-income consumers are harmed by the subsidy because they must pay a higher price. Because their demand is unchanged, they curtail consumption to Q_H'. Unsubsidized consumers may also bear an additional cost if they pay some or all of the taxes needed to finance the subsidy. The benefits of the subsidy accrue to the subsidized consumers, who now pay a net

[8]This assumes that the income effect of the tax on demand is small enough to be ignored.

price of P_L and consume Q'_L. In addition, sellers benefit because the price they receive has increased from P to P'. Note, however, that we have assumed an increasing cost industry. If the supply curve were horizontal, the product price would not rise, and the entire benefit of the subsidy would accrue to low-income consumers.

This analysis suggests how the incidence of a subsidy may be spread widely and unevenly throughout society. And the analysis is of more than academic interest. It is precisely this combination of circumstances that, in the opinion of many economists, contributed to the surge in medical care costs (prices) following the enactment of Medicaid and Medicare in the mid-1960s. Medicare and Medicaid are subsidies that apply to the elderly and poor, so an analysis that distinguishes subsidized from unsubsidized consumers is appropriate.

Taxation and the Analysis of Expenditures

In this chapter, our emphasis has been on the analysis of expenditure policies, and we have given little attention to the way in which these policies are financed. By concentrating on the effects of the expenditure policies by themselves, we can work out many of the consequences of the policies. However, in evaluating the efficiency effects of government spending, it should be kept in mind that the fundamental issue is whether the spending program together with its financing method leads to a more or less efficient resource allocation. Normally, taxes will provide the funds that are spent, and we need to consider somewhat more carefully how taxation is integrated into the analysis of an expenditure program. (A much more detailed analysis of taxes will be given in later chapters.)

The central point is that *every dollar the government spends imposes a cost on taxpayers of more than a dollar.* There are several reasons for this. First, there are administrative costs associated with collecting tax revenues. When taxpayers pay $1 in taxes, the administrative costs must be paid out of this amount before any spending program can be financed. For example, if administrative costs are 1 percent of tax revenues, taxpayers must pay $100 in taxes to finance a $99 expenditure program; each $1 spent costs taxpayers approximately $1.01. In fact, administrative costs are fairly small. The federal government's Internal Revenue Service collects taxes at a cost of about 1 percent. There are, however, other more important costs borne by taxpayers over and above the funds remitted to the government.

A second reason for higher costs is the compliance costs borne by taxpayers—the time and resources required to comply with the tax laws. For the federal individual income tax, these costs have been estimated to be about 6 percent of revenues. Taken together with administrative costs, this means that each $1 spent by government imposes a cost of about $1.07 on taxpayers.

A third reason is likely to be even more important. Most real-world taxes lead to distortions in resource allocation themselves; that is, they have welfare costs. We will examine how this occurs and evaluate the likely quantitative importance later. For now it is enough to realize that there is an adverse impact due to taxes that makes their cost to taxpayers greater than the revenue raised.

These costs (and possibly others) can be combined and referred to as the *marginal welfare cost* of taxation. Their meaning is, as already stated, that each dollar spent by the government has a cost of greater than $1 on taxpayers. For example, if marginal welfare cost is 25 percent of revenue, then each dollar spent costs the public $1.25—$1 of which is the direct cost of the revenue and the other $0.25 of which is the marginal welfare cost.

The marginal welfare cost of taxation has important implications for evaluating the efficiency of expenditure policies. For example, we ignored this cost when we discussed Figure 4–2. There we argued that if the recipient of the fixed quantity subsidy paid the tax, he or she would end up after the tax and the subsidy with the same consumption mix (at point E' in the graph) as before, and thus there would be no effect on well-being. If there is a marginal welfare cost associated with the tax, however, the taxpayer cannot be returned to his or her original indifference curve; he or she will be worse off than before the tax and spending policy. (In terms of Figure 4–2, the $300 tax burden might finance only a $250 fixed quantity subsidy, so the final budget line will be lower than $M'N'$.)

Recognizing the marginal welfare cost of taxation does not, however, mean that all expenditure policies will lead to net reductions in efficiency. If there are external benefits associated with production of some good, it may still be worthwhile to subsidize production of the good. But it is important to take appropriate account of the marginal welfare cost in determining the size of the subsidy. Exactly how that should be done depends on the type of subsidy, but we can illustrate the general principles involved by considering once again an excise subsidy.

Suppose that there are external benefits associated with production of a good that is provided by a constant cost competitive industry. In Figure 4–9, the consumers' private demand curve is D_P and the supply curve is S, so the competitive output is Q_1. The marginal social benefit curve is the vertical summation of the marginal external benefit and the demand curve. In our earlier analysis of this situation, we ignored the marginal welfare cost of taxation and concluded that the efficient output was Q_3 and that this output could be achieved with an excise subsidy. We now want to see how recognizing the marginal welfare cost of taxation affects this analysis.

We must first determine how much the government must spend on the subsidy to increase output. It is easiest to figure this out if we make the simplifying assumption that the demand curve is unit elastic, as it is drawn in the graph. Recall that this means that total consumer outlays remain unchanged when the price consumers pay changes. Thus, if the excise subsidy lowers the price enough so that consumers purchase Q_3, their total outlays

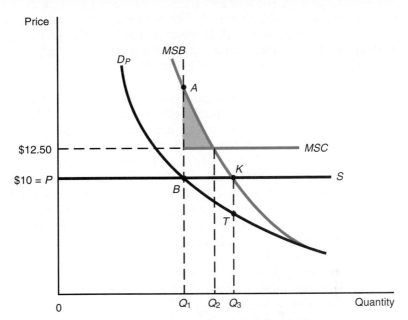

Figure 4–9 *An excise subsidy with costly taxation*

will still be equal to the area PBQ_10, their original value (though now composed of a lower price and a higher quantity). How much will the government be spending on this subsidy? Since total outlays (consumers' outlays plus the government subsidy) must equal PKQ_30, that amount less consumer outlays equals the amount spent on the subsidy. In other words, the total cost of the subsidy would equal BKQ_3Q_1, which is just equal to the market cost of the extra output stimulated by the subsidy. With a unit elastic demand curve, this reasoning shows that the total cost of the subsidy equals the cost of producing the extra output. Thus, if an excise subsidy is used to expand output by one unit, the total cost will be $10; if a larger per unit subsidy is used to expand output by two units, the total cost will be $20, and so on. In short, total government spending will also measure the market value (at cost) of the additional output stimulated. (This simple relationship holds only for a unit elastic demand curve.)

Therefore, to expand output by one dollar's worth requires the government to spend one dollar. This is what we need to know because the marginal welfare cost of taxation is the additional real cost associated with each dollar of spending. In terms of Figure 4–9, this means that the marginal social cost of expanding output is $12.50 per unit of output. The *MSC* is composed of the cost of the resources necessary to produce each unit ($10, as shown by the height to the supply curve) plus the marginal welfare cost of the tax revenue necessary to stimulate each additional unit, or $2.50, on the assumption that marginal welfare cost is 25 percent. (It requires spending $10 worth of taxes to stimulate each unit of extra output, so the marginal welfare cost related to output is 25 percent of that amount.) In the graph, the marginal social cost of expanding output with an excise subsidy is shown as *MSC*. It relates only to output in excess of Q_1 since that quantity is produced without a subsidy.

In our previous analysis of externalities, we assumed implicitly that there were no welfare costs associated with raising taxes, and so treated the supply curve as the *MSC* curve. Now we see that when we take account of the costs of raising tax revenue, the real cost of expanding output with a subsidy is greater than just the cost of production; we must also account for the costs of raising tax revenue, and that is done with the *MSC* curve.

Armed with the *MSC* curve, it is easy to determine the efficient output; it is Q_2 where marginal social cost and marginal social benefit are equal. Thus, it is still efficient to use a subsidy in this case even though there are welfare costs associated with raising the tax revenue. There are, however, several important implications of recognizing the welfare costs of taxation. First, the most efficient subsidy will be smaller when these costs are taken into account. (If the marginal welfare cost is zero, for example, the efficient subsidy is *KT* per unit, resulting in output of Q_3.) Second, it is no longer true that the mere existence of external benefits implies that some subsidy can result in a welfare gain. If the marginal external benefit was less than $2.50 per unit of output at Q_1, for example, it would be best not to use a subsidy at all. The marginal social benefit of any expansion of output would be less than the marginal social cost. Third, the potential gain from using a subsidy is smaller the larger the marginal welfare cost. In the graph, the net gain from the excise subsidy is shown by the shaded triangle; if the marginal welfare cost were zero, the potential gain would be shown by the much larger triangle *BAK*.

Although the exact effects of incorporating the marginal welfare cost of taxation into the analysis of government expenditures depend on the type of spending program, the general principle that these costs of taxation are part of the cost of the expenditure program remain true.

A P P E N D I X   T O   C H A P T E R   4
Benefit-Cost Analysis

Benefit-cost analysis is a technique that can be used to evaluate government projects. The basic concept is quite simple: Identify the benefits and costs of a project and then measure them in comparable units (such as dollars). If the benefits exceed the costs, the project will lead to a more efficient resource allocation. If the costs exceed the benefits, the project will lead to a poorer allocation of resources.

Because the benefit-cost technique is a logical method to use in appraising alternatives, it is not surprising that it is occasionally used to analyze government expenditure programs. Some government agencies, notably the Bureau of Reclamation and the Army Corps of Engineers, have employed benefit-cost analysis since the 1930s to evaluate alternative potential projects. In recent years the technique has been used by other agencies and practitioners outside government to analyze policies in such diverse areas as health, transportation, education, and social welfare programs. Such studies are sometimes available to Congress and provide information that is useful in its deliberations. Our main concern, however, will not be with how benefit-cost analysis has been employed within government but instead with the nature of the technique itself. A study of the nature and limitations of the benefit-cost approach provides further insight into the application of economics to government policy analysis.

Identifying and Measuring Benefits

Suppose that we are trying to ascertain what benefits will result from a particular government project. Obviously, the first step is to determine the impact of the project: What goods or services will we have more of as a result of the project? Second, these effects must be expressed quantitatively; that is, the value of these effects to the public must be calculated. Usually this second step causes the greatest difficulty. An example will illustrate why.

Consider the construction of a dam to control flooding. One obvious benefit is a reduction in the probability of flood damage. How do we measure this effect in dollars? The generally correct theoretical answer is that the dollar value of the benefit equals the maximum amount that people would be willing to pay to secure this service. Because of the free rider problem, however, we are unable to survey the potential beneficiaries to determine this figure. Instead an alternative means of estimating the benefit must be found, and that is the difficulty. Frequently there is no way to do this accurately.

Although it may be impossible to measure the benefit with perfect accuracy, analysts have shown considerable ingenuity in devising ways to approximate the magnitudes involved. Consider how this might be done in the present case. If flooding destroys farmers' crops, then we could estimate the average annual volume of crops destroyed and multiply this amount by their market price (the value to consumers). For a variety of reasons, this approach is unlikely to yield exactly the correct answer (i.e., how much farmers would be willing to pay), but it may be a fair approximation. In any event, it is likely to be better than relying on pure guesswork.

For some projects, the valuation of benefits is easier than for others. If, for example, the output is a good or service that is already produced and sold in private markets, we can use the market price to estimate the benefit. The production of electricity by nuclear power plants falls in this category. However, in many, perhaps most, cases the output of a government expenditure project is not sold and so is not valued directly in some market. In these situations, we must devise alternative methods to estimate benefits if benefit-cost analysis is to be used.

Benefit-cost studies usually distinguish between the direct and indirect benefits of a project. In the case of the flood control project, the direct benefit might be the reduced probability of flooding. An indirect benefit might be the recreational services provided by the lake behind the dam (e.g., swimming, fishing, camping, boating). The value of these services is as real a benefit as flood control and should also be counted as a benefit in a benefit-cost analysis.

In principle, there is no clear-cut distinction between direct and indirect benefits. All the effects of a project that are considered desirable by those affected are benefits and should be counted as such. Admittedly, some benefits are likely to be quantitatively less important than others; the recreational value of the lake may be very small in comparison with its flood control services. In addition, some benefits are likely to be much more difficult to estimate with any accuracy than are others: How much is it worth to homeowners overlooking the lake to have a better view? What we call these indirect or intangible benefits is irrelevant as long as we generally recognize that all real benefits should, in principle, be counted. (In practice, however, many benefits may be too small or too costly to measure.)

One error frequently made in benefit-cost studies (especially in the past) was to count pecuniary externalities as benefits. Any government project is likely to affect the prices and quantities of other goods. It is important to distinguish between effects that provide clues to the net benefits and those that represent only transfers. For example, providing a recreational area may lead to higher prices for boats and fishing tackle, which benefit sellers of these items. At the same time, however, the higher prices are costs to people who purchase these items. Consequently, there are no net benefits. These effects may be treated in two ways. One is to recognize that a benefit accrues to the seller and include it along with other benefits. If this is done, the burden placed on the purchasers must also be entered as a cost. Alternatively, these effects can be disregarded altogether. In either case, the net effect is zero. The error arises when the benefit to sellers is included and not the cost to consumers, or vice versa.

Another common error is to double-count benefits. An estimate of how much the view of the lake is worth to a nearby homeowner might be included as a benefit. But what about the higher property value of his home? The increased value of his home is not a separate benefit because the increase in the property value is a result of the house's commanding a better view. It might be possible to use the increment in property value as an estimate of the value of the view, but to include both is to count the same benefit twice.

The identification and measurement of the benefits of a government project constitute a difficult task, one that is likely to be even more difficult when we consider such complex areas as national defense, education, health insurance, or welfare programs. When externalities or public goods are involved, there is no accurate way to determine benefits. (This does not mean that the benefit-cost approach is faulty but only that its practical implementation is difficult.) Perhaps this explains why benefit-cost analysis has been limited to areas in which benefits are relatively easy to measure, such as irrigation, flood control, and transportation projects. Nonetheless, as our technical ability to estimate benefits improves, benefit-cost analysis is likely to find applications in other areas.

Identifying and Measuring Costs

The consequences of a project that involves burdens or sacrifices for people are its costs. In the case of a dam, manpower, concrete, equipment, energy, and other productive resources must be used for its construction and maintenance. Using these resources involves an opportunity cost because productive services in other sectors of the economy must be sacrificed. The task of placing a dollar figure on these costs is generally thought to be much simpler than valuing the benefits of the project. As a first approximation, the costs are what must be paid to attract the required resources into employment on the dam. Insofar as the economy is competitive, these payments will equal the value of sacrificed output elsewhere.

When the economy is not fully competitive, however, the payments necessary to attract resources into employment on the dam may either underestimate or overestimate the true costs. For example, the wage necessary to bid a worker away from a monopoly will underestimate the costs because the monopoly pays a wage below the marginal value product of the workers. On the other hand, bidding workers away from subsidized industries requires wages above their marginal value products and overstates the costs. It will seldom be possible to identify exactly where the resources employed by the government come from, so there may be little option but to use the actual payments as an estimate of their resource cost. Because there are biases in offsetting directions, this figure may in many cases be approximately correct.

Some analysts have suggested that if the project employs previously unemployed resources, the opportunity cost of using these resources is zero. As explained earlier in this chapter, this is generally incorrect. Not only are there practical problems (the value of leisure is not zero; a worker who is unemployed when hired may not remain unemployed very long even if the project were not undertaken), but also the basic point is that unemployed resources can be reemployed in a variety of uses. Using an unemployed worker to construct a dam means that the worker cannot be used elsewhere, and that involves an opportunity cost.

Although the costs of using resources to construct and maintain the dam will normally be the most important costs associated with the project, there may be additional costs. For example, damming a river might cause environmental damage. The lake could become a breeding ground for disease-carrying insects. In addition, the dam could break and cause a flood more severe than the floods it was built to prevent. Costs such as these should also be included, although clearly it would be difficult to measure them.

The funds to finance a project are normally raised through taxation. However, the burden on taxpayers is not (with a qualification noted later) a cost in addition to the payments to productive factors. Using taxes is simply a way of distributing the burden of diverting resources to the project; it is not a separate or additional cost. The owners of the resources that are used in constructing the dam do not necessarily bear any burden, because they are paid by the government. The income they receive is a measure of the opportunity cost, but taxpayers are the ones who ultimately bear the burden.

There are, however, additional costs arising from the use of tax revenues to finance a project. As discussed earlier in this chapter, to secure $100 in revenue to fund some government project, a burden greater than $100 must be placed on taxpayers due to the marginal welfare cost of taxation. Therefore, the welfare costs associated with raising the tax revenue should be counted as costs in benefit-cost analyses. Unfortunately, until quite recently, almost no benefit-cost studies included these important costs, and even today many still do not.

Another cost can be produced by the tax financing of a project. If the taxpayers whose incomes are reduced by the tax spend part of their incomes in ways that generate external benefits, then there will be a reduction in such external benefits as a result of the tax. In this case, collecting the tax involves another cost. (The opposite case is also possible; expenditures that generate external costs may fall.) For example, the tax may lead some families to spend less on their children's education, and if education is an external benefit, others will be harmed indirectly. This type of effect would generally be expected to be small, if not insignificant, in most practical situations. Benefit-cost analysts generally have little option but to ignore effects this remote and hard to measure.

This last point brings us to another of the real difficulties in conducting a benefit-cost study. Benefits are generally concentrated in a certain area or sector of the economy and are often highly visible. The costs, on the other hand, are spread widely throughout the economy by taxation and may be hard to perceive. As an example, consider this list of alleged benefits from a low-income housing project: reductions in crime, juvenile delinquency, and marital instability; reductions in fire and police protection costs; improved sanitation and reduced health-related costs; reduction in traffic congestion (dependent on location); more attractive neighborhoods and increased property values; improved access of tenants to jobs; and improved competition in the housing market. It is easy for anyone familiar with housing projects to list these and other possible benefits—and some may conceivably be quantitatively important. However, a little thought concerning the effects of the reduction in disposable incomes that result from the higher taxes needed to finance the project will also produce a similarly lengthy list of potentially harmful effects. The difference is that on a per taxpayer basis the costs are so small and uncertain that they will be neglected, even though in the aggregate (because there are more taxpayers than beneficiaries) they may be significant.

In general, the more important costs are probably the use of resources by a project and the administrative, compliance, and welfare costs of taxation. Other costs may be important in specific instances.

Comparing Costs and Benefits

Once all the costs and benefits have been identified and measured, our task is almost over. Now we must decide if it is efficient to undertake the project. Because benefits and costs are reckoned in dollars, the magnitudes can be compared. (In this section, we will assume that the benefits and costs occur in one year; the next section considers the issues involved when the effects occur over a period of several years.) The results are generally presented as a ratio. If the benefits are estimated to be $1.5 million and the costs to be $1.0 million, the benefit-cost ratio will be 1.5. This means that, on average, each dollar of expenditure on the project provides services worth $1.50 to the public.

Note that a benefit-cost study usually results in an estimate of the total benefit and total cost of a project of a specific scale. If the benefit-cost ratio exceeds 1, undertaking the project will lead to a more efficient allocation of resources than doing nothing. This does not mean, however, that such a project is the most efficient. To clarify this point further, consider Figure A4–1. The diagram plots the total benefits and costs for varying scales of a particular type of project. For example, the size of the dam used for flood control might be measured on the horizontal axis.

A benefit-cost study will generally estimate the costs and benefits of a specific project. For example, the project identified by the scale of V in the diagram has a benefit-cost ratio of AV/BV. Because total benefits exceed total costs, this project is more efficient than is none at all. It is not, however, the most efficient scale. The most efficient dam size is where total benefits exceed total costs by the greatest amount because this yields the largest possible net gain. The most efficient project is shown by point W in the diagram, where benefits exceed costs by CD, a larger amount than for any other scale of project. This occurs where the marginal benefits of changing the scale of the project equal the marginal costs. Although the results of a benefit-cost analysis are often summarized as a ratio of benefits to costs, the most efficient project is not the one with the largest ratio. The project of scale V, for example, has total benefits of, say, $4 million (equal to AV) and total costs of $1 million (equal to BV), for a ratio of 4/1. The project scale W, on the other hand, produces total benefits of $8 million ($CW$) and total costs of $4 million ($DW$), a ratio of only 2/1. Nonetheless, the project of scale W is more efficient because its net benefit is $4 million, compared with a net benefit of only $3 million for the project of scale V. Consequently, choosing the project with the highest benefit-cost ratio is not the appropriate strategy.

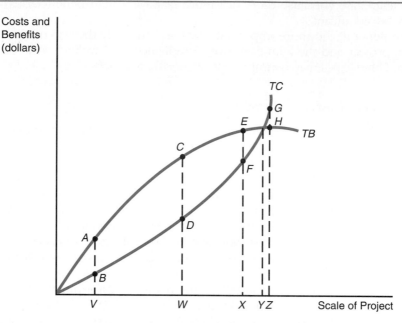

Figure A4–1   *Benefit-cost ratios*

Clearly, if benefit-cost studies could be prepared costlessly, we would like to have one for each possible size of the project, for scales *V, W, X, Y, Z,* and all intermediate points, in Figure A4–1. With this information we could readily identify *W* as the most efficient project. Because of the cost and difficulty of preparing a benefit-cost study, however, we will generally have studies of only a limited range of options, frequently only one. Even in this case it can provide useful information—although there is no guarantee that a policy with benefits greater than costs is better than some alternative policies that were not analyzed.

Time and Discounting

With many, perhaps most, government expenditures, the benefits received by the public are experienced at approximately the same time that the costs are incurred. This, however, is not always true. In the case of our dam for flood control, for example, during the first few years (while the dam is being constructed) there are heavy costs and no benefits. During later years, there are benefits and much lower costs (only maintenance costs). For such projects, the time at which benefits and costs are experienced becomes an important consideration.

A benefit-cost study typically estimates the benefits and costs of a project over a number of years. We should realize, however, that a dollar in benefits received 10 years in the future is not worth as much as a dollar in benefits today. You would not be willing to pay a dollar today to receive a dollar 10 years from now because you could put the dollar in a savings account and it would grow to more than a dollar in 10 years. Thus, it is not correct to add the dollar value of benefits or costs that extend over a period of years in the future. Instead, all of the benefits and costs must be evaluated at their worth in today's dollars. To do this, benefits and costs to be experienced in the future are discounted using a discount (or interest) rate to arrive at a present value measure.

The term *discounting* refers to the fact that future benefits and costs are worth less (must be discounted) today. If the discount rate is 5 percent, a dollar in benefits today is equivalent to $1.05 in benefits to be received 1 year later; that is, a person would be indifferent between receiving $1 today and $1.05 next year. Thus, the present or discounted value of $1.05 in benefits received next year is only $1 today. Putting this in a benefit-cost perspective, to consider an expenditure of $1 today, the project would have to produce a benefit of at least $1.05 a year from now (if next year's benefits were the only benefit). The present value of the benefit can be calculated from $B_1/(1+i)$, where B_1 is the benefit 1 year from now and i is the discount rate. Similarly, the present value of a dollar in benefits to be received 14 years from now is only 50 cents today: $B_{14}/(1+i)^{14}$, or $\$1/(1.05)^{14}$ equals $\$0.50$.

When costs and benefits occur over a period of years, the total benefit of the project is the present value of the stream of benefits. Similarly, costs must be evaluated at their present value. Having done this, we once more arrive at a single figure for the total benefit and for the total cost, and the project can be evaluated as we did earlier.

A major issue in discounting future costs and benefits concerns what discount rate to use. The results of a benefit-cost study can depend critically on the discount rate used to calculate the present value of benefits and costs. Consider a simplified example of a government project that has costs in the first year of $1 million and no benefits until 14 years later when there are $2 million in benefits; there are no other costs or benefits. If the discount rate is 3 percent, the present value of $2 million in benefits to be received 14 years in the future is $1.32 million, and the present value of $1 million in costs incurred in this year is, of course, $1 million. The benefit-cost ratio is 1.32, and the project looks attractive. Alternatively, suppose that we use a discount rate of 6 percent; then the present value of the $2 million benefit is only $0.89 million today, and the benefit-cost ratio if 0.89. If the discount rate is instead 10 percent, the present value of benefits is $0.53 million, so the present value of costs is almost double the present value of benefits.

This example illustrates that the desirability of a project can depend heavily on what discount rate is used. The higher the discount rate is, the smaller the present value of future benefits and costs will be. (We are discounting the future more heavily with a high discount rate.) Most government projects that yield benefits and costs over many years are similar to our example; there are high initial costs with benefits accruing later. This would be true, for example, of many irrigation, environmental, energy, and job training policies. In cases like these, the higher the discount rate used, the less favorable the project will appear.

What is the appropriate discount rate to use? The answer to this question turns out to be a highly complex issue. Intuitively, it seems that the discount rate should be related to two different variables. One is the rate at which people are willing to sacrifice present consumption for future consumption. If the public is willing (at the margin) to give up $1 today in return for $1.05 a year from now, the 5 percent rate tells us how much the public discounts future benefits. This is sometimes called the *time preference rate*. On the other hand, public investment projects use resources that can alternatively be employed in private investment projects. If private investment projects yield (at the margin) 10 percent, then diverting resources from private investment to public projects entails an opportunity cost in the form of a sacrificed return of 10 percent. The return on private investments is sometimes called the *opportunity cost rate*. Which of these two rates should be used?

Frequently prices (in this case interest rates) determined in private markets can serve as a guide. If capital markets were perfectly competitive, and there were no risk associated with investments,[9] a single interest rate would be determined. This is illustrated in Figure A4–2, where the investment demand curve is I and the saving supply curve is S. The equilibrium rate of return (interest rate) is 6 percent. At the equilibrium level of investment, I_1, the interest rate measures both the marginal return to private investments (the height of the I curve) and the return the public requires to sacrifice present consumption (the height of the S curve). The opportunity cost rate and the time preference rate are equal to each other at the competitive equilibrium. If this model were an accurate description of reality, most economists would agree that 6 percent would be the appropriate discount rate to use for discounting future benefits and costs.

For a variety of reasons, the real world differs from this model. Perhaps the most important difference is that the government taxes the return to private investments with the corporation income tax and property taxes. These taxes will be considered in detail in Chapters 12 and 13, but their relevance to the discount rate issue deserves mention here. Briefly, if a private investment yields a return of 10 percent and the government taxes this yield, then less than 10 percent is left to be paid to investors (savers). The effect of a 50 percent tax is shown in Figure A4–2 by a pivoting downward of the I curve to I'. The I' curve shows the after-tax return that can be paid at each rate of investment; the I curve continues to show the before-tax return. The new equilibrium is at I_2. At this equilibrium, the net return to investors is 4 percent, in contrast with the before-tax return of 8 percent.

---

[9] When investments differ in their degree of risk, there is a wide range of interest rates in markets reflecting the varying risks of different projects. This is ignored in the text but is yet another reason why it is difficult to agree on a single interest rate to use in discounting.

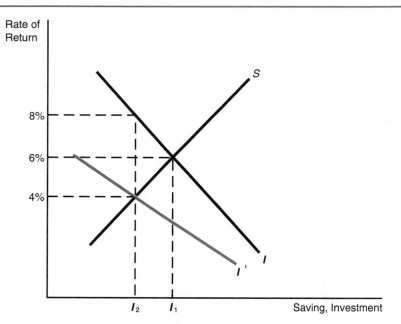

Figure A4–2   *Taxation and discount rates*

Note that this means that the time preference rate differs from the opportunity cost rate. The time preference rate is now 4 percent and the opportunity cost rate is 8 percent. (These figures are intended only as illustrations; actually, empirical evidence suggests that the opportunity cost rate is around 10 percent.)

We now face a dilemma because we cannot choose one discount rate that simultaneously reflects the time preference of the public and the opportunity cost of private investments. Which rate, 4 percent or 8 percent, should be used? This question has been widely debated by economists, but no one answer seems to produce a consensus. Most economists seem in limited agreement that the 4 percent rate is too low and that either the opportunity cost rate of 8 percent or some weighted average of the two rates should be used. In practice this means that many of the earlier benefit-cost studies have used discount rates that were far too low.

Our discussion thus far has not distinguished between real and nominal rates of interest, but this distinction is quite important in inflationary periods. If the future benefits and costs of a project are estimated in dollars of constant purchasing power, then it is the real rates of interest that are relevant. The numbers that we have used for illustrative purposes are closer to the level of the real rates that have prevailed in recent years. Because of inflation, nominal rates have been much higher.

Whose Benefits and Whose Costs?

Generally, people receiving benefits from a project are not the same ones bearing the costs. The tax system usually distributes the costs widely among the public, and it would be only a coincidence if the benefits were distributed in a similar way. When this is true, exactly what meaning should be attached to the final benefit-cost ratio? To take an extreme case, suppose that wealthy yacht owners receive $2 million in benefits from an irrigation project that imposes $1 million in costs on middle- and low-income families. Should this project, with a benefit-cost ratio of 2/1, be undertaken? Can we really compare the benefits and costs as evaluated by different people?

This issue has troubled many analysts. The problem is that the project has both efficiency and distributional (equity) implications, and benefit-cost analysis has evaluated only the efficiency implications. Therefore, one must avoid thinking that any project with benefits greater than costs is necessarily desirable, irrespective of its distributional implications. Value judgments must still be made concerning distributional effects of government policies.

An estimate that a project's benefits exceed its costs has a definite meaning: It means that the beneficiaries *could* pay the entire cost and still be better off. If this were actually done, beneficiaries would be better off, and no one else would be affected—a clear efficiency gain. When other people bear some of the costs, there is still an efficiency gain, but it is coupled with a redistribution of income. Thus, benefit-cost analysis, like any other economic analysis, cannot demonstrate desirability.

Some economists have suggested that the benefit-cost technique be modified to permit an evaluation of distributional as well as efficiency effects. This could be done by using distributional weights that specify, for example, that a dollar benefit to a wealthy person could be counted only as $0.80, whereas a dollar of benefit to a poor person should be counted as $1.20. Such a procedure is an attempt to combine efficiency and distributional effects in one measure of "desirability." This would mean that an inefficient policy could be adjudged desirable if it redistributed income to low-income persons. For example, if the government places a tax burden of $1 on a wealthy person and transfers $0.80 to a poor person ($0.20 being used up in administrative costs), the benefit-cost ratio will be $0.96/$0.80, or 1.2 (using these weights).

There are several practical and conceptual problems with this procedure. For example, there is no objective way to choose a set of distributional weights. People would disagree over what weights to use; to select one particular set of weights would require a value judgment. More important, many policies are available that provide alternative means of redistributing income, and these should be explicitly compared if it is decided that the government should redistribute income. Using distributional weights in benefit-cost analysis could easily lead to enactment of policies that help the poor, but do so less than would an alternative policy of the same cost to other people.

For these reasons, most benefit-cost analysts have not attempted to apply distributional weights. This does not imply a judgment that distributional effects are unimportant but only that the benefit-cost analysis is more useful if it concentrates on efficiency considerations.

Benefit-cost Analysis: Not a Panacea

Benefit-cost analysis provides a technique that is helpful in weighing the advantages and disadvantages of government policies. Our discussion has only touched on the major problems in applying this technique, notably identifying and measuring benefits and costs and discounting to obtain present value measures. In particular, the difficulty of measuring benefits and costs has been emphasized because this is the real problem in most attempts to grapple quantitatively with policy issues.

The remainder of this book deals with many policy issues that are, in principle, amenable to benefit-cost analysis. Unfortunately, the problems of measuring benefits and costs are extremely difficult for many of the most important government policies. No attempt is made to construct a formal benefit-cost analysis of any of the policies discussed later, but the reader should find the benefit-cost approach a helpful guide in thinking about the economic effects that will be identified.

Review Questions and Problems

1. "Government defense expenditures created 300,000 jobs in Texas in 1993. A reduction in defense spending thus would cost Texas thousands of jobs and produce much hardship." Discuss.

2. Identify and explain why some types of government expenditures could have no effect at all on the allocation of resources. What actual government expenditures do you think are likely to be of this type and have very little effect on the composition of output?

3. What are the essential characteristics of a fixed-quantity subsidy? Under what conditions would such a subsidy have no effect on a recipient's consumption pattern?

4. Explain how a fixed-quantity subsidy can lead to underconsumption. Does the subsidy always have this effect, or could it lead to underconsumption for some recipients and to overconsumption for others? Support your answer with a graphical analysis.

5. Is it better for a subsidy to lead to overconsumption or to underconsumption?

6. What is an excise subsidy, and how does it differ from a fixed-quantity subsidy? Can an excise subsidy ever lead to underconsumption?

7. Compare the effects of an excise subsidy and a fixed-quantity subsidy (in which the consumer can supplement the quantity provided by government). Which subsidy will lead to greater consumption of the subsidized good, and which will make the consumer better off? (Be sure to compare subsidies of equal cost to the government.)

8. Senator Throckmorton, arguing for federal funds to build a dam in his district, observed: "Not only will the dam benefit the area, it will also create much needed jobs in the area. As a matter of fact, I wouldn't consider the $200 million price tag of the project as a 'cost' at all, given that we will be using unemployed workers and resources. I mean the people and resources weren't being used to do anything, right? Therefore, society doesn't give up anything to get the dam. The correct economic phrase would be the opportunity cost of the dam is zero." Evaluate the senator's reasoning.

9. If you were to conduct a benefit-cost analysis of an excise subsidy granted to a single consumer, how would you measure the policy's benefits? How would you measure its costs? (Try to do this using a graph.) Can you say which will be larger, or will this depend on the particular good and the consumer being subsidized?

10. Why is the choice of a discount rate often important to conducting a benefit-cost analysis? Why is it difficult to determine what discount rate should be used?

11. Should the public be satisfied if it gets a dollar's worth of benefits for every dollar spent by the government?

12. What is the marginal welfare cost of taxation? How does it affect the analysis of externalities and public goods?

13. If the private demand curve in Figure 4–9 is of less than unit elasticity (an inelastic demand curve), how would this affect the position of the *MSC* curve in the graph?

Supplementary Readings

BROWNING, EDGAR K. "Subsidies Financed with Distorting Taxes." *National Tax Journal* 46 (June 1993).

GRAMLICH, EDWARD M. *Benefit-Cost Analysis of Government Programs,* 2nd ed. Englewood Cliffs, N.J.: Prentice-Hall, 1990.

HARBERGER, ARNOLD C. "On the Use of Distributional Weights in Social Cost-Benefit Analysis." *Journal of Political Economy,* 86(2):S87–120, Part 2 (Apr. 1978).

HAVEMAN, ROBERT H., and JULIUS MARGOLIS, eds. *Public Expenditure and Policy Analysis,* 3rd ed. Boston: Houghton Mifflin, 1983.

Food Stamps, Unemployment Insurance, and College Subsidies

*C*HAPTER 4 DEVELOPED THE ANALYTICAL FRAMEWORK NEEDED to study the effects of different types of subsidies. Two categories of subsidies, fixed quantity and excise subsidies, were emphasized. In this chapter we adapt this analytical framework to examine more thoroughly three actual policies that fall into these two general categories: the food stamp program, unemployment insurance, and subsidies to higher education.

The Food Stamp Program

President John F. Kennedy's first executive order in January 1961 directed the secretary of agriculture to establish pilot food stamp programs for needy families. After several years of experience with the pilot programs, Congress enacted the Food Stamp Act of 1964. In 1965, federal expenditures were only $30 million, but growth was rapid in the next several years as coverage of the population widened. By 1975 the program had achieved nationwide coverage, and expenditures reached $4.6 billion. In 1991, total expenditures were $18.7 billion, but most of the growth after 1980 has been due to inflation. As shown in Table 5–1, total spending in constant 1991 dollars rose only from $15.1 billion in 1980 to $18.7 billion in 1991. The program has provided benefits to about 20 million persons annually in recent years.

The food stamp program provides benefits to low-income households. To establish eligibility to receive the food stamp subsidy, a household's net income and total assets must fall below specified amounts. In 1992, for example, a family of four had to have a monthly net income below $1,100 and total assets below $2,000 (not including home or up to $4,500 in automobile

Table 5–1   *Food Stamp Program: Total Expenditures and Participation, 1965–1991*

Year	Total Federal Outlays ($ billions)	Federal Outlays in 1991 Dollars	Participation (millions)
1965	$ 0.03	$ 0.13	0.4
1970	0.58	2.04	4.3
1975	4.60	11.65	17.1
1980	9.12	15.07	21.1
1985	11.70	14.81	19.9
1990	14.99	15.62	20.0
1991	18.68	18.68	22.6

Source: Office of Managment and Budget, The Budget of the United States Government, Fiscal Year, 1993. Table 11.3, *Social Security Bulletin, Annual Statistical Supplement,* 1991, Table 9.H.1.

equity). The benefit levels depend on *net* income, or total income minus certain allowable deductions, so families with higher total incomes can receive benefits. The most important deductions are a standard deduction of $127 a month, shelter costs in excess of specified levels, and 20 percent of earned income. As a result of these deductions, a family of four could have had a total income as high as $18,405 in 1992 and still have received some benefits.

If households meet the eligibility requirements, they can receive food stamps. Food stamps can be thought of as checks signed by the government that can be used only to purchase food; some government publications, in fact, refer to food stamps as "food money." The dollar amount of food stamps that a family can receive is called the *coupon allotment*; it depends on the family's net income and the number of persons in the family. Larger families receive a bigger coupon allotment, and families with higher incomes receive a smaller allotment.

Table 5–2 shows how the coupon allotment varies with net income for four-person families. For example, a family with a zero monthly net income would receive $370 in food stamps. *Note that for each dollar of net income the family earns, food stamp benefits are reduced by 30 cents.* Thus, a family with a net income of $100 receives $340 in food stamps, $30 less than a family with zero income receives. The rate at which benefits fall as income rises is called the *benefit reduction rate*, and in the food stamp program it is 30 percent. The benefit reduction rate ensures that the poorest households get the largest benefits.

The basic coupon allotment, the dollar amount of food stamps given to a family with zero net income, is based on the "Thrifty Food Plan" of the Department of Agriculture, a low-cost plan for achieving a nutritionally adequate diet. Since 1974 the basic coupon allotments (one for each family

Table 5–2 **Food Stamp Benefits, Family of Four, 1992**

Monthly Net Income	Food Stamps
$ 0	$370
100	340
200	310
300	280
400	250
500	220
600	190
700	160
800	130
900	100
1,000	70
1,100	40

size) have been tied to a price escalator that increases the allotments to reflect changes in the prices of food items.

Some Economic Effects of the Food Stamp Program

The food stamp program is an example of a fixed-quantity subsidy, which we examined in the last chapter. There are several special features that we need to take into account, notably the way the amount of the subsidy varies with income, with poorer families receiving more assistance.

In Chapter 4 we noted that this form of subsidy can be equivalent to a cash transfer or result in overconsumption, producing a welfare cost. Both of these possibilities are illustrated in Figure 5–1. As we will see, we expect food stamps to be equivalent to a cash transfer for most of the recipients, with only the poorest households likely to have their consumption patterns distorted. To see this point clearly, we will make one special but not too unrealistic an assumption: that at any given level of cash income, low-income families have preferences implying they would choose to spend 30 percent of their income on food.

Given this assumption, Figure 5–1(a) shows the effects of food stamps for a family with a gross income of $850 per month—toward the middle of the eligibility scale after deductions are taken into account. The family is assumed to have deductions of $250 per month, so its net income is $600 and its coupon allotment is $190 (Table 5–2). With food measured in units that cost $1 each, the presubsidy budget line is MN, and food consumption is 255 before the subsidy. The food stamp subsidy causes the budget line to become MM'N'. The new equilibrium is at point E', with consumption of

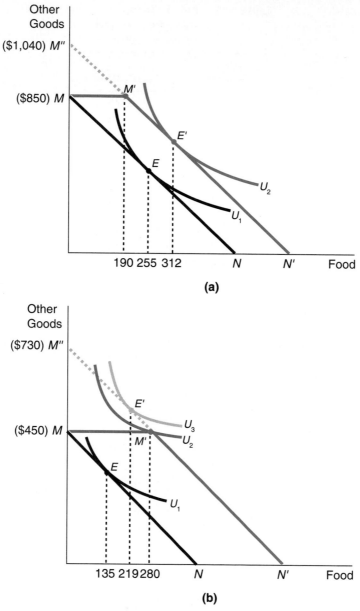

Figure 5–1   *Food stamps: two possible outcomes*

312 units of food. (We know the family will choose to consume 312 units of food on *MM'N'* because, if they were given $190 in cash, their income would be $1,040, and they would spend 30 percent on food.) In this case, the food stamp program has the same effect as an unrestricted cash transfer.

Part (b) of Figure 5–1 shows the results for a lower-income family with a gross income of $450 per month and $150 in deductions, which makes it eligible to receive $280 in food stamps. In this case, equilibrium occurs at point M' on the postsubsidy budget line, where the family uses only food stamps to finance all of its food consumption, leaving its entire income to be used to purchase other goods. Note that the family would be better off if it received $280 in cash, since that would generate a budget line of $M''N'$. In that case, the family would reach a higher indifference curve, U_3, by spending 30 percent of its income ($730) on food and purchasing 219 units of food at point E'.

In Figure 5–1(b) the food stamp program produces a welfare cost by leading to overconsumption of food: The family attains indifference curve U_2 with food stamps, but it could reach U_3 at the same cost if the family were given cash instead. In effect, the food stamp program forces an inferior consumption pattern on the family by requiring that the subsidy be consumed as food.

Which type of outcome, the one shown in Figure 5–1(a) or 5–1(b), is more common under the food stamp program? There have been a number of studies dealing with this question, and they have all concluded that the overwhelming majority of food stamp recipients are in positions like (a).[1] This is not particularly suprising since earlier budget studies have found that low-income families spend about 30 percent of their incomes on food, but the lowest-income families spend an even higher proportion. (The significance of this latter point can be seen by noting that if the family in (b) had preferences implying that 40 percent would be spent on food, the subsidy would be equivalent to a cash transfer for it also.)

Families with very low incomes could still find themselves in the situation shown in (b), but it appears certain that *the subsidy is equivalent to a cash transfer for almost all recipients*. This conclusion is significant because it means that the impression most people have—that the food stamp program is distinctly different from cash welfare programs—is incorrect. Food stamps no more encourage food consumption than would cash assistance.

It is also worth noting that, regardless of whether (a) or (b) is the appropriate analysis, *the food stamp program has the effect of increasing nonfood consumption as well as food consumption*. This finding is particularly interesting since many proponents of food stamps emphasize that the subsidy should not be used to finance consumption of "unnecessary" goods (such as liquor or cigarettes?). In practice, however, the food stamp subsidy unavoidably helps to finance the consumption of goods other than food; in

---

[1]See, for example, Lois Blanchard, J. S. Butler, T. Doyle, R. Jackson, J. Ohis, and B. Posner, *Final Report, Food Stamp SSI/Elderly Cash-out Demonstration Evaluation* (Princeton, N.J.: Mathematica Policy Research, 1982); and Thomas Fraker, Barbara Devaney, and Edward Cavin, "An Evaluation of the Effect of Cashing Out Food Stamps on Food Expenditures," *American Economic Review*, 76:230 (May 1986).

fact, it is difficult to conceive of a subsidy that will only increase consumption of the subsidized good.

Although its impact on food consumption is perhaps the most widely emphasized effect of the food stamp program, the program does have other significant effects. The most important of these is probably the way the program affects the work incentives of the recipients. The feature in the program that bears most directly on work incentives is the benefit reduction rate. With a benefit reduction rate of 30 percent, when a family increases its net earnings by $100, its food stamp benefits go down by $30, so its net income rises by only $70. The benefit reduction rate acts like a marginal tax rate on earnings. The work incentives issue is extremely important in evaluating a number of welfare programs, but we will defer a fuller consideration of this issue until Chapter 9. It should be noted here, however, that in the analysis of Figure 5–1, we implicitly assumed that the program did not affect the level of earnings, although in practice it probably does result in some reduction.

As explained earlier, the dollar amount of food stamps a family receives is related to net income, or total income less allowable deductions. One interesting implication of the deduction of shelter costs is that this deduction acts as an excise subsidy for housing-related expenditures. Shelter costs (including rent, insurance, and utilities) in excess of 30 percent of income are deductible from total income in determining the net income figure on which food stamp subsidies are based. To illustrate how this can act to subsidize housing, consider a family on food stamps spending 30 percent of its income on housing. If the family increased its housing outlays by $50 per month, its "monthly net income" used to determine the food stamp subsidy will fall by $50. With a lower net income, the food stamp subsidy is larger (see Table 5–2), in this case by $15. The deduction thus acts to reduce the net cost of additional housing by 30 percent (from $50 to $35 in our example) in the same way as an excise subsidy would. Thus, the food stamp program also acts to subsidize the consumption of housing of families that spend more than 30 percent of their income on shelter. As we will see in Chapter 11, this is similar to the way deductions in the federal income tax operate as implicit subsidies.

Other Factors in an Evaluation of Food Stamps

Considerations that influence congressional decisions are often different from those emphasized by economists. Food stamps are a case in point. Consider, for example, the testimony of the late Senator Hubert Humphrey in congressional hearings on food stamp reforms. Senator Humphrey summarized three arguments in favor of food stamps that are still often heard in Congress:

> The food stamp program plays a very critical role in enabling millions of low-income families to have a better diet.
> It plays a very important role in the support of American agriculture.

It also plays a very important role in keeping the economy from sliding into a deeper recession.[2]

Because these three arguments are frequently mentioned in discussions of food stamps, we shall consider each in turn.

Nutrition   Improving the nutritional adequacy of the diets of poor families is frequently stated as the primary objective of the program. As we have already seen, it is inappropriate to think of the food stamp program as a food subsidy since it really is equivalent to a cash transfer for most recipients. So if it affects nutrition, it does so indirectly by increasing the incomes of recipients. A relevant question is whether the small increases in income accomplished by the food stamp program have a significant effect on the nutritional adequacy of diets.

Perhaps surprisingly, the evidence suggests that the food stamp program has had little or no effect on the nutritional adequacy of the diets of recipients. Although food expenditures are certainly increased, that does not translate into better-quality diets. This finding is not as tragic as it sounds because low-income American families on average have diets that already meet or exceed the recommended dietary standards of most nutrients. In fact, one interesting finding of studies of nutrition is that there is very little difference in the nutritional adequacy of the diets of low- and high-income American families.[3] This suggests that increases in the incomes of low-income families will not lead to more nutritious diets.

If improving nutrition were an important goal, it would be possible to restructure the program in a way that would promote it more effectively. All we would have to do is restrict the use of food stamps to food items that are highly nutritious per dollar of cost. Instead of allowing food stamps to be used to purchase frozen dinners, candy, soft drinks, coffee, sugar, and so on, they could be restricted to the purchase of items like soybeans, nonfat dry milk, vitamin pills, and fresh fruits and vegetables. This reform would certainly be more effective in improving nutrition, but it would also make food stamp recipients worse off according to their preferences (i.e., the reform would lead to a welfare cost from distorted consumption patterns).

Claiming that nutritional improvement is a goal of the food stamp program implicitly seems to adopt the position that we do not want the program to cater to the needs of the recipients as they themselves evaluate their needs. For if the food stamp program did significantly improve nutrition (more than a cash transfer would), it would do so at the expense of other

[2]Statement of Senator Hubert Humphrey, *Food Stamp Hearings*, Subcommittee on Agriculture and General Legislation of the Committee on Agriculture and Forestry, U.S. Senate, *Food Stamp Reform*, Part 1 (Washington, D.C.: U.S. Government Printing Office, 1975), p. 107.

[3]See Robert Rector, Kate O'Beirne, and Michael McLaughlin, "How 'Poor' Are America's Poor?" *Backgrounder,* 791 (Washington, D.C.: Heritage Foundation, 1990), for a discussion of some of the relevant evidence.

food or nonfood items considered more desirable by the recipients. This position is, of course, defensible (perhaps especially in regard to children), but it is a paternalistic position and should be evaluated as such. In any case, as it now stands, the food stamp program does not do much to promote better nutrition.

Effect on the Agricultural Sector   Senator Humphrey argued that food stamps "support American agriculture." In recent years, food stamps have accounted for approximately 3 percent of total food expenditures, but that does not mean that the demand for food has increased by 3 percent as a result of the program. Since food stamps are like an increase in income for most recipients, food purchases by recipients will increase by less than the dollar amount of food stamps. It is unlikely, for example, that the recipients of the $18.7 billion in food stamps in 1991 increased purchases of food by more than $4 billion. (Our earlier assumption that 30 percent is spent on food is reasonable as an average, but the *marginal* propensity to spend on food is less than 20 percent.) In addition, the taxes needed to finance the program would probably reduce food purchases by taxpayers by at least $2 billion. Thus, the net increase in food purchases would be about $2 billion. Since total outlays in the United States on food products were about $620 billion in 1991, a $2 billion increase would imply an increase in demand of 0.3 percent resulting from the food stamp program.

No detailed study is required to see that the impact of a 0.3 percent increase in demand for food on the agricultural sector will be trivial. Less than half of the retail food dollar reaches the agricultural sector; costs of retailing, transportation, and processing account for the remainder. Most, if not all, of what reaches agriculture covers the costs of producing the small increment in output that results. Although the exact effects depend on the nature of the market (see Figure 4–8 in Chapter 4 for the relevant analysis), the quantitative impact is clearly very small.

Suppose, however, that food stamps really did lead to a significant increase in the demand for agricultural sector products. *To the extent that the food stamp program increases the demand for food, it reduces the demand for other goods and services.* Any increase in incomes, wages, or profits in agriculture is therefore accompanied by a reduction in income, wages, or profits in other parts of the economy. In short, any advantages derived by food producers reflect a redistribution of income away from other people; what farmers gain, others lose. So even if the agricultural sector does benefit, we need to question why this result is considered desirable.

Employment and Business Expansion   Senator Humphrey buttressed his preceding remarks concerning the stimulative effect of food stamps by referring to a Department of Agriculture study on the impact of the program in Texas in 1972:

> The study found that $63.9 million in bonus food stamps provided in Texas that year generated $232 million in new business in Texas and appeared to generate at least $89 million in business elsewhere in the United States. In addition, the

$63.9 million provided in bonus food stamps created 5031 jobs. Translated nationwide, this could mean that the food stamp program is now responsible for $27 billion in business in the United States each year and 425,000 jobs.... Furthermore, consider how much money we would have to spend to support those 425,000 workers and their dependents if they did not have the jobs that the food stamp program has apparently generated.[4]

Such arguments, frequently presented in Congress, represent a basic misunderstanding of the significance of the effects of the program on employment and output. The opportunity cost of the expansion of business and employment resulting from the expenditure on food stamp subsidies is a contraction of business and employment elsewhere. This expansion, if it occurs, is not a net effect because it involves drawing resources from other uses. This is easily seen when we recognize that the taxes that finance the program reduce taxpayers' demands for goods and services, reducing output and employment via multiplier effects through other markets.

At the end of his statement, Senator Humphrey seemed to suggest that the workers were not bid away from other jobs, so the effects described represent a net increase in economic activity. This is highly unlikely; even if it were true, the implications drawn by Senator Humphrey would be wrong. As will be recalled from the previous chapter, the opportunity cost of using these resources is that they could have been employed in other jobs producing different goods and services. Had the government spent the $63.9 million on a different subsidy or had it cut taxes, these resources would have been drawn into the production of other goods. The food stamp subsidy simply leads to a different pattern of employment and output than alternative policies. Adding up the employment and output related to food stamp subsidies ignores the fact that employment and output elsewhere could have been higher with different policies. There is, therefore, no net gain in output and employment attributable to food stamps.

Of course, we made this last point earlier: Impacts, if any, on the level of aggregate economic activity (macroeconomic effects) are irrelevant to the analysis of specific expenditure programs. The use of arguments like the one quoted, however, is so prevalent in discussions of many expenditure programs that we thought it useful to examine this one in somewhat greater detail.

Has the Food Stamp Program Hurt the Poor?

The food stamp program is one of several policies that provides benefits to low-income households. In some cases, there are important interactions among the policies for households that receive benefits from more than one policy. We have ignored this fact so far in our analysis of food stamps, but in this case there is a very interesting possibility suggested by the way food stamps interact with another welfare program, Aid to Families with Dependent Children (AFDC).

---

[4]Statement of Senator Humphrey, *Food Stamp Hearings*, p. 107.

AFDC is a policy that provides benefits primarily to single-parent households with children (in practice, usually female-headed households). The level of benefits is determined by individual state governments, although the policy is partially financed with a federal matching grant. (AFDC is, in fact, the policy usually referred to as *welfare* in popular discussions, although as we will see later, it is not the largest spending program providng benefits to poor households.) One of the most noted changes in U.S. welfare policies has been the decline in real AFDC benefits over the last two decades. The first row in Table 5–3 documents this decline; it gives the average (across states) maximum AFDC benefit (payable to those with no other income) in constant 1991 dollars. Note that the maximum AFDC benefit declined by almost 25 percent between 1972 and 1987.

Why has this decline occurred? Since state governments individually determine their benefit levels, there are many factors that could be responsible. One interesting possibility that has been emphasized by several economists is that the introduction of the federal food stamp program on a nationwide basis in the early 1970s may have been responsible.[5] The argument is basically a public choice analysis applied to state governments.

To understand the argument, think of how a particular state determines the level of benefits for AFDC recipients. Based on the neediness of poor single-parent families, state taxpayers decide to tax themselves to provide a basic AFDC benefit to these families. (We are here essentially applying the majority voting model, assuming that some upper-income households wish to help lower-income households and so vote to tax themselves. Other approaches to the analysis might well yield the same results, however.) Here it is important to note that the AFDC program existed for many years before the food stamp program was enacted. Up to the late 1960s, AFDC benefits were the major form of welfare available to single-parent, low-income households.

Then in the early 1970s, the federal government expanded the food stamp program to a nationwide welfare program providing benefits to all low-income households, including single-parent households that also received AFDC benefits. With the federal government now providing benefits to the AFDC population, consider how this situation would affect the decision of state taxpayers regarding the level of AFDC benefits to provide. For example, suppose that you are the "median voter-taxpayer" in a state. You have determined to give $700 a month to AFDC recipients. Then the federal government starts providing food stamps worth $300 a month to these households. How would this decision affect the level of AFDC benefits you decide to provide? If you respond as our basic consumer choice model suggests, you would cut back on the level of AFDC benefits you give to the poor because the poor are no longer as needy as they were due to the receipt of food

---

[5]Christopher B. Colburn, "A Public Choice Explanation for the Decline in Real Income Transfers," *Public Finance Quarterly*, 18:123 (Jan. 1990); and Robert Moffitt, "Has State Redistribution Policy Grown More Conservative?" *National Tax Journal*, 43:123 (June 1990).

Table 5–3   *Monthly Welfare Benefits, Family of Four,*
1969–1987 (1991 dollars)

	1969	*1972*	*1977*	*1982*	*1987*
Maximum AFDC	726	722	684	556	551
Maximum food stamps		320	347	329	320
Combined benefit	726	825	825	718	706

Source: Robert Moffit, "Incentive Effects of the U.S. Welfare System: A Review," *Journal of Economic Literature* (Mar. 1992), Table 3. Figures converted to 1991 dollars using the Consumer Price Index.

stamp benefits. In fact, if there were a target level of income you were trying to achieve for the AFDC recipients, say $700 per month, you would cut your AFDC benefits by $300 when the federal government starts providing $300 in food stamp benefits. (The formal analysis is just like the one developed for a fixed-quantity subsidy in the last chapter. In this case, the fixed-quantity subsidy is the food stamp benefit, and the outcome is reduced private purchases of AFDC benefits by state taxpayers.)

There is another feature of the food stamp program that increases the likelihood that state governments would cut AFDC benefits in response to the food stamp program. Recall that the food stamp program reduces its benefits (the coupon allotment) by 30 cents for each dollar of other income of households. According to the provisions of the food stamp program, AFDC benefits are counted as income in determining the amount of food stamps payable. For example, in 1992, if net income from the AFDC program had been $600 a month, food stamps would have been $190, but if AFDC benefits had been reduced to $500 a month, food stamp benefits would have been increased to $220 (see Table 5–2). *For each dollar in AFDC benefits state taxpayers provide, federal food stamp benefits are reduced by 30 cents.* This reduction has the effect of increasing the cost, or price, to state taxpayers of increasing the income of the AFDC population. Before food stamps, each dollar in AFDC increases the income of recipients by a dollar, but after food stamps, each dollar in AFDC increases the income of recipients by only 70 cents (because food stamp benefits fall by 30 cents). Confronted with a higher price (of providing income to the AFDC population), we would expect state taxpayers to choose to provide lower AFDC benefits.

Thus, there are two ways the food stamp program could affect the decision of state taxpayers regarding the level of AFDC benefits. First, the basic benefit from food stamps reduces the neediness of the AFDC population, which would tend to reduce AFDC benefits. Second, the way in which the programs interact increases the price to state taxpayers of helping the AFDC population, and this would also tend to reduce the level of AFDC benefits they would provide. Taken together, these features of the food stamp program suggest that state taxpayers would reduce AFDC assistance. As can be seen in Table 5–3, AFDC benefits did in fact decline following the introduction of the food stamp program. Indeed, the combined benefits have declined. (Combined benefits are not the sum of the *maximum* benefits of AFDC and food stamps individually because of the interaction noted in the previous paragraph.)

It should be emphasized that this analysis only suggests the possibility that the federal food stamp program has caused state governments to reduce AFDC benefits; it does not prove that this is the case. Other factors may also have played a role. Nonetheless, it is an interesting application of public choice theory, and it shows how policies may have effects quite different from those intended or commonly realized. It should also be pointed out, however, that there are other welfare programs that we have ignored in this analysis. When all programs are considered together, the combined benefit package available to the AFDC population has grown somewhat since the early 1970s. We will take a closer look at all of the policies constituting the welfare system in Chapters 8 and 9.

Unemployment Insurance

Government-provided unemployment insurance has been a part of American life since it was enacted into law in the Social Security Act of 1935. Systems providing unemployment compensation are operated by the states under federal guidelines. These guidelines ensure that the state systems are quite similar, although some significant differences exist.

Workers who *lose* their jobs receive financial support from the unemployment insurance system while they remain unemployed. In most states, new entrants into the labor force and persons who quit their jobs are not eligible to receive unemployment benefits. Cash benefits are provided to eligible unemployed workers, typically at a level of about 50 percent of previous wages up to some maximum amount. Some states replace as much as two thirds of an individual's previous wages, and several also use dependents' allowances, which provide an additional income supplement based on the number of family members. These benefits are normally payable up to a maximum of 26 weeks. Supplementary federal programs have in recent years generally provided additional benefits to jobless persons after they have exhausted their regular 26 weeks of benefits. In most years, only about half of those counted as unemployed actually lost their jobs; the remainder either voluntarily quit or are new entrants or reentrants into the labor force. This accounts for the fact that many unemployed persons do not receive unemployment benefits, since generally one must lose a job to be eligible. The insured unemployment rate in Table 5–4 shows the unemployment rate of those who actually receive benefits. The insured unemployment rate is typically between 40 and 60 percent of the overall employment rate.

Table 5–4   *Expenditures on Unemployment Insurance, 1960–1991*

Year	Total Outlays ($ billions)	Unemployment Rate	Insured Unemployment Rate	Average Weekly Benefit
1960	$ 3.0	5.5%	4.8%	$ 32.87
1965	2.4	4.5	3.0	37.19
1970	4.2	4.9	3.4	50.34
1975	16.8	8.5	6.0	70.23
1980	16.2	7.1	3.9	98.92
1985	15.1	7.2	2.9	128.23
1990	19.6	5.5	2.4	161.56
1991	25.6	6.7	3.0	170.08

Source: *Economic Report of the President,* 1992, Tables B-37, B-40.

Earmarked payroll taxes are used to finance unemployment insurance. In most states, the tax is levied on employers only (rather than being split between employers and employees, as is the social security payroll tax) and is based on the total taxable wages paid to workers. Not all of a worker's wages are taxable; there is a ceiling amount beyond which there is no additional tax liability. Federal law requires that states tax at least the first $7,000 of each worker's earnings, but almost three fourths of the states use a higher ceiling. There is also some variation in tax rates, but the average rate is about 4 percent.

To understand how this tax works, consider a state where the ceiling is $10,000 and the tax rate is 4 percent. Then an employer must pay $320 in taxes when employing a worker for $8,000, $400 for a worker earning $10,000, and $400 for every worker earning over $10,000: there is no additional tax for earnings beyond the tax ceiling. Even though employers are responsible for paying this tax, economists believe that employees bear the actual cost in the form of lower wages.

Distribution of Benefits

Our discussion of food stamps observed that virtually all of the benefits go to families with low incomes. Because unemployment insurance (UI) benefits are paid to the unemployed, it is widely believed that this program also concentrates benefits on those who would have low incomes without the program. This, however, turns out not to be the case. In one of his several studies of unemployment insurance, Martin Feldstein found that in 1970 only 17 percent of total UI benefits paid went to families whose incomes were below one half of the median income level. In contrast, more than half of the benefits went to families with incomes (even before receiving UI benefits) that were greater than the median family income. More than 15 percent of benefits went to families with incomes of more than double the median level.[6] The distribution of benefits is probably much the same today.

It is not really surprising that UI benefits do not disproportionally benefit low-income families since the nature of the program guarantees this result. Since UI benefits are related to previous earnings, unemployed workers who had higher earnings receive higher UI benefits. In addition, most unemployment tends to be of fairly short duration (as we will see later), so a high-wage worker who is unemployed for one month will still receive UI benefits, even though his or her annual income may be quite sizable. Well-paid union members, for example, can receive benefits while temporarily laid off. In contrast, many low-income persons may be ineligible for benefits for a variety of reasons. For instance, they may not be involuntarily unemployed at all (i.e., they may be retired or on welfare), they may have just entered the labor force, or they may have been unemployed so long that their UI benefit payments have ceased.

UI is therefore not a redistributive program (at least among income classes) to the same extent as food stamps. Instead, unemployment insurance tends to provide temporary assistance to persons who have lost their jobs, without regard to how needy their families are.

Replacement Rates

In analyzing unemployment insurance, a key concept is the *replacement rate*, which refers to the extent to which UI benefits replace lost earnings. For example, if a person's earnings were previously $300 per week and his or her UI benefit is $100 per week, the replacement rate is one third. In practice, replacement rates vary widely from one worker to another. They depend on the state of residence, type of family, number of dependents (several states have dependents' allowances that serve to increase the replacement rate), whether the spouse is working, and other factors. There are also usually minimum and maximum UI weekly benefits. A minimum weekly benefit serves to increase the replacement rate for low-paid workers and a maximum benefit to reduce it for high-paid workers.

Given this variation, it is difficult to generalize regarding the typical replacement rate, but it is important to have some understanding of the general level involved. One approach is to simply compare the average weekly benefit (as given in Table 5–4) with average weekly earnings for the economy as a whole. For 1991, this calculation suggests that replacement rates were 48 percent of average wages. The problem with this approach is that unemployed persons typically have previous wages that are somewhat below the national average, generally about 75 percent of the national average. This suggests that replacement rates are on average about 60 percent of previous wages.

---

[6]Martin Feldstein, "Unemployment Compensation: Adverse Incentives and Distributional Anomalies," *National Tax Journal*, 27(2):231 (June 1974).

This calculation, however, may understate replacement rates for two reasons. First, it ignores the tax status of UI benefits. Prior to 1986, most UI benefits were nontaxable, which meant that these benefits relative to after-tax earnings—the relevant replacement rate, sometimes called the *net replacement rate*—were substantially higher than the preceding calculations suggest. In 1986, however, UI benefits were made taxable under the federal income tax, which tended to reduce net replacement rates. But UI benefits are still not taxed under the social security payroll tax, which falls at a rate of 7.65 percent on an employee's earnings. To see the importance of this situation, suppose that a worker receives UI benefits of $180 based on previous earnings of $300. That represents a 60 percent replacement rate, but the $180 actually replaces 65 percent of the $277 the worker has after paying the social security payroll tax. (Note that the fact that income taxes apply to both previous earnings and the UI benefit does not affect the ratio of the two, that is, the replacement rate.)

A second reason replacement rates may be somewhat higher, at least for some unemployed persons, is that people may receive food stamps while unemployed, and the food stamps also serve to replace lost earnings. Consider a worker whose regular pay is $2,000 a month and who is ineligible for food stamps while employed. If unemployed, this worker might receive, say, $1,000 a month in UI benefits, a gross replacement rate of 50 percent. However, with deductions of $300, he or she might also receive $160 in food stamps (see Table 5–2). (A person whose annual income is too high to receive food stamps can still get them if income in any month is low enough.) The combined UI and food stamp benefits of $1,160 would represent a net replacement rate of 63 percent, after also taking account of the payroll tax. Food stamps thus serve to increase the replacement rate for some unemployed persons. Not all of those who receive UI benefits also receive food stamps, however, but one study found that 12 percent of UI recipients did receive food stamps in 1983.

As mentioned previously, given the many factors that influence a given worker's replacement rate, replacement rates can vary significantly among workers. It appears that, on average, net replacement rates are probably at least 60 percent of previous earnings, but somewhat higher for low-wage workers and somewhat lower for high-wage workers.

Duration of Unemployment

The most important potential effect of UI on the allocation of resources is its impact on the unemployment rate. UI does not, of course, often cause people to lose jobs; instead, it creates an incentive for workers, once unemployed, to extend the duration of their unemployment. The replacement rates of UI are the key to this effect. *The greater the replacement rate* (including food stamps), *the lower the cost to the worker of extending the duration of unemployment.*

When a worker is unemployed and does not receive UI benefits, the cost the worker bears is the sacrifice of net income earned if he or she were employed. UI substantially reduces this cost by replacing a large fraction of lost net earnings as long as the worker is unemployed. Given the general level of replacement rates, many workers find that they have two thirds of their net income while not working; that gives little incentive to try to locate a new job as promptly as possible. Indeed, if the unemployed worker believes that it is impossible to find a job that pays as much as the previous one, or if there are expenses associated with the job (such as transportation), the gain from finding a job will be reduced even further. It is understandable, then, that a worker who has lost a job would feel no great urgency in finding a new one, and could delay making a concerted effort because the cost of postponing the job search is so low. Such reactions on the part of unemployed workers add to the unemployment rate.

In understanding this effect, it may help to recognize that UI is really a type of excise subsidy. UI reduces the price to the worker of a certain good—lengthening the duration of unemployment—and the law of demand reminds us that people generally consume more at a lower price. Not all people can be expected to react to this incentive in exactly the same way, but the general direction of the effect is clear.

It can now be seen that the replacement rate is significant for two different reasons. First, a higher replacement rate means that workers are provided greater security against the temporary loss of income because of unemployment. Second, a higher replacement rate lowers the cost to workers of remaining unemployed. The critical policy question is how to strike a balance between providing security and undermining incentives.

Although the beneits paid by UI give workers an incentive to extend spells of unemployment, there are several ways in which the UI system attempts to counter this effect. As mentioned earlier, UI benefits are normally payable for 26 weeks. Because benefits cease after that period, there is no incentive to remain unemployed indefinitely. (There is also no security provided for very long periods of unemployment.) In addition, UI benefits are generally (but not in all states) restricted to workers who have lost their jobs through no fault of their own. Workers who quit or who are discharged for misconduct are ineligible for benefits, although some states do permit such workers to collect benefits after a waiting period of four to six weeks.

In addition, unemployed workers are required to register for work at the State Employment Service and to accept a suitable job if one is offered or lose their UI benefits. These features of the program are attempts to offset the financial incentive of workers to remain unemployed, but how effective they are is uncertain. Workers are required to accept "suitable work," but what constitutes suitable work is nowhere precisely defined and is largely left to administrative discretion. In practice, suitable work is sometimes interpreted to mean a job paying the same wage rate as the one lost, with the same working conditions, and in the same location. This requirement, of course, robs the provision of much of its force.

It is probably true therefore that these practices frequently fail to offset the financial incentive of workers to extend the duration of unemployment.

No doubt, major abuses are avoided, and some workers lose UI benefits because of these practices, but it is not easy to induce people to behave in a way they perceive as contrary to their best interests. Indeed, to make these provisions fully effective would probably lead to workers' having little freedom to choose among alternative jobs.

The analysis suggests therefore that a major effect of UI is to increase the nation's unemployment rate. Many people find it hard to believe this because they have an erroneous view of the nature of unemployment, thinking of it as an unchanging pool of workers who will remain out of work unless economic conditions are improved. Nothing could be further from the truth. Actually, in most years more than 40 percent of those counted as unemployed are out of work for less than five weeks, and the median duration of unemployment seldom exceeds seven weeks.

Table 5–5 provides some information concerning the duration of unemployment in recent years. As mentioned, Table 5–5 shows that most unemployment is of short duration. If the unemployment rate is 6 percent over one year, this means that many more than 6 percent of members of the labor force are out of work at some time during the year, but each person is unemployed for only a relatively short period of time. *Reducing the unemployment rate is largely a problem of reducing the average duration of unemployment.* What appears to be a small reduction in the duration of unemployment can have a significant effect on the unemployment rate. Suppose, for example, that in 1991, when the average duration was 13.8 weeks, it would have been 11 weeks in the absence of UI. The unemployment rate would then have been 5.3 percent instead of 6.7 percent. (Obviously, we are

Table 5–5 *Unemployment Rates and Duration of Unemployment, 1960–1991*

Selected Years	Unemployment Rate	Duration of Unemployment (in percent)		Average Duration in Weeks	Median Duration in Weeks
		Less Than 5 Weeks	26 Weeks or More		
1960	5.5%	45%	12%	12.8	
1965	4.5	48	10	11.8	
1970	4.9	52	6	8.7	4.9
1975	8.5	37	15	14.1	8.4
1980	7.1	43	11	11.9	6.5
1985	7.2	42	15	15.6	6.8
1990	5.5	46	10	12.1	5.4
1991	6.7	40	13	13.8	6.9

Source: *Economic Report of the President,* 1992, Tables B-37, B-39.

not suggesting that this is the actual impact of UI; we are only trying to illustrate how a small reduction in the average duration of unemployment would affect the unemployment rate.)

In our discussion of UI so far, its macroeconomic effect on unemployment as an "automatic stabilizer" has been conspicuously absent. At the risk of belaboring what is perhaps by now obvious, let us turn to Feldstein on this point:

> it is really irrelevant to argue that the program reduces unemployment because it automatically increases government spending when unemployment rises. We have come to accept the government's general responsibility for maintaining a high level of demand through variations in spending, taxation, and monetary policy. The fiscal stimulus now provided by unemployment compensation would alternatively be provided through other government expenditure increases or tax cuts.[7]

We should note that a tax cut rather than an expenditure increase (as with UI) would increase the incentive of unemployed workers to return to work because their potential take-home (after-tax) pay would be higher.

Job Search

Contrary to popular opinion, many economists have emphasized that the longer duration of unemployment produced by UI is not unequivocally bad. An unemployed person may devote time to "job search," that is, to looking for a new job. The longer an unemployed worker looks for a job, the more likely it is that a good job will be found. UI reduces the pressure on an unemployed worker to take just any job that comes along and allows a more thorough search for a job that could make better use of the person's skills. If a greater duration of unemployment leads to a better matching of job and person, it may represent a productive investment.

It is important to determine whether longer spells of unemployment do lead to higher wages (implying, presumably, a better job) when workers ultimately return to work. Ehrenberg and Oaxaca found that longer periods of unemployment raise postunemployment wages. These effects, however, were statistically significant only in the cases of older males and females aged 30 to 44.[8] By contrast, Kathleen Classen found that longer durations of unemployment had no effect on postunemployment wages.[9] Thus, it is uncer-

---

[7]Martin S. Feldstein, "Unemployment Insurance: Time for Reform," *Harvard Business Review* (Mar./Apr. 1975).

[8]Ronald G. Ehrenberg and Ronald I. Oaxaca, "Impact of Unemployment Insurance on the Duration of Unemployment and Post-Unemployment Wage," Paper presented at the Meetings of the Industrial Relations Research Association, Dallas, Texas, December 30, 1975.

[9]Kathleen Classen, "The Effects of Unemployment Insurance: Evidence from Pennsylvania," The Public Research Institute of the Center for Naval Analysis, PRI 166–175, April 1975.

tain whether people find better jobs as a result of the longer duration of unemployment caused by UI.

Even if the longer spells of unemployment caused by UI do lead to higher postunemployment wages, it is not clear that this increase is efficient. There is an efficient level of job search that involves equating the marginal return from the additional search to the marginal cost of continuing to look for a job. This does not generally involve waiting for the best possible job offer because there is a substantial cost—sacrificed earnings—to waiting. The problem with UI is that it greatly reduces the marginal cost of looking for a job, as perceived by workers, and encourages the unemployed to wait too long to take a job. The marginal cost of looking for a job is the earnings that an unemployed worker sacrifices while searching, but as we have seen, UI makes the net sacrifice to the worker much lower by replacing a large fraction of his or her potential earnings. Workers receiving UI benefits have an incentive to hold out for a better job as long as there is almost any hope, however small, because they are sacrificing very little income by not returning to work.

An example may clarify this point. Suppose that an unemployed person can return to work for $300 a week, but believes that by searching or waiting for four weeks, a job paying $320 can be found. The marginal cost of waiting for the $320-a-week job is $1,200—the worker's earnings at the $300 job for those four weeks. The marginal return is $20 extra per week for (we will assume) 50 weeks, or $1,000. In this case, the marginal cost is $1,200 and the marginal gain $1,000, so it is inefficient to wait for the higher-paying job. If the worker receives $150 a week in UI benefits, however, the net cost of remaining unemployed for those four weeks is $600, because he or she could get only $150 more per week by returning to work. The costs and gains as the unemployed person perceives them have changed; to wait for the higher-paying job would cost $600 in forgone earnings compared with a gain of $1,000. Because the worker does not bear the entire cost of waiting with UI, he or she would then be led to wait for the better-paying job even though such a decision is inefficient.

Thus, UI could be expected to lead to an excessive job search. Only if people would, in the absence of UI, tend to underestimate substantially the prospects of finding a better job by additional searching and thus search too little would encouraging job search be an appropriate policy. Even if this were the case, UI is not well designed to deal with the situation because it reduces not only the cost of the job search but also the cost of all other ways an unemployed person may use his or her time.

Empirical Evidence

Economic theory predicts that UI tends to increase unemployment, but empirical research is necessary to determine the size of the impact. In recent years, economists have devoted much attention to this issue. Dozens of studies have been published.[10] Some studies have emphasized the effects of increasing the level of UI benefits (by increasing replacement rates), and others have focused on how lengthening the duration of benefits (say from 26 to 39 weeks) would affect the duration of unemployment. Almost without exception, these studies do find that the UI program increases the duration of unemployment, that is, it increases the unemployment rate. After surveying 14 of the earlier studies, Daniel Hamermesh concluded: "There should be no doubt whatsoever that UI benefits in the U.S. do induce longer spells of unemployment."[11] That conclusion has been supported by more recent research.

Thus, there is a consensus that UI does increase the unemployment rate. Understandably, there is less agreement about exactly how large the effect is. Hamermesh's best guess of the overall impact is that UI adds 0.7 percentage points to the unemployment rate. Feldstein's best guess is an addition of 1.25 percentage points. If UI adds as much as 1.0 percentage point to the nation's unemployment rate, this is highly significant, for it suggests that in most years the unemployment rate would be about 15 percent lower in the absence of UI. Putting this in terms commonly (and misleadingly) used by the news media, it would mean that UI results in more than 1 million workers being out of work each year.

In interpreting the significance of the effect of UI on the unemployment rate, it is important to recall that the measured unemployment rate cannot feasibly be reduced to zero. In the best of times, there will always be people between jobs and people who have entered the labor force but have not yet located the best job available. Much unemployment is of this sort and is sometimes referred to as the "frictional" unemployment that will always exist in a dynamic society. There is also some structural unemployment that cannot be eliminated without changing government policies (like UI and minimum wage laws) or labor market institutions. Building on these ideas, economists have developed the concept of a "full employment unemployment rate," intended to be the rate below which unemployment cannot fall except possibly for short periods of time. In the 1960s, the full employment unemployment rate was widely believed to be around 4.0 percent. Solely as a result of changes in the age-sex-race composition of the labor force, the full employment unemployment rate had risen to between 5.5 and 6.0 percent by the mid-1980s.[12] Since much unemployment is unavoidable, if UI adds one percentage point to the overall rate, that would represent a large part of the avoidable unemployment in most years.

[10]For a recent survey of many of the studies, see Anthony B. Atkinson and John Micklewright, "Unemployment Compensation and Labor Market Transitions: A Critical Review," *Journal of Economic Literature*, 29:1679 (Dec. 1991).

[11]Daniel Hamermesh, "Transfers, Taxes and the NAIRU," National Bureau of Economic Research Working Paper No. 548, p. 15 (Sept. 1980).

[12]Ronald G. Ehrenberg and Robert S. Smith, *Modern Labor Economics*, 3rd. ed. (Glenview, Ill.: Scott, Foresman, 1988), p. 606.

Why Not Give Loans Instead of Subsidies?

Martin Feldstein has proposed a radical form of the UI program.[13] He suggested that the government lend unemployed workers 60 percent of their previous wage rather than giving them benefits. These loans would be repaid after the worker returned to work. Only after a worker has been unemployed for a long period, three to six months, would he or she be eligible to receive nonrepayable benefits.

A loan program to provide support for the unemployed would virtually eliminate any incentives for a worker to extend inefficiently the duration of unemployment. Each week the worker borrowed money, his or her indebtedness to the government would increase, and consequently the worker would bear the entire cost of remaining unemployed. This would be a strong incentive to avoid extending unemployment unnecessarily and would also encourage the worker to search more actively for a job. On the other hand, workers unemployed longer than six months would receive nonrepayable benefits and find unemployment subsidized thereafter.

In evaluating this proposal, it is important to recall that most unemployment is short-lived (see Table 5–5). Most unemployed workers would never become eligible for nonrepayable benefits. Only those with very long spells of unemployment would receive an outright subsidy, and this group would be more likely to be the most needy among the unemployed. (To avoid possible abuses in these few cases of extended unemployment, there would probably have to be some limitation on the duration of benefits.) Therefore, Feldstein's proposal would almost completely eliminate the adverse incentives inherent in the present system.

Would the repayment of loans be a great burden on workers after they return to work? Perhaps in some individual cases, but two points should be recalled. First, under the current distribution of benefits, most of the outlays are received by middle- and upper-income families. Second, using loans rather than nonrepayable benefits would allow the government to reduce the tax used to finance UI benefits, increasing after-tax income and the ability of reemployed workers to repay the loan.

Actually, this proposal is a large step in the direction of eliminating UI altogether. Most unemployed persons would probably not borrow the money even if they could, but instead would finance their unemployment out of their own savings (at least, unless the government lent at below-market interest rates). In that event, workers would be using savings to "self-insure" against unemployment. Indeed, people do not need a very large nest egg to provide the same degree of insurance currently provided by UI. Recall that the average duration of unemployment seldom exceeds 12 weeks. At a

---

[13]Feldstein, "Unemployment Insurance: Time for Reform." Actually, Feldstein's reform contains two additional proposals. The first, to make UI benefits taxable, has already been enacted. The second is intended to deal with what is known as *experience rating*. We have ignored experience rating because it is very complex and does not materially affect the analysis in the text.

replacement rate of 50 percent, UI provides on average benefits equal to six weeks of wages. Thus, a worker requires savings of less than one eighth of his or her annual income to provide the same average protection as afforded by UI.

Since converting UI to a loan program shifts the costs of being unemployed to the worker, why not simply eliminate UI altogether? The obvious reason is that some people would be too poor to have accumulated any savings. Yet if this is the reason, the real problem is a distribution of income with too many poor families, and that problem could be resolved by a welfare system that raised the incomes of low-income families. Feldstein's proposal is a compromise that guarantees that those who cannot or simply do not provide for emergencies will be supported during periods of unemployment.

Subsidies to Higher Education

Nearly half of all high school graduates go to college, and about 90 percent of them receive some form of subsidy from their state government or the federal government, or both. Two major types of subsidies are involved. The first is a *tuition subsidy* reflected in the fact that the tuition charged to students does not cover the costs of the educational services they receive. This subsidy is of long standing; for many years, states have operated colleges and universities, financing them largely out of state tax revenues and thereby enabling the schools to charge low tuitions.

The second type of subsidy is *student aid*, or direct financial assistance to students. There are many different programs in this category, including direct grants, student loans, and work-study arrangements. Total spending on these subsidies rose from $15.6 billion (1991 dollars) in the 1970–71 academic year to $29.9 billion in the 1989–90 academic year. In recent years, nearly three fourths of total spending on student aid has been financed by the federal government.

Tuition Subsidies

Table 5–6 provides estimates indicating the importance of tuition subsidies for undergraduate students at various types of institutions in 1985–86. At public universities and colleges, expenditures per student exceeded the tuition charged by more than $6,000. Taxpayers are effectively paying more than 80 percent of the cost of educating students at state-supported institutions. It should also be noted that tuition does not cover costs at private institutions. (About 25 percent of college students attend these schools.) Charitable contributions to the private institutions provide most of the funds to finance tuition subsidies there. As a percentage of costs, tuition subsidies are smaller at private institutions.

Table 5–6   *Undergraduate Tuition Subsidies,*
             1985–1986 (1985 dollars)

	Public University	Public College	Private University	Private College
Education expenditures per student	$8,183	$7,302	$14,861	$8,319
Average tuition	1,536	1,157	7,374	5,641
Tuition subsidy	6,647	6,145	7,487	2,678
Subsidy as a percent of cost	81.2%	84.2%	50.4%	32.2%

Source: U.S. Congress, Congressional Budget Office, *Student Aid and the Cost of Postsecondary Education* (Jan. 1991), Table 1.

The total value of tuition subsidies in 1985–86 has been estimated at $44.6 billion. In addition, student aid subsidies were about $20.7 billion in that year. It is clear that subsidies to college students in the aggregate are much larger than the other two subsidies examined in this chapter.

To analyze some of the consequences of tuition subsidies, let us begin by looking at how they affect the educational choices of a family considering sending a son or daughter to college. Suppose that we simplify our analysis by assuming that "education" can be purchased in the private market at a constant price per unit. The budget line showing the private unsubsidized alternatives is *MALN* in Figure 5–2(a). (In practice, the choice is likely to be among a number of schools, with the higher-priced ones offering better— that is, more—education. Combining all the choices to form a straight line, however, seems a reasonable simplification.) Next, let the state government operate a college that provides E_G units of education. Suppose that it costs $7,500 to provide E_G units of education; this is shown by distance MM_2. At the public college, however, the students will pay a tuition of only MM_1 ($1,500, for example), with the remaining cost, M_1M_2 ($6,000), financed by tax revenues. The budget line confronting the family then changes to *MARLN*. Point *R* indicates the option of attending the public college, and the *RLN* portion of the line shows that to get more education the student must forgo the public college subsidy and bear the entire cost of an unsubsidized college. Thus, the subsidy available at public colleges is a form of fixed-quantity subsidy where it is difficult for the student's family to supplement the subsidized quantity (compare the discussion of Figure 4–4).

For such families, there are a number of possible outcomes. Figure 5–2 identifies two of them. Figure 5–2(a) shows a family that would choose a private college providing E_1 units of education in the absence of the subsidy. But given the availability of the subsidy, the family can attain a higher indifference curve by sending its son or daughter to the public college, although

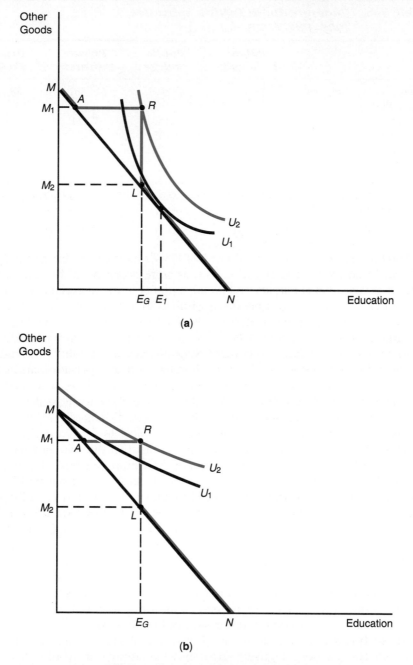

Figure 5–2   *Effects of state-supported higher education*

that choice means consuming a lower quantity of educational services. Figure 5–2(b) illustrates a second outcome, in which the student decides not to attend any college without a subsidy; the highest indifference curve attainable is U_1 at point M, a corner equilibrium. With the subsidy, however, the student will attend the public college, and the equilibrium will be at point R. There are also two other possibilities, not shown in the graph. First, the equilibrium could be along the MAL portion of the budget line without the subsidy; the subsidy produces a new equilibrium at point R, with the family consuming more education than they would have chosen without the subsidy. Second, the equilibrium could be along the LN portion of the budget line without the subsidy and remain at the same point when the subsidy is available: This outcome occurs when the family chooses an unsubsidized college and forgoes the subsidy available at the public college.

In all likelihood, there are many instances of each of these four possible outcomes. On theoretical grounds, we cannot predict the relative importance of each possibility, as the actual choices made will depend on incomes, preferences, and other factors. We do know, however, that approximately 25 percent of all college students currently attend private colleges. The important question is, therefore, how the choices of the remaining 75 percent of college students attending public colleges have been affected by the existence of state-supported public colleges.

Sam Peltzman investigated this question and estimated that if public colleges were eliminated, total expenditures on higher education would fall by somewhere between zero(!) and 25 percent. At the same time, Peltzman found that enrollment in colleges would fall by about 25 percent.[14] In other words, he concluded that there would be fewer students in college but that the students that did remain would, on the average, receive more education. This accords with our analysis because Peltzman's findings imply that some students would choose more education without subsidies [Figure 5–2(a)] and that others would choose less or none [Figure 5–2(b)].

Initially, it may seem surprising that our system of state-supported higher education has such a small effect on the allocation of resources to higher education, but Peltzman's results are quite plausible when we think about the extent to which public colleges reduce the cost of education. Although public colleges reduce the tuition cost to students by more than 80 percent, tuition is not the only cost of attending college, nor is it even the most important cost. The largest cost is the earnings that college students forgo when they attend college. The decision to attend college means sacrificing four years of earnings, and those sacrificed earnings are an opportunity cost of attending college. (Note that students' living costs while in college are not an additional cost because such costs would be incurred whether or not they attended college.)

[14]Sam Petzman, "The Effect of Government Subsidies-in-Kind of Private Expenditures: The Case of Higher Education," *Journal of Political Economy*, 81:1 (Jan./Feb. 1973).

The cost that a student (or his or her family) bears from attending college is largely the sum of tuition and sacrificed earnings. (There are, of course, some other costs, such as books and the subjective disutility from studying, and some offsets, such as summer earnings, that for simplicity we shall ignore.) To see the practical importance of these factors, we can estimate sacrificed earnings by using the average earnings of male high school graduates between the ages of 18 and 24 in 1985: approximately $14,000. College students probably sacrificed about that much each year they attended college. In addition, the average cost of educational services at public colleges were about $7,500, so the total (social) cost of a student attending college was about $21,500 per year. When students attending a public university paid a tuition of only $1,500 instead of $7,500, however, the cost falls from $21,500 to $15,500, or by 28 percent. Given this moderate reduction in the true cost, together with the restricted nature of the subsidy that leads some students to consume less education, Peltzman's results appear plausible.

Student Aid

By *student aid* we mean direct financial assistance to students. This assistance comes in a variety of forms and is financed by federal, state, or institutional sources. In total, student aid is about half as large as tuition subsidies, but for some students it is more important than this overall figure suggests.

About three fourths of all student aid is provided by the federal government. The two most important federal programs are Pell Grants and Stafford Loans. Pell Grants provide outright cash subsidies to eligible students; Stafford Loans are federally guaranteed loans, usually from private lenders. It should be noted that the loan program is, in part, a subsidy because students are not charged interest on the loan until six months after they leave school, and the interest rates then charged are below-market rates. For these reasons, it has been estimated that about 40 percent of the value of the loans represents subsidies.

Under most programs, the amount of aid a student can receive is based on financial need. While the exact determination of the amount is often complicated, generally both the cost of the college attended and the financial resources available are involved in determining eligibility and the amount of aid. If a given student attends a more expensive school, he or she will typically be eligible for more aid. Other things equal, most programs (especially the federal programs) explicitly attempt to provide greater assistance to more needy students.

A recent study by the Congressional Budget Office has provided a great deal of information concerning who gets student aid. Some of the results are presented in Table 5–7. For students who are financially dependent on their parents, the table shows how total assistance (from all programs together) varied among family income classes in 1986. For example, 88 percent of students from families with incomes below $11,000 received some

Table 5–7 *Student Aid, 1986*

Family Income	Public Four-Year Institutions		Private Four-Year Institutions	
	Percent of Students Receiving Aid	Average Aid per Recipient	Percent of Students Receiving Aid	Average Aid per Recipient
$ 0–11,000	88%	$3,929	98%	$7,614
$11–17,000	82	3,359	96	7,050
$17–30,000	66	2,790	91	6,460
$30–50,000	48	2,261	84	5,351
Over $50,000	25	1,986	51	3,845

Source: U.S. Congress, Congressional Budget Office, *Student Aid and the Cost of Postsecondary Education* (Jan. 1991), Figures 2 and 4.

form of aid at public four-year institutions (universities or colleges), and the average amount of aid was $3,929.

One striking feature of these estimates is the extent to which students from upper-income families receive financial assistance. It should be noted that in 1986, median family income was just under $30,000. Thus, the $30,000–$50,000 and over-$50,000 income classes constitute the upper half of the income distribution. In the $30,000–$50,000 class, nearly half of the students at public institutions received student aid, and more than four fifths received it at private institutions. The amount of aid per recipient was about 60 percent (public) and 70 percent (private) of the amount for students from the lowest family income class. On the other hand, a larger percentage of students from lower-income families do receive assistance, and the amounts are somewhat larger.

Turning to the allocative consequences of these programs, it should be mentioned that a major goal of these programs, especially the federal ones, was to increase college attendance by students from low-income families. In 1970, before the federal programs were enacted, the percentage of college-age children from families with incomes below the median who attended college was about half the percentage for families with incomes above the median. It was thought that by reducing the net cost to students from low-income families that ratio could be increased. However, this has not occurred: Families with above-median incomes still have about twice the percentage of college-age children in college that lower-income families do.

Why these subsidies have failed to achieve their primary goal is not entirely clear, but part of the reason is probably that financial considerations (at least over the range of amounts involved) may not play that crucial a role in the decision to attend college. This is particularly true given the size of the subsidies involved. Recall from our earlier example that the net cost of attending college (after the tuition subsidy) may have been about $15,500 in 1985. Even the large subsidies to students from low-income families would not reduce that cost by much more than 25 percent; this reduction may not be enough to induce more students to attend college.

It is still possible that student aid programs could have increased college attendance from both low- and high-income families, leaving the ratio unchanged. College attendance did increase somewhat over this period, but it was increasing before the federal subsidies were enacted as well, so it is not clear whether they had any independent effect. Statistical studies have not resolved this issue. As the Congressional Budget Office observed: "Some of [the] models indicate that financial aid has increased total postsecondary enrollment. . . . Other researchers, however, continue to doubt that student aid has produced those effects."[15] It seems clear from the evidence that if there has been any effect on enrollment from student aid programs, it has been small.

From this analysis, tuition subsidies and student aid programs appear to have a rather limited effect on the allocation of resources to higher education. Most students attending college today would probably be attending even if there were no subsidies at all. While it is difficult to doubt that some students are induced to attend college as a result of these subsidies, the increase in attendance may be rather small. It is also probably true that some students attend more expensive colleges than they would without the subsidies, but on the other hand, according to Peltzman, some students actually get less education.

Distributive Effects

Since the analysis suggests that the allocative effects of higher education subsidies are fairly limited, let us now take a look at how they affect the distribution of income. There are two different ways to look at the distributional effects. One is to focus on the families that have students in college. Since higher-income families send a larger proportion of their children to college, it is to be expected that tuition subsidies disproportionately benefit these families. That outcome is magnified by the tendency of these students to attend more expensive schools, where tuition subsidies are larger. Operating in the other direction are student aid subsidies, which dispense more aid on a per student basis to those from lower-income families.

Table 5–8 presents estimates of the distributional effects of tuition subsidies and student aid programs together. (Loans are valued at 40 percent of the value of the loan.) On a per student basis, larger subsidies do go to students from lower-income families. However, because there are so many more students from higher-income families, the total subsidies going to stu-

---

[15]U.S. Congress, Congressional Budget Office, *Student Aid and the Cost of Postsecondary Education* (Jan. 1991), p. 4.

Table 5–8 *Total Student Subsidies, 1986*

	Public Four-Year Institutions		
Family Income	Number of Students (thousands)	Subsidy per Student	Total ($ billions)
$ 0–11,000	146	$ 9,405	$1.4
$11–17,000	166	8,771	1.5
$17–30,000	484	7,977	3.9
$30–50,000	615	7,488	4.6
Over $50,000	617	7,157	4.4

	Private Four-Year Institutions		
Family Income	Number of Students (thousands)	Subsidy per Student	Total ($ billions)
$ 0–11,000	64	$11,058	$0.7
$11–17,000	71	10,389	0.7
$17–30,000	209	9,416	2.0
$30–50,000	293	8,407	2.5
Over $50,000	398	7,290	2.9

Source: U.S. Congress, Congressional Budget Office, *Student Aid and the Cost of Postsecondary Education* (Jan. 1991), Figure 8 and Table 9.

dents from higher-income families are larger. For example, students from families with incomes above the median level receive $14.4 billion in subsidies, about 60 percent of the total subsidies received by all students. (This table does not include independent students—those who are financially independent and receive aid based on their own financial resources rather than their parents'. Approximately 22 percent of undergraduate students have independent status.)

Some economists have argued that this is not the proper way to evaluate the distributional effects of subsidies to higher education. They contend that we should consider the subsidies as benefiting the students themselves rather than their parents. From this perspective, the distributional effects of subsidies to higher education are even more pro-rich (or at least, favor those who are well off). All college-caliber students are wealthy in terms of their lifetime earning potential, regardless of the current incomes of their parents. In 1991, for example, the average earnings of male college graduates over the age of 25 was $42,000, whereas the comparable figure for high school graduates was $24,000. Subsidies to higher education thus effectively benefit the brightest and most ambitious young people, and this group will, on the average, have the highest lifetime incomes even without assistance.

Who Should Pay for Higher Education?

Is there a rationale for government involvement in higher education, and if so, what is it? This is a difficult question, and there is no consensus regarding the justification for subsidies to higher education. Thinking about the issues involved is worthwhile, however, because it can provide some insight into the types of policies that are appropriate. In this section, we shall discuss three of the most common arguments supporting government subsidies to higher education.

1. *Families cannot afford to send their children to college.* College is expensive, and in recent years costs have risen slightly faster than the overall price level. Government subsidies, however, do not reduce the cost of education to society; they only reduce the cost to the recipient by shifting part of the expense to someone else. (In fact, government subsidies actually increase the cost of education to society because of the additional marginal welfare cost of the taxes.) So the real issue is why people other than those who receive the educational services should bear part of the cost.

Why can't families afford to pay the full cost of college? Students who can succeed in college will, on the average, have high lifetime incomes. The fact that their current earnings are low is not relevant to their ability to pay for college. College enhances earning capacity, and the costs of college could be financed out of the higher future earnings that college makes possible. In other words, students (or their families) could borrow to finance college and repay the loan out of their future earnings. If college is really worthwhile as an investment in human capital, the higher future earnings that a college education makes possible should be more than adequate to repay the loan.

There are, however, problems with borrowing to finance college education. Although the average expected return to college education may be substantial, there is a wide variation around the average, so not all students who graduate from college will realize higher lifetime earnings. This, together with the current bankruptcy laws that have enabled some students to rid themselves of their debt by declaring bankruptcy, make such student loans risky. Consequently, some economists have suggested that government facilitate educational loans, possibly by guaranteeing repayment to private lenders. Note, however, that this argument does not require that the government offer subsidized loans (as it now does) or run state-supported colleges and universities, but only that the government ensure that students can borrow at market interest rates to finance their college educations. If loans are available at unsubsidized interest rates, the fact that a student's family has a low income would not affect his or her ability to attend college.

2. *We must have equal opportunity in higher education.* An ideal widely held in our society is that anyone capable of succeeding in college should be able to attend; that is, financial considerations should not keep talented young people from going to college. But is it necessary to subsidize college education with low-interest loans or public colleges to realize this goal? The

availability of guaranteed loans at market interest rates would provide educational opportunity without subsidizing students. Educational opportunity would seemingly be provided if any person who thinks that he or she can benefit from attending college is able to do so despite small or nonexistent current earnings.

This argument is usually raised in connection with students from low-income households where financial considerations might deter them from attending college. Even if the student's family is poor, however, loans provide a method of paying for college. The important point is that any college-caliber student, whether from a poor or a wealthy family, can expect to have income in the future that is well above the national average. To subsidize college students is to make individuals with higher expected incomes in the future even wealthier at the expense of the less fortunate.

Many believe, however, that there are reasons to offer special assistance to students from low-income families to attend college. For persons raised in an environment that does not stress the benefits of education, the availability of loans may not be enough to make college attractive. This consideration may be the basis for an argument that some type of special encouragement, perhaps a subsidy, be made available to students from disadvantaged backgrounds, but this would not seem to justify subsidies to 90 percent of college students.

3. *There are external benefits associated with higher education.* When economists evaluate the appropriateness of government action, they generally first consider whether any externalities are involved. As the analysis in Chapter 2 suggests, if the production of college-trained persons generates external benefits for other people, private markets will lead students to purchase less than the efficient quantity. In this case, a subsidy that lowers the price to students (i.e., with someone else paying part of the cost) can induce students to acquire the efficient quantity of education.

What types of external benefits are associated with higher education? One common argument holds that education increases the productivity of workers, increasing national output and improving the welfare of everyone. On inspection, however, this does not describe any external benefits from education. Education generally improves students' productivity, enabling them to produce more and, therefore, increasing the national output. However, in a market system, the student is the one who receives the benefit of this higher productivity in the form of a higher wage rate. Wages are related to productivity, and insofar as education improves productivity, it increases the wage rate that students can command in job markets.

A related argument holds that an increase in the supply of trained workers leads to lower wage rates, and lower wage rates benefit the rest of society as consumers. For instance, subsidies to education may increase the supply of engineers and lead to lower prices for engineering services. Again, however, this does not describe a true external benefit but only a pecuniary externality. If an increase in supply leads to lower engineers' wages, this will benefit consumers, but at a cost to the engineers who were previously employed at a higher wage. This, therefore, is a transfer of real income from engineers to consumers, not a net benefit to society.

Having considered these fallacious, externality-sounding arguments, what are the real external benefits of higher education? External benefits from education might include speaking a common language that facilitates communication with others; knowledge of laws and customs that facilitates interactions with others; acceptance of a common set of values that improves the stability of the system; and improved understanding of social processes that leads to better informed political decisions. These consequences of education can benefit people other than the student.

We should, however, realize that such general benefits from education are largely realized at lower levels of schooling. Are there really more external benefits if a high school graduate extends his or her education? Many economists feel that the answer to this question is probably no, contending that the marginal external benefits become smaller as the person becomes more educated. In other words, the primary benefit of a college education is likely to be the benefit that the student receives in the form of increased earning capacity.

Of course, certain types of higher education may generate external benefits, whereas others may not. Much of higher education today is technical training that prepares students for careers, and this type of education seems unlikely to involve external benefits. For instance, how does the general public benefit from the nearly 25 percent of college students who take their degrees in some form of business administration? Perhaps economics courses lead to better-informed citizens and ultimately to better public policies—but it is difficult to see that this has happened, even though tens of millions of people have taken basic courses in economics.

We do not mean to deny the existence of external benefits associated with higher education. Perhaps there are some difficult-to-articulate and difficult-to-measure external benefits involved. Exactly what they are and how important they are, however, remain unclear. Moreover, we should recall from Chapter 2 that the external benefits are relevant only to the extent that there are *marginal* external benefits from obtaining more education than students would gain without a subsidy. If Peltzman's findings are correct, most college students would go to college even without subsidies and would, in fact, receive slightly better educations. Whatever the strength of the externality argument is in principle, existing subsidies have not significantly increased the consumption of college education, according to Peltzman. Consequently, if education produces external benefits, the current system of subsidies has been poorly designed to increase the quantity of education consumed.

The Voucher Alternative

States now subsidize college students by providing funds directly to public colleges, enabling them to charge tuition that is below the actual cost of educating students. There is nothing in the arguments defending subsidies for higher education, however, that requires the subsidy to take this particular form. So let us consider an alternative way of subsidizing higher education, *vouchers*. Under a voucher scheme, public colleges would no longer receive any funds directly from the government; instead they would have to charge tuitions that were sufficient to cover the cost of providing educational services to students. Students would continue to be subsidized, but now they would receive the assistance directly with a voucher, to be used at any college they choose to attend.

An example will help clarify how the voucher subsidy might be structured. Recall our earlier example in which the public college incurred costs of $7,500 per student but charged tuition of only $1,500, with the remaining $6,000 paid by the government. With a voucher program the college would have to charge tuition of $7,500, but the students would be given a voucher by the government that could be used to cover $6,000 of the tuition cost at any college. In effect, the voucher would be much like food stamps because it could be used only to purchase the targeted good. From the student's point of view, the cost of attending the public college is unchanged. The out-of-pocket cost is still $1,500 to attend the public college, because $1,500 plus the $6,000 voucher will cover the $7,500 tuition. Now, however, the student can use the subsidy at any college or university. To attend a private college with a tuition of $10,000, for example, the out-of-pocket cost would be $4,000. In contrast, it would cost the student $10,000 to attend the private college under the current arrangement, because the implicit subsidy available at the public college could not be used to purchase educational services elsewhere.

Figure 5–3 illustrates how this program would affect the options open to the student. The original budget line is shown as *MARLN*, as explained previously. Given those options and the indifference curves shown, the student would attend the public college and be in equilibrium at point R on indifference curve U_2. The voucher changes the budget line to $MM'N'$. With the preferences shown, the student would choose a school with a higher tuition that provides E_1 units of education; equilibrium would be at point A, with the student reaching a higher indifference curve at no greater cost to the government. Of course, the actual outcome would depend on the student's preferences, and Figure 5–3 shows only one possible result. Some students, faced with the same options but having different preferences, might choose to purchase less education under the voucher arrangement. In this case, the equilibrium would be along the $M'R$ portion of the budget line. In either case, however, the student would attain a higher indifference curve.

In addition to the effects on students' options, the voucher arrangement is also likely to affect the types of education provided by colleges. Under the present arrangements, public colleges are sheltered to a large degree from competition with other (out-of-state) public and private colleges. Because students will lose the subsidy if they go elsewhere, public colleges do not have to offer an education that caters as fully to the students' interests in order to retain them. In contrast, under the voucher plan, every college

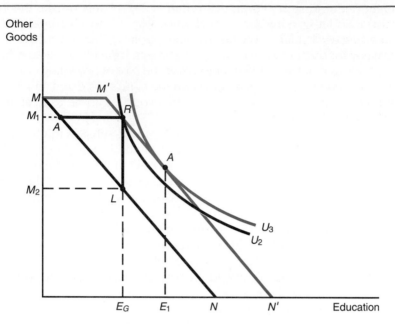

Figure 5–3   *Vouchers versus subsidies through state-supported colleges*

would have to compete on the same basis by offering an education that is attractive to students. Greater competition among colleges would result, advocates of vouchers believe, in a better-quality education at many colleges.

Opponents of the voucher plan argue that placing more power in the hands of students might lead to a lower quality of education. Some students might select colleges on the basis of how easy the coursework was or how attractive the social life was. We doubt that this would be a serious problem, however. Students now clamor to get into the colleges generally acknowledged to be the best and toughest, for they apparently recognize that their future prospects depend on the quality of the education they receive and not just on getting a degree.

Another concern is that the voucher plan might lead to greater segregation in colleges by income, religion, or race. Quite possibly a poor family would use the $6,000 voucher to purchase an education costing $6,000 and no more, but wealthier families would supplement the voucher and send their children to more expensive schools. The voucher plan, however, can be adapted to avoid this problem by giving larger vouchers to poorer families. Just as poorer families receive more food stamps and more Pell Grants, vouchers could be adjusted to offer more assistance to low-income families. In addition, the use of vouchers could be limited to schools enrolling students from all social backgrounds or schools offering approved courses of instruction. The basic point is that the voucher approach is quite flexible and can be adapted to subsidize some kinds of students or some types of education more than others.

Review Questions and Problems

1. Of the three subsidies discussed in this chapter, food stamps are a pro-poor subsidy, unemployment insurance is a pro-middle-class subsidy, and support for higher education is a pro-rich subsidy. Do you agree? Explain.

2. Food stamps are a type of fixed-quantity subsidy. Can the food stamp subsidy lead to underconsumption? Why or why not?

3. "The average four-person family on food stamps receives about $150 in food stamps a month. You can't feed four people on $5 per day, so food stamp benefits should be increased." Comment. (Does the average family referred to here have to finance its food purchases entirely with food stamps? See Table 5–2.)

4. Before 1979, the food stamp subsidy operated differently. Although the subsidy at each level of income was approximately the same, the family had to pay something to receive food stamps. For example, instead of receiving $150 in food stamps outright, the family had to pay $50 to receive $200 in food stamps. The food stamp subsidy costs the government $150 in both cases. This feature was called the *purchase requirement*. Explain how a family's budget line changes with this type of food stamp program.

5. Would you expect food consumption to be greater or less when the food stamp program had a purchase requirement, as explained in question 4? Do you think eliminating the purchase requirement in 1979 was a good idea?

6. If the replacement rate in the unemployment insurance program is increased, how will this change the nation's unemployment rate?

7. Could the adverse effect of UI on unemployment be avoided if unemployed persons were given a lump-sum payment when they became unemployed, so that the subsidy would be the same regardless of the duration of unemployment? What adverse incentives, if any, would such a UI program produce?

8. Explain Feldstein's proposal to convert UI from subsidies to loans. Who would be benefited and who would be harmed if this change in the program were made?

9. Explain why you believe that government support of higher education is or is not justified. If you believe it is justified, do you think that the way that higher education is now subsidized is the best way? (In other words, what type of subsidy do you favor?)

10. Show how state-supported colleges can lead some students to consume less education than they would without this subsidy. If a voucher program were used and tuition were raised to cover the full cost of college education, how would your analysis be affected?

Supplementary Readings

ALCHIAN, ARMEN A. "The Economic and Social Impact of Free Tuition." In Armen A. Alchian, *Economic Forces at Work*. Indianapolis: Liberty Press, 1977.

ATKINSON, ANTHONY, and JOHN MICKLEWRIGHT. "Unemployment Compensation and Labor Market Transitions: A Critical Review. *Journal of Economic Literature*, 29:1679–1727 (Dec. 1991).

CLARKSON, KENNETH W. *Food Stamps and Nutrition*. Washington D.C.: American Enterprise Institute, 1975.

CONGRESSIONAL BUDGET OFFICE. *Promoting Employment and Maintaining Incomes with Unemployment Insurance*. Washington, D.C: U.S. Government Printing Office, (Mar. 1985).

CONGRESSIONAL BUDGET OFFICE. *Student Aid and the Cost of Postsecondary Education*. Washington, D.C.: U.S. Government Printing Office, (Jan. 1991).

FELDSTEIN, MARTIN S. "Unemployment Compensation: Adverse Incentives and Distributional Anomalies." *National Tax Journal*, 27(2):231–244 (June 1974).

———. "Unemployment Insurance: Time for Reform." *Harvard Business Review* (Mar./Apr. 1975).

HAMERMESH, DANIEL. *Jobless Pay and the Economy*. Baltimore: Johns Hopkins University Press, 1977.

Financing Health Care

*C*ONCERN ABOUT THE HEALTH CARE SYSTEM in the United States has been increasing in recent years. Indeed, no other economic issue played a more prominent role in the 1992 presidential campaign. Two major problems are widely believed to plague the health care system. The first is high and rapidly rising costs. In 1990, more than $1 of every $9 spent in the United States was devoted to the purchase of some form of health care, and the Congressional Budget Office predicts that the figure will become $1 of every $6 by the year 2000. The second problem concerns health insurance coverage. Roughly 14 percent of the population has no insurance coverage, and many of those who do have coverage fear they may lose it.

Numerous proposals have been made to deal with these and other perceived problems of the health care system. We will examine some of the major reform options at the end of this chapter. First, however, it is necessary to examine how health care and health insurance markets function and how they are affected by current governmental policies.

◆──

Public and Private Expenditures on Health Care

Expenditures on health care have not always absorbed such a large share of national income as they do today. As Table 6–1 shows, in 1950 total health care expenditures were only 4.2 percent of the GNP. Both private and government spending have risen rapidly since that time, with the total outlay on health care nearly tripling as a proportion of GNP by 1990, when it reached $614.5 billion. To put that figure in perspective, note that it is more

Table 6–1   *Expenditures on Health Care (in $ billions)*

Fiscal Year	Total Spending	Total as a Percentage of GNP	Private Spending	Government Spending	Government Spending as a Percentage of Total
1950	$ 12.0	4.2%	$ 9.0	$ 3.1	25.5%
1960	25.9	5.1	19.5	6.4	24.7
1965	38.9	5.6	29.4	9.5	24.5
1970	69.2	7.0	43.8	25.4	36.7
1975	124.7	8.0	72.4	52.3	42.0
1980	232.1	8.7	132.3	99.8	43.0
1985	392.9	9.9	221.3	171.6	43.7
1990	614.5	11.3	343.0	271.5	44.2

Source: Ann Kallman Bixby, "Social Welfare Expenditures, 1963–1983," *Social Security Bulletin,* 49(2) (Feb. 1986), Table 7. For 1980 to 1990, *Social Security Bulletin, Annual Statistical Supplement, 1991,* Table 3.A1, p. 101, and Table.3.A4, p. 103.

than twice as large as total spending on national defense and nearly twice as large as all spending on education.

Later in this chapter, we will consider why public and private spending on health care have increased so rapidly. Here it should be noted that government spending has been rising faster than private spending, as indicated by the growing share of government outlays shown in the last column of Table 6–1. By 1990, more than $2 of every $5 spent on health care was spent by government, but as we will see later, even this figure understates the role that government now plays in this industry. Much of the growth of government spending in this area has resulted from the enactment of Medicare and Medicaid in 1965 and their subsequent rapid growth. (Note the jump in the government share between 1965 and 1970, reflecting the introduction of these two policies.) By 1990, expenditures on Medicare and Medicaid alone totaled about $170 billion, more than 60 percent of total government expenditures in the health care area. The remainder of government spending was devoted to a wide variety of purposes: public health, medical research, veterans' hospitals, child health programs, hospital construction, and others.

Another significant development in the post–World War II financing of health care has been the growth of private health insurance. Table 6–2 provides a percentage breakdown of personal health expenditures by sources of funds. In 1990, private insurance covered 31.8 percent of health expenditures, more than three times its share in 1950. Both government and private insurance are sources of *third-party payments* for health care. Third-party payments are so called because they are expenses covered by someone other than either the provider or the consumer of health care (the two parties involved in the market exchange). Of course, the public does ultimately bear the cost of third-party payments in the form of insurance premiums or

Table 6–2   *Percentage Distribution of Personal Health Care Expenditures*

Fiscal Year	Total	Private Direct Payments	Private Insurance Benefits	Government	Third-party Payments
1950	100	65.5%	9.1%	22.4%	34.5%
1960	100	54.9	21.1	21.8	45.1
1965	100	51.6	24.2	22.0	48.4
1970	100	40.5	23.4	34.3	59.5
1975	100	32.5	26.7	39.5	67.5
1980	100	27.1	29.8	67.6	72.9
1985	100	25.5	30.8	40.1	74.5
1990	100	23.3	31.8	41.3	76.7

Note: Personal health care expenditures are about 10 percent smaller than the total expenditures shown in Table 6–1 because the former do not include medical research, public health activities, and so on.

Source: 1950–74 data, U.S. Department of Health, Education, and Welfare, Social Security Administration, *Compendium of National Health Expenditures Data,* Office of Research and Statistics Pub. No. 76-11927 (Jan. 1976), Table 2. 1980–90 data, Katharine R. Levit, Helen C. Lazenby, Cathy A. Conan, and Suzanne W. Letsh, "National Health Expenditures, 1990," *Health Care Financing Review* (Fall 1991), Table 11.

taxes, but the fact that the consumer (patient) does not bear these costs in proportion to his or her own use of health care resources has important implications for the functioning of health care markets.

Roughly speaking, the share of health care spending covered by third-party payments measures the extent to which consumers are subsidized at the time they utilize health care resources. As shown in the last column of Table 6–2, third-party payments have risen steadily over the period, until in 1990 they covered more than three fourths of all health costs. The mirror image of the third-party share is, of course, the share borne by private parties. By 1990, direct private payments covered only 23.3 percent of total health care expenditures.

Health Care and Health Status

In discussions of the U.S. health care system, it is common to contrast the mammoth costs of health care with the health status of the American people. Although the United States spends more on health care than any other nation, both absolutely and as a percentage of national income, its people are far from being the healthiest in the world, at least as measured by some commonly used indices. For example, of the 16 advanced economies comprising the Organization for Economic Cooperation and Development (OECD), the United States ranks in the bottom half in terms of life expectancy and 14th in terms of infant mortality. Does this imply that our health care system is generally inefficient? Perhaps surprisingly, it does not. A wealth of empirical evidence strongly suggests that differences in the quantity or quality of health care among developed countries are *not* significantly related to differences in health. Put another way, health levels in a country reflect a wide variety of factors; medical care is only one of these factors, and its independent contribution to the general level of health seems rather minor.[1] Thus, spending more on health care or reorganizing the system is not likely to improve greatly the international standing of the United States.

With respect to life expectancy, it is easy to understand why additional health care expenditures are unlikely to increase longevity. The three leading causes of death in the United States are heart disease, cancer, and accidents (mainly automobile), accounting for 7 of every 10 deaths. More or better medical care is unlikely to prevent many of these deaths. In general, the health of a people depends heavily on other factors such as heredity, nutrition, smoking, drinking, exercise, education, environmental influences, and general lifestyle. Provision of additional medical care will not alter these other influences and so cannot be expected to transform us into a healthier nation.[2]

A striking example of the importance of nonmedical factors is provided by two adjacent states in the western United States, Utah and Nevada. These states enjoy similar levels of income and medical care, but the inhabitants of one state are apparently far healthier than those of the other. Death rates at all age levels, for males and females, are substantially higher in Nevada, typically 20 to 40 percent higher. What explains these huge differences? Although we are not certain, the answer probably lies in the fact that Utah is predominantly Mormon. Devout Mormons lead temperate lives, neither smoking nor drinking.

No intent to disparage the contributions of health care to health and well-being should be inferred, however. Here, as elsewhere, it is important to distinguish between the *total* and *marginal* benefits of an economic use of resources. The total contribution of medical care to health in the United States is doubtless immense, at least at the present time. (It is now generally agreed that "it was not until well into the twentieth century that the average patient had better than a 50-50 chance of being helped by the average phy-

---

[1] This theme is stressed in Victor R. Fuchs, *Who Shall Live?* (New York: Basic Books, 1974), Chapter 2. This section draws heavily on Fuchs's interesting work.

[2] That defects in the U.S. health care system are not responsible for the relatively high infant mortality rate is persuasively argued in Nicholas Eberstadt, "America's Infant-Mortality Puzzle," *The Public Interest,* 105:30 (Fall 1991). The U.S. infant mortality rate in 1986 was 10.4 per 1,000 births (compared to 69.0 in 1925–29). Had it been 8.0, the United States would have ranked in the top half of the OECD countries; only small differences separate most of these countries.

sician."[3]) One need only imagine what would happen if we had to do without any medical care to realize its importance. All or nothing, however, is not the relevant issue. Instead, the issue is more correctly posed as a question of reorganizing the use of existing medical resources or of devoting more or fewer resources to the provision of health care. The contention here is that such *marginal* changes will not produce major differences in the average level of health.

If there is a health care "crisis," it is not demonstrated by our international standing. Our ranking internationally probably tells us more about the lifestyles we have chosen (usually individually and voluntarily) than about our health care system.

Is Health Care Special?

Just as with other goods and services, the provision of health care requires the use of scarce resources that have alternative uses. To provide more health care means that less of other desired goods and services can be produced. In this sense, there is an opportunity cost associated with the provision of health care, just as there is with other goods and services. This raises the question of whether there are any special characteristics associated with health care that require government intervention. Many economists believe that there are. Certain types of health care have a public good or externality characteristic, implying that private provision would be inefficient. This is especially true of medical research (where production of knowledge is a public good) and the treatment of contagious disease (where there are external benefits for those not treated). A role for government in these areas can be rationalized. However, only a small share—less than 5 percent—of health expenditures falls in these two categories.

Another, more subtle type of externality is suggested by statements such as "Health care is a right" and "No one should have to go without needed medical attention because of inability to pay." These statements imply that the general public takes an interest in the consumption of health care by those who are ill. Insofar as this is true, there may be external benefits from consumption of general types of health care. But for the vast bulk of the population that is nonpoor, these benefits are probably inframarginal because adequate levels of care would be purchased privately without subsidization. This argument, then, may constitute a reason for subsidizing consumption of health care by the poor.

Apart from such fairly conventional externality considerations, two other peculiarities about health care are often stressed. First, health expenses are irregular and unpredictable. In contrast to expenditures on goods like food

[3]Fuchs, *Who Shall Live?* p. 30.

and clothing, which tend to be steady and easily predicted, some types of health expenses are incurred only in the uncertain event of illness. This particular characteristic of health care accounts for the demand for insurance protection, and requires that we analyze the provision of health insurance and how it affects health care markets.

The second and probably most frequently noted characteristic of health care is the difficulty the consumer has in evaluating the service received. In general, consumers do not know the consequences of different medical treatments, nor are they able to determine whether they require any treatment at all. This situation arises because knowledge is a scarce good, and it is not unique to health care; education, legal services, and auto repairs share this characteristic. However, the lack of knowledge on the part of the consumer may be more pronounced and more important in the medical field. As a result, the consumer's demand for health care depends in part on advice given by his or her doctor and raises the problem of whether individual demand reflects the true marginal value of the service. Although this "knowledge imperfection" is widely acknowledged, its implications for public policy are far from clear.

Finally, we should emphasize that health care markets cannot reasonably be characterized as competitive in the United States today. In part, this situation reflects the features already mentioned, but to a far larger degree it is due to government intervention in this industry. The federal and state governments have numerous laws, regulations, tax policies, and spending policies that affect the way health care markets function. There is probably no other industry in the country where government intervention is so ubiquitous. This means that it is very difficult to understand the way these markets function since decisions are as likely to be affected by government policies as by market forces.

Some Principles of Health Insurance

We live in a risky world, and one of the major risks is the probability of illness. This risk of illness carries with it the risk of incurring heavy medical expenses. Most people do not like to bear risk and are willing to pay to avoid it. Insurance provides this service. By pooling the risks of many people, insurance companies are able to provide insurance on favorable terms. A simple example can be used to show why insurance markets develop.

Suppose that there is 1 chance in 100 of contracting an illness that costs $20,000 to treat. An insurance company sells policies agreeing to cover this expense. If it sells a large number of policies, say, 10,000, the statistical law of large numbers implies that the insurance company can be nearly certain of having to pay almost exactly 100 people (1/100 of 10,000). The number may be a few more or less than 100, but it is very unlikely to be far from 100. In effect, by pooling the risks of a large number of people, the risk borne by the insurance company is quite small. This makes it possible for the company to sell the insurance policy at a price (premium) slightly above $200 (1/100 times $20,000), which is the expected value, or average expense, incurred by the company for the people it insures. The price will have to be somewhat above $200 because the company must cover not only the expenses of those who become ill but also other costs (processing claims, selling costs, administrative costs, etc.).

Most people are what economists call *risk averse*. Technically, this means that a person prefers to bear a given cost with certainty rather than an uncertain prospect of a greater cost with the same expected value. For example, most people would prefer to pay $200 for insurance than to remain uninsured and to take one chance in a hundred of losing $20,000. When people are risk averse they are willing to pay more, sometimes much more, than $200 for an insurance policy that covers the $20,000 medical cost if they become ill. Because businesses are able to provide this service at a cost of slightly more than $200 by pooling the risks of many people, insurance policies can be supplied at a price that consumers find attractive. Thus, markets for insurance will emerge.

It is not efficient, however, to insure against all medical expenses. To take an extreme case, suppose that you know with certainty that you will have a physical checkup costing $100 next year. An insurance company would be willing to sell you a policy to cover this expense, but only at a price of $110, for example, because it has to cover its own costs in addition to the cost of your physical. You would, of course, be better off paying the $100 bill directly and saving $10. In this case, there would be no insurance protection against risk because there is no risk, and the additional $10 payment to the insurance company would provide no service.

This simple example suggests some important principles. It is generally inefficient to insure against *predictable* expenses (where the risk is small). In addition, it is generally inefficient to insure against *small* expenses because one can provide one's own insurance more cheaply, simply by saving a small sum. Thus, it is rational for people to bear many of the risks involved in living in an uncertain world. Insurance makes the most sense (is the most beneficial) in highly risky situations in which the costs may be quite large (consider life insurance, home insurance, and automobile liability insurance). This does not imply that there is one level of insurance coverage that is most suitable for everyone. People's abilities and willingness to bear risks vary greatly, so they prefer different types of insurance coverage.

The Problem of Moral Hazard

Payment of health expenses by a third party, either an insurance company or the government, encounters a problem when the size of the loss a person suffers depends partly on the individual's own behavior. Consider an

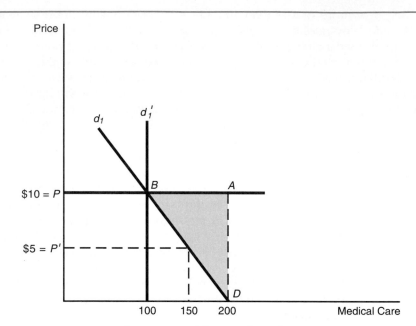

Figure 6–1   *Moral hazard and insurance*

insurance policy that covers *all* hospital expenses. When a person is hospitalized, the patient bears no financial cost if his or her stay is prolonged. *In effect, full insurance coverage means that the insured pays a zero price for hospital care at the time treatment decisions are made.* This is likely to lead the person to overconsume hospital services: Any medical care that has any benefit, no matter how slight, would seem worthwhile if the insurance company incurs the expense. The patient's doctor is more likely to prescribe expensive tests and sophisticated treatments, knowing that no financial responsibility falls on the patient. Although the value of the health care to the patient is less than its actual cost, it seems worthwhile because the patient bears no out-of-pocket cost.

In insurance terminology, this is called the *moral hazard* problem. It has nothing to do with morality; to an economist it simply represents the resource misallocations caused by a particular method of finance. Figure 6–1 illustrates the moral hazard problem. Curve d_1 is a representative consumer's demand curve for a particular type of medical care if he or she becomes ill. (If the consumer does not become ill, there will be a zero demand.) At a price of $10 per unit, consumption would be 100 units, for a total cost of $1,000 in the absence of insurance. If the person is fully insured (all expenses covered), the net price of care the patient will bear at the time illness strikes is zero and consumption will be 200 units. Consumption will be greater because of the law of demand; in fact, the moral hazard problem exists because the economic behavior of people is responsive to prices. Note that there is a welfare cost because of overconsumption of medical care, which is measured by triangle *BAD*. In effect, insurance that covers all costs is identical to an excise subsidy that reduces the consumer's price to zero.

In this way, insurance induces increased consumption of medical care. *Because the out-of-pocket cost is so modest, insured patients (or their doctors) have little incentive to economize on the use of medical resources.* This effect of insurance has several important consequences for an analysis of health care financed by insurance. First, because the effective demand of patients is increased, the price of health care is likely to rise. Many economists believe that the rapid growth in public and private insurance (third-party payments) is directly responsible for the rapidly rising costs of health care over the past several decades.

Second, when the moral hazard problem exists, insurance coverage of all health expenses, even large ones, is no longer likely to be an efficient policy. Instead the welfare gain from having insurance protection must be weighed against the welfare cost of overutilization of medical resources. Note that the induced increase in consumption increases the total cost of health care, and hence will increase the insurance premium needed to finance the policy. In Figure 6–1, if there is a 1-in-10 chance of being ill, the premium (ignoring the loading factor caused by administrative costs) for full insurance coverage would be $200 (one tenth of the $2,000 cost of 200 units of care). Because the cost is $1,000 if uninsured, a person might prefer to remain uninsured and take a one-tenth chance of bearing a $1,000 cost rather than pay $200 for the insurance policy. Either may be efficient depending on the consumer's attitude toward risk.

The severity of the moral hazard problem depends on how sensitive consumers are to medical care prices, that is, on the price elasticities of demand. Figure 6–1 shows that if the demand curve were perfectly inelastic—the vertical curve d_1'—consumption of health care would not increase even at a zero price. If people's consumption of health care is completely unresponsive to price, there is no moral hazard problem, and full insurance coverage will not distort economic choices. In general, the more elastic the demand for medical care, the more severe is the problem of moral hazard and the more inappropriate full insurance coverage is.

Much popular discussion of medical care issues implicitly assumes vertical demand curves—"needs" that do not depend on price. In life-threatening and other serious situations, price is probably not a major consideration. Most health care is not of this sort, however, and the doctor and patient frequently have a broad range of discretion in selecting treatments. In the past several years, a considerable body of evidence has accumulated suggesting that people consume more medical care at lower prices. For example, Feldstein estimated the price elasticity of demand for hospital care to be about 0.7, and Rosett and Huang's estimates are even higher.[4] (An elasticity of 0.7 means that a 10 percent reduction in price increases quantity demanded by 7 percent.)

Coping with the Moral Hazard Problem

The moral hazard problem can be dealt with in several ways. Because moral hazard implies inefficiency associated with overconsumption, it is in the interest of insurance companies (as well as of insured parties) to devise ways to avoid the problem. One way to deal with the moral hazard problem is to make a fixed payment to the insured party in the event of a specified illness. For example, the insured party might be given $1,000 as a lump-sum payment; this completely avoids the incentive to overconsume because the insurance benefit is fixed and does not depend on the quantity of health care purchased. (This is, in fact, the way home fire insurance policies are written. The insurance benefit does not cover *all* costs incurred in purchasing a new house to replace a burned one but is fixed in amount.) In the health care field, this approach is sometimes difficult. For adequate protection, it would be necessary to specify a different payment for each illness, but because there are many possible complications and severities of illness within each category, this would be a complex and costly way of writing insurance. Nonetheless, some policies do place upper limits on the liability of the insurance companies, which tends to place an upper limit on the moral hazard problem.

A second approach is to require the insured person to pay part of the costs. The patient might be required to pay half of the cost, for example. In Figure 6–1, the price would then be P', or $5, and overconsumption would be reduced. The share of the cost borne by the insured person is called the *coinsurance rate,* a device that is widely used in insurance programs. It has the advantage of reducing the welfare cost of overconsumption but the disadvantage of requiring the insured party to bear some of the risk of illness. Focusing on where to set the coinsurance rate is a good way to understand the trade-off between providing insurance protection and weakening the economic incentives necessary for efficient utilization of health care resources.

A third approach is the use of *deductibles.* Using a deductible means that a patient must pay, for example, the first $200 of hospital costs, and then the insurance company will cover all additional costs (full insurance), if any, or some fraction of these costs (using coinsurance rates). A deductible gives insured patients an incentive to be economical in the event of minor medical problems; it avoids, for example, the incentive for a person to enter a hos-

---

[4]Martin S. Feldstein, "Hospital Cost Inflation: A Study in Nonprofit Price Dynamics," *American Economic Review,* 61:853 (Dec. 1971); and R. Rosett and L. Huang, "The Effects of Health Insurance on the Demand for Medical Care," *Journal of Political Economy,* 81(2):281 (Mar./Apr. 1973).

pital for a brief treatment that could be just as easily provided at home or in a doctor's office. In addition, insurance itself is generally not efficient in the case of small expenses, as explained earlier, so deductibles are generally appropriate in any insurance policy.

Much of the discussion on how to structure a government policy of health insurance such as Medicare and Medicaid centers on the size of the deductibles and the level of the coinsurance rates. It is generally accepted that both features have a place in any program of health insurance, but their exact specification remains controversial. The basic issue should by now be clear: how to provide adequate insurance protection and preserve incentives at the same time.

Tax Policy and Private Health Insurance

Most workers are covered by health insurance that is provided by their employers. In 1990, 70 percent of the U.S. population under the age of 65 was covered by employment-based health insurance.[5] (Another 15 percent is covered by a variety of public and private forms of insurance.) This represents a dramatic increase in insurance coverage over the past several decades. In 1940, only 10 percent of the U.S. population had any form of health insurance.

Under employer-provided health insurance, employers select the health insurance policies that cover their workers and pay all or part of the premium costs to insurance companies. Employers do not, however, bear the costs of the insurance coverage. It is well established, both in economic theory and by empirical evidence, that workers ultimately pay for this fringe benefit with lower cash wages. Thus, when an employer "pays" for a $1,000 policy covering a worker, that worker's cash wages will be $1,000 lower. Employers, of course, have an incentive to provide fringe benefits that workers want and are willing to pay for with reduced cash wages, just as they have an incentive to provide products that consumers want and are willing to pay for. It is appropriate, therefore, to think of workers choosing to take part of their pay in the form of health insurance and to pay for it with reduced cash wages. (The individual worker does not have this choice since generally the same policy must cover all workers of a given employer, but workers as a group do have this choice.)

Why would workers choose to take part of their wages as employer-provided health insurance rather than as cash? After all, with cash they could purchase their own policies, ones presumably better tailored to their individual circumstances. One reason is that there are cost savings associated

---

[5]U.S. Congress, Congressional Budget Office, *Economic Implications of Rising Health Care Costs* (Washington, D.C.: U.S. Government Printing Office, Oct. 1992), p. 30.

with the provision of health insurance to large groups of persons. Group health insurance—which is what employers purchase from insurance companies—is less expensive on a per capita basis the larger the size of the group. For businesses with between 2,500 and 10,000 employees, administrative expenses of health insurance plans averaged 8 percent of benefits actually paid out in 1988. For businesses with between 10 and 20 employees, administrative expenses averaged 30 percent, and for single individuals purchasing health insurance, they averaged 40 percent.[6]

A second reason for the prevalence of employment-based health insurance is even more important. *Employers' contributions to group health insurance plans are not subject to federal income, state income, or payroll taxes.* This means that workers can purchase employer-provided health insurance with before-tax wages, but they have to use after-tax wages to purchase medical care or individual insurance. To see how this works, consider a worker in a 20 percent tax bracket. If the worker is paid $100 in cash by the employer, after paying taxes there will be $80 left to purchase health insurance or medical care. In contrast, the employer can devote the $100 to the purchase of health insurance for the worker, and there will be no tax liability. From the worker's point of view, the choice is between $80 in cash or $100 in health insurance. Thus, by not taxing health insurance "paid for" by the employer, the government effectively lowers the net price of insurance to workers; they can purchase $100 in health insurance by giving up only $80. In effect, this tax provision acts as an excise subsidy for the purchase of health insurance, lowering workers' net prices by a percentage equal to their combined marginal tax rates under the income and payroll taxes.

In this way, the tax system subsidizes the purchase of health insurance. The rate of the subsidy varies with the combined marginal tax rate of the worker. For a low-wage worker who does not have enough income to be subject to federal or state income taxes, the social security payroll tax rate (15.3 percent) is the effective rate of subsidy. Most workers, however, are in the 15 percent bracket of the federal income tax. They receive a subsidy that is at least 30.3 percent, and higher if there is a state income tax. For high-income workers in the 28 percent bracket, it is likely that the rate of subsidy exceeds 45 percent. It should be noted that the implicit tax subsidy tends to rise with income because income tax rates are higher for those with more income.

Employer-provided health insurance leads to lower taxable wages for workers and hence lower tax revenues for government. In fact, the cost of the subsidy to the government is best measured by the amount of tax revenue not collected as a result of the tax provision. On that basis, the cost of the health insurance tax subsidy in 1993 was $65 billion in lost revenues

---

[6]Congressional Budget Office, *Rising Health Care Costs,* p. 32.

from the income and payroll taxes of the federal government.[7] Revenue losses to state governments would probably add at least $10 billion more.

Consequence of the Tax Subsidy

As mentioned earlier, there are many public policies that affect health care markets. Many analysts believe that the tax subsidy is the most significant policy of all, with dramatic implications for the functioning of this sector of the economy. Among the many effects of this policy, two will be emphasized here.

The first effect is that the policy encourages workers to buy employer-provided health insurance. Since it is a form of excise subsidy, it is not surprising that more insurance will be purchased at a lower price. In general, we expect the result to be that workers will purchase more insurance than is efficient. But the policy does more than just encourage additional consumption of a standardized product; it also affects the nature of the insurance coverage purchased. As we explained earlier, it makes no economic sense to have insurance cover small and predictable medical expenses. Yet employer-provided health insurance often covers such things as annual physical checkups, routine dental care (cleaning), and maternity benefits.

It is inefficient to cover small and predictable medical expenses with insurance because of the necessary *loading rate*. This refers to the administrative costs of providing insurance, which form a wedge between premium costs and medical benefits paid. For example, on average, policies pay $1 in medical benefits at a premium cost of about $1.12. For risky events it may be worthwhile to pay this loading rate of 12 percent, but not for small and predictable ones. In the absence of a subsidy, a predictable medical expense would never be covered by insurance. However, when the rate of subsidy exceeds the loading rate, it becomes cheaper for workers to cover *any* medical expenses with employer-provided insurance. Since the rate of subsidy equals the combined tax rate, which almost always exceeds 12 percent, the tax subsidy gives all workers a strong incentive to have extensive coverage of medical services for which insurance is inefficient.

The tax subsidy therefore probably leads most workers to overconsume health insurance and to have many medical expenses covered that should not be covered by insurance at all. It accounts for the fact that most employer-provided health insurance uses very low deductibles (often only $250) and low coinsurance rates (often 20 percent) and covers fully medical care costs below a low ceiling (for example, pays 100 percent of the costs in excess of $1,000).

Not only does the tax subsidy directly affect the purchase of health insurance, but it also has a strong indirect effect on the operation of medical care markets. With insurance covering most medical costs, patients and health

---

[7]Congressional Budget Office, *Rising Health Care Costs,* p. 32.

care providers have no incentive to keep costs down. Patients, for example, have no incentive to seek out the hospitals or doctors who offer care for the lowest prices. In prescribing treatments, doctors do not have to be concerned about the costs falling on the patient since insurance covers those costs. Full-coverage insurance is like giving patients and health care providers a blank check. Any medical care, even if its benefits are only a few cents per dollar of cost, becomes attractive when the insurance company is bearing all the costs.

In short, the tax subsidy encourages excessive insurance coverage, and that, in turn, leads to a great increase in the demand for medical care, which increases health care costs. Higher health care costs also mean higher premiums for health insurance. The only countervailing force is the incentive insurance companies have to keep their payments from becoming excessive. They have adopted a number of procedures in an attempt to control costs (such as requiring the insurance company to approve medical procedures before they are undertaken), without much apparent success. When health care providers and patients have an incentive to utilize the best treatments possible, regardless of cost, it is understandably difficult for insurance companies to keep costs down.

Publicly Financed Health Care

The federal and state governments indirectly subsidize health care through provisions in the tax laws, as we have just seen. They also directly subsidize health care through a variety of spending programs. The two most important ones are Medicare and Medicaid. Combined government outlays totaled $184 billion in 1991, $104 billion for Medicare and $80 billion for Medicaid. Both programs were enacted in 1965, Medicare as Title 18 and Medicaid as Title 19 of the 1965 amendments to the Social Security Act. Medicare subsidizes health care for the elderly, and Medicaid subsidizes health care for low-income persons. Approximately one fifth of the U.S. population (50 million people) is covered by one or both of these programs.

Medicare is a federal government program. It is composed of two parts. Part A (Hospital Insurance, or HI) is a program of mandatory hospital insurance that is provided to all elderly persons (with minor exceptions) and is financed as part of the social security system by a 2.9 percent payroll tax. Part B is called Supplemental Medical Insurance (SMI) and covers physicians' costs and other related services. Participation in SMI is voluntary, but it is so heavily subsidized that almost all the elderly participate. To receive benefits from SMI, the elderly must pay a monthly premium, which was $36.60 in 1993 (scheduled to rise to $46.10 in 1996). That sounds like a lot, but it covers only one fourth of the costs of the program; the other three fourths are covered by a subsidy from general federal revenues.

Medicare can best be thought of as government provision of health insurance for the elderly. Part A, covering hospital costs, uses a deductible ($676 in 1993) and thereafter covers *all* hospital expenses for a stay of up to 60 days. For stays from 61 to 90 days, patients pay a coinsurance rate of about 25 percent, but many of the elderly have Medigap private insurance policies to cover this cost. (Most hospital stays are less than 60 days.) Part B uses a $100 per year deductible and then pays 80 percent of the cost of physicians' and most other services (a 20 percent coinsurance rate). One type of medical care that Medicare does not cover is nursing home care, but the elderly poor can have this paid for by Medicaid.

Medicaid is a joint federal-state program, with the federal government paying at least 50 percent of the costs and states picking up the remainder. Medicaid is actually administered by individual states under federal guidelines. To receive federal subsidies, states must provide Medicaid services to all persons receiving public assistance; states may also choose to cover other low-income people who are considered medically indigent. In addition, the range of medical assistance provided to recipients varies from state to state. All states are required to cover hospital, physicians', and nursing home services. Other types of medical care may be provided at the option of the states. With few exceptions, Medicaid covers *all* the costs of covered medical services provided to eligible persons.

In recent years, Medicaid has become the largest government welfare program, at least if we interpret "welfare program" to mean a program that provides benefits almost exclusively to low-income persons. Total Medicaid outlays are more than triple those of the food stamp program or AFDC. Not all poor persons are eligible to receive Medicaid, however. Eligibility is generally restricted to those with low incomes who are also elderly, blind, or disabled or who are members of families with dependent children (the AFDC population). Single persons and families without dependent children are frequently ineligible for Medicaid even if they are poor.

Price, Output, and Usage

Medical care prices have risen rapidly over the past four decades, and economists believe that a major reason is the growth in third-party payments by both public and private insurance, especially when the insurance covers a large share of the costs. Let us focus initially on the publicly provided insurance, namely, the Medicare and Medicaid programs. Figure 6–2 will help us analyze the effects of these programs.

In the absence of Medicare and Medicaid, the demand for medical care by potential recipients is shown as D_P, and the demand by all others is D_N. Total demand, D_T, is the horizontal sum of these curves, and the intersection of D_T and the supply curve determines price and output, P and M_T. Consumption levels of the two groups are M_P and M_N. As we have indicated, Medicare and Medicaid cover virtually all costs of medical care for recipients.

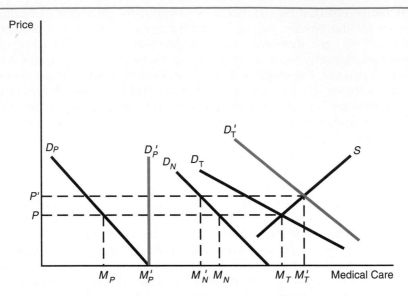

Figure 6–2 *Economic effects of Medicare and Medicaid*

In Figure 6–2 these policies have the effect of shifting the demand curve of recipients to the vertical curve D'_P, indicating that subsidized groups would choose to consume M'_P, whatever the market price, because the government pays it, and their net price is zero. Thus, there is a large increase in effective demand by subsidized parties, and this, coupled with an unchanged demand by the other group, causes the total demand curve to shift to D'_T. With an upward-sloping supply curve, the price increases to P' and the total quantity to M'_T. As a result, consumption by the unsubsidized group falls to M'_N, and consumption by the subsidized group rises to M'_P.

This is a highly simplified exposition of the way government subsidies affect medical care markets. Since it is based on the competitive model, it no doubt does not do justice to the complexity of the effects that can be produced. (For example, many hospitals are nonprofit institutions, and they may respond differently than private, for-profit competitive firms.) It also ignores the fact that the tax laws act to subsidize medical care usage by many members of the unsubsidized group in Figure 6–2. These tax subsidies have a demand-increasing effect on the D_N curve similar to that produced by Medicare and Medicaid. Thus, a fuller analysis of the medical care sector would also have D_N shifting outward in response to subsidized private health insurance.

A general implication of this analysis is that prices and costs (price times quantity) will be higher because of the direct and indirect subsidies. More to the point, more resources will be employed to produce more health care, such that output will be expanded to a point where marginal benefit is far below marginal cost. In other words, welfare costs will be produced because of the subsidies.

It would be a mistake to conclude that all of the rise in health care costs over the past several decades is due to excessive output of health care stimulated by subsidies. There have been dramatic improvements in the quality of many types of health care, but the higher quality does come at a higher price. It seems likely that people would spend more on health care today even if the subsidies did not exist. Nonetheless, some of the increase in health costs is certainly due to the effects of the subsidies. It is possible to have too high-quality a product (if its higher costs are larger than the additional benefits), and hospitals in particular may have been induced to produce excessively high-quality care. By 1990, hospital patients were paying only 5 percent of hospital costs, and because out-of-pocket expenses are so low, doctors and patients were likely to choose the most sophisticated and expensive treatments available.

An example will show clearly why such a heavy subsidy is likely to lead to better-quality, more expensive products. Suppose that the government pays 95 percent of the cost of the automobiles consumers purchase. It is possible that some consumers would respond by purchasing more of the Chevrolets, Fords, or Hondas they use now. But another plausible response would be to move up to a better-quality car, to purchase a Cadillac or Lincoln Continental instead of a Chevy or Ford, or a Mercedes or BMW instead of a Honda. We suspect that most people would purchase not only more cars but also more expensive cars. (We know we would!) Statistics would then show a sharp rise in automobile costs because the higher-quality cars cost much more.

Something like this probably has happened in the field of health care. It is a source of concern because many experts believe that consumers would not want more expensive hospital care if they had to pay for it: To most people, the higher quality of "Cadillac" care is not worth the extra cost. Patients and doctors choose this high-quality care now only because its direct cost at the time of treatment is so low, even though the actual marginal benefit of the more expensive care is below the marginal cost of providing it. This, of course, is simply a statement of the welfare cost resulting from overconsumption—but here the emphasis is on the quality dimension rather than on the more familiar quantity dimension.

Controlling Costs

When third-party payments cover most or all health care costs, there are diminished incentives for health care providers or consumers to keep costs down. In fact, when third-party payments cover *all* of the costs, there would seem to be *no* incentive for the market participants to keep costs down. What difference does it make to you if a doctor charges you $500 or $5,000, as long as you bear a zero cost in either case (and in many instances will not even see the bill)? Thus, as the rate of subsidy approaches 100 percent, market forces to contain costs within reasonable bounds become increasingly weaker. As a result, health costs go up.

Medicare and Medicaid, as well as private health insurance influenced by the tax laws, have substantially increased the demand for health care. Third-party payers, the government and insurance companies, have effectively replaced consumers as the purchasers of health care. As long as we remain with this system whereby third-party payments cover most of the costs, there will be strong upward pressure on costs from the behavior of consumers and health care providers. The only way costs can be controlled within this system is by direct actions taken by the actual purchasers, the insurance companies and government. The third-party purchasers have, in fact, already tried a variety of ways to control health care costs.

Prior to 1983, the government reimbursed hospitals on the basis of "reasonable and customary" fees for various treatments. *After* the actual costs had been incurred and the bill presented to the government, it would be determined whether the charges were reasonable. If they were judged so, the government would pay; otherwise, it would not. A similar process was often used by private insurance companies. In practice, this came pretty close to being a blank check for health care providers, although it probably did avoid the worst abuses and excesses. It is generally agreed that health care costs were not held in check.

In 1983, the federal government introduced a major new policy governing payment of hospitals for Medicare patients. This policy, the Prospective Payment System, determines how much will be paid to the hospital *before* treatment is given. The payment depends on the diagnosis of the patient's ailment. Each patient is classified into one of 470 different *diagnosis-related groups* (DRGs), and then payment is based on what is considered reasonable for that type of medical problem. For example, the payment for an appendectomy might be $2,000. Then a hospital providing this service knows it will be paid $2,000 by Medicare, regardless of its costs.

One implication of this payment approach (which many states now use for Medicaid reimbursements and which some private insurance companies also use) is that it gives a hospital an incentive to hold costs down for each patient. The lower the hospital's actual costs, the greater its profits will be (if it is a for-profit hospital) or the greater the resources it will have to devote to other purposes (if it is nonprofit). Hospitals no longer have an incentive to conduct every conceivable laboratory test or to keep patients for excessive periods of time in order to increase revenues; that will not work under the DRG system of payment.

There is no doubt that the DRG system is potentially capable of reducing budgetary costs. Recognizing that it is nothing more than an elaborate system of price controls cautions us against being too optimistic. As with any other price controls, problems arise if the specified price is set at the wrong level. As long as it is set at or above the cost to the hospital of providing the service, the problems are fairly minor. (The potential for reducing costs is also rather minor.) When the price is set below the hospital cost, however, there are bound to be some repercussions, possibly undesirable ones. For example, the hospital may reduce the quality of treatment in order to reduce its costs to the payment it will receive. (During the first five years under the DRG system, the average length of stay of Medicare patients in hospitals declined 10 percent.) A second option is to treat the patient at a loss and attempt to make up the loss by overcharging someone else, presumably private insurance companies. This practice, called *cost shifting*, has been observed to occur. In that case, the apparent cost savings from the DRG system are illusory. A third option is to refuse to treat the patient at all. Thus, budgetary costs can be controlled but hidden costs will often be incurred as a result of the price controls, often taking the form of reduced quantity or quality of care.

Beginning in 1992, Medicare adopted a fee schedule (similar to the DRG system for hospitals) to reimburse physicians, who previously were reimbursed based on "reasonable and customary" charges. Again, this is just a form of price control. A clue to the effects it can have is suggested from experience with Medicaid, which has used reimbursement rates for physicians significantly lower than those of Medicare. One consequence has been that only about 75 percent of physicians are willing to treat Medicaid patients, while nearly all treat Medicare patients. In some specialties, treatment of Medicaid patients is even less: Only 55 percent of physicians providing reproductive health services treat Medicaid patients.[8]

Governments and private insurance companies have used these and other strategies in an attempt to reduce budgetary costs. Because of the extensive subsidies in health care markets, there are reasons to think that budgetary costs are excessive, so some method of reducing these costs may be desirable. However, it is clearly not easy to design procedures that actually hold down costs, as is apparent from the experience of the last 10 to 15 years when health care costs soared despite numerous attempts to control them.

Why Have Health Costs Risen So Much?

As pointed out earlier in Table 6–1, health costs have risen dramatically over the past several decades, both absolutely and as a percentage of GNP. We have already examined two of the reasons for this growth: tax subsidies for health insurance and government expenditures on health care. Table 6–3 shows the combined effect of these third-party payments on the share of health costs borne as out-of-pocket expenses by consumers. As can be seen, the consumer's share of total health care expenses decreased from 45.7

---

[8]U.S. Congress, Congressional Budget Office, *Rising Health Care Costs: Causes, Implications, and Strategies* (Washington, D.C.: U.S. Government Printing Office, Apr. 1991), p. 42.

Table 6–3   *Consumer Out-of-Pocket Spending on Health Care as a Percentage of Total Spending, 1965–1989*

	1965	*1970*	*1980*	*1989*
Hospital	19.6%	9.0%	5.2%	5.5%
Physician	60.4	42.6	26.8	19.0
Nursing homes	63.6	47.8	43.2	44.5
Drugs and other nondurables	95.8	90.5	79.2	72.4
Other	38.6	36.3	26.6	22.5
Total	45.7%	34.4%	23.5%	20.6%

Source: U.S. Congress, Congressional Budget Office, *Rising Health Care Costs: Causes, Implications, and Strategies* (Washington, D.C.: Apr. 1991), Table A-1.

percent in 1965 to just over 20 percent in 1989. Of particular interest is the dramatic reduction in the share of hospital and physician costs (which together account for more than 60 percent of all health costs). Out-of-pocket costs to consumers for hospital care fell from 19.6 percent of total costs in 1965 to a mere 5.5 percent in 1989. In view of the near-zero price to consumers, it is perhaps not surprising that hospital costs have been the most rapidly rising type of health care cost. There has also been a significant reduction in the net price of physicians' services. In 1965, consumers paid for most (60.4 percent) of the costs of physicians' services, but this had fallen to 19 percent by 1989.

Some economists believe that the increased importance of third-party payments, and the consequent reduction in the net price of health care to consumers, are the major causes of the increase in health care costs. Others disagree, pointing out that the price elasticity of demand for most types of medical care is relatively low, so even large price reductions would not lead to great increases in the quantity demanded. For example, if the elasticity of demand for hospital care is 0.2, a 50 percent reduction in its price would increase the quantity demanded by only 10 percent. However, there may be other cost-increasing effects of extensive subsidies, such as the possibility that consumers would begin to demand "Cadillac" care instead of "Chevy" care.

Although it is not clear exactly how quantitatively important the system of third-party payments has been in driving costs up, it is certainly not the only factor. Another factor has been government regulations that require insurers to provide specific benefits. Health insurance policies are regulated by the states, and every state requires certain benefits to be provided. In 1970, there were only 48 laws mandating specific benefits, but by 1991 there were nearly 1,000 such laws. These laws effectively make it illegal for an insurance company to offer a bare-bones, low-cost insurance policy, even if that is what consumers want. The mandated benefits vary from state to state but include such things as maternity care, drug abuse treatment, mental health care, chiropractic, marriage counseling (in California), pastoral counseling (in Vermont), and sperm bank deposits (in Massachusetts). Obviously, these mandated benefits increase the cost of health insurance.[9]

Another factor that has contributed to rising health care costs is the aging of the American population. In 1950, 8 percent of the population was age 65 or over, but by 1990, 12.6 percent were in this age group. Because elderly persons incur more health care costs, on average, than do younger persons, this change in the age distribution of the population itself increases health care costs. One estimate is that this change alone can account for an increase of 15 percent in national health care spending.[10]

Other familiar economic factors, changes in income and price, may also have played a role. As real incomes rise, people will generally spend more on health care. Whether they choose to spend an increased proportion of income, however, is less clear; most estimates of the income elasticity of demand are 1 or less. As for price changes, if the real price of medical services rises and the demand is inelastic, desired total expenditures will increase. There is reason to think that demand is inelastic, but it is not clear how much price has risen. Measuring prices in a dynamic sector where the nature of the product changes rapidly is notoriously difficult, so it is hard to determine how much the relevant prices have changed. (The relevant price is not the cost of a day in the hospital but the cost of treating specific ailments.)

A final factor in contributing to higher health care costs is the most important of all, in the view of some economists. It is technological change. Almost all of today's diagnostic procedures and treatment options were unknown 40 years ago. Consider a very selective list: magnetic resonance imaging, computed tomography scanning, coronary artery bypass grafting, renal dialysis, artificial joints, drugs for mental illness, polio vaccines, arthroscopic surgical techniques. The list could be extended for pages. These all represent increased medical capabilities. Often they increase the cost of treating specific ailments, but they also provide significant benefits. We must consider the possibility that people would wish to spend an increased portion of their incomes on medical care today, given the new, albeit costly, options available.[11]

On the other hand, it can be argued that the extensive subsidies in health care markets have been the cause of the development of some of this

---

[9]A detailed discussion of state government regulations can be found in John C. Goodman and Gerald L. Musgrave, *Patient Power* (Washington, D.C.: Cato Institute, 1992), Chapter 11.

[10]Joseph P. Newhouse, "Medical Care Costs: How Much Welfare Loss?" *Journal of Economic Perspectives,* 6:3 (Summer 1992).

[11]Newhouse, "Medical Care Costs." Newhouse argues that this is the major factor increasing health care costs.

technology. With third parties paying for virtually all hospital treatments, those engaged in developing new technology are given a strong message: Any new technology you develop that provides any medical benefits, no matter how small, will be purchased, regardless of the cost. Thus, the explosive growth of medical technology may have been fueled by the system we have been using to finance medical care.[12] It is certainly possible to overinvest in new technology if it produces only small benefits at high costs. When patients choose to use costly new medical treatments but pay only 5 percent of the costs, it is difficult to determine whether it was worthwhile to develop the techniques in the first place.

Thus, we do not know exactly what contribution each of these factors has made to increasing health care costs. The issue of what has caused the cost increases is extremely important. If, for example, we determine that costs increased because of the subsidies, we would have reason to believe that the increase was inefficient and that it would be desirable to curtail spending on health care substantially. Alternatively, if the cost increases resulted solely from aging of the population and efficient new technologies, the increased health costs represent a desirable adaptation to changed economic circumstances. In that event, efforts to reduce health care costs would have costs greater than benefits.

The Problem of the Uninsured

Some people do not have any health insurance coverage. Estimates vary but typically suggest that there were about 33 million uninsured persons in 1989, about 15.7 percent of the population under the age of 65 (those over 65 are covered by Medicare). The number of the uninsured has been rising in recent years; in 1978 about 12.2 percent of the under-65 population was uninsured. To put these figures in some perspective, recall that 90 percent of the entire population was uninsured in 1940. The uninsured population declined steadily until around 1978 and for some reason has climbed since then.

It is important not to equate lack of health insurance with lack of health care. Few uninsured people go without needed medical care. They can pay for medical care out of pocket, or if they cannot afford it, access to care is guaranteed by numerous federal and state laws. For example, federal law requires hospitals treating Medicare patients to accept all patients with emergency health problems, regardless of their ability to pay or insurance status. (Each year, hospitals provide about $4 billion in medical services to unin-

[12]This possibility is examined in Burton A. Weisbrod, "The Health Care Quadrilemma: An Essay on Technological Change, Insurance, Quality of Care, and Cost Containment," *Journal of Economic Literature,* 29:523 (June 1991).

sured patients without receiving payment.[13] Physicians probably provide similar amounts.) One study found that, after adjusting for differences in age, family size, education, and other relevant factors, the uninsured population consume about half as much health care as the insured population.[14] (Recall that the insured population almost certainly overconsumes health care.)

The uninsured population is a diverse group. Some characteristics are worth noting. First, uninsured persons tend to have lower incomes than insured persons. This is not surprising, but what may be surprising is that most of the uninsured population are not poor. In 1989, nearly 40 percent of the uninsured had family incomes greater than twice the poverty line, 25 percent had incomes above $30,000, and 10 percent had incomes above $50,000.[15] Second, the uninsured tend to be young. About 60 percent are under the age of 30. This is significant because health care expenses tend to be low at younger ages, so those uninsured are bearing smaller risks of incurring large health care costs. Third, most of the uninsured, about 81 percent, are employed or are dependents of employed persons. However, about half of this group is employed by (or are dependents of those employed by) small firms, those employing fewer than 25 workers. (Only about one fourth of insured workers are employed by small firms.) Fourth, there is a lot of turnover in the uninsured population, just as there is in the unemployed population. While 15 percent of the nonelderly population are uninsured at a point in time, only 4 percent are uninsured for two years or more.

Now let us consider why so many persons lack health insurance. One reason is that some are uninsurable. These are persons who have serious preexisting medical conditions, such as cancer or AIDS, or who belong to very-high-risk groups (drug abusers). Understandably, insurance companies do not wish to insure persons who are certain to have heavy medical expenses. Uninsurable persons, however, constitute only about 1 percent of the total population, so this is not the major reason for lack of insurance.

Most of the uninsured choose not to purchase health insurance because the price is higher than they are willing or able to pay. Among the uninsured, many have incomes high enough to pay for health insurance, but they judge that the price is higher than the expected benefits. There are reasons why the price may be artificially high. We have already mentioned state-mandated benefits in insurance policies, and these benefits increase premiums significantly. Since many of the uninsured are in a low-risk (young)

[13]Goodman and Musgrave, *Patient Power,* p. 101.

[14]Stephen H. Long and Jack Rodgers (Congressional Budget Office), "The Effects of Being Uninsured on Health Services Use: Estimates from the Survey of Income and Program Participation," unpublished paper cited in Goodman and Musgrave, *Patient Power,* p. 358.

[15]*Economic Report of the President,* 1991, p. 138; Jill D. Foley, *Uninsured in the United States: The Nonelderly Population without Health Insurance* (Washington, D.C.: Employee Benefit Research Institute, 1991), Table 5.

group, these mandated benefits may make the coverage seem particularly unnecessary. (One study estimates that as many as one fourth of the uninsured lack health insurance because of the effects of state regulations on insurance costs.[16]) A second factor is that many of the uninsured are employed by small firms where administrative costs add more to premiums. (Recall that administrative costs are 30 percent of health benefits paid for firms employing between 10 and 20 people.) A third factor is that the uninsured tend to be in lower tax brackets, and so get less advantage from the tax subsidies. This combination of factors can easily lead to insurance costs that seem excessive relative to the likely benefits they will provide.

Another factor is relevant for the uninsured who have very low incomes. That is the expectation that someone else will pay for their health care costs should they incur large expenses. While some of the uninsured are not now covered by Medicaid, if they face large medical bills they may become eligible. Even if Medicaid does not cover the costs, someone else surely will.

The large number of people lacking insurance, and the many others who fear they may lose it, is considered to be one of the most serious problems with our health care system. Why is this a problem? Shouldn't people be free to not purchase insurance, just as they are free to take innumerable other risks in life? There are at least two reasons why we might consider lack of insurance a problem. First, some lack insurance because of the inflated costs produced by public policies, and these costs are most likely to deter those with the lowest incomes from purchasing coverage. In other words, the uninsured are disproportionately bearing some of the costs of policies that are generally inefficient. Second, because society will not permit people to go without needed medical care, those who do not have insurance and then incur large medical costs they cannot pay impose costs on the rest of society, which will pay these costs. Just as there is a reason for requiring drivers to have liability coverage (to protect other people), it may be desirable to see that all people have at least basic health insurance.

Reforming the Health Care System

Wide agreement exists that the present health care system is in need of reform. On the other hand, there is little agreement over exactly how it should be reformed. Indeed, in 1992 there were over 200 bills pending in Congress dealing with the health care system. Many of the specific proposals that have been made, however, fall into a few general categories. We consider three of the most common ones in this section.

---

[16]Cited in *Economic Report of the President* (Washington, D.C.: U.S. Government Printing Office, 1991), p. 141.

Comprehensive National Health Insurance

Under a comprehensive national health insurance (NHI) program, the federal government pays for all (or most) of the health care received by the entire population. All people, regardless of employment status or income, would be covered, thereby achieving universal coverage. Exactly what health services would be covered, and what share of costs would be borne by consumers in the form of deductibles or coinsurance, vary with the particular proposals. In effect, comprehensive NHI would generally be much like extending Medicare and/or Medicaid to cover the entire population.

Several other countries have comprehensive NHI systems, with Canada and England often cited as examples we might emulate. One frequently claimed advantage of having the government as one big insurer is that there would be substantial savings in the administrative costs of operating the system. As we pointed out earlier, administrative costs of private health insurance average about 12 percent. By contrast, administrative costs of Medicare and Medicaid are about 5 percent of outlays; similar estimates have been made for the Canadian and British systems. With total spending on health care of more than $600 billion, a 7 percent saving in administrative costs is a great deal of money.

The argument that it would be less costly to have the government finance health care rather than private insurance is, however, almost certainly wrong. It ignores the cost to the government of acquiring the funds to spend. As we discussed in Chapter 4, there are various welfare costs associated with raising tax revenue, and these costs are incurred under NHI but not under private health insurance. Although the exact magnitude of the marginal welfare cost of tax revenue is in dispute, almost all estimates are much larger than 7 percent, often several times larger. There is little doubt that it would cost more to finance health care through NHI than through private insurance when we take account of the marginal welfare cost of taxation.

Taxes would have to be increased substantially to finance comprehensive NHI. A rough idea of how much can be gotten from Table 6–1 by subtracting current government spending from total spending on health care; the difference, private spending on health care, is approximately how much more the government must spend under NHI. This calculation suggests that in 1990 comprehensive NHI would have involved an increase in government spending of about $340 billion. Of course, if deductibles and coinsurance rates are used, and if there is some administrative cost savings, the sum would be somewhat less, so let us say that the required outlay would have been about $300 billion. If this were financed through the federal individual income tax, each taxpayer's tax liability would, on average, have to increase by 67 percent. If it were financed through payroll taxes, like the social security payroll tax, rates would have to nearly double.

Supporters of comprehensive NHI argue that there is no *net* cost from these higher taxes because we are already paying the costs in the form of out-of-pocket outlays on health care or insurance premiums. This again ignores the marginal welfare cost of taxation, which is a new cost. It also tends to ignore who pays the taxes and gets the benefits under the two systems. Under the present private system, each person pretty much pays for his or her health care or insurance through premiums (sometimes paid with lower wages when employer provided) or cash. Under comprehensive NHI there will be a massive redistribution of income. Exactly how much depends on what tax is used to finance it, but consider that under the federal income tax the poorer half of the population contributes only 7 percent of total revenue. Under NHI, they would get about half of the benefits, some (those with incomes below the exempted level) without paying any of the taxes. By contrast, the wealthiest 10 percent of taxpayers currently pay about 60 percent of federal income taxes; they would get back only about 10 percent of NHI benefits. One prominent economist has stated that the redistribution produced by comprehensive NHI would exceed that produced by any other single national policy now in existence.[17]

Turning to how health care markets would be affected, the most obvious effect of comprehensive NHI would probably be an increase in the demand for health care. Basically, NHI simply pushes the current third-party payment system to the limit by having government pay for virtually all health care. Taken by itself, this would put even more pressure on health costs to rise.

This is widely recognized, and consequently all comprehensive NHI proposals include some form of cost controls. Obviously, consumers could not be permitted to have all the highest-quality health care they want at a zero price; there would have to be rationing. Any subsidy paying the full costs of some activity must of necessity be accompanied by a regulatory mechanism to limit the cost and the quantity actually provided. This might be done by giving hospitals a fixed budget to operate within or by reimbursing doctors according to a governmentally set schedule of fees. The overall division of the total health care budget among hospitals, physicians, dentists, and so on would have to be determined by some agency.

How this cost control regulatory mechanism would actually operate is the greatest uncertainty encountered in an attempt to analyze comprehensive NHI. Controls could easily lead to shortages, waiting lines for some medical procedures, misallocations among regions or types of care, and so on. How much health care costs go up over time and who gets care of what quality and on what terms cannot be predicted in advance. It is certainly possible for cost controls to keep monetary health care costs from rising as rapidly, but the real issue is how this would be accomplished.

The important point here is that the choice between comprehensive NHI and a system in which the patient bears a larger part of the cost is not really a choice between free and unfree care. Rather, the choice is between a government regulatory mechanism to ration care and allocate health care re-

[17]Henry J. Aaron, "Health Care Financing," in *Setting Domestic Priorities,* edited by H. J. Aaron and C. L. Schultze (Washington, D.C.: Brookings Institution, 1992), pp. 23–61.

sources and a market system to perform these functions. In either case, the patients will ultimately bear the costs, either in the form of prices (or insurance premiums) or in the form of taxes.

Catastrophic National Health Insurance

Catastrophic health insurance refers to health insurance that covers only extraordinarily large medical expenses, not moderate or small ones. For example, the insurance might only cover medical costs in excess of $4,000 a year; the first $4,000 would have to be paid out of pocket. The basic rationale for this particular type of health insurance follows from our discussion of the economic rationale of insurance: It makes sense to insure only large and unpredictable expenses. The most important, that is, most valuable insurance to any person will be that covering catastrophic costs; insurance covering relatively small costs has little value. As we have seen, many people have coverage of relatively small and predictable expenses, but that is a consequence of the tax laws, not of the true benefits of this form of insurance.

Catastrophic national health insurance is the name given to a variety of approaches that attempt to ensure universal coverage of the population, but coverage that is limited to large expenses. The basic idea is to ensure that all people have the type of insurance that is most valuable. If they want to supplement this basic insurance with a more comprehensive type of coverage, they are free to purchase it, but only in unsubsidized markets.

How this goal would be achieved varies among specific proposals. A basic problem that has to be confronted, however, is that what is considered a catastrophic medical expense depends on the financial resources of the family. A family with an annual income of $40,000 (about the median family income in 1993) can certainly afford medical expenses of $3,000 or $4,000 a year; a deductible of that amount would not be onerous. However, for a family with an income of $10,000, medical expenses of that size would be catastrophic. Clearly, what is a financial catastrophe depends on one's income and wealth. The way in which catastrophic NHI proposals deal with this issue is to make the size of the deductible depend on family income. For example, it might be decided that the deductible is to be 10 percent of the family income. Then the deductible would be $1,000 for a family with an income of $10,000 but $4,000 for a family with an income of $40,000. It might also be desirable to have some coinsurance, or cost sharing, beyond the deductible. For example, families might have to pay 20 percent of the costs in excess of the deductible, up to some maximum amount beyond which insurance would cover all costs.

Supporters of catastrophic NHI want to see consumers more directly involved in the medical marketplace. In particular, they want to see third-party payments reduced or eliminated for most medical expenses since that form of payment system is seen as a major source of inefficiency. To achieve this outcome, it is essential that the tax subsidies granted to employer-provided health insurance be terminated. In addition, it is frequently advocated that

Medicare and Medicaid be reformed to resemble more closely catastrophic health insurance.

If everyone had this sort of health insurance coverage, three major advantages would ensue, according to supporters of catastrophic NHI. First, we would achieve universal coverage of the type of insurance that is most important to people. Second, efficient use of health care resources will be encouraged. Patients, as well as physicians, will have an incentive to take account of costs as well as benefits in determining appropriate treatment. Medical care practices will be determined by comparing the expected benefits of more expensive care with the actual costs of providing that care, instead of largely ignoring costs, as is frequently the case under present financing arrangements. (Note that this argument only holds fully for expenditures under the deductible amounts.) Third, the rate of increase in health care costs would be reduced. This follows directly from the removal of the subsidies applying to a large part of medical care purchases in current markets.

There are a variety of approaches to achieving universal coverage with catastrophic health insurance. One approach is simply to require every person to have this sort of coverage. Since the cost of acquiring this coverage would be excessive for low-income households, it is usually proposed that their purchases be subsidized in some way. Tax credits, which are subsidies operated through the federal income tax, are one popular option. The basic idea is to provide a subsidy large enough to purchase this type of insurance coverage for very-low-income households. The size of the subsidy would decline at higher income levels, just as the food stamp subsidy declines. For instance, all families (of a given size and composition) might be required to have a policy that costs $3,000 a year. The tax credit could be $3,000 for low-income households, declining to, say, $1,000 for families with $20,000, which would have to pay $2,000 of the cost of the policy.[18]

Within this general approach there are, of course, many possible variants. It should be noted, however, that they do involve additional budgetary costs for the government, and so likely imply some degree of income redistribution. The amounts involved would be substantially less than with comprehensive NHI, however, because low-income families would contribute something to the cost of the insurance coverage. In addition, the insurance coverage would be less comprehensive, and thus far less costly.

Critics have raised two significant objections to this type of reform. First, it will not bring market-like incentives to control costs to bear on all medical decisions; for expenditures in excess of the deductibles, the same incentives to ignore costs would still exist. There is no way to avoid the fact that there is a difficult trade-off between the extent of insurance protection and preserving incentives. Second, some proponents of comprehensive national

---

[18]A particular proposal along these lines is explained in detail in Mark V. Pauly, Patricia Danzon, Paul J. Feldstein, and John Hoff, *Responsible National Health Insurance* (Washington, D.C.: American Enterprise Institute, 1992).

health insurance worry that with only catastrophic coverage, monetary considerations might deter some people from receiving medical care. Of course, the fact that people would have to incur some out-of-pocket expenses would lead to less medical care being consumed (demand curves would slope downward), but whether this would adversely affect the health of the population is not clear. Moreover, it should be emphasized that even "free" comprehensive NHI will have barriers to care that will prevent people from getting all the medical care they want (at a zero price). With comprehensive NHI, the barriers will take the form of bureaucratic rules, waiting lines, and quantity and quality limits. With catastrophic NHI, the barrier to the use of medical resources (at least up to the deductible amount) is the price, the same barrier that limits consumption of most other goods and services.

Mandatory Employer Health Insurance

In recent years, another type of reform has gained popularity. It attempts to build on the extensive employer-provided health insurance system already in place. Since most members of the uninsured population are employed, it would be possible to expand insurance coverage by simply requiring businesses to provide health insurance coverage to all workers (and possibly their dependents). The government would have to specify the types of insurance benefits that must be provided and then let firms choose from among private insurance companies to provide this coverage.

A major problem with this approach is that it would increase greatly the labor costs of firms hiring predominantly low-wage workers. In 1992, the average cost of standard health insurance for large firms (which would be higher for small firms) was $5,000 for family coverage ($1,925 for individual coverage).[19] As we pointed out earlier, a large share of the uninsured population is employed by small firms and at low wages. In general, fringe benefits, whether government mandated or not, are ultimately paid for by lower wages for workers. For low-wage workers this can be a real burden, if not illegal because of the minimum wage law. An insurance policy that costs $5,000 represents a labor cost of $2.50 an hour for full-time workers (2,000 hours a year). For firms hiring workers at the minimum wage ($4.25 in 1993), it is not possible to reduce cash wage payments in order to pay for the mandated health insurance costs. For these firms, the effective minimum wage would rise from $4.25 to $6.75 an hour, $4.25 in cash and the required fringe benefit costing $2.50 an hour. This would be devastating to small firms, not to mention the many low-wage workers who would be unemployed because they were priced out of the market.

[19]Aaron, "Health Care Financing," p. 31.

This problem is addressed in versions of this approach referred to as "pay or play." Firms are given an option of either providing health insurance to their workers or paying a new payroll tax of a certain percentage of their wage costs, typically suggested to be about 8 percent. Firms with higher-wage workers would then provide the health insurance and avoid the tax. Firms with lower-wage workers then can avoid providing insurance by paying the tax. In this way, their labor costs cannot be increased more than 8 percent, rather than by the nearly 60 percent in the previous example (from $4.25 to $6.75). This avoids the most drastic negative labor market effects of the outright mandate. The basic idea is that revenues from the tax could be used to provide some governmental insurance to those not privately insured, perhaps using Medicaid as a guide.

The "pay or play" approach still involves some significant problems. First, it does nothing to deal with the inefficiencies in the current system that result from too much third-party payment. In fact, by extending open-ended insurance coverage to even more people, it will only intensify the pressures on costs. Second, if "pay or play" applies only to full-time workers (and their dependents), only about 54 percent of the uninsured will be covered. Achieving universal coverage will still require additional government expenditures that must be coordinated with the employer mandates in some way. Third, low-wage workers who do receive the new employer-provided insurance will find their wages reduced to pay for it, and they will generally find themselves worse off as a result. (If the insurance was worth what it cost to them, they would have gotten it without the government's requiring them to do so.)

The appeal of this approach is that it might involve very little budgetary cost for the government, possibly a major consideration in this era of large deficits and citizen unwillingness to pay higher taxes. Mandated employer health insurance also involves less redistribution of income than either of the two other approaches we have discussed since most low-wage workers will be paying for their own health insurance in the form of reduced money wages from their employers.

Review Questions and Problems

1. For what reasons, if any, should medical care be subsidized?

2. Why is it usually economically inefficient to insure against *predictable* and/or *small* medical expenses?

3. How does the tax system encourage people to insure themselves against small and predictable medical expenses even when it is inefficient to do so?

4. What is the relationship between the level of marginal tax rates and the incentive of individuals to purchase health insurance through their employers?

5. What are third-party payments? Why have they grown, and how do they affect the operation of medical markets?

6. How does Part B of Medicare affect the budget line of an elderly person in regard to insurance coverage of physicians' services and all other goods? Could this subsidy lead to overinsurance? If so, show the results in your graph.

7. In recent years, various types of cost controls have been used extensively to deal with rising medical care costs. Could changes in the tax laws and a greater use of deductibles and coinsurance rates have accomplished the same thing? Which alternative is preferable?

8. Consider two ways to reduce the tax subsidy to medical insurance. First, employer contributions up to a maximum of $2,000 per worker are nontaxable; anything above $2,000 is taxed under the income tax. Second, only employer contributions in excess of $1,000 are nontaxable; the first $1,000 is fully taxable. Assume that these two alternatives cost the government the same amount. Which one will reduce the extent of overinsurance more?

9. A recent book is entitled *What Has Government Done to Our Health Care?* Does this title suggest a valid diagnosis of the ills of the health care system?

10. Why have medical care costs been rising so rapidly over the past several decades? Is this phenomenon a social problem that requires government action to deal with it?

11. What reasons account for the large number of people without health insurance? Is the existence of people without health insurance evidence of market failure in the health care market?

12. Suppose that the government knows the number of kidney dialysis machines people use per year in the United States and the number of days people stay in a hospital per year. Assume that the government decides to provide "free" kidney dialysis machines for those who need them and "free" hospital care for anyone who stays in a hospital. The government would, of course, try to estimate the cost of providing each service "free." Is the government more likely to underestimate the cost of providing free kidney dialysis machines or free hospital care? Why?

13. If comprehensive NHI were introduced and financed by a flat rate tax on wage earnings, what groups would likely be benefited and what groups harmed? In particular, how would NHI affect the groups now covered by Medicare and Medicaid?

14. Medicare and Medicaid are much like comprehensive NHI for the elderly and poor. Had the catastrophic approach to health insurance been used instead, how would the effects of these programs have differed? Which approach is preferable? Can you give a public choice explanation of why the comprehensive rather than the catastrophic approach was selected?

Supplementary Readings

AARON, HENRY J. "Health Care Financing." In H. J. Aaron and C. L. Schultze, eds., *Setting Domestic Priorities.* Washington, D.C.: Brookings Institution, 1992.

CONGRESSIONAL BUDGET OFFICE, *Economic Implications of Rising Health Care Costs.* Washington, D.C.: U.S. Government Printing Office (Oct. 1992).

ECONOMIC REPORT OF THE PRESIDENT 1993. Washington, D.C.: U.S. Government Printing Office, 1993, *Chapter 4.*

FELDSTEIN, MARTIN S. "A New Approach to National Health Insurance." *Public Interest,* 23:93–105 (Spring 1971).

FUCHS, VICTOR. *Who Shall Live?* New York: Basic Books, 1974.

GOODMAN, JOHN C., and GERALD L. MUSGRAVE. *Patient Power.* Washington, D.C.: Cato Institute, 1992.

MEYER, JACK A., and ROSEMARY G. KERN. "The Changing Structure of the Health Care System." In P. Cagan, ed., *Essays in Contemporary Economic Problems.* Washington, D.C.: American Enterprise Institute, 1986.

NEWHOUSE, JOSEPH P. "Medical Care Costs: How Much Welfare Loss?" *Journal of Economic Perspectives,* 6:3–21. (Summer 1992).

PAULY, MARK V. "Taxation, Health Insurance, and Market Failure in the Medical Economy." *Journal of Economic Literature,* 24:629–675 (June 1986).

Social Security

*T*HE SET OF PROGRAMS POPULARLY KNOWN AS *social security* actually has a far more imposing official designation: Old Age, Survivors, Disability and Health Insurance, or OASDHI for short. Enacted as part of the Social Security Act of 1935, social security was originally designed to provide only old-age or retirement benefits; it was then known as OAI. Survivors benefits were added in 1939, and the system became OASI. In 1954 disability benefits were included, and the system was thus OASDI until 1965, when Medicare was enacted and it evolved into OASDHI. Today social security is perhaps the most important, *and certainly the largest,* expenditure policy in the United States.

Table 7–1 summarizes information relating to the growth in social security since 1945. Total expenditures rose from $0.3 billion in 1945 to $352.4 billion in 1990. Because the rate of growth in expenditures was more than double the rate of growth in the nation's output, social security outlays have grown rapidly relative to net national product (NNP). Whereas social security outlays were a scant 0.1 percent of the NNP in 1945, they had grown to 7.1 percent by 1990. Three factors largely account for this growth. First, an increased proportion of the elderly has become eligible to receive benefits. In 1945, only 8 percent of those over 65 received benefits, but today more than 94 percent receive benefits. (Most of those who do not receive benefits under social security today receive benefits under other federal retirement programs or welfare programs.) Second, a larger proportion of the population is now elderly. In 1945, only 8 percent of the population was aged 65 or older; today the proportion is nearly 13 percent. Third, the level of real benefits per retired person has risen. This third factor has been especially important since 1970, as we shall see later.

Table 7–1   *OASDHI System, Selected Data*

Year	Spending on OASDHI ($ billions)	Spending as a Percentage of NNP	Maximum Taxable Earnings	Payroll Tax Rate	Percentage of People 65 or Over Receiving Social Security
1945	$ 0.3	0.1%	$ 3,000	2.0%	6.2%
1950	1.0	0.4	3,000	3.0	16.4
1955	5.0	1.4	4,200	4.0	39.4
1960	11.0	2.3	4,800	6.0	61.6
1965	17.0	2.6	4,800	7.3	75.2
1970	36.8	4.0	7,800	9.6	85.5
1975	78.4	5.5	14,100	11.7	90.4
1980	152.1	6.3	25,900	12.3	91.4
1985	257.5	7.2	39,600	14.1	91.7
1990	352.4	7.1	51,300	15.3	94.2

Note: Figures include cash payments plus Medicare.

Source: Social Security Bulletin, *Annual Statistical Supplement, 1991,* Tables 2.A1, 3.A3, 3.C5; *Economic Report of the President, 1991,* Table B-20.

Social security outlays are financed by an earmarked tax on earnings. (An *earmarked tax* is one whose revenues must be used to finance a specific program, in this case social security.) Workers in jobs covered by social security (almost all jobs today) pay a flat-rate tax on *earnings* (other types of income, such as capital income and government transfers, are not subject to tax) up to a maximum amount. There are, in fact, separate taxes for the various components of the system; for example, in 1992, the OASDI rate was 12.4 percent and the HI (Medicare) rate was 2.9 percent, which together produce the combined rate of 15.3 percent shown in the table. In 1992, the ceiling on taxable earnings for OASDI (it is higher for Medicare) was $55,500. Thus, the combined rate of 15.3 percent applied to the first $55,500 in earnings in 1992. For Medicare, the ceiling was $130,200 in 1992, so only the 2.9 percent rate applied to earnings between $55,500 and $130,200. The taxable ceilings are adjusted upward each year with changes in average earnings in the economy.

Actually, the social security tax is composed of two equal levies, one paid by the employer and the other by the employee. In 1992, the employer and employee rates were 7.65 percent, up to the $55,500 ceiling. Beyond $55,500 up to the Medicare ceiling, the separate rates were 1.45 percent. Whatever the intention of Congress may have been in levying separate rates, there is little doubt that the economic effects would be the same as if workers paid a tax equal to the combined rate. We will analyze this tax more carefully in

Chapter 13; in this chapter, we will simply assume that employees ultimately bear the full cost of the taxes that finance social security benefits.

Social security is still primarily a system providing retired persons with benefits both in cash (in the form of pensions or annuities) and in kind (Medicare). To receive social security benefits, a retired person must have worked in a covered job and paid social security taxes for a sufficient number of years to establish eligibility. The exact size of the benefits received depends on previous covered earnings, in addition to other factors. As a result of legislation enacted in 1972, retirement benefits are automatically adjusted upward with increases in the consumer price index. Benefits can be increased still further by congressional action, but no additional legislation is required to ensure that benefits keep pace with inflation.

Other details concerning the working of social security will become clear as we proceed with the analysis. Although our emphasis will be on the provision of retirement benefits, we should also note that the program includes disability and survivors benefits. The analysis can easily be extended to include these programs.

Pay-as-You-Go Financing

It is important to understand that social security does not operate like private insurance. When a person pays premiums to a private insurance company to purchase an annuity, the premiums are invested and build up a fund that will be adequate to finance the annuity, or pension. Social security functions in a different way. Over most years of its operation, the tax revenues collected in each year were immediately paid out as benefits to currently retired persons. In other words, there was no fund accruing in each taxpayer's name; the only way the taxpayer could receive benefits when he or she retired was from taxes levied on workers employed at that time. This type of financing arrangement is called *pay-as-you-go financing* to distinguish it from the procedures employed by private companies. Alternatively, it is sometimes referred to as an *unfunded* system to emphasize the absence of a retirement fund.

Following reforms enacted in 1983, however, the social security system has begun to accumulate a sizable trust fund, at least for OASI. For the past few years, the tax revenues collected each year have been about 15 percent larger than the benefits paid out each year, with the excess accumulating in a fund. This is still a far cry from full funding, which would require all tax revenues to go into the fund; some refer to the present system as one of *partial funding*. We will explain why this shift to partial funding occurred and what the consequences will be later in the chapter. Until then, we will analyze social security as if it were on a pay-as-you-go (unfunded) basis, which has been true for most of its existence, is about 85 percent true now, and will be true again in about three decades (as we will explain later).

The trust fund that has accumulated as of 1992 is enough by itself to pay social security benefits for only a little more than 12 months. Recognition that the trust fund is inadequate to finance future benefits has led many people to conclude that the system is "bankrupt." It is true that social security would be considered insolvent if judged according to the same standard applied to private insurance companies. A private insurance company must have a reserve fund sufficient to finance its obligations even if it never sells another insurance policy. If the social security system required a fund capable of meeting its already accumulated obligations, that fund would have to be about *$7 trillion*. Judged by private insurance standards, the social security system is bankrupt because its fund was only about $300 billion in 1991 instead of $7,000 billion.

Fortunately, it is not necessary to judge social security by private insurance standards. A *governmental* system of providing retirement benefits does not require a large fund to finance future benefits; these benefits can be financed out of future taxes. Pay-as-you-go financing is a viable method for the government to use to provide retirement benefits. Workers currently in the labor force can expect to receive pensions when they retire because the government is able to tax the working generation at that time to finance these pensions. Social security is simply a different method of providing for retirement, and this does not imply that it is an inferior method.

How a Pay-as-You-Go System Operates

Social security is different in a number of respects from private insurance. Let us consider the economic effects of these differences. To understand its consequences, it is necessary to understand how the system functions over time. A simple arithmetic example will be helpful. Assume that the adult population consists of only three people: one young, one middle-aged, and one retired. There is zero population growth, and each person has a three-year life span: young in the first year, middle-aged in the second, and retired in the third. The retired person dies at the end of each year and is replaced by a new young person the following year. Each year the young and middle-aged persons have equal earnings, and these earnings grow over time at the rate of 100 percent per year (in other words, the growth rate of the economy is 100 percent annually). These assumptions are obviously unrealistic but are made to simplify the computations and to allow us to highlight some basic relationships in the simplest possible way.

Table 7–2 shows an economy growing over time according to our assumptions. Individuals are denoted by the letters *A, B, C,* and so on. In year 1, individuals *C* and *B* are young and middle-aged, respectively, and have incomes of $250 each. In the same year, individual *A* is retired and has zero current income. In the following year, *C* becomes middle-aged, *B* retires, and a new young person, *D,* joins the labor force. *C* and *D* have incomes of $500 in year 2, double the per worker incomes of the previous year. We can

Table 7–2 *Pay-as-You-Go Financing of Social Security*

Year:	1	2	3	4	5
Tax Rate:	0	10%	10%	10%	10%
Young	C250	D500	E1000	F2000	G4000
	(0)	(−50)	(−100)	(−200)	(−400)
Middle-aged	B250	C500	D1000	E2000	F4000
	(0)	(−50)	(−100)	(−200)	(−400)
Retired	A(0)	B(+100)	C(+200)	D(+400)	E(+800)

follow an individual through his or her lifetime by looking along a diagonal: *C* is young in year 1, middle-aged in year 2, and retired in year 3. Now let us introduce a system of pay-as-you-go social security in year 2. A tax of 10 percent is levied on the incomes of the young and middle-aged workers each year, and the proceeds are transferred to the retired person. The tax payments and retirement benefits are shown by the figures in parentheses. Thus, *C* and *D* pay taxes of $50 each in year 2, and *B* receives $100. With the same tax rate in subsequent years, the total tax revenue and retirement benefits will grow with the economy over time.

Now let us see how people fare under this system. Initially, consider individual *D*, because *D* is the first person to spend an entire lifetime under the system. *D* pays taxes of $50 and $100 in years 2 and 3 and receives retirement benefits of $400 in year 4. *D*'s retirement benefits are substantially larger than the taxes paid. This is also true for later generations, such as *E*, *F*, and *G*, who also receive retirement benefits exceeding previous taxes paid. This would be true too if they saved privately, because they would earn interest on their savings. The relevant question is how large the rate of return is under social security. In other words, for individual *D*, what rate of interest would produce a $400 sum if $50 were invested for two years and $100 for one year? The answer is 100 percent: $50 invested at 100 percent for two years will grow to $200, and $100 invested for one year will also grow to $200, for a total of $400. Thus, individual *D* is effectively receiving an annual rate of return of 100 percent under social security. This is also true of *E*, *F*, *G*, and later individuals, as long as income continues to grow at 100 percent per year and the tax rate remains 10 percent.

It is no accident that the rate of return on taxes paid is equal to the rate of growth in national income. *An important implication of pay-as-you-go social security is that it can provide pensions that represent a rate of return on taxes paid equal to the rate of growth of the tax base*—in this case, national income. In a sense, social security allows people to "share in the growth of the economy." Of course, in reality, income grows less than 100 percent per year. Taking a long-term perspective, the U.S. economy has grown at an average *real* (adjusted for inflation) rate of about 3 percent per year over the past 60 years. This growth has resulted from an increase in output per person of about 2 percent and a growth in population of about 1 percent per year. (In a more elaborate model, the rate of return under social security depends on the sum of the rates of growth of earnings per worker and the number of workers, a sum that gives the total rate of growth of national income.)

Recent trends suggest that the rate of growth in the social security tax base will be lower in the future. Both the population growth rate and the rate of growth in real wages have fallen relative to long-run averages. Thus, an annual real growth rate in the tax base of 2 percent per year may be a more reasonable prediction of the long-term prospect. As a rough average, this suggests that persons retiring in future years may expect to receive social security benefits that represent a 2 percent rate of return on taxes paid. (Some qualifications are noted later.)

Two Types of Redistribution

Social security is a method of providing retirement benefits to the population. If each person's pension were strictly related to the taxes he or she paid earlier in life, the system would not tend to redistribute income among people. But as it actually operates, social security redistributes income in two different ways.

The first type of redistribution is called *intragenerational* redistribution, which refers to a redistribution among members of a given generation. For example, suppose, referring to Table 7–2, that there are two people in each age group. The two *D*s both can receive benefits of $400 in year 4; alternatively, the government could provide a benefit of $500 to one *D* and $300 to the other *D*. This would effectively redistribute $100 from one *D* to the other. Members of the same generation can therefore receive different rates of return on taxes paid, some above and some below the average rate of return. As explained in more detail later, the social security system contains several features that produce intragenerational redistribution.

The second type of redistribution is called *intergenerational* redistribution, which refers to the ways some generations of retirees receive higher benefits in relation to taxes paid than other generations. Table 7–2 shows that individual *D* and all subsequent generations would receive a rate of return on their taxes equal to the rate of growth. Now, however, consider individuals *B* and *C*, who did not pay the 10 percent tax over their entire working lives. Individual *C* received a pension in year 3 after paying taxes for only one year, and individual *B* received a pension without ever paying taxes. The rate of return that individuals *B* and *C* received on their tax payments is far greater than the rate of growth of the economy.

Generations that retire in the early years of a pay-as-you-go social security program receive much better returns than later generations do. In the start-up phase of social security, retired persons pay taxes for only part of their working lives and fare extremely well. The same is true for people who work and pay taxes during years when the tax rate is low and who then retire and receive benefits based on a higher tax rate enacted later on. Table 7–1 shows how low the tax rate was until recent years. People who retired in 1992 spent a majority of their working years in the work force when the payroll tax rate was under 10 percent and yet were entitled to receive benefits financed by the 15.3 percent tax rate in effect in 1992.

Both types of redistribution are illustrated by the data in Table 7–3. This table gives estimates of projected social security benefits expressed as an annual real rate of return on the projected taxes paid for several demographic categories and income levels. In effect, the estimates are like the real interest rates that different groups can expect to receive on their social security taxes. For example, a married couple, composed of a high-earning male (earning at the taxable earnings ceiling each year) and a median-earning female, who retired in 1980 is estimated to receive retirement benefits that represent a real rate of return on their lifetime taxes of 6.0 percent.

The *intergenerational* redistribution of social security is illustrated in the table by the decline in the rate of return in later years for each household category. All households retiring in 1970 receive high rates of return, but the rates are much lower for those retiring in later years. For example, a high-earning single male retiring in 1970 has a rate of return of 5.4 percent, but the return declines steadily until it reaches 0.7 percent for individuals retiring in 2020. Comparisons between earlier and later years in the table illustrate the important difference between the way the system affects people

Table 7–3   *Projected Real Rates of Return by Household Type and by Age Cohort*

Demographic Status	Earnings Profile	Year in Which Head of Household Becomes 65					
		1970	1980	1990	2000	2010	2020
Single men	Low	7.5%	5.3%	3.2%	2.4%	2.2%	2.1%
	Median	6.3	4.5	2.4	1.6	1.3	1.3
	High	5.4	4.0	2.3	1.4	.9	.7
Single women	Low	10.7	7.7	5.9	5.0	4.5	4.4
	Median	9.1	6.6	4.6	3.8	3.4	3.3
	High	6.7	5.1	3.5	2.6	2.1	1.8
Married couples	Low/zero	9.7	7.4	5.3	4.3	4.1	4.0
	Median/zero	8.5	6.7	4.5	3.6	3.3	3.2
	High/zero	7.5	6.0	4.4	3.5	2.9	2.6
Married couples	Low/low	8.8	6.4	4.4	3.5	3.3	3.2
	Median/low	7.7	6.0	3.9	3.1	2.7	2.6
	High/median	6.7	5.1	3.4	2.6	2.2	1.9

Source: Michael D. Hurd and John B. Shoven, "The Distributional Impact of Social Security," NBER Working Paper No. 1155 (June 1983), Table 11.

who retired in the start-up phase of the system and those who will retire later.

The *intragenerational* redistribution of social security is shown in the table by the differences in the rates of return for different household types retiring in the same year. In 1980, for example, a married couple with a low/zero-earnings-profile received a 7.4 percent rate of return, whereas a high-earnings-profile single man received only 4.0 percent. In general, married couples fared better than single persons did, and low-income households fared better than high-income households did. These differences reflect the way social security benefits are calculated, which will be discussed in more detail later in the chapter.

Do not make the mistake of thinking that there is little difference in the rates of return shown in Table 7–3. A small difference in the annual rate of return compounded over a lifetime makes a substantial difference in the level of retirement benefits. To give a simple example, consider the effect of compound interest over a 30-year period—which is about the average time between paying taxes and receiving benefits under social security. At a 7 percent rate of return, $1,000 will grow to $7,612 after 30 years; at a 2 percent rate of return, $1,000 will grow only to $1,811. The 7 percent return produces more than four times the benefit of the 2 percent return! From this example, it is clear that persons retiring in 1970 received substantially higher benefits relative to the taxes they paid than will those retiring in the next century.

Two important qualifications to the estimates in Table 7–3 should be mentioned. First, the projected benefits and taxes are based on the social security law as it existed in 1980, but scheduled taxes in 1980 were not sufficient to pay for the scheduled benefits, especially for the later years covered by the table. In 1983 Congress made major changes in the system intended to balance benefits and taxes, and these reforms will significantly reduce the rate of return for individuals retiring after the year 2000. Thus, the expected rates of return for the later years are even lower than those shown in the table and are probably negative for some household groups.

Second, the rates of return in the table compare the social security pensions only with the lifetime taxes paid. This procedure ignores the possible adverse effects of the system on labor supply and saving, which would make the system less attractive on balance than the rates of return suggest. These effects will be discussed later in the chapter.

Is Social Security a Good Deal?

Perhaps the most basic question to ask about social security is whether it is a more attractive way of providing retirement benefits than the alternative methods available. Could we do a better job of providing for retirement by saving privately? In answering this question, it is essential to distinguish between the start-up phase of the system and all subsequent years. Workers who retired in the early years of the start-up phase received extremely favorable returns—generally much more than they could have gotten by saving privately. Younger workers and all future generations, however, will not do as well.

As a long-term, permanent mechanism, social security can offer retirees, after the start-up phase, an annual rate of return, on average, equal to the real rate of economic growth (which we take to be about 2 percent). Could people earn more than 2 percent by saving privately? Over the past 60 years, real annual rates of return on long-term government bonds have averaged about 1 percent, while common stocks have averaged about 7.0 percent.[1] Corporate bonds and home ownership have yielded only slightly more than 2 percent. These comparisons may suggest that a real return of 2 percent from social security over the long run is not bad.

However, it may not be appropriate to compare these market yields with the implicit return under social security. These market rates of return are lower than the real rate of return to capital investment because the government taxes the return to capital investment heavily. (See Chapter 15.) A more appropriate comparison of the relative rates of return is the before-tax return to capital investment relative to the rate of return provided by social security. The before-tax return is a measure of how much private saving that is channeled into capital investment contributes to future output; it is a measure of the real productivity of private saving. Even though an individual does not realize the before-tax return, the society does. Estimation of the before-tax return to capital investment suggests that it has averaged about 10 percent in the post–World War II period.[2]

Thus, private saving for retirement yields a real annual return of 10 percent, whereas social security yields 2 percent. The significance of this difference in returns can be appreciated from the following example. Suppose that a person saves $2,000 a year for 41 years at a 2 percent interest rate. At the end of that time, the accumulated sum would be $124,740. However, $2,000 a year for 41 years at 10 percent grows to $1,072,390. The sum available for retirement is more than eight times as great at 10 percent than it is at 2 percent; such is the power of compound interest over long periods. *Young workers and future generations could do a much better job of providing for their retirement by investing in real capital than by relying on social security.* Not surprisingly then, this difference in yields has led several economists to urge that we rely less on social security and more on real capital accumulation to provide retirement benefits.

---

[1]Robert Kaplin, "A Comparison of Rates of Return to Social Security Retirees Under Wage and Price Indexing," in Colin Campbell, ed., *Financing Social Security* (Washington, D.C.: American Enterprise Institute, 1979), Table 4.

[2]See Martin Feldstein, James Poterba, and Louis Dicks-Mireaux, "The Effective Tax Rate and the Pretax Rate of Return," National Bureau of Economic Research, Working Paper No. 740 (Sept. 1981); Alicia Munnell, *The Future of Social Security* (Washington, D.C.: The Brookings Institution, 1977), p. 128; and Michael Boskin, "Taxation, Saving, and the Rate of Interest," *Journal of Political Economy,* 86(2) Part 2:S 3 (Apr. 1978).

Social Security, Retirement, and Work Incentives

Social security can have important effects on the labor supply decisions of the elderly. If the provision of retirement benefits creates work disincentives that lead older people to retire earlier or work less, the elderly will have lower earnings. Thus, granting the elderly retirement benefits will not raise their money incomes by as much as it would without a work disincentive effect.

Social security affects the labor supply of the elderly in two distinct ways. One way is through the earnings test, which applies until retirees reach the age of 70. Under the earnings test, a person's pension is reduced if earnings exceed a certain amount ($10,200 in 1992). The pension is reduced by one-third of the amount of earnings in excess of $10,200. For example, if a person would receive a pension of $12,000 if fully retired and then earns $15,000, the pension would be reduced by $1,600 (one-third of the difference between $15,000 and $10,200). In effect, the earnings test is like a 33⅓ percent tax rate on earnings above $10,200, up to the point where the pension is exhausted.

The earnings test is effectively a tax on earnings, and so may discourage the elderly from working. The effect on work incentives is intensified by the interaction with other tax policies. For example, social security taxes must be paid on earnings, and perhaps other taxes (federal and state income taxes) as well. In addition, part of social security benefits is directly taxable under the federal individual income tax for elderly persons with high incomes (above $32,000 for a married couple). As a result, the combined tax rate on earnings above $10,200 can easily exceed three fourths, leaving little incentive to earn beyond that amount (unless the retiree can earn substantially above the cutoff point where the pension is exhausted, which is $46,200 in this example). If part-time work is not readily available, some workers must stop working in order to receive their social security pensions.

A second way in which social security can encourage earlier retirement is by providing a pension that is large relative to the taxes paid. As we saw, in the start-up phase of the program, pensions are several times larger than the taxes paid plus a reasonable interest rate. In effect, this large unpaid-for net benefit produces an income effect: It increases the lifetime income of early retirees and enables them to afford an earlier retirement than they otherwise would have chosen. This situation, of course, is relevant only for workers who retire in the start-up phase and can be expected to diminish in importance in the coming years.

Taken together, these two effects can be expected to lead to earlier retirement, especially for generations retiring in the start-up phase. The evidence tends to support this expectation. Labor force participation among men over 65 fell from 47.8 percent in 1947 (when only about 12 percent of the elderly received social security benefits) to 14.8 percent in 1991, a reduction of 69 percent. In addition, the retirement rate for males aged 60 to 64 doubled, from 15 to 30 percent, between 1960 and 1978 following legislation permitting social security benefits to be paid (at reduced levels) beginning at age 62.

The fact that people have retired earlier since the introduction of social security, however, does not prove that social security caused it to happen. There had been a trend toward earlier retirement for many years before social security, reflecting growth in real income and the ability to afford earlier retirement. In 1900, for example, about 60 percent of men over 65 were in the labor force, and the decline to 47.8 percent in 1947 cannot be attributed in any significant degree to social security. The trend toward earlier retirement has, however, accelerated since 1947, suggesting that social security did play a role. In addition, a number of statistical studies have concluded that a significant part of the reduction in labor supply by the elderly since 1947 is directly attributable to social security.[3]

The earnings test, which restricts benefits to those who withdraw partially or completely from the labor force, has been one of the most unpopular features of the social security system. Today its rationale is explicitly redistributive.[4] With a given amount of revenue available for social security payments, a reduction in benefits for higher-income wage earners makes it possible to settle larger benefits on those without earnings—many of whom are poor. If the earnings test were eliminated, about $8 billion in additional benefits would have to be paid to those over 65 still working. Such a change would necessitate an equivalent reduction of $8 billion for those not working or for those working and earning under $10,200.

Social Security and Saving

In the absence of social security, people have strong incentives to save part of their incomes during their working lives to provide financial support for themselves during retirement. Social security, by promising pensions to

[3]See Colin Campbell and Rosemary Campbell, "Conflicting Views on the Effect of Old-Age and Survivor Insurance on Retirement," *Economic Inquiry,* 14(3):369 (Sept. 1974); Michael Boskin, "Social Security and Retirement Decision," *Economic Inquiry,* 17 (Jan. 1977); Michael Boskin and Michael Hurd, "The Effect of Social Security on Early Retirement," *Journal of Public Economics* 7 (Dec. 1978); and Louis Esposito and Michael Packard, "Social Security and the Labor Supply of Aged Men: Evidence from the U.S. Time Series," Working Paper No. 21, Social Security Administration (Dec. 1980).

[4]When originally enacted in the depression of the 1930s, the rationale for having an earnings test was to encourage older workers to leave their jobs and make room for younger workers. This rationale commits the "lump of labor" fallacy, which holds that there are a fixed number of jobs, so to have more jobs for younger workers requires older workers to quit their jobs.

retired workers, alleviates the need to save privately and may therefore lead to a reduction in saving. Consider a person who would normally set aside 10 percent of his or her income for retirement purposes. If the social security tax rate is 10 percent, and if he or she believes that the pension promised by the system is comparable to what his or her private savings would produce, then that person will stop saving altogether. Social security pensions would simply replace privately provided support for retirement.

Figure 7–1 shows the impact of social security on private saving in a more rigorous fashion. Assume that Caroline has a total income of OM over her working life. If she consumed her entire income, her consumption before retirement would be OM, and she would have no resources available to finance her consumption during retirement. By consuming less than her total income before retirement, that is, by saving, Caroline can accumulate resources for consumption after retirement. The budget line MN shows the combinations of before- and after-retirement consumption attainable; its slope reflects the interest return received on saving. With preferences shown by indifference curve U_1, Caroline would choose OC_1 consumption before retirement and OC_2 consumption after retirement. By saving MC_1 of her be-

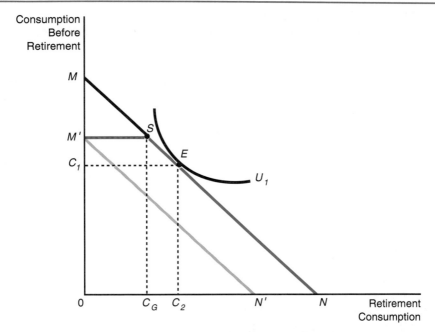

Figure 7–1   *Effect of social security on saving: individual taxpayer*

fore-retirement income, Caroline can finance consumption of OC_2 during retirement.

Now consider how social security will affect this individual. The social security tax of MM' will produce an after-tax budget line of $M'N'$. In return for paying the tax, Caroline is also promised a pension: We will assume that the government pension is OC_G, or the same after-retirement consumption that Caroline would receive if she had saved MM' privately. As a result, her after-tax-and-pension budget line is $M'SN$. Caroline remains in equilibrium at point E but reduces private saving to $M'C_1$. In other words, her saving has fallen by the amount of the social security tax. (Note that it is not the tax alone that reduces her saving, but the tax combined with the promise of a future pension from the government.)

It might be thought that total saving is unchanged. After all, isn't the government now saving MM' for this individual? The answer to this question is no. Recall that social security is financed on a pay-as-you-go basis, so current taxes are not invested but instead finance current benefits. Thus, the reduction in Caroline's saving is not offset by any increase in saving by the government, and the result is a net reduction in total saving. We will consider the consequences of a reduction in saving in the next section, but it should be noted now that Figure 7–1 is an incomplete analysis because it fails to show all the effects of a net reduction in saving. All it illustrates is the incentive a person has to curtail his or her own saving when the government promises to provide retirement benefits.

Possible Offsets to Reduced Saving

There are some other factors, however, that suggest social security may not cause saving to fall by as much as the preceding analysis indicates. One of these is the effect of social security on retirement; by inducing the elderly to retire earlier, the system produces a separate force that tends to increase saving. An extreme example will illustrate this clearly. Suppose that social security forced you to retire at age 40 on a very meager pension—because it would have to be paid for perhaps 35 years. In this case, you would have only about 20 years to accumulate sufficient assets to provide for a lengthy period of retirement. Consequently, you would increase your saving dramatically during your working years, much more so than if you did not plan to retire until age 65. Although this is an extreme example, it clarifies how lengthening the period of retirement (fewer working years to provide for longer retirement) tends to increase saving.

As we saw in the previous section, social security has had the effect of encouraging earlier retirement for some of the elderly. The size of this offsetting effect on saving, however, is almost certain to be quite small. Recall that labor force participation among men over 65 fell from 47.8 percent in 1947 to 14.8 percent in 1991. If half of this decline is a result of social security, then the system has led to earlier retirement for 16.5 percent of the elderly. It is only for this 16.5 percent that the offsetting effect on saving previously described is relevant. Even for this group, there is no reason to suspect that the positive effect on saving of induced early retirement will offset the negative effect associated with the provision of retirement benefits. Moreover, if the earlier retirement is the result of the temporary windfall gains of the start-up phase, this effect will become increasingly unimportant in future years. Therefore, the positive stimulus to saving due to induced earlier retirement will clearly be minor in comparison with the negative effect, so the net result is now, or soon will be, a substantial fall in saving.

A second factor that mitigates the depressing effect of social security on saving is the fact that in its absence some people would save less than the social security tax. If a person normally saved 5 percent of income for retirement and the tax is 10 percent, then saving will not fall by the amount of the tax. Saving will fall to zero, but that reduction is equal to half the tax liability. For people who would save very little in the first place, saving would fall by less than the tax liability. This is likely to be true for those with low incomes (and perhaps for those who optimistically expect to be supported by relatives when retired). Many people, however, would probably save more than the social security tax in its absence. Supportive evidence lies in the fact that large numbers of people continue to save even after paying social security taxes.

A third factor suggesting that saving will not fall so sharply is the possibility that voluntary transfers of funds between the young and the old may change in response to social security. Suppose, for example, that the social security benefits to the elderly are not used for consumption but instead are set aside and left as bequests to their descendants, who in turn leave it to their descendants, and so on. In that event, social security would reduce saving by the young but increase saving by the elderly, possibly producing no net change in total saving.[5] If it is correct, this analysis implies that the retirees in the start-up phase do not really benefit: The elderly just increase bequests to offset what they perceive as harm done to their descendants by social security taxes. In this view, social security could be eliminated overnight without harming the elderly. Judging from the reactions of the elderly to proposals to cut their social security benefits even slightly, this is not the case. The importance of this possibility therefore seems dubious.

Evidence of the Effect of Social Security on Saving

On balance, the analysis seems to suggest that social security will substantially reduce saving, but what does the evidence indicate? If you have followed the analysis closely, you may be surprised to learn that saving as a percentage of national income has shown only a slight decline since World War II. This, however, does not mean that social security has not strongly

---

[5]Robert Barro, "Are Government Bonds Net Worth?" *Journal of Political Economy,* 82:1095 (Nov./Dec. 1974).

depressed saving. The relevant question is what the saving rate would have been without social security. If the saving rate would have increased in the postwar period without social security, then social security has significantly depressed saving by keeping the rate from rising. This is what some economists believe has happened.

There are several reasons why the saving rate would have been expected to rise in the postwar period. Not only was the retirement age falling, life expectancy was rising. There were also fewer working years in which to save for retirement because people were staying in school until a later age. With a trend toward longer retirement and fewer working years, saving for retirement would automatically have risen. In addition, rising real incomes over the period should have reinforced this tendency. Therefore, the small reduction in the rate of saving since 1945 may mean that social security has strongly reduced saving in a situation in which otherwise there would have been a rising trend.

A number of sophisticated econometric studies in recent years have attempted to measure the effect of social security on saving. Martin Feldstein, in his seminal work in 1974, estimated that personal saving was 50 percent lower in 1971 than it would have been without social security.[6] In another study, Feldstein presented evidence that countries with larger social security systems tended to have lower private saving rates, other things being equal.[7] Most other studies, however, have concluded that the magnitude of the effect is smaller than Feldstein's estimates, and some have even concluded that social security has had no effect on saving.[8] At the present time, there is no consensus that social security has had a large negative effect on saving; there is also no consensus that it has not. The issue remains controversial. Given the apparent strength of the theoretical argument, however, it is difficult to believe that saving has not been negatively affected by social security to a significant degree.

---

[6]Martin Feldstein, "Social Security, Induced Retirement and Aggregate Capital Accumulation," *Journal of Political Economy,* 92(5):905 (Sept./Oct. 1974).

[7]Martin Feldstein, "Social Security and Private Savings: International Evidence in an Extended Life Cycle Model," in M. Feldstein and R. Inman, eds., *The Economics of Public Services,* an International Economic Association Conference Volume (New York: Halsted Press, 1977).

[8]See Alicia Munnell, "The Impact of Social Security on Personal Savings," *National Tax Journal,* 27(4):553 (Dec. 1974); Robert Barro, *The Impact of Social Security on Private Saving* (Washington, D.C.: American Enterprise Institute, 1977); Michael Darby, *The Effects of Social Security on Income and the Capital Stock* (Washington, D.C.: American Enterprise Institute, 1979); Louis Esposito, "The Effect of Social Security on Saving: Review of Studies Using U.S. Time-Series Date," *Social Security Bulletin* (May 1978); Selig Lesnoy and Dean Leimer, "Social Security and Private Saving: New Time Series Evidence," *Journal of Political Economy,* 90(3):606 (June 1982); and Martin Feldstein, "Social Security and Private Saving: A Reply," *Journal of Political Economy* 90(3):630 (June 1982).

Effects of Reduced Saving

It may not be clear why we have devoted so much attention to the way social security affects saving. If, however, social security does reduce saving, the consequences are of tremendous importance for an evaluation of the system.

The act of saving, that is, consuming less than one's income, represents a reduction in the demand for consumer goods. When the funds that would have financed current consumption are put in a bank or used to purchase bonds or stocks, they eventually provide financing for borrowers to purchase capital goods such as factories, machines, computers, and so on. Savings ultimately tend to be channeled into productive investment in real capital goods. As a result, saving tends to increase society's stock of productive capital, and this, in turn, increases the future productive capacity of the economy. The rate of saving is consequently one important determinant of the growth in real income over time.

We explained earlier the analysis suggesting that pay-as-you-go social security tends to reduce the saving of individual workers. The effect on national saving is a little more involved. Total national saving is the sum of the savings of all persons, workers and retirees alike. In the absence of social security, retirees often have negative saving, that is, they dissave. For example, a retired person might own corporate stock worth $100,000 that has a real return (dividends plus real capital gains) of 5 percent. Thus, the retiree's income is $5,000, but he or she may well consume beyond that amount by selling some of the stock each year. For example, $10,000 might be consumed by selling $5,000 worth of stock in addition to realizing the $5,000 real return on the stock. In that case, this retiree contributes a negative sum to national saving; he or she is dissaving. This is fairly common among the elderly, and for anyone who receives a fixed private pension that terminates at death, it occurs automatically.

Now consider how social security affects national saving in a society where workers are saving and retirees are dissaving. Social security will reduce the saving of workers, as we saw, but how will it affect the retirees? When first introduced, social security pensions would probably just add to consumption by retirees without affecting the amount of dissaving. For example, in our previous example, the retiree would receive a social security pension and add that amount to his or her consumption of $10,000. After several decades, the situation will be different, however, because retirees then will own less capital than they would have had without social security. A person anticipating a $10,000 social security pension might never accumulate the $100,000 in corporate stock (this is the result of the earlier reduction in the worker's saving). There will then be a smaller amount of negative saving by the elderly. So at that time, retirees have less negative saving and workers have less positive saving; the overall saving rate may not be affected. Thus, when social security is first introduced, we expect national saving to fall (workers save less, but dissaving by the elderly is not much affected), but it will slowly rebound to a higher level as later retirees have less capital and therefore dissave less.

Figure 7–2 illustrates how this effect of social security on national saving affects the economy. The logarithm of GNP is measured on the vertical axis and time on the horizontal axis. In the absence of social security, we assume that GNP will grow at a constant rate, say, 3 percent per year. This is shown by the line *ABC*. (The significance of measuring GNP in logarithms is that a constant annual rate of growth is then shown by a straight line.) Now suppose that social security begins in 1940. This reduces national saving in that year, and the real capital stock of the economy will be lower the following year. Thus, output (GNP) will be lower than it would have been the following year, so the rate of growth of the economy falls somewhat. National saving remains lower than it would have been for a number of years, as explained earlier, and during this time the rate of growth of GNP is below 3 percent; this is shown by the *BD* portion of the curve. In 1990, however, dissaving by the elderly has been reduced enough so that the saving rate is no longer lower than it was, and the rate of growth has returned to 3 percent per year. From that time on, the economy grows at 3 percent per year, as shown by the *DE* line (parallel to *ABC*), *but the level of GNP in every*

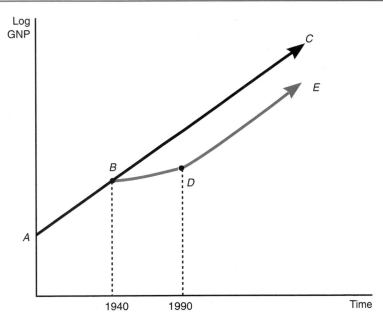

Figure 7–2   *Economic growth and social security*

subsequent year is lower than it would have been had social security never been implemented.

The important point is that although the rate of growth of the economy is only temporarily lower (from 1940 to 1990 in our example), the level of output is permanently reduced below what it would have been. This occurs because the reduced saving during the 1940–90 period leads to a permanently lower capital stock for the economy. If social security does reduce the saving of workers by the amount of taxes collected, this effect on GNP is quite large. For example, Feldstein estimated that GNP is 10 to 20 percent lower than it would have been in the absence of social security. Of course, what this suggests is that workers living today and all those in the future will have lifetime real incomes that are 10 to 20 percent below what they would have been. Even if the effect on saving is only half this large, there is probably no other policy that has had such a large effect on living standards. That is why we have spent so much time considering how social security affects saving.

We have been considering the effect of reduced saving on aggregate output; now let us see how it affects individuals under the social security system. Consider Table 7–4a. This table illustrates consumption and saving behavior in the absence of social security. Thus, individuals save 10 percent of their incomes during their working years and consume the accumulated sums when they retire. (It is assumed that the annual interest return on private saving is 100 percent, equal to the rate of growth of the economy.) Thus, individual *C* saves \$25 and \$50 in years 1 and 2 (and consumes \$225 and

Table 7–4   *Distributional Effects of Reduced Saving*

a. Without Social Security

Year	*1*	*2*	*3*	*4*	*5*
Young	*C*250	*D*500	*E*1000	*F*2000	*G*4000
	(−25)	(−50)	(−100)	(−200)	(−400)
Middle-aged	*B*250	*C*500	*D*1000	*E*2000	*F*4000
	(−25)	(−50)	(−100)	(−200)	(−400)
Retired	*A*(+50)	*B*(+100)	*C*(+200)	*D*(+400)	*E*(+800)

b. With Social Security

Year *Tax Rate:*	*2* *10%*	*3* *10%*	*4* *10%*	*5* *10%*
Young	*D*500	*E*950	*F*1800	*G*3500
	(−50)	(−95)	(−180)	(−350)
Middle-aged	*C*500	*D*950	*E*1800	*F*3500
	(−50)	(−95)	(−180)	(−350)
Retired	*B*(+100)	*C*(+190)	*D*(+360)	*E*(+700)

$450 in these years) and consumes the accumulated sum of $200 in year 3. In this way, Table 7–4a shows what the lifetime consumption patterns of people would be without social security.

The introduction of social security temporarily reduces the rate of growth in incomes. The consequences are illustrated in Table 7–4b. Suppose that the system begins in year 2, with individuals C and D paying taxes of $50 each to finance a retirement benefit of $100 for individual B. Social security does not reduce incomes in year 2, but the following year the capital stock is lower than it would have been, and the incomes of D and E are $950 rather than $1,000, a reduction of 5 percent. A tax of 10 percent then finances a transfer of $190 to individual C. The reduced saving in year 3 results in the capital stock in year 4 falling further behind what it would have been, and total incomes are $1,800 rather than $2,000, a reduction of 10 percent. In this way, social security gradually causes incomes to fall below the level they would have attained if saving had not fallen.

Now consider how individual D fares under social security. D's consumption in years 2, 3, and 4 is $450, $855, and $360. Compare this with what D's consumption would have been without social security (from Table 7–4a)— $450, $900, and $400; D's lifetime consumption is lower under social security. For individual E, consumption is $855, $1,620, and $700 with social security but $900, $1,800, and $800 without it. Because social security causes real national income to grow less slowly, the lifetime incomes of people are lower under this system. After year 5, incomes may again double each year, but note that this will leave all subsequent generations with lower lifetime incomes. If Feldstein is correct, young people beginning to work now will have, roughly speaking, 10 to 20 percent less income every year of their lives.[9]

Note, however, that many people retiring during the start-up phase will still benefit from social security even if it reduces saving and the rate of growth in real income. As shown in Table 7–4b, for example, individuals B and C clearly gain. They receive retirement benefits without suffering a reduction in income before retirement. Because the effect of reduced saving on output and on real incomes is small at first and gradually grows, the negative impact on preretirement income will be more than offset by the windfall gains of early retirees. Workers who retire later are not so fortunate and will have lower lifetime consumption. When the negative effects will begin to prevail is not clear, since it depends on the unknown magnitude of the saving effect and its impact on real incomes. If the saving effect is as large as Feldstein believes it to be, quite possibly all those who have benefited from the system are already retired or deceased, and everyone working now and in the future will have lower lifetime standards of living.

It should now be clear why simply comparing retirement benefits and taxes paid, as is done in Table 7–3, does not tell the full story. Even if people

---

[9]A reduction in saving will tend to increase the interest rate and reduce wage rates (because there is less capital per worker). Thus, there may also be some redistribution of the smaller total output from workers to investors.

receive a favorable rate of return on their tax payments, they can still be harmed by the system because it reduces before-tax incomes.

Equity-Related Issues

Individual Equity versus Social Adequacy

The terms *individual equity* and *social adequacy* recur frequently in official discussions of social security. Individual equity refers to the degree to which an individual's benefits are related to taxes paid. If the retirement benefits were strictly proportional to taxes paid, so that a person who had paid twice the taxes of someone else would receive twice the benefits, then the system would embody individual equity. Social adequacy, on the other hand, refers to the welfare objective of ensuring adequate benefits, regardless of the taxes paid.

These two objectives are competing goals that cannot be fully realized simultaneously. If benefits were strictly related to taxes paid, low-income families that paid low taxes would receive very small benefits—a violation of social adequacy. On the other hand, if everyone received a sizable benefit, regardless of the taxes paid, then the goal of individual equity would be sacrificed.

The present structure of the social security system represents a compromise between these two conflicting objectives. Retirement benefits are related to previous earnings (and hence to taxes paid), but the relationship is not proportional. To illustrate the relationship, let us consider how benefits are calculated for a single worker retiring at age 65 in 1993. The first step in calculating the benefits is to determine the average monthly taxable earnings over a period of 35 years. To figure the average monthly earnings, the worker's earnings in each year are indexed by the average annual covered wages in the economy in that year. For example, suppose that the worker's earnings at age 40 (in 1968) were $5,000 but that the average covered wages in the economy had tripled (owing to increases in real wages and inflation) by 1993. When the worker's benefits are calculated at age 65, his or her earnings at age 40 are counted as $15,000, triple the nominal wages actually earned at age 40. This "wage indexing" of earnings effectively counts wages at younger ages relative to economywide wages and thereby protects workers from inflation eroding their average earnings and hence benefits.

Once the worker's average (indexed) monthly earnings have been determined, the initial monthly retirement benefit is calculated using the benefit formula. In 1993, this formula figures the monthly benefit as 90 percent of the first $401 in average monthly earnings, plus 32 percent of any monthly earnings between $401 and $2,420, plus 15 percent of any monthly earnings in excess of $2,420. For example, with average monthly earnings of $3,000, the monthly benefit would be 0.9 ($401) + 0.32 ($2,420 − $401) + 0.15

($3,000 − $2,420), or $1,094. (The formula determines the first-year retirement benefits. Thereafter, the benefit is automatically increased by the rate of increase in the consumer price index, thereby preserving the real value of benefits in later years.) The *bend points* in the formula, at $401 and $2,420, are indexed to the average covered earnings and so will increase automatically as average wages in the economy rise. The marginal replacement rates, the 0.9, 0.32, and 0.15 ratios, however, are not scheduled to change in the future.

Figure 7–3 illustrates the benefit formula with the schedule 0*ABC,* which identifies the monthly benefit at each level of average indexed monthly earnings. The slope of 0*ABC* along the 0*A* segment is 0.9; along the *AB* segment, 0.32; and along the *BC* segment, 0.15. Note that this benefit formula makes benefits a larger proportion of previous earnings for low-wage workers than for high-wage workers. For example, workers with average monthly earnings of $401 receive benefits that are 90 percent of their average monthly earnings, whereas workers with average monthly earnings of $4,800 (the maximum ultimately possible, because this is the ceiling amount of taxable

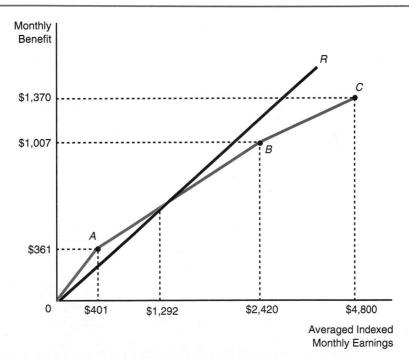

Figure 7–3   *The social security benefit formula for single workers, 1993*

earnings, or $57,600 a year in 1993[10]) receive benefits of less than 30 percent of their average monthly earnings.

In effect, *the benefit formula redistributes income among the retired population from individuals who had high earnings to people who had low earnings.* This is an attempt to achieve social adequacy and represents an intragenerational redistribution of income. This redistribution is why low-wage workers receive a higher rate of return on their taxes paid than do high-wage workers, as shown in Table 7–3. Individual equity, on the other hand, would call for workers to receive benefits proportionate to their average monthly earnings. If this were done, the benefit formula would be the straight line $0R$ in Figure 7–3, with a slope of approximately 0.5. With the $0R$ schedule, all workers retiring in a given year would receive the same rate of return on their taxes paid, but with the $0ABC$ schedule, workers with average monthly earnings below approximately $1,292 receive a higher than average rate of return, whereas workers with higher earnings receive a lower than average rate of return.

How to draw a balance between individual equity and social adequacy is unclear. Another government policy, however, has weakened the case for trying to achieve social adequacy through the social security system. In 1974 the federal government began a program called Supplemental Security Income (SSI). This is a welfare program that provides cash assistance to elderly persons (as well as the blind and disabled) who have little income or assets. In effect, SSI guarantees a minimum income, with the level of support approximately equal to the poverty line for a married couple. SSI therefore serves the welfare function of providing income support for the elderly poor. With this program in place, there is less reason for social security to be concerned with social adequacy. Indeed, SSI has weakened the ability of social security to help the aged poor. Under SSI, if an elderly poor person receives a dollar more from social security, his or her assistance payment under SSI falls by a dollar. Raising social security benefits for those also covered by SSI therefore does not help them at all.

Single- and Two-Earner Families

Under the present law, retirement benefits for married couples are calculated in one of two ways. First, the husband and the wife each can receive the benefits they are separately entitled to using the benefit formula for single workers we discussed earlier. Second, the couple can choose the "dependent-spouse" option, in which the couple's benefits are equal to 150 percent of the retirement benefit due one of them according to the single-worker benefit formula. Note that this second option means that a couple

---

[10]No one retiring in 1993 could have average index monthly earnings as high as $4,800, however. This is because the ceiling on taxable earnings went up faster than average covered earnings did before the ceiling itself was indexed in 1977, and many of the years when the ceiling was lower had to be counted by those retiring in 1993.

with only one working spouse can receive 150 percent of the benefits of a single person with the same earnings. In other words, a working wife can receive benefits based on her own earnings or benefits equal to 50 percent of her husband's retirement benefits, or vice versa, with the choice usually determined by which alternative leads to greater combined retirement benefits for the couple.

This treatment often results in a working wife's finding that the family's total retirement benefits are no higher than they would have been had she never worked and paid taxes at all. For a wife with low earnings relative to her husband's, the total retirement benefits will be greater if she takes a benefit equal to 50 percent of her husband's benefit rather than the benefit she is entitled to based on her own earning record. Note that she would receive this 50 percent benefit even if she had not worked, so the social security taxes she paid did not increase the family's total retirement benefits. Many working wives view this as unfairly discriminating in favor of non-working wives. (We are referring to work in the paid labor force; obviously, wives not in the labor force provide valuable services at home.)

Another consequence of this treatment is that retirement benefits can differ between two-person families with the *same* total earnings. In 1993 a family retiring in which only one spouse worked, with average indexed monthly earnings of $2,000, could receive monthly retirement benefits of $1,309–$873 based on the working spouse's earnings and 50 percent of that sum in the form of a dependent-spouse benefit. However, a family with the same combined average indexed monthly earnings, but with 75 percent received by the wife and 25 percent received by the husband, would have smaller monthly retirement benefits, regardless of how they calculated them. If the benefits were figured separately, they would receive $1,106 ($713 + $393); if the dependent-spouse option were used, the benefits would be $1,070 ($713 plus 50 percent of $713). So two couples with the same combined earnings would receive different retirement benefits. Outcomes like this are fairly common under the social security system. Again, they reflect a compromise between social adequacy and individual equity. Two-person families need more income than one-person families do, so the goal of social adequacy suggests that they be given larger retirement benefits unrelated to their taxes paid. This, however, immediately produces situations like those just discussed, which are widely viewed as violating the standard of individual equity.

These provisions in social security are another instance of intragenerational redistribution. Single-earner families benefit at the expense of two-earner families and single individuals. When social security began, the favored single-earner families were quite common. In 1940 in only 3 of 20 households did both the husband and the wife work; in 1993, however, in over one half of households, both the husband and wife worked. The increased prevalence of two-earner families has strengthened the support for reform to end this inequitable (in the sense of individual equity) treatment.

Any move to increase benefits to two-earner families would, however, mean a relative decrease in benefits for single-earner families, thereby sacrificing social adequacy.

The General Level of Retirement Benefits

Are social security benefits too high? This question is difficult because its answer depends on what the system's objective is thought to be. To those who prefer to provide privately for their own retirement, almost any level of social security benefits will seem too high. But to those who view social security as part of the welfare system and want social security by itself to provide adequate standards of living for all the elderly, almost any level of benefits will seem too low. Nonetheless, there are some points regarding the general level of benefits that should be made, especially since there are serious questions about our ability to continue financing benefits at their current levels (as we will discuss in the next section).

One measure of the adequacy of social security benefits is suggested by their replacement rates. The *replacement rate* is the ratio of the benefit amount payable to a worker in the first year of retirement to his or her earnings in the year before retirement. (Recall that benefits are indexed to the consumer price index in subsequent years.) Table 7–5 shows the replacement rates for selected years at different levels of earnings for single workers. Two points should be observed. First, in every year the replacement rate is greater for low-wage workers, reflecting the tilt in the benefit formula favoring low-wage workers. Second, replacement rates have risen sharply for low and average earners since 1970 and have fallen somewhat for high earners. Between 1970 and 1990, the replacement rate rose by 63

Table 7–5　Replacement Rates Under Social Security (in percentages)

Year	Low Earnings Individual	Average Earnings Individual	Maximum Earnings Individual
1950	44.7%	30.0%	26.8%
1960	45.0	33.3	29.8
1970	42.7	34.3	29.2
1980	64.0	51.1	32.5
1990	69.7	42.3	24.7

Note: For the average-earnings individual, earnings are assumed to be equal to national average earnings in each year. Earnings for the low earner are assumed to be half the average, and for the maximum earner they are equal to the taxable ceiling in each year.

Source: Henry J. Aaron, Barry P. Bosworth, and Gary Burtless, *Can America Afford to Grow Old?* (Washington, D.C.: The Brookings Institution, 1989), Table 2-4.

percent for a low-wage worker and by 23 percent for an average-wage worker, and it fell by 15 percent for a maximum-wage (at the ceiling on taxable earnings) worker.[11] This means that the amount of intragenerational redistribution has been increased in recent years. (If there were no intragenerational redistribution, all workers in each year would have approximately the same replacement rates.)

The recent rise in replacement rates was the result of deliberate congressional decisions to increase benefits, as well as congressional error. The deliberate decisions were to raise benefits by 15 percent in 1970, 10 percent in 1971, and 20 percent in 1972. These increases were far in excess of the 5 percent inflation rate during these years, so the real benefits that retirees received rose. The error resulted from the congressional attempt in 1972 to index benefits to inflation; at that time, benefits were not automatically indexed, as they are now. However, the indexing provision Congress enacted in 1972 double-counted inflation and increased benefits faster than the price level. This mistake was corrected in 1977 (when the current benefit formula was enacted), but during the intervening years, the real benefit levels increased and were then locked in at the higher levels they attained in 1977.

In judging the adequacy of these benefit levels, it should be kept in mind that the elderly's standards of living are generally much higher than suggested by these replacement rates alone. There are several reasons. First, the figures in Table 7–5 do not include Medicare benefits (enacted in 1965), which are now 40 percent as large as the cash benefits, on the average. Second, the replacement rates for married couples are higher than those for single workers; they would be 50 percent higher, for example, if one spouse did not work. Third, social security benefits are nontaxable for most retired persons. Replacement rates relative to after-tax earnings would therefore be higher than those shown in the table. Fourth, almost three out of four elderly households own their own homes (half with no mortgage at all) and therefore have lower housing expenses than do younger households. Fifth, retired persons do not have work-related expenses, expenses that have been estimated to be between 6 and 13 percent of earnings for workers.

When these factors are taken into account, it is clear that many retired households have standards of living as high as those they enjoyed before retirement. In fact, on average, the elderly population appears to be better off than the nonelderly population. One recent study adjusted the income figures to take account of the fact that elderly households have fewer

---

[11]Do not make the error of equating the replacement rate with the extent to which a person benefits from the system. The replacement rate relates benefits to earnings, not to taxes paid. People retiring in 1950 had paid taxes of only 2 and 3 percent for only 13 years. In fact, retirees in 1990 who had worked since 1937 had paid an average tax rate of only 8 percent, although workers paying for their benefits were then paying a rate of 15.3 percent. The windfall gains to retirees in the start-up phase are not indicated by the level of replacement rates.

persons, pay less in taxes, and receive Medicare. After these adjustments, it found that the average elderly household in 1979 had an income 28 percent greater than the nonelderly household.[12] And this comparison does not take into account work-related expenses or home ownership, which would raise further the incomes of the elderly relative to the nonelderly. Although many of the elderly are still poor, the poverty rate among the elderly is lower than among younger persons, and as a group the elderly are not poor.

These facts do not by themselves, however, help us much in determining whether social security benefits are too high. Making that determination involves evaluating the effects of changing the level of benefits in light of the desired objectives. Even if we decide that benefits are too high, we must understand that reducing benefits quickly would be difficult, if not impossible. Many retired persons have withdrawn from the labor force expecting to continue receiving their benefits at their current levels, as promised under the current law. Thus, reducing the benefits for those already retired, at least if the reductions were substantial, could impose major hardships and would certainly be viewed by many as unfair. If social security benefits are to be reduced, then, they should be lowered gradually by decreasing benefits for new retirees in some future year so that workers can effectively plan now for retirement.

Apart from questions of the adequacy of retirement benefits, benefits at their current levels heighten concerns about how the system affects incentives to save. Are low- and average-income households likely to save much to supplement social security benefits that already provide for a standard of living that is, for many, comparable to their preretirement years?

The Future Crisis in Social Security

An important factor affecting the viability of a pay-as-you-go system of social security is the population's age distribution. The smaller the number of people working, relative to the number of people who have retired, the higher the tax burden will be per worker in order to finance a given level of retirement benefits. The ratio of workers to retirees is largely determined by two demographic factors: the longevity of elderly persons and the birthrate. Recent trends in these factors suggest that the number of workers per retiree will fall sharply in the first half of the twenty-first century, and this decline is likely to cause serious financing problems for the system.

The longevity of retirees has an obvious effect on social security: The longer retirees live, the higher the tax rate that will be needed to finance a

[12]Michael D. Hurd, "Research on the Elderly: Economic Status, Retirement, and Consumption and Saving," *Journal of Economic Literature,* 28:577 (June 1990). Hurd gives several estimates, based on different ways of adjusting for household size differences, and the figure reported here is the one he considers best.

given level of annual benefits. In 1940, the remaining life expectancy at age 65 was 11.9 years for males and 13.4 years for females. The corresponding figures in 1989 were 15.2 years for males and 19.0 years for females, improvements of 28 and 42 percent, respectively. If longevity continues to improve, as expected, the number of elderly persons will rise compared with the number of working-age persons, requiring higher tax rates to finance the system.

The pattern of birthrates over time is of perhaps even greater importance to the ratio of workers to retirees. The total fertility rate (the average number of babies born to each woman during her lifetime) is a convenient measure of the birthrate. Following a downward trend begun a century and a half ago, the fertility rate stood at 2.42 in 1945; then it started to rise as a result of the postwar baby boom, reaching a peak of 3.77 in 1957. After 1957 the fertility rate declined more or less steadily until it reached 1.80 in 1983. It increased slightly in the following years, reaching 2.0 in 1989. (A fertility rate of 2.1 is required for zero population growth, ignoring immigration.) We thus have had a baby boom followed by a "baby bust," a bad combination from the perspective of social security financing. *When the baby-boom generation retires, the number of retirees will grow rapidly, and they will have to be supported by taxes on the relatively small baby-bust generation.*

Prospects for the social security system in the next century depend heavily on demographic developments in the future as well as on the economic performance of the economy. Obviously, future events cannot be predicted with great accuracy. It is possible, however, to make forecasts based on assumptions regarding demographic and economic factors, and that is what the board of trustees of OASDI does each year. Their 1992 *Annual Report* contains projections based on three sets of alternative assumptions about demographic changes and economic growth. Alternative I is the optimistic one (from the standpoint of social security financing) and assumes a prompt reversal in the downward trend in the fertility rate, with the fertility rate rising to 2.2 by the year 2016 and then stabilizing. Strong economic growth is also assumed in this alternative. Alternative II is based on intermediate economic and demographic assumptions. It assumes a fertility rate of 1.9 and moderate economic growth. Alternative III is the pessimistic forecast, assuming that the fertility rate will decline to 1.60 and that economic growth will be weak.[13]

Although the consequences for the social security system depend on both demographic and economic assumptions, the demographic factors are the more important, because they largely determine the number of workers per retiree in each year. To illustrate what the various alternatives imply, let us

---

[13]For a more detailed discussion of the economic and demographic assumptions underlying these alternatives, see the *1992 Annual Report of the Board of Trustees of the Federal Old Age and Survivors Insurance Trust Funds* (Washington, D.C.: U.S. Government Printing Office, 1992).

begin with the current ratio of workers to retirees: there are now 3.3 workers paying social security taxes to finance benefits for each retiree. Under Alternative I, this ratio will fall to 2.4 in the year 2040, but it will fall to 2.10 and 1.6 under Alternatives II and III, respectively. Thus, the number of workers supporting each retiree is predicted to fall under all three alternatives, but with larger declines for the more pessimistic demographic assumptions. These changes thus have important implications for the future financing of social security.

Now let us consider what these demographic factors imply for the future financing of social security. Table 7–6 gives the projected payroll tax rates required to finance future benefits as determined under present law for each of the three alternative sets of assumptions. Note that these rates are the ones required if social security is financed in each year on a pay-as-you-go basis; they are not the legislated rates in each year. Let us begin by looking at Alternative II, which is considered by many to be the "best guess" about a highly uncertain future. In 1992, the required rates are 11.5 percent for OASDI and 2.8 percent for HI (Medicare). Recall that these are actually lower than current rates (12.4 percent and 2.9 percent)—more on this later. The current combined tax rate, 15.3 percent, actually exceeds the required rate until shortly after the year 2000. Starting at around 2020—about the time the baby boom generation is retiring in full force—the rates go up sharply. By 2030, the required combined rate is 25 percent, and it reaches 30 percent in 2070.

Table 7–6 *Projected Tax Rates Required to Finance OASDI (HI) Benefits, Various Demographic and Economic Assumptions (in percentages)*

Year	Alternative I		Alternative II		Alternative III	
	OASDI	HI	OASDI	HI	OASDI	HI
1992	11.38%	2.77%	11.50%	2.80%	11.62%	2.83%
1995	10.79	2.99	11.42	3.18	11.97	3.36
2000	9.96	3.24	11.24	3.76	12.58	4.35
2010	10.05	3.55	11.66	4.87	13.56	6.71
2020	12.14	4.01	14.25	6.58	16.78	10.88
2030	13.57	4.60	16.58	8.62	20.23	16.17
2040	13.03	4.96	16.86	9.71	21.94	19.11
2050	12.48	5.18	17.02	10.13	23.63	19.97
2060	12.53	5.54	17.84	10.82	26.17	21.35
2070	12.48	5.99	18.35	11.66	28.07	23.11

Source: *1992 Annual Report of the Board of Trustees of the Federal Old-Age and Survivors Insurance and Disability Trust Funds* (Washington, D.C.: US Government Printing Office, 1992), B24, Table III.A.2.

Under the intermediate assumptions, the required payroll tax rate is nearly double its present level by the middle of the next century. Thus, under a pay-as-you-go system, the country will face a difficult choice. If it maintains the present payroll tax rate, benefit levels will have to be cut in half when the baby-boom generation retires. Alternatively, if benefit levels are maintained as in current law, the payroll tax rate on workers at that time will have to be doubled. The prospect of a doubled payroll tax rate raises two important questions. Is it fair for future workers to pay a 30 percent tax rate to support the baby-boom retirees when these retirees only had to pay a 15.3 percent rate when they were younger? Second is the issue of efficiency: Would future workers, paying a payroll tax rate of 30 percent plus other taxes that would probably be an additional 30 percent of their income (about the current level of nonpayroll taxes), continue to work as hard and be as productive when facing a total tax rate of 60 percent?

Making very long-term projections is difficult, and it makes a lot of difference which set of alternatives more closely resembles the future. Under the optimistic Alternative I the future payroll tax rate rises only to 18.5 percent, but under the pessimistic Alternative III it increases to a mind-boggling 51 percent. In the past, the intermediate assumptions have turned out to be too optimistic; we may hope that this is not the case with the most recent estimates.

The Move to Partial Funding: Will It Help?

The impending crunch in social security financing has been anticipated for at least two decades. Following several years of active public debate, Congress enacted the Social Security Act Amendments of 1983 in an effort to deal with the situation. Many changes were made in the law that affected the future financial integrity of social security. Two of these changes had the effect of reducing the future benefits that had to be paid: raising the retirement age and taxing part of social security benefits.

Under the 1983 amendments, the age at which full retirement benefits are available will gradually rise from 65 to 67 between 2000 and 2027. This will reduce the number of retirees receiving benefits and therefore reduce the tax rates required to finance benefits. This represents, of course, a reduction in benefits, but given the fact that longevity for the elderly has increased, this may be the best way to reduce benefits. Even with a retirement age of 67, people retiring in the next century will probably receive benefits for a longer period of time than those retiring in recent years.

Before the 1983 amendments, social security benefits were not taxed under the federal individual income tax. Under the 1983 law, up to one half of social security benefits are taxable for individuals with incomes above $25,000 and for couples with incomes above $32,000. The revenues raised are channeled back directly into the social security system, so the net effect is the same as a cut in benefit levels for wealthy retirees. Only about 20 percent of retirees had incomes high enough to be affected by this law in

1992, but that fraction will increase over time because the threshold income levels of $25,000 and $32,000 are not indexed to inflation.

These two changes are already incorporated into the estimates in Table 7–6, so obviously they were not enough to restore financial balance to the system. The other major change in 1983 was to schedule payroll tax rates that were higher than necessary to finance current benefits in the late 1980s and for several years thereafter. Thus, as can be seen in Table 7–6, the 15.3 percent current rate (and it is scheduled to remain at that level) is higher than necessary to pay benefits each year until sometime after 2000. Thus, the current social security system is running a surplus, with revenues exceeding outlays, and this surplus is being used to build up a reserve fund. This fund can then be used in later years to pay some of the benefits, thereby obviating some of the higher tax rates that would otherwise be needed. In effect, the baby-boom generation is paying higher taxes than necessary now in order to prepay some of their retirement benefits, rather than sticking the baby-bust generation with the full tab (as would be the case with a pure pay-as-you-go system).

Table 7–7 provides some estimates about the buildup and subsequent rundown in the trust fund. (The estimates refer to OASDI and HI together and pertain to the Alternative II case.) As can be seen, the annual excess of revenues over outlays (the surplus) peaks at about $120 billion (constant 1989 dollars) in 2010. By the year 2020, annual taxes fall short of estimated benefits, in increasing amounts through 2060. (This was already suggested

Table 7–7   Social Security Surpluses, Deficits, and Reserves.

	Annual Surplus or Deficit		Total Reserves
Year	1989 Dollars ($ billions)	As a Percent of GNP	1989 Dollars ($ billions)
1990	$ 79	1.49%	$ 280
2000	115	1.74	1,022
2010	120	1.49	1,765
2020	− 32	− 0.34	1,753
2030	− 332	− 3.10	− 247[a]
2040	− 658	− 5.29	− 4,279
2050	− 1061	− 7.41	− 9,896
2060	− 1625	− 9.83	− 17,790

[a]The reserve fund is exhausted. Negative figures show the cumulative amount of money that would have to be borrowed to pay benefits.

Source: Carolyn L. Weaver, "Introduction" to C. L. Weaver (ed.), *Social Security's Looming Surpluses* (Washington, D.C.: A.E.I. Press, 1990), Tables 1–1 and 1–2.

by our discussion of Table 7–6.) The last column in the table shows the accumulated reserves in the trust fund; the total reaches $1,765 billion ($1.765 trillion) in 2010. Even though the system goes into annual deficit between 2010 and 2020, the funds in the trust fund can be used to make up the shortfall for several years, until some time between 2025 and 2030, at which time the trust fund will be completely exhausted.

Basically, the accumulation of reserves in the trust fund allows us to postpone for 10 or 15 years the difficult decision on whether to increase payroll tax rates sharply or reduce benefits. By 2030, however, there will be no remaining trust fund, and then we will face the harsh reality suggested by Table 7–6.

One potential benefit of the accumulation of reserves is that it may increase real saving and investment in the economy, thereby increasing the output of the economy and making it easier to finance the changes that will be required in the middle of the next century. This can occur even though the social security trust fund is simply accumulating IOUs from the federal government (the trust fund cannot acquire corporate stocks or bonds). For a given amount of federal debt, the more that is held by the social security trust fund, the less private sector savings are required to finance the debt. Thus, private sector saving is freed up to finance investment in real capital. This scenario does assume that the surplus in social security does not lead to even larger federal deficit financing of other programs; if it does, then there would be no real capital accumulation achieved by the buildup of the social security trust fund. It is very difficult to determine whether this has happened, and economists are uncertain about whether the accumulating reserves are promoting real capital accumulation.

It seems clear, however, that the current buildup and later rundown of reserves in the social security trust fund will only delay the financing crisis. At some point before 2030, there will have to be major changes in tax rates or benefit levels.

Social Security and Public Choice

Social security has always enjoyed broad public support. Even in recent years, when concerns over the ability of the system to pay all of its future benefit obligations have grown, there has been little support for changing the system in any significant way. Social security seems to have great political appeal, and this presents us with a puzzle. We have seen that as a permanent institution for providing retirement benefits, social security offers an annual return of perhaps 2 percent, although the rate of return to private investment is much higher. What accounts for the political support of a retirement system that yields such a lower rate of return? The answer probably largely lies in the peculiar distributional effects of a pay-as-you-go system.

Consider how the introduction of a pay-as-you-go social security system affects the well-being of different age groups. Retired persons will benefit, since they will receive pensions without paying taxes. Persons near retirement will also secure large gains, since they pay taxes for only a few years. (Consider individuals *B* and *C* in Table 7–2.) In its start-up phase, social security will be a good bargain for middle-aged and older persons, and they would be expected to support it politically. Only very young workers and future generations (who do not vote) receive the low 2 percent rate of return. In general, *starting the system or expanding its size will be more attractive the older a person is at the time the change occurs.* If the tax rate is increased today, only the very young and subsequent generations will have to pay the higher rate over their entire lifetimes to get the larger pensions. In contrast, a person aged 55 will pay the higher tax rate for only 10 years before receiving the larger pension yielded by the higher tax rate. From his or her perspective, the larger retirement benefit may be well worth paying higher taxes for 10 years. This explains why older age groups support a pay-as-you-go system.

After the start-up phase, subsequent generations receive only the rate of economic growth as a rate of return under social security. As younger workers grow older, won't they reject the system? It is important to see why they are unlikely to do so. The low 2 percent return you may receive over your lifetime is an average rate of return. However, it is the marginal return from changing the size of the social security system that is the dominant consideration, and this increases as a worker becomes older. A person who is young today will be better off if the social security system is expanded when he or she is retired and worse off if it is contracted. Similarly, when a young person today reaches age 55, continuing the system for the remainder of his or her lifetime will then be more attractive than doing away with it; the retirement benefits relative to the remaining 10 years of taxes will be large. As people become older, they will increasingly favor continuing or expanding the system. At each point in time, the older portion of the population will favor pay-as-you-go social security, so there is no reason to expect political support for the system to diminish over time.

For this reason, society may find itself locked into a pay-as-you-go social security system. Even if every young person today and all future generations would be better off providing for retirement privately, political support from the older members of the population in every future year may perpetuate the system.

Should Social Security Be Phased Out?

Whenever fundamental reforms of social security are seriously considered, the possibility of eliminating the system altogether and letting people provide for their retirement privately is certain to come up. Although the prospects for such a reform are remote, we should consider it carefully because it forces us to try to understand the rationale for the social security system.

The present social security system contains two potentially separate features: the requirement that people set aside a certain fraction of earnings each year for retirement and the requirement that these sums be channeled through a pay-as-you-go system. Arguing that people should be required to save for retirement is not enough to justify social security, since the government could still force people to save but allow them to choose the form of assets to hold. Both features must be defended to justify social security.

Why should people be required to save for their retirement? Two reasons are most frequently mentioned. The first is paternalistic: People may underestimate retirement needs when they are young, and by the time they are approaching retirement age, it is too late for them to remedy the situation. The second is based on the possibility that some people will not save and will go on welfare when they are older, placing an extra cost on workers who do save. In this view, people should be forced to provide for their own retirement needs so that they do not impose the burden of their support on others.

Both of these arguments are logically sound, but their relevance depends on how many people would, in fact, fail to make provision for retirement if they were not forced to. Unfortunately, there is little evidence on this point one way or another. (The fact that many retired persons today have no means of support except social security does not mean that they would not have saved in its absence. The expectation of social security benefits may be why they did not save.) What if people do not save? Will they have to be supported by someone else at age 65? Usually there is the option of continuing to work. Only for those who reach age 65 without savings and who are at the same time unable to work would it be necessary to provide welfare. The number of people in this category may be quite small, in which case a welfare program for the elderly who are unable to work and who have no savings might be less costly than a social security system for everyone.

If, however, the argument for requiring people to save is accepted, the next step in defending social security is to justify its pay-as-you-go format. Here the critical question seems to be whether pay-as-you-go financing provides a better return than private saving. Over the long run, the scales tip decisively in favor of private saving. The 10 percent rate of return to private capital accumulation far exceeds the expected 2 percent rate of economic growth associated with social security. We must not forget, however, that people retiring in the start-up phase of social security receive much more than a 2 percent return. Early retirees—those retiring in the 1950s, 1960s, and 1970s—received windfall gains that exceeded what they could have earned by saving privately. Under pay-as-you-go financing, early retirees benefit, whereas later generations lose. This suggests a possible defense of social security if a redistribution in favor of early retirees is considered desirable. Sometimes it is argued that early retirees are likely to be poorer than future generations, so that such a redistribution favors those with lower incomes. But the largest windfall gains went to those who were not particularly poor: Recall that higher benefits went to those with higher earnings.

These brief remarks only touch on the major issues, but they do suggest why some people find the rationale for social security to be far from conclusive. As an alternative, let us consider private provision for retirement. The first point to note is that social security would have to be phased out very gradually, for the same reason noted in our discussion of the level of benefits. If people no longer had to pay social security taxes, retirement benefits to those who were already retired could no longer be paid. An abrupt termination of benefits would be unfair to workers who had already retired, as well as to individuals approaching retirement who had made plans based on the expectation of social security benefits.

Milton Friedman proposed a gradual transition to a private voluntary system that would work in this way.[14] Retirement benefits already accumulated would be paid, but there would be no further accumulation of benefits in the future. People already retired would continue to receive their existing pensions (including cost-of-living adjustments). People near retirement would receive a sizable pension because they had already accumulated benefits implicitly owed them as a result of paying taxes over many years. Their pensions, however, would be smaller than if the social security system continued on its present course. At the other extreme, young people just entering the labor force would receive no retirement benefits under social security because they would not have accumulated benefits as a result of paying taxes. Thus, there would be a gradual reduction in the level of retirement benefits, and after 50 or 60 years, social security benefits would have fallen to zero. Note what this implies for taxes. Social security taxes would also gradually fall, but very slowly at first. Because retirement benefits to those already retired would be fixed, the required taxes would fall only slowly as retired persons died and were replaced by new retirees receiving lower benefits. The taxes paid after the adoption of Friedman's proposal, however, would *not* entitle one to added benefits on retirement; only the taxes paid before that time would be accompanied by promises of future benefits.

Such a gradual phasing out of social security is feasible, but would it be beneficial? Phasing out social security should increase private saving as younger workers save more for retirement, and that implies greater output and real income in subsequent years. Future generations would be better

---

[14]Milton Friedman, "Second Lecture," in Wilbur J. Cohen and Milton Friedman, *Social Security: Universal or Selective?* (Washington, D.C.: American Enterprise Institute, 1972), pp. 44–49.

off as they receive the high rate of return on real capital accumulation rather than the 2 percent return on social security. Workers who are young when the reform is implemented will also probably benefit, but to a lesser degree. Although they will pay (declining) social security taxes over their working lives, the increasing capital stock will gradually raise their before-tax incomes. Middle-aged workers are the ones who are most obviously harmed. They will continue to pay fairly high social security taxes until they reach retirement age, but their social security pensions will not reflect these taxes (only past taxes). Although there is also an offsetting feature from the greater capital accumulation leading to higher before-tax incomes, this offset will be small for those near the end of their working lives because it occurs only gradually over time. They are too old to receive much benefit from slowly rising before-tax incomes.

Thus, phasing out social security and relying on private provision for retirement would tend to harm middle-aged groups and benefit the young and future generations. Basically, it would reverse the process of introducing pay-as-you-go social security, which, as we saw, benefits those relatively old at that time and harms the young and future generations. Whether this reform is desirable is debatable, but it is one way to alleviate the future crisis in social security financing. Because of the political factors discussed earlier, however, such a reform seems unlikely to be adopted.

Review Questions and Problems

1. How does an unfunded, or pay-as-you-go, social security system differ from a funded system?

2. In what two ways does the social security program redistribute income? Who are the main beneficiaries of each type of redistribution? Who is harmed by each type of redistribution?

3. Viewed as a method of providing for retirement, does social security offer an attractive rate of return?

4. How social security affects saving is a controversial issue. What are the various reasons why it might or might not affect saving? How do you think it affects saving? Defend your answer.

5. If social security does affect saving adversely, this effect will be important in determining who benefits and who is harmed by the system. Explain why.

6. One proposal for reforming social security is to have all retirees receive the same retirement benefits, instead of having the benefits depend on past earnings. What advantages and disadvantages would this reform have?

7. A common proposal for changing social security is to permit people who provide for their own retirement through private saving to resign from the system (and not pay social security taxes or receive social security benefits). Why not let all workers choose between staying in or resigning from the system?

8. Analyze the consequences of a further increase in the retirement age from 67 to 70 under social security. Is this reform a desirable one for the system?

9. One proposal to reduce social security benefits is to have benefits inversely related to the level of income of retirees, i.e., to have lower social security benefits for those who have higher private pensions or other sources of income. Analyze the effects of this proposal.

10. Does the political process produce too large a social insurance system? If so, what reforms would lead to a better political outcome?

11. From a public choice perspective, describe the problem social security creates when the ratio of retirees to workers increases as is expected to happen in a couple of decades.

12. At the time you retire, how do you think the social security system will differ from the way it now operates? *Why* do you think it will have been changed?

Supplementary Readings

AARON, HENRY J. *Economic Effects of Social Security.* Washington, D.C.: The Brookings Institution, 1982.

AARON, HENRY J., BARRY P. BOSWORTH, and GARY BURTLESS. *Can America Afford to Grow Old?* Washington, D.C.: The Brookings Institution, 1989.

AUERBACH, ALAN J., and LAWRENCE J. KOTLIKOFF. "Simulating Alternative Social Security Responses to the Demographic Transition." *National Tax Journal,* 38:158–168 (June 1985).

CAMPBELL, COLIN, ed. *Controlling the Cost of Social Security.* Washington, D.C.: American Enterprise Institute, 1982.

COHEN, WILBUR J., and MILTON FRIEDMAN. *Social Security: Universal or Selective?* Washington, D.C.: American Enterprise Institute, 1972.

FELDSTEIN, MARTIN S. "Social Security, Induced Retirement and Aggregate Capital Accumulation." *Journal of Political Economy,* 82(5):905–926 (Sept./Oct. 1974).

—— "Toward a Reform of Social Security." *Public Interest,* 40:75–95 (Summer 1975).

HURD, MICHAEL D. "Research on the Elderly: Economic Status, Retirement, and Consumption and Saving." *Journal of Economic Literature,* 28:565–637 (June 1990).

LESNOY, SELIG D., and DEAN R. LEIMER. "Social Security and Private Saving: Theory and Historical Evidence." *Social Security Bulletin,* 48(1):14–30 (Jan. 1985).

WEAVER, CAROLYN L., ed. *Social Security's Looming Surpluses.* Washington, D.C.: AEI Press, 1990.

Government and the Distribution of Income

*W*E HAVE EXAMINED SEVERAL GOVERNMENT EXPENDITURE PROGRAMS that have significant effects on the distribution of income, not always to the advantage of low-income households. However, it is clear that among the major goals of government policies—expenditure policies especially—are the provisions of financial and other forms of assistance to the poor and possibly the redistribution of income from upper-income groups to middle-income groups as well. Have government policies reduced economic inequality and the number of persons living in poverty? There are many policies that have important effects on the distribution of income, and it is necessary to take a broad perspective and evaluate their combined effect as we examine that fundamental question.

We begin, however, with a consideration of perhaps an even more fundamental question: *Should* the government redistribute income? Then we review the major expenditure policies affecting the income distribution, and we conclude by investigating how economic inequality and poverty are measured. In the next chapter, we take a more careful look at some of the economic effects of redistributive policies.

Arguments for Government Redistribution

The Utilitarian Argument

If the government is deciding whether to give $100 to Ms. Rich or Mr. Poor, do you think the needier person should get the funds? If so, you are probably basing your position instinctively on what economists call *utilitarian-*

ism. Utilitarianism holds that the desirability of a social policy is to be judged by its effects on the well-being, or *utility,* of individuals in society. *Social welfare* is thought to depend on the utilities of all members of society. Historically, the utilitarians of the nineteenth century saw social welfare as the sum of the utilities of the individuals. Social arrangements were to be judged on how they affected the sum of utilities, and the goal was to make that sum as large as possible (i.e., to "maximize social welfare"). If $100 added more to the utility of Mr. Poor than it would to the utility of Ms. Rich, utilitarianism called for the money to be given to Mr. Poor.

To give more concrete content to the utilitarian argument for redistribution, it is necessary to make some assumptions: (1) Each individual's utility (well-being) depends on his or her income. Specifically, total utility increases as income increases but at a diminishing rate; the marginal utility of income is declining. This result means that $100 will add more to your well-being if your income is $10,000 than if it is $50,000, because your marginal utility will be higher in the former case. (2) All individuals have the same utility function relating income to utility. Two people with the same income are equally well off (same total utility), while a third person with a higher income is better off. (3) There is a fixed total amount of income in society. This means that the amount of income is not affected by how it is divided among persons.

These three assumptions imply that social welfare is increased when income is taken from someone with a higher income and given to someone with a lower income. Taking $1,000 from a millionaire reduces his or her utility by less than it adds to the utility of an impecunious person (because marginal utility is lower for the millionaire) and therefore increases the sum of utilities. Indeed, the logic of the utilitarian position implies that *income should be redistributed until all persons have equal incomes.* As long as there is any inequality, those with higher incomes will have lower marginal utilities, and a redistribtuion to those with lower incomes will raise social welfare.

One major objection to this argument is that total income is not fixed but is reduced by the policies used to redistribute income. This is probably true, obviously so if we consider complete equalization of incomes. In that case, a person's income does not depend on whether he or she works or not, so why work? If none work, there will be no income to distribute. While this argument destroys the presumption in favor of complete equality of incomes, it is possible to use utilitarian logic to argue for some redistribution even if total income falls somewhat. Another objection is that there is no way to verify objectively that individual utility functions are the same, and therefore it is not permissible to compare one person's utility loss with another's gain. This issue is complicated further when we recognize that utility does not depend solely on income but also on age, health, job, friends, hobbies, and so on. One can argue, however, as an ethical position that social policy should treat people *as if* they have the same utility functions.

Despite the criticisms that can be leveled against utilitarianism, it seems likely that much support for redistributive policies is ultimately based on exactly such considerations, whether it is called utilitarianism or "fairness." Many people instinctively feel that moderating income inequalities will increase social welfare as they individually view it.

The Contractarian Approach

The philosophical approach known as *contractarian theory* dates back at least to the seventeenth century, but we will focus on its more recent incarnation in the work of John Rawls,[1] who uses it to develop strong egalitarian conclusions. In attempting to derive principles that should guide a just society, Rawls asks us to think of what principles people would agree to (contract to) if they were in an "original position." In this imaginary situation, people do not know what their places in society will be. The idea is to get people to abstract from considerations of personal advantage that may tinge our judgments when we already know our position in society and therefore help us arrive at more unbiased conclusions. Thus, you are to imagine that you might be born healthy or sickly, intelligent or retarded, male or female, have wealthy or poor parents, and so on. Given that choice setting, what types of social policies would you like to see operating in this society?

When it comes to distributional issues, Rawls argues that people would opt for arrangements that reduce income inequalities. The basic motivation is the same as for the purchase of insurance. In the original position, operating behind a veil of ignorance as to your actual position, you run the risk of being a person lacking the ability or skills necessary to earn much income. In order to guard against that eventuality, you would like to see mechanisms that provide income to such persons, presumably a government redistribution policy. Rawls actually goes on to argue that all people will agree to a specific amount of redistribution: that which maximizes the well-being of the worst-off person in society. That particular argument has been widely criticized, but one can reject it and still conclude that most people in the original position would choose social policies embodying some redistribution.

In effect, contract theory invites us to try to put ourselves in other people's shoes as we decide whether redistribution is desirable. Aside from the practical difficulty of doing that, it seems clear that people would not all agree on the amount or type of redistribution considered desirable. Nonetheless, many do find this approach an appealing way to arrive at relatively impartial decisions, and they conclude from it that some degree of redistribution is desirable.

Redistribution as a Public Good

Raising the incomes of the poor by making transfers to them may have the characteristics of a public good. If many of the nonpoor feel (for whatever reason) that higher incomes for the poor are desirable, then the income level of the poor is a good that simultaneously affects the well-being of many

---

[1]John Rawls, *The Theory of Justice* (Cambridge, Mass.: Harvard University Press, 1971).

nonpoor persons. It is quite similar to national defense because actions that raise the incomes of the poor benefit not only the poor but also some (or all) of the nonpoor. If the nonpoor have a sufficiently large demand for helping the poor, a redistribution of income from the nonpoor to the poor *will benefit both groups.* Under these circumstances, there is an efficiency case to be made for government redistribution.

If the nonpoor want to help the poor, however, why not make private transfers individually on a voluntary basis rather than have the government perform this function? Where is the case for redistribution *by government*? The answer, of course, is the free rider problem. Too small a volume of voluntary transfers—just as with national defense—would be supported by private contributions. Suppose, for example, that each of 10 million nonpoor persons would be willing to pay $1,000 if the combined incomes of the poor were increased by $5 billion. No single nonpoor person would voluntarily make a transfer because a $1,000 transfer by itself would not make a dent in the extent of poverty—just as one car equipped with pollution controls would not perceptibly clean up the environment. Yet all the nonpoor would be better off if the government levied a tax of $500 on each and transferred the revenue ($5 billion) to the poor; each of the nonpoor would obtain an outcome worth $1,000 at a cost of $500. As this example suggests, there can be benefits to both the nonpoor and the poor from redistribution by government.

Exactly why nonpoor persons have these altruistic feelings about helping the poor is immaterial; it is enough that they do. And opinion polls do indicate a willingness on the part of many nonpoor persons to pay taxes to help the poor. However, the critical question is not the existence of altruism by the nonpoor but how quantitatively important it is. The nonpoor may genuinely care about the poor, but if each nonpoor person was willing to pay only $250 (rather than the $1,000 in our previous example), then collectively they would receive benefits of only $2.5 billion if $5 billion is transferred to the poor; the nonpoor would be worse off, and the public good argument would hold that the redistribution should not take place. Just as with other public goods, it is difficult to determine the position of the demand curve.

Arguments Against Government Redistribution

Justice of Market Outcomes and Processes

Any evaluation of the desirability of redistribution should begin with an explanation of how incomes are determined in the absence of government redistributive policies. In a competitive market economy, personal incomes are generated through the sales of productive inputs (e.g., labor, capital). A well-established result of economic analysis is that input prices in competitive markets tend to equal the marginal value products of the inputs; each input is paid an amount equal to the value consumers place on that input's contribution to output. In short, each person gets an income equal to what he or she contributes to the total income "pie." If it is considered fair for a person to take out of the total income pie an amount equal to what he or she adds to it, then the distribution of income generated by competitive markets would be equitable and any government redistribution would be inequitable.

Few people accept this conclusion without qualifications. The problem centers on whether the initial distribution of resources (in a broad sense, including human abilities) is just. A person born mentally retarded, with chronic health problems, raised by a single alcoholic parent, may well be paid his or her marginal value product in competitive markets, but does that small income constitute fairness? The ultimate unfairness suggested here is in the distribution of resources people bring to the market, which perhaps can be changed very little, but we can alter the market outcome to alleviate nature's unfairness to some degree.

A related argument focuses on the market *process* rather than on the results. Most arguments tend to focus on the results; whether the distribution of income is just is evaluated without reference to the process that generated that distribution. However, it can be argued that the fairness of the distribution of income should be judged by whether the process that produced it is fair. In markets, that process is based on voluntary exchange. People do not acquire their incomes coercively; other people choose to give them those incomes. Many people see voluntary exchange as a just process. Nonetheless, there is still the possibility that a just process can produce unjust results if the starting positions of people—what they bring to the market to exchange—are unjustly distributed.

It would probably be going too far to reject completely these arguments showing that markets are fair. After all, the market does tend to reward ambition, hard work, foresight, honesty, and perseverance and to penalize (or reward less) laziness, ineptitude, and dishonesty. For people in reasonably comparable initial circumstances, the proposition that the market distribution is just seems reasonable. (Would you accept market-determined incomes as fair for students in a college class?) Where the arguments fail is for those people severely disadvantaged by nature or circumstances.

Welfare Costs of Redistributive Policies

Virtually all redistributive policies produce inefficiencies in resource allocation, that is, they have welfare costs. The exact form of the inefficiency varies with the policy. Minimum wage laws produce unemployment, social security may encourage early retirement and reduce saving, welfare benefits reduce incentives to work, and so on. These adverse effects provide the basis for an argument against redistribution, especially if they are large enough.

Unless efficiency is our only goal, however, the fact that redistributive policies entail welfare costs is not a strong enough reason to oppose all redistribution. To see this, note that although the inefficiencies can take many forms, they all boil down to increasing the true cost of raising the well-being of those who benefit from the redistribution. If there were no inefficiency, increasing the income of the poor by $1 would necessitate a $1 reduction in the income of the nonpoor; the cost to the nonpoor of raising the income of the poor by $1 is $1. When there are inefficiencies from the redistributive policy, the cost to the nonpoor of increasing the income of the poor by $1 will be greater than $1. The cost might be, for example, $1.50, with the extra $0.50 being the welfare cost of the redistributive policy.

Thus, to say that a redistributive policy is inefficient is just to say that the cost of redistribution is greater than $1 per dollar of benefit to the poor. That does not prove that the policy is undesirable. If the cost is $2, for example, a utilitarian would still favor the redistribution if he or she believes that the marginal utility of income for the poor is more than twice as large as the marginal utility of income for the nonpoor, for then the utility gain to the poor would exceed the utility loss to the nonpoor.

Of course, there is an extreme case where the welfare cost is so large that all would agree redistribution is undesirable. That occurs when the attempt to redistribute undermines efficiency so much that it leaves both the poor and the nonpoor worse off. This possibility highlights the importance of having some idea of how large the welfare costs of redistribution are, something we will discuss in the next chapter.

Government Failure

In discussing public choice, we introduced the concept of government failure, the possibility that imperfections in the political process will tend to produce inefficient and/or inequitable policies. To the extent that this outcome applies to redistributive policies, it constitutes an argument against relying on government to redistribute income. In its extreme form, the argument is that the redistributive policies adopted by the political process may be worse than doing nothing.

Government redistributive policies can have two undesired effects. The first is that such policies are inefficient, as just explained. Of course, all policies are inefficient to some degree, but the possibility emphasized by this public choice argument is that the actual policies may be more inefficient than is necessary. The other undesired effect is that government redistribution may not concentrate the benefits on the right people. All of the arguments for redistribution suggest that those at the bottom of the income distribution should be the primary targets for assistance. Despite these arguments, many policies actually redistribute substantial sums to nonpoor persons. Social security has redistributed to the nonpoor retirees in the start-up phase, subsidies to higher education benefit disproportionately wealthy and middle-class students and their families, and agricultural subsidies provide most of their benefits to wealthy farmers. These outcomes suggest that relying on government to redistribute income will not always result in policies that target benefits on the poor.

This is a difficult argument to evaluate because it suggests that we have to evaluate how well government functions by considering all policies at once.

The fact that some policies actually hurt the poor is not conclusive, for there are obviously several that do benefit the poor. But clearly, the more we view the political process as flawed, the less we would wish to rely on it to redistribute income (or do anything else, for that matter).

Weighing the Pros and Cons

Economics cannot demonstrate that one distribution of income is "better" than another. Indeed, the concept of an "optimal" or "best" distribution of income must be firmly rejected. Different distributions of income involve gains in well-being for some at the expense of others; to judge such changes requires relying in part on value judgments that cannot be objectively demonstrated to be true or false. This does not imply that economics cannot aid people in making better-informed decisions in this matter. Many factual and analytical questions can be resolved, at least in part, through the use of economics.

In view of the many factors to be considered, it is difficult for an individual to arrive at a well-reasoned and consistent view of what his or her values suggest is an appropriate redistributive policy by government. In weighing the benefits and costs of redistribution, one piece of advice can be offered: Remember to evaluate these benefits and costs at the margin. The marginal benefit you perceive from the government's redistributing the first $5 billion to the poor is likely to be quite large: It could literally be a life-or-death matter. The marginal benefit of increasing the volume of redistribution from $200 billion to $205 billion will probably be much smaller. The opposite is true for the marginal costs. At low levels of redistribution, the marginal costs due to efficiency losses or inequities in government programs are likely to be small. The marginal costs of moving to complete equality will rise at increasing rates. Thus, marginal benefits fall and marginal costs rise with increased amounts of redistribution.

No suggestion is being made, however, that there is an objectively best amount of redistribution where marginal benefits and costs are equal. We are only considering what is a logical framework for an individual to utilize: The marginal benefits and costs are those factors that, according to your values, are advantages and disadvantages. Other people's values will differ. Still, recognizing the importance of thinking in terms of marginal changes will forestall much unproductive speculation about whether the arguments for government redistribution are better or worse than the arguments against it. The relative importance of the arguments depends on how much redistribution is being contemplated. If the government were not now redistributing any income to the poor, we suspect that virtually everyone would agree that some redistribution is desirable; marginal benefits are undoubtedly greater than marginal costs at low levels of redistribution. With the government already redistributing billions of dollars annually, however, there would likely be much less agreement that a further increase is desirable.

This brings us to the question of how government is currently affecting the distribution of income. How unequally are incomes distributed, and how does government policy affect the degree of inequality? The remainder of this chapter is devoted to this surprisingly complex question.

Major Income Transfer Programs

There are many government expenditure programs that affect the distribution of income, but here we focus on those generally acknowledged to have the most pronounced effects. Thus, Table 8–1 identifies the most important income transfer programs and gives total expenditures (federal plus state, where applicable) for four years beginning in 1965, the time President Lyndon Johnson declared a "War on Poverty." The programs are divided into two categories: social insurance and welfare programs.

Social insurance programs base benefits at least partly on past contributions. This category includes social security, unemployment insurance, and Medicare, all of which we have discussed. As you recall, people do not have to be poor to receive benefits under these programs, and in fact a large share of the outlays do benefit nonpoor persons. Nonetheless, these programs do tend to redistribute income to some degree, as we saw in discussing the formula that determines social security benefits. Although the extent to which social insurance programs actually redistribute income is not completely clear, there is little doubt that they differentially benefit those with low incomes to some degree.

With the second category of transfer program, welfare programs, it is clear that benefits are concentrated on low-income persons. In fact, the distinguishing characteristic of a *welfare program,* as we use the term, is that the eligibility for benefits depends on having a low income. In this category we list the six programs that form the core of the U.S. welfare system. Four of these (AFDC, SSI, Medicaid, and food stamps) have been referred to in previous chapters. The two new programs are housing assistance (not a single program, but several that together provide or subsidize housing) and the earned income tax credit, which is a transfer program for working low-income families that we will examine in the next chapter.

Looking first at the bottom of the table, we can see that in 1991, total expenditures on all of these income transfer programs together amounted to $593.4 billion, or 11.5 percent of NNP. This is more than twice the share of NNP devoted to these programs in 1965. Note that social insurance programs account for (in 1991) more than two thirds of the total expenditures. This, however, is significantly lower than their share in 1965, when social

Table 8–1   *Expenditures on Major Income Transfer Programs (in $ billions)*

	1965	1973	1980	1991
Social insurance:				
Cash benefits				
Social security (OASDI)	$16.5	$ 48.3	$117.1	$269.0
Unemployment insurance	2.5	5.4	18.0	27.1
Veterans' benefits	4.1	12.0	21.2	31.3
Railroad retirement	1.1	2.4	4.7	7.5
In-kind benefits				
Medicare	NE	9.5	35.0	105.5
Subtotal	24.2	77.6	196.0	440.4
Percentage of NNP	4.0%	6.8%	8.7%	8.5%
Welfare				
Cash benefits				
Aid to Families with Dependent				
Children (AFDC)	1.7	7.0	14.0	20.4
Supplemental Security Income (SSI)*	2.7	3.3	6.4	14.7
Earned income tax credit	NE	NE	1.3	4.9
In-kind benefits				
Medicaid**	0.5	9.1	25.2	77.1
Food stamps	0.0	2.5	9.1	18.7
Housing assistance	0.3	1.6	5.3	17.2
Subtotal	5.2	23.5	61.3	153.0
Percentage of NNP	0.9%	2.1%	2.7%	3.0%
Total expenditures	29.4	101.1	257.3	593.4
Total expenditures as a percentage of NNP	4.9%	8.9%	11.5%	11.5%

NE = Nonexistent.
*Aid to the Blind, Aid to the Permanently and Totally Disabled, and Old Age Assistance in 1965 and 1973. SSI was implemented in 1974.
**Medical Aid to the Aged in 1965.

Source: Office of Management and Budget, *The Budget of the United States Government and Appendix* (Washington, D.C.: U.S. Government Printing Office), fiscal years 1975, 1982, and 1993; 1965 data from Robert Plotnik and Felicity Skidmore, *Progress Against Poverty* (New York: Academic Press, 1975).

insurance spending was more than 80 percent of the total. The change has occurred because of the more rapid growth in spending on welfare programs, which has risen from $5.2 billion in 1965 to $153 billion in 1991, or from 0.9 to 3.0 percent of NNP. Note that about half of total welfare spending in 1991 was on Medicaid alone.

A significant development since 1965 has been, therefore, rapid growth in income transfer spending, especially on programs that concentrate their benefits on low-income persons. Another notable change has been the increasing importance of in-kind transfers. Table 8–1 also subdivides the programs into those providing cash benefits and those providing in-kind transfers. (Recall that in-kind transfers are subsidies for the consumption of specific goods and services, like food stamps and Medicaid.) In 1965, less than 3 percent of total income transfer expenditures were on in-kind transfers, but by 1991 in-kind transfers represented 37 percent of the total. The change is even more dramatic in the welfare category. In-kind welfare benefits were 16 percent of the total in 1965 but nearly 75 percent in 1991. *Welfare assistance was mostly in the form of cash in 1965, but today the bulk of the much larger welfare spending takes the form of subsidies for the consumption of particular goods and services.*

It should also be noted that the rate of increase in spending has been slower since 1980. Although much popular discussion suggests that welfare spending in particular was slashed during the Reagan–Bush years, the table shows that this is untrue. Not only did real expenditures on welfare rise, from $101 billion in 1980 (in 1991 dollars) to $153 billion in 1991, but as a percentage of NNP spending went up from 2.7 to 3.0 percent.

There are many other smaller income transfer programs that are not listed in Table 8–1, especially in the welfare category. In fact, in 1990 there were 15 additional programs (that restrict benefits to those with low incomes; most are in-kind programs) with expenditures in excess of $1 billion each.[2] These include programs such as Head Start ($1.9 billion), low-income energy assistance ($1.6 billion), Pell grants ($4.5 billion), and training for disadvantaged adults and youth ($1.7 billion). Total spending on these programs was $50 billion, and the figure for 1991 is at least $55 billion (of which about $45 billion provided in-kind benefits). Combining this with the $153 billion figure from Table 8–1 gives us an estimate of $208 billion for expenditures on welfare programs in 1991, or 4.1 percent of NNP.

To provide some perspective on just how large a commitment to helping low-income persons an expenditure of $208 billion is, we note that there were 35.7 million persons counted as officially poor in 1991 (as we discuss further later). The figure of $208 billion is more than enough by itself to provide incomes to these 35.7 million to remove them from poverty. In fact, it is enough to provide each poor family with an income that is 37 percent above its poverty threshold, and this does not count any other sources of income, like social security or earnings. For each four-person poor family, for example, we could provide a transfer of more than $19,000 (in comparison with the poverty threshold of $13,924 for a family of four), and similarly for different-sized poor families. Why there were still 35.7 million poor persons after spending this $208 billion is a question we will look at later. The point here is that this sum is a sizable commitment of resources relative to the number of low-income persons.

[2]Congressional Research Service, The Library of Congress, *Cash and Noncash Benefits for Persons with Limited Income: Eligibility Rules, Recipient and Expenditure Data, FY 1988–90* (Washington, D.C.: U.S. Government Printing Office, September 30, 1991), Table 2.

Income Distribution and Poverty

The U.S. Bureau of the Census each year surveys a sample of about 60,000 households, and the results provide much of the information we have about the distribution of income and the number of persons in poverty. In this section we will discuss the most widely used estimates provided by the Census Bureau. First, however, we should note that the definition of *income* used includes only income received as money. It includes not only wage and salary income, dividends, and interest, but also government cash transfers such as social security, unemployment insurance, and AFDC. Income received in noncash form is not counted, including such important items as in-kind transfers, employer-provided health insurance, and the value of owner-occupied housing. In addition, it should be noted that incomes are measured before payment of direct personal taxes such as income taxes and the employee portion of social security payroll taxes.

Table 8–2 is a very common way of summarizing information about the distribution of income. This tabulation covers only families (two or more related persons living together)[3] and is constructed by grouping families into five income classes, each containing 20 percent of all families. The lowest fifth, or *quintile,* of families therefore contains the 20 percent of families with the lowest incomes. The total income of all families in each quintile is then expressed as a percentage of the total income of all families.

To see how to interpret the resulting percentage shares of income, consider the last row in the table, which gives the distribution for 1991. In 1991, the lowest fifth had a combined income of 4.5 percent of total income for the entire population of families, the second fifth had 10.7 percent, and so on up to the top fifth, with 44.2 percent; the shares sum to 100 percent. It is possible to manipulate these shares to get a better understanding of how much inequality they represent. For example, the average income of families in the lowest fifth was 22.5 percent of the average income of all families. (This is equal to 4.5/20, since if 20 percent of the families have 20 percent of the income, their average income equals the overall average.) Similarly, the top quintile had an average income of 2.2 times the average of all families (44.2/20) and had an average that was nearly 10 times the average for families in the lowest fifth (44.2/4.5). Most people interpret these numbers as showing that there is a substantial degree of economic inequality in the United States.

---

[3]The Census Bureau also publishes distributions of income for households, which include not only multiperson families but also single persons. The household distribution can be somewhat misleading, however, because there are large differences in the number of persons per household in different income classes. For example, the top income class has 65 percent more people in it than the bottom, even though they both have the same number of households. In the family distribution, the top income class has only 12 percent more people, so the classes are more comparable.

Table 8–2   *Distribution of Money Income Among Families*

	Percentage Share					Median Income (1991 dollars)*
Year	Lowest Fifth	Second Fifth	Third Fifth	Fourth Fifth	Highest Fifth	
1929	3.5%	9.0%	13.8%	19.3%	54.4%	NA
1947	5.0	11.9	17.0	23.1	43.0	$17,004
1960	4.8	12.2	17.8	24.0	41.3	23,767
1970	5.5	12.2	17.6	23.8	40.9	32,540
1980	5.2	11.5	17.5	24.3	41.5	34,790
1991	4.5	10.7	16.6	24.1	44.2	35,939

*Converted to 1991 dollars using CPI-UX1.

Source: The 1929 data are from Herman Miller, *Income Distribution in the United States* (Washington, D.C.: U.S. Bureau of the Census), 1966, p. 21. Other data from U.S. Bureau of the Census, Current Population Reports, Series P-60 (Washington, D.C.: U.S. Government Printing Office), various issues.

The range of absolute incomes in each income class may also be of interest. In 1991, the lowest quintile was composed of families with total incomes below $17,000. The second quintile includes incomes up to $29,111, the third up to $43,000, and the fourth up to $62,991. Thus, families with incomes above $62,991 were in the wealthiest fifth of families in 1991. This often surprises many people, because most families with incomes in the $60,000–$100,000 range do not think of themselves as particularly wealthy. It should also be mentioned that most families in the top quintile have incomes below $100,000; only 5 percent of all families (one fourth of the top quintile) have incomes in excess of $100,000.

Table 8–2 also gives estimates for a number of earlier years, so we can examine the trend over time. First, note from the last column how real median income has changed. Between 1947 and 1992, real median income more than doubled, but most of the increase occurred by 1970. In the 23 years between 1947 and 1970, real median income rose from $17,004 to $32,540, an increase of more than 90 percent. In the 21 years between 1970 and 1991, by contrast, real median income rose by only 10 percent. *This slowdown in the growth rate of real incomes is one of the most important economic events in recent decades,* and one we will refer to several times later on.

Now consider the degree of inequality over the years covered in the table. There was a significant movement toward greater equality between 1929 and 1947, but since 1947 there has been relatively little change. Comparing 1991 and 1947, for example, we find that no quintile's share had changed by more than 1.2 percentage points. Looking more closely, however, you can see that there has been an increase in inequality in more recent years. Between 1980 and 1991, for example, the top-to-bottom quintile share ratio rose from 8 to

1 to 10 to 1. It may be too much to call this a "surge in inequality," as one prominent economist has done, but there is no doubt that inequality has been rising in recent years. Taking a longer view, however, the distribution is still more equal than in 1929 and not greatly different than in 1947.

The quintile share that concerns many people the most is, of course, the lowest one, since that quintile contains the families with the lowest incomes. That this share is lower today than in 1960 is bothersome. It is also surprising in view of the enormous increase in government income transfer programs that has occurred since that time.

Poverty

Few statistics emanating from Washington attract more attention than the estimated number of persons living in poverty. The same Census Bureau survey that gives us estimates of incomes of all persons and families (as discussed earlier) also classifies a certain number of Americans as poor. Poverty-level incomes, or poverty *thresholds,* are set for families of various sizes and compositions. There are, in fact, 48 different poverty thresholds (or poverty lines) that vary with family size, age of householder, and number of children. For example, the weighted average poverty threshold for a family of four in 1991—the most frequently cited figure—was $13,924. For a single nonelderly person, the poverty line was $7,086, and for a family with nine or more persons it was $27,942. The poverty thresholds are adjusted upward each year to reflect increases in the cost of living; the real poverty thresholds are not intended to change over time.

Table 8–3 gives the Census Bureau estimates of the number of poor persons for several years, as well as their proportion of the total population. The total number of poor persons declined from 39.9 million in 1960 to 35.7 million in 1991. Since the population grew over this period, the reduction is greater when expressed as the percentage who were poor, falling from 22.2 to 14.2 percent. Poverty did not fall at a steady pace over this period,

Table 8–3   *The Poverty Population*

Year	Number (millions)	As a Percentage of the Population
1960	39.9	22.2%
1966	28.5	14.7
1970	25.4	12.6
1980	29.3	13.0
1991	35.7	14.2

Source: U.S. Bureau of the Census, Current Population Reports Series P-60, *Poverty in the United States: 1991* (Washington, D.C.: U.S. Government Printing Office, 1992).

however. Most of the decline took place between 1960 and 1966. The rate did reach a low of 11.1 percent in 1973, but since 1980 it has never been below 12.8 percent (in 1989). The increase between 1989 and 1991 is largely attributable to the fact that 1991 was a recession year.

What is striking about these figures is the relationship between the poverty rates and government spending on income transfer programs. There has been a major increase in income transfers since the mid-1960s, yet the poverty rate was scarcely lower in 1991 than in 1966. The decline between 1960 and 1966 was not due significantly to government programs but rather to the economic growth that raised real wage rates and earnings during this period. Since 1970, economic growth has slowed considerably, and that is one reason why poverty has been so persistent. Nonetheless, it is surprising that the growth in spending on income transfer programs has had such a small apparent effect on the poverty rate. We will consider why this has been the case later.

Table 8–4 provides some information about the composition of the poverty population in 1991. (The poverty rates given are for the poor in each category as a percentage of all persons in that category.) Among the poor in families, note that more than half were in families headed by a female (no

Table 8–4   *Portrait of Official Poverty, 1991*

Person Category	Number (millions)	Poverty Rate (percent)
All persons	35.7	14.2%
White	23.7	11.3
Black	10.2	32.7
Hispanic*	6.3	28.7
Persons under 15 years old	12.5	22.4
Persons 65 years and older	3.8	12.4
All persons in families	27.1	12.8
Married-couple families	12.2	7.2
Families with female householder, no husband present	13.8	39.7
Number of persons in family		
One	7.8	21.1
Two	5.0	8.8
Three	5.4	11.6
Four	6.6	11.8
Five or more	10.1	18.8
Seven or more	3.0	33.3

*Persons of Hispanic origin may be of any race.

Source: U.S. Bureau of the Census, Current Population Reports Series P-60, *Poverty in the United States: 1991* (Washington, D.C.: U.S. Government Printing Office, 1992).

husband present). Of the 13.8 million poor persons in female-headed families, 8.1 million—nearly one fourth of the total poverty population—were in families where the female householder was under 18 years old. Female-headed families have not always represented such a large proportion of the poverty population. In 1960, three fourths of the poor in families were in married-couple families. It should also be noted that while the average size of poor families is not much different from the average size of all American families, one-person families and large families are disproportionately represented in the poverty population. In 1991, 10.1 million poor persons were in families with five or more persons, and 3.0 million were in families with seven or more persons.

How Much Economic Inequality Exists?

The Census Bureau's figures on money income distribution provide the factual basis for most discussions of economic inequality. In other words, the degree of inequality in money incomes is often interpreted as equivalent to the degree of economic inequality in standards of living. This is almost certainly untrue, and it is important to understand the shortcomings in the Census estimates because they are so often referred to in the news media and even in many scholarly analyses. At the outset, it should be stressed that we are not claiming that the Census figures are wrong; there is every reason to believe that *they accurately measure what they claim to measure.* However, there are two problems: (1) there are many components of income that are not measured (some of which would be extremely difficult to measure), and (2) there are unresolved conceptual problems about how to measure what we ultimately want: how well off people are, that is, what their "real" incomes are.

Let us begin by considering taxes and income in-kind. As we mentioned, the usual Census figures, such as those reported in Table 8–2, do not include income in-kind and measure incomes on a before-tax basis. Most analysts agree that a better measure of the standard of living people enjoy is provided by including income in-kind and subtracting taxes. Making these adjustments to the before-tax money income figures has the effect of lowering incomes at the top and raising incomes at the bottom. Indeed, there are now estimates from the Census Bureau itself that make these adjustments. Starting in 1988, the Census Bureau began to issue reports that develop these new estimates of income distribution and poverty. Unfortunately, the estimates in these reports are still not widely known, even though they are a definite improvement over the usual numbers.

The new estimates are available only for the incomes of *households,* as distinct from the family distribution discussed earlier. Households include families and unrelated (single) individuals; by incorporating single persons, who have lower incomes than families, the distribution is seen to be more unequal than that reported in Table 8–2. For example, in the family distribution, the ratio of top-quintile income to bottom-quintile income is 10 to 1; in the household distribution, it is 12 to 1. In this discussion, we will emphasize this ratio as indicative of the degree of inequality since estimates are not available for the middle three quintiles.

Table 8–5 begins, in the first row, with the current measure (before-tax money income) of the average income of households in the lowest and highest quintiles. The Census Bureau then makes a series of 14 adjustments to these numbers, which are here consolidated into four. Row 2 starts with the current measure, subtracts *all* transfers, and then adds *market* income in-kind (most importantly, employer-provided health insurance and annual income value of owner-occupied housing). The result can be thought of as the level of market income, before any taxes or transfers are incorporated. Note that on this basis, the top quintile has nearly 36 times the income of the bottom quintile. The next step is to subtract federal and state income taxes and payroll taxes. This reduces the average income of the top quintile by nearly $23,000 but reduces that of the bottom quintile by only $146; the result is that the ratio falls to 29 to 1. Then in row 4, cash transfers are added back, and in row 5, in-kind transfers are added. At this point, the top quintile has 8.4 times the income of the lowest quintile, a substantial reduction from the original 12 to 1 ratio.

The Census Bureau stops at this point, but there is one other adjustment that can and probably should be made. This relates to differences in household size. There are 1.95 persons per household in the lowest quintile

Table 8–5 Adjusted Income Measures for Households, 1991

Income Measure	Average Income, Lowest Quintile	Average Income, Highest Quintile	Ratio of Quintiles (highest/lowest)
1. Current measure	$7,272	$88,101	12.1
2. Adjusted market income before taxes and transfers	2,778	99,244	35.7
3. (Row 2) less taxes	2,632	76,494	29.1
4. (Row 3) + cash transfers	7,878	78,146	9.9
5. (Row 4) + in-kind transfers	9,416	78,825	8.4
6. (5)/persons per household	4,829	24,480	5.1

Source: U.S. Bureau of the Census, Current Population Reports, Series P-60, No. 182RD, *Measuring the Effect of Benefits and Taxes on Income and Poverty: 1979 to 1991* (Washington, D.C.: U.S. Government Printing Office, 1992), Tables F and G. Row 6 calculated by the author.

(many single persons here) but 3.22 persons per household in the top quintile. Thus, the income reported for the top quintile in row 5 supports 65 percent more people than the income of the bottom quintile. Row 6 adjusts for this difference by giving the average income per person for the quintiles, and on this basis the top quintile has only five times the income of the bottom quintile. (This adjustment is not as important quantitatively for the family distribution, where the top quintile has only 12 percent more persons than the bottom quintile.)

There is at least one basic problem with these adjustments, and that concerns the treatment of in-kind transfers. Note that the addition of in-kind transfers adds just over $1,500 to the average income in the lowest quintile. Excluding Medicare, the figure is $1,082, which amounts to only $20.7 billion for all households in the bottom quintile. Contrast this with the more than $160 billion in government spending on in-kind *welfare* programs in 1991 (see the discussion of Table 8–1). Even though some of this $160 billion goes to higher quintiles (e.g., Pell Grants), there is little doubt that at least half goes to the bottom quintile. For all quintiles together, only one fourth of the total spending on in-kind welfare programs (excluding Medicare) is counted as income by the Census Bureau.[4] The Census Bureau does not count many of the smaller programs, and for the major medical care programs it uses a procedure that counts as the income value an amount substantially less than it costs the government to provide the services. (In some cases, this results in estimating that Medicaid and Medicare have zero value to some recipients.) While there is controversy over exactly how to value medical subsidies, a good case can be made for using their market value. If this were done, and if all in-kind programs were included, the final household income figure for the lowest quintile would probably be at least $3,000 higher. This would result in the top quintile having only four times the income of the bottom quintile on a per person basis.

Even without adjusting the amount of in-kind transfers, Table 8–5 suggests that the combined effect of taxes and transfers redistributes income downward. Figure 8–1 shows this more clearly by giving the average net tax paid or transfer received for each quintile of households in 1990, where the estimates are based on the same procedures just described for Table 8–5. (Thus, only a small part of spending on in-kind transfers is included as income in the figure.) Households in the highest quintile paid $22,022 more in taxes than they received back in transfers, while households in the lowest quintile received $8,808 more in transfers than they paid in taxes. These estimates do not reflect, however, the full distributional effect of all taxes and expenditures. Only payroll and income taxes (which amount to about two thirds of all taxes) are included and only expenditures on cash and

---

[4]This is based on the report for 1989 (Census Bureau, *Measuring the Effect of Benefits and Taxes on Income and Poverty: 1989*), Table A, which shows total income from in-kind transfers (excluding Medicare) as $29.5 billion, and Congressional Research Service, *Cash and Noncash Benefits for Persons with Limited Income,* Table 1, which gives total spending on welfare in-kind programs of $136 billion for that year.

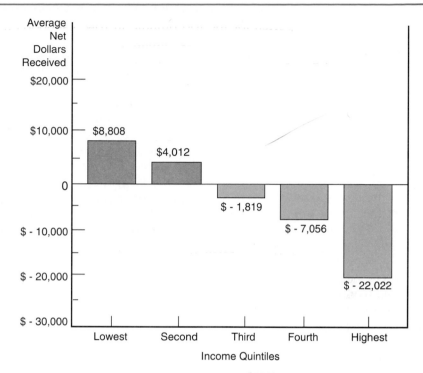

Figure 8–1 *Effects of taxes and transfers on income, 1990*
Source: *Economic Report of the President* (Washington, D.C.: U.S. Government
Printing Office, 1992), p. 137.

certain in-kind transfers (as discussed earlier). Nonetheless, the pattern suggested in the figure is almost certainly generally true: Taxes and transfers taken together redistribute income from high-income to low-income households.

Other Problems in Measuring Inequality

So far, we have only considered shortcomings in the official Census figures due to the treatment of taxes, income in-kind, and differences in household size. Adjusting for these things does make a major difference, but there are many other problems in trying to interpret the results as accurate measures of economic inequality. For example, there are a number of other government expenditure programs that provide benefits to households that are not counted at all. These include public schools and colleges, highways, police, defense, medical research, and many others. Arguably, the benefits from these programs should be counted as income to households, but the problem is how to do this. Another difficult conceptual issue is how to deal with differences in labor supply. There are great differences in how much house-holds in different income classes work for the incomes they receive. For example, annual hours of work for the highest quintile of households are more than five times greater than for the lowest quintile.[5] Since leisure has value (and work involves costs), some account should be taken of this pro-nounced difference. It is not clear exactly how that should be done, but it would presumably lead to a more equally distributed measure of income.

There is one other fundamental problem that a number of economists have emphasized, and that is the one-year accounting period that is empha-sized in conventional treatments. People's incomes change greatly over the course of a lifetime, and most move around quite a bit within the income distribution. College students, for example, may be treated as households falling in the lowest quintile, but in middle age they are likely to find them-selves in the highest quintile. According to one study, fully one third of all families move from one quintile to another from one year to the next.[6] Mo-bility is even greater over longer periods of time.

Many economists believe that in evaluating the degree of inequality, it is important to measure incomes over periods of time longer than a year; some feel that a lifetime measure would be the best. There are great difficulties in estimating lifetime incomes, but a couple of attempts have been made. One relates to income distribution in Canada, but since the Canadian annual dis-tribution is similar to the U.S. distribution, the results may be relevant for the United States. Table 8–6 gives the results. A word of warning: Lifetime incomes were not measured, but they were estimated using a computer model. Nonetheless the outcome is certainly provocative. Based on after-tax lifetime incomes, the share of the lowest quintile is 11.6 percent, 56 percent of the average lifetime income of all households. Moreover, the top quintile received less than three times the income of the bottom quintile, whereas on the basis of annual data the ratio is 9 to 1.

Another study used a unique data set that followed the same families over several years. Focusing on families headed by someone between 25 and 34 years of age in 1969, the study tabulated the incomes of these families over the next 16 years. Though this is not a full lifetime, the results are suggestive. Using the average income of each family over the 16 years, the study found that families in the top quintile received 35.8 percent of total income, while families in the lowest quintile received 8.6 percent, a ratio of about 4 to 1.[7]

---

[5]There are many reasons for this difference, mainly resulting from the different types of households that occupy the various quintiles. A large part of the lowest quintile con-sists of either elderly and retired persons or female-headed families on AFDC, whereas the top quintile is disproportionately middle-aged married couples with two earners. There are also more adults in the highest quintile than in the lowest quintile.

[6]Cited in *Economic Report of the President,* 1992, p 124.

[7]Edgar Browning, John Horowitz, and John Bishop, "Long-Run Economic Inequality," paper presented at the 1990 Annual Meetings of the Southern Economic Association, Orlando, Florida.

Table 8–6   *Annual versus Lifetime Income Distribution in Canada*

Income Class	Before-tax (percent)		After-tax (percent)	
	Annual	Lifetime	Annual	Lifetime
Lowest quintile	4.1%	10.4%	4.6%	11.6%
Second quintile	11.2	15.6	12.4	16.5
Third quintile	16.7	18.8	17.9	19.3
Fourth quintile	22.5	22.7	23.6	22.4
Highest quintile	45.5	32.4	41.5	30.2

Source: James Davies, France St.-Hilaire, and John Whalley, "Some Calculations of Lifetime Tax Incidence," *American Economic Review,* 74 (Sept. 1984). Calculated from Tables 1 and 2.

The incomes were measured on a before-tax basis and did not include in-kind transfers, so presumably the inequality in final incomes was even less.

One strong conclusion is suggested by the evidence we have discussed. *The degree of economic inequality among American households is substantially less than implied by the commonly used Census Bureau figures.* This is important because many policies are intended to reduce inequality, and our perception of how important it is to do this is strongly affected by our perception of how much inequality now exists. It also appears likely that government taxes and (especially) transfers, do tend to produce greater equality, although this judgment is not certain because we do not know what the income distribution would look like if these policies did not exist.

Up to this point we have been considering the degree of inequality that exists at a specific point in time. A conceptually separate issue is whether there has been a trend toward greater or less inequality over time. Frank Levy has investigated this question by adjusting the Census family income distributions in 1949 and 1984 for taxes, major forms of in-kind income, and family size differences. The results are given in Table 8–7. As can be seen, the adjustments result in diminished inequality in both years, but the reduction is greater in 1984. Thus, there is evidence of reduced inequality over this period, with the share of the bottom quintile rising from 5.8 to 7.3 percent, a 26 percent gain. The ratio of top to bottom incomes fell from 6.8 in 1949 to 5.0 in 1984. A study by Robert Haveman, which examined the effects of cash and in-kind transfers without adjusting for taxes or household size differences, found that the share of the lowest quintile in the household distribution increased by 3.5 percentage points between 1950 and 1985.[8]

Thus, it also seems clear that the conclusion of virtually unchanged inequality from the late 1940s to the present, suggested by the official Census figures in Table 8–2, is also incorrect. There has been a movement toward greater equality. This does not deny that there has been a disequalizing trend

[8]Robert Haveman, *Starting Even* (New York: Simon and Schuster, 1988), p. 111.

Table 8–7   *The Trend in Income Inequality*

	Family Income Distribution in 1949 (percent)				
	Lowest Quintile	*Second Quintile*	*Third Quintile*	*Fourth Quintile*	*Highest Quintile*
Census measure	4.5	11.9	17.3	23.5	42.7
Adjusted measure	5.8	13.1	18.6	23.2	39.3

	Family Income Distribution in 1984 (percent)				
	Lowest Quintile	*Second Quintile*	*Third Quintile*	*Fourth Quintile*	*Highest Quintile*
Census measusre	4.7	11.0	17.0	24.4	42.9
Adjusted measure	7.3	13.4	18.1	24.4	36.8

Source: Frank Levy, *Dollars and Dreams* (New York: Russell Sage Foundation, 1987), Tables 3.4 and 9.1.

in recent years, but the gains prior to that time have exceeded the losses since then.

How Much Poverty Exists?

The official poverty statistics suffer from many of the same shortcomings as the income distribution figures. Income is measured on a before-tax basis, and in-kind transfers are not counted. In addition, there is another significant problem. The poverty lines were intended to be increased in line with prices, so that they would represent unchanged real levels of income over time. Adjustments in the poverty thresholds are based on the consumer price index (CPI). During the periods of high inflation in the 1970s and early 1980s, however, the CPI overstated the rate of inflation because of the way it counted housing costs. Since the poverty thresholds were tied to the CPI, they were raised faster than increases in the real cost of living. This defect in the CPI was corrected in 1983, and since that time, inflation has been measured more accurately. However, the excessive increases in the poverty lines prior to 1983 were not rolled back; it is estimated that today the poverty lines are 8 percent higher than they would be if the earlier inflation had been measured using the new methodology. Thus, the poverty lines today represent a higher real income than they did when they were originally formulated in 1965.

As with the income distribution data, the Census Bureau has attempted to make adjustments to deal with these issues in recent years. Making the adjustments described in Table 8–5 (for taxes and in-kind income) and correcting the poverty lines for the mismeasurement of inflation, it estimates an adjusted poverty rate of 8.9 percent in 1991. (That was a recession year, and poverty rises during a recession; the comparable poverty rate for 1989 was 7.6 percent.) The official poverty rate, as reported in Table 8–3, was 14.2 percent in 1991. Even though the 8.9 percent figure is probably a better measure of the poverty rate, the higher figure continues to be the official poverty rate since poverty is officially defined based on before-tax money incomes. That in-kind transfers were not counted as income in defining poverty originally in 1965 is probably due to the fact that in-kind transfers were almost nonexistent at that time (see Table 8–1). Now that they constitute three fourths of welfare spending, there is no doubt that they should be counted as income.

There are two reasons for thinking that even the 8.9 percent figure overstates the poverty rate. The first is one discussed earlier: The Census counts as income only about one fourth of welfare spending on in-kind transfers. Counting all in-kind transfers would probably have significantly reduced the poverty rate. Second, there are problems with underreporting of income in the Census survey, especially transfer income. This may be due to the fact that households are surveyed in March and asked to recall their incomes for the previous year. How severe this underreporting is can be suggested by another income survey conducted by the Census Bureau, the Survey of Income and Program Participation (SIPP), which interviews households each month. Estimates from the SIPP survey are widely regarded as more reliable, and they routinely show poverty rates that are 25 percent lower than the official Census estimates.

Thus, there is reason to think that the 8.9 percent poverty rate is too high. One can only speculate what the poverty rate would turn out to be if all the income of the low-income population could be accurately measured. Our guess is that the poverty rate for 1991 would, on that basis, be under 6 percent. In any event, it is clear that it would be significantly lower than the official 14.2 percent rate.

There are critics who claim that the official poverty estimate is too low. One concern is that the homeless population is not counted at all. Only three national studies have attempted to measure the homeless population, with estimates ranging from 228,000 to 600,000.[9] Even using the higher figure, however, this would not significantly increase the official poverty count.

More generally, these critics argue that the poverty thresholds themselves are too low. It is sometimes suggested, for example, that the poverty thresholds be set at one half of median family income. If this definition is used, many more persons, of course, would be counted as poor. But arguing that

[9]See Gordon Berlin and William McAllister, "Homelessness," in *Setting Domestic Priorities,* ed. by H. J. Aaron and C. L. Schultze (Washington, D.C.: Brookings Institution, 1992), pp. 63–99.

the poverty lines should be raised is quite different from contending that estimates of the poverty population are too low given the real standard of living stipulated in the original definitions of poverty. The evidence strongly suggests that the official poverty rate greatly overstates the number of people who fall below the original poverty thresholds. Whether these thresholds themselves should be raised is a different issue, and in evaluating it we should consider exactly what it means to have a poverty-level income.

Many people have a perception of the poor as hungry and malnourished, and as living in dilapidated, rat-infested, overcrowded housing. This is not the case, at least for the average poor person. Consider that low-income households (the bottom quintile, actually a larger group than the official poverty population) spent 80 cents on food for every $1.00 spent by the median American household in 1988 (and 32 cents of that was spent in restaurants). There is, in fact, little difference in calorie consumption or in the nutritional adequacy of diets between the poverty population and other households.[10]

In terms of housing, nearly 40 percent of officially poor households own their own homes, with a median value of 58 percent of the national average. Considering all the poor, only 8 percent live in overcrowded conditions, according to the Census Bureau, with nearly two thirds having more than two rooms per person. Poor Americans average 1.8 rooms per person, compared to 1.25 for the *average* (not poor) Italian, 1.4 for the average Swiss, and 1.25 for the average Japanese.

Moreover, the homes and apartments of the poor are typically in good condition, with only 5 percent of all housing reported as having "moderate upkeep" problems by the Census Bureau (only 1 percent had severe upkeep problems) compared to 2 percent of the housing of the nonpoor. Fifty-three percent of poor households have air conditioning. Only 3 percent of the housing of the poor lacks a full kitchen, compared to 1 percent for the nonpoor. Toilets were broken two or more times over the previous three months in only 2 percent of poor households (0.6 percent for the nonpoor).[11]

These points are not intended to suggest that the poor live as well as average Americans, for that is certainly not the case. They do suggest that the poor are not as destitute as they are frequently portrayed, at least in material terms, and this is partly a consequence of our welfare programs.

---

[10]Nick Eberstadt, "Economic and Material Poverty in the U.S.," *The Public Interest,* 90:50 (Winter 1988). See also Robert Rector, Kate O'Beirne, and Michael McLaughlin, "How 'Poor' Are America's Poor?" *The Heritage Foundation Backgrounder* (Sept. 21, 1990).

[11]The information in this and the previous paragraph is reported in Robert Rector, "How the Poor Really Live: Lessons for Welfare Reform," *The Heritage Foundation Backgrounder* (Jan. 31, 1992), and all data are taken from government publications.

Table 8–8   Mean Family Incomes (1991 dollars*)

Year	Lowest Fifth	Second Fifth	Middle Fifth	Fourth Fifth	Highest Fifth	Top 5 Percent
1970	$ 9,963	$22,343	$32,305	$43,577	$74,936	$114,108
1980	10,199	22,904	34,695	48,140	82,433	121,726
1990	10,247	23,900	36,808	52,935	98,377	154,357
1991	9,734	23,105	35,851	51,997	95,530	147,817

*Converted to 1991 dollars using CPI-UX1.

Source: U.S. Bureau of the Census, *Current Population Reports,* Series P-60 (Washington, D.C.: U.S. Government Printing Office, 1991), Table B-7.

The Recent Trend Toward Inequality

As we pointed out earlier, there has been an increase in inequality in the distribution of incomes over the last 15 or 20 years. Table 8–8 presents some information that may help to indicate the magnitudes of some of the changes involved. It gives average income for each quintile and for the top 5 percent of *families* for several recent years. (These are the unadjusted Census figures, so they are before-tax and do not include in-kind transfers.[12]) Recall that 1991 was a recession year, with the consequences of this shown in the table as lower real incomes for all income classes than in the previous year.

Between 1970 and 1990, real average income rose for every income class. What is apparent, however, is that incomes rose proportionately more for the higher-income classes. In the bottom quintile, the increase from 1970 to 1990 was only 3 percent, but it was 7 percent for the second quintile, 14 percent for the third, 21 percent for the fourth, 31 percent for the fifth, and 35 percent for the top 5 percent. (These increases understate the increases in income per person because average family size fell by 12 percent over the period.) The larger increases for the higher-income classes mean that there is greater inequality in the relative positions of the quintiles, as shown by the quintile shares in Table 8–2.

---

[12]The adjustment to constant 1991 dollars, however, uses the corrected CPI (known as CPI-UX1) that corrects for the overstatement of inflation in years prior to 1983. If the uncorrected CPI, which is still considered the official CPI for years prior to 1983, were used instead, all the income figures for 1980 and 1970 would be higher. This makes the growth in real incomes, especially for the lower-income classes, appear lower than it really was.

The question that has most intrigued economists is *why* inequality has increased. This question needs to be answered before we can determine what, if anything, can or should be done about the situation. Unfortunately, it is very difficult to isolate the underlying causes. One popular culprit, however, can be largely exonerated: the policies of the Reagan–Bush years. Although popular discussion often presumes that these policies have been responsible for the growing inequality, there are at least three reasons to doubt that this is so. First, the incomes that are becoming more unequally distributed are market incomes, incomes before taxes and in-kind transfers. (Except for the bottom quintile, most of the incomes shown in Table 8–7 are market earnings.) Thus, the changes in tax and expenditure programs during the Reagan–Bush years would affect them only indirectly.[13] Second, it is now clear that the trend toward inequality began in the mid-1970s, if not earlier, and therefore predated the Reagan–Bush years. Third, a similar trend has been noted in a number of other industrialized countries, suggesting that whatever is producing more inequality transcends national boundaries.

A number of factors have played some role in producing greater income inequality. One is the changing composition of families and households: There are more elderly households (21.6 percent of all households in 1990 versus 19.3 percent in 1970), and there are more female-headed families (16.5 percent of all families in 1990 versus 10.8 percent in 1970). These demographic changes would make the family and household distributions more unequal. In addition, there has been an increase in two-earner families, especially among families with higher incomes. Another factor has been increased immigration of persons with lower skills.

Although these factors have played some role in producing an increase in measured income inequality, they explain only part of the increase that has occurred. Underlying the changes in incomes is a change in the distribution of wage rates. Specifically, those with greater skills are increasingly commanding higher wage rates relative to those with fewer skills. This can be seen, for example, in the change in the "college premium." In 1975, the average male college graduate had earnings that were 45 percent greater than those of the average male high school graduate; by 1990, college graduates' earnings were 75 percent higher. This is but one bit of evidence that the highly skilled are commanding higher relative wages now than in the past.

Of course, a greater dispersion in wage rates by skill levels does not explain why this dispersion occurred. Although this issue remains controversial, the leading current candidate seems to be a change in production

---

[13]Some economists do believe that the reductions in tax rates on those with high incomes may have induced them to earn and report more income, but whether this accounts for some of the increase in the higher-income classes remains controversial. We will discuss this issue in Chapter 11.

technology.[14] Modern production techniques are believed to require workers with greater skills. The rise and spread of computer technology is an example of this trend (but not the only example) as more and more workers need to be computer literate.

Whatever the ultimate cause of the recent trend, policymakers have used it as justification for new government policies. President Bill Clinton, for example, based his proposal to increase sharply taxes on those with high incomes and to increase transfers to low-income working families (through an expanded earned income tax credit, discussed in the next chapter) squarely on the fact that the real incomes of the well-off had increased the most in recent years. Before assuming that the recent trend calls for such actions, it should be noted that unchanged tax and transfer policies automatically ameliorate increases in the inequality in market earnings. If incomes rise at the top, unchanged tax rates collect more in tax revenue from them, and if incomes fall at the bottom, most transfer programs automatically increase transfers to them (recall how the food stamp program operates). This increased redistribution is not registered in figures like those reported in Table 8–8.

Another factor to remember is that the recent change may be self-correcting. Workers with lower skills now have a much larger incentive to improve their skills. If workers respond to the change in incentives (and this can take a number of years, of course), the result would be a reduction in the supply of workers for low-skill jobs (raising wages in these jobs) and an increase in the supply of higher-skilled workers (lowering wages there). Indeed, there is a very tentative suggestion in recent data that these changes are under way. The share of income going to the top quintile of families fell from 44.6 to 44.2 percent between 1989 and 1991, and it increased by 0.1 percent for the second and third quintiles. Economists and others will watch the evidence closely to see if this is the beginning of a reversal of the trend toward greater inequality.

Review Questions and Problems

1. Is there one distribution of income that is most efficient?

2. Explain the public good argument for redistribution. Does this argument offer any reason to favor government redistribution over private charity?

---

[14]For a discussion of the evidence supporting technological change as the major cause of increased inequality in the wage rate distribution, see John Bound and George Johnson, "Changes in the Structure of Wages in the 1980's: An Evaluation of Alternative Explanations," *American Economic Review*, 82:371 (June 1992).

3. Travis thinks that a competitive economy produces a poor distribution of income. Yet Travis does not favor any type of government transfer programs. Is Travis being inconsistent? Explain.

4. Which of the three arguments supporting government redistribution that were discussed do you think is the most convincing? Why? Does this argument help in determining how much should be distributed?

5. Which of the three arguments opposing government redistribution that were discussed do you think is the most convincing? Why? Does this argument imply that there should be no redistribution by government?

6. The United States is a welfare state. True or false? Explain.

7. What are the major in-kind transfer programs, and how much have they grown since the mid-1960s? Why is it important to take account of this growth when evaluating economic inequality and poverty?

8. Many presentations of information about income distribution rely on the use of quintile shares. Explain this construction. How would the quintile shares be affected if every household's income were to increase by $5,000? How would the quintile shares be affected if every household in the lowest quintile had $5,000 more in income and every household in the higher quintiles had $10,000 more in income?

9. Interpreted as a measure of economic inequality, what are the major defects in the widely used Census Bureau figures (as in Table 8–2)?

10. What factors are relevant to determining whether there is too much inequality in the United States?

11. How does the distribution of lifetime income differ from the distribution of annual income? What accounts for the difference? Which measure is a better indication of the degree of economic inequality?

12. The Census Bureau publishes separate estimates of income distribution for households and for families. How do these differ? Which is a better indication of the degree of economic inequality?

13. How would you expect the social security system to affect the Census Bureau's estimates of the income distribution? In other words, does it lead to a more or less equal distribution of money income? Why might this be misleading?

14. The official poverty rate was nearly the same in 1991 as in 1966. Does this demonstrate the failure of our welfare programs?

15. Rank the following households according to which has the higher real standard of living over whatever time period you consider relevant:
a. A single graduate student majoring in engineering (and getting straight A's). Current money income $10,000, in the form of a fellowship.

b. A middle-aged married couple, both working full time, with two children in college. Current money income $60,000.

c. A young married couple, with one preschool-aged child, only the husband working. Current money income $30,000.

d. An elderly retired couple who own their own home and receive $10,000 in real interest income (from $200,000 in financial assets) and $10,000 in social security benefits, for a total money income of $20,000.

16. Does the recent trend toward economic inequality justify increased government redistribution?

Supplementary Readings

BURTLESS, GARY. "The Economist's Lament: Public Assistance in America." *Journal of Economic Perspectives,* 4:57–78 (Winter 1990).

DANZIGER, SHELDON, ROBERT HAVEMAN, and ROBERT PLOTNICK. "How Income Transfers Affect Work, Savings and the Income Distribution." *Journal of Economic Literature,* 19(3):975–1028 (Sept. 1981).

HAVEMAN, ROBERT. *Starting Even.* New York: Simon and Schuster, 1988.

KAUS, MICKEY. *The End of Equality.* New York: Basic Books, 1992.

LILIA, MARK. "Why the Income Distribution Is So Misleading." *Public Interest* (Fall 1984).

MEAD, LAWRENCE M. *The New Politics of Poverty.* New York: Basic Books, 1992.

MURRAY, CHARLES. *Losing Ground: American Social Policy, 1950–1980.* New York: Basic Books, 1984.

OKUN, ARTHUR. *Equality and Efficiency: The Big Trade-off.* Washington, D.C.: The Brookings Institution, 1975.

SAWHILL, ISABEL V. "Poverty in the U.S.: Why Is It So Persistent?" *Journal of Economic Literature,* 26:1073–1119 (Sept. 1988).

WAGNER, RICHARD E. *To Promote the General Welfare.* San Francisco: Pacific Research Institute for Public Policy, 1989.

Analyzing Income Transfer Programs

IN THE LAST CHAPTER, WE EMPHASIZED certain factual dimensions that are relevant to the impact of redistributive tax and transfer policies. In this chapter, the emphasis shifts to the way economic theory can be used to evaluate the effects of various income transfer programs. Neither economics nor economists can objectively demonstrate that one type of income transfer policy is best, or how much redistribution is desirable, because such conclusions must reflect in part value judgments concerning the effects of those policies. Economics can, however, determine some of the effects that most people would consider relevant to an evaluation of redistributive plans. For example, economic theory can be used to investigate how various income transfer programs will affect the work incentives of recipients; this is a question of considerable importance that is covered in detail in this chapter.

We begin with a discussion of a transfer program known as the *negative income tax* (NIT). At this time, the United States does not have a comprehensive NIT program. Nonetheless, the NIT program is probably the most important type of transfer program, and one that should be understood fully, because several existing programs essentially operate like an NIT and because most welfare reform proposals build on certain features of the NIT. After a discussion of the NIT, we turn to an analysis of several other programs and issues, including the trade-off between equality and efficiency.

The Negative Income Tax

The negative income tax, also known as a *guaranteed annual income,* is a program of cash transfers to families, with the size of the transfer depending on the family's income and size. The distinguishing characteristic of this program is that for families of a given size, the transfer is larger the lower their income. The poorer the family is—at least in terms of its money income— the more assistance it will receive. Table 9–1 illustrates how a hypothetical NIT transfer would vary with income for a four-person family. In this exam- ple, if a family's income (pretransfer income) is zero, the transfer will be $5,000. At higher income levels, the transfer is smaller, ultimately reaching zero at $10,000.

For families of a given size, an NIT can be concisely described by its three policy variables. First is the *income guarantee,* which is the transfer received by a family with no income of its own—$5,000 in Table 9–1. The *marginal tax rate* is the second policy variable. The marginal tax rate indicates how much the transfer payment declines as pretransfer income rises; because it identifies the rate at which benefits are reduced, it is sometimes called the *benefit reduction rate.* In our example the marginal tax rate is 50 percent because the transfer falls by $0.50 for each $1 that pretransfer income in- creases. The third policy variable is called the *breakeven income* and is the level of income at which the transfer falls to zero—$10,000 in Table 9–1.

A NIT can also be illustrated graphically. In Figure 9–1, which shows sev- eral alternative plans, pretransfer income is measured horizontally and disposable income (pretransfer income plus the transfer) is measured ver- tically. The 45-degree line indicates the equality between pretransfer and disposable income in the absence of the NIT (and other transfers or taxes). It has a slope of unity, implying that an additional $1,000 in pretransfer in- come adds exactly $1,000 to disposable income. The line *RB* illustrates the relationship between pretransfer income and disposable income for the NIT just described. The transfer is the vertical distance between *RB* and the 45- degree line. The distance *OR* ($5,000) is the income guarantee, and *BL*

Table 9–1 *Hypothetical Negative Income Tax*

Pretransfer Income	Transfer	Total Disposable Income
$ 0	$5,000	$ 5,000
1,000	4,500	5,500
2,000	4,000	6,000
3,000	3,500	6,500
4,000	3,000	7,000
5,000	2,500	7,500
6,000	2,000	8,000
7,000	1,500	8,500
8,000	1,000	9,000
9,000	500	9,500
10,000	0	10,000

($10,000) is the breakeven income. The slope of RB shows that disposable income rises by only $500 for each $1,000 in pretransfer income under this NIT (because the transfer falls by $500). The marginal tax rate is equal to 1 minus the slope of the transfer schedule RB. The other NIT plans shown in Figure 9–1 are considered in the following section.

The transfer received at any income level below the breakeven income can be calculated from the following equation:

$$T = r (B - Y_i) \tag{1}$$

where T is the transfer payment, r is the marginal tax rate, B is the breakeven income, and Y_i is the family's pretransfer income. If r is 50 percent, then we can say that the NIT fills 50 percent of the gap between the family's income and the breakeven income.

The Conflict Among Competing Goals

The three policy variables of the NIT are not independent of one another. If the income guarantee is set at $5,000 and the transfer falls by $0.50 for each $1 of pretransfer income (a marginal tax rate of 50 percent), then the transfer

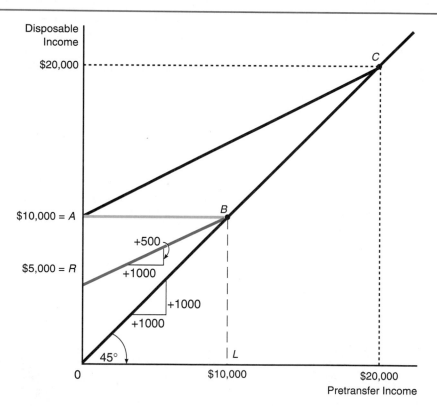

Figure 9–1   Hypothetical NIT plans

will fall to zero at $10,000. Thus, the breakeven income is already determined when the income guarantee and the marginal tax rate are set. Put concisely, *the income guarantee equals the marginal tax rate times the breakeven income;* in our example, $5,000 = 0.5 × $10,000. This relationship is also apparent from equation (1), because if we set pretransfer income (Y_i) equal to zero, the transfer (the income guarantee) will be equal to rB. Therefore, specifying any two of the policy variables implicitly determines the third.

The relationship among the policy variables poses a difficult policy choice. First, consider the significance of each policy variable. The income guarantee will represent the total disposable incomes of families with no other income, so it is important that the guarantee be high enough to permit an adequate standard of living. A low marginal tax rate is desirable to preserve work incentives because a high rate means that disposable incomes will rise only slightly when earnings increase, which would give recipients little incentive to increase their earnings. (More on marginal tax rates and work incentives is presented later.) A low breakeven income appears desirable because it restricts transfers to those with low incomes and, at the same time, keeps the costs manageable (because those above the breakeven income must bear the cost of financing the NIT).

It seems desirable, then, to have a high income guarantee, a low marginal tax rate, and a low breakeven income. Because of the relationship among these policy variables, however, this is impossible: A "low" marginal tax rate multiplied by a "low" breakeven income cannot equal a "high" income guarantee. The difficult trade-off among policy variables can be clarified by reference to Figure 9–1. Suppose that the poverty line is $10,000 and the income guarantee is set at this level (0A) to ensure that no family is in poverty. If the breakeven income is also kept relatively low at $10,000, the entire transfer schedule will be AB. This implies, however, a marginal tax rate of 100 percent, because disposable income does not rise as pretransfer income increases between zero and $10,000. This plan would leave no financial incentive for low-income families to work because a family would have the same disposable income when it earned nothing as when it earned $10,000.

How can we avoid destroying the incentives that families have to support themselves? To make earning an income worthwhile, the marginal tax rate must be lowered to well below 100 percent. There are two distinctly different ways to do this, and each way has drawbacks. One method is to maintain the income guarantee at $10,000 and lower the marginal tax rate, but this implies a higher breakeven income. For example, if the tax rate were lowered to 50 percent, the breakeven income would have to be $20,000, and the entire relationship would be shown by line AC. This program would not completely destroy work incentives, but it would weaken the incentives of a much larger number of people—all those with incomes below $20,000—and many (in the $10,000 to $20,000 range) would then be subject to a marginal tax rate under an NIT that excluded them before. Perhaps more important, it would be exorbitantly costly because it would involve transfers to about 25 percent of the American people!

A second way to lower the marginal tax rate is to hold the breakeven level of income at $10,000 and lower the income guarantee. With a 50 percent tax rate, an income guarantee of $5,000 is implied, and we are back with the schedule shown as *RB*. This method of reducing the tax rate would substantially improve the financial rewards from working for low-income families (compared with the *AB* schedule, which removes all incentives), and it would reduce the cost of the program. However, these effects come at a cost: The level of assistance for low-income groups is reduced, and the income guarantee is now only half the poverty line.

Harsh choices must be made in setting the policy variables of an NIT. A high guarantee and a high tax rate (implying a low breakeven income) restrict transfers to those with low incomes but weaken incentives to work. A high income guarantee and a low tax rate (implying a high breakeven income) produce a large number of transfer recipients and impose a high cost that must be borne by those taxpayers remaining above the breakeven income. A high tax rate must be applied to the remaining taxpayers to finance such an NIT, and this would weaken their work incentives. Alternatively, a low income guarantee and a low or moderate tax rate (say, 50 percent) keep costs down and maintain work incentives, but the level of assistance will be modest.

The NIT and Actual Welfare Programs

It is important to understand that many of the most important existing welfare programs are simply variations on the basic NIT theme. The food stamp program, for example, is nothing more than an NIT in which the subsidy is in the form of food coupons rather than cash. Refer back to Table 5–2 and note that the food stamp subsidy declines as the monthly income of the recipient rises. This inverse relationship between the transfer and income is the defining characteristic of the NIT. In the case of the food stamp program, the implicit marginal tax rate on net income is 30 percent.

Other welfare programs are also NITs in disguise. Aid to Families with Dependent Children (AFDC) is a program of cash assistance for female-headed households with children. Because the transfer is smaller when the family's income is higher, it is essentially an NIT restricted to a particular demographic group within the population. The nominal marginal tax rate has varied between 67 and 100 percent, but administrative practices often operate to make the effective rate somewhat lower. Supplemental Security Income (SSI) is another NIT that is restricted to a particular demographic group, primarily the aged poor, but also the blind and disabled. Its marginal tax rate is 50 percent. Some housing subsidies, such as public housing, are also similar to the NIT combined with a restriction on housing consumption. The earned income tax credit, a program that is becoming an increasingly important part of our welfare system, also has similarities to the NIT, as we will see when we examine it later in the chapter.

In fact, if you refer back to Figure 8–1 in the previous chapter, you will see that the combined effects of major transfers and taxes produce effects much like those of an NIT. In that figure, we saw that the average net transfer to the lowest quintile of households was $8,808, falling to $4,012 for the second quintile and to − $1,819 for the third quintile. This inverse relationship between the transfer and household income is the defining characteristic of an NIT. On average, the United States already has something close to an NIT, although it is important to recognize that the "average" conceals a lot of variation due to the many different programs with varying eligibility requirements.

Therefore, studying an NIT is not merely an academic exercise; it helps us understand the workings of several existing welfare programs. For example, the food stamp program involves the same trade-off among policy goals that was previously discussed. In one form or another, many actual and proposed welfare programs entail this same type of trade-off. Careful attention is thus given to the NIT not only because in its pure form (benefits in cash available to all low-income families) it is a reform proposal that has been widely debated but also because in its several variations it is already an integral part of the U.S. welfare system.

The NIT and Work Incentives

Much attention has been given to the question of how an NIT affects the work incentives of transfer recipients. In principle, any transfer program will affect work effort in two ways: first, through an *income effect* and, second, through a *substitution effect*. By providing a transfer to families, the NIT makes them better off and able to afford to work less. Having a higher real income, the recipient will increase his or her consumption of normal goods, including leisure or time spent not working. (Recall that an increase in leisure is the same as a reduction in work effort.) This is the income effect of the NIT, and it is related to the size of the transfer payment: The larger the transfer, the greater is the income effect favoring less work.

The NIT affects work incentives another way by reducing the net wage rate of recipients. Reducing the transfer received when a person earns more income has the effect of lowering the recipient's net hourly compensation for work. For example, if a person is employed at $4 per hour and works an additional hour, the extra $4 in earnings will reduce the NIT transfer by $2 (assuming a 50 percent marginal tax rate), so the net increase in income is only $2 for an extra hour's work. The net wage rate is cut in half by this NIT, so a person sacrifices less disposable income by working less. Thus, the relative price of consuming leisure—the sacrificed net income—has fallen from $4 per hour to $2 per hour, and this lower relative price encourages greater consumption of leisure (less work). This is the substitution effect of the NIT, and its magnitude is related to the marginal tax rate of the program. The higher the marginal tax rate, the lower the net wage and the greater the incentive to substitute leisure for money earnings because leisure will cost less in sacrificed money income.

Since both its income and substitution effects operate to reduce work effort, on balance the NIT can be expected to lead to a reduction in work effort. Some consequences of this diminished incentive to work are illustrated in Figure 9–2. An individual's budget line relating money income and leisure in the absence of the NIT is shown as YN, which has a slope of $4 per hour, the market wage rate of the individual. In the absence of any subsidy, equilibrium occurs at point E, with a money income of $0Y_1$ and leisure of $0L_1$ (so work effort is NL_1).

Introduction of the NIT shifts the budget line from YN to YRM. The break-even income, OB, is $10,000, and the income guarantee, MN, is $5,000. The vertical distance between the subsidized portion of the budget line, RM, and the unsubsidized budget line equals the transfer. The transfer is larger when the individual works and earns less: It equals MN with zero work effort, $E'K$ if work effort is NL_2, and SE if work effort is NL_1. The slope of the budget line has become flatter, $2 per hour, rather than the previous $4 per hour, reflecting the 50 percent marginal tax rate that cuts the net rate of pay in

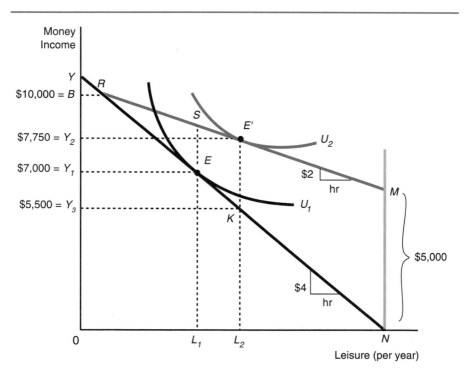

Figure 9–2   *Effect of a NIT on work effort*

half. Note that the rotation of the budget line at point R lowers the price of leisure: Less money income must be sacrificed when more leisure time is consumed.

Confronted with the YRM budget line, the individual's new equilibrium position occurs at point E', with total money income of OY_2 (or $7,750, equal to the sum of earnings of $5,500 and the transfer of $2,250), and leisure of OL_2. The reduction in work effort from NL_1 to NL_2 shows the total effect of the NIT on work effort—the combined influence of the income effect and the substitution effect. (These effects are discussed separately later.)

Figure 9–2 also illustrates several other significant points. First, note that the cost of the program depends on the work response of the recipient. Had the individual continued to work NL_1, the transfer would have been $SE,$ or $1,500, but because of the reduction in earnings from $7,000 to $5,500, the transfer rises to $2,250. Second, the incomes of recipients do not rise by the amount of the transfer: In this example, the recipient's income increases from $7,000 to only $7,750, although the transfer is $2,250. Third, if the transfer is given in kind, the money incomes of recipients—which is all the Census Bureau normally counts—actually falls. In Figure 9–2, if the $2,250 transfer takes the form of food stamps and housing assistance, the individual's money income will fall from $7,000 to $5,500. This means that it is possible for an in-kind transfer actually to increase the number of persons counted as poor at the same time that it raises their standards of living.

Even when given as cash, the NIT transfer can lead to a reduction in the recipient's total money income if the reduction in work effort is large enough. Figure 9–3, which illustrates this possibility, shows that total money income falls from OY_1 or OY_2 because the reduction in earnings, Y_1Y_3, is greater than the transfer received, Y_2Y_3. Even so, the recipient ends up with a higher real income (on a higher indifference curve) as a result of the transfer. Most scholars believe that work effort will rarely fall enough to reduce total money income, but it is a theoretical possibility.

Evidence on Work Incentives

Economic theory predicts that there will be some reduction in work incentives from an NIT, but it does not allow us to predict its size. A growing number of empirical studies have been designed to estimate its quantitative impact and its relationship to the policy variables. The empirical evidence is of two types: (1) studies of the reactions of low-income families to existing welfare programs similar in nature to the NIT and (2) studies of the results of experimental NIT programs funded by the government.

In reviewing the nonexperimental evidence, Irwin Garfinkel concluded that the evidence supports the view that work effort will fall under an NIT. However, there is no consensus about the size of the reduction. For an NIT with a moderate income guarantee and a 50 percent marginal tax rate, the estimated reduction in work effort ranges from 3 percent to 40 percent for prime-age married men (the group in which the disincentive problem is

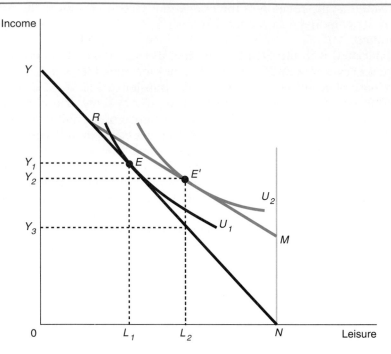

Figure 9–3   *A NIT may reduce total money income*

expected to be the smallest).[1] Estimated reductions for other demographic groups are generally somewhat larger.

Perhaps the most fascinating evidence on work incentives is based on the results of actual experiments in which random samples of low-income families were granted NIT transfers for several years and their work responses were recorded. The first of four experiments, carried out in New Jersey and Pennsylvania, was completed in 1972; the last, and largest, experiment was carried out in Seattle and Denver and ended in 1978. The experiments utilized a variety of NIT plans, but on the average, the income guarantee was set at the poverty level and the marginal tax rate was set at 50 percent.

These experiments have not, however, resolved the question of just how large the labor supply effects of an NIT would be. Responses in the four experiments varied somewhat, and there are statistical problems in evaluating the results. For husbands, labor supply reductions (in hours of work) ranged between 1 and 8 percent; for wives, labor supply varied from an

[1]Irwin Garfinkel, "Income Transfer Programs and Work Effort: A Review," *Studies in Public Welfare,* U.S. Congress, Joint Economic Committee, Subcommittee on Fiscal Policy, Paper No. 13, 93rd Congress, 2nd Session (Washington, D.C.: U.S. Government Printing Office, Feb. 1974), pp. 11–32.

increase of 1 percent to a reduction of 55 percent; and for female family heads, the reductions varied from 12 to 26 percent.[2]

Among these experiments, attention has centered on the Seattle–Denver sites because this experiment involved more participants than the other three programs combined and because some participants were enrolled in a five-year program, in contrast with the three-year duration for the other experiments. For the Seattle–Denver experiment as a whole, Robins and West estimated labor supply reductions of 7, 25, and 15 percent for husbands, wives, and female family heads, respectively.[3] For participants in the five-year experiment, however, the response in the third year involved reductions of 13, 21, and 23 percent for husbands, wives, and female family heads, respectively. These results suggest that a permanent program might produce larger labor supply responses than the three-year experiments implied.

As this brief review of the evidence makes clear, we are not yet in a position to make definitive statements about the actual size of the work disincentive effects of NIT programs.

The Welfare Cost of the NIT

By artificially lowering the net wage rates of the transfer recipients, the NIT will distort decisions on work effort. Consider the example of an NIT recipient, Cleo, who can earn $4 an hour but whose net wage rate is $2 under the NIT. Cleo will give up leisure (supply labor) as long as she considers an extra $2 in income worth more than the sacrificed value of an hour of leisure time. At the equilibrium level of work effort under the NIT, leisure would have a value of $2 per hour, and Cleo would be willing to work an additional hour if she received anything more than $2 in compensation.[4] Because her market wage rate is $4, her employer would be willing to pay $4 for additional hours of work. The marginal benefit from additional work—$4 per hour—is greater than the marginal cost—$2 worth of leisure given up—so there are efficiency gains from working longer hours. Yet under the NIT, Cleo will not work longer hours because her *net* wage rate is $2 per hour due to the reduction in the transfer payment that occurs when she earns the additional $4. Cleo will be led to work too little because the marginal *private* benefit from working that she receives—$2 per hour—is less than the marginal *social* benefit of her labor services—$4 per hour.

[2]Robert Moffit, "The Labor-Supply Effects of an NIT: The Findings of the Income Maintenance Experiments," unpublished paper, Rutgers University, Mar. 1980.

[3]Phillip K. Robins and Richard W. West, "Program Participation and Labor Supply Response." *Journal of Human Resources,* 15:499 (Fall 1980). The entire issue of the journal is devoted to analysis of the Seattle–Denver experiment.

[4]In other words, in equilibrium the marginal rate of substitution between income and leisure is equal to the net wage rate. This is shown by the tangency in Figure 9–2 between the recipient's indifference curve and the budget line.

Because the marginal tax rate makes market and net wage rates diverge, the NIT produces a welfare cost. This is illustrated in Figure 9–4, in which the equilibrium under the NIT occurs at E' on the subsidized budget line YRM. To see the loss in potential welfare, imagine that the government gives Cleo an unrestricted, or lump-sum, cash transfer instead of the NIT transfer. Because the cost of the NIT is $E'K$, a lump-sum transfer of equal cost will produce the budget line Y_2N_2 parallel to the original YN budget line, implying that the transfer is not reduced when more is earned; hence the net wage rate is unaffected by the lump-sum transfer. This budget line permits Cleo to reach a higher indifference curve, U_3, at point L. Thus, Cleo can be made better off at no additional cost to the taxpayers.

Alternatively, a smaller lump-sum transfer can make the recipient just as well off as under the NIT. With a lump-sum transfer of YY_1 (producing the budget line Y_1N_1), Cleo can reach U_2 at point T, the same level of welfare as under the NIT. Note that the cost of this lump-sum transfer is only JK, or $E'J$ less than the NIT. *$E'J$ is a measure of the welfare cost of the NIT:* It shows

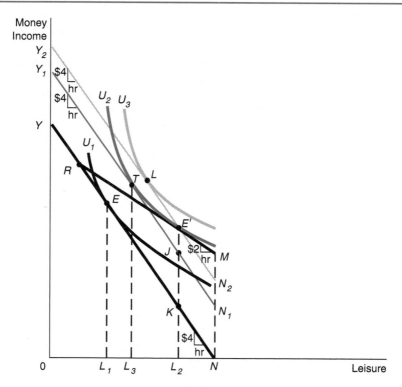

Figure 9–4 *Welfare cost of a NIT*

that the NIT costs $E'J$ more than is necessary to permit the recipient to attain the level of welfare indicated by U_2.

We have seen that the recipient can be made better off with a lump-sum transfer than with an NIT of the same cost or (what amounts to the same thing) equally well off at a lower cost. This happens because the NIT lowers the net wage and encourages the recipient to consume too much leisure (work too little). This distortion of the NIT is caused by the marginal tax rate that induces the recipient to substitute leisure for money income.

Figure 9–4 can also be used to show the income and substitution effects of the NIT. The income effect is the increase in leisure from $0L_1$ to $0L_3$ that results from giving the recipient enough income to attain U_2, but without affecting the net wage rate received. The substitution effect is the increase in leisure from $0L_3$ to $0L_2$ that results from the lower net wage rate when the recipient is kept on the same indifference curve, U_2. The welfare cost of the NIT is due to the substitution effect alone: $0L_2$–$0L_3$ measures the overconsumption of leisure. The income effect of the transfer is not a distortion; it is simply the increase in consumption of leisure—and other normal goods—that results from a pure, nondistorting change in the income distribution. Economists emphasize the importance of the size of the marginal tax rate of the NIT because it lowers the net wage rate and causes the uneconomic substitution of leisure for money income.

If the welfare cost of the NIT (and of other transfer programs as well) can be avoided by using lump-sum transfers, why don't economists favor such transfers? That is a reasonable question, and the answer involves understanding the nature of a lump-sum transfer more precisely. A lump-sum transfer is one in which the amount transferred does not depend on income, consumption, work effort, education, family size, or any other economic characteristics under the control of the recipient. It is simply fixed in amount, totally independent of any individual's actions. By its very nature, it is impossible to restrict a lump-sum transfer to those with low incomes because, by definition, it is unrelated to any of the characteristics associated with being poor. If given only to people with low incomes, it would not be a lump-sum transfer because it would give incentive to others to reduce their incomes to become eligible for the transfer and would thereby create a distortion. Thus, in the interest of *equitably* relating assistance to need, we may choose to use transfers related to income despite the efficiency cost.

For this reason, lump-sum transfers and taxes are not generally considered practical policy tools. Nonetheless, they serve a highly useful role in analysis as a conceptual benchmark against which to view the allocative effects of real-world taxes and transfers. They provide a means of understanding how other policies may distort the allocation of resources and the factors that determine the size of these distortions. In the present context, even though the NIT produces a welfare cost, that cost may be smaller than those of alternative practical policies. This is precisely what many economists believe.

Aid to Families with Dependent Children

When most people use the phrase "on welfare" or think of the U.S. welfare system, they really have one program in mind: Aid to Families with Dependent Children (AFDC). As we have seen, this is not the largest welfare program in terms of either recipients or outlays. In recent years, outlays have averaged about $20 billion, and there have been about 12 million recipients in 4 million families. In terms of outlays, Medicaid is much larger, and in terms of recipients, there are almost twice as many persons receiving food stamps. (Of course, AFDC recipients are automatically covered by both Medicaid and food stamps, so total benefits going to the AFDC population are much larger than the outlays on it alone.) Nonetheless, in many respects, AFDC is the centerpiece of the welfare system.

Everyone seems to agree that the welfare system, especially as it affects the AFDC population, is "a mess." Four out of the last five presidential administrations have proposed sweeping overhauls of the system. In the first three instances (Nixon, Carter, and Reagan), Congress rejected the proposals; the fate of the fourth (Clinton) has not been resolved at this time. What are the defects of the current system that make it such a prime candidate for reform efforts? Consider these charges commonly leveled against it: It discourages work; it allows or encourages long-term dependence; it encourages family dissolution and illegitimacy; benefits are too low; costs are too high; benefits are unfairly distributed; it is too complicated for anyone to understand; administrative and compliance costs are excessive.

Before evaluating some of these criticisms and reform options to deal with them, a brief description of AFDC is in order. AFDC is a joint federal–state program of cash benefits to families with dependent children (under age 18). Until 1990, it was generally restricted to single-parent families, but federal legislation required states in that year to offer benefits to two-parent families if the primary earner was unemployed or worked less than 100 hours a month. This has had only a small effect, since in most two-parent families at least one adult works. Thus, AFDC has remained primarily a program for female-headed families, and it is appropriate to think of it as restricted to that demographic group.

AFDC is similar to an NIT restricted to a particular demographic group. States are free to set the income guarantee at whatever level they select, and there is wide variation in the levels chosen. The federal government sets the marginal tax rate that must be used in all states; currently that rate is 100 percent. However, because of earnings-related deductions and other administrative practices, the effective (as distinct from the statutory) marginal tax rate is thought to be closer to 70 percent.

In considering how AFDC affects work incentives, we are first struck by the high marginal tax rate. Actually, the marginal tax rate can be even higher because of the way that AFDC interacts with other programs. Consider the hypothetical situation described in Table 9–2 for a single parent with two

Table 9–2   *Options for AFDC with a Single Parent and Two Children, 1986*

Level of Work and Wages	Earnings	Day Care	Taxes and Earned Income Tax Credit	AFDC and Food Stamps	Disposable Income
No work[a]	$ 0	$ 0	$ 0	$6,284	$6,284
Half time at the minimum wage*[a]	$ 3,350	− $1,000	$229	$4,577	$7,156
Full time at the minimum wage[a]	$ 6,700	− $3,000	$373	$2,744	$6,816
Full time at $4.00 per hour[a]	$ 8,000	− $3,000	$171	$1,624	$6,795
Full time at $5.00 per hour[b]	$10,000	− $3,000	− $172	$ 970	$7,798
Full time at $6.00 per hour[b]	$12,000	− $3,000	− $515	$ 538	$9,023

[a]Eligible for Medicaid
[b]Not eligible for Medicaid

*The minimum wage was $3.35 in 1986.

Source: David T. Ellwood, *Poor Support* (New York: Basic Books, 1988), Table 5–2.

children in 1986. Although hypothetical, it was constructed by David Ellwood to faithfully reflect a fairly typical situation for someone on AFDC. Note that if the recipient's earnings go up, disposable income does not rise commensurately because child-care expenses must be paid and AFDC and food stamp benefits are lost (due to the marginal tax rates in those programs). (In addition, there is a small adjustment due to the earned income tax credit and taxes; we discuss the earned income tax credit later.) As a result, unless the AFDC recipient earns more than $8,000 (1986 dollars), disposable income scarcely rises at all; the *combined* effective marginal tax rate is just about 100 percent up to that level. And even if more can be earned—say, $12,000—disposable cash income is only $2,739 more than if nothing at all is earned, but earning that much also makes the family ineligible for Medicaid, and that loss may more than offset the cash gain.

Faced with options like these, is it surprising that AFDC recipients don't work very much? And they don't. In recent years, only 5 to 6 percent of recipients have worked at all, and only 1 to 2 percent have worked full time. Indeed, for many years, mothers with dependent children were not expected to work. It is only in the last two or three decades, which have seen more and more married women with children continue to work, that nonwork by the AFDC population has come to be widely viewed as a serious problem.

Almost everyone agrees that we should not penalize work by AFDC recipients so much, so why isn't the program changed? Consider Figure 9–5, where schedule *AB* represents the present AFDC program (plus other subsidies), with its approximately 100 percent marginal tax rate. Suppose that we lower the rate to 50 percent to produce schedule *AC*. This *may* cause some current AFDC recipients to work more, but even that isn't certain; they may continue not to work at all, although presumably some would be encouraged by the lower tax rate. (Note that there is an income effect that discourages work for those already working.) On the other hand, consider the single-parent households that had incomes between Y_1 and Y_2; they had earnings above the breakeven level and were supporting themselves before the policy change. But now they are eligible to receive AFDC, and *this group definitely has an incentive to reduce its work effort* because of both the income effect of the transfer and the substitution effect of the 50 percent marginal tax rate that now applies to them. So the total work effort of the entire low-income, single-parent population is almost certain to decline. There will be more people on AFDC, and it will be even harder to get off

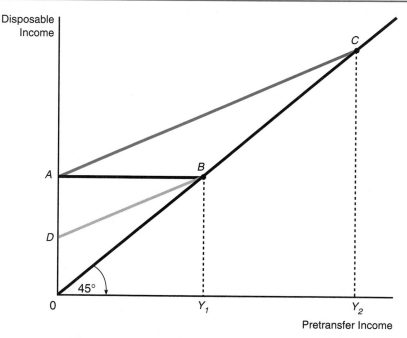

Figure 9–5 *AFDC reform options*

the program entirely because the breakeven level is so much higher. In addition, budgetary costs will go up because of the expanded coverage.

The only other way to improve financial incentives to work is to reduce the marginal tax rate *and the income guarantee,* producing schedule *DB,* for example. That does improve incentives to work for the original AFDC population, but it also reduces the basic benefit level sharply for those who do not work, and even those who do will end up with lower disposable incomes. A major concern here, of course, is the well-being of the children; they seem certain to suffer under this option.

What we have just been discussing is, of course, the trade-off imposed by every NIT program (as we explained earlier), in this case as it applies to AFDC.

There are other ways to encourage work, and the federal and state governments have been trying some of them. Mandatory work requirements, for example, have been tried, but with little success. Training programs to increase the earning capacity of AFDC recipients have been tried, and we will discuss this approach further in the next section. President Clinton also has a proposal directed to the problem. He has proposed limiting receipt of AFDC benefits to a maximum of two years. About half of all AFDC recipients already leave the program in less than two years (usually because of marriage, not increased earnings), so for them the two-year limit poses no problem and also has no effect. Since many of the hard-core recipients who stay on AFDC for long periods are high school dropouts with limited labor market skills, the two-year limit could impose significant hardship. To ease matters, Clinton proposes to have new job training and child-care programs to try to equip this group with the skills necessary to obtain decent-paying jobs. Whether this approach will work is unclear. Some states have already provided job counseling, training, and child-care support (but without the mandatory two-year limit), with little success.

One implication of the Clinton proposal should be emphasized, however: it makes the initial total benefit package even more attractive. In other words, with this reform, a single parent could get higher benefits for two years than under the current system (the same cash, food stamp, and Medicaid benefits, but now job training and child care as well). That makes it likely that the number of people going on the program will increase, and even if they are moved off at the end of two years, the total caseload and total costs could well increase.

Training and Education Programs

Most of our welfare programs attempt to improve the standard of living of recipients by supplementing their incomes with cash or in-kind assistance. A fundamentally different approach attempts to improve the ability of the poor to support themselves: a "hand up, not a handout." Education and training programs exemplify this approach. Their goal is to increase the earning capacity of low-income persons and therefore make it unnecessary, or less necessary, to supplement their incomes with cash or in-kind assistance. Programs designed to increase the labor market skills and earning capacity of the poor are sometimes described as treating the causes of poverty rather than its symptoms.

Starting around 1964, when President Lyndon Johnson declared a "War on Poverty," the government began to use a variety of compensatory job training and education programs. Since that time, literally dozens of different programs have been enacted. To name a few: Neighborhood Youth Corps, Job Corps, Talent Search, Adult Education Act of 1966, Job Opportunities in the Business Sector, Manpower Development Training Act, Pell Grants, Head Start, Comprehensive Education and Training Act, AFDC Work Incentive Program, and the Employment Opportunity Pilot Project. In 1990, about $18 billion was spent on programs of this sort.[5]

The basic question is whether programs of this sort really work. How effective are they in increasing the earnings of poor persons? That turns out to be a very difficult question to answer, despite the fact that hundreds of evaluations have been completed. Before reporting some of the results of these evaluations, the reason why it is difficult to determine the actual consequences of these programs should be noted. It is that participants in the programs are usually either volunteers or selected by the program operators. This suggests that they may be the more highly motivated or able persons among the eligible pool, so positive results for this group might not generalize to the entire population. For example, suppose that job training is made available to AFDC recipients, and 10 percent volunteer to participate in the program. It is likely that this 10 percent would have done better than the other 90 percent even in the absence of the training program (because they are more willing to work, more ambitious, etc.), so comparing subsequent earnings for the volunteer group with earnings for the 90 percent who did not volunteer would overstate the effectiveness of the training program. This problem, and others as well, makes it difficult to determine the effects that are attributable to the training programs themselves.

Early experience with education and training programs was analyzed by Henry Levin in 1977.[6] Levin's basic conclusion was a gloomy one: "There are few who would deny the basic failure of existing approaches toward education and training for alleviating poverty." The general belief, based on studies done at that time, was that "nothing worked." That was not exactly true, since a number of studies did estimate that some programs resulted in

---

[5]Vee Burke, "Cash and Noncash Benefits for Persons with Limited Income: Eligibility Rules, Recipient and Expenditure Data, FY 1988–90," Congressional Research Service, *CRS Report for Congress* (Sept. 30, 1991), p. 2.

[6]Henry M. Levin, "A Decade of Developments in Improving Education and Training for Low-income Populations," in *A Decade of Federal Antipoverty Programs: Achievements, Failures, and Lessons,* ed. by R. H. Haveman (New York: Academic Press, 1977). The quotation is from p. 179.

increased earnings. Nonetheless, relative to the optimistic early expectations, the results showed clearly that training and education programs did not offer a panacea for poverty.

More recent studies have suggested that perhaps a more positive assessment is in order. Robert Moffitt surveyed about a dozen studies that focused on programs for welfare (AFDC) recipients and found a clear indication of positive effects on earnings: "This constitutes a rather new finding, for the conventional wisdom in this area for many years was that 'nothing works,' that is, that no training program has significant effects on earnings."[7] However, there was still wide variation in the estimated effects on earnings, ranging from zero to as high as $1,500 per year. Another survey of studies dealing with Comprehensive Employment and Training Act programs found that most studies estimated that these programs raised earnings by $200 to $600 annually.[8] It also found the programs to be more effective for women than for men.

What is clear from these studies is that even the programs that were estimated to have a positive effect on earnings did not increase earnings very much. As Moffitt put it, one has to be "relatively optimistic" to believe that these programs can consistently increase earnings by as much as $1,000 *per year* for female heads receiving AFDC. While increases of this magnitude may be cost effective, they will not reduce poverty very much.

One reason not to be too optimistic about the potential of compensatory training and education programs is that private markets already offer opportunities for workers to improve their labor market skills. For workers with the motivation and ability to benefit from more training and education, the expectation is that they will upgrade their earning skills to the level that is efficient for them. While many doubt that the private sector is fully efficient in this area, the small gains estimated for government education and training programs do support the view that the big gains (if there are any) have already been realized by people before they are subsidized, leaving little scope for further improvement.

The Earned Income Tax Credit

The earned income tax credit (EITC) was introduced in 1975 as a modest program intended to offset the burden of social security payroll taxes on the working poor with children. Total expenditures were only $1.3 billion in 1980. It proved to be a popular program with both Democrats and Republicans, and a series of expansions resulted in an increase in expenditures to

[7]Robert Moffitt, "Incentive Effects of the U.S. Welfare System: A Review," *Journal of Economic Literature,* 30 (Mar. 1992), especially pp. 42–51. The quotation is from p. 49.

[8]Burt S. Barnow, "The Impact of CETA Programs on Earnings," *Journal of Human Resources,* 22:157 (Spring 1987).

$6.3 billion by 1991. Legislation passed in 1990 schedules further major increases that will raise spending to about $12 billion by 1994, when the new law is fully in effect. In a world of tight budgets and retrenchment, this welfare program has succeeded in becoming the focal point of many welfare reform and expansion efforts.

EITC provides cash assistance to *working families with children* who have relatively low earnings. Both single-parent and two-parent families are eligible. This is one of the few welfare programs that provides benefits to low-income married-couple families. The only other major program that covers married-couple families is food stamps (although Medicaid provides coverage in some states). In a sense, the working poor with children are the target group. One of the reasons for the popularity of this program is that it provides benefits only to those who are working; those with zero earnings receive no assistance under EITC.

Technically, EITC is a *refundable tax credit* that operates through the federal individual income tax. This means that the subsidy is subtracted from federal income tax owed, if any, and if the subsidy is larger than the tax owed, the difference is given as a cash transfer to the recipient family. In either case, it is equivalent to a cash transfer given to the family after it has paid any federal income taxed owed.

Figure 9–6 helps to illustrate how the amount of assistance is determined. It shows how the EITC will operate when the new law is phased in in 1994 for a family with two or more children. (Families with one child receive benefits that are about 10 percent lower.) The graph shows how the program operates in the absence of any other tax or transfer programs that affect families; we will consider the interaction between EITC and other policies later. For families with earnings below the earnings threshold Y_1 ($7,520 in 1992), the EITC acts as an earnings subsidy that provides a benefit equal to 25 percent of earnings. Thus, if the family has total earnings of $1,000, it receives an EITC grant of $250; if earnings are $2,000, it receives a grant of $500, and so on up to earnings of $7,520, where the grant is $1,880. Each dollar of additional earnings up to $7,520 increases the family's disposable income by $1.25.

For families with earnings between Y_1 and Y_2, that is, between $7,520 and $11,840, the EITC grant is equal to its maximum amount, $1,880. In other words, if earnings increase from $8,000 to $9,000, there is no change in the benefit received; it remains at $1,880. Over the Y_1–Y_2 earnings range, the EITC is like a lump-sum grant, with the size of the benefit being independent of earnings.

For families with earnings in excess of Y_2, or $11,840, the size of the benefit is reduced as earnings increase. This is necessary, of course, to restrict the benefits to those with relatively low earnings. Benefits are reduced by about $18 for every $100 of earnings until the benefit reaches zero at an earnings level of $22,370. *Note that over the Y_2–Y_3 earnings range, the EITC operates exactly like an NIT.* Thus, the EITC is an earnings subsidy at low

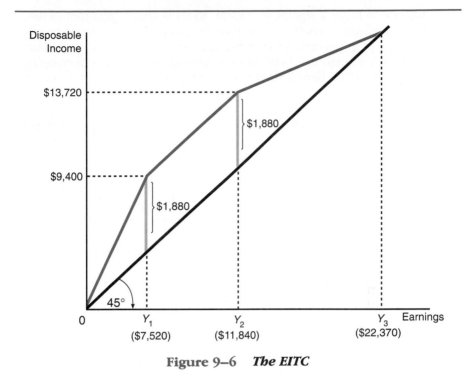

Figure 9–6   *The EITC*

earnings levels, a lump-sum transfer over an intermediate range, and an NIT at higher earnings levels. (The three earnings thresholds, by the way, are indexed to the CPI and so increase over time with inflation.) One final point about the way benefits are calculated: Benefits depend on total family earnings, not on an individual's earnings. If there are two earners in the family, each earning $6,000, the benefit is calculated for family earnings of $12,000, and if either person earns $1 more, the benefit is reduced by $0.18 because the family is in the Y_2–Y_3 range.

Before examining the way the EITC affects work incentives, let us consider the distribution of benefits under the program. In 1991, about 10 million families (not persons) received EITC benefits. Of these, about three fourths had incomes above the official poverty lines even before receiving assistance![9] That is not really surprising since it is clear from Figure 9–6 that benefits extend well beyond the poverty line for families with only one or two children. In fact, only about one third of the poverty population is eligible to receive EITC benefits since many officially poor persons are in nonworking families (the AFDC population and elderly retired persons) or do

[9]Saul D. Hoffman and Laurence S. Seidman, *The Earned Income Tax Credit* (Kalamazoo, Mich.: W. E. Upjohn Institute, 1990), p. 25.

not have children. To a significant extent, EITC is thus a program of assistance to the near-poor who work and have children. (That is, of course, what is intended: to help low-income working families with children.) In addition, it should be mentioned that EITC will not remove any persons from *official* poverty because EITC benefits are not counted as income in determining poverty status.

In considering how the EITC affects work incentives, it is important to recognize that the effects differ among the three income ranges shown in the graph. For families with earnings below Y_1, the EITC is like an earnings subsidy that acts to increase the effective wage rate workers are paid. If the worker has a market wage of $5 and works one hour more, the family receives an additional $1.25 in EITC benefits, so the effective wage rate is increased from $5 to $6.25 by the program. This is intended to encourage work effort. However, the program results in both income and substitution effects on labor supply. By providing cash assistance, there is an income effect that discourages work, while the higher wage rate results in a substitution effect that encourages work. On balance, it is not clear whether work effort will rise or fall for those in this range of earnings. Compared to other ways of subsidizing low-income families, however, the EITC is certainly more favorable to work incentives in this low earnings range. Recall that programs like the NIT definitely reduce work effort.

For families with earnings between Y_1 and Y_2, the EITC has only an income effect that tends to reduce work effort. There is no substitution effect here because additional earnings neither increase nor reduce the $1,880 grant that is received, so there is no change in the effective wage rate.

Finally, over the Y_2–Y_3 earnings range, the EITC produces income and substitution effects that both result in lower work effort. Since the EITC operates exactly like an NIT over this range of earnings, our earlier analysis of the way an NIT affects work incentives applies here.

Although the EITC is often popularly referred to simply as an "earnings subsidy" that "rewards work," it is clear that this is misleading; at best, this characterization applies only to the lowest earnings range. Moreover, it turns out that *nearly 70 percent of EITC recipients have earnings in the Y_2–Y_3 range where the program operates like an NIT.*[10] This is not really so surprising since full-time employment at the minimum wage results in earnings in excess of the Y_1 threshold. Thus, it is probably more accurate to think of the EITC as an NIT for the bulk of those receiving benefits from it, and to expect the adverse work incentives effect associated with the NIT to be the predominant outcome of the EITC.

We have concluded that the EITC will reduce labor supply for most recipients, but we have not determined how large the reduction will be. Given that the marginal tax rate of the EITC is only 18 percent in the upper earnings range, and that the amount of the transfer is not very large relative to

[10]Hoffman and Seidman, *The Earned Income Tax Credit,* p. 21.

income, it is probable that the reduction would not be too large. However, in assessing the impact on work incentives, it is extremely important to consider the combined impact of all the policies that affect families receiving EITC transfers. All families receiving EITC are subject to social security payroll taxes, some will also receive food stamps (with its 30 percent marginal tax rate), and some will be in the first bracket of the federal individual income tax and subject to its 15 percent marginal tax rate. State income taxes may also apply.

The combined, or effective, marginal tax rate will vary from family to family, depending on what other tax and subsidy programs apply to them. To consider a common outcome, however, we note that families of four persons are subject to federal income tax at a marginal rate of 15 percent if their income exceeds about $15,000 in 1992. (The federal income tax is examined in detail in Chapter 11.) Thus, a family with earnings of $18,000 is subject to a combined marginal tax rate of about 30 percent from the income and payroll taxes even before the EITC subsidy. The EITC program pushes the combined marginal tax rate up to about 48 percent for this family: An additional $100 in earnings results in an additional payroll tax of $15, an additional income tax of $15, and a loss in EITC benefits of $18, so the family's disposable income rises by only $52 when it earns an additional $100.

For many families in the Y_2-Y_3 earnings range, the EITC pushes the effective marginal tax rate on earnings up to about 50 percent. In the lower part of this range, families do not pay federal income taxes but are eligible to receive food stamps, and the effective marginal tax rate will then be close to 60 percent. Effective marginal tax rates of this level do suggest that the impact on work incentives may be significant.

Redistribution: An Overview

As we have seen, most welfare programs relate the size of the transfer to the recipient's level of income, just like the NIT. Reducing the transfer as income rises ensures that the largest transfers go to the neediest families, but at the same time this relationship results in marginal tax rates on the recipients— and these marginal tax rates are largely responsible for the adverse incentive effects of the programs. Of course, the incomes of higher-income families must also be subjected to marginal tax rates in order to produce the revenue needed to finance the transfers to lower-income families. There may also be adverse effects on the work incentives of taxpayers from higher marginal tax rates on them. We now present a broad overview of tax and transfer policies that takes account of the effects on transfer recipients and taxpayers alike.

It is difficult, if not impossible, to describe concisely the combined effects of all taxes and transfers, given their variety and complexity. We will examine a hypothetical tax-transfer policy that is roughly similar to the overall effect of taxes and transfers. This hypothetical policy is called a *linear income tax* and is illustrated in Figure 9–7. The 45-degree line shows the equality between earnings and disposable income in the absence of any tax or transfer, as in our earlier graphs. The schedule *ABC* shows the relationship when a linear income tax is used to redistribute income. Note that a linear income tax is just like an NIT for incomes below $35,000 (in this example). The new feature is that the NIT schedule *AB* extends as a straight line, *BC,* below the 45-degree line to show that families with incomes above $35,000 are paying taxes to finance the transfers. The fact that the entire schedule *ABC* is a straight line indicates that the marginal tax rate is the same for all households, taxpayers and recipients alike; that is the defining characteristic of a linear income tax. (The marginal tax rate is equal to 1 minus the slope of *ABC.*) Suppose that the common marginal tax rate is 40 percent. Then a household with an income of $40,000 pays a tax of 40 percent of its income in excess of $35,000, that is, 40 percent of $5,000, or $2,000.

A linear income tax is a straightforward redistributive policy that combines an NIT for low-income households with a positive tax on incomes above the breakeven level to finance it. Just as we do not have an outright NIT in the United States, we do not have an outright linear income tax, but

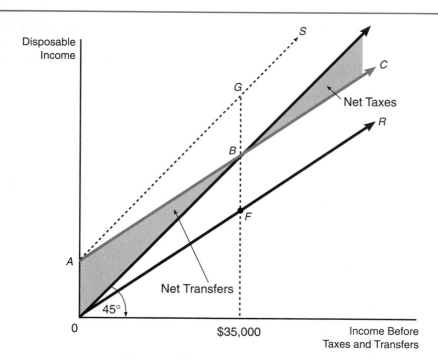

Figure 9–7 *Linear income tax*

what we do have is close enough so that we can understand many of the implications of tax-transfer policies by studying it. In particular, it forces us to take account of how the financing of transfers to low-income households affects the higher-income households that pay the taxes.

It is important to note that a linear income tax result can be produced with two separate policies that appear quite different. Suppose, for example, that we apply a flat rate tax of 40 percent on *all* incomes; this is shown in Figure 9–7 by the schedule *OR* (with the same slope as *ABC*). Then the revenue collected is returned in the form of an equal per household grant to *all* households; this is shown by the schedule *AGS*. The combined effect of these two policies is schedule *ABC*, which now shows the *net* transfer received or the *net* tax paid. At an income of $35,000, the transfer of *BG* equals the tax of *BF*, so net income is unaffected. For households above $35,000, the tax paid exceeds the grant received, and the net tax paid is shown by the vertical distance between *BC* and the 45-degree line at each income level; similarly, for lower-income households, the transfer received exceeds the tax paid, and the net transfer received is indicated in the same way by *AB*. Thus, these two separate policies combine to produce a linear income tax, with everyone subject to a 40 percent marginal tax rate in our example. Recognizing that these two separate tax and transfer policies combine to produce a redistributive linear income tax is helpful, as we will see.

Let us see how a linear income tax would work if it were added to the present U.S. tax-transfer system. In Table 9–3, the first row shows the percentage shares of income for families in the United States in 1991 (from Table 8–2). The second row gives the average incomes of families within each quintile (from Table 8–8); we can imagine, in fact, that there is one family in each quintile with income equal to the quintile average. Now suppose that we add a linear income tax with a 10 percent marginal tax rate. We will assume that the separate tax and transfer policies are used to implement this policy. Furthermore, we will initially assume that there are no disincentive effects; family incomes remain unaffected by the tax and transfer. (We

Table 9–3 *Redistribution and Income Shares, 1991 (no disincentive effects)*

	Lowest Quintile	Second Quintile	Middle Quintile	Fourth Quintile	Highest Quintile
(1) 1991 shares	4.5	10.7	16.6	24.1	44.2
(2) Mean incomes	$ 9,734	$23,105	$35,851	$51,997	$95,530
(3) 10 percent tax	−973	−2,311	−3,585	−5,200	−9,553
(4) Transfer	4,324	4,324	4,324	4,324	4,324
(5) New mean income	13,085	25,118	36,590	51,121	90,301
(6) New shares	6.1	11.6	16.9	23.6	41.8
(7) Change	1.6	0.9	0.3	−0.5	−2.4

will want to examine the effect of dropping this assumption later.) Then the 10 percent tax will collect as tax revenue the sums shown in row (3); a total of $21,622 is collected from the five families. This amount is returned as equal per family transfers of $4,324 to each family, as shown in row (4). Then the new average incomes (after the tax and transfer) in each quintile are given in row (5); total income of all five families is, of course, unchanged.

This example allows us to see some of the quantitative effects of a redistributive tax-transfer policy. In particular, we can see how much marginal tax rates must be increased to change the quintile shares. Note that the lowest quintile share has been increased from 4.5 to 6.1 percent (6.1 percent is equal to $13,085/$216,215, where $216,215 is the sum of the five incomes in row (5)). In fact, from the change in shares, we see that 2.9 percent of total income has been redistributed from the top two quintiles to the bottom three. What is interesting about this effect is that it required an increase in the marginal tax rate on *all* families of 10 percentage points to redistribute just 2.9 percent of total income. For each 1 percent of national income redistributed, marginal tax rates on everyone had to increase by about 3.5 percentage points. This is significant because the increase in marginal tax rates is the source of most of the adverse incentive effects of redistribution. *Redistributive programs require greater increases in the marginal tax rates needed to finance them than other expenditure programs.* For example, by raising everyone's marginal tax rate by one percentage point, it would be possible to spend 1 percent more of national income on defense. But we cannot redistribute 1 percent of national income with just an increase of one percentage point in everyone's marginal tax rate; the required increase is much greater.

Everyone's marginal tax rate goes up by 10 percentage points, but the result is an increase in the lowest quintile share of only 1.6 percentage points.[11] This also illustrates how difficult it is to increase the share of the lowest quintile, for a 10 point increase in marginal tax rates is a large change. To put it in perspective, the average marginal tax rate of U.S. families is now about 40 percent (counting all taxes and, for low-income families, all transfers). A 10 percent tax on income added to the present system thus increases everyone's effective marginal tax rate by 25 percent, from 40 to 50 percent.

It is sometimes thought that there must be some simple modification in the redistributive policy that could avoid such sharp increases in marginal tax rates. For example, suppose that in Table 9–3 we did not give transfers

---

[11]Actually, the share of the lowest quintile cannot feasibly be increased even this much by a linear income tax. The reason is that in practice, the transfer would have to be an equal per capita transfer rather than an equal per family transfer, as we assumed in the table. If all families got the same transfer, there would be a strong incentive for families to break up into smaller units to be eligible for more money, something that would not work if the transfer depended only on the number of persons. Since family size is smaller in the lower quintiles, they would get smaller transfers than would the higher quintiles with an equal per capita transfer.

to the higher quintiles so that we could give larger transfers to the lower quintiles. But a little thought will indicate that the only way to concentrate larger transfers on those with lower incomes and not make transfers to the higher quintiles is to reduce the transfer as income rises, thereby instituting an additional marginal tax rate on those with low incomes. This increases the net transfer to the bottom of the distribution, but it does so by increasing the marginal tax rate at the bottom even further. There is simply no way to avoid sharply increased marginal tax rates when redistributing income, and thinking about redistribution accomplished by a linear income tax brings this important point out clearly.

The arithmetic underlying redistribution demonstrates how difficult it is to increase significantly the share of income going to the lowest quintile. Many people think that it must be simple to augment the small (in the Census tabulations) percentage of income received by the lowest quintile by two or three points. The harsh reality, however, is that the policies required to accomplish this would increase marginal tax rates by 15 to 20 points or more, resulting in marginal tax rates of over 60 percent for most households. To the extent that higher rates reduce incentives to earn—a matter we shall consider further in the next section—the actual gain for low-income households would be even smaller.

The Cost of an Income Guarantee

We can arrive at the same general conclusion by approaching the problem from a different direction. Let us focus on the marginal tax rates necessary to establish a given effective income guarantee, or *floor,* for all people. Using the example involving equal transfers for all households again, the size of the transfer then effectively becomes a guaranteed income because it is the total income received by a household with no earnings of its own. Suppose that we wish to have an income guarantee equal to one half of the average household income: What marginal tax rate is required? Since each household will receive a transfer equal to half of the average household income, total outlays on transfers will equal half of total household income. Thus, tax revenue must equal half of total household income, so the required tax rate is 50 percent. *In general, the necessary tax rate is equal to the income guarantee divided by average income when using a linear income tax.* So to have an income floor of 50 percent of average income requires a tax rate of 50 percent.

Once we recognize that the government also requires tax revenues for nonredistributive purposes, the marginal tax rate necessary to establish an income floor at half of the average income can be seen to be even higher. Suppose, not unrealistically, that 20 percent of national income is required to finance defense, schools, police, payments on the national debt, roads, and so on and that these outlays necessitate a tax rate of 20 percent. To have an income floor of 50 percent of the average would require an additional 50 percent marginal tax rate and, therefore, an effective marginal tax rate on all households of 70 percent.

These arithmetical relationships, simple as they are, are extremely important to understanding how limited our ability is to achieve a substantially
more equal distribution of income through redistribution. Yet most people
discussing these matters seem completely unaware of how difficult it would
be for tax and transfer policies to alter materially the distribution of income
further. For example, a common suggestion of scholars is that an income
floor of half the average or median income level be established or that the
official poverty line be set at half the median-income level and then poverty
eliminated. Such ideas are always proposed as if they would be easy to accomplish; yet our discussion shows that transfer and tax programs that established an income floor of half the average would require marginal tax
rates on all households to be increased by perhaps 20 percentage points, a
50 percent increase for the average household.

The Equality-Efficiency Trade-Off

The sensitivity of the level of marginal tax rates to the amount of redistribution would be no obstacle to income redistribution except that economic
incentives are affected by the level of marginal tax rates. Higher marginal tax
rates are likely to diminish the quantities of labor and capital supplied, so
redistributing additional income will reduce society's total income. This relationship does not mean that redistribution is undesirable, but it does imply
that greater equality may be achieved only at the cost of a lower average
income. Put differently, raising the income of low-income households will
result in larger reductions in the incomes of upper-income households.
The magnitude of this trade-off between equality and efficiency is of
obvious importance in determining the appropriate amount of government
redistribution.

The size of the trade-off between equality and efficiency depends on a
number of factors, such as the current level of marginal tax rates, how responsive people's work and saving decisions are to tax and transfer programs, and the types of policies used to redistribute income. Since we
cannot measure some of these factors with much precision, we cannot estimate the trade-off exactly. Nonetheless, it is possible to use plausible values
for the various important factors and to show how they interact to determine
the cost of raising the income of low-income households.

Let us reconsider the redistributive policy we examined in Table 9–3, but
now let us evaluate the consequences when incomes fall in response to
higher marginal tax rates. In order to work this out, we make the following
assumptions. First, each family is initially confronting a marginal tax rate of
40 percent as a result of existing tax and transfer policies, that is, before the
linear income tax with its 10 percent rate is added. Second, all income is
labor earnings. Third, we assume that each family's labor supply elasticity
with respect to the net wage rate is 0.3. This is the crucial assumption since
it determines how much labor supply, and hence earnings, will decline as

Table 9–4 *The Marginal Cost of Redistribution*

	Lowest Quintile	Second Quintile	Middle Quintile	Fourth Quintile	Highest Quintile	Total
(1) Mean incomes	$ 9,734	$23,105	$35,851	$51,997	$95,530	$216,217
(2) Reduction in incomes	− 487	− 1,155	− 1,793	− 2,600	− 4,777	− 10,812
(3) Additional tax revenue	730	1,733	2,689	3,900	7,165	16,216
(4) Transfer	3,243	3,243	3,243	3,243	3,243	16,215
(5) Net transfer	2,513	1,510	554	− 657	− 3,922	0
(6) Change in net income	2,026	355	− 1,239	− 3,257	− 8,699	− 10,814
(7) New mean income	11,760	23,460	34,612	48,740	86,831	205,403
(8) New shares	5.7	11.4	16.9	23.7	42.3	100

the marginal tax rate rises.[12] Recall that an elasticity of 0.3 means that a 10 percent reduction in the net wage rate will reduce labor supply by 3 percent. This 0.3 figure is selected to reflect the available empirical evidence in the economics literature. It should be emphasized, however, that there is no consensus regarding just how large this value should be; some studies have estimated higher values and others have estimated lower values.

Now let us consider the effects of the 10 percent linear income tax in Table 9–4, which uses the same initial family incomes as the previous table. The linear income tax increases everyone's marginal tax rate from 40 to 50 percent. This implies that each worker's net wage rate falls from its initial 60 percent of the market wage (when the marginal tax rate was 40 percent) to 50 percent of the market wage, a reduction of 16.7 percent. With a labor supply elasticity of 0.3, labor supply and earnings will fall by 5 percent (0.3 × 16.7 percent). The implied reductions in earnings are shown in row (2) of Table 9–4.

The additional tax revenue collected from each family by the 10 percent tax is shown in row (3) (figures are rounded to the nearest dollar). Comparing these figures with those in Table 9–3, you will note that additional tax revenue is significantly smaller in this case, because earnings are reduced in response to the higher rate. A major reason for this effect on tax revenue is that when earnings fall, the government loses some of the revenue it

[12]Our example has earnings depend only on the marginal tax rate, but economic theory implies that the average tax rate (determined by the size of the net tax or transfer) also matters. Marginal tax rates govern substitution effects, whereas average tax rates govern income effects. For the transfer recipient, both effects operate in the same direction, but for the taxpayer they operate in opposing directions. We neglect this complication here, but in later chapters we examine in greater detail the way taxes affect taxpayers.

formerly collected with the previous 40 percent rate, and this loss must be made up before it has any additional revenue to redistribute.[13]

The additional $16,216 in revenue finances transfers of $3,243 per family as shown in row (4). Row (5) shows the net transfer, that is, the difference between the transfer received and the additional tax revenue collected. Taking taxes and transfers into account, the policy redistributes about $4,579 from the top two quintiles to the bottom three. Note that this is only about 2.1 percent of total income redistributed by the 10 percentage point increase in marginal tax rates. (The figure was 2.9 percent when there were no disincentive effects from the higher tax rates.) Thus, marginal tax rates rise by nearly 5 percentage points for each 1 percent of income redistributed, with the disincentive effect incorporated into the analysis.

The net transfers shown in row (5) do not indicate how much each family's income has been changed by the policy, however, because each family's earnings have also fallen. The change in disposable income is given by the sum of the net transfer, row (5), minus the reduction in earnings from row (2). The final effect on each family's net income is shown in row (6).

Overall, the linear income tax has raised the net incomes of the lowest two quintiles by $2,381, but at a cost of reducing the incomes of the top three quintiles by $13,195; the difference is how much the total income of the community has fallen due to the aggregate reduction in earnings. In other words, the cost to the top three quintiles per dollar increase in the income of the lowest two quintiles is $5.54. This is sometimes called the *marginal cost of redistribution,* and it is one way to express the magnitude of the trade-off between equality and efficiency. Repeating a point made earlier, this calculation does not tell us whether the additional redistribution is desirable; it only identifies some of the relevant effects that should be weighed in making that judgment.

Row (7) of Table 9–4 gives the new quintile shares after the redistribution. Note that the share of the lowest quintile is increased only to 5.7 percent, rather than to 6.1 percent when we assumed that the higher tax rates caused no reduction in earnings. (In addition, the shares are calculated relative to a lower total income, so they overstate the absolute gain in income at the bottom.)

Obviously, the exact numbers should not be taken too seriously; they are only meant to be illustrative. What they suggest is that it does not require a large disincentive effect for the marginal cost of redistribution to be substantial. The reason is that marginal tax rates rise sharply relative to the amount of income actually redistributed, and the disincentive effects are produced by the higher marginal tax rates. There is, however, one factor that we have ignored, which implies that the actual cost may be higher than suggested by this example. We have used the *annual* income figures from the Census

---

[13]The additional tax revenue can be calculated by first computing 10 percent of initial mean incomes; this is given in Table 9–3 and indicates how much revenue would rise if earnings did not decline. From this we must subtract the revenue loss when earnings do decline, and this loss is equal to 50 percent of row 2. Alternatively, take 50 percent of the difference between row 1 and row 2, and subtract from this 40 percent of row 1.

data, but as we saw in the last chapter, *lifetime* incomes are probably more important in determining how the well-being of people is affected. Lifetime incomes are more equally distributed than annual incomes, and starting with more equal incomes (all other things the same) results in an even higher marginal cost of redistribution.[14] (You might try using initial incomes that imply the lifetime share estimates in the last chapter, and then go through the steps in Table 9–4 to work out how this assumption will affect the gains and losses for the various quintiles.) On the other hand, in our numerical example, we have measured the marginal cost of redistribution in terms of its effect on disposable money incomes alone. If we include the value of additional leisure time (all quintiles are working less, and so have extra leisure), the marginal cost would be lower.

The NIT as a Reform Option

Over the past two decades, a number of economists of widely differing political persuasions have advocated an NIT as a replacement for most, if not all, federal welfare programs. At issue is whether a single transfer program with uniform nationwide standards would be more equitable and efficient than the current system, which is composed of a large number of separate— but overlapping and interacting—programs. Given the complexity of the existing system and the numerous factors that are relevant, arriving at a balanced judgment is difficult. Nonetheless, the major advantages and disadvantages of an NIT are fairly clear.

At the outset, it should be emphasized that we are considering an NIT of total cost equal to the programs it replaces. Thus, there would be no increase in the cost to taxpayers. The volume of redistribution is considered fixed, so we can focus on different ways of effecting this redistribution. As just noted, adding an NIT (in the form of a linear income tax) to the present system to increase substantially the amount of redistribution would be costly. Here we are concerned with welfare *reform,* not with an *expansion* of the system.

The principal advantages of an NIT as a replacement for existing welfare programs include the following:

1. Assistance would be in the form of cash; as shown earlier, recipients would generally be better off, according to their own preferences, if they could spend the transfers as they saw fit. This advantage supposes that the NIT would replace the in-kind transfer programs now in use. Although recognizing that several arguments favor in-kind transfers, proponents of the NIT find them generally unconvincing.

2. Administrative and compliance costs of an NIT would be lower. Although there is little firm evidence on this point, it seems generally agreed

---

[14]For a detailed analysis of the various factors that affect the size of the marginal cost of redistribution, see Edgar K. Browning, "The Marginal Cost of Redistribution," *Public Finance Quarterly,* 21:3 (Jan. 1993).

that the cost of administering a single, fairly simple program would be lower per dollar of transfer than for the present system, which is composed of many potentially overlapping programs. In addition, the costs borne by recipients in terms of filling out forms, establishing and maintaining eligibility, and so on would probably be lower under the NIT. Lower administrative and compliance costs mean that more resources can be made available to the poor at no extra cost to taxpayers.

3. Assistance would be objectively and uniformly related to need. Under the present system, there are wide differences in the level of assistance given to families with the same incomes. These differences reflect in part the fact that current programs grant assistance primarily to the poor who are elderly, in female-headed families, unemployed, and so on. What this means, for example, is that a poor person age 65 can receive assistance under SSI, but an equally poor elderly person age 64 may receive no assistance. Proponents of the NIT view disparities of this sort as inequitable; these disparities would be avoided by an NIT because a low income—for whatever reason—would entitle an individual to assistance. Families of the same size and income would receive equal transfers.

4. The NIT would concentrate transfers on those with low incomes. Recall that under the present system many programs confer a large share of their benefits on the nonpoor. Unemployment insurance, in which over 80 percent of the benefits go to families in the upper four fifths of the income distribution, is an example. Under an NIT, larger transfers would go to those with lower incomes. Although some of the transfers under the NIT would probably go to the nonpoor, depending on where the breakeven income is set, these transfers would be small compared to those received by lower-income families.

5. The NIT would be easier to understand than the present system. Not only would it be simpler to determine how much is being transferred and who is benefiting from it (which is quite difficult to determine with current programs), but the various trade-offs among the policy goals would also become more apparent. Existing programs require trade-offs of much the same type as the NIT, but this is often not understood because of the number of interacting programs involved.

Note that many of the advantages claimed for the NIT simply reflect perceived disadvantages of the present system. Proponents of the NIT view current programs as constituting a welfare mess, with severe inequities in the distribution of transfers among the poor, avoidable distortions in consumption patterns, high administrative costs, and a complexity that makes rational decision making impossible. Although the NIT is not presented as a panacea, it is viewed as an improvement over the status quo.

There are, at the same time, a number of disadvantages to substituting an NIT for existing programs. These disadvantages should be reviewed.

1. Money income is not always an accurate indication of need. We have already emphasized the inadequacies of annual income as a good measure of a family's standard of living. Because transfers under the NIT would be based on money incomes, they would not necessarily be related to need.

For example, a family may have a child who requires expensive medical treatment and is poorer in a meaningful sense (unless they have insurance) than another family with an equal money income. Of course, an NIT could allow medical expenses to be deducted, but the more special circumstances it tries to take into account, the more complex it becomes. In any event, the relevant question is whether standards under existing programs constitute a better definition of need than would the income measure employed by an NIT—not whether the NIT's measure is imperfect. Opinions on this point differ.

2. Work incentives would be impaired by the NIT. This contention is far from obvious because we are using the NIT as a replacement for existing programs that already imply high effective marginal tax rates. On the average, marginal tax rates need not rise under the NIT when it replaces other programs. What would happen is that marginal rates would rise for some low-income families and fall for others. Those families currently facing very high rates would generally have lower rates under the NIT, whereas the opposite would be true of families with unusually low rates now. Whether the net effect would be a reduction in work effort is therefore unclear, but it obviously could be.

3. The NIT would treat the symptoms but not the causes of poverty. It would give money to the poor but do nothing to help them become more self-supporting. This argument is usually advanced by those who advocate job training and educational subsidies to increase the earning capacity of the poor. The NIT would do nothing directly to increase earning capacity, but it would provide the means to finance job training if the recipient chose to use the subsidy in that way. It can be argued, however, that this is not enough. Unfortunately, evidence from the several manpower training and compensatory education programs that have been tried in the past leaves considerable doubt about the effectiveness of such policies.

4. Many poor families would find their benefit levels reduced under an NIT. No one likes the thought of reducing assistance to needy families, but some low-income families would clearly be worse off under an NIT. Families receiving unusually large benefits under the present system would have lower benefits under the NIT, just as those with unusually low benefits now would receive larger benefits. The average benefit level would go up somewhat because of the saving in administrative costs, but some would still be worse off. The real question is whether existing differences in benefit levels for families with equal incomes are equitable or inequitable. If these differences are inequitable, some people are getting too much and others too little now, and a move to the NIT would seem fair. In other words, would the distribution of benefits under the NIT formula be more or less fair than under the present system? The answer probably depends on whether the income definition of the NIT corresponds to one's view of need, as mentioned earlier.

5. It is sometimes argued that the taxpayers would not support so large a volume of redistribution under the NIT as they now do under present programs. Taxpayers, it is argued, are willing to pay taxes if the funds are

used to subsidize obviously needy groups (the elderly poor, female-headed households) or support consumption of necessities (food, housing, medical care). They might not, however, be willing to bear so large a tax burden when cash transfers are made to everyone with low incomes. This argument is difficult to evaluate because we do not understand precisely how the political process functions. Some have expressed the opposite concern: that by making the redistribution open and aboveboard, political pressures would push up the benefit levels of an NIT. After all, recipients vote, too. It is certainly possible that the politically determined volume of redistribution could differ under an NIT, so this is a legitimate concern in evaluating the proposal.

Replacing the current system with an NIT therefore raises a number of issues. Although we, along with many other economists, find considerable merit in the proposal, it is important to consider both its advantages and disadvantages.

Review Questions and Problems

1. Tom favors an NIT with a 50 percent marginal tax rate. Dick believes that no family should receive any cash if their income is about $12,000. Harry feels that no family's income should fall below $6,000. Can these goals be achieved simultaneously? Explain.

2. If an NIT causes a recipient to reduce her earnings so much that her disposable income does not change, the welfare cost of the NIT will be equal to the total amount spent: It will be entirely wasted. True or false? Explain.

3. Suppose that we now have an NIT with an income guarantee of $5,000, a marginal tax rate of 50 percent, and a breakeven income of $10,000. Then the policy is changed so that the income guarantee remains $5,000 but the marginal tax rate is reduced to one third. How will this change affect the work incentives of low-income households? (*Note:* Consider separately how it affects families with earnings below $10,000 and those with earnings between $10,000 and $15,000.)

4. How could a reform of AFDC that limited receipt of benefits to a maximum of two years result in a larger number of people receiving AFDC benefits? Do you think this outcome is likely?

5. "We can avoid the work disincentive problems of transfer programs just by requiring welfare recipients to work in public employment programs." Discuss.

6. In our welfare system, should greater reliance be placed on training and education programs and less reliance on outright income transfers?

7. Explain, using graphs, the income and substitution effects on labor supply for each of the three segments of the earned income tax credit schedule of benefits. Based

on this analysis, how do you think the total labor supply of recipients is affected by this program?

8. In what way, if at all, does economic analysis help you evaluate the desirability of the government's taking $10 billion from the nonpoor and giving it to the poor?

9. What is the marginal cost of redistribution, and what are the factors that determine its magnitude?

10. Table 9–4 illustrates the calculation of the marginal cost of redistribution for certain assumptions. How would the result differ if the initial marginal tax rate were 50 percent rather than 40 percent? How would the result differ if the labor supply elasticity were 0.5 rather than 0.3? Calculate the marginal cost of redistribution for each of these cases.

11. Calculate the marginal cost of redistribution based on the lifetime income distribution data in Table 8–6. (Use the before-tax figures, and make the same assumptions regarding labor supply and marginal tax rates that were made in Table 9–4.) How and why do the results differ from those given in Table 9–4? Which is a better measure of the economic effects of redistributing income?

12. Why is the effect of transfer programs on the work incentives of recipients important in evaluating these programs? In other words, why should we be concerned about the magnitude of disincentive effects?

13. What would be the major advantages and disadvantages of replacing all existing welfare programs with a single universal negative income tax?

Supplementary Readings

BROWNING, EDGAR K. "The Marginal Cost of Redistribution." *Public Finance Quarterly* (Jan. 1993).

BURTLESS, GARY. "The Economists's Lament: Public Assistance in America." *Journal of Economic Perspectives,* 4 (Winter 1990), pp. 57–78.

DANZIGER, SHELDON, ROBERT HAVEMAN, and ROBERT PLOTNICK. "How Income Transfers Affect Work, Savings, and the Income Distribution." *Journal of Economic Literature,* 19(3):975–1028 (Sept. 1981).

ELLWOOD, DAVID T. *Poor Support.* New York: Basic Books, 1988.

HOFFMAN, SAUL D., and LAURENCE S. SEIDMAN. *The Earned Income Tax Credit.* Kalamazoo: W. E. Upjohn Institute, 1990.

MEAD, LAWRENCE M. *The New Politics of Poverty.* New York: Basic Books, 1992.

MOFFITT, ROBERT. "Incentive Effects of the U.S. Welfare System: A Review." *Journal of Economic Literature,* 30 (Mar. 1992), pp. 1–61.

MURRAY, CHARLES. *Losing Ground: American Social Policy, 1950–1980.* New York: Basic Books, 1984.

OKUN, ARTHUR. *Equality and Efficiency: The Big Trade-off.* Washington, D.C.: The Brookings Institution, 1975.

CHAPTER 10

Principles of Tax Analysis

*T*O A LARGE EXTENT, THE ANALYSIS OF TAXES parallels the analysis of expenditures. Our major concerns remain how the policy affects the pattern of output of goods and services (allocative effects) and who bears the cost (distributional effects). As with expenditures, the exact consequences depend on the particular tax employed, but some general principles are helpful to keep in mind.

Tax Incidence

The questions "Who pays the tax?" and "Who bears the burden of the tax?" can have different answers. Determining who pays the tax is a simple matter of tax liability as defined by the tax statutes. Locating the economic units responsible for writing the checks covering the tax is not of much interest to economists because these units may not be the ones that actually bear the burden of the tax. Everyone knows this fact and believes, for example, that the federal excise tax on liquor, although paid by liquor producers, is actually passed on to consumers in the form of higher prices. *Tax incidence theory is concerned with determining who bears the real burden of taxation.* More generally, the incidence of a tax refers to its effects on the distribution of income.

All taxes ultimately result in a reduction in the real disposable incomes of some people. To refer to "business" or "property" bearing the burden of a tax is potentially misleading because businesses and property are owned by individuals, and it is these individuals who *may* suffer reductions in their real incomes as a result of business and property taxes. (Whether or not

306

these individuals actually *do* bear the burden of these taxes refers to the actual incidence of the taxes.) Do not be misled, therefore, by references to "businesses paying their fair share" of taxes because businesses per se do not bear the burden of any tax. It makes more sense to ask whether business *owners* bear a fair share of the tax burden.

Before proceeding we should consider the meaning of incidence more carefully; it is not as unambiguous a concept as might be thought at first glance. Possible ambiguity results from the necessity of accounting for what the government does with the tax revenues raised. The consequences of any tax obviously depend to some degree on how the government uses the revenue, because the government may tax individuals and then use the revenue to provide goods and services that benefit those who originally paid the taxes. Two different concepts of incidence are widely used by economists; these concepts differ in what is assumed to happen to the tax revenue.

Balanced-budget Incidence

Balanced-budget incidence refers to the distributional effects of a tax combined with the expenditure program it finances. In other words, it considers how the opportunity cost of a given spending policy is distributed among the public by the tax. Figure 10–1 illustrates this concept of incidence. ZZ is the production possibility frontier relating the outputs of food and clothing, assumed for simplicity to be the only two goods produced by the private sector. Initially, equilibrium is at point E, with outputs of food and clothing equal to F_1 and C_1.

Now let the government undertake an expenditure program to provide a public good. Because productive resources must be employed to produce the public good, a smaller quantity of resources will be available to produce food and clothing. The resources remaining in the private sector can produce the output combinations shown by $Z'Z'$. Suppose that an excise tax on clothing is used to finance the expenditure, and the final equilibrium on $Z'Z'$ occurs at point E_1.

The balanced-budget incidence of the tax-and-expenditure program compares the distributions of private income (here just food and clothing) associated with points E and E_1. Of course, Figure 10–1 does not show how the lower private income of the community at E_1 is divided among persons: we must go beyond the aggregate effects shown in the diagram to determine this. When we do so, however, we will be comparing the distributions of income implied by points E and E_1.

Balanced-budget incidence seems to be what most people think of as the incidence of taxation: It tells us how the cost of spending programs is divided among the population. It has the defect, however, of making the incidence of a tax depend on how the revenue is spent.[1] In other words, there

---

[1] A change in the expenditure program financed by the tax will normally have an effect on consumer demand. Thus, the point on $Z'Z'$ that will be an equilibrium under a given excise tax on clothing will depend in part on how the revenues are spent.

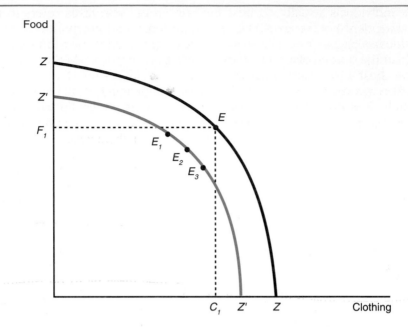

Figure 10–1 *Nature of tax incidence*

is no such thing as *the* balanced-budget incidence of a particular tax because the final effects depend on how the revenue is spent. In addition, it is usually impossible to say that a particular tax finances a particular spending program when the government utilizes many different taxes. For example, what expenditure does the federal excise tax on liquor finance? It is not possible to say, because the revenue goes into a general fund along with the revenue from dozens of other taxes, and thousands of spending programs are financed out of the general fund.

Despite these difficulties in applying balanced-budget incidence, this concept is useful in many contexts. It has the advantage of reminding us that taxes are the way we pay for government expenditures, and a comprehensive view of tax incidence often requires that both policies be considered together.

Differential Incidence

The concept of *differential incidence* assumes that government expenditures are held constant and then compares the distributional effect of substituting one tax for another. In other words, differential incidence compares alternative ways to finance a given government expenditure. Figure 10–1 can also be used to illustrate differential incidence. As we saw, point E_1 shows the equilibrium with an excise tax on clothing used to finance the expenditure on the public good. If an income tax were used instead of the excise tax, equilibrium might be at E_2. The differential incidence of the income tax relative to the excise tax involves a comparison of the distributions of disposable income implied by the alternative equilibria at points E_1 and E_2. The alternative method of financing could include more than two taxes; for example, E_3 might be the equilibrium under an excise tax on food.

Differential incidence avoids the necessity of considering the effects of expenditure programs by assuming that expenditures remain unchanged as one tax is substituted for another. It is still not an entirely unambiguous concept because the differential incidence of a tax depends on what other tax it is compared to. There is no such thing as "the" differential incidence of an excise tax because the effects differ, depending on whether it is compared to an income tax or a property tax. Generally, when this concept is employed, some tax is selected as a benchmark against which all other taxes are compared. A proportional tax on income is frequently used as the reference point.

Differential incidence and balanced-budget incidence are the two major concepts of incidence used by economists. Although neither concept is entirely unambiguous and without problems, they force us to be careful in defining clearly what is meant by the burden of a tax. Which concept to use depends largely on the purpose of the study. For example, if you are concerned with tax reform or with determining the "best" (according to some criteria) method of financing an expenditure, then the use of differential incidence is dictated by the subject of the investigation. However, if you are concerned with the impact of government on the distribution of income, balanced-budget incidence is the natural selection.

Incidence of Excise Taxes

A good way to begin to study tax incidence is to examine the effects of excise taxes. Although excise taxes are only moderately important as sources of revenue (in 1992 only $67 billion out of a total of $1,092 billion in federal revenue came from excise taxes), they permit many important principles of tax incidence to be illustrated. The incidence of the personal income tax and the social security payroll tax, the two most important sources of tax revenue, are examined in later chapters.

Let's consider the effect of a per unit excise tax on margarine. Assuming that the margarine industry is a constant-cost competitive industry, the pretax equilibrium is shown in Figure 10–2 by the intersection of the supply and demand curves at a price and quantity of P_1 and Q_1. An excise tax of $0.30 per pound of margarine is levied *on all firms* in the industry. This means that the minimum price at which firms will supply any given quantity of margarine to consumers will be $0.30 higher than before. Thus, the supply curve confronting consumers shifts vertically upward by $0.30 to $S + T$, and a new equilibrium is established at a price of $1.30 and quantity of Q_2.

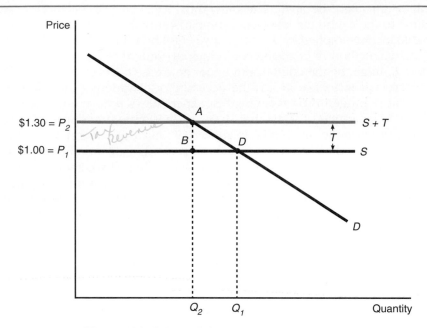

Figure 10–2   *Incidence of an excise tax*

With a constant-cost industry, the price to consumers ultimately rises by the amount of the tax per unit. In this case, the tax is said to be *shifted forward* to consumers because they bear the burden of the tax in the form of a higher price. In the final equilibrium, firms are receiving $1.30 per unit from consumers, but since the firms must remit $0.30 of this to he government, their net, or after-tax, price is $1, the same as it was befc re the tax. Consequently, factors of production engaged in producing margarine bear no tax burden.[2] Total tax revenue received by government is shown by the rectangle P_2ABP_1.

The term *shifting* refers to the process by which markets adjust to a tax. This process may permit the incidence of the tax to differ from the point of legal liability. In the present example, firms are legally liable for the tax, but the actual burden has been shifted to consumers through a higher price. *Unless a tax leads to a change in some market price or prices (including input prices), it cannot be shifted.* If the tax is not shifted, the economic units that are legally liable for the tax will also bear the incidence of the tax. Thus, determining the incidence of a tax actually involves ascertaining if and how market prices change in response to the tax.

---

[2]Here we are considering the long-run effects of the tax. In the short run, an excise tax may lead to a temporary reduction in the net price received by producers even in an industry in which the long-run supply curve is horizontal.

Shifting a tax is not a conscious process that occurs just because firms wish to avoid the tax. Firms as well as all other taxpayers would like to avoid the burden of taxation, but whether or not they can depends on the nature of the market as well as the type of tax. Consider an excise tax levied on only one firm in a competitive industry. If this firm raises the price, its consumers will purchase from other, untaxed firms, so the taxed firm must leave its price unchanged. Although the taxed firm would like to shift the tax to someone else, it cannot. The situation is entirely different when all firms are taxed, as in Figure 10–2. Therefore, shifting does not occur just because someone wants to avoid a tax; instead, the extent to which it occurs depends on the nature of the tax and the market to which it applies.

The analysis depicted in Figure 10–2 is not a complete analysis of the reaction of the economy to the tax. It is a *partial equilibrium analysis* that emphasizes the effects in the market directly affected by the tax and ignores secondary effects that may occur in other markets. Because markets are interdependent, other markets will be affected. For example, a tax that raises the price of margarine will increase the demand for butter (because butter and margarine are substitutes), and this enhanced demand may also increase the price of butter. Secondary effects such as this one are also relevant in determining the incidence (distributional effects) of the margarine tax but are generally ignored because they are thought to be much less important than the direct effects in the market where the tax is levied. Incidentally, a higher price of butter is not a *net* cost to the public because the higher price paid by consumers benefits the producers: It is a redistribution of income from butter consumers to butter producers. By contrast, the higher price paid by margarine consumers because of the tax does *not* benefit producers, so in this case the higher price does reflect a net cost on the public.

We have referred to the incidence of the tax on margarine as falling on margarine consumers, but which concept of incidence is being used here? Actually, the partial equilibrium analysis of an excise tax can be made consistent with either balanced-budget or differential incidence if appropriate assumptions are made. To interpret the analysis as balanced-budget incidence, it is necessary to assume that the revenue is not spent in a way that affects the supply or demand curves of margarine. To interpret the analysis as differential incidence, it is necessary to assume that the reduction in the other tax that the margarine tax replaces has no effect on the supply of or demand for margarine. In making either of these assumptions, we are clearly ignoring some conceivable secondary effects, but that is inevitable if we are to make the problem manageable. As a first approximation, then, the analysis of Figure 10–2 is probably accurate enough for most purposes.

Excise Tax Levied on Consumers

An *excise tax* is a tax on the sale of some product or service, and it can be collected from either the buyer or seller of the product. In practice, excise taxes are always collected from the seller as a matter of administrative convenience; there are fewer firms to deal with than there are consumers. It is instructive, however, to consider the effects of an excise tax that is collected from consumers.

Using our previous example, assume that there is a tax of $0.30 per pound of margarine that is levied on consumers. (We will ignore the administrative and compliance costs of this tax.) In Figure 10–3, the before-tax equilibrium is shown as Q_1 and P_1. In this analysis, it is important to recall that the height to the demand curve at each quantity is the maximum amount per unit that consumers will pay for that quantity. Thus, at quantity Q_1, consumers are willing to pay DQ_1, or $1.00, for that quantity. The fact that consumers must now pay a tax of $0.30 per unit does not change the amount they are willing to pay for margarine. What it does is to reduce the price that producers will receive, since the tax must come out of the unchanged price that consumers will pay. This reasoning holds for every point on the demand curve, so we can analyze the excise tax on consumers as a downward shift in the demand curve, with the curve shifting downward by the amount of the tax per unit. This result is shown in the graph by the demand curve $D - T$.

The new equilibrium produced by the tax on consumers is therefore at the intersection of $D - T$ and the unchanged supply curve at point B. In interpreting the equilibrium, note that the original demand curve, D, continues to show the total price per unit paid by consumers (including the tax), while the shifted demand curve, $D - T$, shows the corresponding price received by firms (net of the tax). Thus, at the equilibrium, consumers are

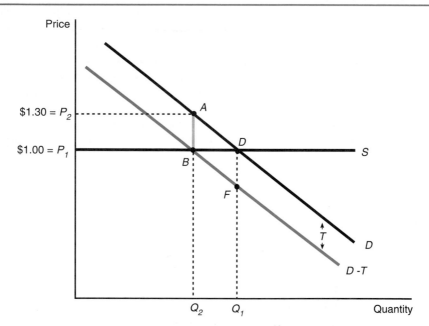

Figure 10–3   *An excise tax levied on consumers*

paying a price of AQ_2, or $1.30, and firms are receiving a price of BQ_2, or $1.00—the difference being the $0.30 tax per unit. This is exactly the same outcome produced when the tax is levied on firms, as we saw in Figure 10–2. In both cases, the tax per unit enters as a "wedge" between the buying and selling prices, as shown by the original demand and supply curves. (The tax wedge is shown by distance AB at the final equilibrium in both graphs.)

Therefore, the economic effects are the same whether the tax is collected from firms or from consumers. Of course, we made the same point about an excise subsidy in Chapter 4, so it is not particularly surprising that it remains true for an excise tax. One implication of this analysis is that an excise tax can be analyzed either as an upward shift in the supply curve or as a downward shift in the demand curve, regardless of which side of the market the tax is collected from. Thus, we could use Figure 10–3 to analyze an excise tax on firms, as long as we are careful to remember that one demand curve shows the price gross of tax (the price paid by consumers) and the other shows the price net of tax (the price received by sellers). This is helpful to keep in mind because in some cases it is easier graphically to use one approach than the other, as we will see in later examples.

Incidence and Elasticities of Supply and Demand

Our conclusion that an excise tax leads to an increase in the price paid by consumers equal to the tax per unit is valid when the industry is a *constant-cost* competitive industry. In general, the extent to which an excise tax leads to a higher price depends on the price elasticities of supply and demand, that is, on how responsive consumption and production are to a change in price. As we shall see, an excise tax may not always be passed on to consumers in the form of a higher price.

In Figure 10–4(a) we show the supply and demand curves for an increasing-cost (upward-sloping supply curve) industry, with an initial equilibrium at P_1 and Q_1. A per unit excise tax of $0.30 shifts the supply curve to $S + T$, but in this case, as firms cut back output, their reduced demand for productive resources leads to lower input prices. Thus, unit costs of production fall as output is reduced, and the price does not have to rise by the full amount of the tax to cover the now lower unit costs of production. The final equilibrium is at Q_2, with a price to consumers of $1.20, but with an after-tax price of $0.90 to producers. The final consumer price is higher than the production cost by $0.30, the amount of the per unit tax, but the production cost has fallen from the original equilibrium. In this case, the tax is said to be partially shifted forward to consumers (their price is $0.20 higher) and partially shifted backward to producers (their price is $0.10 lower). Both consumers and producers bear a burden from the excise tax when the supply curve is upward sloping.

When we speak of producers as bearing part of the burden of an excise tax in this case, we are using the term *producers* to refer to owners of some or all inputs used in producing the good. In fact, without knowing more about supply conditions, it is impossible to determine which input owners

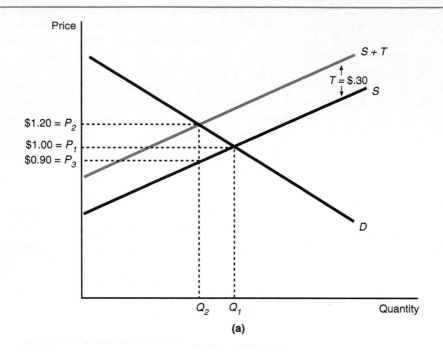

(a)

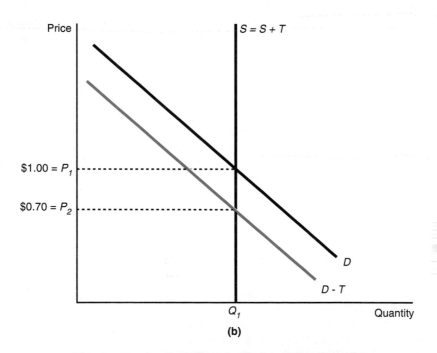

(b)

Figure 10–4   *Incidence of an excise tax with different supply elasticities*

are burdened. For example, workers in the industry, investors in the firms, or suppliers of raw materials could be the groups that bear the burden of the tax. Which group or groups are affected depend on the elasticities of supply of the inputs to the industry.

Figure 10–4(b) shows what happens if the industry supply curve is perfectly inelastic, that is, vertical. Under this condition, firms will not reduce output if taxed. The same level of output placed on the market will fetch the same price, so the price to consumers does not rise. Producers simply accept the reduced after-tax price and continue producing at the same level of output. Formally, this is shown by the fact that a vertical upward shift in a vertical curve does not alter the supply curve ($S = S + T$ in the diagram), so the market price remains unchanged at P_1. This result can perhaps be seen more easily by analyzing the tax as a downward shift in the demand curve to $D - T$, where the $D - T$ curve indicates the after-tax price that consumers are willing to pay for the product. As far as the firms are concerned, demand has simply fallen, but with a vertical supply curve a reduced demand leads to a lower price and no change in output. An excise tax on a good with a vertical supply curve therefore is borne entirely by producers.

This analysis suggests an important general principle: *The more inelastic the supply curve (with a given demand curve) is, the greater will be the share of the tax that will be borne by producers of the good.* This is a significant proposition, and it explains why economists believe that taxes on wages and salaries tend to be borne largely by workers (because labor supply is very inelastic), whereas taxes on particular products are often shifted forward to consumers (because product supply curves are generally highly elastic). A similar analysis will show that the incidence can also depend on the elasticity of demand: *The more inelastic the demand curve (with a given supply curve) is, the greater will be the share of the tax that will be borne by consumers of the good.* Taking these two principles together allows us to state that the incidence depends on the relative elasticities (or slopes)[3] of the demand and supply curves.

Significance of Tax Incidence

Determination of the incidence of taxation is important for a very simple reason: We want to know whether a tax leads to a just division of the cost of government expenditures. To determine whether the tax burden is shared fairly, we need to know the real burden placed on various economic groups by the tax; that is the subject of incidence analysis.

Economics cannot ascertain whether a tax is fair because "fairness" must reflect a value judgment about the incidence of the tax. Economics can, however, help us make more informed value judgments by determining

---

[3]Formally, the division of the burden between consumers and producers depends on the ratio of the slopes of the demand and supply curves, but this is exactly equal to the ratio of the elasticities of the curves. See John F. Walker, "Do Economists Ever Agree? The Case of the Teaching of Excise Tax Shifting and Incidence." *National Tax Journal,* 27:351 (June 1974).

the actual incidence of taxes. Still, many economists have attempted to formulate and refine the value judgments that are widely used to evaluate the fairness of the incidence of taxes. Our discussion of incidence would be incomplete without at least a brief mention of the criteria commonly used to evaluate the incidence of taxes.

Taxation According to the Benefit Received   Because the government expenditures financed by taxes provide benefits to people, the magnitude of these benefits could be used to determine the size of the tax burden various people should bear. To say that taxes should be levied in accordance with benefits received is to make a value judgment explicitly about the proper division of the tax burden.[4] The great advantage of the benefit principle is that it emphasizes the essential two-sidedness of government tax-expenditure decisions. If people do not receive benefits commensurate with their tax burden, then perhaps the expenditure should not be undertaken at all.

Even if we make this value judgment (and clearly not everyone would), its practical application in many cases is virtually impossible. As we have emphasized, there is usually no way of determining the benefits to specific people from expenditures on public goods such as national defense. In addition, applying this principle would be self-defeating in some instances. For example, if some people are taxed to provide funds to redistribute to other people, we cannot then tax the recipients according to the benefits they receive, for that would completely negate the effects of the redistribution.

Despite these practical problems in applying the benefit principle universally, there are cases in which people seem to approve of its selective application. Highway finance through taxes on gasoline is a case in point. Because the benefits from public provision of highways are probably correlated fairly well with gasoline use, a tax on gasoline places a tax burden on those who benefit from expenditures on highways. Another example is the payroll tax that finances social security benefits. Although taxes are not proportionate to retirement benefits received, there is some connection, as we saw in Chapter 7. Some believe that public support for social security is based in part on the perception that it is fair to base people's benefits on the taxes they pay, in effect suggesting that many feel that taxation according to the benefits received is equitable.

Taxation According to Ability to Pay   A second principle of fairness in taxation ignores the benefits from government spending altogether and considers how tax burdens should be allocated independently of who benefits from spending the revenues. This principle holds that taxes should be levied in accordance with the taxpayer's ability to pay, and it is often considered by

---

[4]The *benefit principle* holds that people should be taxed according to the *marginal* benefits they receive from government spending. Taxation according to *total* benefits means that taxpayers would receive *no* net benefit as a result of government spending and taxation. The discussion on pp. 32–34 of Figure 2–1 indicates how the taxes financing a public good should be divided among taxpayers according to the benefit principle.

many to be the basic criterion of justice in taxation. It suggests that those who have an equal ability to pay should bear the same tax burden and those who have a greater ability should bear a heavier tax burden.

Although "ability to pay" provides a convenient slogan, to implement it we must be more precise about its meaning. Under what conditions do two taxpayers have an equal ability to pay? In practice, many economists have assumed that income is the best measure of ability to pay. (As we will see, however, the definition of income is not exactly uncontroversial.) If this assumption is granted, then an equal tax burden for those equally able to pay (sometimes called *horizontal equity*) means that those with the same income should bear the same tax. By making these value judgments, we arrive at a criterion that can actually be applied as a benchmark to judge a tax. Note that an excise tax (constant-cost case) would fail the test of horizontal equity except in the unlikely event that all those with the same income purchased the same quantity of the taxed good.

What constitutes *vertical equity*—the treatment of those with different abilities to pay—is even more controversial. Although it is generally agreed that those with higher incomes have a greater ability to pay and should therefore bear a heavier tax burden, the principle does not tell us how much heavier the tax burden should be. (For example, if we decide to use an income tax to finance government expenditures, should a proportional or a progressive tax be used? In both cases, taxpayers at higher income levels would pay a larger tax than would taxpayers with lower incomes, but with a progressive rate the higher-income individuals would pay relatively more as well as absolutely more.)

Note that the ability-to-pay principle is simply an attempt to make an explicit value judgment about the distributional effects of taxes. Insofar as our concern is with the distribution of income, however, we should not forget that expenditure policies also have a major impact on the distribution. It is not clear whether it is appropriate to make judgments about the equity of a tax, regardless of the pattern of benefits from spending the revenue. For example, could we say that a tax is unfair if it takes $1,000 from a poor person while at the same time the person receives a $1,500 transfer from the government?

Partial versus General Equilibrium Analysis

We employed partial equilibrium analysis in our examination of the incidence of an excise tax. *Partial equilibrium analysis* refers to the study of a specific market, such as the market for the output of some industry. It examines the direct effects of the tax within this market and tends to ignore the secondary effects occurring in other markets. For example, we saw that the output of the taxed industry tends to fall. This means that productive resources leave the taxed industry and find employment in other industries, thereby increasing output and possibly depressing prices in other sectors. This secondary effect on other industries is ignored in a partial equilibrium analysis, which concentrates only on the taxed industry. Why do we employ an analysis that ignores some effects? Basically, it is because economists believe these secondary effects are usually sufficiently small, uncertain, and spread over so many other industries that we may legitimately ignore them and concentrate on the taxed industry, in which the effects are likely to be the most significant. More important, the secondary effects are unlikely to have a feedback effect on the taxed industry that would upset our conclusions concerning that market.

Partial equilibrium analysis provides an appropriate framework for the analysis of many problems, but there are some cases in which its application is inappropriate. *For a policy that directly affects one industry or market, partial equilibrium analysis gives reasonably accurate results, but for a policy that directly affects many or all markets, it can be misleading.* Let's consider one example to see why. A general sales tax is a tax on the sale of all goods and services in the economy; that is, it is an excise tax applied to all goods.[5] It is tempting to generalize on the basis of the results of our earlier partial equilibrium analysis of one excise tax in order to deduce the effects of a general sales tax. If we did this, we might conclude that a general sales tax tends to raise all product prices and is therefore borne by consumers. This, however, is unlikely to be so. Our earlier analysis of an excise tax in effect assumed that other industries were not taxed; when other industries are taxed—as with a general sales tax—the effect in any given market can be quite different, as we shall see next.

Incidence of a General Sales Tax

General equilibrium analysis is intrinsically difficult, since we must take account of what happens in several markets simultaneously. To make the analysis manageable, it is necessary to make some simplifying assumptions. Thus, we assume that there are only two products produced in the economy, X and Y, and they are produced by competitive industries. Only one input, labor, is used to produce these goods, and the total supply of labor is fixed (i.e., a vertical supply curve). We will also measure the output of X and Y in units such that marginal costs of production are equal, so that under competitive conditions the prices will be equal. (A unit of X might be an automobile, for example, and a unit of Y might be 15 refrigerators.)

With these assumptions, we can employ the open-topped box graph in Figure 10–5 to examine what is happening in both product markets. The origin for measuring the output of X is the left corner, 0_X, with output measured from left to right, and the origin for measuring the output of Y is the right corner, 0_Y, with output of Y measured *from right to left*. Thus, a point on the horizontal axis simultaneously measures both outputs; point E, for

---

[5]To qualify as a general sales tax, the tax must be the same percentage of the market price for all goods and services.

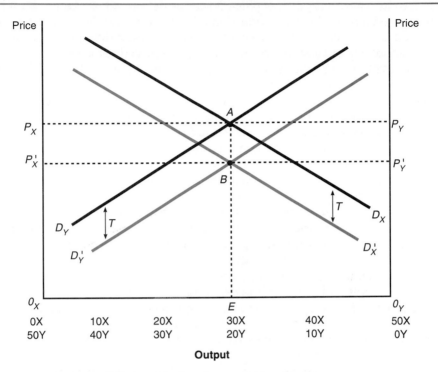

Figure 10–5   *A general sales tax*

example, indicates that the output of X is 30 units and the output of Y is 20 units. A movement to the right along the horizontal axis shows the output of X increasing and the output of Y decreasing (i.e., a movement along the production possibility frontier).

The demand curves are shown as D_X and D_Y, drawn relative to their respective origins. With units defined so that marginal costs are equal, the equilibrium before the tax is shown by the intersection of the demand curves at point A, since this point indicates the output mix where the prices are equal. (If the output of X was lower and that of Y was higher, the price of X would be higher and the price of Y lower, indicating profits in the X industry and losses in the Y industry.) In this simple economy, GNP is equal to the rectangle $P_X P_Y O_Y O_X$, or combined total outlays on the two goods. This area is also equal to the total wage income for workers, since with competitive industries there are no profits and all revenues are paid to providers of the single input, labor.

When we introduce a general sales tax, it is particularly important to be specific about what happens to the tax revenue collected. We will assume that the tax revenue is simply returned as lump-sum transfers to the consumers. This assumption makes it plausible to suppose that the demand curves are not affected by the tax because the public has the same total purchasing power after the tax-plus-transfer as before. All workers will continue to be employed in the production of X and Y; no public good is being financed by the sales tax. (Alternatively, we could use a differential tax-incidence approach and assume that the sales tax replaced some other tax.)

Now a sales tax of T per unit of both X and Y is imposed. We will analyze this situation by shifting both demand curves downward by T dollars, as shown in Figure 10–5 by D'_X and D'_Y. As with our analysis of an excise tax, the original demand curves continue to show the price including the tax, while the shifted demand curves show the price net of tax received by firms. The new equilibrium is indicated by point B where the shifted demand curves intersect, showing that the net prices received for both goods remain equal. Thus, the outputs of X and Y are not changed, and neither are the prices consumers pay (P_X and P_Y). The prices received by producers are lower by the amount of the tax per unit, AB; they become P'_X and P'_Y. Total tax revenue is shown by the rectangle $P_X P_Y P'_Y P'_X$. Total outlays on both goods together (GNP) is unchanged at $P_X P_Y 0_Y 0_X$, but after paying the tax, producers have net sales revenue of only $P'_X P'_Y 0_Y 0_X$. What this means is that firms have reduced revenues with which to pay workers, so wage rates must decline. (Recall that the supply curve of labor is vertical, so this reduction in the wage rate does not change employment.) Total wage income, in fact, declines to $P'_X P'_Y 0_Y 0_X$, so it falls by the amount of tax revenue collected. *In this situation the incidence of the general sales tax is on workers.*

Although workers have lower wage income as a result of the tax, they can continue purchasing the same quantities of X and Y at the unchanged (gross of tax) prices because we have assumed that the tax revenue is returned to them as lump-sum transfers. Total wage income falls by the amount of the tax revenue, $P_X P_Y P'_Y P'_X$, but this same sum is returned as transfers so the total purchasing power of the public is unchanged.

Although a general sales tax is just an excise tax applied at equal rates to all industries, note how the results differ. For a single excise tax, we expect the price of the taxed product to rise significantly because a single product supply curve tends to be highly elastic. But with a tax on all products, the relevant supply curve is the supply of all inputs to all industries together; that supply curve we have assumed to be perfectly inelastic, that is, vertical. (In practice, the labor supply curve may not be exactly vertical, but there is no doubt that it is quite inelastic.) Resources, labor in our example, do not have an incentive to move to an untaxed industry, as they do with an excise tax, since all industries are taxed and thus the wage rate goes down in all industries. In a sense, this conclusion has already been anticipated in our discussion of Figure 10–4(b), where we examined the effect of a tax in a market with a vertical supply curve.

Thus, in some cases it is important to utilize a general equilibrium analysis, which takes explicit account of interactions among all markets. It is not possible to lay down an ironclad rule concerning when it is appropriate to use partial and when to use general equilibrium analysis. Ideally, we would like to be able to trace out all the effects in any analysis, but no general equilibrium model has been developed that is capable of accomplishing such a gargantuan task. Instead, we try to use the simpler partial equilibrium approach when it seems plausible that we can get approximately correct results by focusing on a single market.

Absolute and Relative Prices

In our analysis of a general sales tax, we found that the tax burden fell on workers in the form of lower wage rates. This result seemingly contradicts the widespread view that sales taxes burden consumers by raising the prices consumers pay for products. In fact, we cannot rule out the possibility that absolute (dollar) prices will rise. It is not clear why the imposition of a tax would lead to an increase in the overall price level, but conceivably it could, especially if the monetary authorities follow an expansionary policy. Do these ambiguities mean that the incidence of the tax depends on whether the price level rises in response to the tax, something that would be very difficult to ascertain (since there are so many other factors affecting the price level)?

Suppose that product prices (inclusive of the sales tax) rise enough so that the net prices received by firms are unchanged. How would this outcome change our analysis? In fact, very little. In Figure 10–5, we could imagine *both* sets of demand curves shifting vertically upward so that the D' curves intersect at the original product prices. Both product prices (inclusive of tax) would still be equal, so relative product prices are unchanged, just as before. How about wage rates? Since net sales revenues in dollar terms for the firms are the same as before, the money wage rate does not have to change. But the *real* wage rate has then declined, since an unchanged money wage rate represents less purchasing power when the price level has increased. Therefore, workers are receiving a lower real wage rate, and the incidence of the tax is still on workers.

An important principle of tax incidence analysis is that the incidence of a tax depends on what happens to relative prices, not absolute prices.[6] In our example of a sales tax, workers bear the same burden when the absolute price level does not change (as in our previous discussion) as when it rises. In this case, the relative price change that governs the incidence of the tax is the wage rate relative to product prices, or $w/\mathbf{P}$ (sometimes called the *real wage rate*), where w is the nominal (money) wage rate and $\mathbf{P}$ refers to an index (like the CPI) of the absolute price level. In the last section, $\mathbf{P}$ did not change but w fell, producing a reduction in the real wage rate. Now we see that the same result occurs if w does not change and $\mathbf{P}$ rises.

---

[6]There are some minor exceptions to this proposition. For example, for those who have assets that are fixed in dollar terms, like bonds, it does make a difference whether or not the price level rises in response to a tax. For a further discussion, see Charles E. McLure, Jr., "Tax Incidence, Macroeconomic Policy, and Absolute Prices," *Quarterly Journal of Economics,* 82:255 (May 1969).

In some circumstances, it may not make much difference whether you think of workers or consumers bearing the burden of a sales tax, for they are largely the same people. In our example, workers consume all of their disposable income by spending it on X and Y, so if you think of the tax burden as falling in proportion to consumption, that incidence would give the same result as a tax burden falling in proportion to wage income. In more complex and realistic models, however, it can make a difference, and we will want to examine this issue again later when we consider empirical estimates of the distribution of the tax burden.

Equivalence of Major Broad-based Taxes

There are four taxes that have a tax base that is essentially equal to national income:

1. General sales tax: a tax levied on the sale of all final goods and services in the economy.
2. Individual income tax: a tax levied on all personal income in the form of wages and salaries, interest, dividends, royalties, rents, and any other payments for the services of productive resources.
3. Value-added tax: a tax levied on firms according to the value added by each firm. Value added is simply the firm's gross receipts minus the cost of intermediate goods that have already been taxed at an earlier stage of production.
4. Expenditure tax: a tax levied on the total outlays of households on goods and services.

These taxes are "broad-based" taxes because the tax base includes all of national income. Income and sales taxes are well known in the United States, and value-added taxes are used in a number of European countries. Expenditure taxes are rare.

Now we can state a proposition that at first glance is remarkable: All four of these taxes have identical economic effects. This proposition concerns the differential incidence of these taxes, and it means that substituting a general sales tax, for example, for an income tax leaves the real disposable incomes of all people unchanged. After our analysis of a general sales tax, this result can be understood easily. Recall that a sales tax tends to reduce wage rates and other resource prices. If an income tax were substituted for a sales tax, the wage rates paid by firms to workers would be higher, but the workers would have to pay part of their wages to the government. The workers' *net* wage rates would thus be reduced by either an income tax or a sales tax, and similarly for other resource prices.

Actually, this proposition of equivalence is simply an application of the result obtained earlier in our discussion of excise subsidies and excise taxes. It makes no difference on which side of the market (buyers or sellers) the subsidy (or tax) is levied. The tax base of all four of these broad-based taxes is national income, but each tax is levied at a different point in the circular flow of income. Figure 10–6 illustrates this point with the familiar circular flow diagram for a simple economy composed of households and firms. At point 1, national income is measured by the total sales of goods and services; a general sales tax is imposed at this point. At point 2, national income is measured as the sum of wages, rents, interest, and other factor payments; an income tax is imposed here. At point 3, national income is measured as the sum of value added by all firms; a value-added tax is levied on this sum. At point 4, national income is measured as the total expenditures of households on goods and services; an expenditure tax is levied on this base. Thus, all four of these tax bases are equal to national income, but the taxes are collected at different points in the circular flow.

These taxes can be shown to be *perfectly* equivalent to one another *only under certain strong assumptions*. For example, the tax base must be defined in a consistent way. Clearly, an income tax with numerous "loopholes"—deductions or exclusions—will not be equivalent to a general sales tax that strikes all goods and services. In addition, the equivalence holds only for taxes levied at a flat rate on each tax base. A progressive income tax using graduated rates will not be equivalent to a sales tax using a uniform rate.

In view of these and other possible qualifications, it is clear that real-world versions of these taxes will not be exactly identical. Nonetheless, recognizing their general similarity is quite helpful, as it allows us to see, for example, that there is likely to be little, if any, difference between a sales tax and a value-added tax in terms of their economic effects.

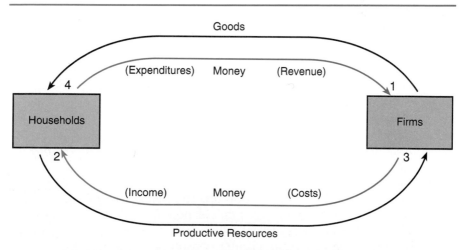

Figure 10–6 *Equivalence of major broad-based taxes*

The Welfare Cost of Taxation

All methods of financing government expenditures, including taxation, place a burden on people because they are part of the process that diverts control over resources to the government. In some cases, however, a tax will produce a burden that is larger than necessary to raise a given amount of tax revenue. This additional burden occurs because the tax leads to a misallocation of the resources that remain in the private sector. This welfare cost of taxation is also frequently referred to as the *excess burden* of taxation, to emphasize that it is a cost in addition to the direct burden as measured by the tax revenue raised.

It is important to distinguish clearly between the welfare cost of a tax and its direct cost as reflected in the withdrawal of resources from the private sector. This distinction can be seen most clearly with an example. Suppose that an excise tax is levied on vacuum cleaners, but the tax is set at such a high level that the output of vacuum cleaners falls to zero. In this case there is no direct cost due to the tax because no tax revenue is collected (and thus no resources are diverted to the public sector), but there is clearly a burden resulting from the tax. Resources are misallocated: Too few vacuum cleaners are produced and too much of other goods. We know that consumers would prefer to have more (than zero) vacuum cleaners and less of other goods because they chose that pattern of production through their purchases in the absence of the tax. Thus, consumers are worse off (they bear a burden) with the resource allocation produced by the tax. Note that this welfare cost exists even though there is no tax revenue (no direct cost), so the two types of burdens are conceptually quite different.

When an excise tax is levied at a rate that yields some positive amount of tax revenue, there is both a direct cost and a welfare cost. We can examine this case with the aid of Figure 10–7, in which it is assumed that the vacuum cleaner industry is a constant-cost competitive industry. An excise tax of $25 per vacuum cleaner raises the supply curve to $S + T$, so output falls from Q_1 to Q_2 and the price rises from P to P'. Tax revenue—the direct cost of the tax—is equal to $PP'BA$. Note that the price to consumers ($75) is now above the true marginal cost of production ($50); this difference is the source of the misallocation of resources that causes the welfare cost. *The tax has driven a wedge between the price that guides consumer decisions and the price (net of tax) that guides producer decisions.*

The welfare cost is reflected in a misallocation of resources involving too low an output of vacuum cleaners and too large an output of other goods. The reduction in the output of vacuum cleaners from Q_1 to Q_2 means that consumers sacrifice cleaners that are worth more than the cost of producing them. The reduction in vacuum cleaner consumption means a loss of benefits equal to BDQ_1Q_2—the sum of the marginal value of units from Q_1 to Q_2. This area BDQ_1Q_2 is *not* the welfare cost because it is not a *net* loss in

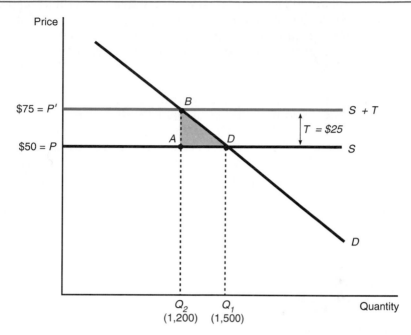

Figure 10–7 ***Welfare cost of an excise***
tax: constant-cost industry

welfare. The resources that were producing the Q_1–Q_2 units can be used to produce more of other goods. Thus, the tax restricts production of the taxed good and diverts resources to other uses, so that we get more of other goods. The value of the other goods produced, however, is less than the loss in value caused by the smaller output of the taxed good. The resources that produced the Q_1–Q_2 units have a market cost of ADQ_1Q_2, which is a measure of how much these resources are worth in the production of other goods. Thus, consumers sacrifice BDQ_1Q_2 in benefits because of restricted production of vacuum cleaners but gain ADQ_1Q_2 as a result of stimulated production of other goods. The loss exceeds the gain by the area BAD: *This triangular area is a measure of the net loss or welfare cost caused by the misallocation produced by the excise tax.* It is simply the difference between the demand curve (giving marginal value) and the supply curve (giving marginal cost) over the range of the output restriction that results from the tax.

Welfare Cost: An Alternative Perspective

An excise tax leads to an inefficient restriction in output of the taxed good. This distortion in resource allocation is, as we have mentioned, a cost in addition to the direct cost as measured by the tax revenue. The nature of this welfare cost can be further clarified by considering the effect on a single

consumer's welfare. In Figure 10–8, *MN* is the initial budget line, with vacuum cleaner consumption measured horizontally and consumption of other
goods measured vertically. Before the tax, the consumer was in equilibrium
at point *E*. An excise tax raises the price of vacuum cleaners and pivots the
budget line to *MN'*. The consumer's most preferred point on *MN'* is at point
E_1, consuming q_2 units of the taxed good. Total tax revenue is equal to E_1R.

To identify the welfare cost caused by this tax, we must show how the
same tax revenue could be raised by another type of tax and yet leave the
consumer better off. To do this, we assume that the tax revenue is raised
with a *lump-sum tax*. A lump-sum tax is a tax with a total tax liability that is
fixed and independent of the taxpayer's consumption pattern, income, or
wealth. For example, the taxpayer might be assigned a tax of $1,000 that
must be paid; it cannot be avoided by not earning income, not consuming
vacuum cleaners, and so on. Governments typically do not use lump-sum
taxes, and they are used in our analysis only as a benchmark against which
to compare the other taxes. Lump-sum taxes are a particularly good benchmark because they have no welfare cost: They do not interfere with the

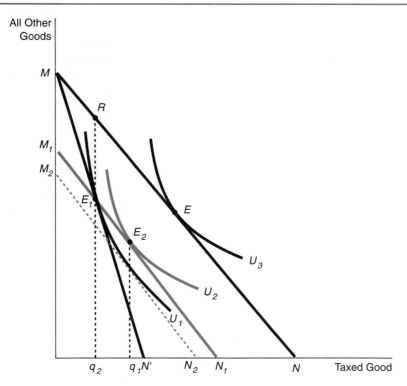

Figure 10–8 *Welfare cost of an excise
tax: individual perspective*

operation of any market by driving a wedge between prices on the two sides of the market.

A lump-sum tax that raises the same revenue as the excise tax (equal to E_1R) would shift the original budget line, MN, parallel and downward to M_1N_1. It would reduce the income of the consumer by MM_1 (equal to E_1R) but would not affect the relative prices of goods. Confronted with the M_1N_1 budget line, the consumer would be in equilibrium at point E_2, consuming more vacuum cleaners and less of other goods. Note in particular that the consumer would be better off (on a higher indifference curve) with the lump-sum tax, even though the tax revenue is the same as with the excise tax. The same amount of revenue raised by the excise tax could therefore be obtained without harming the consumer as much. The extra loss in welfare (the difference between U_2 and U_1) caused by the excise tax is the welfare cost.

The size of the welfare cost in dollars can also be shown in Figure 10–8. A lump-sum tax that produces the same level of welfare as the excise tax for the consumer is shown by the budget line M_2N_2 (tangent to U_1). This tax yields MM_2 in revenue, and MM_2 is a measure of the total (direct plus welfare) cost of the excise tax. Because the direct cost (tax revenue) of the excise tax is only MM_1, the difference, M_1M_2, is the welfare cost of the excise tax. In more advanced courses, the conditions under which M_1M_2 in Figure 10–8 (summed over all consumers) is equal to the area BAD in Figure 10–7 are spelled out. For our purposes, it is sufficient to note that both diagrams show the same distorting effect of the tax, but from different points of view. The q_1q_2 restriction in consumption shown in Figure 10–8 corresponds to the Q_1Q_2 restriction shown in Figure 10–7.[7]

Welfare Cost: Increasing-cost Industry

So far, our analysis has been confined to an excise tax levied on a constant-cost competitive industry. The welfare cost for an increasing-cost-competitive industry is shown as the area BAD in Figure 10–9. It is still measured by the area between the original demand and supply curves over the output restriction. Note in particular that the welfare cost is not equal to the area BAC—a fairly common error.

An excise tax therefore produces a hidden cost in the form of a misallocation of resources that remain (after the tax) in the private sector. The total

[7]The careful reader will note that the q_1q_2 reduction in consumption in Figure 10–8 is not the difference in consumption before the tax and after the tax. It is instead the difference in consumption under the excise tax and under a lump-sum tax that does not distort the consumer's decisions. For Figure 10–7 to be perfectly consistent with this result, the demand curve must be constructed on the assumption that consumers stay on the same indifference curves at all points on the demand curve. Such a demand curve is called a *compensated* demand curve and is the relevant one in estimating welfare costs. In most cases, this complication is a theoretical subtlety that has little practical significance; in the case of an income tax, however, it is of some importance, as seen in the next chapter.

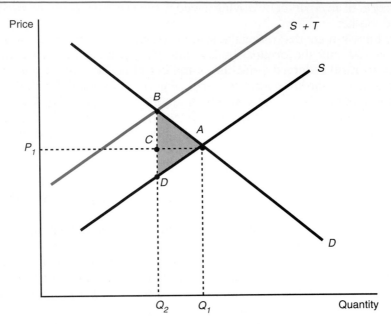

Figure 10–9   *Welfare cost of an excise*
                  tax: increasing-cost industry

sacrifice borne by people is greater than would be anticipated by considering only the tax revenue. This result is also true of all other real-world taxes.
Note, however, that this analysis says nothing about whether the expenditures financed are worthwhile. The expenditures may provide benefits that
are greater than the sum of the direct and welfare costs of the taxes. We are
now restricting our attention to the tax side of the budget in an attempt to
understand the nature of the costs of taxation.

One significant qualification to the analysis should be mentioned. It was
implicitly assumed that the taxed market was efficient in the absence of the
tax. When the taxed market is inefficient, the analysis becomes more complex. For example, an excise tax levied on a good whose production generated external costs might not produce a welfare cost. In fact, in this setting,
as we saw in Chapter 2, a tax might actually improve resource allocation.
However, an excise tax on a monopoly would be doubly inefficient because
it would restrict production of a good that is already being produced in too
small a quantity.

Other Sources of Welfare Cost

Economists usually emphasize the distortions in resource allocation that
taxes produce by driving a wedge between buying and selling prices in one
or more markets. There are, however, other types of welfare costs that can
be important on occasion.

Administrative Costs Government administrative costs are a type of welfare cost because these costs reduce the *usable* revenue received by government. If the government collects $100 billion in revenue but $1 billion must be spent in keeping records, auditing, printing and mailing forms, and so on, then the government will have only $99 billion to spend. Thus it will cost the public $100 billion (plus the other welfare costs) to provide $99 billion in revenue that can be used to finance desired expenditures. The size of the administrative costs will vary from one tax to another. For all federal taxes taken together, the administrative cost of the Internal Revenue Service typically is only 0.5 percent of tax revenues.

Compliance Costs Administrative costs recorded by the government do not include all collection costs because individual taxpayers bear significant costs in complying with tax laws. Compliance costs include the time used in reading, understanding, and filling out tax forms; using tax lawyers and accountants; keeping records in order to fill out (and possibly defend) the tax forms; mailing the completed returns; and using the banking system to transfer funds. Complying with the tax laws can be quite costly. For example, a recent study estimated that taxpayers devoted about 2,000 million hours to filing tax returns in 1982.[8] Even though this cost is not recorded as a monetary outlay, it makes the burden on the public greater than the revenue received by government. Valuing this time cost using market wage rates, Slemrod and Sorum estimated that the compliance cost was between 5 and 7 percent of the revenue collected from income taxes. This evidence suggests that compliance costs are substantially larger than the administrative costs recorded by the government.

The Magnitude of Welfare Costs

We have discussed the nature of the welfare cost produced by the "tax wedge." It is also important to understand under what conditions this welfare cost will be high. In other words, what determines the size of the welfare cost? Two important determinants are considered here.

Price Elasticities of Supply and Demand

In Figure 10–10, the original demand and supply curves are D and S. As we have seen, a tax of $25 per unit produces a welfare cost that can be measured by the triangular area *BAD*. Now suppose that we keep the tax per unit fixed and see what happens to the welfare cost if the price elasticity of demand for the taxed good is greater. A more elastic demand curve—which implies the same before-tax price and quantity—is shown by D'. With this demand curve, the tax would reduce output to Q_3, and the welfare cost would be

[8]Joel Slemrod and Nikki Sorum, "The Compliance Cost of the U.S. Individual Income Tax System," *National Tax Journal,* 38:461 (Dec. 1984).

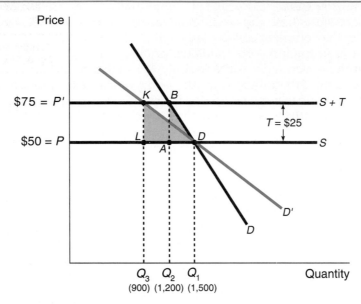

Figure 10–10   ***Effect of demand elasticity***
on welfare cost

equal to area *KLD*. Note that *KLD* is larger than *BAD:* Both triangles have the same height (*KL = BA* = tax per unit), but the base of *KLD* (*LD*) is greater than the base of *BAD* (*AD*). (Recall that the formula for the area of a triangle is one half the base times the height.)

This illustrates an important proposition: *The more elastic the demand curve for the taxed good is, the greater will be the welfare cost of a given per unit tax.* In other words, taxing goods with an inelastic demand will produce a smaller welfare cost. An inelastic demand means that consumption is *less responsive* to the higher price, so the reduction in output produced by the tax will be smaller. Thus, resource allocation is less distorted because it depends to a smaller degree on relative prices in this case.

Other things being equal, then, taxes on goods with inelastic demand are to be preferred. Unfortunately, other things are not always equal. Goods with inelastic demands are often "necessities" that are consumed heavily by low-income households. Cigarettes, for example, are in inelastic demand, but a tax on cigarettes would place a relatively heavier burden on low-income smokers compared with high-income smokers. In short, we must be concerned with the distributional effects (incidence) of taxes as well as their welfare costs, and this fact frequently involves unpleasant trade-offs.

On the supply side, a similar analysis can be employed to show that the welfare cost of a given per unit tax will be smaller the more inelastic is the supply curve of the taxed good. (The reader may wish to verify this result.)

Thus, goods in inelastic demand or supply are good bases for taxes. Because labor supply (in the aggregate) is thought to be very inelastically supplied, a tax on labor income would produce a relatively small welfare cost. Indeed, the belief that the supply of productive resources (land, labor, and capital) is relatively inelastic is in part the basis for support among economists for broad-based taxes such as income taxes. Because the demand and/or supply elasticities of specific goods are generally high relative to the elasticity of labor supply, for example, economists believe that taxes on labor income will produce smaller welfare costs than excise taxes.

The Tax Rate

By now it is probably obvious that the welfare cost will be greater the larger the tax per unit (with given demand and supply curves). The exact relationship between the tax rate and the size of the welfare cost is, however, not obvious and requires careful consideration.

In Figure 10–11, the welfare cost of a $25 per unit tax is equal to area *BAD*. Now consider a larger tax per unit of $50. This tax shifts the supply curve to $S + T_2$, and equilibrium is established at Q_3 and P_3. The welfare cost is equal to area *KLD*. Triangle *KLD* can be decomposed into four triangles of equal size: *KRB, RBL, LBA,* and *BAD*. Thus, the welfare cost of the $50 per

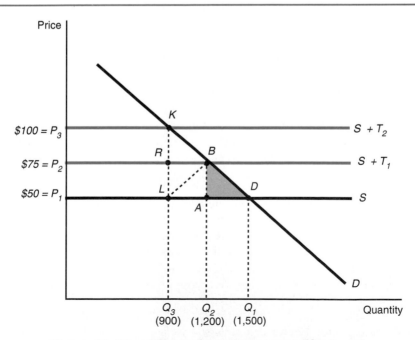

Figure 10–11   *Effect of tax rates on welfare cost*

unit tax is four times as great as the welfare cost of the $25 tax per unit. *Doubling* the tax per unit *quadruples* the welfare cost.

The reason why the welfare cost increases faster than the tax rate can be understood by considering what happens as the tax is gradually increased. Raising the tax curtails consumption that is increasingly worth more than its cost. The additional (marginal) welfare cost is equal to the excess of the marginal value of curtailed consumption over its marginal cost. For example, if the tax is $25 per unit and is increased slightly, the 1,200th unit will not be produced (consumed). This unit has a marginal value of $75 and a marginal cost of $50, so forgoing this unit of output causes a *net* loss of $25. If the tax is $50 per unit, a small increase will lead to the 900th unit's not being produced, and that unit is worth $50 more than its cost. In other words, as the tax is increased, the additional consumption that is choked off has a higher and higher net benefit (excess of demand over supply price). The marginal damage done by the tax increases with the tax rate, which implies that the total welfare cost increases more than in proportion to the tax per unit.

One implication of this conclusion is that a number of low-rate taxes can produce the same revenue at a lower welfare cost than one tax levied at a higher rate. Instead of doubling one tax rate (and quadrupling the welfare cost), we can use a second tax and raise the additional tax revenue by only approximately doubling the welfare cost. As we tax more goods at low rates, we begin to approach a broad-based tax like a general sales or income tax. Thus, this analysis also suggests that broad-based taxes are likely to have a smaller distorting effect than a high tax rate levied on a few goods.

Estimation of the Welfare Cost of Taxation

Our analysis of the determinants of the magnitude of the welfare cost of an excise tax can be summarized by deriving a general formula for estimating the welfare cost. Referring back to Figure 10–11, the welfare cost of the $25 excise tax is given by the triangular area *BAD*. The height of the triangle (*BA*) equals the tax per unit, and the base (*AD*) equals the quantity reduction. Thus, the welfare cost can be expressed as

$$W = 1/2\ T\Delta Q \qquad (1)$$

where W is the total welfare cost (area *BAD*), T is the tax per unit, and ΔQ is the reduction in quantity caused by the tax. The quantity reduction depends on the elasticity of demand, and we can express the ΔQ term in terms of the demand elasticity. Recall that the price elasticity of demand is defined by

$$\eta = \frac{\Delta Q/Q}{\Delta P/P} \qquad (2)$$

By solving equation (2) for ΔQ, we get

$$\Delta Q = \frac{\eta(\Delta P)Q}{P} \qquad (3)$$

which shows how the change in quantity depends on the elasticity of demand and the change in price. For an excise tax on a constant-cost competitive industry, the change in price caused by the tax (ΔP) is equal to the tax per unit (T), so the right side of equation (3) can be rewritten as $\eta TQ/P$. Substituting this expression for ΔQ in equation (1), we get

$$W = 1/2 \left(\frac{\eta T^2 Q}{P} \right) \tag{4}$$

This formula shows that the welfare cost varies in proportion to the elasticity of demand and with the square of the tax per unit, conclusions we have already explained. Equation (4) has been derived for a per unit excise tax; actually, most excise taxes are *ad valorem,* levied as a certain percentage of the market price rather than as a fixed sum per unit of output. Equation (4) can easily be modified to yield the formula for an ad valorem tax. The tax rate of an ad valorem tax (t) is equal to the tax per unit (T) divided by the price, or $t = T/P$. Thus, we can substitute tP for T in equation (4) to obtain

$$W = 1/2 \ \eta t^2 PQ \tag{5}$$

Equation (5) is the most commonly used formula for estimating the welfare cost of an excise tax. As we now understand, the welfare cost depends on the demand elasticity, the tax rate, and the total expenditures on the taxed good (PQ). Variations of this formula have been used to estimate the welfare costs of monopolies, tariffs, and other taxes: It is a general formula and well worth understanding thoroughly.

The derivation of equation (5) was based on the assumption that the taxed good was produced under constant-cost conditions. For an increasing-cost industry—one with an upward-sloping supply curve—the formula is slightly different because the welfare cost depends on both supply and demand elasticities. The formula is[9]

$$W = 1/2 \left(\frac{\eta \varepsilon}{\eta + \varepsilon} \right) t^2 PQ \tag{6}$$

where ε is the price elasticity of supply. Equation (5) is the one most frequently used because constant costs are thought to be a reasonable approximation in many cases.

Now let us apply equation (5) to a few hypothetical examples to get a feeling for the likely quantitative significance of the welfare cost of an excise tax. Suppose that an ad valorem excise tax of 20 percent is applied to a good with total expenditures (PQ) of $1 billion and a demand curve of unitary elasticity. By applying equation (5), $W = \frac{1}{2}(1)(0.2)^2 \times \$1$ billion, or $20

---

[9]For a derivation of this formula, see Robert L. Bishop, "The Effects of Specific and Ad Valorem Taxes," *Quarterly Journal of Economics,* 81:198 (May 1968). Note that as ε becomes larger and approaches infinity, $\left(\dfrac{\eta \varepsilon}{\eta + \varepsilon} \right)$ approaches η as a limit. Thus, for high elasticities of supply, equation (6) approaches equation (5) as a limit.

million. Because the tax revenue would be $200 million, the welfare cost in this example would be 10 percent of the tax revenue. For a tax rate of 40 percent, the welfare cost would be $80 million, equal to 20 percent of the tax revenue. Whether or not these welfare costs are considered large depends on one's viewpoint, but they are far from insignificant. (Recall too that the formula does not measure the welfare costs due to administrative and compliance costs.)

Incidentally, equation (5), or equation (6) if appropriate, can be used to estimate the welfare cost caused by externalities. In this case, the term t in the formula is interpreted to be the marginal external effect at the market equilibrium as a percentage of the market price. For example, suppose that the marginal external benefit is 10 percent of the market price of some good. If total expenditures on the good are $1 billion and the demand elasticity[10] is 1, then $W = \frac{1}{2}(1) \times (0.1)^2 \times \$1$ billion, or $5 million. The welfare cost is only 0.5 percent of the $1 billion market.

Importance of the Welfare Cost of Taxation

The welfare cost of taxation is significant for the analysis of two different problems. First, it is useful in comparing taxes with one another to determine what tax or taxes can raise a given revenue at the smallest welfare cost. Although all real-world taxes produce welfare costs, the distortions produced by different taxes are likely to vary considerably. For example, both theory and evidence suggest that an income tax produces a smaller welfare cost than does an excise tax yielding the same revenue.[11] Unless distributional considerations suggest otherwise, this analysis implies that an income tax is better than an excise tax. The welfare cost of taxes is significant for another, probably more important reason: *The welfare cost of taxation is part of the cost involved in carrying out government expenditures.* If the government spends $1 billion on some project, the cost to the public is the direct cost of sacrificing $1 billion in tax revenue *plus* any welfare costs resulting from the taxation. We made this point briefly in our discussion of expenditure analysis in Chapter 4, and now we are in a position to consider the matter further. What is relevant as part of the cost of government spending is the *marginal welfare cost* of taxation—the additional welfare cost associated with raising the revenue to finance the expenditure. The triangular areas we have identified in our graphs as welfare costs refer to the *total*

---

[10]The demand elasticity relevant for this computation is the elasticity of the marginal social benefit curve including the external benefits, not the consumers' private demand curve.

[11]Arnold C. Harberger, "Taxation, Resource Allocation, and Welfare," in his *Taxation and Welfare* (Boston: Little, Brown, 1974).

welfare cost of the tax, and that cost is often not directly relevant to expenditure analysis.

To clarify the distinction between total and marginal welfare cost, consider Figure 10–12. Suppose that the tax per unit is currently T, and the revenue raised by this tax is used to finance several expenditure policies (just as the revenue from a small number of federal taxes finances thousands of programs). As we have seen, the total welfare cost of raising all this revenue is shown by the area *BAD* in the graph. But now suppose that we are analyzing a proposal for a new expenditure policy: How does the welfare cost of the tax affect the cost of the expenditure policy? Assume that the tax per unit must be raised to T' to raise the additional revenue required for the new expenditure. With a tax per unit of T', the total welfare cost is now area *FGD*. Thus, raising the tax revenue for the new program has increased the welfare cost from *BAD* to *FGD,* or by the trapezoidal area *FBAG.* This trapezoidal area is the *marginal* welfare cost associated with financing the expenditure policy, and it is this magnitude that should be added to the tax revenue to give us the total social cost of the expenditure policy.

A simple numerical example can illustrate how marginal welfare cost can be measured in principle and how it relates to expenditure analysis. We will consider an excise tax on a constant-cost competitive industry where the quantity is 1,000 units and the price is $1.00 before any tax is applied. Assume that the demand curve is linear such that for each $0.10 increase in

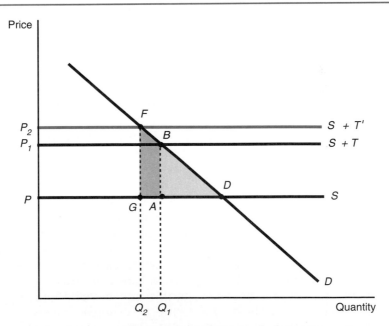

Figure 10–12 *Marginal welfare cost of an excise tax*

price the quantity purchased will fall by 50 units. This is all the information we need to construct Table 10–1.

In Table 10–1, when the tax per unit is $0.10, the quantity consumed falls to 950, so the total tax revenue is $95 (950 × $0.10), as shown in column (3). Similarly, if the tax per unit is $0.20, the quantity consumed is 900 and the total tax revenue is $180. Raising the tax per unit from $0.10 to $0.20 thus increases the tax revenue by $85 ($180 − $95), as shown in column (4). Column (5) gives the *total* welfare cost associated with each tax per unit. For example, when the tax is $0.20, the height of the triangle (*BA* in Figure 10–12) is $0.20 and the base is the reduction in quantity, or 100 units (1,000 − 900), so the area of the triangle, the total welfare cost, is $10.

Marginal welfare cost is, of course, the increase in total welfare cost as the tax is raised. For example, when the tax is increased from $0.20 to $0.30, the total welfare cost rises from $10.00 to $22.50, or by $12.50: This is the marginal welfare cost of increasing the tax from $0.20 to $0.30, as shown in column (6). To see how this relates to expenditure analysis, suppose that the current tax is $0.30. There is an expenditure policy proposed that requires an outlay of $65, so the tax per unit must be increased to $0.40 to finance it. The marginal welfare cost is $17.50, so the total social cost of financing this expenditure is $65 (the direct tax burden) plus $17.50, or $82.50. The expenditure program must therefore provide benefits of greater than $82.50 from the $65 in spending if it is to be worthwhile on efficiency grounds.

A convenient way to measure marginal welfare cost is as a percentage of the additional tax revenue raised when the tax per unit is increased. This is done in column (7). For the example just considered, with the tax increased from $0.30 to $0.40, the marginal welfare cost is 26.9 percent of the additional revenue ($17.50/$65). This calculation means that each dollar of spending over that range has a cost of $1.269, $1.00 as a direct tax burden and $0.269 in added welfare cost. The *marginal welfare cost per dollar of (additional) revenue* thus indicates how much more than $1 each dollar of revenue really costs, and that is what we need to know in analyzing an expenditure policy.

One important implication of this analysis is that the marginal welfare cost of taxation is larger the higher the current level of tax rates. Figure 10–13 shows how to incorporate this conclusion into an analysis of government spending. Government spending is measured on the horizontal axis, and the marginal benefits and costs per dollar of expenditure are measured on the vertical axis. The marginal cost of spending depends on how large the marginal welfare cost per dollar of revenue is. For example, if a tax with no welfare cost, like a lump-sum tax, is used to finance all spending, then the marginal cost per dollar of spending would be exactly $1—equal to the direct tax burden plus the zero marginal welfare cost. This result is illustrated by the MC_D curve in the figure. In this case, the efficient rate of government spending would be S_2, where the government spends up to the point at which the marginal benefit equals the marginal cost of $1.

Table 10–1 *Marginal Welfare Cost of an Excise Tax*

Quantity (1)	Tax (2)	Tax Revenue (3)	Additional Tax Revenue (4)	Welfare Cost (5)	Marginal Welfare Cost (6)	Marginal Welfare Cost as a Percent of (4) (7)
1,000	$ 0	$ 0		$ 0		
950	0.1	95	$95	2.5	$ 2.5	2.6%
900	0.2	180	85	10.0	7.5	8.8
850	0.3	255	75	22.5	12.5	16.7
800	0.4	320	65	40.0	17.5	26.9
750	0.5	375	55	62.5	22.5	40.9
700	0.6	420	45	90.0	27.5	61.1

When the government uses taxes producing welfare costs, the marginal cost of spending $1 is greater than $1. This is shown by the *MC* curve, where the vertical distance between the *MC* and *MC_D* curves at each level of spending equals the marginal welfare cost per dollar of revenue. The *MC* curve

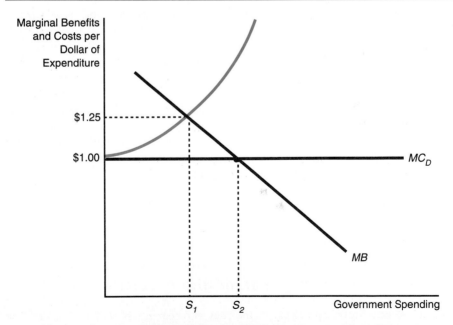

Figure 10–13 *Efficient level of government expenditures financed with distorting taxes*

slopes upward because marginal welfare cost per dollar of revenue increases with the level of tax rates, as shown by our numerical example. With the upward-sloping MC curve, the most efficient level of government spending is at S_1. At this point, the marginal benefit from spending at $1.25 is equal to the marginal cost of $1.25, where the marginal cost is the sum of the direct tax burden ($1) and the marginal welfare cost per dollar of additional tax revenue ($0.25).

Although the marginal cost curve slopes upward, it is often appropriate to treat marginal cost as a constant in analyzing expenditure policies. To see why, suppose that government spending in Figure 10–13 is applied to hundreds of separate policies. Each policy is a small part of total spending, and therefore the increment in the tax rate required to finance it is also small. For example, if the tax rate is 40 percent, it might be possible to reduce it only to 39.9 percent by eliminating any single expenditure policy. Thus, there would be very little change in marginal cost over this range. In other words, in Figure 10–13, *the* marginal cost is $1.25 when considering any one of the hundreds of expenditure policies, since eliminating any of them would produce only a tiny movement along the MC curve. *Every* policy must produce benefits of more than $1.25 per dollar spent if it is to be efficient.

One implication of this analysis is that *it is not efficient for the government to correct all inefficiencies in resource allocation.* There must be some inefficiency in resource allocation whenever it is possible for the government to provide benefits of more than $1 by spending $1. But if the marginal benefit is less than $1.25 (in our example), the public would be worse off if government undertook the expenditure because of the even greater inefficiency produced when tax rates are increased to finance the program.

Clearly, the magnitude of the marginal welfare cost is therefore of the utmost importance. Many factors interact to determine the size of the marginal welfare cost, and some of these factors are not known with much certainty, although there has been a great deal of research in trying to estimate marginal welfare costs for various taxes in recent years. We will report the results of some of this research in later chapters.

Review Questions and Problems

1. "Those who pay the tax may not be the ones who bear the tax burden." Explain what this means, and give an example of a tax where such a distinction is important.

2. "In the presence of excise taxes, the price received by producers will differ from the price paid by consumers, and both of these prices may differ from what they would be in the absence of the tax." Give an example to illustrate the point made in this

statement, and explain how the relationships among these three prices are used to ascertain the incidence of the tax.

3. In applied tax incidence analysis, economists often assume that excise taxes are borne entirely by consumers. Under what conditions is this assumption appropriate?

4. Suppose that the demand curve for a product is perfectly horizontal and that an excise tax of $1 per unit is levied on suppliers. Use supply and demand curves to illustrate who pays the tax.

5. Explain why it is not inconsistent to hold that excise taxes are shifted forward to consumers in the form of higher prices, but to argue that a general sales tax does not lead to higher product prices but instead to lower input prices.

6. Why is it important to use general equilibrium analysis when analyzing a general sales tax, whereas a partial equilibrium approach is generally considered adequate for the analysis of an excise tax?

7. The real burden of a tax is the sum of the revenue it raises plus the welfare cost it creates. True or false? Explain.

8. Why does an excise tax produce a welfare cost? Describe this welfare cost. Would there be a welfare cost if the excise tax were placed on an industry with external costs?

9. Explain why a lump-sum tax is used as the reference tax when evaluating the welfare cost of an excise tax.

10. The excise tax on cigarettes is generally thought to produce a smaller welfare cost (per dollar of revenue) than does the excise tax on wine. Why? Does this conclusion imply that the excise tax on cigarettes is better than the excise tax on wine? Why or why not?

11. Assume that the government has to raise a given amount of revenue by taxing two goods with different elasticities of demand. What policy advice would you provide that would minimize the welfare cost of the taxation?

12. Why is it important to recognize the welfare cost of taxation when analyzing a government expenditure policy? What role does the welfare cost play in the analysis?

13. A product has a demand curve given by $Q = 2,500 - 50P$, and it is produced by a constant cost competitive industry with a supply curve horizontal at a price of $10. Construct a table that shows the tax revenue and total welfare cost with an excise tax of $1 per unit, $2 per unit, and so on up to $10 per unit. What is the average welfare cost per dollar of tax revenue for each tax? What is the marginal welfare cost (the additional welfare cost per dollar of additional revenue) at each tax rate? Do your results conform to the relationships shown in Figure 10–13?

14. "Successive equal increments in a per unit excise tax represent smaller and smaller percentage increases in the tax. Therefore, the additional welfare cost of each increment gets smaller and smaller." True or false? Explain.

Supplementary Readings

BARZEL, YORAM. "An Alternative Approach to the Theory of Taxation." *Journal of Political Economy,* 84(6):1177–1198 (Dec. 1976).

BLUM, WALTER J., and HARRY J. KALVEN, JR. *The Uneasy Case for Progressive Taxation.* Chicago: University of Chicago Press, 1953.

DAVIES, DAVID G. *United States Taxes and Tax Policy.* Cambridge: Cambridge University Press, 1986.

KOTLIKOFF, LAURENCE, and LAWRENCE SUMMERS. "Tax Incidence." In *Handbook of Public Economics,* eds. Alan J. Auerbach and Martin Feldstein, Vol. 2, pp. 1042–1092. Amsterdam: North-Holland, 1987.

MIESZKOWSKI, PETER. "Tax Incidence Theory: The Effects of Taxes on the Distribution of Income." *Journal of Economic Literature,* 7(4):1103–1124 (Dec. 1969).

MUSGRAVE, RICHARD. *The Theory of Public Finance.* New York: McGraw-Hill, 1959.

The Federal Individual Income Tax

*W*HEN MOST PEOPLE THINK OF TAXES, they think first of the federal individual income tax—*the* income tax. This reaction is not surprising, since the individual income tax raises more revenue than any other tax in the United States. Revenues from this tax totaled $476 billion in 1992 (about $4,500 per taxpayer) and accounted for 44 percent of total federal tax revenues. The second largest source of federal tax revenue is the social security payroll tax, but its revenue can only be used to finance social security benefits. Thus, as a source of revenue to finance general (non–social security) federal spending, the individual income tax is even more important, providing 70 percent of nonpayroll tax revenue.

Given its dominant role as the centerpiece of the federal revenue system, we shall consider the federal income tax in some detail.

What Is Income?

The popularity of the income tax as a revenue source stems from the wide agreement that income is the best measure of a person's ability to pay taxes. The credibility of income as a measure of taxpaying capacity depends critically on the way it is defined. Any definition of *income* is of necessity somewhat arbitrary, but the definition most widely accepted by economists is the following: *Income is the monetary value of consumption plus any change in real net worth over a period of time* (usually taken to be a year).[1] An

[1]An early case for the use of this general definition was made by Henry Simons, *Personal Income Taxation* (Chicago: University of Chicago Press, 1938).

equivalent way of expressing this definition is that income is the net increase in the power to consume during the period. This net increase equals actual consumption plus net additions to wealth (saving); saving is included because it represents potential consumption, even if it is not actually consumed during the current period.

As a general matter, income can be defined in terms of where it comes from (on the *sources* side of the budget) or where it goes (on the *uses* side of the budget). The formal definition just given is in terms of the uses of income; that is, income is either consumed or saved (thereby affecting net worth). In terms of the sources side of the budget, anything that permits consumption or adds to net worth would be considered income. This would include wages and salaries, dividends, interest, government transfers, rents, royalties, and gifts (among other things), since all of these either finance consumption or are saved. Hence, the economic definition accords with common usage of the term. Further examination of this definition will show, however, that other, less obvious, items are considered income by economists.

Although income, according to our definition, is measured in monetary units, it need not be received as cash. Fringe benefits provided by an employer, such as free lunches, health insurance, or contributions to pensions, are income, just as are wages paid in cash. Fringe benefits are an example of income in kind rather than cash. Government in-kind transfers (as well as cash transfers) also count as income because the source of income is irrelevant.

There are other important types of income in kind. A person who owns a home consumes housing services, and the monetary value of these housing services should be treated as income. Similarly, goods and services that are produced and consumed within the home qualify as income. Food preparation, growing of foods at home, house cleaning, and child rearing provided by the husband or wife all constitute services that have a monetary value to the family and hence are income. Even leisure can be considered a consumer good and thus part of income.

The second dimension of our definition of income concerns changes in the value of capital assets. If the value of an individual's home rises from $80,000 to $88,000 over a year, the $8,000 increase in value (or capital gain) is income because it represents an increase in net worth. Two points should, however, be noted. First, only the real increase in the value of the home constitutes income: If the price level rises by 10 percent because of inflation over the year, and at the same time the dollar value of the home rises by 10 percent (from $80,000 to $88,000), this nominal gain is not income, since it does not augment the homeowner's ability to consume. Second, the house need not be sold for this appreciation in value to be considered income. Thus, our definition counts income as it *accrues,* not when it is realized through a market sale.

The definition of income is explored further later in the chapter. Before proceeding, however, it should be stressed that *the definition discussed here is not the one embodied in current tax laws.* Instead, we have developed a broad, comprehensive concept of income that can be used as a benchmark against which the actual definition of taxable income in the tax laws can be compared. There are two reasons why a broad concept of income is important. One is to ensure that the tax is equitable. Income, broadly defined, is a comprehensive measure of the resources available to pay taxes; it is also a primary determinant of an individual's standard of living. Unless income is broadly defined, people who receive income in nontaxable forms will pay lower taxes, which would be unfair.

A second reason to use a broad measure of income is to promote economic efficiency. If certain types of income are not taxed, people will have an incentive to convert their income into these nontaxable forms, and such a reallocation of resources, induced by tax considerations, would be inefficient. As explained in the previous chapter, a broad-based tax leaves few avenues that allow tax liabilities to be reduced by rearranging the use of resources, and therefore the welfare cost of the tax is likely to be small.

Although equity and efficiency criteria seem to favor a broad definition of income, other factors should be considered. In particular, in some cases it is administratively difficult to tax some forms of income. This situation is especially true when the goods or services consumed are not purchased in the market and therefore have no easily measured monetary value. Consider the value of the services of a stay-at-home spouse: How much are they worth? Although these services have a monetary value, it would be difficult and costly, if not impossible, for the tax collector to measure their value accurately. In such cases, the cost of measurement and the inequities and inefficiencies resulting from incorrect measurement make the exclusion of some items from the tax base the wisest course of action. Thus, our comprehensive definition of income is not intended to be an assessment formula but instead a guiding principle to be considered along with other factors.

Definition of Taxable Income in Practice

The Internal Revenue Code does not explicitly define income; instead, it enumerates items to be included in and excluded from the tax base. Altogether the tax laws and regulations, and interpretations based on them, total more than 40,000 pages. It would clearly not be possible or worthwhile to describe the tax provisions in detail. In fact, since reforms of the income tax laws are frequently made—ten major reforms were made between 1969 and 1993—any detailed discussion of the tax laws would probably become dated fairly quickly. However, some enduring features of these laws are worth focusing on.

Most of the provisions in the tax laws are rules that instruct taxpayers how to compute their *taxable income.* Taxable income is the tax code's definition of income, and it is this amount that is actually subject to tax. As defined in the tax laws, taxable income is far smaller than the comprehensive measure of income described in the last section. The fact that taxable income deviates substantially from a comprehensive measure of income has important economic effects, as we will see later in this chapter. To get an idea of how far short of comprehensive income actual taxable income falls, we can use the most comprehensive measure of income reported in the National Income and Product Accounts; it is called *personal income*. It is the broadest and most comprehensive measure of the total income of households that is routinely available from annual statistics; even so, it is smaller than comprehensive income as defined in the last section. *In recent years, just under half of personal income has been subject to tax under the federal income tax laws.*[2]

The enormous gap between personal income and taxable income represents the combined effect of multitudes of special provisions in the tax laws that specifically exclude some items from taxation. These provisions, which are sometimes called *tax preferences* and sometimes *tax loopholes* (depending on whether or not you approve of them), fall into several general categories, the most important of which are exclusions, exemptions, deductions, and tax credits.

Exclusions

Some types of real income for taxpayers do not have to be reported on the taxpayer's federal tax return at all. These are called *exclusions* because they are income that is officially excluded from the tax base. For example, most government transfer payments do not have to be reported as income. Except for unemployment insurance benefits and part of social security benefits for wealthy taxpayers, other cash and in-kind transfers are not subject to income taxation. Other important exclusions include interest income on bonds issued by state and local governments; most types of fringe benefits of employment (most important, employer contributions for health insurance and retirement plans); and the rental value of owner-occupied housing. Note that all of these items would count as income under our definition of comprehensive income, but they are not defined as income by the tax laws. How large these exclusions are in the aggregate is not known with great accuracy, but they probably amounted to more than $700 billion in nontaxable income in the early 1990s.

Exemptions

When taxpayers complete their federal tax returns, the first step is the calculation of their *adjusted gross income* (*AGI*). It is arrived at by adding together all the items constituting income from taxable sources—including, most importantly, wages and salaries, interest, dividends, and realized capital

---

[2]Jon Bakija and Eugene Steurele, "Individual Income Taxation Since 1948," *National Tax Journal,* 44:451 (Dec. 1991).

gains—and then subtracting certain allowable business expenses incurred in earning income (for most taxpayers the allowable expenses are zero). AGI is the broadest measure of income entered on tax returns, and most taxpayers think of AGI as their total income, but it is already substantially below a comprehensive measure of income because it does not include the exclusions noted previously. In 1989, the aggregate AGI was $3,256.4 billion.

Several adjustments to AGI are made before taxable income is determined. One of the most important adjustments is the subtraction of personal exemptions from AGI. Taxpayers are allowed a personal exemption for the taxpayer, spouse, and each dependent. The personal exemption is a fixed sum that is subtracted from AGI. In 1992, the personal exemption was $2,300 for each person in the family. (This amount is adjusted annually for inflation.) Thus, a family of four is allowed to subtract $9,200 in personal exemptions from its AGI. In 1989, aggregate personal exemptions removed about $500 billion from the potential tax base.

Deductions

One other major adjustment is made in determining taxable income: The taxpayer either may itemize certain expenditures and deduct them from AGI or may subtract from AGI a fixed sum known as the *standard deduction*. Which alternative the taxpayer chooses normally depends on which option provides the larger tax saving. If the standard deduction is larger than the sum of allowable itemized deductions, the taxpayer would simply take the standard deduction and avoid having to list (and potentially verify) the itemized deductions. In general, lower-income taxpayers find it advantageous to use the standard deduction. In 1992, the standard deduction was $6,000 for a married couple filing jointly and $3,600 for a single taxpayer. The standard deduction is adjusted annually for inflation. About 70 percent of taxpayers now use it.

In combination with personal exemptions, the standard deduction has the effect of removing millions of low-income families from the tax rolls. For a family of four, for example, the sum of personal exemptions and the standard deduction in 1992 was $15,200, so families with AGIs below this had no tax liability at all.

The most important allowable itemized deductions are interest paid on home mortgages and certain other loans ($169.5 billion in 1989); state and local income and property taxes ($129 billion); charitable contributions ($55.5 billion); and unreimbursed medical expenses that exceed 7.5 percent of AGI ($20.9 billion). As mentioned, higher-income families typically have expenditures on these items that are larger than their standard deductions, so itemizers are generally those in the upper part of the income distribution.

Subtracting personal exemptions and deductions from AGI yields taxable income. The relevant schedule of tax rates (more on this in the next section) is applied to taxable income to determine the amount of tax liability. There is, however, one other special feature of the tax law that deserves brief mention.

Tax Credits

Tax credits permit some specified amount to be subtracted directly from the amount of tax paid. Note that they differ from deductions, which are subtracted from the amount of taxable income, not from the tax owed. Whereas the tax savings from a deduction depend on the marginal tax rate of the taxpayer (as explained more fully later), the tax savings from a credit are independent of the marginal tax rate.

There are two major tax credits in the current tax law. One is the earned income tax credit (EITC), which we described in Chapter 9. The other is the child-care credit, which is available to some employed taxpayers who pay someone to care for their children while they work. For taxpayers with AGIs above $28,000, the credit rate is 20 percent, which means that the amount of the credit is equal to 20 percent of allowable child-care expenses. There is, however, a maximum credit of $480 (for one dependent) or $960 (for two or more dependents).

Tax Rates and Tax Revenues

Any tax can be described by defining the tax base (taxable income in the case of the federal income tax) and the tax rate, or structure of rates, that is levied on the base. Before describing the rate structure of the federal income tax, it is important to identify the different types of rate structures that may be used. There are three major alternatives: *proportional, progressive,* and *regressive.* The distinction among these rate structures relates to how the average tax rate (total tax liability divided by the tax base) varies with the tax base. *If the average tax rate is the same at all levels of the tax base, the tax is proportional; if the average tax rate rises with the tax base, the tax is progressive; and if the average tax rate falls as the tax base increases, the tax is regressive.*

Table 11–1 shows examples of each type of rate structure. The proportional tax is levied at a flat rate of 10 percent on taxable income. The average tax rate is 10 percent at all income levels. The marginal tax rate—the rate applicable to additional taxable income—is also constant at 10 percent. Under the progressive tax, tax liability is a higher percentage of taxable income at higher income levels. This arrangement implies that the marginal tax rate is above the average at each income level (beyond the minimum level). When taxable income rises from $2,000 to $3,000, or by $1,000, the tax goes up by $250, so the marginal rate is 25 percent over this range—greater than the average rate. To achieve a rising average tax rate—a progressive tax—it is an arithmetical necessity for the marginal rate to be above the average rate. Under the regressive tax, tax liability is a lower percentage of taxable income at higher income levels. A falling average tax rate implies that the marginal rate at each income level is below the average rate.

Table 11–1   *Tax Rate Structure*

		Taxable Income					
	$0		$1,000		$2,000		$3,000
Proportional tax							
Tax liability	$0		$100		$200		$300
Average tax rate	—		10%		10%		10%
Marginal tax rate		10%		10%		10%	
Progressive tax							
Tax liability	$0		$ 50		$150		$400
Average tax rate	—		5%		7.5%		13.3%
Marginal tax rate		5%		10%		25%	
Regressive tax							
Tax liability	$0		$150		$200		$250
Average tax rate	—		15%		10%		8.3%
Marginal tax rate		15%		5%		5%	

Some additional points concerning this classification of tax rate structures should be mentioned. First, note that the absolute size of the tax liability is larger at higher income levels under all three taxes. At least this is true of the hypothetical examples in Table 11–1; it is possible for a regressive tax to impose a higher absolute tax liability at lower income levels, although no real-world taxes are structured this way. Thus, it is somewhat misleading to view a regressive tax as one in which "the poor pay more" despite the common use of this description. The poor would pay a higher *percentage* of their income as taxes than would the nonpoor under a regressive tax, but generally not higher *absolute* taxes than those with higher incomes.

Second, the rate structure influences the distribution of after-tax income in a particular way. *The more progressive the rate structure is, the more equal will be the distribution of after-tax income.* (A possible exception arises when the incentive effect of the tax changes the before-tax distribution of income. For the moment, this will be ignored.) Under a proportional tax, if taxpayer *A* has twice the taxable income of taxpayer *B* before the tax, taxpayer *A* will have twice the disposable income of taxpayer *B* after the tax. In this sense, a proportional tax leaves the relative distribution of income unchanged. (For example, the quintile shares of income are not affected by subtracting proportional tax liabilities.) In contrast, with a progressive tax, taxpayer *A* will have less than twice the after-tax income of taxpayer *B*. Therefore, a progressive tax makes the relative after-tax distribution more equal. The opposite happens under a regressive tax because taxpayer *A* will end up with more than twice the income of taxpayer *B*.

Third, and perhaps most important, the technical distinction between rate structures is defined in terms of the average tax rate and the tax base. A flat rate tax of 30 percent on the price of cigarettes is a proportional tax, as is a 4 percent sales tax or a 2 percent tax on property values. In this technical sense, there are no regressive taxes in the United States: All taxes are either proportional or progressive with respect to their own tax bases.

These terms, however, have come to be used in a different, but not necessarily incorrect, way to refer to tax burdens in relation to income—regardless of the legal bases. For example, if the tax burden of a consumer under an excise tax is considered relative to the individual's income (rather than to the person's purchases of the taxed product), then a tax that is proportional with respect to its own base might be either regressive or progressive with respect to income. Consider the excise tax on cigarettes. Cigarette expenditures are a higher fraction of the incomes of low-income families, so an excise tax proportional to cigarette consumption will be regressive relative to income.

There is no reason why the terms *progressive, proportional,* and *regressive* should not be used in this way; indeed, most economists, as well as other interested persons, typically use this designation, so perhaps this is the strongest indirect evidence that income is considered a good tax base. If people did not feel that income was the most appropriate tax base, why compare tax burdens under nonincome taxes with income? If income is considered the best possible tax base, however, why bother to use any other tax? If we wish to have tax burdens bear a definite relationship to income, there is only one way to do so with certainty, and that is by taxing income explicitly rather than indirectly through the use of excise, sales, and other taxes.

Rate Structure

Having identified the various categories of possible tax rate structures, let us look at the actual rate structure of the federal individual income tax. The rate schedules are given as marginal rates that apply to specified ranges of taxable income, and there are four different rate schedules. Table 11–2 gives

Table 11–2   *Schedule of Official Marginal Tax Rates, 1992*

Single Returns		Joint Returns	
Taxable Income	**Marginal Tax Rate**	**Taxable Income**	**Marginal Tax Rate**
$0–$21,450	15%	$0–$35,800	15%
$21,450–$51,900	28%	$35,800–$86,500	28%
$51,900 and above	31%	$86,500 and above	31%

the rate schedules that apply to single taxpayers and married couples filing joint returns in 1992. (The other two schedules apply to single heads of households and married couples filing separate returns.)

In 1992, there were officially only three marginal tax rates—15, 28, and 31 percent—and these same rates are used for all four schedules. The difference in the schedules is the range of incomes over which each marginal rate applies. To illustrate the calculation of tax liability, consider the schedule for single taxpayers. If taxable income is less than $21,450, the tax liability is simply 15 percent of total taxable income. When taxable income exceeds $21,450, the higher marginal rates apply only to income in excess of the specified amounts. For example, suppose that taxable income is $60,000. Then the tax equals 15 percent of the first $21,450 *plus* 28 percent of the taxable income in the second bracket ($51,900 − $21,450, or $30,450) *plus* 31 percent of income in the third bracket ($60,000 − $51,900, or $8,100). Thus, the tax equals $3,217.50 + $11,743.50 + $2,511, or $17,472. Note that this taxpayer's taxable income places him or her in the 31 percent bracket, but that rate applies only to the taxable income in excess of $51,900; the first $51,900 is taxed at the two lower marginal rates.

Although the top marginal tax bracket officially identified in the tax law was 31 percent in 1992, it was possible for certain high-income taxpayers to have effective marginal rates that exceeded this level. The reason is that at high income levels taxpayers can lose some or all of their itemized deductions and personal exemptions. For example, allowable itemized deductions are reduced by 3 percent of the amount by which AGI (not taxable income) exceeds $100,000. Similarly, the value of personal exemptions is phased out at AGI levels over $150,000. The effect of these phase-outs is to impose a higher real marginal tax rate on some high-income taxpayers. The exact effects depend on the individual circumstances of the affected taxpayers, but typically these phase-outs add 2 to 4 percentage points to the effective marginal tax rate. Thus, it is more accurate to say that the income tax has a top marginal tax rate of around 35 percent rather than the 31 percent identified in Table 11–2.

The marginal tax rate structure of the federal income tax in 1992 differs in three major respects from the way it was structured in earlier years. First, before the Tax Reform Act of 1986, there were larger numbers of tax brackets and tax rates. In 1985, for example, there were 14 separate bracket amounts subject to 14 different marginal tax rates. (The range of income covered by each bracket was, however, much smaller. For example, some marginal rates only applied to a $5,000 range of taxable income.) A second difference was that the top marginal rates were substantially higher than they are now. For example, in 1985, the top marginal tax rate was 50 percent. It was even higher, at 70 percent, in the 1970s, and in 1961 it was an incredible 91 percent. The large reduction in the top marginal rates has led many people to conclude that the wealthy have benefited disproportionately from the tax law changes in recent years. Surprisingly, this turns out to be largely untrue, as we will see later.

A third major difference in the current tax rate schedules is that the bracket amounts are indexed for inflation. In other words, the $21,450 and $51,900 dividing points that separate the three marginal tax rates (for single taxpayers) are increased each year in line with the general price level. If prices rise by 10 percent, the 15 percent rate will apply to taxable income below $23,595 ($21,450 + $2,145). This indexing provision was enacted in the Economic Recovery Tax Act of 1981 and went into effect in 1985.

Indexing has the effect of imposing the same *real* tax burden on taxpayers with the same *real* taxable incomes year after year, regardless of how their nominal incomes have been affected by inflation. (Recall that personal exemptions and the standard deduction are also indexed.) Before indexing, the tax code was subject to what is called *bracket creep*; that is, inflation pushed taxpayers into higher rate brackets and increased their real tax burdens even if their real incomes did not rise at all. This was a major problem in the 1970s, when rapid inflation resulted in millions of taxpayers moving into higher tax brackets and paying a larger share of their incomes in taxes. If the tax law is not changed further, the indexing provisions in the current law will "inflation-proof" the personal income tax in the future for most taxpayers. However, the phase-out ranges for personal exemptions and itemized deductions are not indexed, so some high-income taxpayers will find themselves elevated into higher marginal tax brackets as a result of inflation.

Where the Revenue Comes From

In 1989, 112 million individual federal tax returns were filed, resulting in total tax revenues of $432.8 billion. Table 11–3 provides some detailed information on how income tax liabilities were distributed among various AGI classes in that year. Of the 112 million tax returns, almost 80 percent reported AGIs between $5,000 and $75,000. At the extremes, 15.7 percent had AGIs under $5,000 and 5.3 percent had AGIs of more than $75,000.

The last column in Table 11–3 gives taxes as a percentage of taxable income for each AGI class. Note that this average tax rate is nearly the same for the approximately two thirds of taxpayers in the under-$30,000 AGI classes. This is so because the majority of taxpayers have taxable incomes that place them in the 15 percent tax bracket. At higher AGI levels, taxes as a percentage of taxable income rise.

A better indication of the progressivity of the tax is afforded by relating taxes to AGI, since AGI is a broader and more comprehensive measure of income than taxable income. Taxes as a percentage of AGI are shown in the next to last column, which demonstrates smoothly rising average tax rates. The rates rise from 1.4 percent for the lowest AGI class to 23.7 percent for the over-$200,000 AGI class. The very low rates at the bottom are the result of the personal exemptions and standard deductions, which together exempt most of the AGI of low-income persons from taxation. Note that a very small percentage of AGI is subject to tax at lower AGI levels (less than 10 percent in the lowest AGI class), but this percentage rises with AGI until taxable income is 84 percent of AGI for the top AGI class. Thus, the rising

Table 11-3 *Distribution of the Tax Burden, 1989*

AGI Class	Percentage of All Returns	AGI ($ billions)	Taxable Income ($ billions)	Taxes ($ billions)	Taxes as a % of: AGI	Taxes as a % of: Taxable Income
Under $5,000	15.7%	$ 41.6	$ 3.4	$ 0.6	1.4%	16.4%
$5,000–$10,000	13.4	111.9	24.1	3.6	3.2	14.9
$10,000–$20,000	23.2	382.3	175.6	24.6	6.4	14.0
$20,000–$30,000	15.1	418.2	254.3	38.9	9.3	15.3
$30,000–$40,000	10.8	420.2	278.3	45.6	10.9	16.4
$40,000–$50,000	7.7	383.7	263.1	44.0	11.5	16.7
$50,000–$75,000	8.8	594.5	424.6	81.3	13.7	19.1
$75,000–$100,000	2.7	261.1	193.0	42.7	16.3	22.1
$100,000–$200,000	1.9	276.3	212.2	54.5	19.7	25.7
$200,000 or more	0.7	409.1	344.7	97.1	23.7	28.2
All returns	100.0%	$3,298.9	$2,173.3	$432.8	13.1%	19.9%

Source: Statistics of Income Division, Department of the Treasury, Internal Revenue Service, *Individual Income Tax Returns 1989* (Washington, D.C.: U.S. Government Printing Office, 1992), Table 1.2.

average tax rates (as a percentage of AGI) result from a combination of two factors: higher marginal rates apply to higher taxable income, and taxable income is a larger share of AGI for high-income taxpayers.

Considering how average tax rates vary by income level conveys some feeling for how the income tax burden is distributed among the population. Another perspective is provided by looking at the share of total taxes paid by selected income classes, which can be calculated from the fourth column. For example, we find that the 52.4 percent of taxpayers with AGIs under $20,000 paid only 6.7 percent of the $432.8 billion in taxes. At the other extreme, only 2.6 percent of taxpayers reported AGIs above $100,000, but this small group paid more than 35 percent of total income taxes. The top 5.3 percent of taxpayers, those with AGIs over $75,000, paid almost half (45 percent) of all income taxes in 1989.

Table 11-3 suggests that high-income taxpayers pay a substantially larger share of their incomes in taxes than other groups do and, in fact, provide most of the revenue. This evidence contrasts sharply with the apparently widely held perception that wealthy persons avoid paying their "fair share" of taxes as a result of tax loopholes and the reductions in top marginal tax rates in the 1980s. There is, however, another possibility. Recall that AGI itself is not a comprehensive measure of income, so the tax rates in the table do not show tax burdens relative to "true" incomes. Thus, if high-income taxpayers have true incomes larger than their AGIs, then the average tax rates in the table will overstate the true burden of taxes on the wealthy.

Taxes Relative to "Family Income"

The Congressional Budget Office (CBO) publishes estimates of tax burdens relative to a broader measure of income than AGI; it calls this measure "family income." In addition to including all income counted as AGI, family income includes all government cash transfers (only some of which are counted in AGI), the employer portion of social security payroll taxes, and a few other smaller items. On average, family income is about 20 percent larger than AGI, so it does represent a more comprehensive measure of income. However, it still does not include in-kind income.

Table 11–4 presents some of the CBO estimates for the federal individual income tax in 1993. Results are given for quintiles of families (with single persons counted as a family), except at the top of the distribution, where more detail is given. Taxes as a percentage of family income for each quintile (average tax rates) are given in the first column. It is clear that the income tax is quite progressive, with average rates rising significantly throughout the income distribution. (The negative rate for the lowest quintile is due to the CBO's counting the earned income tax credit as a negative tax, which was not done in Table 11–3.) The middle quintile, which includes the median taxpayer, pays only 6.2 percent of its family income as income taxes, while the top 5 percent of families pay more than three times this percentage, at 19.0 percent.

The second column in the table gives each income class's total taxes as a percentage of income taxes for all income classes together. What is most striking about these estimates, as we suggested earlier, is the share of total

Table 11–4   *Income Tax Distribution and Family Income, 1993*

Income Class	Tax as a Percentage of Family Income	Percentage of Total Tax Paid
Lowest quintile	− 3.2%	− 1.1%
Second quintile	2.8	2.4
Third quintile	6.2	8.4
Fourth quintile	8.7	17.3
Highest quintile	15.5	73.1
Top 10%	17.3	57.1
Top 5%	19.0	44.5
Top 1%	22.0	25.5
Total	10.9	100

Source: Committee on Ways and Means, U.S. House of Representatives, *Overview of Entitlement Programs, 1992 Green Book* (Washington, D.C.: U.S. Government Printing Office, 1992), Table 29.

taxes that is paid by high-income families. The top quintile pays nearly three fourths of total federal income taxes, with the top half of that quintile, the top decile, paying 57.1 percent of total federal income taxes. The lowest 60 percent of families pay less than 10 percent of total federal income taxes.

Thus, the available evidence indicates that the federal income tax is a highly progressive tax, with high-income taxpayers confronting an average tax rate that is two to three times as high as that of taxpayers with average income. This is not the same, of course, as concluding that the distribution of tax burdens is fair; it is still possible to make the value judgment that the wealthy should pay even more in taxes. President Bill Clinton certainly made that value judgment in the 1992 presidential campaign, when he argued that taxes on the wealthy should be increased to make them pay their "fair share." We will examine the effects of increased taxes on the wealthy later in the chapter.

Recent Evolution of the Income Tax

There were two major reforms of the federal income tax in the 1980s: the Economic Recovery Tax Act of 1981 and the Tax Reform Act of 1986. Many specific provisions of the tax were changed, including the exemptions, the standard deduction, and the tax rates themselves. Most notably, the top marginal tax rate was reduced from 70 percent to 50 percent by the 1981 law, and further to 28 percent by the 1986 law, before being increased to 31 percent by legislation in 1990. Given these apparently momentous changes, it is important to examine how the distribution of the tax burden has changed in recent years.

Table 11-5 gives the CBO estimates of tax burdens as a percentage of family income by income class for four recent years. Note first, in the last row of the table, that the overall burden of income taxes did not change very much between 1977 and 1993: Total taxes were 11.1 percent of family income in 1977 and nearly the same, at 10.9 percent, in 1993. Now compare the distribution of the tax burdens for 1977 and 1993. The tax burden on the top decile is nearly the same in both years, and it is 0.5 percentage points lower for the ninth decile. Comparisons for the lower deciles are complicated by the fact that the estimates for 1993 are available only for the quintiles, but the 1977 quintile tax rates can be calculated as weighted averages of the decile rates; these rates are given in parentheses. As you can see, the average tax rates for all lower-income classes have been reduced, with the largest reduction for the lowest quintile, due in large part to the expansion of the EITC.

Overall, however, the distribution of tax rates is remarkably similar in 1977 and 1993. In the intervening years, however, there were some more noticeable changes. For example, in 1984, just after the 1981 tax act was fully implemented, the tax rate for the top decile was significantly reduced compared to 1977, from 17.0 to 15.1 percent, with larger reductions for the top

Table 11–5   *Income Tax as a Percentage of Family Income, Selected Years*

Decile	1977		1984	1988	1993
			Year		
First	−0.5	} (−0.02)	−0.4	−0.8	} −3.2
Second	0.0		0.3	−0.4	
Third	1.8	} (3.3)	2.8	1.7	} 2.8
Fourth	4.3		4.8	4.1	
Fifth	6.3	} (7.1)	6.3	5.9	} 6.2
Sixth	7.8		7.8	7.2	
Seventh	9.2	} (9.9)	8.7	8.3	} 8.7
Eighth	10.5		9.7	9.0	
Ninth	11.7		10.9	10.4	11.2
Tenth	17.0		15.1	15.5	17.3
Top 5%	18.8		16.3	16.9	19.0
Top 1%	23.2		18.8	19.7	22.0
All deciles	11.1		10.6	10.4	10.9

Source: Congress of the United ates, CBO, *The Changing Distribution of Federal Taxes: 1975–1990* (Washington, D.C.: U.S. Government Printing Office, Oct. 1987), Table 7.

5 percent and top 1 percent of families. This was the result of the famous Reagan tax cut. Subsequent changes in the law, however, largely erased the gains for high-income taxpayers, except for the top 1 percent of all families. In 1993, the tax burden on the top 1 percent stood at 22.0 percent, 1.2 percentage points lower than in 1977. In percentage terms, of course, the reduction in the tax rate for the top 1 percent was smaller than for most of the lower-income classes.

In terms of the overall distribution of tax burdens, it is difficult to avoid the conclusion that not much has changed in recent years. One question raised by this situation is: How could these major tax reforms, reducing the top marginal rate from 70 to 31 percent, have so little apparent effect, especially at the top? There are several reasons. First, the top marginal rates applied to a tiny fraction of high-income taxpayers in the first place, so the quantitative effects of reductions on the entire top 10 percent or so of taxpayers were muted. Second, much of the revenue collected from high-income taxpayers is due to the tax rates applied to lower brackets, and these rates were not reduced as sharply. Finally, there were also changes in the tax base, with a broadening of the tax base by eliminating tax preference items, especially for the wealthy. Overall, the result was very little change in effective tax rates, even though statutory marginal rates were reduced sharply at the top.

Proportional Income Taxation

Incidence

As our discussion of tax incidence in Chapter 10 indicated, the person responsible for paying a tax may not be the economic unit that actually bears the burden. In our discussion of tax liabilities among income classes, however, we implicitly assumed that the size of tax payments measured the size of the tax burdens. Now we need to examine whether a person who pays $5,000, for example, in federal income taxes actually bears a tax burden of precisely that size.

If the income tax changes before-tax incomes—for example, by causing a reduction in labor supply, which, in turn, increases wage rates—then a person's tax liability will tend to overstate his or her actual tax burden because part of the total burden is shifted to others in the form of a higher wage rate. Clearly, it is *possible* for an income tax to be shifted in this way, but the relevant question is whether it *actually* is shifted. To begin our examination of this question, we analyze the incidence of a proportional tax on labor income and defer consideration of the more relevant case of progressive taxation until the next section. Although the income tax applies to other types of income as well as labor income, *wage and salary income accounts for 85 percent of AGI,* so an emphasis on labor supply effects is not misplaced. A proportional tax on labor income (e.g., wages and salaries), wherever earned, is a broad-based tax that cannot be avoided by workers' moving from one industry to another. In contrast, recall the method of shifting in response to an excise tax on one industry—in which productive resources move to untaxed industries. With an income tax, workers can reduce their tax liabilities only by reducing the quantity of labor supplied, that is, by working and earning less. Leisure is not taxed, only money income is, so workers might be led to consume more leisure and less money income in response to a tax on money income.

Consider a flat 40 percent tax on labor income. As a first approximation, this tax rate reduces a worker's net rate of pay by 40 percent. If the worker's market wage rate is $10 per hour, a 40 percent tax means that the individual's net, or take-home, wage rate will be $6 because the government receives $4 of every $10 earned. The primary question is whether a lower net rate of pay will lead workers to reduce the quantity of labor services supplied. According to economic theory, the answer is unclear. A reduction in the net wage rate influences labor supply decisions in two opposing ways. One is through the income effect: Workers are made poorer and thus will tend to work more to offset partially the income loss due to the tax. The other influence is the substitution effect: The net rate of pay is lower, so consuming leisure (working less) involves a smaller sacrifice in income. *The income effect of an income tax thus favors more work, whereas the substitution effect favors less work*; hence, the net effect is uncertain.

The net effect of a change in effective wage rates on the quantity of labor supplied is reflected in the slope of the labor supply curve. If the income effect of a lower wage rate exactly offsets the substitution effect, the labor supply curve will be vertical. In this case, a proportional income tax does not change the quantity of labor supplied and therefore has no effect on market wage rates. The income tax will not be shifted, and the final incidence will fall on workers whose take-home pay falls by exactly the amount of the tax.

Figure 11–1 illustrates this case. D_L is the market demand for labor services: It shows the maximum wage rate that employers are willing to pay for alternative quantities of labor. S_L is the supply curve, drawn as vertical under the assumption that income and substitution effects exactly offset one another in the aggregate. Before the tax, $10 is the market wage rate. A proportional tax of 40 percent can be analyzed in one of two equivalent ways: an upward shift in the supply curve or a downward shift in the demand curve. With a vertical supply curve, it is simpler to view the tax as shifting the demand curve. Thus, D_L' shows the maximum net (after-tax) rate of pay associated with alternative quantities of labor. The net rate of pay is 40 percent (rather than a fixed amount) lower than the market wage rate at each quantity, so D_L' is determined by pivoting the original demand curve downward rather than by a parallel shift. The new equilibrium under the income tax occurs where S_L intersects D_L' because workers make labor supply decisions in response to their net rates of pay. With the vertical supply curve, the quantity of labor is unchanged, and the effect of the tax is to reduce the net

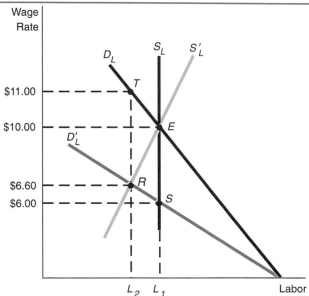

Figure 11–1   *Proportional tax on labor income*

rate of pay from $10 to $6. Employers, of course, are still paying $10 ($4 of which goes to the government), so their productive activities are not influenced by the tax. *When the supply curve is vertical, the incidence of a proportional tax on labor income falls on workers who bear the full burden of the tax in the form of lower net rates of pay.*

If the supply curve is upward sloping, which will be true if substitution effects outweigh income effects, market wage rates will rise and workers will not bear the full burden of the tax. In Figure 11–1, if the supply curve is instead the upward-sloping S_L' curve, equilibrium under the tax will occur at point R. In this case, at the lower net rate of pay, $6.60, workers have reduced their labor supplied, so with labor scarcer, it commands a higher market wage rate, $11. The wage rate actually received by workers has fallen from $10 to $6.60, or by $3.40, but the tax per unit of labor is $4.40. With an upward-sloping supply curve, the incidence of the tax lies only partially with workers because their net rate of pay does not fall by the full amount of the tax. Unless labor supply is quite elastic, however (i.e., unless the quantity of labor falls sharply with a change in net pay), the major part of the tax is still borne by workers.

Economists generally believe that the quantity of labor supplied is fairly insensitive to moderate changes in net wage rates. Empirical evidence (to be considered later) as well as common sense suggests that this conclusion is plausible. Many factors other than the monetary return influence work effort decisions (such as prestige, a desire to get away from home, to avoid boredom, to feel that one is making a contribution, or to associate with congenial co-workers), and it may be that the independent effect of the wage rate is relatively modest. If this is true, then the assumption of a vertical supply curve is reasonably plausible, and the incidence of a proportional income tax falls on the workers. This is an important conclusion, and it strengthens the case for using an income tax because it means that the true burden of the tax can be divided among people according to a reasonable, comprehensive measure of their taxpaying capacity, namely, their income. On the other hand, if an income tax is shifted capriciously through the economic system, it would be difficult to use it and achieve an equitable distribution of the true tax burden by this means.

Welfare Cost

Now let us consider the welfare cost, or excess burden, of a proportional tax on labor income. It is sometimes argued that an income tax will have no welfare cost if it leads to no change in the quantity of labor supplied. This belief is untrue. As indicated earlier, an unchanged quantity of labor reflects two opposing influences of equal size: an income effect that stimulates more work effort and a substitution effect that stimulates less. Any tax will have an income effect because it reduces after-tax income; this is not an excess burden, however, but rather an unavoidable effect of the tax. *It is the substitution effect of the tax that is responsible for the welfare cost,* and this exists even if the net effect of the income and substitution effects together is zero.

Figure 11–2 illustrates this point. The budget line relating money income and leisure before the tax is YN, and a worker, Rufus, is initially in equilibrium at point E, working NL_1 hours and earning EL_1. A proportional tax lowers the net wage rate, confronting Rufus with the $Y'N$ budget line. Assuming that Rufus prefers to work the same number of hours, his new equilibrium is at point E_1; he is still working NL_1 hours, but with a lower after-tax income of E_1L_1 and a tax liability of EE_1. The move from point E to point E_1 reflects the combined effect of the income and substitution effects of the tax.

To show the welfare cost, assume that a lump-sum tax is used instead to raise the same amount of revenue. A lump-sum tax equal to EE_1 dollars shifts the budget line downward to KK', parallel to the original budget line but

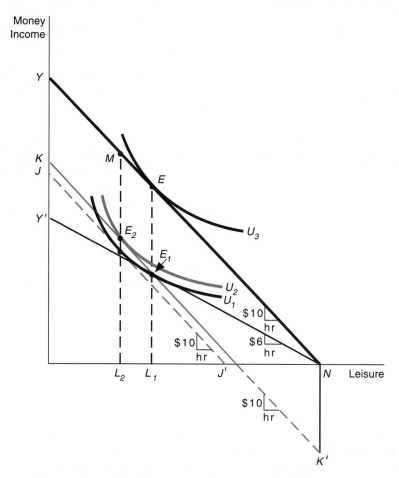

Figure 11–2   *Welfare cost of a tax on labor income*

lying below it at all points by the amount EE_1. The KK' budget line passes through point E_1, but it is steeper than the $Y'N$ budget line produced by the income tax because the net rate of pay (at the margin) is not reduced by a lump-sum tax. With the KK' budget line, Rufus's preferred point is E_2 where KK' is tangent to indifference curve U_2. At point E_2, Rufus is working more and is better off despite paying the same tax ($ME_2 = EE_1$) as under the income tax. Thus, it is possible to raise the same revenue as the income tax without harming Rufus so much; the income tax has a larger burden (an *excess* burden) than is necessary to generate any given amount of revenue. The size of the welfare cost is measured by the difference in welfare under the income tax (U_1) and under an equal-yield, nondistorting tax (U_2) equal to KJ measured in dollars.

An income tax distorts labor supply decisions by leading taxpayers to work less (NL_1 rather than NL_2) than is economically efficient. Even though work effort may be the same before and after the tax (comparing points E and E_1), the relevant comparison is between work effort under the income tax and under an equal-yield, nondistorting tax such as a lump-sum tax. Work effort and welfare will always be greater under a lump-sum tax, which is an indication of how the income tax stifles productive labor effort.

The reason an income tax produces a welfare cost is that work effort decisions are guided by the after-tax return to working, whereas the actual productivity of working is indicated by the higher before-tax return. If a person's market wage rate is $10 an hour, this is a measure of the value of the worker's labor services. With a 40 percent tax, the taxpayer will work up to the point where $6 just compensates for giving up the last hour of leisure (at point E_1 in Figure 11–2). The marginal cost of working an additional hour is then $6 (the value of the leisure sacrificed), and the marginal social benefit is $10. Even though the marginal social benefit of greater work effort exceeds the marginal cost, the worker will not work longer hours because, as a result of the tax, the individual receives only $6 for his or her efforts, not a wage equal to the $10 marginal social benefit. Thus, taxpayers are led to undersupply labor services by an income tax because of the tax wedge that separates market and net wage rates. (Compare this analysis with our discussion of the welfare cost of the NIT: Note that both a positive and a negative income tax produce the same type of welfare cost.)

Progressive Income Taxation

The qualitative analysis of a progressive tax on labor income is quite similar to that of a proportional tax. In both cases, the tax reduces the net rate of pay to workers and so may influence the quantity of labor supplied. Like a proportional tax, a progressive tax has opposing income and substitution effects, so the net effect is uncertain on theoretical grounds. If a progressive tax does not lead to a change in the quantity of labor supplied, then market wage rates will be unaffected, and the incidence of the tax will be borne by workers, just as with the proportional tax.

In considering a progressive tax, however, it is important to understand the roles played by the marginal and average tax rates. Under a proportional tax, the marginal and average rates are equal; furthermore, they are equal for all taxpayers. Under a progressive tax the marginal tax rate exceeds the average tax rate, and the rates vary from one taxpayer to another (because they vary with income). This is significant because *the size of the income effect depends on the average tax rate, whereas the size of the substitution effect depends on the marginal tax rate.*

The average tax rate of any type of income tax for a taxpayer indicates how large a share of income is sacrificed to the tax collector. The greater the share of income paid in taxes, the larger the incentive will be to work more to recoup some of the loss. Hence the income effect favoring more work is related to how much tax is paid, and this amount depends on the average tax rate. The marginal tax rate determines the reward associated with changes in work effort and is therefore related to the substitution effect. *Welfare costs reflect substitution effects and so are dependent on the marginal rate of tax.*

Table 11–6 will clarify these remarks. Assume that we have a taxpayer with an income of $10,000 and we want to compare three alternative ways of raising $2,000 in tax revenue. One way is to use a proportional tax of 20 percent. A second way is to use a progressive tax that exempts the first $5,000 in income and taxes income in excess of that amount ($5,000 for a taxpayer with a total income of $10,000) at a rate of 40 percent. A third way is to use a progressive tax that exempts the first $7,500 in income and taxes income above that amount ($2,500 for our taxpayer) at a rate of 80 percent.

Table 11–6   *Taxpayer with a $10,000 Income*

Tax Structure	Tax	Average Tax Rate	Marginal Tax Rate	Sacrificed Disposable Income If $1,000 Less Is Earned
1. *Proportional:* 20% tax on all income	$2,000	20%	20%	$800
2. *Progressive:* exempt $5,000; 40% tax on income above $5,000	$2,000	20%	40%	$600
3. *Progressive:* exempt $7,500; 80% tax on income above $7,500	$2,000	20%	80%	$200

A taxpayer with $10,000 in income will pay $2,000 in taxes under all three taxes. This loss in income implies an income effect to work more, with the size of the effect being roughly equal for all three taxes because they have the same average tax rate. The substitution effects will differ greatly among these taxes, however. The marginal tax rate determines how any change in earnings affects disposable income. Under the proportional tax, if the taxpayer earns $1,000 less, disposable income will fall by $800 (taxes fall by $200). Because disposable income would have fallen by $1,000 with the same reduction in earnings in the absence of the tax, the tax lowers the cost of reducing earnings (working less) by $200, from $1,000 to $800. It thus becomes less expensive to consume leisure rather than work; this is the reason for the substitution effect favoring less work. Note, however, that the relative cost of earning less is reduced more by the progressive tax alternatives. With the most progressive tax, the taxpayer sacrifices only $200 by earning $1,000 less because the *marginal* rate of tax is 80 percent. It is clear that the taxpayer will be more likely to work less under the progressive taxes because the net rate of pay for work at the margin (in the neighborhood of $10,000) is lower, so the incentive to substitute leisure for money income is greater.

These remarks do not prove that people will work less under a progressive tax, because there is still an income effect favorable to work effort. We are only pointing out the respective roles of the average and marginal tax rates. The size of the marginal tax rate governs the strength of the incentive to work less (as well as the other adverse incentive effects of the tax to be considered later). Because the marginal tax rates are above the average tax rates for a progressive tax, adverse incentive effects due to the substitution effects of the tax are likely to be of greater significance. Still, in comparison with a no-tax situation, the income effect on work effort might be (and probably is for many taxpayers) large enough to produce no change in work effort.

Comparison of Progressive and Proportional Taxes

In general, it is not possible on theoretical grounds to predict how work effort will be affected by a progressive tax relative to no tax at all. Although it is true that the higher marginal tax rates are relative to average rates, the more likely work effort is to fall, we cannot be certain of the net effect of opposing income and substitution effects. Somewhat more can be said, however, when we compare a progressive tax with an equal-yield proportional tax.

Figure 11–3 illustrates this analysis. The budget line under a progressive tax is shown as the truncated line Y_1BN. The tax illustrated exempts a small amount of income (along BN) and then taxes increments in income above that level at successively higher marginal rates. The budget line becomes flatter as the taxpayer works more, indicating that disposable money income rises by successively smaller amounts as the taxpayer works (and earns)

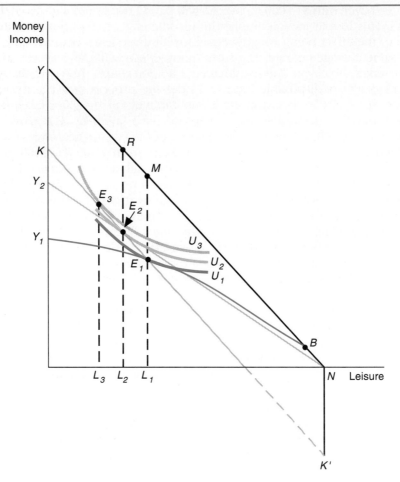

Figure 11–3 *Comparison of proportional and progressive taxes on labor income*

more and moves into successively higher marginal rate brackets. Equilibrium under the progressive tax occurs at point E_1 where U_1 is tangent to Y_1BN. Tax liability equals ME_1, the difference between gross earnings and after-tax disposable income. For reference purposes, line KK' shows the budget line produced by an equal-yield lump-sum tax. The taxpayer would be in equilibrium at point E_3, working more and on a higher indifference curve under the lump-sum tax. The fact that the taxpayer is better off under the lump-sum tax illustrates the welfare cost of the progressive tax, which is qualitatively similar to that of a proportional tax.

A proportional tax that raises the same revenue is shown by the budget line Y_2N. Confronted with Y_2N, the taxpayer is in equilibrium at point E_2, where U_2 is tangent to Y_2N. Note that point E_2 also lies on KK', indicating that the tax revenue is the same as under the progressive tax. (Tax revenue under the proportional tax equals RE_2, which is equal to ME_1.) The only difficulty in making this comparison is that one must imagine varying the tax rate under the proportional tax (pivoting Y_2N about point N) until an equal tax yield equilibrium is found. A little experimentation will confirm that there must be such an equilibrium somewhere between E_1 and E_3 on KK'. Exactly where this equilibrium occurs does not matter for the qualitative conclusions.

An equal-yield proportional tax leads to more work effort and a higher level of welfare than a progressive tax does. Greater welfare under the proportional tax means that it has a smaller (but not zero) welfare cost than the progressive tax does. Although the diagram may seem complicated, the reason for these findings is simple. Because both taxes are designed to yield the same revenue, the income effects are approximately the same. Marginal tax rates are higher under the progressive tax, however, so the incentive to work less is greater. The higher the marginal tax rate is for any given amount of revenue, the greater will be the labor supply distortion. (In fact, the reason a lump-sum tax has no welfare cost is that its marginal tax rate is zero; the tax liability does not increase if a person earns more.)

The conclusion that work effort is greater under a proportional tax of equal yield cannot be fully generalized for a group of taxpayers with different incomes. Figure 11–3 shows that one taxpayer *who pays the same tax under the two alternatives* will work more under a proportional tax. If a flat-rate tax on all taxpayers is used instead of a progressive tax, some taxpayers will pay larger taxes under the proportional tax, and others will pay smaller taxes. (Refer to Table 11–1.) For example, higher-income taxpayers pay larger taxes under a progressive tax, so substituting a proportional tax will lower their marginal and average tax rates. A lower marginal tax rate produces an incentive to work more, but a lower average tax rate produces an incentive to work less, so the net effect on this income group is uncertain. For some groups of taxpayers, therefore, we cannot state definitely that total work effort will be greater under a proportional tax. Only for taxpayers who have lower marginal tax rates and the same or higher average tax rates under a proportional tax can we be reasonably sure that work effort will be greater than under a progressive tax. It may be greater for other taxpayers (if the substitution effect is larger than the income effect), but we cannot demonstrate that effect on theoretical grounds.

Empirical Evidence on Labor Supply Effects

In 1991, 117 million persons were employed in the United States, for an average of about 34 hours per week, and received total labor compensation of $3,390 billion. Labor income, in fact, is about 70 percent of net national product. It is clearly important to determine whether, and by how much, taxation of labor income may affect this crucial productive input. As we have seen, in theory the effect depends on both income and substitution effects, and these effects operate in opposing directions, so the direction of the effect, as well as its magnitude, is open to question.

It is not easy to determine how taxes affect labor supply. Many factors other than tax rates affect labor supply, and these factors change over time. In addition, it is necessary to recognize that the federal individual income tax is not the only tax on labor income; there are also state income taxes, payroll taxes, and, for low-income workers, welfare programs. Moreover, variations in labor supply can take a variety of forms, some of which may be difficult to measure: longer vacations, less intense effort while on the job, earlier retirement, or less labor force participation by married women.

One approach is to compare trends in hours worked with changes in the tax laws to see if there is any obvious correlation. One study found that average hours of work for men fell by 6.8 percent from 1967 to 1978 and then by a further 1.5 percent from 1978 to 1989. For women, there was a rise in average hours of 18.6 percent in the first period and a larger rise of 25.6 percent in the later period. The fact that the labor supply for men fell by less in the 1980s and increased more for women in this period is suggestive of a positive effect on labor supply from the reduced income tax rates in the 1980s. The authors conclude: "By 1989, average male work effort was 105 hours per year—or 6.0 percent—above the level it would have attained if the trend before 1981 had continued through the 1980s. For women . . . [the gain was] 5.4 percent in average hours above the previous trend."[3] Given the relatively small reductions in income tax rates in the 1980s (see Table 11–5), these increases in labor supply represent significant responses. But the crucial question is whether the changes in the trends were the result of income tax changes or other factors in the economy.

Another approach is to use econometric methods to estimate equations that isolate the effects of various factors on labor supply. There have been many studies of this type, and they often generate estimates of wage elasticities of labor supply for various subgroups within the population.[4] The wage elasticities relate hours of work to net wage rates, and this relationship is relevant since income taxes affect labor supply by depressing net wage rates. Although the results vary, it seems fair to conclude that two generalizations can be made. First, for prime-age men (from about 25 to 60 years of age), the estimated labor supply elasticities are typically close to zero. Second, for women, the estimated elasticities are generally positive and large, often as high as 1.0. If we had to pick an overall figure for aggregate labor supply, it would lie somewhere between the low or zero value for men and the higher value for women. On surveying the evidence, Don Fullerton concluded that

[3]Barry Bosworth and Gary Burtless, "Effects of Tax Reform on Labor Supply, Investment, and Saving," *Journal of Economic Perspectives,* 6:11–12 (Winter 1992).

[4]For a survey of these studies, see Ingemar Hansson and Charles Stuart, "Tax Revenue and the Marginal Cost of Public Funds in Sweden," *Journal of Public Economics,* 27:331 (Aug. 1985).

a value of 0.15 is a reasonable estimate of the aggregate labor supply elasticity, although clearly we cannot rule out somewhat higher or lower values.[5]

Note that the labor supply elasticities estimated are intended to show how a change in net wage rates affects the quantity of labor supplied. As such, they identify the *combined* income and substitution effects. Thus, they are not relevant for evaluating the welfare cost of income taxation, which depends only on substitution effects. We will discuss the determinants of the welfare cost of taxes on labor income in a later chapter after examining other taxes that fall on labor income.

To get an idea of the quantitative significance of elasticities of the magnitude suggested by this research, let us suppose for simplicity that taxes on labor income (taking all taxes together) are levied at a flat rate of 40 percent. Note that this rate reduces net wage rates by 40 percent, so an elasticity of 0.15 implies that these taxes would reduce the quantity of labor supplied by 6 percent (0.15 × 0.40) as a first approximation. (It is only a first approximation because if labor supply falls, the market wage rate will rise.) Of course, a world with zero taxation is not a realistic alternative, but suppose, as another example, that we reduced the tax rate from 40 to 30 percent. This increases the net wage rate from 60 to 70 percent of the market wage rate, an increase of 16.7 percent. With an elasticity of 0.15, the estimated increase in labor supply would be 2.5 percent. In short, this evidence suggests that changes in labor supply brought about by feasible changes in income tax rates will be relatively small.

We do not intend to suggest that there is a consensus that 0.15 is the aggregate labor supply elasticity. In fact, there is no consensus, but we suspect that most economists would agree that the relevant elasticity is somewhere in the range 0.1 to 0.3. This range, of course, implies that the aggregate labor supply curve is quite (though not perfectly) inelastic, so the incidence of income taxes is largely borne by the workers themselves.

Tax Preferences

Up to this point our theoretical analysis has assumed that all types of income (except leisure) were subject to tax and that a person's tax liability did not depend on how his or her income was spent. The federal income tax, however, contains numerous exclusions and deductions, and these provisions in the tax law—tax preferences, or tax loopholes—have economic effects of their own. As we will show, in fact, these tax provisions have much the same economic effects as excise subsidies.

---

[5]Don Fullerton, "On the Possibility of an Inverse Relationship Between Tax Rates and Government Revenues," *Journal of Public Economics*, 19:3 (Oct. 1983).

For simplicity, assume that we have a proportional income tax levied at a rate of 50 percent. If there are no exclusions, exemptions, or deductions, our taxpayer, Rufus, with a total income of $10,000, will pay $5,000 in taxes. Now suppose that expenditures on good X can be deducted from total income; the 50 percent rate applies to taxable income, which is now defined as total income less expenditures on good X. If Rufus spends nothing on good X, his taxable income will be $10,000 and his tax will be $5,000, so he will have $5,000 remaining after taxes to spend on other goods (besides X). If, on the other hand, he spends $1,000 on good X, his taxable income will be $9,000, and his tax liability only $4,500. Spending $1,000 on good X reduces his taxes by $500, so the net cost to Rufus of consuming $1,000 of good X is only $500 (i.e., the cost of X minus the tax saving). *For every $1 spent on the deductible item, taxable income falls by $1, so taxes fall by $1 times the (marginal) tax rate*—in this case, 50 percent. This lowers the net cost of consuming the deductible item, just as an excise subsidy does.

To develop this analysis more fully, consider Figure 11–4. The before-tax budget line relating consumption of good X and other goods is MN. It has a

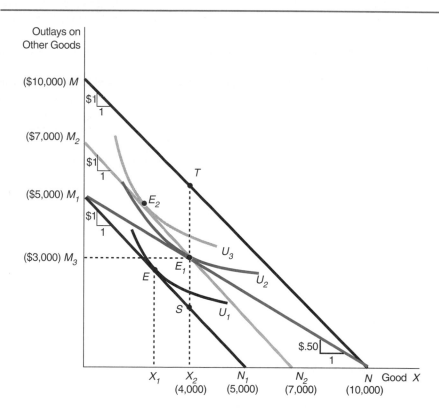

Figure 11–4   *Economic effects of tax loopholes*

slope of $1, assuming that the market price of X is $1 per unit. A 50 percent proportional income tax with *no* deductions shifts the budget line to M_1N_1, parallel to MN but $5,000 below it. (This parallel shift does not mean that the income tax is a lump-sum tax. Rather, we are taking work effort and, hence, before-tax income as given and examining the effects on consumption of various goods with after-tax income. An income tax does not affect the relative costs of consuming different goods, so the M_1N_1 budget line is parallel to MN.) When no deduction is permitted, Rufus must give up $1 in other goods to consume a unit of X, and the slope of M_1N_1 is $1. His equilibrium is at point E, consuming X_1 units of X.

If expenditures on good X are deductible, Rufus's budget line will become M_1N. Because tax liability falls by $0.50 for each unit of X consumed, the net cost of consuming X falls from $1 to $0.50, and the slope of M_1N is $0.50. The tax liability now depends on how much X is consumed. If no X is consumed, Rufus will be at point M_1, consuming $5,000 worth of other goods and paying taxes of $5,000 (equal to MM_1). At the other extreme, Rufus can consume 10,000 units of X and pay no taxes; he will then be at point N. In general, the tax liability equals the vertical distance between MN and M_1N. Confronted with a lower net price of X, Rufus increases his consumption. Equilibrium occurs at point E_1, where M_1N is tangent to indifference curve U_2. At this point, Rufus is consuming 4,000 units of X and $3,000 worth of other goods. His tax liability is $3,000, equal to TE_1 in the diagram. His taxes are therefore $2,000 lower than if the deduction had not been allowed. This tax savings is equal to E_1S because in the absence of the deduction his taxes would have been TS ($= MM_1$, or $5,000); with the deduction they are only TE_1.

Note that the effect of the deduction is the same as when the government uses no deduction and grants an excise subsidy to good X. If the deduction were not permitted, the government would have $5,000 in revenue and Rufus would be confronted by the budget line M_1N_1. If the government then pays half of the unit cost of X, Rufus would face the M_1N budget line, and the cost of the subsidy would be $2,000 ($E_1S$) Rufus would end up at the same point (E_1), and the government would still have $3,000 to finance other expenditures. *It makes no difference whether the government permits the deduction or does not permit it and uses part of the greater tax revenue to subsidize consumption of good X.* This is why the tax savings, E_1S, due to the deduction is sometimes called a *tax expenditure* by economists: The deduction has the same effect on resource allocation as would an outright excise subsidy of the same magnitude. The only difference between subsidizing explicitly and subsidizing indirectly with a deduction is in the size of the government budget. With the deduction, the tax revenue is $3,000, whereas with an explicit subsidy it is $5,000 ($2,000 of which is spent subsidizing good X).

In recent years, the CBO has been required to produce a "tax expenditure budget" that estimates the revenue loss (comparable to E_1S in Figure 11–4, summed over all taxpayers) caused by tax preferences. All together, more than 50 tax preferences have been examined in this way. Table 11–7 provides estimates of the revenue losses in 1991 attributable to some of the more important tax preferences.

These estimates show clearly that the tax preferences in the tax code amount to quite substantial hidden subsidies for certain types of activities. Indeed, some activities are more heavily subsidized through the tax code than through outright spending. For instance, home ownership is encouraged by the deductibility of mortgage interest and property taxes on owner-occupied housing: The combined revenue loss is greater than $40 billion. This is several times larger than the expenditures on housing programs (see Table 8–1). Of course, the tax expenditure primarily encourages housing outlays by middle- and upper-income families (the ones who itemize deductions), whereas outlays on housing programs primarily benefit low-income families.

A major purpose of the tax expenditure budget is to draw attention to the extent to which the tax code affects resource allocation and the distribution of income through its favorable treatment of certain items. Many economists believe we should apply the same criteria to the evaluation of these indirect subsidies that we do to the outright expenditures of government.

The Welfare Cost of Tax Preferences

Because the government permits expenditures on certain goods to be deductible, taxpayers have an incentive to devote more of their incomes to purchasing these goods because the tax deductibility lowers their net prices to taxpayers. The same general analysis applies when some types of income are excluded from the tax base. Because fringe benefits of employment are excluded, workers have an incentive to have employers provide health and life insurance (among other items) for them because it is untaxed. If an employer gives a worker $1,000 in health insurance, it is not taxed; however, if the $1,000 is paid in cash, taxes must be paid. If the worker's marginal rate is 30 percent, he or she will be able to purchase only $700 in health insurance; however, at the same cost to the employer, $1,000 can be provided as

---

Table 11–7   *Selected Tax Expenditures, Fiscal Year 1991 (in $ billions)*

Exclusion of employers' contributions to medical insurance premiums	$37.7
Exclusion of pension contributions and earnings	53.6
Exclusion of social security benefits	20.3
Deductibility of mortgage interest	35.8
Deductibility of state and local taxes	27.3
Deductibility of charitable contributions	13.9

Source: CBO, *The Effects of Tax Reform on Tax Expenditures* (Washington, D.C.: U.S. Government Printing Office, 1988), Table 1.

a fringe benefit. This is one reason for the rapid growth in fringe benefits in the last several decades.

Returning to Figure 11–4, when the deduction is used, tax revenue is equal to $3,000, or 50 percent times taxable income of $6,000 ($10,000 minus the $4,000 expenditure on X). This same revenue could be raised by taxing *total* income, $10,000, at a rate of only 30 percent. This is what much tax reform debate is all about: *Is it better to use lower rates on a more comprehensively defined tax base or to use higher rates on a smaller tax base?* Figure 11–4 can help us understand one factor relevant to making that choice. A tax rate of 30 percent on total income would produce an after-tax budget line M_2N_2, lying $3,000 below the before-tax budget line. This budget line passes through point E_1, the equilibrium when the deduction is allowed, because TE_1 equals $3,000. Although the same tax revenue is raised, Rufus is better off under this tax without the deduction: He is in equilibrium on indifference curve U_3 at point E_2. Rufus is better off with a more comprehensive tax base and a lower tax rate. The reason is that the tax deduction distorts the taxpayer's choices by artificially lowering the price of X and leads to overconsumption of X. The broad-based income tax does not distort choices among different ways of spending income and is therefore more efficient.[6]

What we have just illustrated is the welfare cost of the resource misallocation that results from tax preferences: The same tax revenue could be raised using a tax without preferences, which would place a smaller real burden on the taxpayer.

In addition to distorting the way taxpayers receive or spend their incomes, tax preferences may be responsible for other types of welfare costs. A multitude of special tax provisions adds greatly to the complexity of the tax law. This complexity probably increases the administrative costs of the Internal Revenue Service. Even more important, complexity imposes compliance costs on taxpayers. According to a recent study, the average taxpayer devoted about 27 hours in 1989 to complying with the income tax laws—filling out forms, keeping records, and so on.[7] That figure amounts to a total of about 2.5 billion hours per year, the equivalent of 1.25 million persons working full time preparing tax returns! In addition, about half of all taxpayers pay for professional assistance in preparing tax returns, at a cost of over $7 billion. Valuing the time cost at the taxpayers' net wage rates, total compliance costs are estimated to be between 5 and 7 percent as large as tax revenues collected by the income tax. Not all of this cost is exclusively the result of the complexity produced by tax preferences, but a significant portion undoubtedly is.

---

[6]This conclusion does depend on the assumption that work effort will be the same whether or not a loophole is used, which is plausible in most cases.

[7]Marsha Blumenthal and Joel Slemrod, "The Compliance Cost of the U.S. Individual Income Tax System: A Second Look After Tax Reform," *National Tax Journal,* 45:185 (June 1992).

Efficiency considerations therefore seem to suggest that it would be better to eliminate tax preferences (use a more comprehensive definition of income) and use lower tax rates on a larger tax base. Before accepting this conclusion, however, we should note several arguments in support of tax preferences.

One argument for certain tax preferences is that they produce a more equitable distribution of the tax burden. Tax preferences can be used to increase or reduce the real tax burden across income classes. For example, low-income taxpayers have a larger share of income in nontaxable forms (the exclusion of government transfers, and the personal exemptions and standard deduction) than do higher-income classes, so they benefit at the expense of those with higher incomes. If, however, a comprehensive definition of income is a good measure of taxpaying capacity, as many believe, it would be better to achieve this result by varying tax *rates* that apply to different income levels, thereby avoiding the inefficiencies associated with tax preferences. For this reason, equity considerations do not seem to provide a strong case for tax preferences.

Another argument for some tax preferences is that there are external benefits associated with the tax-subsidized activity. If so, encouraging the activity with special tax provisions (which act like excise subsidies) may produce a welfare gain rather than a welfare cost. For example, the deduction for charitable contributions is sometimes defended on this basis. A problem with this argument is that deductions encourage the activity only for those who itemize deductions, not for the majority who take the standard deduction. In addition, the rate of subsidy will vary with the taxpayer's marginal tax bracket, and it is difficult to see how this fact can be justified in terms of external benefits (is a dollar given to charity by a high-income person more valuable than a dollar given by a low-income person?). In general, it would appear that outright subsidies would potentially be more effective than provisions in the tax code to stimulate activities with external benefits.

Finally, some tax preferences are defended on the grounds that it would be administratively difficult to value them accurately for tax purposes. Income must be valued in money terms to be taxed, and it is difficult to place a monetary value on some types of income. For example, the rental value of owner-occupied housing is income, but what is its monetary value? Another example is unrealized capital gains: How can we measure each year the change in the value of a taxpayer's home? The issues here are, in principle, clear-cut. If any type of income is not taxed, there will be equity and efficiency costs. But the process of placing a money value on some types of income also has a cost that must be weighed against the gains from taxing all income equally. In addition, there is the danger of improper monetary valuation, which can produce inefficiencies and inequities. Thus, whatever the merits of this argument in specific cases, it is valid in principle, and it warns against trying to apply the theoretical definition of income as the sole criterion in defining the tax base.

Taxation of the Wealthy

Following the reductions in the top marginal tax rates achieved by the tax reforms of the 1980s, many commentators felt that the wealthy were not bearing their "fair share" of the tax burden. One of these was Bill Clinton, who in the 1992 presidential campaign argued for raising the marginal tax rate on those with incomes over $200,000 (less than 1 percent of taxpayers) from 31 to 36 percent. This and other similar proposals raise interesting questions about the consequences of increasing the tax burden on those with very high incomes.

Attempting to raise taxes only on those with high incomes means that only the top marginal rates can be increased. Thus, with Clinton's campaign proposal, the 5 percentage point increase in the marginal tax rate would apply only to income in excess of $200,000. This result limits the amount of revenue that such a tax change can produce. For example, in 1989, Clinton's tax proposal would have raised $9.4 billion, assuming that reported taxable income was unaffected. In 1993, the comparable figure would probably be about $12 billion. To put these figures in perspective, the federal budget deficit was around $300 billion that year, and total federal income tax revenue was over $500 billion; $12 billion in extra revenue would obviously be only a drop in the bucket.

Perhaps in recognition of this fact, after the election President Clinton proposed larger increases in taxes on more of the wealthy. Specifically, his plan for higher taxes on the wealthy was composed of three parts. First, the marginal tax rate would rise from 31 to 36 percent on those with taxable incomes exceeding $140,000 (rather than $200,000). Second, the earnings ceiling on the 2.9 percent payroll tax that finances Medicare would be eliminated. Since that ceiling was $135,000 in 1992, this has the effect of an additional marginal tax rate of 2.9 percent on incomes above $135,000. Third, there would be a 10 percent tax surcharge on taxable incomes in excess of $250,000. This has the effect of increasing the new 36 percent marginal tax rate by 10 percent to 39.6 percent for those affected. Taken together, these three tax increases for the wealthy are estimated by the Clinton administration to produce $31 billion in extra revenue in 1994. Since these proposals, or something similar, seem certain of enactment, it will be worthwhile to consider the likely effects in more detail.

It must be emphasized that the $31 billion estimate is based on the assumption that the amount of income earned and reported on tax returns is unaffected by the higher tax rates. We must question whether this scenario is plausible. Will high-income taxpayers continue earning and reporting the same income when there is a 37 percent increase in their marginal tax rate (from 31 percent to 42.5 for those affected by all three tax changes)? High-income taxpayers are often in very good positions to convert taxable income into nontaxable income through the use of various tax preferences when the incentive is great enough. They often can choose to defer more of their income, or invest more in tax-free municipal bonds, or put more into appreciating assets that do not yield current income. And there is always the possibility that some will opt to work and earn less. The end result of all these maneuvers is less taxable income.

What is interesting is that it does not take a very large reduction in taxable income in response to the higher marginal rates to reduce substantially the extra revenue that will be generated. For example, according to Clinton's proposal, half of all taxpayers with incomes over $140,000 have incomes less than $180,000. Suppose that these taxpayers reduced their taxable incomes by 5 percent in response to the 25 percent increase in the marginal tax rate that applies to them (the surcharge would not apply to this group). Consider a taxpayer with taxable income of $180,000 who reduces it by 5 percent to $171,000.[8] From the increased marginal tax rates, the government would then collect an extra $2,594 on the income up to $171,000, but it would lose $2,790 by not collecting any taxes on the $9,000 reduction in income. (This $9,000 was previously subject to a 31 percent rate, and $0.31 \times \$9,000 = \$2,790$.) The net effect of the higher marginal tax rates would be a revenue *loss* of $196 instead of the gain of $3,305 that is estimated on the basis of no change in taxable income. For those with incomes lower than $180,000, a 5 percent reduction in taxable income would produce even larger revenue losses. For those with higher incomes, a 5 percent reduction in taxable income would still result in some additional revenue, but less than estimated in the Clinton plan. (But many of those with higher incomes will have their marginal tax rates increased by 37 percent rather than 25 percent, so they might well reduce their taxable incomes by more than 5 percent.)

This analysis, suggesting that higher marginal rates on the wealthy may not produce much extra revenue, does not apply to all methods of increasing tax rates. For example, if all bracket rates were increased by 5 percentage points, instead of only those applying to taxpayers with incomes above $140,000, a 5 percent reduction in reported income would not result in less revenue; it would take a much larger reduction to produce that outcome. But increasing all rate brackets would increase taxes not just on the wealthy but also on all other taxpayers, and Clinton wished to tax only the wealthy. Thus, it was necessary to tax income only in excess of a high level (so as not to tax any people with lower incomes), and in that case it does not take a very large reduction in the income of those only moderately above the $140,000 level to nullify the effect of the higher rates.

Of course, we do not know exactly how responsive high-income taxpayers are to changes in marginal tax rates. What the previous example shows, however, is that it does not take large responses to make the higher tax rates

---

[8]This instructive example is discussed by Martin Feldstein in "Clinton's Path to Wider Deficits," *The Wall Street Journal* (Feb. 23, 1993), p. A18.

counterproductive. Moreover, a recent study suggests that very-high-income taxpayers may be quite responsive to the level of marginal tax rates.[9] It focused on the top 0.5 percent of taxpayers and found that the minimum reported real AGI in this group increased by nearly 50 percent in the four years 1985–1989, after increasing by only 10 percent in the preceding 15 years. The authors argue that a major reason for this increase was the reduction in the top marginal tax rate from 50 to 28 percent by the Tax Reform Act of 1986. This finding provides some tentative evidence that the incomes reported by very-high-income taxpayers may be greatly affected by the marginal tax rates that apply to these incomes, although whether the changes result from changes in actual earnings or from use of tax preferences, or both, is not clear.

In future years, economists will be looking at the reaction of high-income taxpayers to the higher marginal tax rates that Clinton has proposed (assuming that they are enacted) in a further effort to determine just how responsive these taxpayers are to tax incentives. What does seem clear is that the $31 billion revenue gain estimated for these tax changes is exaggerated, and there is a real possibility that there will be no revenue gain at all.

Capital Income and the Income Tax

Capital income—the income generated by one's assets—is also part of income, according to our theoretical definition of income discussed at the beginning of the chapter. However, under the actual federal income tax, not all capital income is subject to tax, and that part which is tends to be subject to many complicated tax provisions that make evaluation difficult. Let us first consider the effects of an income tax that does tax capital income and then introduce some complications that arise because of the way in which the actual tax treatment differs from this benchmark.

When a tax is applied to capital income, it falls on the rate of return earned by one's accumulated savings. For example, if Sheri has $100,000 invested in corporate bonds yielding 8 percent, her capital income for the year would be $8,000, and that would be the sum subject to the tax. If the tax rate is 25 percent, the tax would be $2,000. Note that the effect of this tax is to reduce the rate of return Sheri receives on her assets. Before the tax, the rate of return is 8 percent, but the after-tax rate of return is 6 percent (after-tax income of $6,000 divided by $100,000). So the 25 percent tax can be thought of as reducing the rate of return by 25 percent, from 8 to 6 percent.

[9]Daniel R. Feenberg and James M. Poterba, "Income Inequality and the Incomes of Very High Income Taxpayers: Evidence from Tax Returns," National Bureau of Economic Research Working Paper No. 4229 (Dec. 1991).

The major potential economic effect of a tax on capital income is to influence the amount that people will save and, therefore, the rate of capital accumulation for the economy. The incentive people have to change their rate of saving is due to the reduction in the net rate of return they receive. But exactly how a reduced rate of return on saving affects the level of saving is unclear. Just as with a tax on labor income, there are income and substitution effects, and once again, they operate in opposing directions. For a saver, a lower rate of return reduces his or her real income, making it necessary to save more to achieve any specific objective; that is the income effect. However, a lower rate of return makes it less worthwhile to save because the payoff is reduced; that is the substitution effect. In theory, the overall effect on saving can go either way, depending on whether the income or substitution effect is larger. The evidence on this issue is mixed, but many economists believe that there is a very small effect of taxation on the amount of saving. It should be emphasized, however, that the welfare cost of a tax on capital income depends only on the substitution effect, which does operate to reduce saving.

One important form of saving that may be affected by income taxation, which is frequently overlooked, is investment in human capital. People can save and increase their future income by undertaking training or schooling that increases their productivity. Spending $50,000 to attend college[10] might result in increased earnings of $10,000 per year thereafter, for example. This increment in earnings, however, is subject to tax. (In fact, note that it is treated as labor income under the income tax, even though it is a return to human capital investment.) If the relevant marginal tax rate is 28 percent, the effect of increasing gross earnings by $10,000 will be to increase disposable income by only $7,200. The incentive a person has to augment his or her earning capacity is therefore diminished in the same way as is the incentive to save by an explicit tax on capital income. Recent research has suggested that the effect of income taxation on human capital investment may be quite important.[11]

What complicates the analysis of the actual effects of the federal income tax on saving is the existence of several provisions in the tax law that treat saving in special ways. For instance, employers' contributions to pension plans (subject to ceiling amounts) and the interest income earned each year from these plans are excluded from taxation. (This income may be taxed when it is received as a pension in retirement, but there is still a tax advantage from allowing the money to accumulate tax free over many years.) Similarly, some workers can make contributions of up to $2,000 per year in *individual retirement accounts* (*IRAs*) that are tax deductible. (Higher-income workers are often ineligible for this tax break.) In addition, it is im-

[10]Earnings that are sacrificed while attending college should also be considered as part of the cost of increasing productivity through schooling.

[11]Philip A. Trostel, "The Effect of Taxation on Human Capital." *Journal of Political Economy,* 101:327 (April 1993).

portant to take into account that much capital income is generated by corporations, and corporations are subject to a separate tax of their own (to be discussed in the next chapter).

Because of these and other provisions in the tax law, some forms of saving are taxed and others are not, or they are taxed at different rates. This situation makes it very difficult to evaluate the overall effects of taxation without also considering the interaction between the federal income tax and the other taxes that may also affect saving and capital allocation (notably the corporation income tax and property taxes). After discussing the corporate and property taxes in the next two chapters, we shall consider the way the tax system as a whole affects saving and capital accumulation in Chapter 15.

Inflation and Mismeasurement of Capital Income

Inflation potentially has two important consequences for the way our income tax laws operate. First, inflation causes bracket creep unless the rate brackets and exemptions are properly indexed. Indexation became part of the tax law in 1985, so inflation-produced bracket creep is a thing of the past, unless the law is again changed. Inflation, however, has another important effect on the operation of the income tax: Inflation causes capital income to be measured incorrectly.

The tax system bases taxes on nominal capital income rather than real capital income, and these two magnitudes differ significantly in inflationary periods. As an example, suppose that you purchase a $10,000 corporate bond that yields 10 percent interest. The $1,000 in annual income is the *nominal* capital income on your investment. If there is a 10 percent inflation rate, however, your *real* capital income will be zero, since the $1,000 interest payment just offsets the loss in purchasing power of the $10,000 bond. Although your real capital income is zero, you will be taxed on the $1,000 in nominal interest income. Similarly, if you purchase corporate stock for $10,000 and sell it for $20,000 10 years later after the price level has doubled, your real capital gain will be zero, but your tax will be based on the $10,000 nominal capital gain.

What this mismeasurement of capital income means is that the rate of taxation on real capital income is greatly affected by the rate of inflation. Table 11–8 illustrates this point by considering the case of a taxpayer who invests $10,000 in a bond. We assume that the interest rate on the bond (column 2) is always two points greater than the inflation rate (column 1), so the real rate of interest is always 2 percent. This means that real capital income (column 4) is always $200 but that nominal capital income (column 3) is greater than $200 whenever inflation exceeds 0 percent. The income tax on the capital income for a 30 percent bracket taxpayer is shown in column (5): The income tax is 30 percent of nominal capital income. The last column shows how the effective tax rate on real capital income varies with the rate of inflation. Even at moderate rates of inflation, taxes on real capital income may exceed 100 percent.

Table 11–8   *Inflation and Tax Burden on a $10,000 Investment:*
30 Percent Rate Bracket

Inflation Rate (1)	Nominal Interest Rate (2)	Nominal Interest Income (3)	Real Income Before Tax (4)	Income Tax (5)	Tax Rate on Real Interest Income (6)
0%	2%	$ 200	$200	$ 60	30%
4	6	600	200	180	90
6	8	800	200	240	120
8	10	1,000	200	300	150

By taxing nominal capital income instead of real capital income, the income tax law levies extremely severe tax rates on capital income whenever the inflation rate is high. In effect, the interaction of inflation and the income tax sharply lowers the net (after-tax) real return to saving, diminishing the incentive of taxpayers to save. In addition to the potential significance of this effect on capital accumulation, it is relevant from an equity standpoint. Those who receive capital income pay higher taxes than do those with equal real incomes derived from other sources. Since high-income taxpayers receive a larger share of their income in the form of capital income, their real tax burdens are increased during inflationary periods by more than other income classes.

Capital Gains

Capital gains—increases in the value of an asset—are an important type of capital income for many taxpayers. For example, if Charlene owns some shares of corporate stock worth $20,000 and the value of the stock rises to $30,000 over the course of a year, she gets a capital gain of $10,000. Note that it is a capital gain whether or not she sells the stock at the end of the year. If she sells the stock, the capital gain is referred to as a *realized* capital gain. If she holds the stock, the gain is *unrealized.* In our theoretical definition of income, it is irrelevant whether or not she sells the stock. Even if she does not, her potential to consume is $10,000 greater, so the unrealized gain is income.

Under the federal income tax, however, capital gains are taxed only when realized. Although it might seem that there is little difference—you are only postponing the tax until you do realize the gain—it turns out to be highly significant. For example, consider a $100,000 investment in stocks that grows in value at a steady rate of 10 percent a year. After 25 years, the stocks are sold for $1,083,471 ($100,000 $\times$ 1.1^{25}). The capital gain is $983,471. If the tax rate is 31 percent, the tax liability is $304,876, and you are left with an after-tax capital gain of $678,595. However, if you are taxed on the accrued gain each year instead of a 10 percent return, you will receive an after-tax return of 6.9 percent each year, and your $100,000 investment will grow to only $530,204. With annual taxation, your investment grows by $430,204, but with taxation only at realization at the end of the 25 years, your investment grows by $678,595. Taxing only realized gains is advantageous to the investor because the investment can grow at the before-tax rate of return (10 percent) rather than at the after-tax rate of return (6.9 percent), and this advantage is greater the longer the investment is held. (Note that this advantage also exists for taxpayers with assets in pension funds.)

Taxation of capital gains only when realized has the effect of applying a lower effective tax rate to this type of capital income, and the tax rate is lower the longer the asset is held. Why should capital gains be given this special treatment in the tax law? One reason is the difficulty of measuring capital gains each year as they accrue. A good example of this difficulty is homes, an important source of capital gains for many families. How can we accurately measure the increase (or reduction) in the value of a home before it is sold? For many types of capital gains, however, this difficulty is much less severe. Stocks, for example, are valued in the stock market whether or not they are sold. But would it be fair to tax unrealized annual capital gains in the stock market and not in homes, real estate investments, or art investments?

A second reason for taxing only realized capital gains is that this arrangement may roughly offset the tendency of inflation to increase tax rates on capital income. It should be emphasized that the tax law subjects *nominal realized* capital gains to taxation. By taxing only realized gains, the effective tax rate is reduced, but by taxing nominal gains, the effective rate is increased, as we explained in the last section. On balance, it is argued, these two distortions might just balance out. Unfortunately, there is no reason to expect this serendipitous result, and in fact the combined effect is often to increase the effective tax rate.[12] The preferred alternative here would seem to be to tax real capital gains, realized or not, by indexing the value of the investment.[13]

A third reason for taxing only realized gains is that much of this capital income is already taxed annually by the corporate income tax, so a second tax on the same income could easily be excessive. There is much merit in this argument, but as we will see in the next chapter, there are other, and probably better, ways to integrate the corporate and personal income taxes to ensure equitable taxation of capital income.

The tax treatment of capital gains is a controversial issue, and it is easy to see why. There are a number of complex and difficult issues involved, and the whole topic is complicated further by the fact that most realized capital gains go to persons with high incomes. Some seemingly sensible reforms,

[12]Martin Feldstein and Joel Slemrod, "Inflation and the Excess Taxation of Capital Gains on Corporate Stock," *National Tax Journal,* 31:107 (June 1978).

[13]In most cases, this tax is entirely feasible. See U.S. Congress, CBO, *Indexing Capital Gains* (Washington, D.C.: U.S. Government Printing Office, August 1990).

such as indexing the value of investments so as to tax only real capital gains, would result in reducing taxes on the wealthy, and that result is clearly contentious (although it would be possible to offset it by increasing the tax rates).

A Flat Rate Tax?

Let us examine a proposal to substitute a flat rate, or proportional, tax on a broad measure of income for the current graduated (progressive) income tax that reaches less than half of total income. If personal income, as defined in the National Income and Product Accounts, is used as the tax base, a flat rate tax of 11 percent would raise the same revenue that the 1989 tax structure raised with tax rates ranging from 15 to 35 percent (including the effects of the exemption and deduction phase-outs) on the narrower base of taxable income. We do not mean necessarily to advocate personal income as the tax base; the important point is that it is feasible to define income broadly enough so that a surprisingly low tax rate is capable of raising the same revenue as the present tax. For example, if AGI were the tax base, a tax rate of 13.3 percent would suffice (see Table 11–3).

Advantages of a Flat Rate Tax

Supporters of a flat rate tax argue that it avoids many of the defects of the present graduated tax. For example, the present tax uses unnecessarily high marginal rates on a narrow tax base. This type of tax undermines economic productivity in two ways. First, it seems likely that total output will be lower than is efficient because of the way high marginal tax rates reduce the incentive to supply labor and capital. A flat rate tax would not avoid this cost altogether, but a lower marginal rate would probably reduce the magnitude of the disincentive effects significantly. Second, high tax rates on a narrow base reduce productivity by inducing taxpayers to channel part of their incomes into nontaxed forms. This is the welfare cost resulting from tax preferences, and a flat rate tax on a broad measure of income would also diminish this problem. (It would probably be impossible in practice to define income so broadly as to completely eliminate this distortion, however.)

In addition to these efficiency advantages, it is claimed that a flat rate tax is simpler. Much of the complexity of the present tax is the result of the numerous special provisions and its graduated rate structure. In principle, most taxpayers could comply with a flat rate tax of 11 percent, for example, by filling in a tax return composed of a single page: Enter all income and multiply by 0.11. Thus, compliance costs borne by taxpayers should be lower under a flat rate tax.

Using a broad base with a flat rate tax would also mean that horizontal equity could be achieved more easily. Currently, taxpayers with the same real incomes bear different tax burdens because of special provisions that some taxpayers can utilize more fully than others.

A flat rate tax also performs better in an inflationary environment. A proportional tax does not require an indexing provision to guard against bracket creep. Note, however, that a flat rate tax does not solve the problem of mismeasurement of capital income; capital income would have to be defined in real terms in the tax laws.

Finally, there may be an advantage to a flat rate tax from a public choice standpoint. One classical indictment of a graduated tax rate is that it is politically irresponsible because "a majority is allowed to set the rates that fall exclusively on the minority."[14] Although the possibility of such an abuse of majority rule arises in other connections, "progression poses difficult problems of equity among taxpayers which need not otherwise arise, so it places strains on the majority rule principle which perhaps need not otherwise arise."[15] Since a flat rate tax represents, in effect, a rule that determines not only how the present tax burden is to be distributed but also how any future increases or decreases are to be allocated, the constant political bickering over how to reform the tax and redistribute its burden may be reduced.

In short, proponents claim that, compared to the present income tax, a flat rate tax on a broad base will be simpler, more efficient, more equitable, more inflationproof, and a politically more responsible formula for apportioning tax burdens.

Disadvantages of a Flat Rate Tax

The flat rate tax proposal combines two potentially separate major tax changes: the elimination of tax preferences (use of a broad base) and taxation of that base at a single flat rate. Thus, the proposal can be criticized on one or both grounds.

In our earlier discussion of tax preferences, we pointed out that certain tax preferences may be defended for equity, externality, or administrative cost reasons, but it is not clear how many of these preferences can be defended in this way. Moreover, if special concessions are granted to certain types and uses of income, even if for legitimate reasons, it may be politically difficult to avoid the spread of tax preferences to any items that are important enough to command a political constituency. For this reason, the real choice we face may be between a broad income measure with no tax preferences and a measure riddled with loopholes, like the existing tax system. Given those alternatives, the broad definition of income—even if it falls short of perfection—may be the preferable option. Most of the objections to a flat rate tax, however, are not over the proposal to use a more comprehensive

---

[14]Walter J. Blum and Harry J. Kalven, Jr., *The Uneasy Case for Progressive Taxation* (Chicago: University of Chicago Press, 1953), p. 19.

[15]Ibid., p. 21

definition of income; instead the controversy centers on the redistributive effects of using a flat rate tax.

Substituting a flat rate tax for the present progressive tax will alter the distribution of the tax burden; it will increase tax burdens on low- and middle-income taxpayers and reduce tax burdens on upper-income taxpayers. For example, under the present tax, taxpayers (families of four) with AGIs of about $15,000 or less pay no income taxes; with a 13.3 percent flat rate applied to AGI, the tax liability on a $15,000 income would be $1,995. At a $30,000 income (AGI) level, tax liability would rise from about $2,250 to $3,990, or by $1,740. A flat rate tax would therefore redistribute income away from low- and middle-income classes.

Whether this change is considered undesirable is largely a matter of whether the income tax is viewed as a redistributive mechanism. In this regard, it should be recalled that government transfer programs are our primary redistributive policies. Even if a flat rate tax is used, the poorest quintile of households would continue to receive three times as much in transfers as they pay in all (federal, state, and local) taxes combined. The net income position of low-income households is largely determined by transfers, and only transfers are capable of actually increasing their net incomes. A case can be made that transfer programs should be the primary redistributive mechanism since they can target benefits more equitably on needier families instead of manipulating the tax rate structure to serve that goal. It is not necessary for every policy to redistribute income since transfers can be adjusted so that the net effect of the system as a whole is to help the poor.

Nonetheless, the distributional consequences of a flat rate tax are likely to be viewed as its major, if not its only, drawback. To some extent, the efficiency gains of the tax will reduce the harm associated with larger tax liabilities for low- and middle-income taxpayers, but it is doubtful that they would offset the additional tax burden completely. As we have seen before, value judgments are necessary to decide whether this proposal for reform is, on balance, worthwhile.

Review Questions and Problems

1. Define *marginal tax rate* and *average tax rate*. Then give an example of an income tax that would result in an average tax rate of 20 percent and a marginal tax rate of 40 percent for a person with income of $20,000. Can the tax be changed so that the average rate falls while the marginal rate increases? If so, give an example.

2. What are the most important differences between the way economists define income and the way the tax code defines income?

3. Describe briefly how the income tax burden is distributed among different income classes. Explain what characteristics of the income tax are responsible for producing this distribution.

4. Have the wealthy benefited unfairly from the changes in the income tax law that occurred in the 1980s? Should tax rates on the wealthy be increased?

5. Explain under what conditions a tax on labor income will be shifted. If it is shifted, who bears the shifted portion of the burden?

6. How does a tax on labor income produce a welfare cost? Use a graph to illustrate the nature of this welfare cost.

7. "It is possible that the benefits a person receives when the government spends tax revenues are larger than the cost the person bears in paying the tax. In this case, the person is benefited by the tax, and there is no welfare cost." True or false? Explain.

8. Is the welfare cost of the income tax system higher for men or for women? In order to minimize the welfare cost for a given amount of revenue, should the marginal tax rates for men and women be the same? Explain.

9. What are the economic advantages of using a more comprehensive measure of income for tax purposes? In other words, why do many economists favor closing tax loopholes?

10. How can the elimination of a tax preference item actually benefit a taxpayer who uses that tax preference? In view of this benefit, why are taxpayers so reluctant to give up their tax preferences?

11. Homeownership receives preferential treatment under the income tax in the form of deductibility of mortgage interest, exclusion of imputed income from owner-occupied housing, and deductibility of property taxes on owner-occupied housing. Defend or attack this preferential treatment, pointing out its implications for efficiency and equity.

12. Define *bracket creep*. Construct an example to show how it can produce a larger real tax burden for a taxpayer whose real income has not changed. How does indexation avoid this outcome?

13. In what way, or ways, does the income tax preferentially treat capital income? In what way, or ways, does the income tax penalize capital income?

14. Explain two sources of reduced welfare costs if the current progressive income tax were to be replaced by a simple proportional tax.

Supplementary Readings

BAKIJA, JON, and EUGENE STEUERLE. "Individual Income Taxation Since 1948." *National Tax Journal,* 44:451–476 (Dec. 1991).

BLUM, WALTER J., and HARRY J. KALVEN, JR. *The Uneasy Case for Progressive Taxation.* Chicago: University of Chicago Press, 1953.

BOSWORTH, BARRY, AND GARY BURTLESS. "Effects of Tax Reform on Labor Supply, Investment, and Saving." *Journal of Economic Perspectives,* 6:3–26 (Winter 1992).

BRADFORD, DAVID F. *Untangling the Income Tax.* Cambridge, Mass.: Harvard University Press, 1986.

BROWNING, EDGAR K., and JACQUELENE M. BROWNING. "Why Not a True Flat Rate Tax?" *Cato Journal,* 5:629–650 (Fall 1985).

DAVIES, DAVID G. *United States Taxes and Tax Policy.* Cambridge: Cambridge University Press, 1986.

FEENBERG, DANIEL, and LAWRENCE SUMMERS. "Who Benefits from Capital Gains Tax Reductions?" *Tax Policy and the Economy* 4, ed. by Lawrence H. Summers. Cambridge, Mass.: MIT Press, 1990, pp. 1–24.

SLEMROD, JOEL. "Optimal Taxation and Optimal Tax Systems." *Journal of Economic Perspectives,* 4:157–178 (Winter 1990).

The Corporation Income Tax

PPROXIMATELY 3.5 MILLION INCORPORATED BUSINESSES FILED federal corporation income tax returns in 1992 and paid, in total, over $100 billion in taxes. In terms of federal tax revenue, the corporation income tax is the third largest federal tax, following the individual income tax and the social security payroll tax. The relative importance of the corporation tax has declined over the past several decades. In 1950, the tax accounted for 27.9 percent of all federal tax collections, but by 1992 this figure was down to 9.2 percent. Most of this decline is due to two factors: the growth in social security payroll taxes, which first surpassed corporate taxes in terms of revenue in 1968 and now produce four times as much revenue, and the reduction in corporate profits as a share of national income. In addition to the federal government, most states use corporation income taxes, although at substantially lower rates than the federal tax. In 1991 corporate tax receipts by state governments were $21.5 billion, just over a fifth as large as federal government receipts. In this chapter, we will emphasize the federal corporation income tax, although much of the analysis is applicable to state taxes as well.

◆

Tax Base, Rates, and Revenues

Businesses can operate as either unincorporated or incorporated entities. Unincorporated businesses tend to be relatively small and take the form of sole proprietorships or partnerships. The income of the owners of unincorporated businesses is subject to tax under the federal individual income tax. A special Schedule C must be filed, which allows for the deduction of the costs of operating the business, and the remaining net profit is included as part of personal income.

Although there are a large number of unincorporated businesses—they are about four times as numerous as corporations—about 90 percent of total business income accrues to corporations. A corporation is a form of business that is established under state laws. It is owned by the stockholders, who hold transferable stock certificates. However, the corporation is treated as an independent legal entity; in many respects the law treats a corporation as if it were a person. Just like a person, a corporation is required to pay tax on its income.

Corporation income taxes are generally described as taxes on the profits of incorporated businesses. In the sense that accountants use the term *profits,* this is roughly correct, but the tax base is not pure profit, at least not as the term is used by economists. In the federal tax statutes, the tax base is defined as the total receipts of the corporation minus certain allowable expenses, or revenues minus costs, for short. Not all economic costs, however, are treated as deductible in the tax law. Although wage and salary outlays, depreciation on capital invested, and interest paid on loans are counted as costs, a normal return for invested capital is not included as a cost. Thus the tax base is really equal to the normal return to capital invested plus any economic profits. (Determination of the tax base is actually more complicated because of special provisions in the tax law that we will examine later.)

An example will clarify this important point. Consider a corporation with $1 million invested in plant and equipment. In one year, its sales revenues equal $2 million, and it pays out $1.9 million in wages. Its taxable net income under the corporation income tax is $100,000, but this amount is not economic profit. If the going interest rate is 10 percent, the $1 million invested in this corporation could have been loaned out and earned $100,000 elsewhere. Thus, the $100,000 realized on the investment in the corporation has an opportunity cost—sacrificed earnings if the capital had been invested elsewhere—of $100,000. In this case, the $100,000 "profit" of the corporation is really only the normal return to capital invested; yet that return is subject to the corporation income tax. To avoid confusion, we refer to the tax base of the corporation income tax as the *net income of equity capital* rather than as *profits.*

Now let us take a look at the source of federal corporation income tax payments. Table 12–1 shows that most corporations are relatively small. More than 3.0 million of the 3.6 million corporations in 1989 had total assets below $500,000, but these businesses paid only $4.0 billion in taxes, or about 4 percent of total corporation income taxes. At the other extreme, 18,000 corporations (0.5 percent of all corporations) had assets above $50 million and contributed $78 billion in taxes (four fifths of the total revenue). In fact, the largest 5,500 corporations—0.15 percent of all corporations—paid more than two thirds of all corporation income taxes. Consequently, in terms of revenue, the corporation income tax is primarily a tax on several thousand large corporations.

Table 12–1 *Corporation Income Tax Returns, 1989*

Size of Total Assets ($ thousands)	Number of Returns (thousands)	Net Income by Class ($ billions)	Tax ($ billions)
Zero	209.2	$ 9.0	$ 2.1
1 under 100	1,833.8	2.5	0.4
100 under 250	617.1	4.0	0.7
250 under 500	364.0	4.5	0.8
500 under 1,000	249.7	5.6	1.2
1,000 under 5,000	261.9	14.5	4.2
5,000 under 10,000	38.2	7.1	2.3
10,000 under 25,000	24.8	9.7	3.1
25,000 under 50,000	10.8	9.2	2.9
50,000 under 100,000	7.3	11.3	3.4
100,000 under 250,000	5.6	19.0	5.8
250,000 or more	5.5	274.6	69.1
Total	3,627.9	371.1	96.1

Source: Internal Revenue Service, *Source Book Statistics of Income 1989,* Corporation Income Tax Returns, All Industries, Returns with and without Net Income (Washington, D.C.: U.S. Government Printing Office, 1989), Lines 1, 75, 89.

The rate structure of the federal corporation income tax is slightly progressive. The first $50,000 in net income is taxed at 15 percent, the next $25,000 at 25 percent, and all income in excess of $75,000 at 34 percent. Nearly 95 percent of total tax revenue, however, is collected from corporations with net income above $75,000. For all practical purposes, most corporate net income is subject to the 34 percent marginal rate. Therefore, in our analysis of the tax, we use the simplifying assumption that the corporation income tax is a proportional tax, an assumption that is not far off the mark for the corporations paying the bulk of the tax revenue.

Incidence

One of the most difficult and controversial issues in tax analysis is to determine who bears the burden of the corporation income tax. Because the tax applies to all corporations and not just to one industry, a general equilibrium analysis must be used to examine its incidence. That is difficult enough, but matters are complicated further by the fact that industries within the corporate sector are of various degrees of competitiveness. In our analysis, it is assumed that the corporate sector, taken as a whole, is generally competitive enough for the competitive model to yield reasonably accurate results.

The corporation income tax is applied to the net income of capital invested in the corporate sector of the economy. There is also a noncorporate sector of the economy that employs capital. Although corporations are perhaps the most highly visible employers of capital, actually the noncorporate sector employs half of all real capital. The noncorporate sector includes most of the agricultural and real estate industries, owner-occupied housing, and a smattering of firms in other industries. Capital invested in this sector is not subject to the corporation income tax. Much of the capital income in the noncorporate sector is, however, taxed under the individual income tax. We will initially ignore this fact.

In competitive markets, the *net* returns to capital invested in different uses will tend to be equal. Investors will invest capital where it yields the greatest return; if the return is higher in some uses, investors will shift capital to (increase investment in) those uses, thus driving down the rate of return until it is equal to the return in alternative uses. *The tendency for capital to be allocated in such a way that the net return is equalized in all sectors is the basic equilibrating force of the economy adjusting to a tax on the return to capital in the corporate sector.*

In the absence of the corporate tax, suppose that the rate of return on capital is 8 percent in both the corporate and noncorporate sectors. Now assume that a 50 percent tax is levied on net income (the return to capital) in the corporate sector. The immediate or short-run effect is to tax away half of the return of investors in the corporate sector, leaving them a net yield of only 4 percent on their investment. This will not be a final equilibrium, however, because the net (after-tax) return on capital is now 4 percent in the corporate sector and still 8 percent in the noncorporate sector. Therefore, investors have an incentive to shift capital into the noncorporate sector, where it will earn a higher net return. As investors reduce the supply of capital to the corporate sector, its gross return there rises, while increasing the supply to the noncorporate sector drives down the return there. This process continues until the net return is the same in both sectors. Assume that this equilibrium occurs when the net return is 6 percent in both sectors.

Note carefully what this equilibrium implies. Because of a reduction in capital employed in the corporate sector, its gross (before-tax) return is now 12 percent, which yields a net return of 6 percent after payment of the corporate income tax. Because the return was previously 8 percent, investors in the corporate sector are receiving a return 25 percent less than their earlier return. *This decline in return also affects investors in the untaxed noncorporate sector;* their return is now 6 percent compared with 8 percent before the tax, even though the tax does not apply to noncorporate investments. In this way, the corporate tax places a burden on *all* owners of capital, regardless of whether their capital is employed in the corporate sector. The net return to all investors has fallen from 8 percent to 6 percent.

We have traced the effects of the corporation income tax on owners of capital, but other persons will also be affected. Because corporations must pay a higher gross return on capital as a result of the tax, the prices of products produced by corporations will rise and their consumption will fall. The opposite occurs in the noncorporate sector; output will rise and prices will fall as capital in this sector becomes less expensive. Does this shift mean that consumers bear a burden because of higher prices of corporate sector products? Not necessarily. Corporate prices are higher but noncorporate prices are lower, and there is no reason for the overall or average price of goods and services to be affected. Only consumers who spend a greater than average percentage of their incomes on corporate products (where prices have risen) will be worse off. On average, consumers are not burdened.

This analysis is a good illustration of a general equilibrium analysis of tax incidence. In a general equilibrium approach, we emphasize not only what happens in the taxed sector but also the repercussions in the nontaxed sector. In addition, attention is given to how the tax affects individuals through changes in input prices (the return on capital in this case) and through changes in output prices that occur in all sectors of the economy. In the case of the corporation income tax, the analysis suggests that owners of capital, wherever their capital is employed, bear a burden as a result of the tax.

Diagrammatic Analysis

A diagrammatic presentation of this analysis as it pertains to capital markets should prove helpful. Figure 12–1 shows the effects of different allocations of a given quantity of capital between the corporate and noncorporate sectors on the rate of return in the two sectors. The curve D_C indicates the

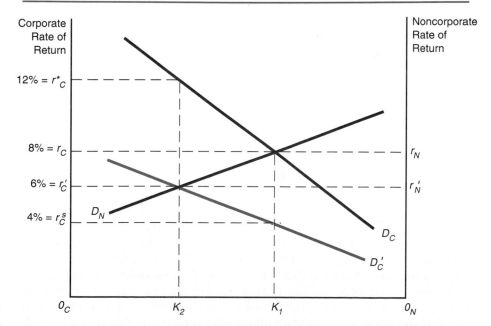

Figure 12–1 *Incidence of the corporation income tax*

productivity of capital employed in the corporate sector, expressed as a rate of return. For example, if 0_CK_2 is employed, the return will be 12 percent, whereas a larger quantity of capital, 0_CK_1, yields a return of 8 percent. The curve D_N shows the productivity of capital in the noncorporate sector, but it is drawn relative to the origin at 0_N. Thus, if 0_NK_1 is employed in the noncorporate sector, the return is 8 percent, whereas if more is employed, 0_NK_2, the return is 6 percent. (The curve D_N is just a reversed demand curve drawn so that the origin lies at the right.)

The horizontal dimension of this boxlike diagram, 0_C0_N, measures the total amount of capital to be allocated between the two sectors. Any point on the horizontal axis indicates the distribution of capital between the sectors. Thus, point K_1 means that there is 0_CK_1 capital in the corporate sector and the remainder, 0_NK_1, is in the noncorporate sector. A movement to K_2 means that 0_CK_2 is now employed in the corporate sector and 0_NK_2 is in the noncorporate sector. Hence a movement from K_1 to K_2 means that there is K_1K_2 less capital in the corporate sector and K_1K_2 more capital in the noncorporate sector; K_1K_2 capital has moved from the corporate to the noncorporate sector.

Before proceeding with the analysis, it may be worthwhile to explain more fully what is meant by capital "moving" from one sector to another. *Capital* refers, of course, to productive resources such as factories, machinery, and trucks. But how can factories and equipment designed to produce automobiles, for example, in the corporate sector "move" to the agricultural industries in the noncorporate sector and produce food? In general, they seldom can move in this sense, but that fact creates no problem for the analysis. Over a period of time the same result—more capital in agriculture and less in automobiles—can occur. Factories and equipment in the automotive industry can be allowed to wear out while new investment expands the capital stock in agriculture. Thus, the passage of time allows the capital stock to be reallocated *in effect* by channeling more new investment to the sector with the higher net return and less to the sector with the lower net return. Although we continue to refer to capital moving from one sector to another, it should be understood that this is a shorthand expression for the process just described.

Returning now to Figure 12–1, in the absence of the corporation income tax, the equilibrium allocation of capital is at K_1, where D_C and D_N intersect, with 0_CK_1 in the corporate sector and 0_NK_1 in the noncorporate sector. With this allocation, the returns to capital in the two sectors, r_C and r_N, are both equal to 8 percent. When the corporate tax is imposed at a rate of 50 percent, the net return to capital in the corporate sector is reduced by half; the new schedule showing the net (after-tax) return is D_C'. In the short run, before enough time has elapsed for capital to "move," the owners of capital in the corporate sector bear the full burden of the tax and receive an after-tax return of r_C^s, or 4 percent. The allocation at K_1, however, is not a long-run equilibrium because the capital in the untaxed noncorporate sector is earning a higher net return of 8 percent. The owners of capital will move it from the corporate to the noncorporate sector until the net returns are equalized. The net returns are equal where D'_C and D_N intersect, with $0_C K_2$ capital in the corporate sector and $0_N K_2$ in the noncorporate sector. Note, however, that this result implies that the before-tax rates of return are not equal. Capital investment is yielding a return of 12 percent before taxes in the corporate sector compared to 6 percent in the noncorporate sector.

Thus, the corporation income tax produces a reallocation of $K_1 K_2$ capital from the corporate sector to the noncorporate sector as investors seek a higher return in the untaxed sector. The final equilibrium is where the net return to all owners of capital is at 6 percent, down from its original 8 percent level. All owners of capital suffer a loss of 25 percent of their pretax capital income, regardless of whether or not they are stockholders in corporations.

The preceding analysis is based on the assumption that capital income in the noncorporate sector is untaxed. Actually, income in the noncorporate sector may be subject to tax under the federal individual income tax and property taxes levied by local governments. The effective rate of tax on capital income in the corporate sector, however, is higher because of the corporation income tax, and differences in tax rates between sectors are all that is necessary for the preceding analysis to hold. Because capital income in the corporate sector is more heavily taxed than in the noncorporate sector, there is an incentive for the reallocation of capital previously described to occur.

To say that all owners of capital bear a burden from the corporation income tax does not necessarily imply that they bear the entire burden (equal to tax revenue raised). The final incidence depends on whether the total *gross* return to capital (the return to capital income in both sectors) is altered by the reallocation of capital produced by the tax. If the total gross return is unchanged, then capital owners will bear the entire burden. For example, if before-tax capital income is $500 billion (8 percent times $0_C 0_N$) and gross (before-tax) capital income after the tax (12 percent times $0_C K_2$ plus 6 percent times $0_N K_2$) is still $500 billion, the after-tax capital income will be less than $500 billion by the amount of the tax [$(r^*_C - r'_C)$ times $0_C K_2$]. Capital owners then bear the entire burden of the tax. Whether or not this outcome is exactly true depends on a number of underlying elasticities in production and consumption. After examining a number of plausible relationships, Arnold Harberger (on whose seminal work this analysis is based)[1] concluded that in all likelihood, owners of capital bear approximately the entire burden of the tax.

[1]Arnold C. Harberger, "The Incidence of the Corporation Income Tax," *Journal of Political Economy,* 70:215 (June 1962), reprinted in his *Taxation and Welfare* (Boston: Little, Brown, 1974), pp. 135–162. For a simplified exposition of the general equilibrium model used by Harberger and its applications to a variety of taxes, see Charles E. McLure, Jr., and Wayne R. Thirsk, "A Simplified Exposition of the Harberger Model, I: Tax Incidence," *National Tax Journal,* 28:1 (Mar. 1975).

What does it mean to accept Harberger's conclusion that owners of capital bear the full burden of the corporation income tax? If Harberger is correct, the incidence of the tax is equivalent to a proportional tax (of 25 percent in the preceding example) on capital income wherever capital is employed. In interpreting this result, it is important to recall that the noncorporate sector actually contains about half of the capital in the United States: The major uses of capital in the noncorporate sector are in agriculture and homeownership. A home represents a way to invest in capital, and it is the major form of capital ownership for millions of families. (The capital income from homeownership is partly in the form of housing services directly consumed, a form of in-kind capital income.) Thus, people who purchase their own homes will realize a lower return because of the corporation income tax. The same is true for savers, who will earn a lower rate of interest on their savings accounts. Stockholders of corporations also bear a burden. In this connection, it should be noted that the millions of workers who own stock indirectly in the form of pension funds are also affected. (In 1990, about 40 percent of all corporate stock was owned by pension funds.) In short, the burden of the corporation income tax is spread widely throughout the population, even though most of the people who bear this burden are unaware of it.

Other Factors Affecting Incidence

The Harberger model is probably the most widely accepted view of the effects of the corporation income tax, but not all economists accept this analysis as a correct or complete analysis of the tax. One frequently criticized feature of the analysis is Harberger's assumption that the corporate sector can be treated as competitive. Not all corporations operate in highly competitive industries; some corporations have some degree of monopolistic market power. In a noncompetitive market, the incidence of the tax could be different than Harberger's competitive model would predict.

Generally speaking, economists who believe that the corporate sector is characterized mainly by monopoly or oligopoly hold that the corporation income tax is really like an excise tax on corporate sector products. Whether that conclusion is correct is far from obvious. Harberger, in his original paper, modified the basic analysis to examine a particular type of monopoly pricing on the part of all corporations. He assumed that corporations set a price that was based on a fixed markup over average cost. Even in this model, however, Harberger found that the incidence of the tax was essentially the same as in the basic competitive model.[2] Anderson and Ballentine extended Harberger's approach further by assuming that all corporations were profit-maximizing monopolies. The incidence results in their model are still almost identical to incidence estimates obtained under competitive

[2] Harberger, "Corporation Income Tax."

assumptions.[3] Thus, although a nagging suspicion may remain that the results will differ in real-world markets, there is some basis for believing that Harberger's basic results may hold even in noncompetitive settings.

A second factor neglected in this analysis was the possibility that the rate of capital accumulation could be affected if the amount of saving changes as a result of the corporation income tax. It is important to note that the analysis of Figure 12–1 focuses on the way the corporate tax affects the allocation of a *given and unchanged amount of capital* between sectors. But one effect of the tax is to depress the rate of return that people receive on their capital investments. If people save less at a lower rate of return, then the total amount of capital will fall or grow more slowly over time with the tax than in its absence. The analysis presented earlier is fully correct only if the rate of saving is unaffected by the corporation income tax.

If the corporation income tax does depress saving (and hence accumulation of real capital), the burden of the tax will be spread even more broadly over the population. A reduction in the amount of capital means that the amount of capital per worker falls so that the marginal productivity of labor and thus wage rates fall (or, perhaps more realistically, grow more slowly over time). Consequently, some of the burden is shifted from capital owners (less capital means a higher rate of return) to workers in the form of lower wages. We shall continue to ignore this possibility here but consider it further in Chapter 15.

Another complicating factor in the analysis of the corporation income tax stems from differences in the tax treatment of investments financed by equity and those financed by debt. If a corporation finances an investment with equity funds (supplied by the owners, or shareholders, either through purchases of new shares of stock or through investment of retained earnings), the return on that investment is subject to the corporate income tax. On the other hand, if the corporation borrows to finance the investment, the interest payments on its debt are considered a cost of operation under the corporation income tax and are therefore deductible. When investments are equity financed, a normal return on capital is not allowed as a cost but is fully subject to the tax. With debt financing, a normal return (as approximated by the interest rate that is paid) is deductible, and the tax applies only to any return in excess of that level.

As a consequence, the corporation income tax leads corporations to favor debt over equity finance. By using debt to finance new investments, corporations reduce their corporate tax liabilities. Thus, the effective tax rate on capital invested in the corporation depends on how it is financed, and as a consequence, the effective tax rate on corporate net income can be below the statutory rates. The significance of this point, however, is a matter of

[3]Robert Anderson and J. Gregory Ballentine, "The Incidence and Excess Burden of a Profits Tax Under Imperfect Competition," *Public Finance/Finances Publiques* 31 (2):157 (1976).

some dispute. In reviewing the literature on this topic, J. Gregory Ballentine concluded that the incidence of the tax is not greatly affected by the favorable treatment given debt finance.[4]

For these reasons, the question of the incidence of the corporation income tax remains a somewhat controversial issue. Accepting for the present, however, the conclusion of our earlier analysis that the tax places a burden on people in proportion to their income from capital, let us consider what this conclusion means for the distribution of the tax burden. A proportionate tax on income from capital is not the same as a proportionate tax on total income. Typically, families with higher incomes receive a larger share of their incomes in the form of capital income. Thus, the burden of the corporation income tax will be a larger fraction of total household income for families in upper-income classes.

Table 12–2 gives the Congressional Budget Office estimates of the distribution of the burden of the federal corporation income tax in 1988 when the tax falls proportionately on all capital income. The second column gives the tax burden as a percentage of "family income" (this is the CBO measure of family income, as described in the last chapter) for each income class. The estimates suggest that the average tax rate rises up to about the fourth decile and then remains more or less constant through the ninth decile before rising significantly for the top decile (and even more so for the top 5 percent and top 1 percent). The tax is, therefore, progressive in its incidence relative to family income. The third column gives each income class's total tax burden as a percentage of the national total tax burden. According to the estimates, the lower 50 percent of the population bears about 10 percent of the total corporate tax burden, while the top decile bears 61.7 percent. The top 5 percent alone bear more than half of the total tax burden. This incidence reflects, of course, the fact that the top 5 percent receives more than half of all estimated capital income.

One major problem with these estimates should be mentioned: It is very difficult to estimate capital income, especially for owners of small businesses and homes. In fact, the CBO estimates of capital income do not include the income from owner-occupied housing at all, even though we expect the corporate tax to place a burden on owners of this form of capital, as we have seen. Given this problem, the estimates should be considered fairly rough, although there is no doubt that the bulk of the tax burden falls on the top income classes, at least if the burden falls on capital income. (Other studies that have included owner-occupied housing have estimated a similar distribution of the corporate tax burden.)

A major reason for considering the incidence of any tax is to determine whether the distribution of the tax burden among families is fair. In considering vertical equity—the treatment of people at different income levels— whether the progressivity of the tax is appropriate is the issue, and clearly

---

[4]J. Gregory Ballentine, *Equity, Efficiency, and the U.S. Corporation Income Tax* (Washington, D.C.: American Enterprise Institute, 1980), Chapter 4.

Table 12–2   *Corporate Tax Distribution and Family Income, 1988*

Decile	Tax as a Percentage of Family Income	Percentage of Total Tax Paid
1	1.1%	0.3%
2	1.0	0.9
3	1.3	1.7
4	1.6	2.9
5	1.6	3.8
6	1.6	4.9
7	1.7	6.3
8	1.6	7.2
9	1.7	9.9
10	4.7	61.7
Top 5%	5.7	53.0
Top 1%	7.7	35.4
All deciles	2.7	100.0

Source: Congress of the United States, CBO, *The Changing Distribution of Federal Taxes: 1975–1990* (Washington, D.C.: U.S. Government Printing Office, Oct. 1987), Tables 7 and B.1

people will make different value judgments about that issue. In terms of horizontal equity—the treatment of people with equal incomes—the corporate tax is clearly inequitable. In comparing two families with the same total income, the family receiving a larger share of its income in the form of capital income will bear a heavier tax burden under the corporation tax. For example, of two families with equal incomes, but one consisting totally of capital and the other totally of labor income, the former would bear a tax burden and the latter none at all. This inequity is one of the objections to having a corporation tax at all. It is possible to avoid this inequity by taxing corporate income as income under the individual income tax, a proposal we will discuss at the end of the chapter.

Welfare Cost

In addition to the direct burden of the corporation income tax, it distorts resource allocation in several important ways. First, it leads to a misallocation of a given stock of capital among competing uses in the economy. Second, it leads to a capital stock that is too small. Since other taxes also interact with the corporate tax to affect the size of the total capital stock, a discussion of this second type of misallocation is deferred to Chapter 15. Third, it biases investment decisions within the corporate sector. This point will be explained later in this chapter. Here we shall discuss only the way the corporate tax distorts the allocation of capital between the corporate and noncorporate sectors of the economy.

Consider Figure 12–2. In the last section, we saw that the equilibrium under the corporation income tax occurred where the net returns to capital in the corporate and noncorporate sectors were equal. This is shown at K_2 with $O_C K_2$ in the corporate sector and $O_N K_2$ in the noncorporate sector. At this allocation, the gross return to capital differs between the two sectors; it is 12 percent in the corporate sector and 6 percent in the noncorporate sector. Capital is misallocated between the two sectors because it is more productive in the corporate sector than it is in the noncorporate sector. Although investors will be guided by the net returns, the gross returns, or true physical productivities, are what are relevant for efficiency considerations. With the allocation at K_2, there are investment projects with yields just below 12 percent in the corporate sector that will not be undertaken because investors are interested in the after-tax yields. The after-tax yield on an investment paying a gross return of 11.9 percent will be only 5.95 percent, less than the return realized in the noncorporate sector. Thus, a reallocation of capital

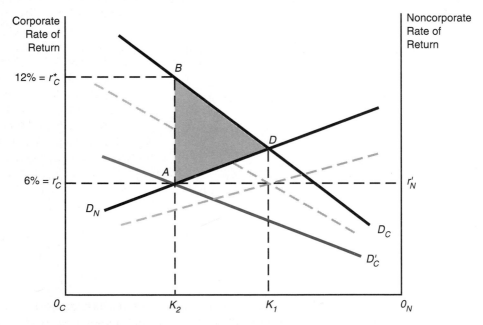

Figure 12–2   One type of welfare cost of the corporation income tax

from the noncorporate sector to the corporate sector will increase the real return on the total capital stock, but the corporate tax will inhibit that reallocation. The result is a welfare cost.

Efficiency requires that the gross yields in the two sectors be equal, and this condition occurs at K_1. The corporate tax produces underinvestment of K_1K_2 in the corporate sector (and overinvestment of K_1K_2 in the noncorporate sector). By reducing capital from K_1 to K_2 in the corporate sector, projects yielding from 8 to 12 percent (along D_C from point D to point B) are sacrificed, and projects yielding from 8 percent to 6 percent in the noncorporate sector (along D_N from point D to point A) are undertaken. The net loss from this reallocation of K_1K_2 between the sectors is the difference between the returns on these projects in the two sectors. This result is shown by area BAD, the loss involved in investing K_1K_2 less in the corporate sector (area DBK_2K_1) minus the gain from investing this capital in the noncorporate sector instead (area DAK_2K_1).

Several economists have developed estimates of the size of the welfare cost as a result of the sectoral misallocation of capital produced by the corporation income tax. Harberger was the first. Using data from the mid-1950s, Harberger estimated the welfare cost to be about 0.5 percent of GNP.[5] John Shoven used a disaggregated model (more than two sectors), corrected a numerical error in Harberger's calculations, and still found a welfare loss of about 0.5 percent of GNP.[6] To put these estimates in perspective, they represent a loss equal to approximately 12 percent of tax revenues.

In addition, it should be recalled that there is a welfare cost caused by the depressing effect of the tax on saving and capital accumulation. Estimates of this resource misallocation vary widely, and since several taxes interact to affect saving and capital accumulation, it is difficult to identify a certain portion of this welfare cost as being exclusively the result of the corporate tax. However, there is some suspicion that this welfare loss is significant, perhaps larger than the welfare cost associated with the misallocation of resources between the corporate and noncorporate sectors illustrated in Figure 12–2. Ballentine, for instance, suggests that the combined welfare cost of both types is at least one third as large as the tax revenue generated by the corporation income tax.[7] Several other studies have also suggested that the distortion in saving and capital accumulation is more important than the welfare cost due to the misallocation among sectors. These studies have estimated the welfare cost due to all taxes on capital income and have

[5]Arnold C. Harberger, "Efficiency Effects of Taxes on Income from Capital," in Marian Krzyzaniak, ed., *Effects of Corporation Income Tax* (Detroit: Wayne State University Press, 1966), pp. 110–117.

[6]John B. Shoven, "The Incidence and Efficiency Effects of Taxes on Income from Capital," *Journal of Political Economy*, 84:1261 (Dec. 1976).

[7]Ballentine, *Equity, Efficiency, and the U.S. Corporation Income Tax*, Chapter 5.

generally concluded that the welfare cost is between 1 and 3 percent of GNP.[8] While the corporation income tax is only one of several taxes responsible for this welfare cost, it is the most important one.

Because of the general perception that the corporation income tax is quite inefficient, many economists have recommended fundamental reforms. One suggested change is capable of reducing, if not eliminating, the inefficiency caused by the sectoral misallocation of capital. Recall that capital is misallocated between the corporate and noncorporate sectors because its return is taxed at different rates in the two sectors. If capital income were taxed at the same rate, regardless of the sector in which the capital is employed, the misallocation could be avoided.

This point is also illustrated in Figure 12–2. Suppose that capital income in both sectors is taxed at a rate of 25 percent, instead of taxing only the corporate sector at a rate of 50 percent. Under this tax, the demand curves identifying the net returns in the two sectors would be shown as the dashed lines in the diagram. With a tax rate of 25 percent of capital income wherever earned, the equilibrium allocation would be at K_1, and capital would be efficiently allocated between the two sectors. With capital taxed equally, no incentive exists for capital to move from one sector to the other. Note that the owners of capital would be no worse off than under the corporation income tax; they would still receive a net return of 6 percent. Resources, however, would be allocated more efficiently between the corporate and noncorporate sectors.

Issues in Tax Base Determination

Thus far, we have given little attention to the tax base of the corporation income tax. In general, special tax preferences or loopholes are not as numerous for the corporate tax as they are for the individual income tax. Nonetheless, some special features of the corporate income tax have important implications and require further discussion.

Depreciation

Probably the most important topic related to the definition of taxable net income for corporations concerns the treatment of depreciation allowances. *Depreciation* refers to the fact that capital equipment frequently lasts for a number of years but tends to wear out gradually over its life span. For tax

[8]Michael Boskin, "Taxation, Saving and the Rate of Interest," *Journal of Political Economy,* 86:S3 (Apr. 1978); Don Fullerton, John Shoven, and John Whalley, "Replacing the U.S. Income Tax with a Progressive Consumption Tax: A Sequenced General Equilibrium Approach," *Journal of Public Economics,* 20:3 (1983); Dale Jorgenson and Kun Young Yun, "Tax Policy and Capital Allocation," *Scandinavian Journal of Economics,* 88:355 (1986).

purposes, the cost of the capital equipment is a legitimate expense that (along with other costs) must be subtracted from revenues in determining net income. Since the equipment contributes to production over a period of years, however, there is a problem in determining how much of the total equipment cost to consider a cost of production each year.

In principle, the apportionment of the cost of real capital assets over the service life of assets should reflect the rate at which they actually wear out. For example, if a piece of equipment costs $100 in year 1 but is worth only $90 a year later, the firm should be able to count $10 as a cost of production in year 1. Over the life of the equipment, the firm should be able to deduct the entire cost of the equipment and pay tax on only the net return to the investment. However, for practical reasons it would be impossible for the tax authorities to determine the true rate of depreciation and apply this principle precisely to all investments. It is not clear how the rate at which equipment wears out can be measured or, when the equipment is acquired, how many years it will last.

The tax treatment of depreciation is important because it influences the effective tax rate that is applied to net income. *If assets can be depreciated faster than they actually wear out, then the effective tax rate will be reduced below the statutory level.* To illustrate, suppose that a corporation purchases equipment with a cost of $100. If the corporation can depreciate the equipment in one year and subtract the entire cost that year (*very* rapid depreciation), its net income subject to tax will fall by $100 and its taxes (assuming a 34 percent rate) will fall by $34. If, alternatively, the asset cannot be counted as a cost until 10 years later and then deducted fully in the 10th year, the corporation will save $34 in year 10. The first method is clearly preferable, since the firm achieves the $34 tax saving in year 1 instead of year 10. The firm could then invest the tax saving in year 1 at the market interest rate, and the sum would grow to much more than $34 by year 10. Put differently, the present value of the tax saving is greater when the portion of the cost that can be written off in the early years is greater. Rapid depreciation allows the firm to postpone paying the tax, which reduces the present value of the tax to the firm. Allowing more rapid depreciation is therefore similar to reducing the effective tax rate on corporate net income.

For purposes of computing depreciation allowances, the tax laws as of 1993 classify all assets into one of eight classes, which differ according to the number of years over which the asset is depreciated. These "tax lives" vary from 3 to 31.5 years. Buildings, for example, must be depreciated over 31.5 years, most equipment over 5 years, and automobiles over 3 years. In addition, three different methods are used to determine how much of the original cost may be written off in each year. The straight-line method is the simplest. Using this method, for an asset in the 10-year class, one tenth of the original cost is taken as an expense in each year. The other two methods, the double-declining balance method and the one-and-a-half-method, allow a larger portion of the cost to be written off in the earlier years than the straight-line method permits. Businesses would always choose the fastest method of depreciation if given a choice, but the tax law specifies the method to be used for each depreciation class.

Congress has frequently changed the rules applicable to depreciation allowances. In the 1981 tax reform (Economic Recovery Tax Act of 1981), for example, depreciation was permitted at a more rapid rate than is allowed now. For example, buildings could be depreciated over 18 years rather than the 31.5 years allowed today. (The Tax Reform Act of 1986 lengthened the tax lives of assets.) Recall that the effect of more rapid depreciation allowances is to reduce the tax paid on new investments. The depreciation allowances introduced in 1981 were intended, in fact, to stimulate corporate investment. Economists generally do not favor altering depreciation allowances as a method of stimulating investment, but prefer instead the use of true depreciation allowances (reflecting, insofar as possible, actual asset lives) combined with lower tax rates. Rapid depreciation has the disadvantages of tending to favor longer-lived investments and of distorting the types of investments undertaken by corporations.

Rapid depreciation, however, has one advantage: liberalizing depreciation practices reduces taxes only on new investments, not on existing assets (which must continue to be depreciated according to the law at the time the assets were acquired). This arrangement implies that tax revenues will fall very little at first, but new investment will be encouraged by the lower taxes that will be paid in the future on that investment. As time passes, however, an increasing portion of investments will be covered by the new depreciation provisions, and tax revenue losses will therefore rise over time. In the long run, there is no advantage to liberalizing depreciation practices rather than cutting tax rates.

Even though the tax lives of assets were lengthened by the 1986 law, they are still generally believed to be shorter than the actual lengths of time most assets last. For example, most buildings have usable lives of 30 to 50 years but are depreciated over 31.5 years, and automobiles certainly are usable longer than the 3 years over which they are depreciated. Thus, depreciation allowances still operate to reduce the effective tax rate on assets below the statutory rate.

Investment Tax Credit

The investment tax credit was introduced at a rate of 7 percent on new investment in 1962, temporarily suspended between 1966 and 1967, "permanently" eliminated in 1969, reintroduced in 1971, and increased to 10 percent in 1975. The 1986 tax reform eliminated the investment tax credit once more, but President Clinton proposed reintroduction of the device on a limited basis in 1993. The phoenix-like characteristic of this tax provision makes it worthwhile to be familiar with its nature.

The investment tax credit permits a corporation to subtract some portion of the cost of new qualified investments from its tax liability. An investment tax credit of 10 percent, for example, means that if a business purchases a computer for $1,000, it can subtract $100 from its corporate tax liability in that year. Thus, the credit has the effect of reducing the net cost of new investments and thereby encouraging them. The effect is again similar to an outright tax rate reduction (which would also encourage new investment), but with the short-run advantage of applying only to new investments rather than to all capital assets already in place. Congress has a penchant for trying to encourage investment without having to pay very much for it in the form of reduced tax revenues.

The investment tax credit can lower the cost of new investments to firms by effectively reducing taxes that apply to new investments without reducing taxes on existing investments. Insofar as it is desirable to stimulate investment, a matter we will examine in a later chapter, the investment tax credit is in principle a cost-effective approach. However, as it has been used in the past, it does have drawbacks. Before its repeal in 1986, for example, the credit applied only to investments in machinery and equipment, not to investments in buildings and structures. It also applied different rates to different types of equipment. This practice had the effect of producing wide variation in the effective tax rates that applied to various investments. This variation, in turn, distorted the investment decisions of firms, leading them to undertake certain types of investments due to their favorable tax treatment.

Inflation and the Measure of Income

As we saw in the last chapter, the individual income tax does not handle inflationary situations well. The same is true of the corporation income tax. With respect to the individual tax, we identified two potential problems: bracket creep (solved by indexing the tax brackets) and mismeasurement of capital income. Since most corporate income is already subject to the highest rate bracket in that tax, bracket creep is not a major problem for the corporate tax, even though the tax brackets are not indexed. But the measurement of income is a problem, and with inflation, real corporate net income is not properly measured.

For the corporate tax to measure net income correctly, all components of costs and revenues must be measured in dollars of the same purchasing power. This measurement, however, does not occur in two important instances. One is depreciation allowances, which are based on the historical cost of the asset, and its historical cost may differ greatly from its real cost when prices are rising. If a piece of equipment costs $100 in 1993, the firm can deduct a total of $100 as depreciation over the allowable years, even though as a result of inflation, it may cost $200 to replace the equipment. Depreciation allowances based on historical cost tend to *understate* true costs in inflationary periods and therefore *overstate* the real net income of the corporation. On this count, inflation increases the real tax burden on corporate net income.

There is, however, an offsetting effect. Corporations are permitted to deduct their nominal interest payments on borrowed funds. In inflationary times, the nominal rate exceeds the real rate of interest, so that firms are permitted to take deductions that are larger than their real borrowing costs warrant. This tax break works to the advantage of corporations.

Considering the corporate sector as a whole, these two factors have been estimated to approximately offset each other, implying that corporation income taxes are not greatly affected by inflation. However, a significant distortion caused by inflation is still present because particular corporations are affected quite differently from the average. Firms that have not borrowed to finance investments find their real tax burdens greatly increased, whereas corporations relying heavily on borrowing find their real tax burdens reduced.

Although corporation income taxes in the aggregate are not greatly affected by inflation, the taxation of corporate income by the tax system as a whole is. Firms gain from being able to deduct nominal interest payments, but those who receive these interest payments pay taxes on the nominal rather than the real interest income and therefore lose from inflation. Feldstein and Summers showed that the higher real taxes paid by the recipients of the nominal interest income are as large as the tax saving to the corporation.[9]

Thus, in a broader sense there is no combined tax advantage from nominal interest deductibility, but the depreciation problem still remains and unambiguously increases the real tax burden on corporate sector income.

What Is the Effective Tax Rate on Corporate Income?

As we saw with the individual income tax, statutory tax rates can differ significantly from effective tax rates due to special provisions in the tax law. The same is true of the corporation income tax. We have, for example, seen how depreciation allowances and the investment tax credit can operate to reduce the tax liabilities of corporations, thereby implying that the effective tax rate is less than the statutory tax rate. There are also other factors that have positive and negative effects on the tax liabilities of corporations that we have not discussed.

Table 12–3 presents estimates of effective tax rates (taxes as a percentage of estimated net income of corporations) for several recent years and contrasts them with the statutory rates. The second column gives the statutory rates (the top rate that applies to most corporate income) in each year. Note that until the last year shown, the statutory rate was nearly 50 percent. The 1986 tax reform reduced the statutory rate to 34 percent. The third column shows the combined effect of depreciation allowances and the investment tax credit. The negative entries there indicate the extent to which these provisions reduced the effective tax rate below the statutory rate. For example, in 1988, these tax provisions were equivalent to a 7.8 percentage point reduction in the statutory tax rate. The fourth column shows the combined effect of five other adjustments, not shown separately. The last column, the

---

[9]Martin S. Feldstein and Lawrence H. Summers, "Inflation and the Taxation of Capital Income in the Corporate Sector," *National Tax Journal,* 32:445 (Dec. 1979).

Table 12–3   *Statutory versus Effective Corporate Tax Rates (in percent), 1970–1988*

Year	Statutory Tax Rate	Depreciation and Investment Tax Credit	Other Adjustments	Average Tax Rate
1970	49.2%	−9.6%	5.3%	44.9%
1975	48.0	−7.4	−1.7	39.9
1980	46.0	−13.3	9.9	42.6
1985	46.0	−25.4	5.4	25.9
1988	34.0	−7.8	4.1	30.3

Source: James M. Poterba, "Why Didn't the Tax Reform Act of 1986 Raise Corporate Taxes?" in James P. Poterba, ed., *Tax Policy and the Economy*, Vol. 6 (Cambridge, Mass.: MIT Press, 1992), Table 7.

sum of the statutory rate and the adjustments in the third and fourth columns, gives the estimated effective tax rates on corporate income.

As you can see, the effective tax rate has varied greatly over time. It was approximately 40 percent during the 1970s, when the statutory rate was 48 percent. In 1985 it was sharply lower at 25.9 percent, *even though the statutory rate was still 46 percent.* This reduction was due primarily to the accelerated depreciation allowances that were adopted in 1981 and phased in over the next several years. Then in 1988 the estimated effective tax rate rose to 30.3 percent, despite the fact that the statutory rate declined from 46 to 34 percent. This tax rate increase was due to the elimination of the investment tax credit and the changes in depreciation allowances in the 1986 tax reform.

One clear message from these estimates is that the statutory tax rate is often not a good measure of the magnitude of the tax burden placed on corporate income.

The R&D Tax Credit

A recent innovation in tax preferences for businesses is the tax credit initially granted in 1981 to spending on research and development (R&D). In the original law, this tax credit was intended to be experimental and was scheduled to expire at the end of 1985. It has been renewed several times since then, so it is beginning to appear that is may become an enduring part of the tax law.

R&D can be thought of as a form of productive investment. As such, the immediate question is why it should be subsidized when most other investments are taxed. One reason, favored by economists, is that spending on R&D may produce external benefits. One outcome of R&D spending is often the production of new knowledge, which later can be used by those who did not share in the cost of producing it. That outcome gives people an incentive to underinvest in R&D. For example, would you spend millions to develop a better mousetrap, knowing that once you succeeded other firms would immediately copy your design and therefore capture part of the benefit of your investment? Although patent and copyright laws attempt to restrict the use of knowledge to those who produce it, at least for a limited time, there are serious problems in enforcing these laws.

Therefore, externality theory provides a rationale for a subsidy to this particular form of investment spending. In fact, a recent survey of the economic research on this topic concludes that the external benefits of R&D spending are quite large, perhaps as large as the private benefits accruing to those who undertake the spending.[10] Note that according to externality theory, if the marginal external benefit is this large, a subsidy of 50 percent would be called for (assuming that the marginal external benefit is still 50 percent of the marginal social benefit at the efficient level of spending). The actual subsidy enacted by Congress in 1981 was a 25 percent tax credit (20 percent after 1985). As we will see, however, that credit did not reduce the cost of R&D spending by 25 percent.

The R&D tax credit was originally applied only to *increases* in R&D spending above the average R&D spending of the firm over the preceding three years. In other words, the subsidy was intended to apply only at the margin, not to pay for R&D spending that was already being undertaken. This restriction was intended to keep the cost of the subsidy manageable. Total R&D spending by industry in 1989 was $67 billion, and if the tax credit had applied to all of this spending, it would have cost the U.S. Treasury nearly $17 billion in lost tax revenue, almost 20 percent of total corporate tax revenue in that year. By restricting the credit to incremental spending, the cost in lost revenue was much lower; estimates suggest that the cost was between $1 and $2 billion per year in the 1980s.[11] Like depreciation allowances and the investment tax credit, the R&D tax credit is an example of an attempt by Congress to stimulate (subsidize) an activity without incurring much cost by restricting the subsidy to incremental spending.

A marginal subsidy of this form should increase spending by lowering the net cost to firms. Estimates of the effect of the credit on R&D spending vary but typically suggest that spending did increase somewhat. Studies suggest that R&D spending may have been increased by $0.2 to $2.0 billion per year. At first glance, these estimates seem to imply that the expansion was very modest. Since total R&D spending by industry averaged about $60 billion a year in the 1980s, if the tax credit was responsible for a $1 billion increase, this would be less than a 2 percent increase in response to a 20–25 percent tax credit.

Analysis of the tax credit has shown that it was not as well designed to encourage R&D spending as Congress thought. Although the statutory sub-

[10]Zvi Griliches, "The Search for R&D Spillovers," National Bureau of Economic Research Working Paper No. 3768 (1991).

[11]Bronwyn H. Hall, "R&D Tax Policy During the Eighties: Success or Failure?" National Bureau of Economic Research Working Paper No. 4240 (Dec. 1992).

sidy rate was 20–25 percent, the effective subsidy rate was much less. There are at least three reasons for this. First, firms must have positive tax liabilities in order to benefit from the credit, since it is nonrefundable. Many firms that actively invest in R&D are young, rapidly growing enterprises, however, and these firms frequently operate in the red in their early years.[12] Second, the likelihood that the tax credit would be temporary (it has been scheduled to expire several times and was then renewed) probably limited its impact. R&D spending is essentially long-term, and few firms would be likely to undertake long-term commitments to research projects on the basis of a tax credit that was scheduled to expire in two or three years.

The third reason is perhaps the most interesting: The incremental form of the tax credit tends to reduce the effective rate of subsidy. For example, suppose that a firm increases its R&D spending by $100 this year and receives a $20 tax credit. The firm's higher R&D spending this year, however, will increase the base used to calculate the tax credit in future years. That is, the additional $100 in R&D spending this year will increase the base by $33 for each of the next three years since the base is the average of R&D spending over the previous three years. Thus, by spending $100 more this year, the firm can lose future tax credits of 20 percent of $33 for each of the next three years, for a total loss of $20 (3 × 0.20 × $33), ignoring the discounting of future loss. Thus, this method of restricting the tax credit to incremental spending greatly dilutes the effective subsidy rate.

For these reasons, the effective rate of the R&D tax credit has been much lower than its statutory level of 20–25 percent. Estimates of the effective credit rate suggest that it was in the range of 2–5 percent during the 1980s. (The method of calculating the base on which incremental spending is calculated, as described in the last paragraph, was changed in 1990, and the effective subsidy rate is expected to increase to about 7 percent.[13]) With that small a reduction in net cost, it is not surprising that increases in R&D spending were rather modest. This experience illustrates once more the difficulties of designing effective tax incentives while simultaneously trying to avoid substantial revenue losses.

Integration of the Corporation and Individual Income Taxes

The corporation income tax turns out to be a complicated levy with a number of undesirable features. As a tax on capital income, it reduces the net (after-tax) return to saving and probably reduces saving and real capital

---

[12]The tax credit can be "carried forward" for up to 15 years, which means that if there is any tax liability in the following 15 years, the tax credit can be used then. However, if the firm is unable to use the credit for several years, the credit's present value will be significantly reduced, especially during inflationary periods, since the credit is not indexed.

[13]Hall, "R&D Tax Policy During the Eighties," Table 3.

accumulation. Since the corporation income tax applies only to capital income generated in the corporate sector, and at different rates to different assets, it is an uneven tax that distorts the allocation of capital among different assets and industries. On equity grounds, the corporation income tax violates the principle of horizontal equity, since taxpayers who receive more capital income bear a heavier tax burden. The vertical equity implications are not as clear. The corporation income tax does result in a higher tax rate for the top decile, but it also applies a sizable tax burden on low-income families with capital income. Under the individual income tax, families with less than about $15,000 in income are considered too poor to pay taxes, but if that income were capital income (such as pension income), it would be subject to a substantial tax burden from the corporation income tax before it reached the family.

For these reasons, a number of economists have for many years urged reform of the corporation income tax. One proposal is simply to eliminate the tax altogether, but that has at least one major disadvantage: Although individuals would still pay individual income taxes on corporate income paid out as dividends, they would pay no taxes on corporate income held within the corporation. Thus, retained corporate earnings would escape taxation, at least until the shareholders realized a capital gain from the sale of the stock.

To ensure that retained corporate earnings do not escape taxation when the corporate tax is eliminated, the individual income tax must be changed. The method generally recommended is to require a corporation to inform each shareholder that it has retained a certain sum of income on his or her behalf; then that sum is taxed as income under the individual income tax on an annual basis. For example, if a corporation has net income of $1,000 that it does not pay out as dividends, and there are 10 shareholders, each owning one tenth of the shares, then each shareholder would be considered to have income from the corporation equal to $100 for individual income tax purposes.

This proposal is commonly referred to as the *integration* of the corporate and personal income taxes. Under this integration, all corporate income (whether paid out as dividends or retained) would be taxed as ordinary income of shareholders. This reform has several advantages. Horizontal equity would be improved: Two taxpayers with the same incomes would pay the same tax even if one received only corporate source income and the other entirely labor income. Vertical equity might also be improved, but this conclusion is more a matter of viewpoint. Low-income families with zero taxable income would no longer pay a sizable tax on their corporate-source income. In general, taxes on lower- and upper-income classes would fall, but the reduction in average tax rates would be larger for those with low incomes.

The integration of the corporate and personal income taxes would also result in efficiency advantages. Integration would end the differences in the tax treatment of corporate and noncorporate income. (In fact, the proposal basically would extend the same treatment to corporate income that is now applied to unincorporated businesses.) This change would avoid the misallocation of capital between the two sectors, as illustrated in Figure 12–2. Integration would also lower the overall taxation of capital income since it would avoid having the same income taxed at both the corporate and personal levels, which could lead to an increase in saving and capital accumulation.

Integration, however, also has some disadvantages. First, it would reduce federal tax revenue. The revenue loss must be offset in some way, so a complete evaluation of the proposed reform should take this factor into account. Second, corporate net income would still have to be defined and measured by the tax authorities, even though it is not subject to a separate tax. Otherwise, the amount of retained earnings allocated among households to be taxed under the individual income tax would not be known. This means, however, that government would still have to specify depreciation allowances and the like.

One different sort of objection to integration holds that it permits corporations to avoid paying their fair share of the nation's tax burden. This objection is based on the notion that corporations have some independent taxpaying ability apart from the taxpaying ability of their workers, customers, or owners. Those favoring integration reject this view. They see the corporation income tax only as an indirect and inefficient means of taxing individual income—but with no attempt made to adjust the tax to the tax-paying capacity of the individuals who are ultimately being taxed.

Review Questions and Problems

1. The rate structure of the corporation income tax is progressive; yet when economists analyze the tax, they often assume that it is proportional. Why?

2. "If the corporate sector of the U.S. economy were really competitive, firms would be earning zero profits, and the corporation income tax would generate no revenue." True or false? Explain.

3. "To corporations, the corporation tax is a cost just like any other cost, and the price of the product must rise enough to cover it. Therefore, the tax is shifted forward to consumers." Evaluate this argument.

4. Explain Harberger's analysis of the incidence of the corporation income tax. In this analysis, does the price of goods produced by corporations rise? If so, why does the analysis not conclude that the tax is at least partially shifted forward to consumers?

5. Harberger's analysis assumes that the nation's capital stock is not affected by the tax. Is this assumption reasonable? If not, how would you expect the capital stock to be affected, and how would this change affect the analysis of the incidence of the tax?

6. If the corporate tax is borne in proportion to capital income, what does this fact tell us about the horizontal and vertical equity of the tax?

7. "The market adjustment to the corporate tax tends to produce equality in after-tax rates of return, implying that the before-tax rates of return diverge. Therefore, there is a misallocation of resources." Does this statement accurately describe how the tax produces a welfare cost in the way it affects the allocation of capital between the corporate and noncorporate sectors?

8. Explain how externality theory provides an economic rationale for the R&D tax credit.

9. How would you change the tax code to stimulate R&D spending, keeping in mind that you would like to minimize the revenue loss?

10. If the corporation and individual income taxes were integrated, who would benefit and who would be harmed? How would the welfare cost of the corporation tax be affected?

11. Compare the effects of complete elimination of the corporation income tax (accompanied by increases in personal income tax rates to keep total revenue constant) to the effects of integration of the corporation and individual income taxes.

Supplementary Readings

BALLENTINE, J. GREGORY. *Equity, Efficiency, and the U.S. Corporation Income Tax.* Washington, D.C.: American Enterprise Institute, 1980.

CONGRESSIONAL BUDGET OFFICE. *Revising the Corporate Income Tax.* Washington, D.C.: U.S. Government Printing Office, 1985.

FULLERTON, DON. "Which Effective Tax Rate?" *National Tax Journal,* 37:23–41 (Mar. 1984).

MCLURE, CHARLES E., JR., and WAYNE R. THIRSK. "A Simplified Exposition of the Harberger Model, I: Tax Incidence." *National Tax Journal,* 28(1):1–28 (Mar. 1975).

Other Major Taxes

*I*N THIS CHAPTER WE EXAMINE SEVERAL OTHER IMPORTANT taxes. We begin with a discussion of the second largest tax (in terms of revenue) in the United States, the social security payroll tax. Sales and excise taxes are then analyzed, with attention also given to a variant of these taxes, the value-added tax, that is frequently proposed as a source of additional revenue. Finally, we consider the property tax, the most important source of tax revenue for local governments.

Social Security Payroll Tax

In our earlier analysis of the social security system in Chapter 7, the expenditure part of the program was emphasized. Now we take a more careful look at the tax side of the social security system. As we shall see, however, it is frequently important to consider both the taxes and the benefits they finance simultaneously. Because the social security tax is an *earmarked tax* with revenues linked to specific expenditures, changes in the tax imply changes in the retirement program and vice versa, so a broad view incorporating both sides of the budget is often required.

The social security (OASDHI) payroll tax applies to the wage and salary income of employees and to the earnings of self-employed persons. For employees, the payroll tax is composed of two equal rate levies, one paid by the employee and the other by the employer. In 1992, each rate was 7.65 percent, for a combined tax rate of 15.3 percent of employees' earnings. This rate applies up to a ceiling amount, $55,500 in 1992. Beyond that amount, there is no further OASDI tax, but as a result of 1990 legislation, the HI

(Medicare) portion of the tax, which is a combined employer-employee rate of 2.9 percent, continues to apply up to a much higher ceiling, $130,200 in 1992. (These ceiling amounts are indexed to average wages and so automatically rise over time.)

To illustrate the determination of tax liability, consider a worker earning $20,000 in 1992. A total of $1,530 (7.65 percent of $20,000), the employee's share of the tax, will be withheld from the worker's paycheck, and the employer will pay an equal amount, for a total tax liability of $3,060 (or 15.3 percent of earnings). For a worker earning at the maximum level of taxable earnings for the OASDI portion of the tax, or $55,500, the combined employer-employee tax liability is $8,492, again 15.3 percent of earnings. For workers earning above $55,500, there is no further OASDI tax liability, but the 2.9 percent marginal rate of the HI portion of the tax continues to apply up to a ceiling of $130,200. For a worker earning $130,200, the total tax liability is $10,658—$8,492 on the first $55,500 in earnings plus 2.9 percent of $74,700 ($130,200 − $55,500), or an additional $2,166, due to the higher ceiling for the HI portion of the tax.

Table 13–1 contains a variety of information about the evolution of the social security tax over time. After the discussion of the growth of social security benefits in Chapter 7, it comes as no surprise that the tax that finances these benefits has also grown rapidly. In 1950, total revenue was $5.9 billion, or 11.8 percent of total federal tax revenues; in 1992, revenue from the social security tax was $488.9 billion, which amounted to more than 40 percent of total federal tax revenues. The tax liability incurred by workers earning at or above the maximum wage base increased more than twentyfold in real terms between 1950 and 1992. In terms of revenue, the social

Table 13–1   *Social Security Tax Data, Selected Years*

Year	Tax Rate	Maximum Wage Base*	Maximum Tax per Earner	Tax Revenue ($ billions)	Social Security Taxes as a Percentage of All Federal Taxes
1950	3.0%	$ 3,000	$ 90	$ 5.9	11.8%
1960	6.0	4,800	288	17.6	18.3
1970	9.6	7,800	749	52.9	27.0
1980	12.26	25,900	3,175	186.8	33.7
1985	14.1	39,600	5,584	309.9	39.4
1990	15.3	51,300	7,849	444.9	40.2
1992	15.3	55,500	8,492	488.9	42.3

*This is the ceiling on taxable earnings for the OASDI tax. The ceiling on the HI (Medicare) portion of the tax has been higher since 1990.

Sources: Department of Health and Human Services, *Social Security Bulletin* (Washington, D.C.: U.S. Government Printing Office, Dec. 1992); and *Economic Report of the President, 1993* (Washington, D.C.: U.S. Government Printing Office, 1993), Table B-79.

security tax is the second largest tax in the United States, following the federal individual income tax, and a majority of taxpayers now actually pay more in social security taxes than they do in income taxes.

Division of the Tax Between Employer and Employee

By splitting the social security payroll tax between the employer and the employee, Congress apparently intended to divide the burden of the tax between them. Whether or not this goal has actually been accomplished is far from clear. Most economists believe that the way the tax is divided into employer and employee portions has no effect on who actually bears its burden. The analysis supporting this view is just an extension of what was discussed in Chapter 10 in connection with an excise tax.

To examine the significance of the division of the tax into employer and employee portions, we compare the two extreme cases, one in which the entire tax is collected from employees and the second in which it is collected from employers. In Figure 13–1, before any tax is levied, the supply and demand curves for labor are shown as S and D, the wage rate is \$10 per hour, and employment is OL_1. Now suppose that a payroll tax is levied on *employers* that requires them to pay \$2 to the government for each hour of labor employed.

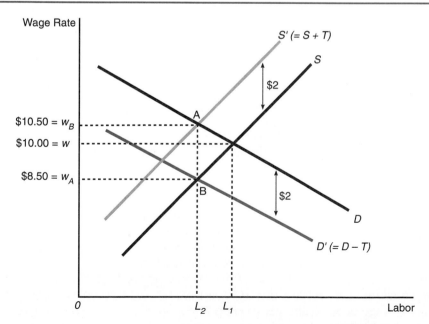

Figure 13–1 *Tax on employers versus tax on employees*

To understand how to incorporate the tax into the analysis, recall that the demand curve for labor shows the maximum amount per hour that the employers will pay for each alternative quantity of labor. For example, the demand curve in Figure 13–1 means that employers will pay a maximum of $10 per hour to hire OL_1 units of labor. With the tax in place, employers will still pay no more than $10 per hour for the quantity OL_1, but since $2 must be paid to the government, the amount that employers will be willing to pay workers for OL_1 units of labor will fall to $8 per hour. In the diagram, the effect of the tax is therefore shown as a vertical shift downward by $2 in the demand curve to D'. The downward shift in the demand curve means that with a $2-per-hour tax, employers will pay $2 less to workers at each level of employment. With the supply curve, S, the tax thus reduces employment to OL_2, and the wage rate paid to workers falls to w_A, or $8.50. To employers, the cost of labor *including the tax* is now $10.50 per hour.

Alternatively, if the $2-per-hour tax is collected from *employees* rather than employers, it will have the effect of shifting the supply curve vertically upward by $2, or to S', without affecting the demand curve. The shift in supply reflects the fact that workers must be paid $2 more per hour to yield the necessary after-tax wage to compensate them for supplying each alternative quantity of labor. For example, if workers must pay the $2-per-hour tax, they will continue to supply OL_1 only if they receive a $12 hourly wage. That is, OL_1 hours of labor will be provided only if workers receive a net (after-tax) payment of $10 per hour. When the tax is collected from workers, the intersection of S' and D determines the new equilibrium, involving employment of OL_2 and a wage rate of $10.50. Since workers must remit $2 to the government, their take-home pay is $8.50.

Note that the real effects of the tax are exactly the same whether the tax is collected from employers or employees. When collected from employers, employment is OL_2, firms pay a wage of $10.50 per hour, but $2 goes to the government, and workers receive the remaining $8.50. When employees pay the tax, employment is again OL_2, and firms pay $10.50 as before; although the workers receive $10.50, they keep only $8.50, since they must remit $2 to the government. In both cases, the $2-per-hour tax, the distance AB, reflects the difference between the gross-of-tax cost of labor to employers and the net-of-tax payment to workers.

The government therefore really has no control over who ultimately bears the cost of the tax by the way the tax is collected. The results are the same whether the employer or employee pays the tax. Although we have shown that the effects are identical for the extreme cases (when the employer *or* the employee pays the tax), it holds for the intermediate cases, too. For instance, if $1 of the tax were collected from employers and $1 from employees, firms would pay $9.50 to workers (plus $1 to the government for a total unit cost of labor of $10.50, as before), and workers would receive a gross wage of $9.50 and get to keep $8.50, since they would turn over $1 to the government.

Incidence

The real effects of the social security payroll tax are thus the same, regardless of how it is divided for collection purposes between employers and employees. This is not the same as saying that workers bear all the burden of the tax. Note that in our example, the $2-per-hour tax led to a $1.50 reduction in the net wage rate ($10.00 to $8.50), so in that case workers did not bear the full burden of the tax in the form of a lower wage rate.

Although the incidence of the social security tax does not depend on how it is divided between employers and employees, it does depend on the elasticities of labor supply and demand. Basically, the tax is a proportional tax on labor income, and as observed in Chapter 11, such a tax falls fully on workers when the labor supply curve is vertical. Since the social security tax applies to almost all industries and workers, it is likely that the relevant aggregate supply curve will be highly inelastic. Figure 13–2 illustrates this case. Since it makes no difference whether the tax is collected from employers or workers, we can analyze the tax by assuming that it shifts the demand curve downward. In addition, we can now treat the tax more realistically as levied at a certain rate on earnings rather than (as in Figure 13–1) as a fixed sum per hour of labor, so the demand curve pivots downward rather than shifting downward in a parallel fashion. With a vertical supply curve, the

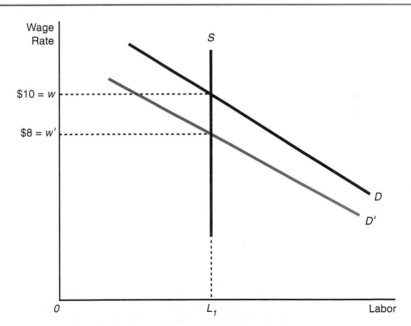

Figure 13–2 *Incidence of the social security tax*

wage rate received by workers falls by $2—the amount of the tax—to $8. When the supply curve is vertical, the net wage rate received by workers falls by the full amount of the tax, so workers bear the entire burden of the tax.

Note that the cost of labor to employers has not risen; it is still $10. Now, however, $2 goes to the government and $8 to workers, rather than $10 to workers. Since the costs associated with hiring labor have not risen, the prices of products are unaffected. Much popular discussion of payroll taxes, especially the employer portion, holds that higher employer payroll taxes add to labor costs and thus contribute to higher prices. This analysis, however, indicates that total labor costs do not rise: When taxes go up, wage rates go down. (Perhaps more plausibly in a dynamic setting, when employer payroll taxes go up, wage rates do not rise over time as much as they would have otherwise. The final result, however, is the same.)

One special feature of the social security tax differs from a proportional tax on labor income and may have some bearing on its effect on labor supply decisions. Under the social security tax, if a worker earns more and incurs an additional tax liability, the tax may not be viewed as a net loss. Because the worker's future social security pension will be larger the more taxes paid, there is an offsetting benefit associated with paying higher taxes. Thus, in Figure 13–2 workers may not believe that their net wage has fallen from $10 to $8 because they will receive a pension when they retire. If this is so, it becomes even more likely that the quantity of labor supplied remains unchanged in response to the tax. This point should not be pushed too far, however, because the link between taxes paid by a worker and the subsequent pension is not very strong.

In all, it seems reasonable to conclude that workers bear the full burden of both the employee and employer portions of the social security tax. This analysis has, however, ignored the expenditure side of the social security system. If saving falls in response to the provision of pensions, then the combined (balanced-budget) impact of the tax and expenditure will produce further effects. Because a reduced capital stock means less capital per worker and lower productivity per worker, the D curve in Figure 13–2 will shift downward (or rise less rapidly over time), reducing wage rates still further. The impact of the entire social security system on saving is usually ignored in an analysis of the tax, which is reasonable if the differential incidence approach is adopted. (Recall that with the differential approach we compare different taxes to finance the same expenditures, here pensions. Then the effect on the capital stock, and hence the position of D, will be the same under alternative taxes.)

If workers bear the full burden of the tax in the form of reduced take-home pay, what is the effect on the distribution of the tax burden among households? One frequently hears the assertion that the payroll tax is regressive. There are two characteristics of the tax that do tend to make it regressive. The first is the ceiling on taxable earnings. Individuals who earn more than the maximum wage base bear the same tax burden as those at the maximum wage base, and therefore the average tax rate will tend to be lower. Recall, however, that more than 90 percent of all workers earn below the OASDI ceiling on taxable earnings (more than 99 percent earn below the Medicare ceiling), which implies regressivity only at the very top of the income distribution. The second factor that contributes to regressivity is that the tax does not apply to capital income, which is a larger part of the total income for high-income households.

Table 13–2 presents the CBO estimates of the distribution of the tax burden for the social security payroll tax. In contrast to the previous argument and widely held views, these estimates show the tax to be progressive, at least up through the eighth decile. (The average tax rate does decline slightly at the ninth decile, and more so at the tenth, for the two reasons just discussed.) The reason is that the tax burden is compared with total income, not just earnings and capital income. It is the existence of government transfer payments, and their concentration in the lower-income classes, that make the social security payroll tax progressive. For example, consider a family with earnings of $5,000 and a government transfer of $5,000. The social security tax will fall at a rate of about 15 percent on earnings but not on the transfer, so the tax rate relative to total income would be 7.5 percent. Transfers become a smaller share of income as we move up the income

Table 13–2 **Social Security Tax Distribution, 1988**

Income Decile	Tax as a Percentage of Family Income	Share of Total Tax Paid
1	5.0%	0.5%
2	5.9	1.5
3	8.6	3.5
4	9.4	5.4
5	9.8	7.3
6	10.4	9.7
7	10.5	12.1
8	10.9	15.7
9	10.6	19.6
10	6.0	24.5
Top 5 percent	4.4	12.7
Top 1 percent	1.8	2.5
All deciles	8.7	100

Source: Congress, of the United States, CBO, *The Changing Distribution of Federal Taxes 1975–1990* (Washington, D.C.: U.S. Government Printing Office, October 1987), Tables 7 and B–1.

distribution, implying that the social security tax as a percentage of income will rise. Thus, the conventional wisdom regarding the incidence of the social security payroll tax is wrong, at least if we evaluate tax burdens relative to total income and not just market earnings. In fact, the tax is more progressive than indicated in Table 13–2 because the CBO measure of family income does not include income in-kind.

It remains true that the social security payroll tax overall is less progressive than the federal individual income tax, and it does become regressive at the very top of the income distribution. Whether it should be more or less progressive is obviously disputable. But it can be argued that the distribution of the social security tax burden should not be evaluated in the same way as other taxes. Because each person pays social security taxes when working and receives retirement benefits later, it may be preferable to take a lifetime perspective and consider the taxes paid and benefits received together. We took this approach in Chapter 7, where we saw that the benefit formula and other provisions favor relatively low-wage earners; that is, low-wage earners receive a higher rate of return than high-wage earners do. Those at the top of the income distribution may pay a very small part of their total income in social security taxes, but when retired, their retirement benefits are smaller relative to taxes paid than those with lower incomes. Thus, viewed from a lifetime perspective, the social security system as a whole is progressive.

Welfare Cost

Since the social security payroll tax is very similar to a proportional tax on labor income, we can analyze it in the same way. Like a proportional tax, the payroll tax produces a welfare cost by distorting labor supply decisions. Taxpayers will work less and be worse off than under an equal-yield lump-sum tax; the graphical analysis would be exactly the same as in Figure 11–2.

The analogy to the welfare cost of a proportional tax must be qualified in two respects, however. First, there is a zero welfare cost as a result of labor supply distortions for workers who earn more than the maximum wage base. The *marginal* rate of the social security tax was zero for workers earning above $130,200 in 1992 (and only 2.9 percent for those earning between $55,500 and $130,200) and it is the marginal tax rate that distorts labor supply decisions. Consider, for example, workers earning $150,000. Their social security tax liability will not be changed even if they earn $1,000 less, so the tax does not give them an incentive to modify their labor supply decisions at the relevant margin. (As an exercise, modify Figure 11–2 to show that the social security tax does not produce a welfare cost for workers earning above the ceiling on taxable earnings.) Although fewer than 10 percent of all workers earn more than the $55,500 wage base, their total earnings are probably about 25 percent of national labor earnings, so the reduced labor supply distortions for this group are far from insignificant.

A second qualification pertains to workers earning below the maximum wage base. To the extent that paying an additional dollar in social security taxes is accompanied by an increase in the pension received in retirement, the distorting effect of the tax is reduced. This effect occurs because workers may not view their net wage as reduced by the full amount of the tax; there is an offsetting future benefit.[1] For this factor to be relevant, however, there must be a consistent relationship between individual taxes paid and future benefits, and workers must recognize the relationship. (But as we have seen, this link is fairly weak.)

Issues in Social Security Tax Reform

As we explained in Chapter 7, in recent years social security tax revenues have exceeded outlays, with the surplus adding to the trust funds. Despite the cushioning effect of the trust funds, as we saw, the system will face severe financing problems early in the next century. Thus, either taxes must be increased or benefits reduced, or both. So let us consider what tax changes could be made to raise additional revenues. In other words, we shall assume that a decision has been made to increase tax revenues flowing into the social security system and compare alternative ways to raise extra revenue.

Using General Tax Revenue

Except for a portion of Medicare, social security benefits are financed exclusively by the social security payroll tax. One common proposal to generate more revenue without raising payroll taxes is to use general federal revenues to supplement the payroll tax. This suggestion is sometimes proposed as if "general revenues" were a free source of funds, which, of course, they are not. Basically, what this approach advocates is the use of the federal income tax instead of payroll taxes to fund the shortfalls in the social security system. Proponents of the use of general revenues emphasize that the income tax is more progressive than the payroll tax, so using general revenues would place a larger share of any additional tax burden on high-income families, who are better able to afford it.

In evaluating this option, as well as others, it is important to look beyond the short-run effect of permitting existing benefit obligations to be financed without increasing payroll taxes. What happens to the future benefits? If benefits go up only for individuals who pay the additional taxes (as "individual equity" requires), that is, mainly for high-income families, then using general revenues would not in the long run increase taxes or benefits for low-income families. This result is not, however, what most proponents of this

---

[1]Note how this result differs from that created by the federal income tax. Under the income tax, if a worker earns more and thereby pays $100 more in taxes, this additional payment is completely a net loss to the worker because it brings with it no additional government benefits. Under the social security payroll tax, paying $100 more in taxes may result in a larger pension in retirement.

approach have in mind. Instead, with this reform, they intend benefits to still be related to taxable earnings under the social security payroll tax, but additional taxes paid under the income tax would not count toward future social security benefits. Consequently, benefits financed by general revenues would apply across the board, regardless of each individual's contribution to general revenues. And because the benefit formula is tilted in favor of workers with low earnings records, most of the benefits financed by general revenues would go to individuals with low earnings, whereas most of the taxes would be paid by workers with high incomes. In short, the proposal to use general revenues is essentially a method to make the system more redistributive.

Raising the Ceiling on Taxable Earnings

Another method of increasing revenues is to continue to rely on the payroll tax as the sole source of revenue but to increase the maximum wage base without increasing the tax rate. For example, the ceiling might be increased from $55,500 to $70,000. (Recall that the ceiling amount is indexed to average wages in the economy and so automatically grows over time. What we are considering here is an increase beyond this automatic increase.) Because the tax rate remains the same, the tax on persons earning below $55,500 would not increase; all of the additional tax burden would be placed on workers earnings over $55,500, with the largest increases falling on those earning $70,000 and above.

This proposal raises the basic issue of why there should be a ceiling on taxable earnings in the first place. After all, the ceiling is what contributes to the regressivity of the tax at high income levels. But once again, we must consider what this change would mean for future benefits. In 1992 a person earning $100,000 paid social security (OASDI) taxes only on the first $55,500, and the retirement benefit is related to the $55,500 in taxable earnings. Thus, the future retirement benefit is only a small fraction of this person's preretirement earnings, and this situation provides a strong incentive to save privately. If the ceiling is raised or eliminated, retirement benefits to high-income persons must be increased sharply (insofar as individual equity is preserved), reducing the incentive to save privately.

The ceiling on taxable earnings serves the function of maintaining incentive for high earners to save privately. Since those with relatively high incomes provide a large share of national saving, removing the ceiling could have a disproportionate effect on saving and capital accumulation. In addition, the ceiling serves to avoid a distortion in the labor supply decisions of workers earning above that level.

As a practical matter, the maximum wage base is already so high that its removal would not provide much additional revenue. Total earnings in excess of the ceiling are now only about 6 percent as large as earnings already subject to tax. Thus complete elimination of the ceiling would increase social security revenues by only 6 percent.

Increasing the Tax Rate

A final option is to increase the tax rate but to leave the ceiling unchanged. If the tax rate is increased, an additional tax burden would be placed on all wage earners. As a percentage of total income, the increase in taxes would be lower at low income levels because of the importance of transfers. In this case, higher retirement benefits could be provided to low-income retirees without violating individual equity because they would bear some of the additional tax burden while they are employed. Even in this case, some further redistribution in favor of low earners would occur because of the nature of the benefit formula. It would, however, be less for an increase in the tax rate than for either of the other two options because workers with low earnings would pay a larger share of the tax increase.

The ceiling on taxable earnings for Medicare is a special case. As mentioned earlier, that ceiling was increased sharply in 1990, and in 1992 it stood at $130,200—with more than 99 percent of workers earning less than the ceiling. But the increase in the Medicare ceiling did not imply increased future Medicare benefits for high-wage taxpayers. In contrast to cash retirement benefits, Medicare benefits are not related to previous taxable earnings or taxes paid. Thus, in increasing the ceiling for Medicare taxes, Congress collected more in taxes from high earners without having to give these workers any greater benefits after they retire.

Taxes on Output

Sales and Excise Taxes

Taxes on output are used by all levels of government, although the relative importance of the various taxes differs, as shown in Table 13–3. The federal government does not use a general sales tax, but it does impose excise taxes on gasoline, tobacco, alcohol, public utilities, and imports (custom duties). In 1990, these federal taxes generated $54 billion, or 6.9 percent of total federal revenue. State governments rely more on general sales taxes, but they also subject the same goods to excise taxes as does the federal government, with the exception of imports. More than a third of state government revenues is generated by sales and excise taxes. Local governments also use these taxes but to a lesser extent; only 9.6 percent of local revenues come from sales and excise taxes. For all levels of government combined, sales and excise taxes produced about $232 billion in revenue in 1990, or 15.5 percent of their total tax revenue.

We have already described the theoretical analysis of sales and excise taxes in our introduction to tax analysis in Chapter 10, and there is no need to repeat that analysis in detail. Here we will emphasize how the theoretical results translate into estimated tax burdens for different income classes. It is

Table 13–3   *Output Tax Revenues by Source and Level of Government, 1990 (in $ millions)*

Source	Total	Federal	State	Local
General sales tax	$121,287		$99,702	$21,588
Motor fuel	33,120	$13,077	19,379	664
Alcoholic beverages	9,223	5,753	3,191	279
Tobacco	10,002	4,268	5,541	193
Public utilities	17,892	6,476	6,514	4,903
Custom duties	16,810	16,810		
Other	23,521	7,586	12,743	3,192
Percentage of own-source revenue from sales taxes	15.5%	6.9%	37.6%	9.6%

Source: U.S. Department of Commerce, Bureau of the Census, *Governmental Finances in 1989–90,* (Washington, D.C.: U.S. Government Printing Office, 1991), Table 6, p. 7.

widely believed that sales and excise taxes impose burdens on consumers and tend to be regressive since low-income families spend a larger portion of their incomes than high-income families. This conventional view turns out to be based on some controversial aspects of tax incidence analysis that we have not yet discussed.

Let us consider a general sales tax that applies to all goods and services. As we saw in Chapter 10, the economy could respond to this tax in two different ways. In one case, if the overall level of absolute (nominal) prices is unaffected by the imposition of the tax, then firms, after paying the tax, will have lower revenues remaining with which to compensate factors of production. Wage rates and other factor prices will therefore decline. (This was the conclusion of our analysis of Figure 10–4.) A second possibility is that product prices will rise by the amount of the tax per unit and that wage rates and other factor prices will remain unchanged. Since we do not have a theory that accurately predicts what determines the absolute level of prices, this possibility cannot be ruled out.

Does it make a great deal of difference which of these alternatives is correct—whether product prices increase and factor prices remain unchanged or whether product prices remain unchanged and factor prices fall? Actually, under certain conditions, the incidence of the tax is the same, regardless of which alternative is correct. The conditions are basically two: (1) Families receive their entire incomes in the form of market earnings, that is, payments for providing factors of production; and (2) families spend the same proportion of their incomes on the taxed goods. Under these conditions, families will bear the same tax burdens, regardless of what happens to the absolute price level. For example, if product prices rise and factor prices are unchanged, the purchasing power of market earnings will be reduced, and families will bear a tax burden in proportion to their market earnings. Moreover, since consumption is the same percentage of market earnings for all families, we could also think of the tax burden as being in proportion to consumption. Alternatively, if product prices are constant and factor prices fall, the purchasing power of market earnings is again reduced, and families will again bear a burden in proportion to their market earnings or consumption.

Thus, when these two conditions hold, it makes no difference whether, or indeed by how much, the absolute prices of goods rise since the real effects of the tax will be the same. To identify the distribution of tax burdens among families, we could allocate the tax in proportion to either consumption or market earnings; both would yield the same result. And in both cases, the sales tax would be proportional to total income.

Problems arise when these two conditions are not met. Let us first consider the significance of the fact that people do receive income in forms other than market earnings. For many families, government transfers are an important source of income, and for many low-income families they are the sole or predominant type of income they receive. For a recipient of a government transfer, it may well make a difference whether or not a sales tax increases prices. If the transfer payment is unchanged and the price level rises, the recipient will bear a burden under the sales tax; if the price level does not rise, there will be no burden on this transfer recipient since the purchasing power of the transfer is unchanged. The view that sales taxes burden consumers, regardless of whether their consumption is financed by market earnings or transfers, must be based on the assumption that sales taxes cause the price level to rise. If the price level does not rise, the consumer whose income is wholly in the form of a government transfer will bear no burden.

It is possible to argue, however, that consumption financed by government transfers bears no burden under sales taxes, regardless of what happens to the price level. If the price level does not change, then clearly transfer-financed consumption will not be affected. Now consider the second alternative, that the price level rises. If the price level increases but the purchasing power of the transfer is maintained by government policy, then once again there will be no tax burden. For example, if the price level rises by 10 percent and a person's transfer also rises by 10 percent, then the transfer recipient will bear no tax burden. This outcome does not necessarily require continued adjustments in government transfer policy. In fact, about three fourths of all government transfers are indexed to the price level, so that the size of the transfer automatically varies with changes in the price level.

In view of this situation, it seems plausible to assume that the real value of transfers is constant when we analyze taxes. This assumption has great significance for the incidence of any tax that is thought to affect consumers through changes in product prices. In the case of sales and excise taxes, it implies that the tax burden falls on market earnings, or on consumption financed by market earnings but not on consumption financed by government transfers. If we continue to assume that consumption is the same percentage of total income for all income classes, the implication is that sales and excise taxes will be progressive. For example, if the tax burden is 10 percent of market earnings and market earnings are only 40 percent of the total income for the lowest income class, the tax as a percentage of income will be 4 percent. Since higher-income classes receive a larger proportion of their incomes as market earnings (a smaller proportion in the form of transfers), the tax rate as a percentage of total income will be higher for them.

Now let us turn to the second condition we specified earlier: that families consume the same proportion of their incomes. In fact, low-income families do consume a larger proportion of their incomes than do high-income families. It is this characteristic that leads many people to believe that sales and excise taxes are regressive. This conclusion may seem obvious, but there are some nagging problems here, too. For example, it now apparently makes a difference whether or not the sales tax causes absolute product prices to rise. If product prices do not rise, the tax burden falls in proportion to market earnings, regardless of what portion of those earnings are consumed. Thus, to argue that the sales tax is regressive due to this factor, it is necessary to assume that the tax causes the absolute price level to rise—which many people unquestioningly accept but which is far from obvious.

Let us tentatively accept the view that absolute prices are increased by sales and excise taxes and consider the way consumption does vary by income class. The second column of Table 13–4 gives estimates of the ratio of consumer expenditures to before-tax total incomes for each quintile in 1984. What is most striking about these figures is that the lowest quintile consumes more than three times its before-tax income. The share of income consumed by the lowest quintile is more than four and half times as large as for the highest quintile, where the share is 69 percent. Note carefully what these figures imply: that any tax allocated in proportion to consumption expenditures will result in an average tax rate for the lowest quintile that is about four and a half times larger (3.17/0.69 times larger, to be exact) for the lowest quintile than for the highest quintile. (The disparity is even greater if we consider income deciles rather than quintiles.) The result would be a highly regressive tax burden distribution.

Most people are surprised by how large the differences are in the proportion of income consumed by income classes, and especially by the fact that the lowest income class consumes more than three times its income. How is it possible for families to consume so much more than their incomes? Indeed, it is impossible for families to consume more than their incomes over prolonged periods of time if income and consumption are properly measured. (There is some suspicion that income is significantly underreported in the lowest income class, leading to an overestimate of the proportion of income consumed.) It is, however, possible for families to

Table 13–4   *Federal Excise Tax Burden by Income Class, 1988*

Income Decile	Percent of Before-Tax Income Consumed (by quintiles, 1984)	Taxes as a Percentage of Family Income When Allocated in Proportion to:	
		Annual Consumption	Market Earnings
1 }	317%	4.5%	0.3%
2 }		2.1	0.4
3 }	130	1.6	0.6
4 }		1.4	0.7
5 }	98	1.1	0.8
6 }		1.0	0.8
7 }	84	0.9	0.8
8 }		0.8	0.9
9 }	69	0.8	0.9
10 }		0.4	0.9

Source: Second column: data U.S. Department of Labor, Bureau of Labor Statistics, *Consumer Expenditure Survey Results from 1984,* (Washington, D.C.: U.S. Government Printing Office, 1986); third column: data from Congress of the United States, CBO, *The Changing Distribution of Federal Taxes 1975–1990,* (Washington, D.C.: U.S. Government Printing Office, October 1987), Table 7; fourth column: calculated by the author.

consume more than their incomes temporarily, and that fact at least partially explains the high ratio at the bottom. Retired persons, for example, may be drawing down their accumulated assets to finance consumption; others may be borrowing to consume above their current incomes. In both cases, of course, such consumption behavior is only temporary, which casts doubt on its relevance for tax incidence analysis.

Generally, people who consume more than their incomes in one particular year do so because their normal, or lifetime average, income is above their annual income in that year. That is why they can afford to consume more in that year. This pattern suggests that those who consume substantially more than their annual incomes really should be thought of as having higher incomes. Many economists believe that tax burdens should be related to longer-run measures of economic status, such as lifetime incomes. This issue also arises with respect to other taxes, but it is most important for sales and excise taxes, where the difference between annual and longer-run, or lifetime, perspectives is enormous. Over a person's lifetime, consumption cannot exceed income if both are properly measured. Indeed, evidence suggests that relative to lifetime income, there is very little difference in the percentage of income consumed among income classes. Thus, in a lifetime tax incidence analysis, any tax allocated in proportion to consumption would be roughly proportional (ignoring the issue of transfers previously discussed). Economists are increasingly questioning the relevance of tax

burden estimates based on annual consumption and income, thinking that
they give a misleading picture of the true effects of the tax.[2]

The quantitative importance of these points is indicated by the estimates
in the last two columns of Table 13–4. The next to last column gives the CBO
estimates of federal excise taxes as a percentage of family income when
these taxes are allocated in proportion to annual consumption. Note that
these figures exhibit a pronounced regressive pattern, exactly as would be
expected from the consumption data in the second column. For many years,
estimates like these have been the basis for the conventional view that sales
and excise taxes are regressive. However, it is now clear that this conclusion
is the result of three assumptions, each of which can be challenged. First,
this approach assumes that sales and excise taxes cause the absolute price
level to rise exactly in proportion to the taxes. Second, it assumes that government transfers fall in real value when the price level rises (unindexed
transfers). Third, it assumes that the annual consumption data provide meaningful indications of how taxes affect people at different income levels.

An alternative approach to the incidence of sales and excise taxes that
reaches a far different conclusion is shown by the estimates in the last column of Table 13–4. Here the taxes are allocated in proportion to the market
earnings of families in each income class. Using the second approach, sales
and excise taxes are found to be progressive because market earnings are a
smaller share of total income for low-income families, who receive proportionally larger transfers. The decline in the importance of transfers as we
move up the income distribution makes the tax burden progressive relative
to total income. This alternative approach reflects two assumptions. First, it
is assumed that real transfers are constant, that is, that transfers will be effectively indexed if prices rise. Second, it is assumed that approximately the
same percentage of income is consumed at each income level, as would be
the case if we measured incomes over a longer period of time than a single
year. *Under these assumptions, sales and excise taxes fall in proportion to
market earnings and will therefore be progressive relative to total incomes.*

Economists do not agree on which of these approaches is more accurate.
The importance of the topic, however, extends beyond the question of the
incidence of sales and excise taxes. Exactly the same issues arise in analyzing
any type of tax that is felt to be partially or wholly shifted to consumers
through higher product prices. If, as some economists believe, corporation
income and property taxes are partially shifted in this way, their incidence
will also depend on resolving the problems discussed here. So too does the
incidence of a value-added tax, which is considered next.

[2]See, for example, James M. Poterba, "Lifetime Incidence and the Distributional Burden of Excise Taxes," *American Economic Review,* 79:325 (May 1989); and Poterba, "Is
the Gasoline Tax Regressive?" in David Bradford, ed., *Tax Policy and the Economy,* Vol.
5 (National Bureau of Economic Research: The MIT Press, 1991), pp. 145–164.

The Value-added Tax

A value-added tax (VAT) is basically a multistage sales tax that is collected from firms at each stage in the production and distribution process. The VAT is an important revenue source in many European countries but not, at the present time, in the United States. Over the past several years, however, the VAT has received much attention as a possible addition to the federal government's tax arsenal. Some of the support for a VAT comes from people who want a new tax to help reduce federal budget deficits, whereas others would like to see the tax replace the corporation income tax or part of the social security payroll tax.

The base on which a VAT is levied is the value added by each firm, that is, the firm's sales less its purchases of material inputs from other firms. Table 13–5 illustrates how a VAT would operate. Suppose that firm A employs only workers as inputs and manufactures a product that is sold to firm B for $500. Firm A's value added is then $500, its sales less its (zero) purchases from other firms. Firm B distributes the product to retail establishments, selling it for $800. Firm B's value added is its sales of $800 less the payment of $500 to firm A, or $300. Firm C sells the product to consumers for $1,000, and since it purchased the product for $800, its value added is $200. Under a VAT, each firm would be taxed on its value added, as shown by the last row in the table. Note that the total tax base, the sum of the value added by each firm, is $1,000 and that this is exactly the retail value of the final product. *The tax base of a VAT is the same as that of a retail sales tax.* If firms are permitted to deduct purchases of capital goods, the tax base essentially becomes total consumption in the economy. (Different treatments of investment goods can transform the VAT into a tax on consumption and saving, but all proposals have specified the consumption type of VAT, on which we focus here.)

A general sales tax on consumption goods and a VAT both have the same tax base and are therefore equivalent in most important respects. Our previous analysis of general sales taxes applies equally to the VAT. What is novel about recent discussions of the VAT in the United States is the proposal that

Table 13–5   *The Value-added Tax Base*

	Firm A (Manufacturer)	Firm B (Wholesaler)	Firm C (Retailer)	Total
	Stage of Production			
Sales	$500	$800	$1,000	$2,300
Purchases	0	500	800	1,300
Value added	500	300	200	1,000

the federal government adopt this form of tax. Forty-five state governments already use general sales taxes, but the federal government does not.

Proponents of a federal VAT cite four main advantages for this tax compared with alternative ways the federal government might raise revenue with its existing taxes. First, the VAT is a broad-based tax utilizing a uniform rate. Since all goods and services would be taxed at the same rate, the tax would not favor the production of some goods over others. In other words, a VAT avoids the sort of welfare cost produced by a selective excise tax on one product. Moreover, as a broad-based tax, it can raise a large amount of revenue using relatively low rates. For example, consumption expenditures in 1992 were over $4,000 billion, so a 5 percent VAT could raise as much as $200 billion.

A second advantage lies in the administration of a VAT. It would be very difficult for firms to avoid paying a VAT since the records of transactions among firms leave a clear trail for auditors. With increasing concern about cheating on income taxes and the belief that substantial amounts of income in the "underground economy" escape taxation, a tax that is relatively easy to administer and collect looks attractive. Third, supporters note that the VAT falls on consumption and not on saving. Because of the desire to encourage investment and saving, a tax that does not penalize saving compares favorably with alternatives like the individual and corporate income taxes.

A final advantage is that the public generally views sales taxes favorably. In recent years, opinion surveys have found that retail sales taxes are a significantly more popular form of taxation than the federal individual income tax is. Even low-income persons, who bear larger burdens under sales taxes than under the federal individual income tax, favor sales taxes by a margin of 1.75 to 1.[3] Whether these findings imply that the public does not understand how the income tax operates (believing, for example, that the wealthy avoid paying income taxes) is not clear. Whatever their source, these attitudes may make adding a VAT more politically feasible than raising some other tax, regardless of the objective merits of the alternatives.

The most commonly stated objection to a VAT is that it would be regressive. Our earlier analysis of the incidence of sales and excise taxes is relevant to this conclusion, since a VAT would have the same pattern of incidence. For reasons explained earlier, it is not at all certain that a VAT would be regressive; it almost certainly would not be regressive when viewed relative to lifetime income. Still, it remains true that a VAT would be less progressive than the federal individual income tax is, so it may suffer by comparison.

The perception that a VAT would be regressive, however, has often led its supporters to favor modifying its structure to make it less so. For instance, instead of applying a VAT to all goods and services, food, housing, and medical care could be exempted from the tax base. Indeed, many European

---

[3]Advisory Commission on Intergovernmental Relations, *Changing Public Attitudes on Governments and Taxes* (Washington, D.C.: ACIR, 1982).

countries go further and tax some goods ("luxuries") at higher rates than other goods. But the evidence suggests that trying to fine-tune the VAT tax base in this way would not significantly increase its progressivity (reduce its regressivity).[4] Using different tax rates or exempting certain goods and services would, however, complicate the tax and increase its distorting effects through the nonuniform treatment of different goods. This result leads to a second disadvantage of the tax: It is susceptible to becoming riddled with special tax preferences, just as the income tax has, which lessens its attractiveness from an efficiency standpoint.

A third disadvantage may simply be the mirror image of the popularity of retail sales taxes. It is argued that because a VAT would be concealed in the prices of goods and services, people would bear more of a burden than they would realize. This is basically a public choice argument made by those who are concerned that taxpayers will agree to more government spending than they really want because they are unaware of how large the costs will be. Since tax rates of more than half a dozen European VATs have risen to 18 percent or more, this concern may be real.

Property Taxation

Property taxation, as it is used in the United States, is used primarily by local governments. Property taxes are levied by almost all local governments and are their major source of revenue. In 1991, property taxes produced more than $167 billion in revenue for local governments, totaling more than 75 percent of all local tax revenue. Because the nature of the tax is determined independently by local governments, there is wide variation in property tax rates and in the definition of taxable property.

In general, the property tax is levied on the assessed value of real property, including land, homes, buildings, and equipment owned by businesses and sometimes consumer durables such as automobiles. Although most people encounter the tax in their role as homeowners, half of the total revenue raised by property taxes accrues from the taxation of business property.

There have long been two conflicting views about who bears the burden of property taxation. One view holds that the tax is eventually reflected in the higher prices of goods produced using taxed property and so would be much like a general sales tax. The other view is that the tax is borne by owners of property, which would make the tax more progressive. These two views have been reconciled and partially incorporated into a third approach in recent years.[5] The "new view" is best explained by first analyzing a

[4]Congress of the United States, CBO, *Effects of Adopting a Value-Added Tax* (Washington, D.C.: U.S. Government Printing Office, 1992), Chapter 4.

[5]Peter M. Mieszkowski, "The Property Tax: An Excise or a Profits Tax?" *Journal of Public Economics,* 1:73 (Apr. 1972).

uniform national property tax and then considering what difference it makes when many local property taxes are levied at different rates.

National Property Tax

Property is simply another name for what economists usually refer to as capital. Property, or capital, is a durable asset that produces a flow of services (income) over a period of time. It is important to understand that taxing the value of property has the same effect as taxing the income generated by that property. Consider a piece of property with a market value of $10,000 that yields an income of $800 per year, a rate of return of 8 percent. A property tax of 2 percent on the market value would yield $200 in tax revenue per year. Similarly, a tax on the property (capital) income of 25 percent would also yield $200 per year. These two taxes have identical economic effects: A 2 percent tax on the market value of an asset that yields 8 percent takes one fourth of the return to the asset, just as does a tax of 25 percent on the income from the asset. Thus, the taxation of property and the taxation of capital incomes (as under the corporation income tax) can be analyzed in the same way.

Let us consider a national property tax levied at a rate of 2 percent on the market value of all capital. Before the tax, the rate of return to capital is 8 percent, so the property tax is equivalent to a 25 percent tax on the income from capital. To prepare for the analysis of different property taxes in different localities, we divide the nation into two geographic localities and call them X and Y. Because the property tax applies at the same rate in both localities, there is no incentive for capital owners to shift capital from one locality to another. If capital is in perfectly inelastic supply, its before-tax return will not change, and capital owners will bear the entire burden in the form of a lower after-tax return.

Figure 13–3, similar to Figure 12–1 used for the corporation income tax, illustrates this analysis. Now, however, capital (property) employed in geographic locality X is measured to the right from 0_X, and capital employed in locality Y to the left from 0_Y, so 0_X0_Y is the total stock of capital. D_Y and D_X show the productivities of capital in the two localities. Before the tax is imposed, 0_XK_1 is employed in X and 0_YK_1 in Y, with the rate of return equal to 8 percent in both localities. A national property tax of 2 percent is equivalent to a 25 percent tax on the return to capital in both localities, making the net return to capital 25 percent below its gross return. D'_X and D'_Y show the after-tax returns available for alternative allocations of capital. Equilibrium still occurs at K_1 because the after-tax returns are equal at 6 percent in both localities.

This analysis implies that the owners of capital bear the full burden of a national property tax; property owners receive an unchanged gross return on their capital but must pay a tax of 25 percent to the government. The prices of goods and services produced using the input, capital, are not affected. Renters pay no higher rents for apartments, whereas the owners of apartments receive the same gross return, and a lower net return, on their

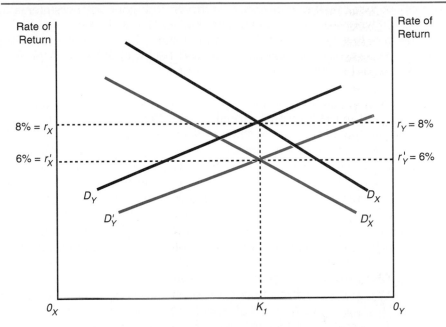

Figure 13–3   *Incidence of a national property tax*

investment. Homeowners pay the same prices for homes and receive the same gross return (partly in the form of housing services directly consumed) but a lower net return because of the tax payment. (Note also that property owners have no incentive to invest less in housing and more in stocks because the net return on stocks is also lowered to 6 percent.) Only owners of capital bear a burden. The incidence will be progressive because capital income is a larger proportion of total income in higher income classes.

System of Local Property Taxes

The United States does not have a national property tax but, instead, a multitude of local property taxes. If all localities taxed property at the same effective rate, the preceding analysis would still be correct. However, localities employ a wide variety of effective rates, ranging from about 1 to 5 percent, with an average around 2 percent. The analysis must therefore be modified to incorporate the diversity of effective rates, but the earlier framework can be easily adapted to accomplish this change.

Suppose that locality X levies a 1 percent tax on property holders and locality Y utilizes a 3 percent tax, or an average for the two localities of 2 percent. These taxes correspond to levies on capital income of 12.5 and 37.5 percent. The effect of these two taxes on the allocation of capital between the localities is easily worked out. In the short run, before the capital can move, the after-tax return to capital in Y will be reduced by more than in X.

The net return available to investors is therefore higher on investments in the locality with lower taxes. In the long run, capital will move from Y to X until the net returns are equalized. In equilibrium, the net returns to capital will be the same in both localities and will be lower than the 8 percent return achieved before the taxes were levied.

Figure 13–4 illustrates this analysis. The heavier tax in Y shifts D_Y down proportionately more than the lighter tax in X affects D_X. The short-run effect would be for the net return in Y to fall to aK_1, but to fall only to bK_1 in X. Thus, capital owners can achieve a higher after-tax return in X and will move capital there. Equilibrium occurs at K_2, where K_1K_2 units of capital have moved from Y to X to produce the same net return of 6 percent in both localities. Equal after-tax returns at 6 percent mean that the before-tax returns diverge: In Y the before-tax return is 9.6 percent, whereas in X it is 6.9 percent.

In terms of their effect on capital income realized by capital owners, these two property taxes at rates of 1 and 3 percent have the same effect as does a national property tax at a rate of 2 percent. In both cases, the net return to all owners falls from 8 to 6 percent. In this sense, a system of hundreds of local property taxes of different rates has an effect on capital income akin to that of a national property tax levied at the average rate of all localities taken together. On the basis of this analysis, many economists now believe that

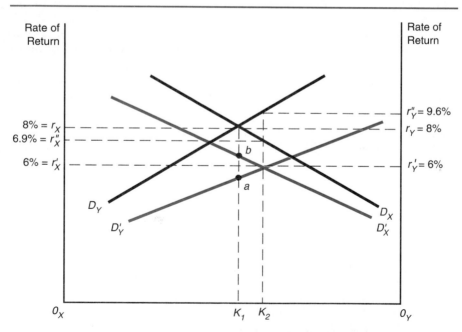

Figure 13–4   Incidence of local property taxes

owners of capital bear the burden of the *combined* effect of many different local property taxes.

There are, however, still other effects to consider. With a national property tax, there are no effects on the prices of goods and services. When local governments use property taxes at different rates, some prices are affected. In locality *Y*, with the higher than average tax rate, the gross return necessary to attract capital has risen from 8 to 9.6 percent. This higher cost will be reflected in higher prices for goods and services produced with capital employed in that locality. Consumers and renters in locality *Y* will therefore bear some burden. The opposite occurs in locality *X*. The gross return has fallen from 8 to 6.9 percent, so lower net prices result in that locality.

With higher prices in localities with above-average tax rates and lower prices in localities with below-average tax rates, the overall price level for the entire nation is not affected. If the aggregate effect on consumers in all areas is considered, there is no net burden; some lose but others gain. Owners of capital bear the full burden of the property taxes taken all together.

This approach reconciles the apparent differences between the view that capital owners bear the burden and the view that output prices are affected. Prices are affected, but in some areas they go up and in other areas they go down. This means that our view of the effects of property taxation depends on whether we are looking at the overall effects for the nation as a whole or at the effects within a specific locality. What is the incidence of the system of property taxes as a whole? The answer is that capital owners bear the burden. Because positive and negative price effects cancel out, consumers, on the average, are not burdened by property taxes. If, by contrast, we consider the effects within a single locality, and if I am a local government official and ask who *in this locality* will be burdened if we raise property taxes here, the answer is that local consumers (who pay higher prices) will bear a large share of the burden. Although prices to consumers in other areas will go down slightly, that result is not relevant when the effects within one locality are being examined rather than those nationwide.

The welfare costs of the system of property taxes are of two types. First, the capital stock is misallocated, with too little capital in high-tax areas and too much in low-tax areas. Second, by driving down the net return on capital, saving may fall and produce too small a total capital stock.

Our brief treatment of property taxes has stressed the broad and general consequences of this tax on investment. A fuller treatment would incorporate more carefully the fact that land is a form of capital that cannot move from one region to another and the distinction between goods produced and consumed in a locality versus those produced in one locality and sold elsewhere.[6] In addition, the way property taxes are administered by local government is a source of concern to many people. Because property (e.g.,

---

[6]For a fuller discussion of these and many other issues related to property taxation, see Henry J. Aaron, *Who Pays the Property Tax?* (Washington, D.C.: The Brookings Institution, 1975).

homes or factories) is not frequently sold and therefore does not have an accurately revealed market value, administrators must rely on assessments to estimate the value of property. A frequent criticism of the tax is that some types of property are assessed at higher ratios of their true market value than others. In fact, some localities apparently intentionally assess business property at higher rates than they do homes, implying that the effective tax rate varies between the different types of properties. This type of treatment, whether intentional or not, raises further questions about equity and efficiency.

Review Questions and Problems

1. "The employer's portion of the social security payroll tax is a cost of hiring labor, and like any other labor cost, it will ultimately be reflected in the price of the product. Thus, increasing the tax will increase prices, and consumers will bear the burden." Discuss.

2. Use a graphical analysis (like Figure 11–2) to determine how the social security payroll tax would affect the labor supply decision of a worker earning above the tax's maximum wage base.

3. Does the social security payroll tax produce a welfare cost? In your answer, be sure to distinguish between how the tax affects workers earning below and above the maximum wage base.

4. Is the social security payroll tax a regressive, proportional, or progressive tax? Does your answer depend on whether each family's tax burden is compared to its earnings or to its total income? Which is the appropriate comparison?

5. It is widely held that sales and excise taxes are regressive. What is the basis for this claim? Do you think it is correct?

6. A general sales tax can either increase the absolute price level or reduce factor prices. Does the incidence of the tax depend on which outcome occurs?

7. What type of welfare cost does a VAT have?

8. One common argument against adopting a VAT is that it would be regressive. Evaluate this argument.

9. In what way is the local property tax similar to the corporation income tax?

10. Some argue that consumers bear the burden of local property taxes since the prices of goods produced using taxed property will rise. Others contend that the entire burden falls on capital owners. Reconcile these differing views.

11. What types of welfare costs are produced by a system of local property taxes?

Supplementary Readings

AARON, HENRY J. *Who Pays the Property Tax?* Washington, D.C.: The Brookings Institution, 1975.

CONGRESS OF THE UNITED STATES, CONGRESSIONAL BUDGET OFFICE. *Effects of Adopting a Value-Added Tax.* Washington, D.C.: U.S. Government Printing Office, 1992.

MIESZKOWSKI, PETER, and GEORGE R. ZODROW. "Taxation and the Tiebout Model." *Journal of Economic Literature,* 27:1098–1146 (Sept. 1989).

POTERBA, JAMES M. "Lifetime Incidence and the Distributional Burden of Excise Taxes." *American Economic Review,* 79:325–330 (May 1989).

ROBERTSON, A. HAEWORTH. *Social Security: What Every Taxpayer Should Know.* Washington, D.C.: Retirement Policy Institute, 1992.

WEAVER, CAROLYN L., ed. *Social Security's Looming Surpluses.* Washington, D.C.: AEI Press, 1990.

Deficit Finance

WE NORMALLY THINK OF THE TAXES WE PAY as providing the funds to finance government expenditures, but there is another important potential source of revenue available to the government: borrowing. When government spending exceeds tax revenues, the difference, called the *deficit,* can be financed by selling government debt obligations and using the proceeds to pay for the excess. The federal government has increasingly relied on this method of paying its bills in recent years. State and local governments also sometimes engage in deficit finance, but it is used more sparingly at these levels of government because of economic (and frequently constitutional) limits on its use.

For more than a decade, the issue of the federal budget deficit has dominated discussions of economic policy. Deficits are universally viewed as bad, but the reason(s) is (are) often unclear. After all, the only alternatives—raising taxes or reducing government spending—also have harmful effects, so the central issue is whether deficit finance is any worse than these alternatives. This chapter develops the economic analysis necessary to compare the alternative methods of finance. We begin with a brief discussion of the nature and evolution of deficit finance in recent years.

Deficits and Debt

At the outset, it is important to distinguish between the concepts of *deficit* and *debt*. The deficit is the excess of government spending over revenues in a given year. In 1992, for example, the federal government spent $1,381.8 billion but took in only $1,091.6 billion in revenue; the difference, $290.2

billion, was the federal budget deficit in that year. The funds to pay for this $290.2 billion in spending were acquired by selling government bonds, Treasury bills, and similar debt instruments to the public. In other words, the federal government borrowed this amount from the public over the course of the year.

By contrast, the federal government debt (the *national debt*) is measured at a point in time and is the sum of all outstanding government debt obligations held by the public. In other words, it is the sum of all past deficits and surpluses. An example will make the distinction between deficits and debt clear. Suppose that the government begins its fiscal operations in year 1 with a clean slate. In year 1, the deficit is $100 billion, followed by deficits of $200 billion and $150 billion in years 2 and 3. At the end of year 3, the public will be holding $450 billion in government debt instruments as a result of the combined borrowing over the three years. Government debt at the end of year 3 is, therefore, $450 billion, the sum of all three of the deficits over the three-year life of our hypothetical government. Budget surpluses will reduce the value of the outstanding debt. For example, if our government had run a surplus of $50 billion in year 3, the debt at the end of year 3 would have been $250 billion.

With that background, Table 14–1 gives historical data on the federal deficits and outstanding debt over a period of years starting with 1950. Let us first consider the deficits. The federal government has actually run a deficit in 39 of the 44 years covered by the table (not all years are shown, of course), so deficits are hardly a recent phenomenon. What is a recent development is the size of the deficits, which became noticeably larger beginning in the 1970s. To compare the sizes of deficits in different years, it is probably most appropriate to consider the deficit relative to the size of the economy, as measured by gross domestic product (GDP) in the table.[1] In the 1950s and 1960s, deficits averaged less than 1 percent of GDP per year, but this figure increased to 2.3 percent for the 1970s and then further to 4.0 percent for the 1980s. In 1993, the deficit was estimated to be 5.3 percent of GDP, second only to the 6.3 percent deficit for 1983.

It is clear from the table that deficit finance has become an important source of funds for the federal government. Indeed, it is now the third most important source of funds, following the individual income tax and the social security payroll tax. In 1993, borrowing provided the funds for 22 percent of total federal government spending.

---

[1]GDP is similar to the more familiar GNP (gross national product), but with this difference: GDP measures the annual output of goods and services produced by labor and property located within the United States (even if foreigners own the property), while GNP measures the output produced by labor and property supplied by residents of the United States, regardless of where the labor and property are located. Several government agencies are beginning to produce GDP estimates rather than GNP estimates, partly because GDP can be measured more accurately and partly because most other countries use GDP measures. Quantitatively, the two measures are very similar; in most years they differ by less than 1 percent.

Table 14-1   *Federal Deficits and Debt*

Fiscal Year	Total Deficit ($ billions)	Total Deficit as a Percentage of GDP	Debt Held by Public ($ billions)	Debt as a Percentage of GDP
1950	$ 3.1	1.2%	$ 219.0	82.4%
1955	3.0	0.8	226.6	58.9
1960	− 0.3	− 0.6	236.8	46.9
1965	1.4	0.2	260.8	38.9
1970	2.8	0.3	283.2	28.7
1975	53.2	3.5	394.7	26.1
1980	73.8	2.8	709.3	26.8
1985	212.3	5.4	1,499.4	37.8
1990	221.4	4.0	2,410.4	44.1
1991	269.5	4.8	2,687.9	47.7
1992	290.2	4.9	2,998.6	51.1
1993*	327.3	5.3	3,309.7	53.7

*Estimates.

Source: *Economic Report of the President* (Washington, D.C.: U.S. Government Printing Office, 1993), Table B–74.

Now let us consider the outstanding public debt, as shown in the last two columns of Table 14–1. At the end of 1950, the public held $219 billion in federal debt obligations, an amount equal to 82.4 percent of that year's GDP. This ratio was actually smaller than that of a few years earlier. At the end of World War II, the public debt actually exceeded 100 percent of GDP. An important reason for this outstanding debt was, of course, World War II. The U.S. government, like other governments before and since, relied heavily on borrowing to finance the war and therefore added substantially to the outstanding debt during the war years.

By 1993, as a result of the combined deficits and surpluses over the intervening years, the national debt had reached $3,309.7 billion, or 53.7 percent of GDP in that year. The national debt has increased greatly (although it should be stressed that the figures are in nominal dollars and therefore, if adjusted for inflation, would display much less growth[2]), but the ratio of debt to GDP has actually fallen. The reason is that GDP, the denominator in the debt/GDP ratio, has increased even more over this time period than has the numerator, the debt. However, the debt has been rising relative to GDP since 1974, when it reached its postwar low of 24.5 percent.

These numbers do not tell us whether deficits or accumulation of outstanding debt are bad. In fact, there are some circumstances in which economists generally believe it is appropriate for the federal government to run a deficit, as we will explain later. It should be clear from the historical rec-

[2]The 1950 national debt of $219 billion would be $1,350 billion in 1993 dollars.

ord, however, that we are not in danger of an imminent catastrophe given the current size of deficits and outstanding debt. After all, deficits were much larger relative to GDP in World War II, and the debt/GDP ratio was higher than in 1993 for all the postwar years up to 1956.

One potential danger arises if the national debt becomes so large that people holding the debt begin to suspect that the federal government will not be able to pay the interest it is legally obligated to pay. Since the government's ability to cover the annual costs of the debt depends primarily on its potential tax base, that is, roughly GDP, it is conceivable that if the ratio of debt to GDP becomes too high, it could trigger some sort of financial panic. However, since that ratio was 53.7 percent in 1993 but exceeded 100 percent in the past without a catastrophe, there seems to be no cause for immediate concern on that account. Moreover, it should be pointed out that it is possible for the government to continue running annual deficits without ever increasing the debt/GDP ratio. For example, if GDP rises by 5 percent from 1993 to 1994, the federal debt could rise by 5 percent and leave the debt/GDP ratio unchanged. Thus, if the federal government runs a deficit of $165.5 billion in 1994 (5 percent as large as the 1993 national debt), the debt/GDP ratio at the end of 1994 would still be 53.7 percent. Projected deficits are actually larger than this amount, so it is probable that the debt/GDP ratio will increase in future years, but the point is that it is possible to stabilize the ratio without reducing the federal deficit to zero.

Evolution of the Deficit Problem

As we have seen, deficits have been growing in size in recent years. Since deficits are the difference between government expenditures and taxes, it is worthwhile to examine how both of these factors have changed over the years. Table 14–2 gives federal taxes, expenditures, and deficits as a percentage of GDP for the years since 1950. For the first four decades, the figures are given as decade averages to highlight the underlying trends.

Federal taxes as a percentage of GDP have not changed very much over this period. Although slightly higher in the 1960s than in the 1950s, since the 1960s the federal tax burden on the American people (relative to their incomes) has been essentially unchanged. In 1993, federal taxes were 18.6 percent of GDP, just 0.2 percentage points above the average for the 1960s. Deficits have therefore not emerged as a result of declining taxes.

By contrast, federal spending relative to GDP has steadily climbed over the period. Averaging 18.1 percent of GDP during the 1950s, federal government spending rose to 23.9 percent of GDP in 1993. The increased deficits, therefore, are the result of government spending rising relative to GDP while taxes have been largely unchanged. Note that these figures do not imply that Congress has been "overspending"; you could just as easily interpret them as showing that the American people are "undertaxed" for the benefits they are receiving from government.

In addition, these figures do not tell us *why* the federal government has increasingly been spending more than it collects in taxes, in contrast to its

Table 14–2   *Federal Taxes, Expenditures, and Deficits*

| Year | As a Percentage of GDP | | |
	Taxes	Outlays	Deficits
1950–59	17.7%	18.1%	0.4%
1960–69	18.4	19.2	0.8
1970–79	18.5	20.8	2.3
1980–89	18.9	22.9	4.0
1990	18.9	22.9	4.0
1991	18.7	23.5	4.8
1992	18.6	23.5	4.9
1993*	18.6	23.9	5.3

*Estimates.

Source: *Economic Report of the President* (Washington, D.C.: U.S. Government Printing Office, 1993), Table B–74.

behavior in earlier years. This question requires a public choice analysis. Some public choice scholars believe the answer is simple. Politicians, they hold, like to spend money since spending provides benefits to their constituents and garners votes to keep them in office. In contrast, they do not like to raise taxes on their constituents for fear of losing votes. Thus, there may be an inherent imbalance in the spending and taxing propensities of politicians, leading them to spend more money than they have available.

The explanation for increasing deficits cannot be quite that simple, however, for it does not show why deficit finance was rarely used in earlier years (except during wartime), when presumably the same political forces operated. Moreover, one should consider the behavior of voters. Voters have repeatedly shown a disinclination to pay higher taxes and have risen up in protest (at least some of them) whenever serious reductions in government spending were contemplated. It appears that voters do not want reduced government spending but they also do not want increased taxes, suggesting that what they really want is for the deficits to continue. So perhaps the behavior of politicians in giving us unprecedented peacetime deficits reflects exactly what the voting public wants. We will be better able to evaluate the plausibility of this explanation once we have examined the actual effects of deficit finance.

Measuring the Deficit

The deficit figures in the two previous tables represent what is called the *unified deficit,* that is, the amount the government must borrow from the public to finance the spending that is in excess of revenues. The proper way to measure the deficit is, however, controversial, and a number of other measures have been proposed. We will discuss only two of the quantitatively more important issues that have been raised in this connection.[3]

One issue concerns the proper treatment of the social security trust funds. Recall that in recent years social security taxes have exceeded current outlays and that the surplus has been used to augment the trust funds. The question is whether this surplus should be subtracted from the deficit due to the rest of the federal government's transactions. In the unified budget, this surplus is subtracted, so it acts to reduce the measured deficit. In 1992, for example, there was a $62 billion social security surplus. The $290.2 billion deficit shown in Table 14–1 for 1992 is composed of a $352.2 billion deficit on non–social security programs that has been reduced by $62 billion when combined with the surplus in the social security system.

In fact, the federal government actually reports "on-budget" and "off-budget" deficits and surpluses, with the social security system off-budget and operating at a surplus, while the remainder of the budget, the on-budget activities, are operating at a deficit. The unified deficit combines these separate budgetary totals to arrive at the overall excess of spending over taxes, taking all programs together. The question here is which deficit measure should be considered as "the" deficit. In large part, the answer depends on what you want the measure to show. If you want it to show how much the federal government has to borrow from the public over the year, the unified deficit is the appropriate measure. However, if you are concerned with the status of non–social security programs, the larger on-budget deficit is appropriate. Most analysts prefer the unified deficit because they are concerned with the effects of government borrowing on capital markets (an issue we examine later), and the unified deficit identifies the magnitude of that borrowing.

Another measurement issue concerns the meaning of the deficit figures when there is inflation. To see the significance of inflation in measuring the deficit, suppose that at the beginning of 1991 the public held $2,410.4 billion in government debt obligations (which it did; see Table 14–1). Then during 1991 the government ran a deficit of $269.5 billion, which it financed by borrowing from the public. Thus, at the end of 1991, the public was holding $2,687.9 billion in government debt. The increase in government debt over the year ($2,687.9 billion − $2,410.4 billion) is the deficit for 1991.

The price level rose by 4.2 percent over 1991. Thus, the $2,410.4 billion in debt held at the beginning of the year fell in value because of inflation; the *real* indebtedness of the federal government on this $2,410.4 billion was thus reduced. Although the government's *nominal* indebtedness rose from $2,410.4 billion to $2,687.9 billion, its *real* indebtedness (measured in end-of-1991 dollars) increased only from $2,511.6 billion ($2,410.4 billion inflated by 4.2 percent) to $2,687.9 billion, or by $176.3 billion. The *real* deficit

---

[3]A discussion of several other problems with measuring the deficit is given by Robert Eisner, "Budget Deficits: Rhetoric and Reality," *Journal of Economic Perspectives,* 3:73 (Spring 1989).

for 1991 was thus only $176.3 billion rather than the $269.5 billion reported as the unified deficit.

During inflationary periods, these calculations imply that the official measure of the deficit overstates the extent to which the government's real indebtedness to the public has increased. In short, the real deficit is smaller than the deficit as officially measured during inflationary periods (which has, in recent decades, been all periods). Many economists contend that it is the real deficit that is responsible for whatever effects the deficit has on the economy.

Correcting the official measure of past deficits for the erosion in the real value of outstanding debt caused by inflation has very significant implications for our understanding of the fiscal stance of government budgets. Indeed, in many years during the 1950s, 1960s, and 1970s when the unified deficit was positive, the inflation-corrected real deficit was negative (i.e., there was a real surplus). But despite this correction, it remains true that the federal government has been running substantial real deficits in recent years, although they are somewhat smaller (as our numerical example suggests) than the official deficits. There is also still a trend toward increasing real deficits after the correction is made. However, this adjustment does suggest that the deficit problem may not be as serious as it is often portrayed to be.

Incidence of Deficit Finance

Although not technically a form of taxation, debt finance raises the same question: Who actually bears the burden of government programs financed by borrowing from the public? Two sharply opposing views are held on the incidence of debt finance. One is that government borrowing, like private borrowing, shifts the burden of paying for current expenditures to the future when the debt is repaid. The other view is that current expenditures impose a burden on the economy at the time the spending and borrowing take place. In trying to disentangle the issues involved, it will initially be assumed that when people buy governmental bonds, their purchases will be financed by a reduction in consumption spending. This means that private savings available for investment and capital formation does not fall. Although such an assumption is probably invalid, it allows us to disregard momentarily the complications that arise when future productive capacity is affected. (That aspect of debt finance is examined in the next section.)

Suppose that the government sells bonds to the public and uses the proceeds to finance the construction of a dam. The argument that this operation imposes no burden in the future runs as follows: To build the dam now, concrete, personnel, energy, and so on will be used today. These resources must be withdrawn from alternative uses in the private sector, thereby reducing the output of private goods and services. Because the output of private goods falls in the present, the sacrifice involved in constructing the dam occurs in the present and is borne by the present generation.

But what happens if the debt is repaid in some future year? If the government raises taxes at some future date to purchase the bonds back from the public (retire the debt), doesn't this impose a burden? Not so, according to this argument. In the future, the taxes are collected from the same groups (the general public) that receive the proceeds. Repayment of the debt is a transfer among those living at the time, and no net burden is imposed on future generations. In particular, debt repayment does not divert resources to the public sector, so private sector output of goods and services is unaffected.[4]

A similar argument applies to taxes used to pay interest on government bonds before the principal is repaid. Citizens pay taxes to finance interest payments, but they also own the bonds and receive the interest payments. There is no net burden, just a transfer of funds among the public.

This view of debt finance, conveniently summarized in the expression "We owe it to ourselves," was almost universally held in the economics profession from the 1930s until 1958. In 1958, James Buchanan published a book that argued that the burden of debt finance was shifted to future generations.[5] No one, according to Buchanan, bears a burden at the time the expenditure financed by debt is carried out. Although it is certainly true that the resources used in the government-built dam must come from the private sector, this does not mean that any person bears a burden in the relevant sense of sacrificed utility or well-being. Citizens who give up control over resources when they purchase bonds do so *voluntarily* in return for the government's promise of interest and principal to be paid in the future. They reduce current consumption in return for bonds, which permit greater consumption later; their lifetime consumption does not fall. Accordingly, it seems correct to say that no one bears a burden at the time the government borrows the money to build the dam.

To determine who does bear a burden, it is necessary to examine what happens in the future. Suppose that the debt is retired in a later year. According to the earlier view, taxpayers lose and bondholders gain, so there is no net burden. In contrast, according to Buchanan, although taxpayers lose, bondholders do not gain, so there is a net burden falling on taxpayers when the debt is retired. Bondholders do not gain because they simply exchange one asset (bonds) for another (money). This exchange represents no more of a gain for bondholders than when a person takes a $100 bill to the bank and exchanges it for five $20 bills. Taxpayers, on the other hand, lose when

---

[4]In the discussion that follows, it is assumed that the government sells the bonds to the general public rather than to other governmental institutions. When the government sells bonds to the Federal Reserve System, the effect is to increase the money supply. This is not really borrowing but a form of disguised money creation.

[5]James M. Buchanan, *Public Principles of Public Debt* (Homewood, Ill.: Richard D. Irwin, 1958).

they pay the higher taxes to retire the debt. Consequently, there is a net burden in the future from debt finance.

A simplified example may help to clarify how deficit finance can result in a burden on future generations. Let us assume that people live for only two years, during which they are young one year and old the next. In Table 14–3, there are two people alive in year 1, A and B. Now suppose that the government spends $100 and issues a bond to finance this spending. Individual A, at the end of his or her life, will not purchase the bond, but individual B does. As we assumed earlier, B reduces consumption by $100 in year 1 to finance the bond purchase. This reduction in consumption frees up private resources so that government spending can bid them away to build the dam (or whatever). We will also ignore interest costs: People are willing to hold the bonds even though they pay a zero interest rate. (We will drop both of these assumptions later.)

To see who bears a burden from the deficit financing of the dam, we must consider what happens in subsequent years. In year 2 suppose that B, who is now old, sells the $100 bond to C in order to finance his or her retirement consumption. C purchases the bond by reducing consumption in year 2 by $100, which makes it possible for B to increase consumption by $100. Now consider carefully how B has been affected over his or her entire lifetime by the government's deficit financing in year 1. B's lifetime consumption has not gone down; it went down in year 1 but was recouped when the bond was sold in year 2. In other words, B bears no burden over his or her entire lifetime as a result of the deficit financing. Of course, neither did A in year 1, so the entire population alive in year 1 (A and B) bears no reduction in lifetime consumption from deficit financing in that year. The population does, however, get the benefits from government spending in that year—so apparently these benefits come at no cost to it.

Let us look further into the future. In year 3 C sells the bond to D, and therefore C's lifetime consumption is unaffected by the earlier deficit financing. This process can continue forever, but to bring it to a conclusion, suppose that in year 4 the government decides to retire the debt. It raises $100 in new taxes—$50 each on D and E in that year—and uses the proceeds to purchase the bond back from D. Now consider how the lifetime consump-

Table 14–3 *The Burden of Deficit Finance*

	Change in Consumption			
Year	*1*	*2*	*3*	*4*
Young	$B(-100)$	$C(-100)$	$D(-100)$	$E(-50)$
Old	A	$B(+100)$	$C(+100)$	$D(+50)$
	(B purchases bond)	(B sells bond to C)	(C sells bond to D)	(Government raises taxes and buys bond)

tion of D and E has been affected. D gave up $100 to purchase the bond in year 3 and sold it for $100 to the government in year 4—a wash—but also paid a new tax of $50, which helped finance the debt retirement. Thus, his or her lifetime consumption has been reduced by $50. E also paid a $50 tax by reducing consumption in year 4 and got nothing in return in year 5; his or her lifetime consumption was also reduced by $50. *The burden of year 1 deficit finance is borne by taxpayers in the future when the debt is repaid.* In this way, deficit finance can result in a burden on future generations.

In this numerical example, it appears possible that deficit finance will never burden even future generations if the government simply decides not to retire the debt. However, this possibility is weakened if we modify the two particularly unrealistic assumptions we made to simplify the example. The first was that the interest rate was zero, so the government could borrow without offering any interest return on its bonds. Assume now that the government must pay a 5 percent interest rate on its bonds to induce people to purchase them. In year 2 and later years, government spending will be $5 a year higher as a result of the $100 borrowing in year 1, at least until the debt is repaid. (In 1993, government spending on net interest on the outstanding national debt was about $203 billion, the third largest expenditure after national defense and social security.) Suppose that the government raises taxes in future years to cover the $5 interest cost.

In this scenario, future taxpayers who pay the taxes to finance the interest costs will also bear a burden. Note that the bondholders who receive the interest do not gain because the promised interest payment was just sufficient to induce them to purchase the bonds in the first place. (Put another way, a bondholder could have purchased a private asset and received the same 5 percent return as on the government bond, so there is no differential advantage to receiving interest on government bonds.) In terms of the numerical example, individual B will receive $5 in interest in year 2, but that is just what he or she could receive on a private asset and therefore represents no gain in lifetime real income. Taxpayers who pay the $5 taxes to finance the interest payment, however, do bear a burden, and their lifetime real incomes will be reduced. (You may want to incorporate the taxes into the example in Table 14–3 to show this effect explicitly.) Thus, even if the debt is never repaid, the higher taxes to cover the interest costs of the debt will place a burden on future generations.

Secondly, we also assumed that people financed bond purchases by reducing consumption. It is probably more realistic to suppose that they reduce their saving to finance purchases of government bonds. Government bonds are, after all, good substitutes for other forms of saving, like savings accounts, certificates of deposit, corporate bonds, and so on. When people finance bond purchases by reducing saving rather than consumption, this will affect future generations in a different way: by reducing capital accumulation and future output of the economy. We will examine this possibility more fully later. The important point made by the numerical example is that future generations are burdened by deficit finance *even if* it does not adversely affect future output.

The Ricardian Equivalence Theorem

Not all economists accept the conclusion that deficit finance places a burden on future generations. A minority of economists believe that a modern version of an analysis originated by David Ricardo in the nineteenth century shows that deficits place a burden on the *current* generation and not on future generations. The argument, however, is more subtle than the "we owe it to ourselves" view that was common several decades ago.

Once again, an example can illustrate the argument. Suppose that the government finances the dam by borrowing in year 1 and announces that it will levy a $100 per person tax in year 2 to purchase the bonds (retire the debt). All persons in year 1 will know that their taxes will be $100 higher in year 2 because of this year's deficit (assume that all of them will be alive one year later). They will then "feel" the burden in year 1 because they know that their lifetime taxes will be higher as a result of the government borrowing in year 1. The act of government borrowing carries the obligation to levy higher taxes in the future, and if taxpayers understand this fact, they will know that the present value of their lifetime disposable incomes has been reduced by the act of deficit finance in year 1. Hence they will feel the burden in year 1, although the actual payment is postponed until year 2.

In this example, the burden is felt by taxpayers in the present because they anticipate the higher future taxes. More formally, the Ricardian equivalence theorem states that deficit finance and tax finance are perfectly equivalent. Borrowing to finance government expenditures today has the same effect as taxing people today to finance those expenditures; people will recognize that their lifetime disposable incomes are reduced by the same amount in either case.

One objection to this view is that people do not live forever and may die before taxes are ever raised. It may be true that deficit finance today means higher taxes in the future, but that fact may not much affect people who are already relatively old. But supporters of the Ricardian equivalence analysis have an answer to this objection. Taxes may be raised only on a later generation, but the later generation is composed of descendants of the present generation. Hilary, for example, may realize that her children or grandchildren will confront higher taxes because of today's deficits, and, because she cares about the well-being of her descendants, she leaves a larger bequest to offset the cost of the higher future taxes.[6] Thus, future generations are not burdened by today's deficits because they will receive larger bequests from their ancestors.

Few economists believe this analysis is entirely valid. There are a number of reasons to be skeptical of its practical importance, including the fact that not everyone has children. In addition, to hold that people generally per-

---

[6]This analysis is developed in Robert Barro, "Are Government Bonds Net Worth?" *Journal of Political Economy,* 82:1095 (Nov./Dec. 1974). A more accessible version of the analysis is Robert J. Barro, "The Ricardian Approach to Budget Deficits," *Journal of Economic Perspectives,* 3:37 (Spring 1989).

ceive a burden when the government borrows, it is necessary to believe that citizens are well informed about current spending and tax policies and about the future consequences of present government policy. It is perhaps more plausible to suppose that few people know how much government spending is financed by borrowing or what borrowing means for future tax policy, much less for their own or their descendants' future taxes. If so, the general public may perceive no burden when the government engages in deficit financing, and the burden may fall on future generations, as we explained earlier.

However, it is probably going too far to completely dismiss the Ricardian equivalence argument. It may hold an element of truth, especially for those who are young when the government is running large deficits. These people may recognize, albeit in an imperfect way, that in later years they will end up bearing some cost because of today's deficits.

On balance, however, we suspect that deficit finance does impose costs on people in later years that are not fully anticipated, as well as on future generations. There is clearly a real burden involved when the government finances expenditures by borrowing, and the real issue seems to be, at what point in time do people recognize that burden?

Impact on Capital Markets

We assumed earlier that government borrowing does not depress private investment but, instead, that people reduce consumption spending to purchase bonds. This assumption is generally untrue. Government must compete with other borrowers when it sells its bonds, and it is likely to bid away funds that would otherwise have financed private investment.

Figure 14–1 shows the results of this process. The S curve shows the amount of current income people will save at alternative rates of interest: It is drawn as very inelastic, in line with our earlier discussion. The I curve shows the demand for funds to invest as related to the interest rate that must be paid. In the absence of government borrowing, equilibrium occurs with $300 billion of investment and saving at a 5 percent interest rate. At any given interest rate, every $1 the government borrows means that the amount of saving that can be channeled into private investment must fall. Government borrowing thus reduces the effective supply of funds available for private investment. If the government borrows $120 billion, the effective supply-of-saving curve shifts to the left by $120 billion. $S-B$ becomes the effective supply schedule confronting private borrowers, and the new equilibrium occurs at an interest rate of 6 percent, with $200 billion in private investment.

In this example, government borrowing bids up the interest rate to 6 percent and induces people to save $320 billion, $20 billion more than before. Of this total, however, $120 billion is used to finance government

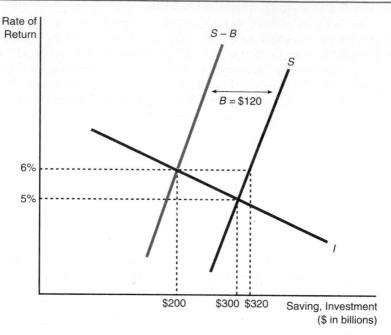

Figure 14–1   *Effect of debt finance on capital markets*

expenditures, leaving only $200 billion for private investment. Government borrowing of $120 billion here leads to a reduction of $100 billion in private investment (and a $20 billion decrease in consumption). The amount by which private investment falls depends on the elasticities of the S and I curves. The more inelastic the saving schedule is, the greater will be the reduction in investment. If the saving schedule is very inelastic, as drawn in the diagram, private investment will fall by almost as much as the government borrows. If the saving schedule is vertical, as some believe, every dollar the government borrows reduces private investment by a dollar. This process, whereby government borrowing reduces funds available for private investment, is sometimes called "crowding out."

It should be mentioned that the analysis in Figure 14–1 is incorrect according to the Ricardian equivalence theorem. One of the implications of the Ricardian analysis is that government borrowing has no more adverse effect on private investment than would occur if taxes were used instead. In other words, the effects of borrowing and taxation are equivalent. In terms of Figure 14–1, when taxpayers become aware of the government borrowing, they will realize that their future taxes will be higher. So in order to pay the higher future taxes, taxpayers will save more in the present. This causes the S curve in the diagram to shift to the right. Thus, according to this argument, private investment will not decline as much as is shown in the graph; it will decline only to the degree that taxation would cause investment to fall.

As we mentioned, for the Ricardian equivalence analysis to be fully appropriate requires a degree of foresight and knowledge on the part of taxpayers that seems unrealistic. As Herbert Stein, former chairman of the President's Council of Economic Advisers, observed: "I have never encountered anyone who says that he has raised his own saving rate because of the budget deficit."[7] Most economists seem to agree and regard the analysis of Figure 14–1 as reasonably accurate.

If deficit finance does lead to a reduction in investment, as suggested by Figure 14–1 (in contrast to our earlier assumption that borrowing came from consumption), a different type of future burden will be produced. The nation's capital stock will grow more slowly, and future productive capacity will be sacrificed. In effect, people will end up owning government bonds rather than real capital that would have augmented productivity. Aggregate output (income) will be lower than it would otherwise have been in subsequent years, so people will bear a burden in the form of lower incomes in the future. The results are quite similar to those produced by the social security system when it reduces saving.

This analysis must be qualified somewhat when we take account of international trade. As a result of the higher interest rates produced by deficit finance, foreigners may be induced to invest more in the United States. This has the effect of moderating, and possibly eliminating, the reduction in domestic investment caused by deficit finance. In effect, as domestic saving available for investment falls, foreign saving for investment here rises. There is some evidence that this process occurred in the 1980s, with the inflow of foreign-owned capital financing substantial amounts of private investment in the United States.

Even if this result occurs, it does not change the conclusion that Americans in the future will be poorer as a result of deficit finance. To understand this outcome, assume that foreign investment in the United States increases enough so that private investment does not fall at all in response to government borrowing. Then future *output* in the United States will not be adversely affected. Future *incomes* of Americans will be reduced, however, because part of the unaffected future output will now go to foreigners in the form of a return (interest, profits) on their investment.

The Welfare Cost of Deficit Finance

So far, we have shown how deficit finance places a burden on people in the future, that is, we have been concerned with the incidence of deficit finance. There is also the important question of the welfare cost of deficit finance: Is there an additional burden that results from some efficiency loss? There is a difficulty in evaluating deficit finance because its consequences depend on

[7]Herbert Stein, "Controlling the Budget Deficit: If Not Now, When? If Not Us, Who?" *The AEI Economist,* :4 (Dec. 1983).

government policy in the future. With government borrowing today, future government policy *must* be affected in some way because of the obligation to pay interest on the debt. The full consequences of deficit finance depend on exactly how these interest costs are financed, and on when and whether the debt is ever repaid.

We shall examine a specific, and perhaps not unreasonable, case in which the debt is never repaid but interest costs are covered by raising future taxes. To use a concrete example, let us suppose that the government borrows $100 this year and the interest rate is 5 percent. Then there will be annual $5 interest costs indefinitely, and we assume that these costs are met by raising an extra $5 in taxes in every future year. (Note that, at a 5 percent interest rate, an infinite stream of $5 payments has a present value of $100. The present value of future interest payments equals the amount borrowed.) Since future tax increases presumably result in welfare costs, and since these tax increases are the consequence of government borrowing this year, one welfare cost attributable to deficit finance is the distortions produced by higher future taxes.

There is also likely to be another sort of welfare cost attributable to deficit finance that relates to its effect on capital accumulation. Actually, the fact that investment and capital accumulation fall in response to government borrowing does not imply that there is necessarily a welfare cost. If capital markets are competitive and efficient, a reduction in investment in response to government borrowing entails no inefficiency; people who make smaller private investments bear the full cost (sacrificed interest return) of those decisions. The situation is different, however, if capital markets are not efficient when government borrowing takes place. For example, suppose that private investment is already too low (inefficient) because of taxes on investment income. Then government borrowing will reduce investment even further, and this situation will be inefficient and the source of a welfare cost.

Figure 14–2 shows the effects of government borrowing in the presence of taxes on the return to capital. The I curve continues to show the real return to private investment, but because some of that return accrues to government, the net return is shown by I'. (It is assumed that the tax rate on the return to capital is 50 percent.) Equilibrium in the absence of any government borrowing occurs at a rate of saving and investment of $300 billion, with a net return to savers of 5 percent, equal to half of the before-tax return of 10 percent realized by the investments. Now when the government borrows $120 billion (as in our previous example in Figure 14–1), investment falls by $100 billion and the net return rises to 6 percent, as before. In this case, however, investment projects yielding between 10 and 12 percent (as shown along the I curve) are sacrificed. Although the government pays an interest rate on its debt of only 6 percent, government borrowing leads private investors to give up investment projects that would have yielded up to 12 percent before taxes.

In this situation, government borrowing crowds out private investment that is more productive than the interest rate government pays on its debt.

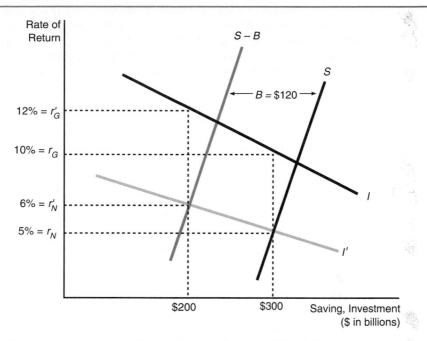

Figure 14–2   *Debt financing in the presence of capital taxes*

(Note that this effect does not occur in Figure 14–1, where there are no taxes on capital income.) This reduction in investment that is already at too low a level because of capital taxes is the source of a second type of welfare cost of deficit finance. In other words, the future losses are greater than the interest payments government must make on its debt. In fact, this future loss will be reflected in lower capital tax revenues collected in the future. Because there is less investment today, there will be less capital income in the future, and revenues collected by corporate, property, and income taxes in the future will be reduced. Thus, future taxes will have to be raised by more than enough just to cover the interest cost of the debt; they will also have to be raised to cover the losses from reduced capital taxes. So there will be more welfare costs from having to replace the lost revenue from taxes on capital income.

This analysis suggests that the welfare cost of deficit finance is likely to be quite high. Indeed, it is almost certain to be higher than the cost of tax finance. In other words, if we are deciding whether to finance given expenditures by either borrowing or taxing today, efficiency considerations suggest that taxation involves lower costs. The reason for this conclusion is the second type of welfare cost produced by deficit finance, related to its effect on private investment in an already distorted market. Tax finance largely avoids this welfare cost. The other welfare cost that results from higher future taxes to cover interest costs is probably about the same as the welfare cost of raising present taxes (the present values of the required taxes are the same), so on that count there is no advantage to taxation over borrowing. But borrowing has the additional effect of reducing capital accumulation and future capital tax revenues, which tips the balance in favor of taxation as the more efficient form of finance.[8]

Should We Reduce the Deficit?

Few topics have attracted more public attention in the past decade than how to reduce the federal budget deficit. It is often taken for granted that it is desirable to reduce, if not eliminate, the deficit. But there may be some circumstances in which it is desirable to use deficit finance, and we should consider whether there may be benefits as well as costs from the deficits.

Some government expenditures involve investments that will produce benefits for many years after the expenditures are undertaken. The beneficiaries of these investments are those living in the future, and fairness may call for them to bear some or all of the cost of providing these government benefits. Deficit finance can do this since it does impose costs in the future. This is one of the arguments favoring deficit finance during wartime, where it is held that future generations will benefit greatly from successful completion of the war. Note that this argument is an application of the benefit theory of taxation, which holds that those who benefit from government spending should bear the cost of it. This argument, however, does not seem to apply to the deficits of the past 15 years or so since the federal government has not used the funds to finance any significant capital investments.

A second argument holds that it may be efficient to finance a large, temporary expenditure by borrowing. The basic idea is that a large expenditure would require a big increase in tax rates to cover the costs in one year, and since the welfare cost rises with the square of the marginal tax rate, this large tax increase can involve a significant welfare cost. In contrast, by spreading out the cost over a number of years of smaller tax increases, the welfare cost may be smaller. (This analysis is similar to the one in Chapter 10 that explained why a number of low-rate taxes are better than one high-rate tax.) However, this argument does neglect the welfare cost due to reduced private investment that results from government borrowing, and when that cost is incorporated into the analysis, it is far from clear that it would be more efficient to finance even an enormous temporary expenditure by borrowing. Moreover, the argument hardly seems applicable to the chronic deficits that the federal government has been running (although some have suggested

---

[8]A more rigorous analysis comparing taxation and debt finance that supports this conclusion is given by Martin Feldstein, "Debt and Taxes in the Theory of Public Finance," *Journal of Public Economics,* 28:233 (Spring 1985).

that it is applicable to the savings and loan bailout and Operation Desert Storm).

A third argument is that the redistribution accomplished by deficit finance is desirable. When expenditures that benefit today's population are financed by borrowing, the burden is placed on future generations, so the net result is to increase the real income of people today at the expense of people in the future. Actually, most people seem to consider this redistribution a disadvantage of deficit finance rather than an advantage ("we should not impoverish our grandchildren"). The redistribution accomplished, however, probably will be from those with higher incomes (future generations will almost certainly be better off than the current generation) to those with lower incomes (the present population), so it accords well with egalitarian sentiments.

A fourth argument for deficits holds that they are necessary to stimulate the economy during recessions. Whether deficit finance actually has the macroeconomic effect of increasing aggregate economic activity is somewhat controversial, but even if it does, there is another way of achieving that end (monetary policy) that does not have the costs of deficits. In any case, this argument would apply only to a small part of the deficits produced in the past 15 years.

Against these arguments for deficits, there are at least four major disadvantages to using deficits as a way of financing government expenditures that should be considered. First, the cost of expenditures financed by deficits is shifted to the future, either to current taxpayers later in their lives or to future generations, or both. If we make the value judgment that fairness requires people to pay for the benefits they receive from government (the benefit theory of taxation), deficit finance is unfair. At least, this is true insofar as government expenditures today provide benefits to today's population (in contrast to being long-term investments), which is characteristic of most government spending.

Second, the welfare cost of deficit finance is quite high, almost certainly higher than welfare cost of raising current taxes to cover current spending. We explained the basis for this conclusion in the last section. It should be noted that the welfare cost of deficit finance is also imposed in the future, so the total (direct plus welfare) costs on future generations are greater than would be the total cost on the present population of paying for its own expenditure policies.

Third, it is arguable that large deficits create political pressures that can lead to inflation. Whether deficits per se are inflationary is debatable, but inflation does reduce the real value of the outstanding national debt and is therefore a way that government can in effect repudiate part of the debt.

Fourth, it can be argued that it is unwise to permit government to utilize deficit finance. Politicians may be tempted to enact expenditure programs that are not really worth what they cost when they can shift the costs to voters not yet born. Put differently, it is politically irresponsible to permit today's voters to (elect representatives who) enact spending programs that benefit them and impose the costs on future generations. There is the possibility that inefficient expenditures will be undertaken because the costs imposed on today's voters are very small or nonexistent. This position is taken by many who favor a constitutional amendment requiring a balanced budget.

It is fair to say that most economists believe that the arguments against deficit finance are more persuasive, at least as regards the chronic deficits of the recent past. According to opinion polls, most of the public also view deficits as highly undesirable, and so do most elected representatives. Why have the deficits persisted in the face of this widespread disapproval? We can begin to understand the reasons when we consider the options for reducing the deficit.

How Can We Reduce the Deficit?

There are basically two ways to reduce the federal budget deficit: increase tax revenues or reduce spending (or a combination of the two). Let us first consider the possibility of reducing expenditures.

When asked how the government ought to cut the deficit, most people immediately answer that expenditures should be reduced. But the problem is: which expenditures? Table 14–4 lists federal expenditures by major categories for 1992. Total federal expenditures were $1,381.8 billion, while the deficit was $290.2 billion, so expenditures would have had to be 21 percent lower to achieve a balanced budget. How would you do this?

Table 14–4   Major Federal Expenditures, 1992 (in $ billions)

Category	Amount
National defense	$ 298.4
Social security and Medicare	406.5
Net interest	199.4
Income security	198.1
International affairs	16.1
Natural resources and environment	20.0
Agriculture	15.0
Transportation	33.3
Education, training, employment	45.2
Health	89.6
Veterans' benefits	34.1
All other	26.1
Total expenditures	$1,381.8
Deficit	290.2

Source: *Economic Report of the President* (Washington, D.C.: U.S. Government Printing Office, 1993), Table B–75.

National defense spending is an obvious target, but it was already 14 percent lower in real terms than in 1989 and is scheduled for further reductions in the future. In a few years, defense spending is likely to be a smaller share of national income than at any time since 1950, and many feel that it is dangerous to cut it much further, even with the demise of the Soviet Union. Social security and Medicare are often considered to be sacrosanct, and some politicians have come to regret even hinting at modest cutbacks in these programs. The third big-ticket item, interest on the public debt, cannot be cut because it is a legal obligation of the government.

Suppose that we agree that spending cannot be cut in these three areas, with total spending of $904.3 billion. That leaves $477.5 billion in federal spending, which we would have to cut by $290.2 billion, or 61 percent, to eliminate the deficit. Welfare programs (the income-security category) would have to be among the likely casualties. If welfare programs were also considered off limits, it would be impossible to eliminate the deficit even if we cut out all remaining government spending programs!

This discussion may convey an idea of the difficulty of eliminating the federal deficit by cutting government spending. Unless substantial cuts are made in the major categories—defense, social security, and welfare—it is virtually impossible. We should mention, however, that we have been considering the official unified budget deficit. As we saw earlier, this deficit is larger than the real deficit because of inflation, so if we are only concerned with eliminating the real deficit, our task will be easier. But in most recent years, the real deficit has been about two thirds as large as the official deficit, so it still would not be simple to find expenditures of that magnitude to cut.

The other option available to eliminate the deficit is to raise taxes. Since total federal tax revenues were $1,091.6 billion in 1992, taxes would have to be increased by about 27 percent to eliminate the deficit. However, since the social security payroll tax is earmarked for social security benefits, the major feasible tax alternatives are the individual income and corporation income taxes. These taxes raised $576.7 billion in 1992, so to eliminate the deficit, they would have to be increased to raise 50 percent more revenue. Indeed, it is not even clear that we could increase revenue that much from these taxes as they are currently structured. Tax rates would have to rise by more than 50 percent because the tax bases would shrink as a result of the disincentive effects of the higher rates. According to a *USA TODAY*/CNN/ Gallup Poll released on April 13, 1993, 55 percent of those polled think their taxes are already too high and only 2 percent think their taxes are too low, so the political difficulty of enacting substantial increases is apparent.[9]

These considerations may suggest why it is not easy to eliminate the federal budget deficit. The most feasible option would appear to be some combination of tax increases and spending cuts, but to make a major dent in the deficit, even these changes would have to be substantial.

---

[9]Richard Benedetto, "2% Say We're Undertaxed," *USA TODAY* (Apr. 13, 1993), p. 1A.

Hidden Deficits and Debt

Our discussion has focused on the official federal budget deficit. There are, however, other government policies that in effect involve deficit finance but are not counted as such in the federal budget. These "hidden deficits" have much the same economic effects as the official budget deficit, but are not even recognized to exist in discussions of "the" deficit problem.

The most important hidden deficit occurs in the social security system. What we want to show is that pay-as-you-go social security is equivalent to outright deficit financing of retirement pensions. The essence of deficit finance is that current expenditures are financed by obtaining funds in return for debt instruments, or promissory obligations—government promises to repay the funds at a later time. Now think of the taxpayer whose current taxes finance social security retirement benefits. That taxpayer does not receive an outright promissory note or government bond in return for taxes, but he or she does receive a promise that in return for these taxes, he or she will receive retirement benefits later in life. In effect, taxpayers receive implicit government bonds in return for their taxes (that are like loans to the government) that they cash in when they retire. In a meaningful sense, government is borrowing from current social security taxpayers to pay current retirement benefits. It is true that the implicit bonds taxpayers receive are not exactly like explicit bonds that underlie the official deficit—the implicit bonds cannot be sold or cashed in before retirement, for example—but the similarities are more important than the differences.

To see how pay-as-you-go social security can be interpreted as a form of deficit financing, consider Table 14–5. (This table is the same as Table 7–2, which we first used to illustrate pay-as-you-go social security.) Recall that the figures in parentheses were interpreted as the taxes and retirement benefits. But we can now see that the consequences are the same as when the government finances the retirement benefits by borrowing from current work-

Table 14–5 *Implicit Deficits in Social Security*

Year: Tax Rate:	1 0	2 10%	3 10%	4 10%	5 10%
Young	C250 (0)	D500 (−50)	E1000 (−100)	F2000 (−200)	G4000 (−400)
Middle-aged	B250 (0)	C500 (−50)	D1000 (−100)	E2000 (−200)	F4000 (−400)
Retired	A(0)	B(+100)	C(+200)	D(+400)	E(+800)

ers. In year 2, for example, the government acquires $50 from individuals C and D, nominally as a form of tax revenue. But in reality, individuals C and D are promised that they will later receive retirement benefits in return for these "taxes"—so they are not really a net loss (like a true tax) after all. Instead, we can think of C and D receiving $50 bonds in year 2 that carry an interest rate equal to the rate of economic growth.

Individual D receives an implicit bond of $50 in year 2 and $100 in year 3. When D retires in year 4, these bonds plus interest are worth $400, which he or she gets as retirement benefits in that year. The government does not, however, raise taxes to pay $400 to D, but instead issues more implicit bonds to E and F to raise the funds. The system continues in this way, presumably indefinitely.

The similarity to deficit finance is very close. That is why many of the economic effects of deficit finance are the same as for social security. For example, we saw that deficit finance benefits the present (current benefits of the expenditure) at the expense of the future. In the same way, social security benefits the start-up generation at the expense of future generations. In addition, we argued that deficit finance reduces the saving available for private investment, and therefore reduces the rate of capital accumulation and results in lower incomes in the future. Social security also probably reduces saving for retirement, with the same consequences.

Recognizing that social security and deficit finance are very similar, it is natural to ask how large the implicit deficit in social security is so we may compare it to the official federal deficit. Unfortunately, there are no estimates of the annual implicit social security deficit. (Note that the implicit deficit of social security is not measured by the difference between current taxes and outlays. In year 2 in Table 14–5, for example, current taxes equal current outlays, yet the entire outlays are really financed by implicit borrowing, so the implicit deficit in that year is $100.) There are, however, estimates of the implicit social security *debt* that are analogous to the official national debt, and this implicit debt is the sum of all past implicit deficits of social security.

The implicit debt of social security is called the *unfunded accrued liability* of the program. It is defined as the present value of future benefits that have already been earned based on taxes already paid. More precisely, this definition is of the *accrued liability,* from which we subtract the amount in the trust funds to arrive at the unfunded accrued liability. Note that this concept is just like that of the national debt. The unfunded accrued liability represents obligations of the federal government to pay future social security benefits that exceed the amount currently available (in the trust funds) to finance these future benefits. The only way to meet these obligations is out of future taxes or future borrowing, as with the explicit national debt. For example, a worker age 30 who has paid social security taxes for 10 years is already entitled to a retirement pension at age 67 even if no further taxes are paid (the pension, of course, is smaller than if he or she continues to pay taxes), and the present value of that pension is the government's accrued liability for this worker.

The unfunded accrued liability of the OASDI program has been estimated at $6,511 billion as of January 1, 1990.[10] This does not include Medicare, which is also financed predominantly in a pay-as-you-go, or unfunded, fashion. The unfunded accrued liability of the Hospital Insurance (HI) portion of Medicare is estimated to be $3,614 billion, and for the Supplementary Medical Insurance (SMI, or Part B) of Medicare, it is estimated at $1,786 billion. All together, there was a total unfunded accrued liability for these social security programs of $11,911 billion at the beginning of 1990. This can be compared to the official national debt at that time, which was $2,189 billion. Amazingly, the hidden debt in social security is more than five times as large as the official national debt!

It is ironic that many people have become nearly hysterical over the dangers of the official federal deficit and national debt without recognizing that the hidden deficits and debt in social security are much larger. It should again be emphasized that the economic effects of outright government borrowing (the official deficit) and implicit government borrowing (the implicit social security deficit) should be much the same. If the official deficit and debt are bad for the economy, it is difficult to avoid the conclusion that unfunded (or underfunded) social security programs are far worse. Yet social security is a very popular program, widely regarded as successful by the public and politicians alike.

Review Questions and Problems

1. Explain the distinction and the relationship between government deficits and debt.

2. Given the record levels of deficits in recent years, why is government debt today a smaller fraction of GDP than it was 50 years ago?

3. Explain how the unified budget deficit is different from the on-budget deficit.

4. The total deficit is projected to be $327.3 billion in 1993, and the inflation rate is predicted to be 2.8 percent. Assuming that these predictions turn out to be correct, compute the real deficit for 1993. (Hint: see Table 14–1.)

5. Economists agree that if debt is used to finance a dam, the resource cost of concrete, labor, energy, and so on occurs in the present. Nonetheless, some economists would argue that a cost is imposed on future generations. Explain their argument. That is, explain how society can incur a burden or cost in periods after that in which the resources are actually used.

---

[10]This estimate, and the following ones for HI and SMI, are reported in A. Haeworth Robertson, *Social Security: What Every Taxpayer Should Know* (Washington, D.C.: Retirement Policy Institute, 1992), Chapter 7. The source of the OASDI figure is "recent unpublished studies made by the Office of the Actuary of the Social Security Administration" (p. 116).

6. If Ricardian equivalence holds perfectly, explain how government borrowing has no effect on private investment. If it does not hold, explain how government borrowing crowds out private investment.

7. How does deficit finance produce a welfare cost? Is the welfare cost of deficit finance likely to be larger or smaller than the welfare cost of tax finance?

8. Explain the circumstances in which it would be appropriate for the government to finance expenditures by borrowing. Does this explanation provide a justification for the large deficits of the last 15 years?

9. If the public overwhelmingly opposes significant tax increases and expenditure reductions, does that decision imply that the current level of deficit finance is desirable? If not, on what basis do you decide what constitutes a desirable level of deficit finance?

10. "Insofar as our current deficits are placing a burden on future generations, this situation is only fair. After all, future generations will be wealthier than we are, so it is in accord with the principle of progressivity in distributing tax burdens that they bear greater costs than we do." Explain why you agree or disagree with this statement.

11. What combination of expenditures cuts and/or tax increases would you use to eliminate the deficit, assuming that it has been decided that the deficit is to be eliminated? Defend your answer.

12. Explain the equivalence of the social security system with government borrowing. What does Ricardian equivalence have to say about people's attitudes on the future of the social security system?

13. Many people are opposed to federal budget deficits yet at the same time support the social security system. Is it logically consistent to take this position? If not, stake out and defend a position that is consistent with respect to deficits and social security.

Supplementary Readings

BERNHEIM, B. DOUGLAS. "A Neoclassical Perspective on Budget Deficits." *Journal of Economic Perspectives,* 3:73–94 (Spring 1989).

BUCHANAN, JAMES M., and RICHARD E. WAGNER. *Democracy in Deficit.* New York: Academic Press, 1977.

CONGRESS OF THE UNITED STATES, CBO. *The Federal Deficit: Does It Measure the Government's Effect on National Saving?* Washington, D.C.: U.S. Government Printing Office, 1990.

GRAMLICH, EDWARD M. "Budget Deficits and National Saving: Are Politicians Exogenous?" *Journal of Economic Perspectives,* 3:23–36 (Spring 1989).

KOTLIKOFF, LAURENCE J. *Generational Accounting.* New York: Free Press, 1992.

The Tax System

 N PREVIOUS CHAPTERS, WE EXAMINED EACH OF THE major taxes in the U.S. tax system separately. In this chapter we consider these components of the tax system together and take a broader view of the way in which taxes affect economic activity. Most households pay, or bear, the burden of several different taxes, and in this situation it is necessary to consider the combined effect of the various taxes to analyze accurately how households will be affected. This situation is analogous to the analysis of income transfer programs, in which we saw the importance of taking into account the overlapping and interacting nature of many transfers.

The first section of this chapter examines the distribution of the tax burden by income class for the tax system as a whole. The next three sections are concerned mainly with the effect of taxes on resource supplies and hence on the level and rate of growth of national output. A proposal for seemingly radical change in the tax system, the taxation of consumption rather than income, is discussed in the last section.

The Distribution of the Tax Burden

Is the overall tax system progressive, proportional, or regressive? That is one of the most fundamental questions concerning the economic effects of taxes. Now that we have examined the incidence of each major tax separately, we are in a position to bring the results together and examine the incidence of the tax system as a whole. We begin by considering the incidence of all federal taxes.

Table 15–1 gives estimates of tax burdens as a percentage of family income by income decile for each of the major federal taxes, and all taxes

Table 15-1 *Federal Taxes and Family Income, 1988 (in percent)*

Income Decile	Individual Income Tax	Social Security Taxes	Corporate Income Tax	Excise Taxes	All Federal Taxes
1	−0.8%	5.0%	1.1%	4.5 (0.9)%	9.7 (5.5)%
2	−0.4	5.9	1.0	2.1 (0.4)	8.6 (6.9)
3	1.7	8.6	1.3	1.6 (0.6)	13.3 (12.3)
4	4.1	9.4	1.6	1.4 (0.7)	16.5 (15.8)
5	5.9	9.8	1.6	1.1 (0.8)	18.5 (18.2)
6	7.2	10.4	1.6	1.0 (0.8)	20.2 (20.0)
7	8.3	10.5	1.7	0.9 (0.8)	21.4 (21.3)
8	9.0	10.9	1.6	0.8 (0.9)	22.3 (22.4)
9	10.4	10.6	1.7	0.8 (0.9)	23.4 (23.5)
10	15.5	6.0	4.7	0.4 (0.9)	26.6 (27.1)
Top 1 percent	19.7	1.8	7.7	0.2 (0.9)	29.3 (30.0)
All deciles	10.4	8.7	2.7	0.9	22.7

Source: Congress of the United States, Congressional Budget Office, *The Changing Distribution of Federal Taxes: 1975–1990* (Washington, D.C.: U.S. Government Printing Office, October 1987), Table 13.3.

together, for 1988. These estimates are taken from the Congressional Budget Office study we have referred to in earlier chapters. Indeed, we have discussed these estimates separately in our analyses of the individual taxes, so here let us focus on the last column, which gives the estimated average tax rates for each income class for all federal taxes together.

Two estimates are given for each income class in the table. The first is the estimate when federal excise taxes are allocated to families in proportion to their annual consumption, and the second (in parentheses) allocates these taxes in proportion to families' market earnings. As we explained in discussing sales and excise taxes in Chapter 13, there are serious questions about the legitimacy of allocation of tax burdens in proportion to consumption, and it is important to understand how that allocation affects estimates of tax burden distribution.

Whichever estimate is used, the federal tax system is progressive with respect to annual income. It is, however, more progressive under the market earnings allocation, with the tax rate rising from 5.5 percent for the lowest decile to 27.1 percent for the top decile, reaching 30.0 percent for the top 1 percent of the population.

One feature of the federal tax system that becomes very clear when we consider all the federal taxes in Table 15-1 is the relative importance of the social security tax for most families. Note that this tax accounts for more than half of the total federal tax burden on the lowest five deciles. Indeed, *the burden of the social security tax exceeds that of the individual income tax for the lowest nine deciles,* and by a substantial margin for lower-income families. Most people are not aware of how important this tax has become because it is entirely withheld by their employers, and only the employee half of the tax is indicated on employees' pay slips.

In interpreting these figures, it should be recalled that the estimates of family incomes do not include in-kind income. If this income were included, the estimated tax rates would be lower for all income classes, but especially for the lowest income classes, for which government in-kind transfers are a substantial share of total income.

Since 1988, there have been three changes in federal taxes (as of mid-1993) that have significant effects on the overall progressivity of the federal tax system. Two of these changes affect tax rates primarily at the top of the income distribution. They are the increase in the top marginal tax rate of the individual income tax from 28 to 31 percent and the increase in the ceiling on taxable earnings for the Medicare portion of the social security payroll tax (both enacted in 1990). These tax changes would add about 2 percentage points to the tax rate shown for the top decile.

The third important change is the expansion of the earned income tax credit. By 1993, this increase reduced the burden of the individual income tax to − 3.2 percent for the lowest *quintile* (see Table 11–5), which probably means a rate no higher than − 4.0 percent for the lowest decile. Note that the effect of this change is to reduce the overall federal tax rate almost to zero for the lowest decile (using the market earnings allocation for excise taxes). However, it can be argued that the EITC should be treated as a transfer rather than as a negative tax. All other government transfer payments increase income in the denominator of the tax/family income ratio, whereas the CBO treats the EITC transfer alone as reducing the numerator. This definitional issue has no substantive effect on the results, properly interpreted, but it can affect the interpretation of numbers like these.

In assessing the distributional effects of taxes, it should, however, be recalled that government transfers are generally (except for the EITC) treated as income and not as negative taxes. That fact is important to remember, especially when evaluating the effect on low-income families. Total government transfers are at least 7 times (using the consumption allocation for excise taxes) the total federal tax burden on the lowest decile and about 15 times the total federal tax burden when the market earnings allocation is used. Therefore, taxes have relatively unimportant effects on the well-being of low-income families in comparison to government transfers. A 10 percent increase in government transfers to the lowest decile would probably increase the disposable incomes of these families by more than if we somehow reduced their federal tax burden to zero.

State and Local Taxes

In the aggregate, state and local taxes are about half as large as federal taxes. Unfortunately, the CBO did not develop estimates of the distribution of state and local taxes in its study, and no other recent studies have done so. We

Table 15–2   *State and Local Taxes and Family*
Income, 1988 (in percent)

Income Decile	Individual Income Tax	Property and Corporate Taxes	Sales and Excise Taxes	All State and Local Taxes
1	0.1%	1.7%	20.2 (1.4)%	22.0 (3.2)%
2	0.3	1.5	9.5 (1.8)	11.3 (3.6)
3	0.5	2.0	7.2 (2.7)	9.7 (5.2)
4	1.0	2.4	6.3 (3.2)	9.7 (6.6)
5	1.2	2.4	5.0 (3.6)	8.6 (7.2)
6	1.6	2.4	4.5 (3.6)	8.5 (7.6)
7	1.9	2.6	4.1 (3.6)	8.6 (8.1)
8	2.3	2.4	3.6 (4.1)	8.3 (8.8)
9	2.7	2.6	3.6 (4.1)	8.9 (9.4)
10	2.7	7.1	1.8 (4.1)	11.6 (13.9)
Top 1 percent	3.1	11.7	0.9 (4.1)	15.7 (18.9)
All deciles	2.4	4.1	4.1	10.6

Source: Estimates made by the author as explained in text.

can, however, use some of the data provided in the CBO study to develop rough estimates of the effects of state and local taxes.

Table 15–2 gives these estimates for the three main categories of state and local taxes: individual income taxes, property and corporate taxes, and sales and excise taxes. Before discussing the figures, let us explain briefly how they were developed. For the individual income taxes, we extrapolated the results of a tax incidence study using 1976 data that did have evidence on the distributional effects of these taxes.[1] Property and corporate income taxes were allocated in proportion to the capital income of families in each income decile, using data from the CBO study. Thus, these taxes have the same pattern of rates as does the federal corporation income tax in Table 15–1, only at higher levels because state and local property and corporate taxes are a larger proportion of total income. Similarly, state and local sales and excise taxes were apportioned among families in proportion to the burden of federal excise taxes (or in proportion to market earnings) from the CBO study. It should be noted that these estimates pertain to average tax burdens across all states and localities. The estimates are too low for those living in locations with higher than average tax rates and too high for those living in locations with lower than average tax rates.

The results of these estimating procedures are shown in Table 15–2. Individual income taxes (levied primarily by state governments) and property

[1]Edgar K. Browning and William R. Johnson, *The Distribution of the Tax Burden* (Washington, D.C.: American Enterprise Institute, 1979), Table 15.

and corporate taxes are generally progressive with respect to family income. In addition, it is not surprising that the tax rates for sales and excise taxes depend heavily on whether they are estimated by allocating the tax burden in proportion to annual consumption or market earnings. But it is striking how large the estimated burdens are on the lowest deciles when these taxes are assumed to fall on annual consumption. The lowest decile is estimated to bear a burden from sales and excise taxes of over 20 percent in this case, despite the fact that the overall average burden is only 4.1 percent. Moreover, that burden is highly regressive, with the rate falling to 1.8 percent on the highest decile. By contrast, when these taxes are assumed to fall in proportion to market earnings, the rates rise from only 1.4 percent for the lowest decile to 4.1 percent for the top decile.

It is clear that one gets an extraordinarily different impression not only of the incidence of sales and excise taxes alone, but even of the overall burden of all state and local taxes, depending on what approach is used to allocate these tax burdens among income classes. That is why we examined the arguments supporting these two approaches in such detail in Chapter 13. Many people believe that state and local taxes overall are regressive, but that conclusion holds only when sales and excise taxes are allocated to annual consumption, where such consumption exceeds income by a factor of more than 3 to 1 for the lowest income classes. As we mentioned earlier, economists have become increasingly skeptical that such estimates give an accurate picture of the burden distribution of these taxes. It is certainly inaccurate for low-income families who have *permanently* (rather than temporarily) low incomes, for these families do not on average consume in excess of their incomes at all.

If sales and excise taxes are allocated to market earnings, which we believe to be the more appropriate procedure, these taxes are progressive, as are all state and local taxes taken together. In that case, the average tax rate for the lowest decile is 3.2 percent, and the rate rises steadily until it reaches 13.9 percent for the top decile.

The Total Tax System

Table 15–3 brings together our earlier results to examine the distribution of tax burdens for federal and state-local taxes together. Once more, two sets of estimates are presented, one when sales and excise taxes are allocated to annual consumption and the other (shown in parentheses) when these taxes are allocated to market earnings.

When sales and excise taxes are assumed to fall in proportion to annual consumption, the overall tax system can almost be characterized as roughly proportional. The tax rate on the bottom decile is 31.7 percent and exceeds that level only for the ninth and tenth deciles, where it is 32.3 and 38.2 percent, respectively. Excluding the lowest decile, there is still a significant degree of progressivity even in this case, with the rate rising steadily from 19.9 percent for the second decile to almost double that level for the top decile. But there is no question about the progressivity of the tax system if

Table 15–3   *Percentage Distribution of the Total Tax Burden, 1988*

Income Decile	All Federal Taxes	All State and Local Taxes	All Taxes	All Taxes Excluding Sales and Excise Taxes
1	9.7 (5.5)%	22.0 (3.2)%	31.7 (8.7)%	7.0%
2	8.6 (6.9)	11.3 (3.6)	19.9 (10.5)	8.3
3	13.3 (12.3)	9.7 (5.2)	23.0 (17.5)	14.2
4	16.5 (15.8)	9.7 (6.6)	26.2 (22.4)	18.9
5	18.5 (18.2)	8.6 (7.2)	27.1 (25.4)	21.0
6	20.2 (20.0)	8.5 (7.6)	28.7 (27.6)	23.2
7	21.4 (21.3)	8.6 (8.1)	30.0 (29.4)	25.0
8	22.3 (22.4)	8.3 (8.8)	30.6 (31.2)	26.2
9	23.4 (23.5)	8.9 (9.4)	32.3 (32.9)	27.9
10	26.6 (27.1)	11.6 (13.9)	38.2 (41.0)	36.0
Top 1 percent	29.4 (30.0)	15.7 (18.9)	45.0 (48.9)	43.9
All deciles	22.7	10.6	33.3	28.0

Source: Tables 15–1 and 15–2.

sales and excise taxes are allocated to market earnings. In that case the tax rate for the bottom decile is only 8.7 percent, and it rises to nearly five times that level for the top decile, reaching nearly 50 percent for the top 1 percent of the population.

Sales and excise taxes provide only about 15 percent of the revenue generated by all taxes in the system, but our perception of the degree of progressivity of the overall system is disproportionately affected by how these taxes are allocated to income classes. It may, therefore, be worthwhile to consider the tax burden distribution for the other taxes that provide 85 percent of the total revenue. These estimates are given in the last column. The distributional effects of these taxes are relatively uncontroversial, and it is clear that the overall burden is very progressively distributed among income classes. The rate rises from 7.0 percent at the bottom to 36.0 percent at the top decile, and reaches 43.9 percent for the top 1 percent of the population. In addition, these taxes have become more progressive since 1988 because of the changes discussed earlier in the federal individual income tax and the social security tax.

One final point in regard to these estimates should be mentioned. All the estimated tax rates are of average tax rates relative to total income. These figures do not tell us how high the marginal tax rates are that apply to labor or capital incomes, and it is these rates that are largely responsible for the welfare costs of the taxes. We expect marginal tax rates to be above average tax rates for progressive taxes, but they can be substantially higher, especially for lower-income families, for whom the implicit marginal tax rates in transfer programs (benefit-reduction rates) are often more important than the marginal tax rates of the taxes. One study estimated that the average value of the marginal tax rates confronting different families was about 43 percent in 1976, and even higher marginal rates applied to many low-income families.

Taxation and Labor Supply

When we take a broad view of the economy and classify all productive resources as either labor or capital, it is clear that the quantities of labor and capital used in production have a pronounced effect on the level of total output. Total output, in turn, effectively equals total real income. If the tax system affects the quantities of labor or capital supplied, it affects the level of real income. For this reason, economists have always been interested in trying to determine exactly how total resource supplies are affected by taxation. In this section, our concern is with the effect of taxation on labor supply.

In 1991, 117 million persons were employed in the U.S. economy. Their combined before-tax labor income was about $3,775 billion, equal to about 75 percent of net national product (or net national income) of $5,069 billion.[2] Of this $3,775 billion in before-tax labor income, about $1,130 billion, or 30 percent, was paid as taxes to federal, state, and local governments. The most important of these taxes were the federal individual income tax, the social security payroll tax, state income taxes, and indirect business taxes (sales and excise taxes). To evaluate the effect of taxes on labor supply correctly, it is necessary to take into account the effect of all these taxes together.

In Chapter 11, we developed a theoretical analysis to describe the way a tax on labor income affects a person's decision regarding labor supply. As we explained, the tax becomes a wedge between the before-tax and after-tax rate of pay, and it is the after-tax rate of pay that guides labor supply decisions. The tax affects labor supply in two different ways. The income effect of the tax, which depends on the average tax rate, encourages greater work effort (labor supply), as the taxpayer attempts to recoup some of the lost income. The substitution effect of the tax, which depends on the marginal tax rate, encourages less work effort, as the taxpayer gets to keep less of each additional dollar earned. In theory, the net effect on labor supply can go either way, depending on the relative sizes of the opposing income and substitution effects.

[2]The *Economic Report of the President, 1993* reports that total compensation of employees was $3,391 billion. To this amount can be added about $184 billion in total proprietors' (self-employed) income of $368 billion (part of which is really capital income). In addition, to arrive at a before-tax figure, we must add in that part of the $228 billion in sales and excise taxes that would have been paid to labor in the absence of these taxes. The result is a total before-tax labor income of about $3,775 billion.

To go much further with this analysis requires information on how responsive people are to tax-induced changes in their wage rates. In making this determination, the wage elasticity of labor supply is crucial. Recall that the wage elasticity of labor supply is defined as the percentage change in labor divided by the percentage change in the wage rate. Letting ε (epsilon) stand for the wage elasticity, we can express the relationship as

$$\varepsilon = \frac{\Delta L/L}{\Delta w/w} \tag{1}$$

Recall that taxes on labor income reduce net wage rates by a percentage equal to the *marginal* tax rate, and it is the wage rate at the margin to which the worker will adjust. So if the marginal tax rate is 40 percent, for instance, the percentage change in the wage rate, or $\Delta w/w$, equals (minus) 40 percent. Thus, if we know the labor supply elasticity and the marginal tax rate, we can calculate the percentage change in labor supply, $\Delta L/L$, from equation (1); that is, $\Delta L/L$ equals ε times $\Delta w/w$, or εm where m is the marginal tax rate.

The problem is that we do not know the magnitude of labor supply elasticities with any precision. Various empirical studies have yielded different estimates. Two surveys of these studies cited in Chapter 11 suggest values of ε in the range of 0.1 to 0.3 and equal to 0.15. (What is relevant here is an average value of ε for the labor force as a whole. Some population subgroups, like married women, are believed to have higher elasticities than do other groups, like married men.) Let us take 0.15 as a reasonable compromise. In addition, suppose that the combined effect of all taxes on labor income produces a marginal tax rate of 40 percent, interpreting this figure as a weighted average of the different marginal tax rates that apply to different people. If these estimates are correct, then taxes can be estimated to reduce labor supply by 6 percent ($\Delta L/L = \varepsilon m$, or 0.15 × 0.4); this figure implies a reduction in labor income of about $240 billion in 1991 when total labor income was $3,775 billion.

A loss of $240 billion due to taxes on labor income sounds substantial, but this estimate, even if it is close, suffers from two defects. First, it compares the level of labor supply (labor income) under the current tax system with a world with no taxes on labor income at all. For almost any conceivable purpose, this is not a relevant comparison since no one is suggesting that we do away with all the expenditure programs that these taxes finance. Second, even ignoring this problem, a reduction of $240 billion in labor income is not a *net* loss to society. The reason for this loss is that people are working less, which means they are enjoying greater amounts of leisure. To determine the net effect on well-being, we must weigh the loss in income against the gain in leisure.

These remarks lead us to consider the sense in which taxation of labor income produces a net loss, or welfare cost. We discussed this topic earlier, but we now take another look as we try to estimate the likely magnitude of the welfare cost from distortions in labor supply.

In Figure 15–1, YN illustrates a budget line for a worker, Wanda, in the absence of any taxes on labor income. With a progressive tax, which we represent for simplicity as a flat rate tax above an exempted amount of earnings, the budget line is $Y'BN$. Wanda's equilibrium is at point E_1, where U_3 is tangent to $Y'B$; this equilibrium implies that Wanda's marginal rate of substitution between income and leisure is equal to the net marginal wage rate (the slope of $Y'B$). As we saw before, the welfare cost is identified by imagining a lump-sum tax that raises the same tax revenue. The lump-sum tax budget line is shown as HH', and Wanda moves to point E_2 and is on a higher indifference curve, although she still pays the same amount of tax. The welfare cost is indicated by the fact that Wanda can be better off (on U_2 rather than U_3) and still pay the same amount in taxes. Stated the other way, the tax places a burden on Wanda by moving her from U_1 to U_3; since it is possible to get the same revenue at a burden of only U_1 to U_2, the difference in well-being between U_2 and U_3 is an avoidable net loss—a welfare cost.

Now let us consider how to measure this welfare cost in dollars. When Wanda moves from E_1 to E_2, she increases her labor supply from NL_1 to NL_3, or by ΔL. (ΔL is also the reduction in leisure time.) In return, Wanda's dis-

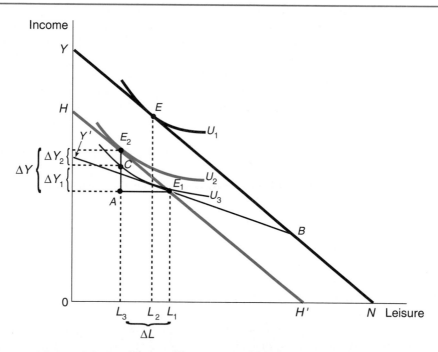

Figure 15–1   *The welfare cost of labor income taxation*

posable income rises by AE_2, or by ΔY. This change in income, ΔY, is not a net gain since part of it just compensates Wanda for the amount of leisure time she gave up to earn the additional income. Wanda would need to receive extra income of AC, or ΔY_1, just to stay on indifference curve U_3 to compensate her for the sacrificed leisure. But she actually receives the larger amount AE_2, or ΔY, which is larger than ΔY_1 by an amount equal to CE_2, or ΔY_2.[3] So ΔY_2 is a measure of the net benefit to Wanda from paying a lump-sum tax rather than the income tax. Conversely, ΔY_2 is the net loss, or welfare cost, resulting from the tax.

To measure this welfare cost, we need to know how much more workers will work when they can keep all *additional* earnings, that is, when they can choose a point on HH'. Recall that along HH' Wanda's tax liability is constant, so working more does not increase her taxes; in effect, the marginal tax rate on additional earnings is zero. In the diagram, this additional work effort is ΔL. To estimate ΔL, we require a particular type of wage elasticity of supply that shows how work effort is affected when the *marginal* tax rate falls from its current value (along $Y'B$) to zero (along HH'), thereby raising the net marginal wage rate that Wanda gets to keep. Note that this elasticity is different from the one discussed earlier, which pertained to the movement from E to E_1. That elasticity, called an *uncompensated* elasticity, identifies the labor supply response taking into account *both* the income and substitution effects of the tax—from NL_2 to NL_1. For purposes of estimating the welfare cost, we need to use a labor supply elasticity referred to as a *compensated* elasticity that identifies the labor supply responses when tax revenue is constant.[4] In effect, the compensated elasticity, which identifies the ΔL change in labor supply, *contains only the substitution effect* since the taxpayer continues to pay the same amount in taxes. And, as long as leisure is a normal good, the compensated elasticity is larger than the uncompensated elasticity. This situation is illustrated in the diagram by the fact that work effort increases more along HH' (by ΔL) than if the worker pays no tax at all (by L_1L_2).

This distinction is subtle, but what is really important is how much more taxpayers will work when they are confronted with a lump-sum tax that is equal in amount to the income taxes they pay.

---

[3]Ideally, a theoretically rigorous measure of welfare cost requires that we locate point C where the slope of U_3 equals the before-tax wage (slope of HH'); and then the distance from C to HH' measures the welfare cost. The measure described in the text is a close approximation to this true measure of welfare cost, and it is adopted here because it permits a more intuitively understandable explanation of what the ΔL term is supposed to measure.

[4]The compensated elasticity is usually measured as the change in labor supply when the worker is kept on the same indifference curve, U_3 in the graph, but confronted with the before-tax wage rate. The interpretation provided here will give about the same result and will allow us to interpret the compensated response as how much more people will work if they do not have to pay taxes on any extra earnings (along HH').

Estimating Total Welfare Cost

To develop a formula that can be used to estimate the welfare cost caused by distorted labor supply decisions, it is convenient to work directly with the labor supply curve. In Figure 15–2, S^* is Wanda's *compensated* labor supply curve, which identifies the substitution effects of tax-induced changes in the wage rate, and it is always upward sloping because as the wage rate rises, leisure becomes more expensive and less is consumed (i.e., more labor is supplied). Wanda's market wage rate is w, and she is subject to a marginal tax rate of m. Thus, Wanda's net-of-tax marginal wage rate is $(1 - m)w$, and at that net wage, her labor supply is L_1. This is a different way of representing the equilibrium shown at point E_1 in Figure 15–1.

If a lump-sum tax is used to raise the same tax revenue, the marginal tax rate on any additional earnings will be zero, thereby raising Wanda's net wage rate from $(1 - m)w$ to w. The increase in the net wage rate induces an increase in labor supply of ΔL (corresponding to ΔL in Figure 15–1). Additional earnings would equal BAL_3L_1 (ΔY in the previous diagram), but in earning that income Wanda would give up leisure time worth DAL_3L_1 (ΔY_1 in the previous diagram). The difference, triangle BAD (ΔY_2 in Figure 15–1),

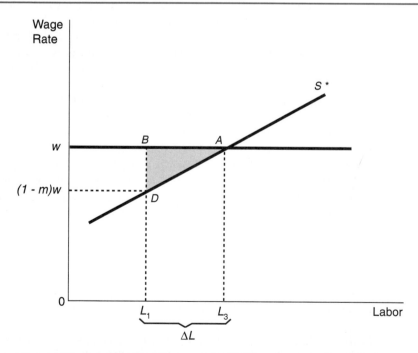

Figure 15–2   *The welfare cost of labor income taxation—a different perspective*

is the money measure of how much better off Wanda is with a lump-sum tax, which is the same as the welfare cost of using the income tax instead of the nondistorting lump-sum tax.

Area BAD is a triangle with a base equal to BD, or $w - (1 - m)w = mw$, and a height equal to BA, or ΔL. Thus, the welfare cost, W, can be expressed as

$$W = 1/2 \ mw\Delta L \tag{2}$$

The compensated change in the quantity of labor supplied, ΔL, can be expressed as the inverse of the slope of the supply curve, $\Delta L/\Delta w$, times the change in the marginal wage rate, wm, so

$$W = \frac{1}{2}\left[\frac{\Delta L}{\Delta w}wm\right]wm \tag{3}$$

If we multiply both sides by $L_1(1 - m)/L_1(1 - m)$, we get

$$W = \frac{1}{2}\left[\frac{\Delta L}{\Delta w}\frac{w(1 - m)}{L_1}\right]\frac{m^2}{1 - m}wL_1 \tag{4}$$

In this expression, the term in brackets equals the elasticity of the compensated labor supply curve evaluated at the net of tax wage rate (point D in Figure 15–2). Thus, equation (4) can be rewritten more simply as

$$W = \frac{1}{2}\varepsilon^* \frac{m^2}{1 - m} wL_1 \tag{5}$$

This formula is similar to the one developed in Chapter 10 for the welfare cost of excise taxes. Here we see that the welfare cost depends on the compensated labor supply elasticity ε^*, the marginal tax rate m, and total labor earnings (wL_1). Total labor earnings and marginal tax rates can be measured with reasonable accuracy, but we have less reliable information about the compensated labor supply elasticity, and that becomes the critical figure.

Ideally, to apply equation (5) we would estimate the welfare cost for each taxpayer separately and then add the costs up, since taxpayers face different marginal tax rates and may have different labor supply elasticities. We can, however, get a rough idea of the size of the welfare cost by using national labor earnings and average values for m and ε^*. In 1991, total before-tax labor earnings were about \$3,775 billion. For m, we will use a value of 43 percent; since the national average tax rate on labor income is about 30 percent and federal and state income taxes apply marginal rates well above the average rates, a figure of 43 percent should not be far off the mark. For ε^*, we will use 0.3; since uncompensated labor supply elasticities have been estimated primarily in the range of 0.1 to 0.3 and the compensated elasticity must be larger, a value of 0.3 seems plausible. Direct empirical estimates of ε^* also suggest that 0.3 is a reasonable value, although lower and higher figures have been estimated.

Using these values, the welfare cost caused by labor supply distortions from all taxes falling on labor income in 1991 is

$$W = \frac{1}{2}(0.3)\frac{(0.43)^2}{(0.57)} \; \$3,775 \text{ billion} = \$184 \text{ billion}$$

An annual loss of \$184 billion is far from negligible, but it should be viewed in comparison with the tax revenues raised. Since all taxes on labor income raised about \$1,130 billion in 1991, the welfare cost is equal to 16.3 percent of tax revenues.

We should emphasize once again that we do not know the compensated labor supply elasticity with great accuracy. When Harberger developed his original estimate of the welfare cost of the federal income tax in 1964, he used a value of 0.125.[5] More recent studies have generally concluded that people's labor supply decisions are more sensitive to taxation than was thought in 1964. By using a value of 0.3 for the compensated elasticity, we are in effect assuming that people would increase their labor supply by about 23 percent $[\varepsilon^* m/(1 - m)]$ if they continued to pay the same tax but faced a marginal tax rate of zero rather than 43 percent. Since a zero marginal tax rate would increase their net wage rate by 75 percent (from 57 percent of the before-tax wage to 100 percent, a 75 percent increase), a 23 percent increase in labor supply seems plausible, but we cannot rule out the possibility that the actual response could be somewhat greater or smaller.

It should be emphasized that this welfare cost only considers the effect on the quantity of labor supplied. Actual taxes on labor income produce other welfare costs, as we have explained in previous chapters. They would have to be added to this \$184 billion figure to give the total welfare cost of the taxes. For example, administrative and compliance costs are also welfare costs. These costs have been estimated to be about 6 percent of revenues for personal income taxes, but the comparable figure for payroll taxes would probably be smaller. Overall, administrative and compliance costs are perhaps 4 percent of the taxes on labor income, which would be about \$45 billion. In addition, human capital investments may be affected, and tax loopholes distort a number of choices concerning the uses of income. How large these welfare costs are is unknown. It does seem clear that the total welfare cost of these taxes is probably at least \$250 billion, or about \$1,000 per person in the United States.

It is unlikely that these welfare costs can be fully avoided; any feasible method of raising this much revenue is certain to distort some economic decisions. However, it may be possible to reduce the loss significantly. Suppose, for example, that we reform the federal and state income taxes so that

---

[5]Arnold C. Harberger, "Taxation, Resource Allocation, and Welfare," *The Role of Direct and Indirect Taxes in the Federal Revenue System* (Princeton, N.J.: Princeton University Press for the National Bureau of Economic Research and The Brookings Institution, 1964), pp. 25–80.

they are proportional taxes applying to a broad measure of income. This change would reduce the overall *marginal* rate of tax on labor income by roughly 10 percentage points, from 43 to 33 percent. We can use our formula to estimate what the welfare cost of distorted labor supply choices would be for the lower 33 percent marginal rate:

$$W = \frac{1}{2}(0.3)\frac{(0.33)^2}{0.67} \; \$3,775 \text{ billion} = \$93 \text{ billion}$$

This welfare cost estimate of $93 billion is almost half of the welfare cost when the marginal tax rate is 43 percent, a gain of $91 billion. In addition, gains in reduced administration and compliance costs, and reduced distortions from eliminating tax preferences (like the nontaxation of employer-provided health insurance), would easily push the total gain to well over $100 billion. That is the efficiency case for the flat rate tax that we discussed in qualitative terms in Chapter 11. Against this gain must be weighed the cost of increasing the tax burden on low-income families—the distributional effect of moving from progressive to proportional taxation.

Estimating Marginal Welfare Cost

As we have emphasized at several points, it is the marginal welfare cost of taxation that is important to consider in analyzing government expenditure policies. The determination of the marginal welfare cost for a tax on labor earnings is illustrated in Figure 15–3. Initially, our representative worker confronts the net wage rate w_1 and is at point D on the compensated supply curve, S^*. The total welfare cost is shown as area BAD. Now suppose that there is a small increase in the marginal tax rate confronting the worker that reduces the net wage rate to w_2. The worker responds by reducing labor supply to point F on the supply curve. Note that the total welfare cost has increased to area GFA. Thus, the increase in the marginal tax rate has caused the total welfare cost to increase by the trapezoidal area $BDFG$. This area, generally expressed as a percentage of the additional tax revenue produced by the tax change, is the marginal welfare cost.

Exactly how large marginal welfare cost is has great importance for the analysis of expenditure policies since its magnitude helps determine whether the policies are efficient and the appropriate level of spending to undertake. The magnitude of marginal welfare cost is affected by three factors. The first is the initial level of the effective marginal tax rate on labor earnings. (Recall that this rate reflects the combined effects of all the taxes and transfers that affect earnings.) *The higher the initial marginal tax rate, the larger the marginal welfare cost.* This relationship can be shown in Figure 15–3 by assuming that the initial marginal tax rate is lower, so the worker is initially at point H on the supply curve. Then a small increase in the marginal tax rate increases the welfare cost by the trapezoidal shaded area at point H, and that increase is smaller than the added welfare cost when the worker originally faces the higher marginal tax rate at point D.

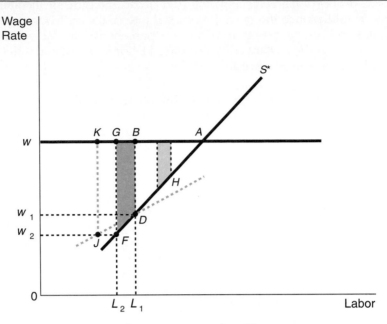

Figure 15–3   *Marginal welfare cost*

The second factor affecting the magnitude of marginal welfare cost is the elasticity of the compensated labor supply curve. *The more elastic the compensated labor supply curve, the larger the marginal welfare cost.* This relationship is illustrated in Figure 15–3 by the dashed supply curve that passes through point D. The dashed curve is more elastic since it shows that a change in the net wage rate will produce a larger change in labor supply than the S^* curve. For the same increase in the marginal tax rate we initially examined, with the more elastic supply curve, the worker would be located at point J, and the added welfare cost is shown by the trapezoidal area $JKBD$, which is larger than the original area $DFGB$. In addition, less additional tax revenue will be produced when labor supply falls further, so on both counts, marginal welfare cost will be higher with a more elastic compensated labor supply curve.

The third factor affecting the magnitude of marginal welfare cost is the progressivity of the change in the tax. *The more progressive the tax change, the larger the marginal welfare cost.* Recall that marginal welfare cost is the ratio of the added welfare cost (the trapezoidal area) to the additional tax revenue. The numerator of this ratio is determined by the change in the *marginal* tax rate, but how much additional tax revenue is produced depends on the change in the *average* tax rate. A progressive tax change is one in which the marginal rate rises more than the average rate, and the more the marginal rate rises relative to the average rate, the larger will be the added welfare cost in comparison to the additional tax revenue generated. Consider a worker earning $20,000. A very progressive tax change would be one in which the marginal tax rate is increased only for earnings in excess of, say, $19,000. Since the average tax rate (relative to total earnings) does not increase very much, this change would not produce much revenue, and the additional welfare cost as a percentage of the added tax revenue would therefore be high.

These three factors interact to determine the magnitude of marginal welfare cost. Table 15–4 illustrates the quantitative importance of these factors. It gives estimates of marginal welfare cost for various combinations of these three factors. The progressivity of the tax change is measured by dm/dt, where dm is the change in the effective marginal tax rate and dt is the change in the average tax rate. For example, if a proportional, or flat rate, tax were added to the tax system to generate extra revenue, dm/dt would be 1.0 since the marginal and average tax rates are equal. A progressive tax change with the marginal tax rate rising by 2 percentage points when the average tax rate rises by 1 percentage point implies that dm/dt equals 2.0.

It is important to realize that we do not know exactly how large the overall marginal tax rate or the compensated labor supply elasticity really is. Empirical estimates are available, but they are inexact and vary over some range—a larger range for the more difficult-to-estimate elasticity. (Both of these figures vary among people, of course, and the numbers in the table should be considered averages across the population.) For these reasons, we use a range of values for these factors. Our best guess is that the elasticity is about 0.3 and the combined marginal tax rate is 0.43, but we have to make allowance for the possibility that these estimates are a bit off.

Table 15–4 Marginal Welfare Cost per Dollar of Revenue (percentages)

| Marginal Tax Rate | dm/dt | Compensated Elasticity | | |
		0.2	0.3	0.4
0.38	1.00	14.2%	23.0%	33.2%
	1.39	20.9	35.1	53.1
	2.00	33.2	59.8	100.0
0.43	1.00	18.0	29.8	44.2
	1.39	27.0	46.9	74.3
	2.00	44.1	85.2	159.7
0.48	1.00	23.0	39.0	59.9
	1.39	35.1	64.1	108.9
	2.00	59.9	128.8	303.1

Source: Edgar K. Browning, "On the Marginal Welfare Cost of Taxation," *American Economic Review,* 77 (March 1987), Table 2.

Consider the estimates for our benchmark values for the marginal tax rate and elasticity (0.43 and 0.3). If additional tax revenue is raised in a way that is equivalent to adding a proportional tax to the system ($dm/dt = 1.0$), then the marginal welfare cost is estimated to be 29.8 percent. Thus, each dollar of revenue imposes a cost of almost $1.30 on the public. (This estimate might be appropriate for evaluating the cost of raising revenue with the social security payroll tax or a VAT.) If a progressive tax change with dm/dt equal to 1.39 is used to generate revenue, then marginal welfare cost is 46.9 percent. This degree of progressivity is actually somewhat less than the average progressivity of the federal income tax, so that raising revenue with that tax may be even more costly, depending on exactly how the rates are changed.

It is clear that we cannot determine a precise figure for the marginal welfare cost of taxing labor income, both because it is necessary to specify how the tax system changes to produce more (or less) revenue and because we are not certain of the exact values for the elasticity and initial marginal tax rate. Nonetheless, the estimates in Table 15–4 do suggest that marginal welfare cost is quite high for reasonable values of the determining factors. Moreover, it should be recalled that these estimates pertain only to the distortion in labor supply; they do not include the additional welfare costs of tax preferences or administrative and compliance costs.

Taxation and Capital Accumulation

By almost any measure, the performance of the U.S. economy over the past 20 years has been disappointing. Perhaps this conclusion is most clearly indicated by the rate of growth of per capita income. Between 1947 and 1973, real GNP per capita grew at an annual rate of 2.4 percent. Since the early 1970s, however, the rate of growth in real GNP per capita has slowed markedly, averaging only 1.3 percent per year over the 1973–1991 period. The reduction in the rate of growth of real per capita income suggests that the average standard of living has been rising only half as fast in recent years, but even this conclusion understates the deterioration in economic performance since more people are working now than ever before. The 1970s and 1980s saw an unprecedented expansion in the number of people working: The baby-boom generation entered the labor force, and the number of married women working rose significantly. But even with an increasing percentage of the population working, GNP per capita grew more slowly than in previous years. In fact, real GNP *per worker* grew at only 0.4 percent per year from 1973 to 1991, although it had been rising at a rate of 1.9 percent per year between 1963 and 1973.

Put differently, Americans' standards of living have increased only slightly since the early 1970s, although living standards grew steadily over previous decades. What caused this slowdown in the growth of productivity is not

Table 15–5   *Capital Formation in the United States, 1951–1991*

| Year | Net Private Investment as a Percentage of GNP | | Growth Rate of Net Capital Stock | |
	Total Investment	Nonresidential Fixed Investment	Per Worker	Per Hour
1951–1955	7.2%	2.9%	3.1%	3.5%
1956–1960	6.1	2.6	3.5	4.1
1961–1965	6.7	2.9	2.5	2.4
1966–1970	7.1	4.0	3.9	4.9
1971–1975	6.4	3.1	2.2	2.6
1976–1980	6.0	2.9	0.4	0.9
1981–1985	5.3	3.0	1.1	NA
1986–1991	4.5	2.2	0.4	NA

Source: *Economic Report of the President 1983* (Washington, D.C.: U.S. Government Printing Office, 1983), Table 4–1, and other sources.

fully understood. No doubt some role was played by the energy price increases of 1973 and 1979, the inflation of the 1970s, and the changing demographic composition of the labor force. Attention has also focused on the rate of investment in productive capital. The amount of capital invested per worker is an important determinant of output per worker. If the stock of capital grows more slowly over time, output per worker will grow more slowly, other things being equal. And there is some evidence of a slowdown in the rate of capital accumulation in recent years.

Table 15–5 gives several alternative measures of capital formation over a period of years. The first two columns focus on the rate of net investment relative to GNP. (Recall that it is net investment, not gross investment, that adds to the nation's capital stock and therefore contributes to economic growth.) As can be seen, there has been a steady decline in this measure of capital formation. Actually, in terms of the effect of capital formation on real wage rates, a more relevant measure is the growth in the amount of capital per worker or per hour of work. These measures are reported in the last two columns, and they suggest a more pronounced decline in this measure of capital formation. For the entire 1974–1991 period, capital per worker grew at an annual rate of only 0.6 percent, substantially below the rate for earlier years.[6] These reduced rates of growth resulted from a lower rate of net investment combined with large increases in the labor force. Whatever the exact cause of the slowdown in capital formation, the fact that capital per worker has been growing very slowly is a major reason why output per worker has been growing so anemically over the past 20 years.

[6]*Economic Report of the President* (Washington, D.C.: U.S. Government Printing Office, 1993), p. 233.

It is not entirely clear how large a contribution real investment makes to economic growth. Table 15–6 suggests, however, that the relationship is likely to be quite important. Several measures of investment for selected developed countries are compared with the annual growth rate in output per hour in manufacturing. Japan has the highest investment rate and also the highest growth rate of productivity, whereas the United States has the lowest investment rate and the lowest growth rate. The table thus implies a strong relationship between investment and the growth in standards of living. Although other factors also contribute to productivity growth, Table 15–6 does suggest that investment in real capital plays an important role, and other evidence supports this conclusion.

What determines the rate of net investment? Ultimately, private saving provides the funds that finance capital investment, so we must consider factors that influence the level of saving. Once again, many factors affect the level of saving and investment, and we do not know exactly how important each factor is. But there are a number of government policies that could affect the level of saving and investment. For example, several taxes fall on capital income that reduce the rate of return received by private savers. These taxes include individual income taxes, corporate income taxes, and property taxes. Insofar as people save less at a lower net rate of return, taxes on capital income tend to inhibit the flow of funds that finance capital investment.

We have also studied two other government policies that can affect the level of saving and investment significantly. As we explained in Chapter 7, the social security system provides retirement benefits largely on a pay-as-you-go basis, and that arrangement probably has reduced individual saving for retirement purposes to some degree. Social security has grown rapidly since the late 1960s, suggesting that this policy may have played some role. In addition, deficit financing tends to absorb funds that would otherwise be

Table 15–6 Capital Formation and Growth Rates in Selected Countries, 1971–1980

| Country | Investment as a Percentage of GDP | | | Growth Rate of Output per Hour in Manufacturing |
	Gross Investment	Gross Fixed Investment	Net Fixed Investment	
France	24.2%	22.9%	12.2%	4.8%
Germany	23.7	22.8	11.8	4.9
Italy	22.4	20.1	10.7	4.9
Japan	34.0	32.9	19.5	7.4
United Kingdom	19.2	18.7	8.1	2.9
United States	19.1	18.4	6.6	2.5

Source: *Economic Report of the President 1983* (Washington, D.C.: U.S. Government Printing Office, 1983), Table 4–2.

channeled into private investment, as we saw in the last chapter. Thus, deficit financing and social security may be part of the explanation for the decline in investment. In addition, nongovernmental factors, such as the rapid rise in energy prices that occurred following the Arab oil embargo in 1973–1974, probably had some effect. In the remainder of this section, however, we shall focus on the way taxation of capital income affects saving, investment, and economic well-being.

Just as with taxes on labor income, it is important to recognize that a number of separate taxes fall on capital income, and it is their combined effect that is relevant. For example, suppose that a corporate investment yields $100 in income. Part of that income goes to pay property taxes, and the remainder is subject to federal and state corporation income taxes. What is left is either reinvested by the corporation or paid out as dividends. If the remaining funds are reinvested, it will lead to a capital gain on the stock held by shareholders that will be taxed under the individual income tax when realized; if they are paid as dividends, they will be immediately taxed under the individual income tax. Inflation may also interact with the tax code to increase the taxation of real capital income.

Table 15–7 presents some of the results of a study that examined how various taxes interact to determine the effective tax rate on capital income generated by investments in the corporate sector. Corporate investment is about 60 percent of total national investment, with residential investment (housing) accounting for 25 percent and noncorporate business accounting for the remaining 15 percent. Columns (1) to (7) show how much each of seven different types of taxation contributes to the total effective tax rate. Except for the federal corporation income tax, the separate rates are moderate, but together they produced a total effective tax rate of 69.4 percent in 1979. Over the entire 1955–1979 period, corporate investments were taxed at rates well in excess of 50 percent, with rates somewhat higher and approaching 70 percent in the 1970s. The increase in the effective rate in the 1970s was in large part the result of the interaction of inflation and the tax system. This result is shown by the sharply higher rates in columns (6) and (7) beginning around 1970, when the inflation rate began its upward trend.

The last two columns in Table 15–7 indicate how taxes on capital income drive a wedge between the before-tax and after-tax real rates of return. During the 1970s, the before-tax real rate of return to corporate investment (including estimates for years not shown in the table) averaged almost 10 percent. With an effective tax rate of about 70 percent, however, the after-tax rate of return was only about 3 percent. Taxes act to reduce the net return, and it is this after-tax return that guides household decisions regarding how much to save. Changes in corporate and individual income taxes in the 1980s probably reduced the effective tax rate on corporate capital income to somewhere between 50 and 60 percent today.

Figure 15–4 illustrates how the taxation of capital income can affect the level of saving and investment. The before-tax rate of return associated with each level of investment is shown by the investment demand curve, *I*. The

Table 15–7   The Taxation of Corporate Capital Income

				Contribution to the Total Effective Tax Rate						
				Individual Income Tax						
Year	Federal Corporate Tax (1)	State and Local Corporate Taxes (2)	State and Local Property Taxes (3)	Tax on Dividends (4)	Tax on Real Capital Gains (5)	Tax on Nominal Capital Gains (6)	Tax on Interest (7)	Total Effective Tax Rate (8)	Before-tax Rate of Return (9)	After-tax Rate of Return (10)
1955	45.0%	2.1%	7.7%	7.7%	1.2%	0.8%	1.0%	65.4%	13.2%	4.6%
1960	40.1	2.3	11.6	8.6	1.0	0.7	2.1	66.5	10.4	3.5
1965	31.8	2.2	9.1	6.2	1.7	0.7	1.9	53.5	14.8	6.9
1970	30.8	3.6	15.4	7.7	1.8	3.5	6.6	69.5	9.8	3.0
1975	28.3	4.6	13.9	6.4	2.6	6.6	7.8	70.3	9.1	2.7
1979	31.7	5.5	10.5	6.9	2.6	4.2	8.0	69.4	9.0	2.7

Source: Martin Feldstein, James Poterba, and Louis Dicks-Mireaux, "The Effective Tax Rate and the Pretax Rate of Return," National Bureau of Economic Research, Working Paper No. 740 (Aug. 1981), Tables 2, 3, and 4.

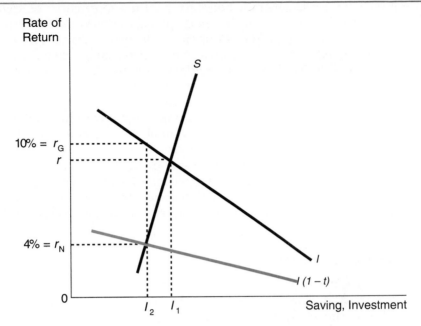

Figure 15–4   *Effects of capital income taxation*

saving supply curve is shown as S. In the absence of any taxes, the intersection of S and I determines the equilibrium with investment of I_1 and a rate of return of r. A tax on the rate of return at a rate of t, however, means that the after-tax, or net, rate of return associated with each level of investment is shown by the curve $I(1 - t)$. Assuming a tax rate of 60 percent means that the $I(1 - t)$ curve will lie 60 percent lower than the I curve does. Equilibrium is determined where the saving supply curve intersects with $I(1 - t)$ curve. With the S and I curves as drawn, the capital income taxes reduce the net return to savers to 4 percent and the level of saving and investment declines to I_2.

The extent to which taxes that fall on capital income reduce capital investment depends on the elasticities of the I and S schedules. Since the I schedule is generally thought to be relatively elastic, the net return will fall by almost as much as the tax. (Note that the return to savers falls from r to r_N, which is not a 60 percent drop because the before-tax return rises to r_G as the level of investment falls.) This result means that the way savers respond to lower rate of return—that is, how elastic the saving supply curve is—is critical. If the saving supply curve were vertical (perfectly inelastic), there would be no reduction in the level of saving and investment in response to taxes on capital income; if instead the saving supply curve were relatively elastic, the level of saving and investment would be reduced sharply.

Until recently, it was generally believed that the supply curve of saving was quite inelastic, if not vertical. Recent empirical evidence and theoretical work, however, have suggested that this view is incorrect. On the empirical side, Boskin argued that earlier studies of the relationship between saving and interest rates did not look at the relevant after-tax rates of return. Correcting for this deficiency, he found an interest elasticity of saving of 0.4.[7] This value implies that capital income taxes reduced saving by perhaps $200 billion in 1991. On the theoretical side, Summers argued that in a multiperiod model in which households save for a number of years to provide for future retirement, theoretical considerations alone strongly suggest that a reduction in the net rate of return received by savers will reduce saving substantially.[8] Since both of these findings contrast sharply with earlier research results, it is understandable that they are controversial. At the present time, the quantitative effect of capital income taxes on saving is best regarded as an open question.

Is the Rate of Investment Too Low?

In recent years, the view that the level of capital investment in the United States is too low has come to command wide respect. But what does it mean to say that investment is "too low"? Before answering this question, let us first evaluate two common arguments made in favor of increasing the rate of investment.

One frequently heard argument advocates increased capital investment as the cure for the sluggish economic growth of recent years. Although it is true that increased investment tends to increase the growth rate of real GNP, the relevant question is how much of an effect it will have on the growth rate. Since the before-tax rate of return is what measures the contribution of investment to output in subsequent years, let us use the 10 percent figure suggested by Table 15–7 to get an idea of the magnitude involved. Suppose that we increase net investment by $150 billion annually, which would be a substantial increase from its late 1980s average level of approximately $250 billion. At a 10 percent return, $150 billion in additional capital investment this year would add $15 billion to annual output in subsequent years. Since GNP is about $6,000 billion, a $15 billion increment in output would add only 0.25 percentage points to the growth rate. In other words, the growth rate of GNP might rise from 2.5 to 2.75 percent. Although this is not negligible, it seems clear that feasible increases in investment will not transform the United States from a slowly growing to a rapidly growing economy overnight. Physical capital investment is only one of a number of factors that

[7]Michael J. Boskin, "Taxation, Saving, and the Rate of Interest," *Journal of Political Economy,* 86(2), Part 2:S3 (Apr. 1978); and Boskin, "Tax Policy and Economic Growth: Lessons from the 1980s," *Journal of Economic Perspectives,* 2:71 (Fall 1988).

[8]Lawrence H. Summers, "Capital Taxation and Accumulation in a Life Cycle Growth Model," *American Economic Review,* 71:533–544 (Sept. 1981).

determine the rate of growth, and its independent role should not be exaggerated.

Another argument for increased investment stresses that business requires more capital in order to increase employment as the labor force expands rapidly. Put differently, capital investment "creates jobs." This argument is almost wholly fallacious. A given level of capital investment is consistent with any level of employment as long as wage rates can adjust. Downward-sloping labor demand curves mean that the level of employment will depend on wage rates—not that there is just one level of possible employment with a given stock of capital. As evidence, recall that the number of persons actually employed increased more rapidly in the 1970s than in any previous decade, despite an unusually low rate of investment.

In deciding whether the rate of investment is too low, economists emphasize that we should compare the costs of increasing investment with its benefits. To increase investment, people must reduce their current level of consumption; that is, they must save a larger portion of their incomes. There is no way to avoid this, and the sacrifice of current consumption is therefore the cost of increasing investment. The benefit associated with reduced current consumption is increased future consumption, since higher levels of investment now make it possible to consume more in the future because they add to the productive capacity of the economy. The magnitude of that benefit is correctly measured by the before-tax real rate of return to capital investment. If the before-tax real rate of return is 10 percent, then giving up $1 in consumption today will make it possible to consume $1.10 one year later, or $2 after only seven years.

The relevant question is whether people would be better off by sacrificing present consumption in return for increased future consumption. Since much saving is done to finance consumption in retirement and since 20 years is the approximate average length of time between when one starts to save for retirement and then consumes during retirement, the size of the trade-off can be illustrated in the following way: At a 10 percent rate of interest, $1 saved now will grow to $6.73 in 20 years, so the present cost of $1 in retirement consumption is $0.15. Would people be better off saving more (consuming less) now in return for that payoff? And if they would, why aren't they saving more? The answer is that households do not get to keep the before-tax return of 10 percent; they only get to keep the lower after-tax return of 4 percent, for example. One dollar saved now at 4 percent will grow to only $2.19 in 20 years, so the present price of retirement consumption is $0.46 per dollar. A tax on capital income of 60 percent triples the present price of retirement consumption, increasing it from $0.15 to $0.46 per dollar of retirement consumption. Faced with that much less favorable rate of exchange, it is understandable that saving remains low, even though the real before-tax return to saving justifies the cost of reduced present consumption.

What we have just described is the way capital income taxation can distort the choice between present and future consumption and lead to a welfare cost. Let us consider this situation further with the aid of Figure 15–5. Consumption by a household before retirement is measured on the vertical axis, and consumption after retirement is measured on the horizontal axis. In the absence of any taxes on capital income, MN is the budget line, with a slope of $0.15 in present consumption per dollar of retirement consumption, reflecting the 10 percent rate of return. Saving is initially MC_1. With a 60 percent tax on capital income, the budget line becomes MN', with a slope of $0.46 in present consumption per dollar of retirement consumption. Because of conflicting income and substitution effects, the effect on saving is uncertain. Let us suppose, however, that the level of saving still remains at MC_1, so the household's new equilibrium after the tax is at point E_1.

To see how the tax on capital income distorts the household's choice between present and future consumption, we perform the familiar experiment of substituting a lump-sum tax that yields the same revenue as the capital income tax. With the equal-yield lump-sum tax, the budget line is HH' and passes through point E_1. Using an equal-yield lump-sum tax means that the household can keep the full 10 percent return on any additional saving in excess of MC_1. Faced with the higher rate of return, the household chooses point E_2, saving an additional C_1C_1' before retirement in return for

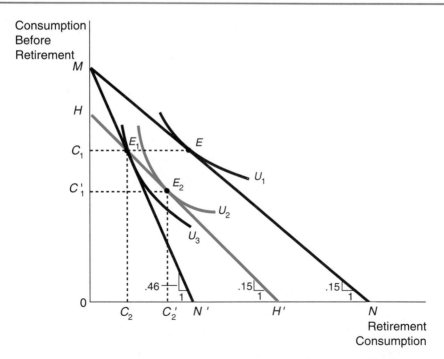

Figure 15–5   *The welfare cost of capital income taxation*

extra consumption of $C_2C'_2$ after retirement. The household is better off under the lump-sum tax than under the capital income tax, reflecting the excess burden or welfare cost of the capital income tax.

It is in this sense that economists claim that investment (saving) is too low. The benefits to the public from the greater future consumption that additional investment makes possible $(C_2C'_2)$ are greater than the sacrifice involved in reducing present consumption $(C_1C'_1)$.

Trying to estimate the size of this welfare cost from capital income taxation is tricky, in part because it requires the use of a dynamic model that can examine how the effects unfold over a long period of time. Recent research does, however, suggest the conclusion that *the welfare cost of capital income taxation is significantly larger than the welfare cost of labor income taxation.*[9] Among other things, this conclusion suggests that reducing the taxation of capital income (say, by eliminating the corporation income tax) and simultaneously increasing the taxation of labor income would result in a net gain for society.

Tax Rates, Tax Revenues, and the Laffer Curve

In the late 1970s and throughout the 1980s, the public became aware of something called *supply-side economics.* At the risk of oversimplifying, *supply-side economics emphasizes the way that government programs, especially taxes, can reduce national output (and hence national income) by reducing the incentive of people to work, save, and invest.* That is precisely the topic examined in the previous two sections. But supply-siders go on to emphasize a novel and often overlooked point: A higher tax rate will not necessarily produce more tax revenue if the base of the tax (income, or whatever) falls significantly in response to the higher rate. Moreover, a lower tax rate might actually increase revenues if enough additional productive activity is stimulated by the lower rate. To be able to lower tax rates and still get more revenue would seem to be the ideal free lunch, and some people thought that the supply-side approach might work in the United States.

To evaluate this possibility, let us examine the relationship between tax rates and tax revenues by considering a proportional income tax on earnings applied to an individual worker. Then we shall examine the implications of this analysis for the economy as a whole. We begin by assuming an income tax levied at a flat rate of 25 percent. As we have seen, the income and substitution effects of this tax are in opposite directions, so the net effect of

[9]Martin Feldstein, "The Welfare Cost of Capital Income Taxation," *Journal of Political Economy,* 86(2), Part 2:S29 (Apr. 1978); Christopher Chamley "Efficient Tax reform in a Dynamic Model of General Equilibrium," *Quarterly Journal of Economics,* C:335–356 (May 1985); Kenneth L. Judd, "The Welfare Cost of Factor Taxation in a Perfect-Foresight Model," *Journal of Political Economy* 95:675–709 (Aug. 1987).

the tax on work effort cannot be predicted on theoretical grounds. It is possible that an income tax would lead people to work more if the income effect dominated. We can, however, go a bit further with the analysis. Although an income tax levied at a low rate might increase the taxpayer's work effort, as the rate becomes increasingly higher, we will ultimately reach a point at which work effort will fall. We know, for example, that a 100 percent tax on earnings, which implies that the worker gets to keep no income, regardless of how much is earned, will lead a person to stop working altogether. Therefore, as the tax rate rises, it is more likely that the substitution effect will dominate and work effort will decline. Predictably, work effort will decline to zero by the time the rate reaches 100 percent.

Panel (a) of Figure 15–6 shows what this implies for the relationship between tax rates and tax revenue. The before-tax budget line is MN. A 25 percent income tax rotates the budget line to M_1N, and the worker chooses to work NL_1 hours. Tax revenue, the difference between before-tax earnings when work effort is NL_1 (BL_1) and after-tax earnings (AL_1), is the distance AB. If the tax rate is increased to 50 percent, the budget line will become M_2N. With the 50 percent tax on earnings, let us assume that the worker reduces his or her work effort moderately to NL_2 so that tax revenue is the distance CD. *Even though the worker's earnings are lower under the 50 percent tax, tax revenue is still higher (CD is greater than AB) because the doubled rate applied to moderately smaller earnings still yields more tax revenue.* (Do not make the mistake of concluding that if a tax rate increase has a disincentive effect, revenues will fall. The disincentive effect must be large relative to the rate increase if revenues are to fall.) However, when the tax rate is increased to 75 percent and the budget line becomes M_3N, work effort drops more sharply to NL_3, and tax revenue, EF, is lower than it was at the 50 percent rate. In this example, if the tax rate is initially 75 percent for the worker, a reduction in the rate will actually increase the government's tax revenue and also benefit the worker—just as the supply-siders predicted.

This suggests a general relationship: At low tax rates, an increase in the tax rate will increase tax revenues, but beyond some point a further increase in the tax rate will reduce tax revenues. This relationship is illustrated in panel (b) of Figure 15–6, where points A, C, and E correspond to the three tax rates depicted in panel (a). The curve in panel (b), well known among economists for many years, is now popularly known as the *Laffer curve* after contemporary economist Arthur Laffer. Rumor has it that Laffer drew the curve on a napkin for some politicians in a posh Washington restaurant sometime in the 1970s, and those politicians have never been the same.

Where Are We on the Laffer Curve?

There is no doubt that a relationship of the general form shown in Figure 15–6(b) exists. The critical question is to determine where we are on the curve. If the current tax system puts us at a point like A, then higher tax rates will produce more tax revenues—despite a reduction in productive activity—and lower tax rates will mean less revenue. If we are at a point like E,

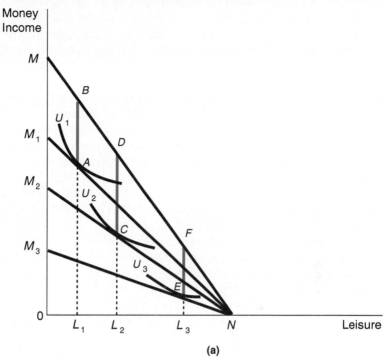

(a)

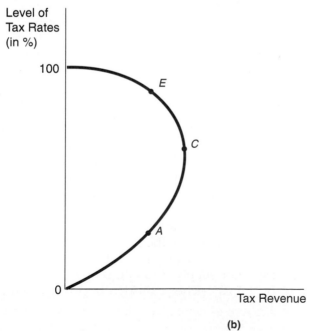

(b)

Figure 15–6   *Derivation of the Laffer curve*

however, taxes have depressed productive activity so far that a reduction in rates will spur sufficiently greater output to increase tax revenues.

In trying to determine whether a reduction in tax rates in the United States would lead to increased tax revenue, we immediately encounter a difficulty. What tax rates would be reduced? Because of the variety of different taxes and, more important, the fact that these taxes apply at different marginal and average rates to different persons and activities, there are innumerable ways in which tax rates can be reduced. We might possibly find some activities so heavily taxed and in such elastic supply that a carefully designed rate reduction could lead to increased tax revenues, but the more important question is whether an economywide reduction in marginal and average tax rates is likely to have this result.

To investigate this question, let us consider the taxation of labor income since our knowledge of how labor supply responds to taxation, imperfect as it is, is better than our knowledge of how saving and capital accumulation respond to capital income taxes. As we explained earlier, a typical person is subject to a marginal tax rate of about 40 percent on labor earnings and an average tax rate of about 30 percent. Suppose that a representative household's current earnings are $30,000, so its tax equals $9,000. Next, let the marginal rate be reduced from 40 to 30 percent and the average rate to 22.5 percent (at $30,000 in earnings[10]), so that the original ratio of marginal to average tax rates is maintained. A bit of arithmetic shows that earnings would have to rise by $7,500 to $37,500 for these lower rates to generate the same revenue. (That is, 22.5 percent of $30,000 equals $6,750, and with a marginal tax rate of 30 percent, if earnings rise by $7,500, an additional $2,250 in tax revenue results, for a total of $9,000.) Thus, a 25 percent increase in earnings is necessary for revenue to remain the same, requiring work effort to increase by at least 25 percent. Larger increases are necessary if tax revenue is to be higher at the lower rates.

Is it likely that work effort will increase by 25 percent if the marginal tax rate is reduced by 10 percentage points? For a person working a 40-hour week, this would mean an increase to 50 hours per week—and the workweek has not been at that level since early in the twentieth century. Intuitively, such a large change in hours worked would seem unlikely to follow from a 10 percentage point reduction in the marginal tax rate. We can also evaluate the possibility of such a large increase in work effort in terms of the wage elasticity of labor supply. Since reducing the marginal tax rate from 40 to 30 percent corresponds to an increase in the net marginal wage rate from 60 to 70 percent of the market wage, the implied increase in the net marginal wage rate would be 16⅔ percent. For a 16⅔ percent increase in the wage rate to increase labor supply by 25 percent, the labor supply elasticity would have to be 1.5 (25 percent divided by 16⅔ percent). As

---

[10]For a progressive tax, the average tax rate is not a fixed number but depends on how much is earned. We assume that the tax structure changes so that the average rate will be 22.5 percent as long as the household continues to earn $30,000.

we mentioned, most evidence suggests that the labor supply elasticity is in the 0.1 to 0.3 range, far below the required value. For an intermediate value, an elasticity of 0.15 would imply increased work effort of 2.5 percent, only one tenth of the 25 percent increase necessary to keep tax revenue from falling.

Reasoning along these lines has convinced most economists that the United States is not on the upper part of the Laffer curve. There are, however, two other ways that might result in higher tax revenues without an increased labor supply. One way is to induce currently untaxed economic activity in the so-called underground economy to move back into the taxed sector. To avoid taxes, some persons do not report their actual earnings. A carpenter or lawyer, for example, may be paid for a job in cash and not report the income. The gain from such activity is the tax saving; the cost is the risk of being caught and prosecuted. When tax rates are lower, the gain from not declaring income is reduced, which might induce some of this income to be reported rather than those individuals' running the risk of legal sanctions.

The best estimates of the size of the underground economy suggest that it is about 10 percent as large as measured GNP.[11] For the hypothetical tax reduction of 10 percent, we saw that taxable earnings would have to increase by 25 percent to keep tax revenue from falling. Allowing for a 2.5 percent increase in earnings from those already taxed, even if the entire underground economy went legal, the increase in taxable earnings would only be about 12.5 percent—still far short of the required 25 percent increase needed. And there is no reason to think that the entire background economy would become legal when marginal tax rates fell by one fourth; at best, probably only a small fraction would.

Another potential source of additional taxable income when tax rates are lower is the reduced use of legal tax preferences. At lower rates, for example, untaxed fringe benefits become less attractive relative to taxed cash income. Consequently, workers might take a larger part of their salaries as cash, and this action would increase their taxable earnings. But the total amount of excluded income under the federal income tax that would be affected by such a change—primarily itemized deductions plus exclusions other than government transfers—is only about 10 percent of GNP. Only a small part of this total could realistically be expected to become taxable income when the marginal rate falls by 10 percentage points, and this amount would not be nearly enough.

Thus, it appears unlikely that a reduction in tax rates would lead to the same or greater tax revenue through an expansion of taxable income. Taking account of the illegal underground economy and the legal use of tax preferences in addition to labor supply responses, however, does increase the probability of such an outcome, but that probability still seems low.

---

[11]Carl P. Simon and Ann D. Witte, *Beating the System: The Underground Economy* (Boston: Auburn House, 1982).

We should recall, however, that we are considering broad tax changes like across-the-board reductions in tax rates. There remains the possibility that some carefully targeted changes in specific taxes might have a different effect. For example, some have argued that the reductions in marginal tax rates that applied to the wealthy in the 1980s may have had the effect of increasing the tax revenue collected from them.[12] Others have argued that reducing the tax rate on realized capital gains might increase revenue. While these remain intriguing possibilities, it is important to recognize that the increased revenue possible from reducing these taxes (assuming that there would be an increase) would be extremely small relative to the total amount of tax revenue generated by the U.S. tax system.

Where Should We Be on the Laffer Curve?

It may be tempting to argue that the point at which tax revenues are as large as possible—point C in Figure 15–6—is somehow special. In fact, one popularizer of the Laffer curve observed: "It [point C] is the point at which the electorate desires to be taxed. [At lower tax rates] the electorate desires more government goods and services and is willing—without reducing its productivity—to pay the higher rates consistent with the revenues at point [C]."[13] Indeed, point C is special, but it is distinct only because government is raising and spending too much revenue at that point.

It is impossible to determine the appropriate (efficient) level of taxing and spending without evaluating the benefits from the expenditures of tax revenues, and these benefits are not identified by the Laffer curve. As we move up the Laffer curve, however, we know that each successive equal increase in tax rates imposes a larger burden (direct burden plus welfare cost) on the public than the previous increment did. At the same time, each successive equal increment in tax rates generates less revenue than the previous increment did. Thus, the marginal welfare cost per dollar of revenue rises as we move up the curve, and it approaches infinity at point C since the denominator—the increase in tax revenue—goes to zero at that point. In other words, as we near point C, an increase in tax rates raises almost no more revenue but continues to increase the burden on taxpayers. Since the marginal burden, or marginal cost, per dollar of revenue is infinite at point C, the only way that point could represent the efficient level of government spending is if the marginal benefit of government spending is also infinite— and that is impossible.

Figure 15–7 clarifies the relationship between the Laffer curve and the efficient level of government taxing-spending activity. Both the upper and lower panels measure total tax revenue—assumed equal to total government spending—on the horizontal axes. In the lower panel, the MC curve shows the marginal cost of raising tax revenue. MC is upward sloping since the marginal welfare cost of taxation rises with the marginal tax rate, whereas

[12]Lawrence B. Lindsey, *The Growth Experiment* (New York: Basic Books, 1990).

[13]Jude Wanniski, "Taxes, Revenues, and the Laffer Curve," *The Public Interest,* 5:5 (Winter 1978).

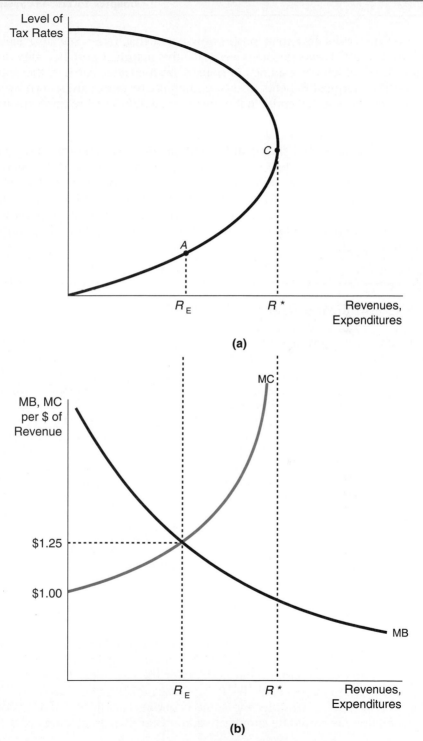

(a)

(b)

Figure 15–7 *The Laffer curve and efficient government taxing-spending activity*

tax revenue rises less than proportionally to that rate. (See also Figure 15–3.) The *MC* curve becomes vertical—the marginal cost becomes infinite—at R^*, which corresponds to point *C* on the Laffer curve in the upper panel. The marginal benefits from spending tax revenues are shown by the downward-sloping *MB* curve in the lower panel. Efficiency requires that taxing-spending be expanded until marginal benefit and marginal cost are equal, at R_E in Figure 15–7.

The efficient level of taxing and spending will always be somewhere on the lower part of the Laffer curve, not at point *C*. Actually, the Laffer curve is not useful in helping us identify the efficient level since it does not tell us the magnitudes of either *MC* or *MB* at different rates of taxation. At least, this is true at all tax rates lower than the revenue-maximizing rate at point *C*. If we were at point *C* or higher, we would know that tax rates were unambiguously too high.

Tax Consumption Instead of Income?

In recent years, there has been growing support among tax specialists for a seemingly radical change in the tax system. Many now advocate that taxes on income be eliminated and that a consumption tax be used instead. Support for such a reform has come from the the U.S. Treasury Department itself,[14] in addition to many private economists.

Consumption taxes in the form of sales and excise taxes have been used for a long time in the United States. The personal consumption tax discussed in this section, however, differs from these taxes significantly since it would be levied at the individual level and would be based on each taxpayer's consumption. That may not seem to be a major difference since we saw in Chapter 10 that the point of collection of a tax—whether from firms or individuals—does not affect its real economic consequences. Indeed, a personal consumption tax levied at a flat rate would have the same general effects as would a national retail sales tax, or VAT, levied on a comparable base. One advantage of a personal consumption tax, however, is that it can be levied at graduated rates, taxing those who consume more at a higher rate, for example. Therefore, the consumption tax can be a progressive tax, if desired—something that is difficult to achieve with sales taxes collected from business firms.

Until recently, personal consumption taxation was thought to be too difficult to administer. The vision of each taxpayer's having to fill out a tax return listing every consumption outlay over the year indicates what an administrative nightmare it could be. Recent research, however, has shown that it is administratively feasible, and some economists believe that a personal consumption tax would be simpler to administer than an income tax is. For

---

[14]U.S. Treasury, *Blueprints for Basic Tax Reform* (Washington, D.C.: U.S. Government Printing Office, Jan. 17, 1977).

example, it would not be necessary for each taxpayer to identify every consumption expense; instead, the tax base could be measured as the difference between income and the amount saved. Recall that consumption plus saving (change in net worth) equals income, so subtracting current saving from income measures consumption. Although it would not be quite that simple in practice, we will proceed on the assumption that a personal consumption tax is administratively feasible.

Equity

One of the strong claims made on behalf of an income tax has always been that income is the best measure of a taxpayer's ability to pay taxes. Consider two taxpayers, Alma and Barney, who each have incomes of $20,000. If Alma consumes her entire income and Barney consumes half and saves half, a consumption tax would require Barney to pay lower current taxes. A proponent of the income tax would argue that Barney must be just as well off as Alma since he had the same options as Alma; therefore Barney should pay the same tax. In this view, horizontal equity calls for the broader income base.

Proponents of consumption taxation have turned this argument upside down, claiming that the consumption tax is fair and the income tax is not. They agree that Alma and Barney are equals but stress that we must examine the taxes over a longer period than a single year. Under a consumption tax, the saver, Barney, does not avoid paying taxes by saving; he merely postpones the tax until he ultimately consumes the funds accumulated through his saving. To judge the fairness of income versus consumption taxes, we must therefore look beyond the current year.

Table 15–8 illustrates three alternatives: no tax, an income tax, and a consumption tax. We assume that Alma and Barney live for only two years; Barney saves part of year 1's income to consume in year 2; the interest rate is 10 percent. The no-tax option shows their preferred consumption patterns over time in the absence of taxes. The consumption tax advocate would argue that these two persons have identical taxpaying capacities because both have the same opportunities to consume; the fact that Barney prefers to consume more in year 2 should not subject him to any tax penalty.

Now notice what happens under a 20 percent income tax. Both Alma and Barney pay a $4,000 tax in year 1, but Barney pays an additional tax of $160 in year 2—20 percent of the $800 in *interest income* earned on his $8,000 savings of the year before. Although both Alma and Barney have exactly the same consumption opportunities, Barney pays a higher tax because the interest return on saving is subject to income taxation. By contrast, under a consumption tax (levied at a 25 percent rate[15]), Barney pays $2,000 in year 1 and $2,200 in year 2. In present value terms, over the two-year period,

---

[15]Since consumption is a smaller tax base than income, a higher tax rate must be applied to consumption. The 25 percent consumption tax raises the same tax revenue from Alma in year 1 as the 20 percent rate applied to income does since Alma consumes $16,000.

Table 15–8   *Income versus Consumption Taxation*

		No Tax	
Person	***Earnings***	***Year 1 Consumption***	***Year 2 Consumption***
Alma	$20,000	$20,000	$ 0
Barney	20,000	10,000	11,000

		Income Tax	
Person	***Earnings***	***Year 1 Consumption (and tax)***	***Year 2 Consumption (and tax)***
Alma	$20,000	$16,000 ($4,000)	$ 0 ($0)
Barney	20,000	8,000 (4,000)	8,640 (160)

		Consumption Tax	
Person	***Earnings***	***Year 1 Consumption (and tax)***	***Year 2 Consumption (and tax)***
Alma	$20,000	$16,000 ($4,000)	$ 0 ($0)
Barney	20,000	8,000 (2,000)	8,800 (2,200)

Barney pays the same amount of tax as Alma, since $2,200 paid in year 2 with an interest rate of 10 percent is equivalent to $2,000 in year 1.

A person's lifetime tax liability under a consumption tax is the same (in present value), regardless of how much is saved. *Savers do not avoid the tax; they just postpone it by saving.* Under income taxation, those who save a larger portion of their incomes end up paying more in lifetime taxes than do those equally situated who choose to save less. Thus, it is argued that consumption is a better base for taxation than income since it treats equals equally. Not all economists accept this argument, but the case is a strong one if you are willing to take a long-run view of tax equity, rather than comparing tax burdens in a single year.

One equity problem in actually adopting a personal consumption tax is the transition from an existing income tax to a consumption tax. How should a newly implemented consumption tax treat those who have saved in the past and expect to consume the principal amount later with no further tax on that sum? Consider Barney's position under the income tax in Table 15–8. If a consumption tax were introduced in year 2, when Barney consumed his saving, he would have to pay a tax of much more than $160 in year 2. This extra taxation only compounds the unfairness of the income tax because Barney already paid $4,000 in taxes in year 1. Since savers have already paid income taxes on the amount they saved, taxing the same sum again when consumed would be unfair under any view of tax equity.

The case for a consumption tax is strongest when we are designing a tax system starting with a clean slate. When an income tax is already in place, however, the transition to a consumption tax raises the difficult issue of equity for those with accumulated savings. Although some provision can be made for this situation, it may be difficult to do so fairly and at low administrative cost.

Efficiency

As we have seen, an income tax distorts two important types of economic decisions. First, it distorts labor supply choices. Second, it distorts the saving decision since the after-tax return to saving is lower than the before-tax rate of return. A consumption tax also distorts labor supply choices since people work not for wages per se but for the consumption that wages make possible. A consumption tax, however, does not distort the saving decision.

Refer back to Table 15–8 and note how the consumption tax affects Barney. Barney could have consumed $16,000 in year 1 and nothing in year 2 (as Alma did), but by reducing consumption by $8,000 in year 1, Barney is able to consume $8,800 one year later. Since the interest rate is 10 percent, each dollar of reduced consumption in year 1 makes possible $1.10 of increased consumption in year 2. Taxing consumption at the same rate in both years does not alter the relative price of future consumption compared with that of present consumption. A consumption tax does not drive a wedge between market and net rates of interest, as an income tax does.

We have already discussed how taxes that reduce the net return to saving produce a welfare cost by distorting the choice between present and future consumption. A consumption tax avoids this welfare cost. We cannot, however, conclude that a consumption tax is thus superior to an income tax. Since consumption is a smaller tax base than income is, higher tax rates must be used to raise the same revenue under a consumption tax. It is possible that this arrangement will make the labor supply distortion of the consumption tax greater than that of the income tax. This result is not certain, however. The consumption tax taxes the labor used to finance current consumption more heavily than the income tax does, but it taxes the labor used to finance future consumption less heavily since the return to saving is not taxed. Since people work to provide both current and future consumption, a consumption tax may not distort labor supply more than an income tax does.

Whether a consumption tax has a lower overall welfare cost than an income tax does depends on the relative degrees of responsiveness of labor supply and saving to taxation. If labor supply is relatively unresponsive to taxation but saving is quite sensitive, then the consumption tax is the more efficient alternative. In view of our earlier discussion, it is clear that we cannot be certain whether this conclusion is correct, given the available empirical evidence. But the recent research findings of large welfare costs from the taxation of the income from saving have convinced many economists that a consumption tax is worth a try.

Review Questions and Problems

1. For each category of tax shown in Table 15–1, explain why it has the particular pattern of incidence shown. In other words, what features of the tax, what theoretical analysis, and what characteristics of the data combine to produce these rates?

2. What tax in the U.S. tax system is the most progressive? What tax is the least progressive? In what ways do your answers depend on the theoretical analysis of the taxes' incidence?

3. One recent study estimated that the compensated labor supply elasticity (an average for all groups) of U.S. workers is approximately 0.7. Do you find this estimate plausible? Why or why not? If correct, what does it imply about the size of the welfare cost caused by the labor supply distortions?

4. Use the formula in the text to calculate the welfare cost caused by the labor supply distortion for each of the following two workers:
   a. Worker A, who earns $25,000, pays total taxes on labor income of $5,000, faces an effective marginal tax rate of 30 percent, and has a compensated labor supply elasticity of 0.3.
   b. Worker B, who earns $75,000, pays total taxes on labor income of $25,000, faces an effective marginal tax rate of 50 percent, and has a compensated labor supply elasticity of 0.3.

5. Can the welfare cost of a tax caused by labor supply effects be greater than the tax revenue collected from a worker? If so, use a diagram to illustrate this result, and also illustrate it using the formula in the text.

6. What factors determine the size of the marginal welfare cost of a tax on labor earnings?

7. "We must cut taxes on capital income in order to get the country growing again." Discuss.

8. How will the incidence of a tax on capital income be affected if the tax leads to a reduction in the level of investment? (Remember that our analysis of the corporation income tax assumed that the amount of capital was not affected by the tax.)

9. The maximum amount of revenue that can be raised is lower for a progressive tax than for a proportional tax. True or false? (Try to adapt Figure 15–6a to compare the two taxes.)

10. Why are tax rate reductions for the wealthy less likely to reduce the tax revenue collected than are tax rate reductions for middle-income taxpayers? Suppose that the tax rates could be reduced by 25 percent for those with incomes above $100,000 without any loss of revenue. Would you favor this tax cut?

11. "A tax on income is fairer than a tax on consumption because income is a broader measure of the taxpayer's ability to pay." True or false? Explain.

Supplementary Readings

BOSKIN, MICHAEL J. "Tax Policy and Economic Growth: Lessons from the 1980s." *Journal of Economic Perspectives,* 2:71–97 (Fall 1988).

BOSWORTH, BARRY P. *Tax Incentives and Economic Growth.* Washington, D.C.: The Brookings Institution, 1984.

BROWNING, EDGAR K. "On the Marginal Welfare Cost of Taxation." *American Economic Review,* 77:11–23 (Mar. 1987).

FELDSTEIN, MARTIN S. "The Welfare Cost of Capital Income Taxation." *Journal of Political Economy,* 86(2), Part 2:S29–S52 (Apr. 1978).

———. *Capital Taxation.* Cambridge, Mass.: Harvard University Press, 1983.

FULLERTON, DON, and DIANE LIM ROGERS. *Who Bears the Lifetime Tax Burden?* Washington, D.C.: The Brookings Institution, 1993.

LINDSEY, LAWRENCE B. *The Growth Experiment.* New York: Basic Books, 1990.

MIESZKOWSKI, PETER. "The Choice of Tax Base: Consumption versus Income Taxation." In Michael J. Boskin, ed., *Federal Tax Reform.* San Francisco: Institute for Contemporary Studies, 1978, pp. 27–53.

PAYNE, JAMES L. *Costly Returns: The Burdens of the U.S. Tax System.* San Francisco: Institute for Contemporary Studies, 1993.

SEIDMAN, LAWRENCE S. "The Personal Consumption Tax and Social Welfare." *Challenge,* 23:10–16 (Sept./Oct. 1980).

SLEMROD, JOEL, ed. *Do Taxes Matter?* Cambridge, Mass.: MIT Press, 1990.

U.S. TREASURY. *Blueprints for Basic Tax Reform.* Washington, D.C.: U.S. Government Printing Office, Jan. 17, 1977.

Federalism

 HE UNITED STATES HAS A FEDERAL FORM OF government, with one central government, 50 state governments, and thousands of local governments. The existence of a multiplicity of government units raises a number of interesting questions. What is the rationale for so many different levels of government? Are some types of economic policies better carried out by local governments than by the federal government? How does the free movement of people and businesses among local government units affect their performance? These are a few of the questions that are considered in this chapter.

◆ ──

Overview of State and Local Expenditures and Taxes

A casual observer of contemporary affairs could easily believe that the federal government overwhelms lower levels of government in terms of its economic impact. In a sense this is probably true: The federal government spends almost 50 percent more than the combined expenditures of all state and local governments. If only domestic expenditures (thereby excluding national defense) are considered, however, state and local outlays are on a par with federal outlays. For many persons, the services provided by subnational levels of government are more important to their day-to-day lives than the services provided by the federal government.

Table 16–1 shows the major expenditures of state and local governments in 1990. Taking state and local governments together, total expenditures were $976 billion, or about $3,900 per person. The general categories of education and social services—income maintenance (generally, redistributive programs) together account for almost half of this expenditure. Other

Table 16–1   *State and Local Government Expenditures,
Fiscal 1990 (in $ billions)*

Function	Combined State and Local	State	Local
Education	$292.2	$ 75.8	$216.5
Grants to local governments	—	175.0	—
Social services and income maintenance	188.3	122.0	63.1
Transportation	70.6	37.8	32.8
Public safety	74.0	23.9	50.0
Environment and housing	70.6	14.3	55.4
Government administration	44.8	17.7	27.1
Interest on debt	49.7	21.5	28.2
Insurance trust expenditures	63.3	54.5	8.9
Utility expenditures	74.9	7.1	67.7
All other	47.4	22.7	25.6
Total expenditures	$975.9*	$572.3	$575.4

*Net of duplicative intergovernmental transactions.

Source: U.S. Department of Commerce, Bureau of the Census, *Governmental Finances in 1989–90* (Washington, D.C.: U.S. Government Printing Office, 1991), Table 8.

major types of expenditures included transportation (mainly highways), public safety (mainly police, fire protection, and prisons), interest on debt, and government administration, but none of these categories accounted for as much as 10 percent of total outlays. When we look at state and local government expenditures separately, we see that grants to local governments and social services–income maintenance expenditures are the largest categories for state governments, together accounting for half of all state outlays. At the local level, education is by far the single largest expenditure function.

Not all expenditures by state and local governments are financed from their own taxes. Some expenditure programs are partially or wholly financed by the federal government through grants (subsidies) given directly to lower levels of government. In 1990 the federal government made grants totaling $137 billion to state and local governments, thereby financing about 15 percent of the total expenditures of subnational governments out of federal taxes. These *intergovernmental grants* have become increasingly important in recent years, and their rationale and consequences are considered later in the chapter.

Sources of revenue for state and local governments are shown in Table 16–2. Although subnational levels of government use many of the same types of taxes as the federal government does, the relative importance of these taxes differs greatly. At the state level, general sales and excise taxes produce nearly half of total revenue. Individual income taxes have also become an

Table 16–2   *State and Local Government Revenue, Fiscal Year 1990 (in $ billions)*

Type of Revenue	Combined State and Local	State	Local
Taxes			
Individual income	$ 105.6	$ 96.1	$ 9.6
Corporation income	23.6	21.8	1.8
Property	155.6	5.8	149.8
General sales	121.3	99.7	21.6
Selective sales (excise)	56.6	47.4	9.2
Payroll	18.4	18.4	0.1
Other	38.9	29.7	9.2
Total taxes	520.1	318.9	201.2
Charges and miscellaneous	375.3	187.0	188.3
Intergovernmental revenue			
From federal government	136.8	126.3	18.4
From state government			172.3
Total revenue	$1,032.1*	$632.2	$580.2

*Net of duplicative intergovernmental transactions.

Source: U.S. Department of Commerce, Bureau of the Census, *Governmental Finances in 1989–90* (Washington, D.C.: U.S. Government Printing Office, 1991), Tables 6 and 15.

important source of revenue in recent years and now produce 30 percent of state tax revenue. By contrast, at the local level, the tax picture is dominated by the property tax, which generates three fourths of local tax revenue.

Taxes actually finance only about half of all state-local expenditures. The remaining funds come from "charges and miscellaneous" and intergovern- mental grants. The "charges and miscellaneous" category includes such rev- enues as college tuition, parking fees, sewage fees, license fees, and receipts from the operation of state liquor stores. Intergovernmental grants are par- ticularly important to local governments. Local governments received $191 billion from the federal and state governments as grants, and that sum was almost as large as the tax revenues raised by the local governments themselves.[1]

One important characteristic of our federal system cannot be shown in tables such as Table 16–1 and 16–2, which combine the accounts of all sub- national governments. This characteristic is the great diversity of tax and expenditure policies employed by the states and localities. Not all subna- tional governments use the same taxes, apply them at the same rates, or spend the same amounts on the various programs; they are independent

[1]For a comparison of expenditure and tax policies of the federal and state-local gov- ernments, see Tables 1–1, 1–2, and 1–3 in Chapter 1.

units making their own individual tax and expenditure decisions, and these decisions can and do vary considerably. Table 16–3 indicates the variation in state expenditures and taxes per capita among selected states in 1990. Taxes per person range from a low of $537 in New Hampshire to a high of $1,696 in Delaware; the national average was $1,211. Expenditures per capita are much higher (recall that charges and miscellaneous and federal grants also finance state expenditures), but there is still wide variation. New York leads the way with per capita expenditures of $3,287, more than double those of Texas. Some of this variation simply reflects the fact that average per capita incomes are higher in some states, so it is not surprising to find per capita expenditures and taxes higher in those states. Yet even when we consider taxes as a percentage of personal income, there is still considerable variation, as shown in the last column of Table 16–3. State taxes range from 2.7 percent of personal income in New Hampshire to a high of 9.1 percent in Delaware.

Even greater differences are found among lower levels of government. Table 16–4 shows taxes and expenditures per capita for selected cities with populations of 75,000 or more in 1990. Gainesville, Florida, and Decatur, Illinois, are apparently tax havens, with taxes per capita of $204 and $254, respectively. (These are city taxes only.) By contrast, New York City clearly deserves its reputation as a high-tax city, since its taxes per capita are $2,063.

The diversity in tax and expenditure policies among subnational governments is quite important. If all subnational governments chose identical

Table 16–3   *State Government Expenditures and Taxes, Selected States, Fiscal Year 1990*

State	*Tax per Capita*	*Expenditure per Capita*	*Taxes as a Percentage of Personal Income of the State*
Alabama	$ 945	$2,006	6.8%
California	1,459	2,650	7.5
Delaware	1,696	3,195	9.1
Florida	1,027	1,679	5.9
Indiana	1,101	1,878	6.9
Michigan	1,220	2,485	7.0
Missouri	965	1,627	5.9
New Hampshire	537	1,778	2.7
New York	1,591	3,287	7.6
Texas	866	1,532	5.5
All states	$1,211	$2,305	6.9

Source: U.S. Department of Commerce, Bureau of the Census, *State Government Finances in 1990* (Washington, D.C.: U.S. Government Printing Office, 1991), Tables 26, 27, and 29.

Table 16–4 **Taxes and Expenditures per Capita, Fiscal Year 1990, Selected Cities with Populations of 75,000 or More**

City	Tax per Capita	Expenditure per Capita
Montgomery, Alabama	$ 349	$ 453
Los Angeles, California	519	963
Hartford, Connecticut	1,376	3,537
Gainesville, Florida	204	1,092
Decatur, Illinois	254	422
Indianapolis, Indiana	533	1,237
Boston, Massachusetts	996	2,593
Albuquerque, New Mexico	318	1,307
New York City, New York	2,063	4,256
Austin, Texas	366	1,164

Source: U.S. Department of Commerce, Bureau of the Census, *City Government Finances in 1989–90* (Washington, D.C.: U.S. Government Printing Office, 1991), Table 6.

policies, there would be little reason to have a multitude of different governments.

Economic Advantages of Subnational Governments

To some people, it is an article of faith that a local government will perform more efficiently than a state government, and a state government more efficiently than the federal government.[2] Other people believe the opposite. Actually, what requires emphasis is that some governmental functions are more efficiently performed by lower levels of government, whereas other functions are carried out better by the federal government. For some types of policies, local government is better, but care is needed in determining exactly what policies are more suitable for local governments.

In our earlier discussion of market failure, we defined public goods and externalities and showed the potential efficiency gains from government policies. It is now time to recognize that there are frequently geographic or spatial dimensions to the provision of public goods. Consider, for example, the public provision of a police force in Richmond, Virginia. This police force provides benefits to virtually all Richmond residents, but very few benefits accrue to residents of Charlottesville, Virginia, and even fewer benefits, if any, to residents of College Station, Texas. There are *nonrival* benefits from the police force in Richmond, but they do not extend over the entire

[2]This section and the following one draw heavily on Wallace E. Oates, *Fiscal Federalism* (New York: Harcourt Brace Jovanovich, 1972), Chapter 1.

U.S. population. Instead, the benefits are concentrated mainly on people living in or near Richmond and diminish rapidly as one moves farther away.

Such a public good, with benefits concentrated geographically, is referred to as a local public good, as distinguished from a national public good such as national defense. Similarly, there are local externalities such as the pollution of a particular lake or stream. Note that whether a good is a local or national public good is really a matter of degree. Not all local public goods benefit only those who live in a specific locality (tourists and shoppers in Richmond may benefit from police protection in that city), and not all national public goods benefit everyone in the nation. Still, the benefits from some goods are far more limited geographically, and that is the essential point.

With respect to the provision of local public goods, it is possible for different communities to provide different levels of output. This is also true of other governmentally provided services that are not, strictly speaking, public goods at all. Because the preferences of residents are likely to vary from one community to another, a federal system of government makes it possible for consumption levels to vary with the preferences of residents. A community that wants (and is willing to pay for) a strong police force but no parks can have such a pattern of services without interfering with another community that prefers the opposite pattern of services. Thus, a federal system is capable of greater efficiency than is a system that provides the same level of government services to all citizens. In principle, a federal system of many subnational governments is able to provide a range of outputs that correspond more closely to differing preferences among communities than could a national government.

Figure 16–1 illustrates this advantage of subnational governments. Suppose that there are three communities, *A, B,* and *C,* and a local public good, X. The curves A_1A_2, B_1B_2, and C_1C_2 show the distribution of quantities of X preferred by the residents of each community. If a national government were to provide a uniform level of X to all communities, it would probably supply a level near the overall median at X_B. This equilibrium would be very unsatisfactory for those residents of communities A and C whose preferences are at the A_1 and C_2 tails of their respective distributions. By contrast, if we have independent governments in the communities, three different levels of output, for example, X_A, X_B, and X_C, would be provided. Community C, whose residents have a large demand for X, would thus get a larger output than would community A, with its smaller demand. This range of outputs possible when X is provided by local governments is likely to be more efficient than is a uniform level of output supplied by a national government.

In comparing the uniform level of provision, X_B, for all communities with different levels for the three communities, note that not all persons will be better off under the latter. In particular, residents of communities A and C whose preferences place them near the A_2 and C_1 tails of their respective distributions will be worse off when X_A and X_C are provided than when X_B is. This point brings us to a second major advantage of a federal system:

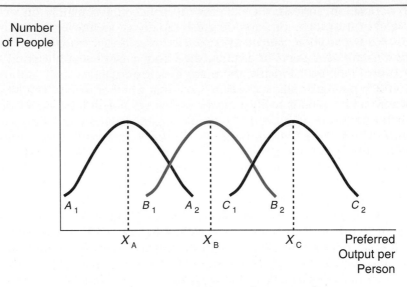

Figure 16–1 *Provisions of services by*
subnational governments

People are free to move from one community to another. In a federal system, it is possible for people to shop around for the community whose tax and expenditure policies are best suited to their needs. This is sometimes called "voting with their feet." Persons in community A who prefer X_B more than X_A (whose preferences are close to A_2) can move from community A to community B. In this way, an element of individual choice among various combinations of government policies is possible, an option that is not possible for federal policies.[3]

As a result of consumer mobility, one would ultimately expect residents of communities to have similar tastes for government policies. Some communities will emphasize good public schools and attract families with school-age children. Others will stress security and hospitals and tend to attract retired persons. Still others may emphasize low taxes (and few government services) for those who prefer private goods to government services. This process of consumers' choosing places of residence in response to differences in governmental services enhances the efficiency advantage of subnational governments. Of course, this process does not guarantee that every person will obtain exactly the type of government he or she would prefer. Within each community there will still be differences of opinion. Moreover, many factors in addition to government policies influence a per-

[3]This advantage of a federal system was first stressed by Charles Tiebout in "A Pure Theory of Local Expenditure," *Journal of Political Economy,* 64:416 (Oct. 1956).

son's choice of a location: The availability of jobs, proximity to friends and relatives, climate, and other factors play a role in a locational decision. Nonetheless, the possibility of "voting with one's feet" clearly enhances to some degree the attractiveness of a federal system as an institutional arrangement for providing government services.

A further advantage is that local government may be more responsive to the needs of its citizens. The political process in smaller government units may be more efficient than in larger units. Logrolling and pressure groups constitute less of a problem, and voters are likely to be more knowledgeable about how their tax dollars are spent. In short, when government is "closer to the people," it may possess fewer inherent defects as a decision-making mechanism. It is not obvious that this conclusion is always true, but it is widely believed to be so.

Finally, experimentation and innovation are likely to be greater in a federal system. With thousands of local governments, some are certain to be experimenting with new policies that are quite different from those used by the bulk of communities. Different approaches to police investigation, instruction in schools, and environmental policies will be tried. This process of experimentation can be beneficial even if some of the new policies prove to be failures. A successful policy innovation in one community can be adopted by other communities. If a new policy fails, other communities benefit from that knowledge too and can avoid a similar error.

Current examples of state and local governments trying new policy approaches are easy to find. In the last several years, a number of states have been modifying the AFDC program, especially with the use of diverse sets of work rules, in an attempt to get AFDC recipients off welfare more quickly. In education, governments are trying different systems for organizing and financing schools, including modified voucher systems and magnet schools. In the environmental area, over 1,000 communities are now using "pay-as-you-throw" garbage collection (up from only a handful in the 1980s), in which households are charged by the can or bag rather than being allowed to discard unlimited amounts of trash at a zero marginal cost. The goal, of course, is to reduce the amount of trash, and apparently this approach works; when consumers must pay to get rid of trash, they generate less.

It is not an easy matter, however, to determine whether a new policy is a "success" or a "failure." (Indeed, since preferences of citizens differ among communities, a policy that is successful for one community might be judged a failure by another community.) Nonetheless, a federal system provides the raw material for more direct comparisons among different policy approaches than is possible in a system in which one policy (of a particular type) applies to everyone.

In summary, a system of subnational governments possesses a number of advantages. Communities can provide different levels and combinations of services more in line with the preferences of their citizens, and citizens are free to move to communities that they feel are doing a better job. The political process may be more efficient at the subnational level. Experimentation and innovation are more likely, and direct comparisons among different approaches to economic problems are facilitated.

Economic Disadvantages of Subnational Governments

Despite its advantages, a system of subnational governments is likely to be ineffective in resolving certain policy issues. For example, if local governments are relied on to provide national public goods, the result is certain to be substantial inefficiency. Each community would be responsible for its own defense against foreign aggression, but all communities taken together would probably be underdefended. The reason is that a large part of the benefits from, for example, a missile system provided by one community accrue to residents of other communities. In determining how much to spend on missiles, each community would consider only the benefits its residents receive and ignore the benefits to nonresidents. The free rider phenomenon is relevant here, just as it is when we consider whether an individual has an incentive to contribute to the financing of a good that benefits other persons in addition to himself or herself. Because each community has an incentive to free ride, fewer resources would be devoted to defense than are justified by the interests of all persons in the nation considered together.

Efficient provision of a public good that benefits persons in all communities thus necessitates a central government. The key issue here is the geographic area over which persons necessarily benefit from provision of the good. Some goods, such as a sewer system or a police force, have benefits that extend over a limited area, and a city or county government can supply the good more efficiently because most, if not all, of the benefits and costs occur within one locality. Some environmental policies may have effects over larger regions and require state governments, but defense is clearly the province of the federal government. Thus, subnational governments will not be efficient in providing all types of government services.

A second area in which subnational governments will be relatively ineffective is in redistributing income. If one community embarks on a redistributive program by taxing its higher-income residents and transferring the proceeds to its poorer residents, two things will happen eventually to hinder the goal of providing assistance to the poor. First, wealthy residents can move to another community where taxes are lower. Second, poor persons in other areas can move to the community providing higher welfare benefits. As a result, the average per capita income in the community will fall, and it will become increasingly difficult to finance high welfare benefits.

Thus, *the very consumer mobility that is beneficial when subnational governments engage in nonredistributive programs tends to limit their use of redistributive measures.* This remains true even if those with higher incomes genuinely wish to help the poor. Each wealthy individual who leaves a community has a negligible effect on the extent to which the poor are helped, so it is in each person's interest to leave. If all wealthy persons leave, of course, there can be no redistribution. Here is simply the free rider problem once again.

Any significant degree of income redistribution must be carried out by a central government. Even in this case, there are limits because wealthy persons can always leave the country, and poorer immigrants may be permitted to enter. Mobility, however, is far more restricted between countries than between regions within a country, so a national government has greater latitude in carrying out redistributive programs. Moreover, insofar as our concern is with poor persons, regardless of where they reside within the nation, only a national program is capable of accommodating this goal by helping the poor in all regions.

This does not mean that local governments cannot adopt policies that benefit some residents at the expense of others, because they obviously do, but there are limits. In addition, the redistribution that occurs often takes a form that cannot be avoided by moving from the region. If a heavy property tax is placed on land owned by a wealthy person, the landowner cannot fully avoid the burden by selling the land; the sale price will be reduced because the buyer will pay less for heavily taxed property. The immobility of property, especially land, makes it possible for local governments to engage in some redistribution, but still only to a limited degree.

A third policy area in which subnational governments are relatively inefficient is in the pursuit of macroeconomic objectives. Although our primary concern here is not macroeconomics, it should be pointed out that subnational governments have little effect on employment and price levels within a specific region. These governments have no power to change the money supply, and any fiscal policies would be greatly diluted through the movement of persons and goods across jurisdictional boundaries. The national government must assume the responsibility for macroeconomic stabilization policy.

Certain government functions can therefore best be performed by a central government. Although we have been referring to the "advantages" and "disadvantages" of subnational governments, it should be clear that it is not necessary to choose between total reliance on one form of government or another. Instead, the real issue should be to determine which functions are best carried out by local governments and which by the national government. The optimal system is obviously one that relies on both types of government, with each performing the functions it does best. Our discussion should provide some guidance in determining what level of government is best suited for the performance of different types of policies. Still, there are many in-between cases that do not fit neatly into the categories we have considered. Some examples are discussed later in this chapter.

Tax and Expenditure Analysis

Principles

In earlier chapters we considered general principles pertaining to the analysis of expenditure and tax programs. Many of the points made remain relevant when we turn to the consideration of the fiscal activities of subnational governments. We still wish to ascertain, for example, how policies affect the distribution of income and the allocation of resources. In the context of subnational government policies, however, the framework of analysis is more complicated. Our earlier models entirely disregarded locational aspects of government policies. For national policies, this approach is generally appropriate: Where a business chooses to operate or where a consumer chooses to live, work, or purchase products is generally not influenced by a national policy. Instead, emphasis is placed on the level of output, consumption, or work effort because locational decisions are not affected. On the other hand, when local government policies are considered, locational decisions must be incorporated into the analysis. Decisions by businesses about where to operate or where to sell, as well as consumers' choices of where to live and work, may be affected and so need to be considered explicitly.

Local government jurisdictions are generally "open" economies in the sense that movement of persons and goods across jurisdictional boundaries is prevalent. In this sense, they are much like small countries engaging in international trade with neighboring countries. Goods produced in one locality are often sold ("exported") to persons in another locality, and residents often purchase ("import") goods produced elsewhere. The policies of local governments can often influence the flow of goods and services, as well as that of people and productive capital, across government boundaries.

If we could assume that people and productive resources were completely immobile among government jurisdictions, most of our earlier analysis would remain valid. For some specific problems, it may be reasonable to assume such immobility, not because people are unable to move but because many policies have little *net* impact. To take an example, if a community raises taxes to finance better public schools, how will this action affect locational decisions? If only the improved school system is considered, an incentive for families with children to move into the community has been created. At the same time, however, the higher taxes considered alone create an incentive for people to move away. With these two opposing influences, what will the net effect be? It is entirely possible that little or no net movement of people to or from the locality will occur: the *net* attractiveness of the community as a place of residence may remain unchanged. If this is the case, an analysis that ignores locational decisions will be a reasonable approach.

This highly simplified example suggests one important general principle: It is especially important to consider both sides of the budgets of local government policies in determining whether locational decisions will be affected. A balanced-budget approach to the study of local taxes and expenditures is frequently essential. It would be a mistake to conclude that a community with better public services is a more attractive place to live; it will also have higher taxes, so it will be more attractive only to those who consider the better services worth the additional tax cost.

Thus, in some situations there may be little net effect on locational decisions from local government policies. The difficulty, however, is to determine in which situations this is likely to occur. Just because the government spends and taxes more, it does not follow that no business or person will be led to relocate. For some individuals, the tax increase may impose costs in excess of the benefits derived from the expenditure, and the community will become a less attractive place. This will be true, for example, for people without children when school spending increases. The opposite may be true for other persons. In other words, it is not only the total benefits and costs for the community as a whole but also the pattern of individual benefits and costs that is relevant to locational decisions.

These remarks suggest that there may be a tendency for local governments to provide benefits to individual taxpayers in proportion to taxes paid. To see why, consider what would happen to a community that provided superb schools out of property taxes levied on all families. Clearly, families without children would be paying taxes and receiving no benefits. They might leave the community, and only those who wanted and were willing to pay the required taxes would stay. Thus, the community would end up with those who felt the schools were at least worth their tax cost. Alternatively, to avoid the departure of dissatisfied taxpayers, the community could use some of the tax revenue to provide services to those without children. In either case, the end result would be that all families would receive benefits roughly in line with their tax costs. This conclusion reflects the difficulty that local governments have in redistributing income, that is, in using taxes from some people to provide benefits to other people. As suggested earlier, there is probably only a weak tendency of this sort, but it does perhaps have some effect on expenditure and tax patterns of subnational government units.

Locational decisions are emphasized basically because they represent the one really new element in the study of state and local government finances. Efficiency requires not only appropriate output decisions but also appropriate locational decisions—and the latter are more strongly affected by policies of subnational governments than by policies of the federal government. As an example, an excise tax at the national level only reduces output, but at the local level it can have additional effects. Consider an excise tax on liquor in one state. A consumer may stock up in a neighboring state or city where liquor is untaxed or less heavily taxed. The cost of time and transportation is then a welfare cost of the local excise tax—a distortion that is quite different from, and in addition to, that produced by a federal excise tax.

Clearly, the analysis of the expenditure and tax policies of subnational governments can be complicated. Although much of our analysis in earlier chapters remains valid, this analysis must sometimes be amended to incorporate influences on locational decisions. There are no simple rules to lead us to the correct conclusions in all cases. Perhaps the best advice is simply always to consider how locational decisions will be affected by any policy being examined.

The mobility of goods and services across governmental boundaries is also relevant because of what it implies for price elasticities of supply and demand for various products and inputs. In general, price elasticities are likely to be higher when submarkets within particular localities are considered. For example, if the price received by producers of ball-point pens in Michigan is reduced sharply by a tax (and the price is unchanged in other states), pen producers have an incentive to leave Michigan. This outcome suggests a high price elasticity of supply within the state. Similarly, if a retail sales tax raises consumer prices sharply in some city, sales will fall significantly if consumers shop in other communities or by mail. Such a result once again implies a high price elasticity of demand.

High price elasticities have important implications for the tax and expenditure policies adopted by subnational governments. Price elasticities are not, however, high for all products and inputs. For example, land cannot move (it is in perfectly inelastic supply), and structures cannot move in the short run. Thus, it is not surprising that local governments rely heavily on property taxes as a source of revenue. Similarly, Texas and Oklahoma have been able to tax oil production at high rates without fear of their tax base's migrating to another state.

The Birth of an (Illegal) Industry[4]

Both state and local governments frequently impose excise taxes, and cigarettes are among the most important items that are most often subjected to these taxes. If all tax rates on cigarettes were the same, the effects would be the same as for a national excise tax, as analyzed in Chapter 10, except that revenue would accrue to states approximately in proportion to the cigarette consumption in each state. States, however, have chosen to tax cigarettes at different rates, and the result is a substantial variation in cigarette prices from state to state.

The differences in cigarette prices among states has another consequence too: namely, to create incentives for consumers in high-tax states to take advantage of the lower prices in low-tax states. One common way for consumers to react to the cigarette tax differential is to load up on cigarettes when they travel in low-tax states. This activity is probably a minor problem,

---

[4]This section draws on Carl P. Simon and Ann D. Witte, *Beating the System: The Underground Economy* (Boston: Auburn House, 1982), Chapter 2.

since few consumers regularly travel from New York (a high-tax state) to North Carolina (a low-tax state). More enterprising individuals, however, have found a way to take advantage of economies of scale in transportation and operate on a larger scale by smuggling cigarettes by the truckload. All that is necessary is to rent a truck, drive to a low-tax state, and purchase cigarettes from a legitimate cigarette wholesaler or retailer. After the individual returns to a high-tax state, the cigarettes are sold to wholesalers or retailers there. Although it is illegal, this activity can be quite profitable. For example, it is possible for the cigarette smuggler to make $8,000 per trip on the New York–North Carolina run using a 1-ton panel truck.

The incentive to engage in cigarette smuggling is related to the spread in tax rates between states. Smuggling on a large scale was not a serious problem in the 1950s, when the tax rate differences were relatively small. By 1965, however, state tax rates on cigarettes varied between $0 and $0.09 a pack, and that offered an opportunity for substantial profit. Apparently, the cigarette smuggling industry began to grow rapidly in the 1960s. By 1976, the differential in tax rates had widened even more, ranging from $0.02 a pack in North Carolina to $0.21 a pack in Massachusetts and Connecticut, spurring greater growth in cigarette smuggling. It is estimated that over 2 billion packs of cigarettes were smuggled in 1975. One expert suggests that cigarette smuggling is second only to selling narcotics as a source of funds to organized crime.[5] Naturally, such estimates of the extent of illegal activity must be recognized to be subject to considerable error, but the evidence suggests that cigarette smuggling is a big business.

Although the price elasticity of demand for cigarettes is low, it is not low for sales within a single state when the price there differs greatly from that in other states. The extent of cigarette smuggling is evidence of this fact. Legal sales of cigarettes in high-tax states have fallen sharply, at an estimated cost in lost revenue of $391 million in 1975. Conversely, tax revenues in three (low-tax) states (Kentucky, New Hampshire, and North Carolina) have increased significantly since smugglers purchase most of their cigarettes there.

Evaluation of this side effect of state tax policies is difficult since some states gain and others lose. From a national point of view, there is a loss in state tax collections, but in part this "loss" is just a transfer of income to consumers and smugglers. To the extent that the smugglers' transportation costs are no higher than the legal transportation costs, there is no welfare cost on this score, and there could actually be a welfare gain if the effective price spread between states were narrowed as a result of the smuggling. But the enforcement costs of government and the costs that smugglers incur to avoid apprehension should not be ignored.

From the viewpoint of the individual states, however, cigarette smuggling should serve as a warning: Taxing goods that are easily transported across

---

[5]Morris Weintraub, "The Bootlegging of Cigarettes Is a National Problem," *1966 Proceedings of the National Tax Association,* pp. 21–22.

state boundaries at rates higher than those of other states may produce little revenue and a great deal of illegal activity.

Washington, D.C., Learns a Lesson

In August 1980 city officials of Washington, D.C., hard pressed for tax revenues, levied a 6 percent excise tax on the sale of gasoline. This tax was added to an already existing $0.10-per-gallon tax. As a result of the added 6 percent levy, the price of gasoline rose by about 6 percent in Washington, making it well above the gasoline prices in the neighboring Virginia and Maryland suburbs.

Not surprisingly, except perhaps to officials in Washington, the higher price of gasoline in Washington led many motorists to fill their tanks outside the city limits. Within three months, the amount of gasoline sold in Washington had fallen by 33 percent. With a 6 percent price increase producing a 33 percent quantity reduction, the implied price elasticity of demand was about 5.5—and this was only the short-run response. (By contrast, the nationwide price elasticity of demand has been estimated to be in the 0.5 to 1.5 range.) Additional tax revenue produced by the 6 percent tax fell well below expectations. Although the 6 percent tax added to the earlier $0.10 per gallon levy represented an 80 percent increase in the tax rate, tax revenues went up only by about 20 percent because of the sharp reduction in quantity. In the longer run, it is quite possible that gasoline tax revenues might actually have declined. For this particular tax, the 6 percent rate increase was apparently enough to move the city close to the revenue-maximizing point on the Laffer curve. (Recall that with high elasticities of demand and/or supply, relatively low tax rates can place you on the upper part of the Laffer curve.)

The 6 percent gasoline tax was repealed in Washington, D.C., in December 1980. At that time Mayor Marion Barry cited "overwhelming evidence" that the tax had not worked and that it has "caused undue hardship both on the consumers of gas . . . and those who operate retail gas businesses."[6]

Special Topics in State-Local Public Finance

Tax Competition

It is helpful to think of subnational governments as being in competition with one another. They provide public services to their residents in return for taxes. Because all communities do this, each community must offer its public services on terms sufficiently attractive to induce people and business to locate there. If any community provided deplorable services in return for exorbitant taxes, it would find its tax base eroding as people moved elsewhere. Each community is therefore subject to competition from other sub-

---

[6]"Barry Asks Gasoline Tax Repeal," *Washington Post* (Nov. 25, 1980), p. A1.

national governments. Just as with competition among private business firms, we would normally expect competition among governmental units to have a beneficial influence by inducing communities to provide a mix of services in line with the preferences of its citizens.

It is sometimes held, however, that one aspect of the competition among governmental units leads to inefficient results. Business investment in a community may be deterred by an excessive level of taxation; consequently, government officials are often reluctant to increase taxes for fear of driving away part of their tax base. Competition among neighboring communities may lead them to hold down taxes to maintain a favorable climate for business. Many local government officials believe that this "tax competition" results in suboptimal expenditures, arguing that tax competition enters into the war between communities for new industrial and commercial activities and that each competing community avoids making otherwise justified tax increases for fear of decreasing its attractiveness to new business.

This oversimplified view of tax competition ignores the expenditure side of the budget. If a tax increase is justified, then the benefits from expanding public expenditures will exceed the costs of higher taxes. How could providing net benefits to the community make it less attractive to business? Generally, one would expect just the opposite. It is possible, however, that the tax increase exceeds the benefits that go to business; the increased expenditures may be on public schools, for example. If this is so, however, then the community is really attempting to redistribute income from business (more specifically, its owners or consumers) to other groups. As we have already seen, subnational governments are constrained in their ability to redistribute income.

If a tax increase is really worthwhile, it should be possible for the local government to raise taxes without driving business away. There are at least two ways to achieve this result. The first is to levy the taxes on the beneficiaries of the proposed expenditure policy. Taxes on business would then be increased commensurate with any benefits received. This approach may be difficult in practice if the government is legally constrained in the form of taxes it may use. For example, it may not be possible to increase property tax rates on homeowners to finance better schools without also increasing business property tax rates. In this case, the second approach may be followed: Combine the school expenditure with another policy that directly benefits business (police services, utilities, highways, and so on). Then businesses, paying higher taxes and receiving commensurate benefits, will not be driven from the community by the higher tax rates.

In principle, tax competition is no barrier to efficiency in local government operations. In fact, it is a spur to efficiency because it forces government officials to keep benefits in line with the taxes paid. It will inhibit localities, however, if they wish to tax some groups in order to finance benefits for other groups, a desirable limitation insofar as redistribution is intrinsically a function of the national government. It is understandable that local government officials do not like tax competition, but the public is probably better off because of the discipline it enforces.

"Impure" Local Public Goods

When considering public services provided by subnational governments, we saw that these services are sometimes local public goods with benefits limited to a certain geographic area. A further distinction should also be made. A good can have nonrival benefits for the residents of a certain area, but the benefits per person may depend on the number of persons in the area. If so, it is called an *impure* local public good. A comparison between weather forecasting and police protection should clarify this distinction. A weather forecast for a particular geographic area provides nonrival benefits for residents of that area. Moreover, more people can enter the area and benefit from the forecast without reducing the benefits to the original residents. The weather forecast is a *pure* local public good.

A police force is clearly different. If more people move into the area, police services will be spread more thinly over a larger population, so the benefits for the original residents from a given police force will decline. (It is sometimes said that this type of good is subject to "congestion costs" from an increased population.) The benefits are still nonrival for the population, but in this case the individual benefits depend on both the size of the police force and the number of people in the area. A police force is thus an impure local public good. It is clear that most of the services provided by local governments are more appropriately described as impure rather than pure local public goods. Fire stations, sewer services, and public schools are clearly impure in the sense that the larger the population is, the smaller the benefits per person will be for a given size facility.

There are important implications for the functioning of a system of subnational governments because of the prevalence of impure local public goods. Consumer mobility may be a mixed blessing in this setting. We have stressed that a person may move from community A to community B when the individual prefers the mix of public policies in the latter. The person will benefit from the move, but the original residents of community B may suffer from the congestion cost that the newcomer's presence imposes. When the welfare of all concerned is considered, it is not obvious that the relocation leads to a better allocation of resources on balance.

This discussion, however, ignores one point: When a person moves into a community, he or she will also normally pay taxes there. For example, the person's taxes may permit the police force to be expanded. If the tax payments are large enough, the expansion in the police force will be sufficient to keep benefits unchanged for the initial residents. The real question is whether the taxes that newcomers contribute to the local treasury are sufficient to cover the costs their presence imposes on the original residents. If so, consumers will take account of the true costs associated with their locational decisions, and consumer mobility will function to enhance the efficiency of a federal system.

Many of the fiscal problems of local governments result from the fact that their tax systems do not require all newcomers to pay taxes commensurate with the cost that their presence imposes on the community. This is because taxes generally are not (and perhaps cannot be) levied in proportion to the benefits received. For example, a family with five school-age children may purchase a modest home in a community, thereby contributing a modest sum in property tax revenues but imposing a much larger cost on the school system. To avoid the influx of newcomers who would consume more public services than they pay for through their taxes, many communities adopt restrictions on entry into the community. These restrictions take the form of zoning ordinances, limitations on the type of home that can be built, and so on. Although these restrictions are, in principle, inferior to taxing persons in proportion to the costs they impose on the other residents, they can contribute to efficiency when such a tax system cannot be implemented. Unfortunately, these restrictive practices can also be used to serve other ends.

Benefit "Spillovers"

Local government spending programs undertaken in one locality will sometimes confer benefits on residents outside its political jurisdiction. This phenomenon is called a *benefit spillover* because some of the benefits of the local expenditure policy "spill over" onto other localities. Benefit spillover is actually just a form of external benefit, but the literature on federalism uses the term *spillover,* presumably to emphasize its geographic aspect.

Pollution programs adopted by one subnational government often create benefit spillovers for people residing outside the community. If actions are taken to reduce pollution in a river and the river passes through a number of communities, persons residing in communities downstream will benefit from pollution-abatement programs adopted by an upstream community. Similarly, a welfare program adopted in one region will benefit the nonpoor in other regions if the nonpoor care about the degree of poverty in all regions of the country. These two examples illustrate how people living outside a community can benefit from the community's policies without bearing any cost. Consumer mobility among localities gives rise to a somewhat different type of benefit spillover. A person may reside in one area but purchase goods or work in another. Thus, tourists or shoppers will benefit from the police and highway services of a town they only visit. In this case, too, nonresidents receive some benefit, at no cost, from the expenditure programs of a community.

Benefit spillovers are significant for much the same general reason as external benefits are. The political process in a community is likely to be influenced only by the benefits received by its own residents. Local voters, in determining how large an expenditure to approve, will consider only the benefits they receive and disregard the benefits accruing to outsiders. Consequently, when benefit spillovers are substantial, expenditures are likely to be too small because they will reflect only the preferences of residents and not all of those who benefit from the policy.

Benefit spillovers often occur because the geographic range of benefits does not precisely coincide with the political boundaries of government jurisdictions. One way to deal with them, therefore, is to define political boundaries in terms of the area over which benefits accrue. Unfortunately, this method would generally require a different boundary for each of many government expenditure programs. Imagine, for example, having a regional government to deal with pollution, a government encompassing a smaller area to provide police services, a still different one for schools, and so on. When the administrative and decision-making costs of operating so many overlapping governments are considered, it seems clear that this approach is far from ideal. In any event, political boundaries have been determined historically and must, for most purposes, be taken as fixed.

Thus, benefit spillovers are to a degree inevitable. Because they imply some inefficiency in local expenditure decisions, the question is whether the inefficiency can or should be avoided. Several approaches are possible. One is to do nothing. If only a small share of benefits accrues outside the community, the magnitude of the inefficiency will be small (for the reasons discussed in connection with the measurement of welfare costs). A second approach is to rely on voluntary negotiation among governmental units. Because an inefficiency implies the possibilities of mutual benefits from coordinated action, neighboring communities often have incentives to undertake joint programs. When the number of affected communities is small, the "Coase theorem" is relevant: Local governments themselves have incentives to bargain until an efficient outcome is achieved. Although relatively rare, such bargaining among neighboring governments does occasionally take place.

If the benefit spillovers affect residents in a large number of communities, however, bargaining will be infeasible because of the free rider problem. In that event, it is possible for a higher level of government, such as the federal government, to improve matters by providing grants directly to lower levels of government. Properly designed, these intergovernmental grants can increase expenditures in cases in which benefit spillovers are important. Intergovernmental grants are considered in greater detail later in this chapter.

Tax "Exporting"

A portion of the taxes levied by a subnational government is sometimes borne by persons living outside the taxing community. In this event, taxes are said to be "exported" to outsiders. There are a number of ways in which locally levied taxes can have an incidence that places part of the tax burden on nonresidents. For example, an excise tax on a product produced in one locality but purchased by consumers in other parts of the country can achieve this result. (Care must be taken, however, not to tax the product so heavily that production will shift to another locality.) Similarly, the property tax may be applied to property owned by nonresidents that places a burden on outsiders. This outcome is commonly the result of business property taxation.

The federal government also facilitates tax exporting through provisions in its income tax laws. For taxpayers who itemize, certain state and local taxes are deductible in computing federal income tax liability. Thus, when a locality levies a tax on its residents, their federal tax payments are automatically reduced. For persons in the 28 percent federal tax bracket, for example, $1 in local taxes costs them only $0.72 because their federal tax falls by $0.28. This loss of $0.28 in available federal revenues is a burden on taxpayers throughout the country, so part of the local tax is effectively exported to federal taxpayers in general. In the same manner, the federal income tax exempts interest on the bonds issued by subnational governments. This exemption allows local governments to issue debt at lower interest cost; local taxpayers pay smaller taxes to finance interest payments on locally issued bonds, with the federal government losing revenue, as in the previous case.

There are a number of important consequences of tax exporting. For instance, the true distribution of the burden of locally supplied government services becomes more difficult to identify. Each person is a citizen of many local and/or state government units that export some of their taxes and so will to that extent gain. At the same time, each person is likely to bear some of the costs of government services supplied in other regions because a portion of these costs is exported to him or her. The net effect of these influences on the distribution of the tax burden is quite complex and uncertain.

Tax exporting also has important allocative effects on the tax and expenditure policies of subnational governments. Each local government, for example, has incentives to rely heavily on types of taxes that are borne largely by nonresidents. Some states have used this approach quite successfully. Take Florida, for example. As one tax expert in Florida observed: "We have done an excellent job of shifting a large portion of the tax burden to tourists—the tax system is designed to tax the service industries quite heavily."[7] More subtle effects also occur; states are encouraged to use progressive rather than proportional income taxes, for example. A progressive state income tax places a heavier nominal burden on those in higher federal tax brackets in which the net burden (after the deduction) is not as great.

Expenditure decisions of local governments are also affected. If 20 percent of local taxes are exported, every $1 in expenditures costs local residents only $0.80. The unit price of supplying government services is reduced, and the tax prices of local voters are 20 percent lower. At a lower price, voters will approve larger government expenditures. Expenditures are likely to exceed the point at which marginal benefits equal true marginal costs because the residents of a community bear only part of the marginal cost.

The tendency to overspend produced by tax exporting may be mitigated by the presence of benefit spillovers. Benefit spillovers alone will lead to a suboptimal level of spending because residents receive only a portion of the true marginal benefits. If benefits spill over to the same degree that taxes are exported, these two distortions, which operate in opposite directions, may exactly offset each other, fortuitously leading the community to make

[7]C. H. Donovan, "Recent Developments in Property Taxation in Florida: A Case Study," in Harry L. Johnson, ed., *State and Local Tax Problems* (Knoxville: University of Tennessee Press, 1969), p. 59.

efficient expenditure decisions.[8] Such a fortunate outcome should not be generally expected because benefit spillovers are restricted to certain policies, whereas tax exporting lowers the cost to residents of all expenditure policies.

Unlike benefit spillovers—where virtually nothing is known about the empirical significance of the phenomenon—tax exporting has been the subject of limited empirical investigation. Charles McLure examined the extent of tax exporting among states, finding that an average of 20 to 25 percent of state tax burdens were borne by nonresidents.[9] A more recent study estimates the degree of tax exporting by states at 17 percent on average.[10] Unfortunately, no study has examined the extent of tax exporting for lower levels of government.

John Bowman explored the effect of tax exporting on locally financed school expenditures.[11] He assumed that property taxes on commercial and industrial property were exported, whereas taxes on residential and farm property were not.[12] In a study of independent school districts in West Virginia, Bowman found that the degree of tax exporting was positively related to locally financed school expenditures. A 10 percent increase in the degree of tax exporting was estimated to produce a 15 percent increase in spending, suggesting a relatively high price elasticity of demand. To the extent that school districts would finance efficient levels of school expenditures if they bore all costs, this finding also implies that tax exporting leads to overly large budgets.

Despite its apparent importance, tax exporting has been given scant attention by economists. There has been little emphasis on how the inequities and inefficiencies introduced by this phenomenon could be overcome. Some partial remedies are obvious, such as eliminating the tax subsidies introduced in the federal income tax. Communities could still, however, adopt taxes that imposed some costs on nonresidents. An approach that might be worth considering is for the federal government to require subnational governments to finance all expenditures with a tax that cannot be easily shifted to nonresidents, such as a personal income tax. We leave it as an exercise for the reader to determine what disadvantages this proposal would have.

[8]This may be true in some cases with respect to tourists. Tourists often receive government services (e.g., police and highways) when they visit an area. If they bear a tax burden just sufficient to finance the services they enjoy, there is no *net* tax exporting.

[9]Charles E. McLure, Jr., "The Interstate Exporting of State and Local Taxes: Estimates for 1962," *National Tax Journal,* 20:49 (Mar. 1967).

[10]Donald Phares, *Who Pays State and Local Taxes?* Cambridge, Mass.: Oelgeschlages, Gunn and Hain, 1980.

[11]John H. Bowman, "Tax Exportability, Intergovernmental Aid, and School Finance Reform," *National Tax Journal,* 27:163 (June 1974).

[12]This assumption is unlikely to be fully true, but it can be argued that property taxes on commercial and industrial property are "hidden taxes" that residents do not realize they bear, even if they do. These hidden taxes would have the same political effects as exported taxes.

Lotteries as a Source of Revenue

A recent innovation in state government finance has been the introduction of state lotteries. Lotteries were prohibited by every state in this century until 1963, when New Hampshire adopted one. By 1990, 33 states were operating lotteries. Because most state constitutions prohibited lotteries, referenda or initiatives were often required to change constitutions so as to permit the states to operate lotteries. Public support for lotteries has been very strong, and the overwhelming majority of referenda have succeeded, with an average level of support of 65 percent of the voters. North Dakota has been the only state to turn down a state-run lottery.

State lotteries operate in different ways and offer a variety of games. The three most common games are instant lotteries, daily numbers games, and lotto. With instant lotteries, the player buys a ticket and scratches off the covering surface to reveal whether a prize has been won. The daily numbers game is a computerized imitation of the illegal game that has long been popular in many cities. With this game, the player selects a three- or four-digit number and a fixed payoff is made daily on a randomly selected winning number. With lotto, the player selects 6 numbers from among 40 to 50 possibilities, and the winning numbers are selected every week or every other week. If there is no winner, the prize money rolls over into the next game period. Jackpots under lotto have sometimes exceeded $100 million, with the winner (or winners; if more than one person selects the winning numbers, the jackpot is divided among them) often receiving front-page newspaper coverage.

Table 16–5 provides some information on the 9 largest state lotteries in operation in 1989, as well as overall figures for all 32 states with lotteries in that year. In 1989, total sales (the total amount bet) in all states together was $19.5 billion, or $108 per capita. Of this amount, 51 percent (the payout rate) was returned to the public in the form of prize money. In other words, the expected value of the prize on each dollar wagered is about 50 cents. The odds set by the states are not very favorable to the wagerers, although you can do somewhat better if you participate in the Massachusetts games, which return 60 cents in prize money for each dollar wagered. The payout rate from state lotteries is much lower than with other forms of commercial gambling. For example, horse racing has a payout rate of 81 percent, slot machines 89 percent, and table games at casinos 97 percent.

States gain revenue from the operation of lotteries by paying out in prize money and operating expenses less than total sales. Operating expenses average 10 percent of gross sales. Thus, on average, of each $1 bet, $0.10 goes to operating expenses, $0.50 to prize money, and the remaining $0.40 is net revenue for the state treasury. For the states that use them, lotteries provide on average between 3 and 4 percent of all state revenue. Thus, they are not a major source of revenue, but they do provide more revenue than

Table 16–5   *Lottery Sales and Distribution of Revenues, 1989*

State	Sales ($ billions)	Sales per Capita	Payout Sizes (percent)	Operating Costs (percent)	Net Revenue (percent)
California	$ 2.6	$ 89	50%	11%	39%
New York	2.0	113	47	7	46
Florida	2.0	156	50	12	38
Pennsylvania	1.7	137	51	8	42
Massachusetts	1.6	262	60	10	30
Ohio	1.5	141	49	12	39
Illinois	1.5	130	55	7	38
New Jersey	1.3	161	49	9	43
Michigan	1.2	126	48	10	42
United States	$19.5	$108	51%	10%	40%

Source: Charles T. Clotfelter and Philip J. Cook, "On the Economies of State Lotteries," *Journal of Economic Perspectives* (Fall 1990), Table 1.

the combined revenue from state excise taxation of liquor and tobacco, two sources of revenue to which lotteries are often compared.

Lotteries as Taxes

Economists tend to view lotteries as simply an implicit form of excise taxation imposed on a certain type of gambling activity. It is sometimes held that this view is incorrect since the introduction of lotteries (in contrast to taxes) does not harm anyone; in fact, the public presumably benefits since it chooses to play the games rather than spending money in other ways. Nonetheless, there is a very close analogy to excise taxation.

We can understand the sense in which a state-operated lottery is equivalent to excise taxation with the aid of Figure 16–2. In this graph, the quantity of output of a specific game is measured in dollar units; that is, the horizontal axis measures the total amount bet by the public. The vertical axis measures the price of placing a bet, defined as the *takeout rate*. The takeout rate is the fraction of the bet that is retained by the state. In other words, it is 1 minus the payout rate. If the government pays out 40 percent of sales as prizes, then the takeout rate is 60 percent; if it pays out 50 percent, the takeout rate is 50 percent. Thus, the higher the takeout rate, the worse are the gambling odds from the point of view of the wagerer. Just as in other markets, we expect people to purchase less (wager less) when the relevant price is higher, and this relationship is depicted with the demand curve in the graph.

We will assume that operating expenses of lotteries are constant at 10 percent of sales. Thus, the government could charge a price of T^* and cover its costs. However, the actual price charged is much higher, typically 0.5, as shown by T in the graph. At that price, Q_1 is the total amount bet. The takeout

Figure 16–2   *Lotteries as tax finance*

rate times this quantity, area TAQ_10, is the net sales after paying prizes but before operating expenses. Operating expenses are shown by area T^*BQ_10, so the net revenue after expenses and prizes is equal to area $TABT^*$. In terms of economic significance, this area is equivalent to excise tax revenue in a market where the tax per unit is set at TT^*.

Critics of the tax analogy emphasize that consumers are better off after the introduction of the lottery than before. This is true and is shown by the area of consumer surplus, CAT, in the graph. However, consumers would be still better off if the takeout rate were lower, and the only reason it is not lower is that states make it illegal for private firms to produce in this market. If private firms were permitted to operate, competition would drive the price down to T^* (or perhaps lower if operating expenses are smaller for private firms than for government-produced output), benefiting consumers with more favorable odds. State lotteries therefore have the same effect as legalizing competition in this market and then levying a tax of TT^* per dollar bet.

Viewed as a tax, how do lotteries stack up? According to critics of lotteries, they are far inferior to other sources of tax revenue. A primary criticism is that lotteries are regressive. The available evidence suggests that low-income households devote a much higher proportion of their incomes to purchasing lottery tickets than do high-income households, which implies that the tax is regressive relative to income.[13] (Some of our reservations regarding the regressivity of sales and excise taxes are relevant here, however, but there is no doubt that lotteries are more regressive than most if not all other taxes.) There is also the issue of horizontal equity; the implicit lottery tax falls only on those who participate in the lottery. According to one study of the Maryland state lottery in 1984, only 50 percent of those with incomes under $10,000 participated in the previous month.[14] Thus, the implicit tax falls heavily on some poor persons and not at all on others; the same is true at other income levels. (This objection, of course, can apply to any excise tax; not everyone consumes cigarettes or alcohol.)

The implicit lottery tax also does not fare well in terms of its efficiency. Although there have been no empirical estimates of its welfare cost (as shown by area *BAH* in Figure 16–2), there is reason to think that it is quite large relative to the revenue raised. One reason is that the implicit tax rate is substantially higher than the tax rate on cigarettes and alcohol. In addition, and perhaps more suggestive, is the fact that state lotteries are guided by one primary objective: to raise as much revenue as possible. This goal is often explicitly stated in state laws and in the annual reports of lottery agencies. If states are successful in achieving that goal, this result implies that they are on the peak of the relevant Laffer curve. As we saw in the last chapter, this outcome implies that the marginal welfare cost of the tax is then infinite, and there is no way to justify a tax that high if the only goal is to raise revenue to finance spending programs.

In our discussion so far, we have treated gambling just like any other commodity, and some people do not accept this evaluation. One line of criticism emphasizes that gambling is a vice and should not be encouraged. This explicitly paternalistic view might justify a higher price than would be appropriate if we accept the preferences of the wagerers as determining what is socially efficient. However, from a paternalistic standpoint, it would be best to outlaw gambling altogether. Moreover, it is clear that state governments do not try to discourage participation in their lotteries. Quite the opposite, in fact: They actively market the products, often in misleading ways. For example, they almost never tell customers what the odds of winning are, and they often overstate the value of prizes by referring only to the undiscounted sum of a series of annual payments. (For example, a prize consisting of 20 annual payments of $50,000 is referred to as a $1 million prize, even though the present value of these payments is worth less than half that sum.) It is clear that state lottery agencies do not try to discourage sales of their products, as they would if they were paternalistically motivated.

Given the number of people who think that gambling is immoral and should not be encouraged by state policy, and those concerned with having

---

[13]Some of this evidence is reviewed in Charles T. Clotfelter and Philip J. Cook, "Implicit Taxation in Lottery Finance," *National Tax Journal,* 40:533 (Dec. 1987); and Clotfelter and Cook, *Selling Hope: State Lotteries in America* (Cambridge, Mass.: Harvard University Press, 1989).

[14]Clotfelter and Cook, "Implicit Taxation in Lottery Finance," Table 2.

a policy that "preys on the poor," lotteries are likely to remain a controversial source of revenue for states. Economists also have objections, especially regarding the putative inefficiency of this source of revenue. Despite all of these objections, lotteries are very popular with a large share of the voters, and they have been growing rapidly in importance as a source of revenue.

Intergovernmental Grants

Intergovernmental grants are subsidies from cne governmental unit to another. Generally, these grants flow from higher to lower levels of government. In 1990, for example, the federal government made grants of $136.8 billion to state and local governments, and state governments made grants of $192.3 billion to local governments, with the bulk earmarked for education. Intergovernmental grants are an important source of revenue to lower levels of government, as documented by Table 16–6. Federal grants increased from $2.5 billion in 1950 to $136.8 billion in 1990 and represented about one tenth of total federal expenditures in 1990. Table 16-6 also shows the extent to which lower levels of government are dependent on grants as a source of revenue. In 1990, nearly one fifth of total state revenues was in the form of federal grants, whereas local governments received almost one third of their revenues from federal and state governments.

Table 16–6 *Intergovernmental Grants, Selected Years ($ billions)*

Year	Federal Grants to State and Local Governments	Federal Grants to States as a Percentage of Total State Revenues	State (and Federal) Grants to Local Governments*	Grants Received by Local Governments as a Percentage of Total Local Revenue
1950	$ 2.5	16.4%	$ 4.2 ($0.2)	27.5%
1960	7.0	19.4	9.5 (0.6)	27.2
1970	21.9	21.6	26.9 (2.6)	33.1
1980	83.0	22.3	81.2 (21.1)	39.6
1985	106.2	19.2	116.4 (21.7)	34.3
1990	136.8	18.7	172.3 (18.4)	32.9

*State grants include substantial amounts of federal funds that are channeled through state governments to localities.

Source: Data for 1950–1970 from Wallace E. Oates, "Fiscal Structure in the Federal System," Table 10–1, in J. Richard Aronson and Eli Schwartz, eds., *Management Policies in Local Government Finance* (Washington, D.C.: International City Management Association, 1981), p. 244. Reproduced with permission of the publisher. Data for later years from Department of Commerce, Bureau of the Census, *Government Finances in 1989–90* (Washington, D.C.: U.S. Government Printing Office, 1991).

Intergovernmental grants are of two basic types: conditional and unconditional. With conditional grants, the granting government restricts the way in which the funds may be used. In fact, conditional grants are analogous to in-kind subsidies that are made to governmental units. In contrast, unconditional grants can be spent any way the recipient government chooses, so they are analogous to lump-sum, or unrestricted, transfers. The overwhelming majority of intergovernmental grants are of the conditional variety, and we will concentrate on them.

Intergovernmental grants provide financing for a wide variety of programs. In the case of federal grants, more than half of the funds go for programs relating to income security (redistribution) and health. For example, Medicaid and AFDC are both operated by state governments but partially financed by conditional federal grants, as we explained in earlier chapters. Other federal grants are used for education, infrastructure, and transportation, among other purposes. In the case of state grants, by far the most important is assistance in financing local public schools.

Conditional Grants

Conditional grants must be devoted to certain specified uses. These grants are of two general types: matching and nonmatching. A *nonmatching grant* is a fixed sum; in contrast, the size of the *matching grant* depends on the recipient government's own expenditures on the specified program. For example, a matching grant formula might specify that the federal government will contribute 40 percent of the cost and the state government the remaining 60 percent. As can be seen, a matching grant is really a form of excise subsidy that is applied to government units rather than to individuals. Similarly, a nonmatching grant is a form of fixed-quantity subsidy.

The analysis of matching and nonmatching conditional grants closely follows our earlier analysis of excise and fixed-quantity subsidies. There is, however, one basic difference: The recipients of conditional grants are government units and not individuals. Thus, the response of the recipient government will reflect the workings of the political processes of the local governments. Consider the following example. Before the grant, local taxpayers had to pay $100 in taxes to receive school services costing $100 (ignoring tax exporting). With a 60–40 matching grant, local taxpayers can receive the $100 in services at a tax cost of $60 because the federal government contributes the remaining $40. Thus, the tax price of each taxpayer has fallen by 40 percent, and taxpayers will prefer a larger quantity at the lower price. Because all taxpayers will be affected in this way, it seems reasonable to suppose that the local political process will approve greater expenditures under the matching grant. In effect, the matching grant lowers the price of school services to residents of the community, so they purchase more—but the decision to consume additional units is a political one.

For ease of exposition, it will be assumed that the choices made by the political process of a recipient government can be represented diagrammatically by a set of community indifference curves. (Although this is a heroic assumption, the conclusions of this analysis can be demonstrated using a

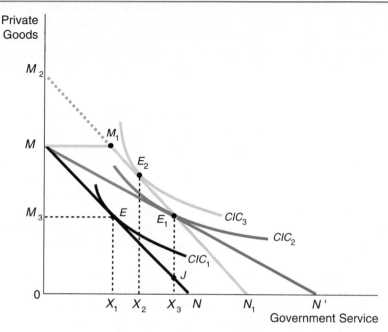

Figure 16–3 *Comparison of matching and nonmatching grants*

majority voting model.[15]) These are shown in Figure 16–3 as the *CIC* curves. The aggregate budget line of the community is *MN*. In the absence of any grant, X_1 of a particular government service is supplied at a tax cost of MM_3. A matching grant applied to this government service lowers its price to the community, and the budget line shifts to *MN'*. At the lower price, the community chooses X_3, and the total subsidy from the federal government is E_1J. A nonmatching grant of the same amount will shift the budget line to MM_1N_1. Under the nonmatching grant, the community will select a lower level of the government service, X_2. A nonmatching grant has the same income effect for the community, but it does not lower the per unit price of the service, as does the matching grant. Thus the matching grant leads to greater output of the goverment service.[16]

The community is better off with the nonmatching grant—at least in this case, in which the nonmatching grant is equivalent to an unconditional grant of MM_2. It should not be thought, however, that every member of the community will prefer the nonmatching grant. Taxpayers who prefer unusually large quantities of the government service will often be better off with a

[15]David Bradford and Wallace E. Oates, "Towards a Predictive Theory of Intergovernmental Grants," *American Economic Review,* 61:440 (May 1971).

[16]Note that this analysis is formally identical to our discussion of an excise subsidy in Chapter 4. The same qualifications and extensions discussed there apply here also.

matching grant. In this case, the use of community indifference curves tends to obscure the distributional effects among different members of the community. Nonetheless, the matching grant results in too much output of the government service, at least if the political process functions to attain the efficient output when residents bear the entire marginal cost of supplying additional units.

Evaluation of Conditional Grants   A major rationale for matching grants is the presence of benefit spillovers. If benefits from a local program accrue to nonresidents, the community may spend too little on its own (ignoring tax exporting). Welfare programs provide a possible example: Assistance provided to the poor by any state may benefit the altruistic nonpoor in other states. Insofar as states are relied on to provide welfare assistance, benefit spillovers provide a rationale for matching grants. In the context of welfare programs, however, the major issue is whether the national interest is sufficiently great to warrant a uniform federal assistance program rather than relying, even partially, on state governments.

To conform to the benefit spillover rationale, federal grants should be matching grants that lower the price to the state, with the federal share being dictated by the percentage of program benefits that accrue to nonresidents. For instance, if 20 percent of the benefits are received by nonresidents, lowering the price by 20 percent to the recipient government would be appropriate on efficiency grounds. Under most federal matching grants, however, the federal contribution is subject to a maximum amount, and if the recipient government spends beyond this level, it must bear the entire marginal cost. (Major exceptions to this rule are most grants for public welfare purposes.) The maximum amounts specified are frequently quite modest, with most states exceeding those levels. Therefore, grants do not lower the price to recipient governments at the margin and so do not induce them to take the spillover effects associated with the program into consideration. In terms of Figure 16–3, this type of grant produces a kinked budget line like ME_1N_1, and for governments that choose a point along the E_1N_1 portion, the grant is equivalent to an unrestricted cash grant.

An additional question is whether benefit spillovers are large enough to justify the share of the cost borne by the federal government. Since benefit spillovers can rarely be measured accurately, we are on uncertain ground. Consider, though, that the federal share of interstate highway construction costs is 90 percent; it seems unlikely that 90 percent of the benefits of an interstate highway in a given state go to nonresidents. Moreover, with respect to sewage waste-treatment systems, it seems unlikely that nonresidents receive 75 percent of the benefits; yet that is the federal share of their construction costs. Since in most federal grant programs the federal government's share of the costs is 50 percent or more, we can question whether spillover benefits are generally important enough to justify so large a share.

For these reasons, it is difficult to justify many existing grant programs on the grounds of spillover benefits. Another possible justification is redistribution. It is certainly true that many grant programs are structured to provide more assistance to poorer states or communities. In this case, the basic question is whether it is better to provide assistance to poor individuals or poor communities. In any nonpoor community there are generally some poor persons, just as there are some nonpoor persons in most communities that have low average family incomes. Thus, any redistribution from wealthier to poorer communities will in part harm the poor living in wealthier communities and benefit the nonpoor living in poor communities. It is arguable that it would be better to transfer income directly to poor persons and avoid this capricious outcome. If income was transferred directly to poor persons, they would still have the option of voting to use part of the transfer to finance improved local government services.

Federal Tax Deductibility and Subnational Governments

Federal taxpayers have been permitted to deduct state and local taxes on their federal individual income taxes since the income tax was introduced in 1913. Today this deduction represents the second largest deduction. A total of $129 billion in state and local taxes was deducted in 1989, at an estimated revenue cost to the federal government of approximately $29 billion. As this tax preference item has grown in importance over time, more attention has been given to the possibility of eliminating it. Many private analysts have recommended its elimination. To a limited degree, this was accomplished in the Tax Reform Act of 1986. That law eliminated the deduction for general sales taxes, but deductibility for income and property taxes remained.

The original justification for this tax preference was that the taxes paid to state and local governments were not really income to the taxpayers, since the funds were not available to pay federal taxes. Put slightly differently, it was (and still is) argued that a taxpayer should not have to pay a tax on a tax. This argument, however, has come under increasing scrutiny. State and local taxes are the costs that taxpayers pay for receiving services from subnational governments; those who pay larger taxes typically receive more in services. Viewed in this way, state and local taxes are not significantly different from taxpayer expenditures on clothes or food, except that tax payments are determined politically rather than individually. If state and local taxes are viewed as payments for government services (which are income to the recipients whether or not they are in the form of cash), equity calls for disallowing the deduction for state and local taxes.

Of course, this argument is not conclusive, so let us consider a specific proposal to end tax deductibility. Since eliminating deductibility would increase federal income tax revenue by about 6 percent, a careful evaluation requires that we specify how this revenue would be used. For the purposes of this analysis, suppose that we assume that the revenue would be used to lower the tax rates of the individual income tax. In other words, we would combine a broader federal tax base with lower rates so that there would be no net change in federal revenue. This result could be achieved in many ways, but let us assume that all marginal tax rates would be reduced proportionately.

In analyzing this proposal, we shall proceed in two steps. First, we shall tentatively assume that state and local government tax and expenditure policies are not changed and consider the effects of the change in the federal tax alone. Then we shall examine the implications of the program for the policies of subnational governments.

If the deductibility ends, federal taxpayers will pay higher taxes because of the broader tax base but lower taxes because of the lower rates. Overall, these effects will cancel out each other, but not necessarily for each taxpayer. In particular, it is important to note who uses the state and local tax deduction. Very few taxpayers with relatively low adjusted gross incomes itemize deductions (they use the standard deduction), but over 90 percent of taxpayers with AGIs over $75,000 deduct state and local taxes. Thus, ending the deduction will increase taxes primarily for upper-income taxpayers, whereas the lower tax rates will reduce taxes for all taxpayers. Taking these two elements of the policy together, it is clear that upper-income taxpayers will lose more when deductibility ends than they will gain from the lower rates, and the reverse will be true at the lower income levels. Thus, the policy will increase the federal tax burden on higher-income taxpayers and reduce it for lower-income taxpayers. However, within the income classes, eliminating the state and local income tax deduction will tend to benefit those who do not itemize at the expense of those who do.

Much discussion of this proposal tends to end at this point, but we must also consider the response of state and local governments to this change in federal tax policy. As noted earlier in this chapter, the deductibility provision in the federal tax results in subnational governments' exporting part of their taxes to the general federal taxpayer. By lowering the net cost of providing local government services to local taxpayers, deductibility probably increases spending by state and local governments. Several empirical studies have suggested that state and local spending may be increased by as much as 10 to 20 percent because of deductibility.[17] Thus, eliminating deductibility would reduce state and local spending and also state and local taxes.

A reduction in subnational taxing and spending is relevant for both efficiency and equity. From an efficiency standpoint, if deductibility leads to overexpansion in subnational spending because the local residents do not bear all of the costs of their local government spending programs, then eliminating deductibility will improve efficiency. From an equity standpoint, the distributional effects of contractions in subnational taxing and spending must be considered. If subnational taxpayers benefit in proportion to the subnational taxes they pay, then the contractions will not change the distribution of income. However, if state and local government policies tend to

---

[17]See Edward M. Gramlich, "The Deductibility of State and Local Taxes," *National Tax Journal,* 38:447 (Dec. 1985), and the other research cited there.

redistribute income downward, on balance, as seems likely, a contraction will redistribute income from low-income to upper-income taxpayers. Note that this shift tends to offset the redistribution accomplished at the federal level.

A second possible response by state and local governments is also worth considering: The governments may make their tax systems less progressive (or more regressive). Since deductibility is utilized mainly by high-income taxpayers, state and local governments may place a larger share of their taxes on these taxpayers, knowing that they will bear only part of the cost. In short, deductibility gives subnational governments an incentive to use more progressive tax structures, so eliminating deductibility will induce them to shift part of their tax burdens to the lower income classes. This shift also tends to offset the distributional effect at the federal level.

Now let us put the two parts of the analysis together. At the federal level, eliminating deductibility tends to resdistribute income in favor of the lower income classes. However, we now see that the responses of the state and local governments are likely to have the opposite effect. Overall, determining how the elimination of deductibility will affect the distribution of income among income classes is not easy. From the point of view of horizontal equity, there is likely to be a gain from using a broader federal tax base. In addition, there may be an efficiency gain from the reduced spending by state and local governments. There is little doubt, however, that taxpayers who prefer more government spending, particularly if they reside in high-tax states, would lose from the reform.

Review Questions and Problems

1. What are the major principles that should be taken into account in deciding whether a particular government function is best handled by the federal, state, or local (city or county) government?

2. For each of the following economic activities, explain whether it should be carried out by the federal government, state government, local government, or private sector: national defense, police protection, fire protection, medical research, elementary education, college education, welfare, and highway construction.

3. How will the analysis of a general sales tax differ if it is used by a local government rather than by the federal government?

4. "Since cigarettes are in inelastic demand, a tax on cigarettes is a good tax for a state government to use." True or false? Explain.

5. Explain how tax exporting and benefit spillovers affect the spending and taxing decisions of subnational governments.

6. Suppose that a locality increases its property taxes and uses the proceeds to increase spending on public schools. What effects is this policy likely to have on the locational decisions of households?

7. What policies of the federal government encourage greater spending by subnational governments? What is the rationale for these policies?

8. Should the federal government use lotteries as a method of raising revenue to reduce the federal deficit?

9. Explain why lotteries are often held to be both inefficient and inequitable ways for state governments to raise revenue. In view of these arguments, why do you think lotteries are so popular with the public?

10. Sometimes matching grants impose limits on the amount of the subsidy. For example, the federal government might cover half of the cost of a certain policy, but only up to $10 million; beyond that, the local government must bear all of the additional cost. How does this type of matching grant affect the budget line of the recipient community?

11. Both the federal government and (more important) state governments provide grants to local governments to help finance public schools. What is the justification, if any, for these grants?

12. How would a community composed entirely of upper-income households be affected by ending the deductibility of state and local taxes?

13. In the absence of federal tax deductibility, suppose that a local community uses the benefit theory of taxation to distribute the costs of local spending policies (see Figure 2–1 and the accompanying discussion in Chapter 2). Then the federal government introduces deductibility, but only a minority of local taxpayers itemize their deductions. Explain how this situation will affect the community's tax and spending policies, assuming that it continues to apply the benefit theory of taxation.

Supplementary Readings

BREAK, GEORGE F. *Financing Government in a Federal System.* Washington, D.C.: The Brookings Institution, 1980.

CLOTFELTER, CHARLES T., and PHILIP J. COOK. "On the Economics of State Lotteries," *Journal of Economic Perspectives,* 4:105–119 (Fall 1990).

FISHER, RONALD C. *State and Local Public Finance.* Glenview, Ill.: Scott, Foresman, 1988.

KENYON, DAPHNE A., and JOHN KINCAID, eds. *Competition Among States and Local Governments.* Washington, D.C.: Urban Institute Press, 1991.

OATES, WALLACE E. *Fiscal Federalism.* New York: Harcourt Brace Jovanovich, 1972.

RUBINFELD, DANIEL L. "The Economics of the Local Public Sector." In Alan J. Auerbach and Martin Feldstein, eds., *Handbook of Public Economics,* Vol. 2. New York: North-Holland, 1987, pp. 571–645.

STIGLER, GEORGE J. "The Tenable Range of Functions of Local Government." In Edmund S. Phelps, ed. *Private Wants and Public Needs,* rev. ed. New York: W. W. Norton, 1965, pp. 167–176.

Consumer Choice Theory

For students unfamiliar with analysis using budget lines and indifference curves, or for those in need of a quick review, this appendix contains some fundamentals.[1] The treatment is brief, with emphasis on certain concepts that are relevant to the analyses developed throughout the text. Our purpose is to present a simple model of consumer behavior that permits us to determine how consumer choices among goods are affected by objective circumstances such as prices, incomes, and subsidies. The goods can be anything—beer, shoes, or public schooling. We begin by explaining the way a consumer's tastes or subjective preferences can be shown using indifference curves, and then we consider how objective conditions such as income can be represented. Next, the consumer's preferences and income are treated jointly in a single model. Finally, several implications of the model are examined.

The Consumer's Preferences

Consumers have different tastes or preferences, which will be reflected in their consumption decisions. The consumption of goods and services provides satisfaction or utility to the consumer, and the consumer will arrange

---

[1]For a more detailed and comprehensive discussion of indifference curve analysis, see an intermediate microeconomics textbook, for example, Edgar K. Browning and Jacquelene M. Browning, *Microeconomic Theory and Applications,* 4th ed. (New York: HarperCollins, 1992).

personal consumption to maximize satisfaction. To understand how the consumer determines what combination of goods will maximize his or her well-being, we begin by making the following assumptions about the consumer's preference patterns:

1. The consumer is able to rank different combinations or bundles of goods in terms of desirability. For example, suppose that the consumer is confronted with three bundles of goods: one hamburger and one beer, three hamburgers and two beers, and two hamburgers and four beers. From among these groupings, the consumer is able to decide whether he or she prefers the third bundle to the second, is indifferent among them, prefers the second to the first, and so on. To say that a consumer is indifferent between two bundles of goods means that either bundle will yield the same level of utility and that the consumer has no preference for one over the other. The consumer will either prefer one bundle to another or be indifferent between them.
2. The consumer's preferences are transitive. If, for instance, there are three bundles of goods, A, B, and C, and the consumer prefers bundle A to bundle B and bundle B to bundle C, then it follows that the consumer will also prefer A to C.
3. The consumer always prefers more of a commodity to less. Referring to the hamburgers and beer in the example, the consumer would always prefer either the second or the third combination to the first because each of these involves more of both hamburgers and beer than the first alternative does.

Having made these assumptions, we can begin to develop our model.

Indifference Curves

Consumer tastes can be represented by indifference curves. To understand this concept, first consider the alternative bundles of goods listed in Table A–1. Assume that the groupings are deliberately arranged so that a con-

Table A–1	*Preferences for Food and Clothing*			
	(a)		*(b)*	
	Food	*Clothing*	*Food*	*Clothing*
A:	10	1	13	2
B:	7	2	10	3
C:	5	3	8	4
D:	4	4	7	5
E:	3	6	6	7
F:	2	9	5	10

sumer, Kimberly, is indfifferent among them. In Table A–1(a), Kim is equally satisfied with 10 units of food and 1 unit of clothing, or 7 units of food and 2 units of clothing, and so on. Similarly, each of the combinations in Table A–1(b) is as desirable as any other. Note, however, in (b) that with the same quantity of clothing, more food is provided compared with (a). So, given the assumption that the consumer always prefers more to less, any combination in (b) will be preferred to any in (a).

These alternative bundles of goods can be represented as points on indifference curves. An *indifference curve* is a locus of points indicating different combinations of goods that yield the consumer the same level of satisfaction. In Figure A–1 an indifference curve, U_1, has been drawn to represent the alternative combinations of food and clothing detailed in Table A–1(a). Food consumed per time period is measured on the vertical axis and clothing consumed per time period on the horizontal axis. Thus, a point such as A represents 10 units of food and 1 unit of clothing. Kim is equally well off consuming any combination of goods shown on U_1.

Indifference curves have the following characteristics:

1. Indifference curves are convex. Typically, an indifference curve is fairly steep at the top and relatively flat at the bottom. Its shape is a function of the relative importance of the two goods to the consumer. Starting at the top of an indifference curve and moving down it, the consumer

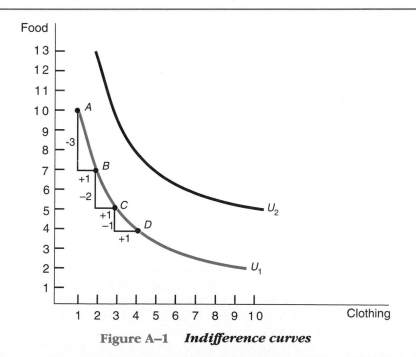

Figure A–1   *Indifference curves*

gives up food for additional units of clothing. At A, for instance, Kim has 10 units of food and 1 unit of clothing; at D Kim has 4 units of food and 4 units of clothing. Recall that at either point she is equally well off.

At the top of the curve Kim has a substantial amount of food and very little clothing; to move from point A to point B (less food and more clothing), Kim would be willing to give up 3 units of food for another unit of clothing. As she moves down the curve to the right, however, the situation changes. Kim has relatively more clothing and relatively less food. To move from C to D, for instance, Kim would be willing to give up a maximum of only 1 unit of food for an extra unit of clothing. If she had more food and less clothing, as at point A, Kim would have traded 3 units of food for another unit of clothing, but at point C she would be only willing to exchange 1 unit. The rate at which the consumer is willing to trade one good for another (while maintaining the same level of utility) is called the *marginal rate of substitution.*

The marginal rate of substitution (*MRS*) is shown in the diagram by the slope of the indifference curve. At point A, for example, the slope is $-3F/1C$, indicating that the *MRS* at that point is 3 units of food per unit of clothing. Note that the *MRS* is a measure of the subjective value of one good in terms of another. At point A, another unit of clothing is worth 3 units of food to Kim because that is the maximum quantity of food she will give up to acquire another unit of clothing.

Assuming that indifference curves are convex is equivalent to assuming that the *MRS* will decline as we move down an indifference curve; that is, the curve will become flatter since the slope measures the *MRS*. Basically, this is an empirical proposition regarding the nature of people's preferences. Although it may not always be true, it makes sense as a generalization. It means, for example, that Kim will give up *more* food to get another unit of clothing when she has a great deal of food and very little clothing (as at point A) than when she has little food and a large amount of clothing (as at point C). At A, clothing is relatively scarce, and Kim will give up 3 units of food for another unit of clothing; at C she has more clothing and less food, so an additional unit of clothing is less important to her, and she will give up only 1 unit of food for it.

2. Indifference curves that lie farther from the origin represent higher levels of utility or well-being than do those lying closer to the origin. So far, only one indifference curve has been discussed. Actually, a complete description of a consumer's tastes would involve an infinite number of indifference curves. Consider Table A–1(b) again. Recall that with all levels of clothing consumption, more food is provided than in Table A–1(a). This combination of goods is represented by the indifference curve U_2 in Figure A–1. Curve U_2 lies farther from the origin than U_1 does and represents a higher level of utility. A utility-maximiz-

ing consumer would prefer to consume *any* combination of goods on U_2 to *any* combination on U_1. Whether the consumer is able to consume at the desired higher level is determined by his or her income and the prices of the two goods, factors that will be considered shortly.

3. Indifference curves cannot intersect. If indifference curves intersected, our assumption of transitivity would be violated. Figure A–2 is drawn *incorrectly* so that two indifference curves cross. Let us examine the implications. Indifference curves U_1 and U_2 intersect at A. On curve U_1, points A and B yield the same level of satisfaction to the consumer because they lie on the same indifference curve. The same is true for points A and C on U_2. Therefore, C is as desirable as A and A is as desirable as B. This seems to imply that C and B are equally desirable. Note, however, that point B is clearly preferable to C because B contains more X and Y than point C does—and we have assumed that the consumer always prefers more to less. Point B cannot be preferred to C and have the same utility as C. Thus, intersecting indifference curves are inconsistent with our assumptions.

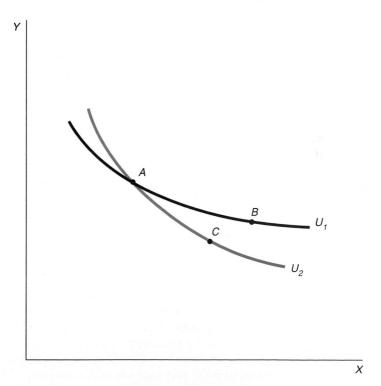

Figure A–2 *Intersecting indifference curves*

The Consumer's Budget

When using indifference curves to explain and predict consumer behavior, we must know more than the consumers' tastes. Because higher indifference curves correspond to higher levels of well-being, a rational utility-maximizing consumer will want to achieve the highest indifference curve possible. In maximizing well-being, however, the consumer is constrained by the level of money income. To want a villa on the French Riviera is not the same as being able to afford it. Even the wealthiest individuals have budget or income constraints because their income is not infinite. In addition to money income, the consumer must consider the prices of all relevant commodities. Price changes as well as changes in the level of the consumer's income will affect consumption patterns.

The Budget Line

Let us begin by assuming that our consumer, Kim, has an income of $1,000 per year and that she is considering the purchase of two goods, X and Y, with the price of X being $5 per unit and the price of Y being $10 a unit. If Kim spent her entire income on X, she could purchase 200 units ($1,000/ $5); if she spent her entire income on Y, she could purchase 100 units ($1,000/$10). In Figure A–3, the straight line MN connecting 200 units of X and 100 units of Y defines Kim's *budget line*. The budget line shows all combinations of quantities of X and Y that Kim can purchase per year. Kim can buy 200 units of X, or 100 units of Y, or various combinations of X and Y (e.g., 50 units of X and 75 units of Y or 100 units of X and 50 units of Y) that lie on the budget line.

The slope of the budget line is equal to the negative of the price ratio, P_X/P_Y (in this example $-\$5/\$10$, or $-0.5Y/1X$). The slope at any point shows how much of one good must be given up to get an additional unit of the other. For the prices assumed, if Kim wishes to consume 1 more unit of X (at a price of $5 per unit), she will have to spent $5 less on Y (and thereby purchase a half unit less because Y costs $10 per unit). Thus, the slope of the budget line is $0.5Y/1X$ at every point because to purchase an additional unit of X always necessitates consuming a half unit less of Y.

The position of the budget line depends on the size of the budget. If Kim's income increases, the budget line will be farther from the origin; if her income falls, it will be closer. This is illustrated in Figure A–4. We begin again with an income of $1,000, and the prices of X and Y at $5 and $10, respectively. The budget line, identical to the one derived in the preceding discussion, is the line MN. If income increases to $1,500, a new budget line will be defined by a line connecting 300X and 150Y, or $M'N'$; similarly, if income falls to $500, another budget line will be drawn joining 100X and 50Y. Note that the three budget lines are parallel. The reason is that the prices of X

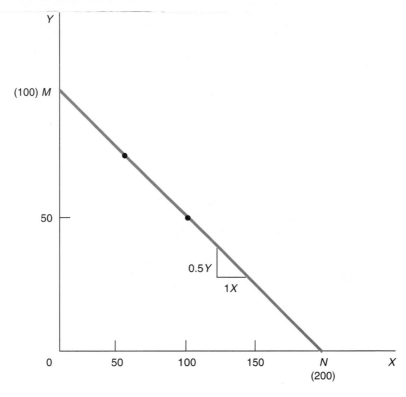

Figure A–3 *Budget line*

and Y have not changed, so the slopes (P_X/P_Y) of all three budget lines are the same.

In addition to changes in income, changes in the prices of goods affect the budget line. To illustrate, again assume that Kim's income is $1,000 and that the price of X is $5 and the price of Y is $10. The initial budget line is shown by the line MN in Figure A–5 connecting $200X$ and $100Y$. Now assume that the price of X falls from $5 to $3 per unit. To reflect this change, the budget line rotates to MN'. Point M ($100Y$) is unchanged because the price of Y is still $10; now, however, if Kim spends her entire income on X, she can purchase 333 units. The slope of the line has been affected, becoming flatter to reflect the lower price of X. (Originally, the slope was $-\frac{1}{2}$; after the price reduction, it becomes $-0.3Y/1X$.) Because the price of X is lower, Kim now has to give up only three tenths of a unit of Y (saving $3) to purchase 1 more unit of X. Alternatively, if the price of X increases to $10, the budget line will rotate toward the origin to MN'', with the steeper slope ($-1Y/1X$) reflecting a higher price for X (1 unit of Y must now be sacrificed

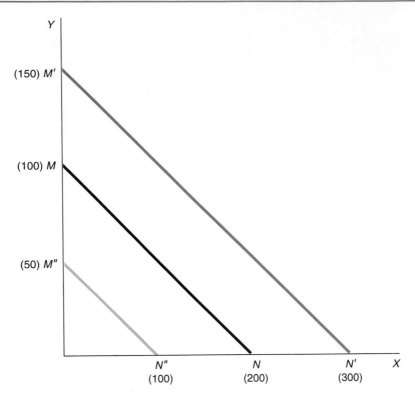

Figure A–4   *Income changes and the budget line*

to obtain an additional unit of *X*). *In this way, the slope of any budget line indicates the price of one good relative to that of the other.* At a lower price of *X,* the budget line is flatter, implying that *X* is now relatively lower priced than before—less *Y* has to be given up to purchase an additional unit of *X.*

The Consumer in Equilibrium

The budget line shows the combinations of goods from which Kim can choose, and the indifference curves show how Kim subjectively ranks all combinations of goods. It is assumed that the consumer will choose the most preferred combination of *X* and *Y* from among the combinations attainable. Consider Figure A–6. The set of indifferences curves, U_1 through U_3, reflects Kim's preferences. Curve U_3 is the most preferred among these three be- cause it represents the highest level of utility. The budget line, *MN,* identifies

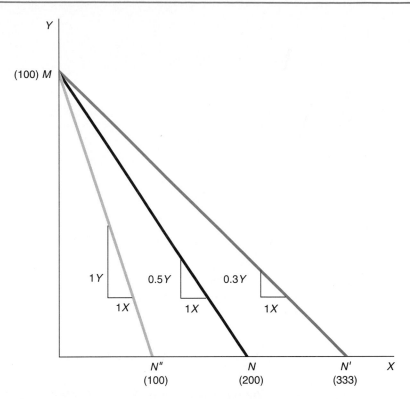

Figure A–5 *Price changes and the budget line*

the consumption options available to the consumer. Any point along *MN* (or below it[2]), such as *A* or *B,* represents a real consumption possibility. Points above the budget line, such as *Z,* are not feasible because Kim lacks the necessary income. Because Kim will seek the highest level of well-being possible given her budget, equilibrium will occur at *B,* where the budget line and U_2 are tangent. Kim will purchase $0X_1$ units of *X* and $0Y_1$ units of *Y.* Note that *A* is also on the budget line but that *A* lies on U_1; *B,* however, is on a higher indifference curve, U_2, so the latter is preferred. Kim's desire to maximize her well-being also rules out the possibility of an equilibrium at a point such as *D;* although *D* is within Kim's budget (in fact, Kim would not be spending all her income on *X* and *Y*), it is not the highest possible level

---

[2]Any point below the budget line implies that the consumer is not spending her entire income; we will assume, however, that the consumer allocates her entire income in some way between *X* and *Y.* In a more general model, saving can be incorporated into the treatment by taking the two goods to be present consumption and future consumption.

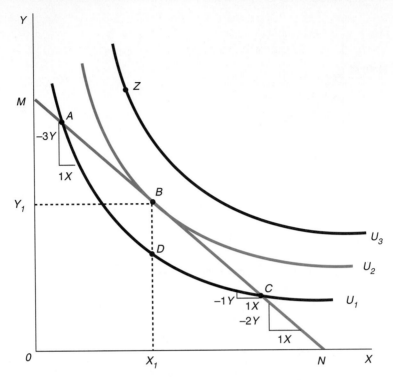

Figure A–6 *The equilibrium of the consumer*

of well-being attainable because it lies on a lower indifference curve. Thus, the combination of X and Y represented by the tangency at B is Kim's equilibrium level of consumption.

It is important to understand the meaning of the tangency between the consumer's indifference curve and her budget line at point B. Recall that the slope of an indifference curve reflects the consumer's subjective valuation of one good in terms of the other, that is, the rate at which she is willing to substitute one good for another—the marginal rate of substitution between X and Y. At A, for example, Kim will be willing to exchange 3 units of Y for 1 more unit of X; at B, $2Y$ for $1X$; and at C, $1Y$ for $1X$. The slope of the budget line at all points is P_X/P_Y, the rate at which X and Y can be exchanged in the marketplace. Assume that the price of X is \$2 and the price of Y is \$1. This price structure means that 2 units of Y can be exchanged for 1 unit of X. The slope of MN is $2Y/1X$. In equilibrium, the marginal rate of substitution between X and Y for the consumer is equal to the price ratio; that is, the rate at which the consumer is subjectively willing to substitute X for Y is just equal to the rate at which market exchange can occur. At B Kim is willing to give up 2 units of Y for another unit of X; at a price of $2 per unit for X and $1 a unit for Y, this exchange rate coincides with the market rate of exchange. Only at B, where the slopes of an indiffference curve and the budget line are equal, does this balance between subjective evaluation and objective terms of trade hold.

Note that Kim *could* consume at point A on her budget line but that she would then be on U_1, a lower indifference curve than at point B. Point A is *not* an equilibrium because the *MRS* is greater than the price ratio. To see that this conclusion is correct, note that at A, Kim is willing to give up 3 units of Y to get another unit of X but *has* to give up only 2 units of Y to consume 1 more X (because X costs twice as much as Y). Therefore, 1 more X costs less (a sacrifice of $2Y$) than Kim is willing to pay ($3Y$), so she will be better off consuming more X and less Y than at point A. This result is shown, of course, by the fact that point B lies on a higher indifference curve than point A does.

Before the analysis is continued, a modification in the model will be made. So far Kim has been choosing between two goods, X and Y, typically dividing her budget between them. From now on we will let the vertical axis measure money spent on all other goods except X for a given time period and let the horizontal axis measure the quantity of X consumed. In effect, the vertical axis measures consumption of non-X items as a group. This modification gives us more flexibility. The indifference curves can now show the trade-offs between good X and money spent on other goods. The slope of an indifference curve will then show how many dollars' worth of other goods Kim is willing to give up to acquire 1 more unit of X. With this modification, the budget line can be constructed as follows: Assume that Kim's income is $1,000 and that the price of X is $2. In Figure A–7, $0M$ ($1,000) is the amount of money available to spend on other goods (i.e., her entire money income) if Kim purchases zero units of X. If she spends her entire income on X, she could purchase $0N$ units of X (500), with no money remaining to purchase other goods. By joining the two points, the budget line MN is derived. Given the preferences reflected by her indifference curves, Kim is in equilibrium at E. She consumes $0X_1$ (200) units of X and has $0M'$ ($600) in income left to spend on goods other than X. Note that Kim's total outlay on X is measured by MM', or $400.

As we did before, let us carefully interpret the tangency at E in Figure A–7 between the consumer's indifference curve U_2 and the budget line. The slope of the indifference curve now represents the rate at which the consumer is willing to trade off expenditures on other goods for additional units of X; the consumer is, in effect, placing a dollar value on the benefits received from a marginal unit of X. At A, for example, Kim is willing to pay $3 for another unit of X (willing to consume $3 less of other goods to consume 1 more unit of X); at B, only $1. The budget line reflects the market rate of exchange between X and other goods. Because the vertical axis now represents expenditures on other goods, it is measured in dollars, and the price of $1 worth of other goods is $1.

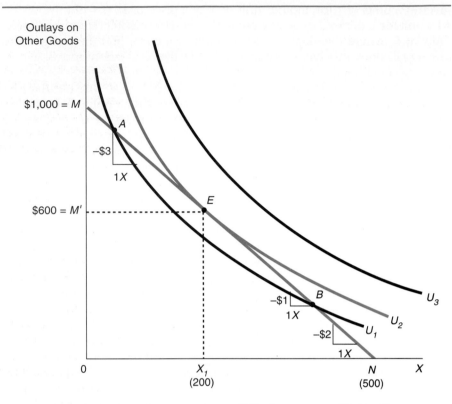

Figure A–7   *Consumer equilibrium—an alternative representation*

To the left of E on the budget line, the consumer places a higher dollar value on X than its market price. For instance, at A, Kim is on U_1 and is willing to pay $3 for an additional unit of X, but she has to pay only the *market price* of 2—the slope of MN. Because the benefit received from the marginal unit is greater than its cost, Kim will purchase the extra unit. Moreover, she will continue to consume additional units as long as this condition persists, that is, until point E is reached, where the additional dollar value of benefits received from consuming 1 more unit just equals its price (in this example, at E the consumer places a value of $2 on an extra unit, which equals its market price). At point E she has attained the highest indifference curve possible. Kim will not purchase any additional units (to the right of E) because the dollar value of benefits received from consuming additional units is less than its price—the marginal benefit is less than marginal cost. Thus, Kim is in equilibrium at E, where the marginal benefit of an extra unit of X is equal to its price. Thus, *when the consumer is in equilibrium, the market price of the good is a measure of the marginal value of the good to the consumer.*

Having changed the vertical axis to money spent on other goods, we can now continue and consider how consumption levels of X are affected by changes in income and prices.

Changes in Income

We noted earlier how changes in income produce parallel shifts in the budget line. Now that indifference curves have been incorporated into the analysis, changes in the consumer's level of income and the corresponding changes in the level of consumption of X can be examined. To illustrate, consider Figure A–8(a). Given the set of preferences reflected by U_1 through U_3, when the budget line is MN, X_1 units of X are consumed. When Kim's income increases to $0M'$ and the budget line becomes $M'N'$, the consumption of X rises to X_2. And finally, when income reaches $0M''$ Kim purchases X_3 units of X. At each income level, Kim chooses the most preferred combination of goods from among the combinations available. A line connecting the consumer equilibria yields the *income-consumption curve,* which identifies the various quantities of X that will be consumed at different income levels. If the curve is upward sloping to the right, X will be considered a *normal good;* that is, as income rises when prices are unchanged, the consumption of X increases.

In contrast to normal goods, there are *inferior goods.* A good is an inferior good if the quantity consumed falls when income rises. Consider Figure A–8(b). In this case, as income rises and the budget line shifts from MN to $M'N'$, the consumption of X declines from X_1 to X_2. The income-consumption curve slopes backward to the left. Typically most goods are normal goods, but it is possible to find examples of inferior goods. Perhaps, for example, as a person's income rises, he or she switches from hamburger to filet mignon; hamburger, in this particular case, would be an inferior good.

Changes in Prices

So far we have considered the effects of changes in consumer income on the quantity of X consumed with prices assumed constant. Now let us hold income constant, vary the price of X, and observe how the consumption of X changes. Recall that a variation in price is reflected by a change in the slope of the budget line; if the price of X falls, the budget line will become flatter, rotating to the right; if the price rises, the budget line will become steeper, rotating toward the origin. To begin, assume that the consumer's income is $100 in a given time period and the price of X is $5 per unit. In Figure A–9(a) the budget line is MN, and given the consumer's preferences, equilibrium occurs with X_1 units of the good being consumed. Now let the price of X fall to $3.50 per unit. A new budget line, MN', results. At the lower price, X_2 is purchased, as indicated by the tangency between U_2 and MN' at X_2 units of X. Finally, let price fall again—this time to $2 a unit. The budget

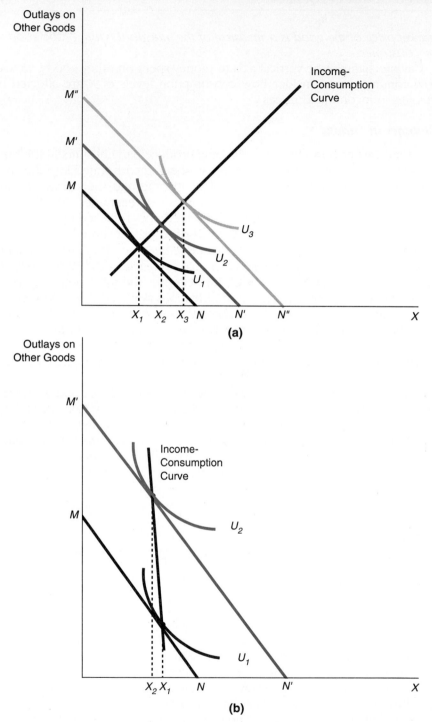

Figure A–8 *Income changes and consumption choices*

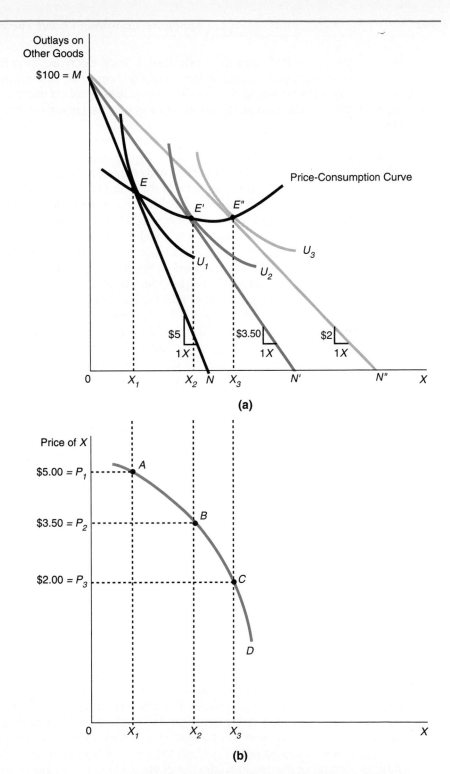

Figure A–9 *Derivation of the consumer's demand curve*

line rotates outward to *MN''*, and X$_3$ is purchased. Each decrease in price establishes a new budget line and a new equilibrium. The line drawn through the tangencies depicting the equilibrium points is called the *price-consumption curve*. It shows how the consumption of *X* varies with changes in its price.

The concept embodied in the price-consumption curve should strike a familiar note. It contains the same information as the consumer's demand curve—how the quantity consumed varies with changes in price when money income is unchanged. So we are now at the point where the demand curve can be derived from the indifference curves in Figure A–9(a). On the axes of a demand curve diagram, price is measured vertically and quantity horizontally, and we need only make a few modifications to translate the information in Figure A–9(a) into a demand curve. The three alternative prices for *X*—$5, $3.50, and $2—are plotted in Figure A–9(b), and the corresponding quantities of *X* consumed are identified. In this way, the demand curve is derived using indifference curves and budget lines.

Because the tangency between an individual's budget line and indifference curve represents the point where the marginal value of the last unit of *X* to the consumer is just equal to its price, and these tangencies in turn define points on the consumer's demand curve, the demand curve must contain the same information. In fact, each point on the demand curve can be interpreted as a measure of the marginal benefit associated with the consumption of the corresponding unit of *X*. Taking this analysis a step further, because each quantity of *X* is associated with a price, the price of *X* can be considered a dollar measure of the marginal benefit of *X* to the consumer: The price reflects the *MRS* between money spent on other goods and good *X*. The vertical distance between the demand curve and the horizontal axis can be taken as a measure of the marginal benefit of *X*. For example, the distance BX_2, or $3.50 per unit of *X*, is a measure of the marginal value, or benefit, of the good when X_2 is the quantity consumed. This way of measuring the marginal value of a good will be useful later in the analysis of many government tax and expenditure programs.

Substitution and Income Effects of Price Changes

When the price of a good changes, the consumer is affected in two distinct ways. One effect is called the *income effect* and the other the *substitution effect*. To illustrate, suppose that the price of beef falls by half. The income effect stems from the fact that the consumer is better off as a result of the price change because his or her budget now goes further. The consumer can buy the same amount of beef as before and still have more income left over to spend on other goods and services. The price change, in effect, raises the consumer's *real* income (in the sense of the level of well-being attainable). With a higher real income, the consumer can now afford to purchase more of all goods—including beef. So when the price of beef decreases, the consumer, as a result of the income effect, will expand his or her purchases of beef if it is a normal good. The substitution effect results from the consumer's decision to substitute the now cheaper good, beef, for other goods such as poultry or pork. To the consumer, beef, because of its lower price, has become a relatively more attractive buy, so the consumer will choose to purchase more beef relative to other types of meat and poultry. The decrease in the price of beef has caused the consumer's purchases of beef to increase for two independent reasons. The income effect makes the consumer better off by increasing real income, which induces him or her to purchase larger quantities of beef. The substitution effect leads the consumer to substitute the cheaper good for the now relatively more expensive ones, and in doing this the consumption of beef increases.

The total effect of a reduction in the price of X from $5 to $3 is shown in Figure A–10 as the increase in consumption of X from X_1 to X_2. The original

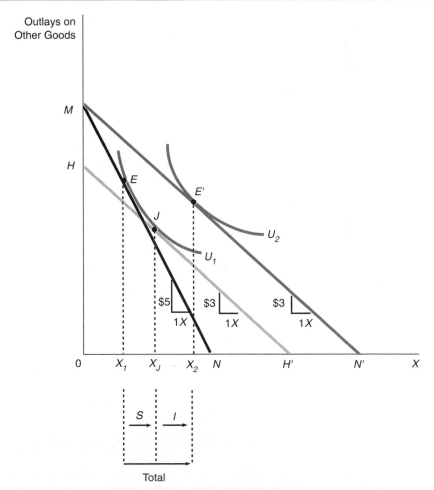

Figure A–10 *Income and substitution effects of a price reduction*

budget line is shown by MN, with our consumer, Kim, in equilibrium at E purchasing X_1 units of X. The lower price of X is reflected by the new budget line MN', with a slope of $3 per unit. The price decline involves a new equilibrium for Kim at E', with X_2 units of X being purchased. The total effect of this price change, X_1X_2, as noted earlier, can be divided into an income effect and a substitution effect. When the price of a good falls, it increases Kim's real income. However, we want to ignore the income effect for the moment and instead concentrate on how much of the increase in the consumption of X can be attributed to the consumer's substituting X for other goods. To make this determination and identify the substitution effect, Kim's real income must be decreased by an amount sufficient to return her to her original indifference curve U_1 in Figure A–10: what is referred to as keeping real income unchanged. To nullify the income effect, a hypothetical budget line, HH', is constructed parallel to MN' and tangent to U_1. The tangency occurs at J. The HH' budget line must be drawn parallel to MN' because we want to keep Kim on her original indifference curve with the *new* price of X to see how the lower price of X—isolated from the income effect—causes Kim to increase her consumption of X. The substitution effect can be identified by comparing the quantity of X consumed at the initial equilibrium, E (where the slope of MN reflects the original price), with the quantity consumed at J, where the slope of HH' indicates the new lower price of X. On the horizontal axis, the quantity X_1X_J is the increase in consumption associated with the substitution effect.

Next, we consider the income effect. Assume now that the budget line HH' shifts to the right to coincide with MN'. The vertical distance between HH' and MN' represents the gain in real income attributable to the decline in the price of X. This rise in income alone is responsible for an increase in the purchase of X by the amount of X_JX_2 because an increase in real income will induce Kim to expand purchases of all goods.[3] Thus, the total effect of the reduction in the price of X, X_1X_2, can be divided into a substitution effect, X_1X_J, and an income effect, X_JX_2.

An Application

To become more familiar with consumer choice theory and at the same time to lay the groundwork for some further analysis, let us examine individual labor supply decisions associated with changes in wage rates. Assume that workers can vary the amount of time they work,[4] and then consider Figure

---

[3]This assumes that X and the other goods purchased by the consumer are normal goods.

[4]Although many workers work an 8-hour day, they can still vary their work effort with overtime or take a second job. In addition, workers can exercise some control over the number of hours worked by the type of job they choose.

A–11. On the vertical axis, money income per week is measured, and on the horizontal axis, reading from left to right, leisure for the same time period is shown. The more hours are worked, the less leisure time will be available; the more leisure consumed, the less time will be available to spend at work. Because time that is not spent working is considered leisure time, the amount of work effort supplied can be read from right to left in Figure A–11. Indifference curves can be drawn representing the preferences of a worker, Kim, for income and leisure. They have a normal shape because both money income and leisure are desirable economic goods. As Kim moves down a curve to the right, money income falls as she consumes additional amounts of leisure. The slope of a curve at any point represents the rate at which the worker is subjectively willing to give up money income for leisure. At A, for example, it would require more income to induce her to work more (consume less leisure) than it would at B.

The worker's wage rate is reflected in the slope of a budget line showing the trade-off between money income and leisure. The flatter the budget line, the lower the wage rate; the steeper the budget line, the higher the wage rate. In Figure A–11, let the slope of MN reflect a wage of $10 per hour. If Kim works a 40-hour week, for example, her weekly income will be $400.

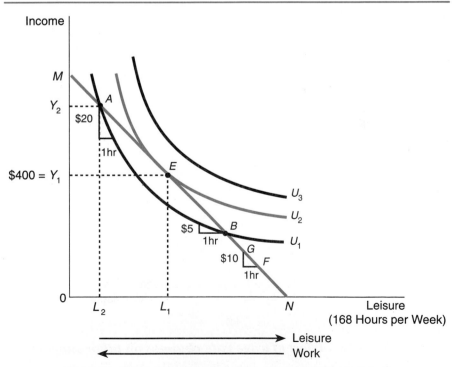

Figure A–11   *Income-leisure choice of the worker*

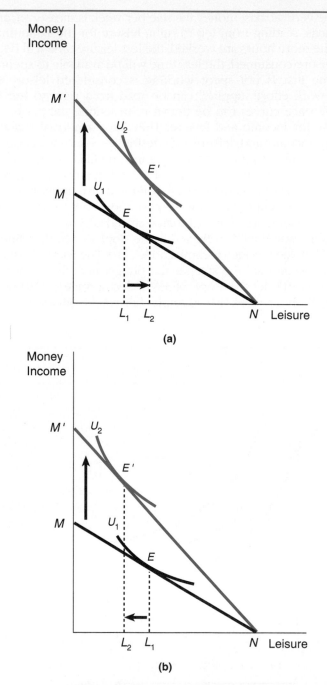

(a)

(b)

Figure A–12   *Effect of wage rate changes on labor supply*

Of course, how many hours Kim chooses to work at the $10 wage rate will depend on her preferences relating money income and leisure, as shown by her indifference curves. In Figure A–11, Kim's equilibrium—showing the most preferred combination of money income and leisure on her budget line—is point E, with weekly earnings of $400 and a labor supply of NL_1, or 40 hours. Note that Kim could earn more by working longer hours, at point A, but she would then be on a lower indifference curve. Her decision means that Kim considers the additional earnings she could earn by working longer hours insufficient compensation for having to give up additional hours of leisure.

So far, this situation describes a worker's equilibrium at a give wage rate. (For most consumers, labor income is the main, and often sole, source of their money income; we assumed money income as given in earlier diagrams.) If the wage rate changes, the budget line will rotate around the horizontal intercept. In Figure A–12, the budget line with a $10 wage rate is shown as MN in both diagrams. If the wage rate rises to $15, the budget line will shift to $M'N$. The slope (equal to the wage rate) is now greater, showing that for every hour of leisure given up (for every hour worked), more money income is received than before. At any given level of work effort, total money income will be higher at a wage rate of $15 than at a wage rate of $10.

How a worker responds to changes in wage rates is an interesting question. An increase in the wage rate has two effects on labor supply decisions: an income effect and a substitution effect. The income effect is a result of the fact that the higher wage rate raises the worker's income for any amount of work effort supplied; at higher income levels, the income effect will lead the worker to consume more of all goods, including leisure. Thus, the higher income associated with higher wage rates encourages the increased consumption of leisure (or reduced work effort).

The substitution effect, on the other hand, encourages greater work effort. If the wage rate rises from $10 an hour to $15, the relative cost of consuming leisure will increase and the quantity consumed will decline. More specifically, when the wage rate is $10 per hour, the cost of consuming an additional hour of leisure is $10 in forgone earnings; when the wage rate rises to $15, the sacrifice in earnings also increases, inducing the worker to consume less leisure and to work more.

Because the income and substitution effects work in opposing directions, it is impossible to predict whether a person will work more, less, or the same amount in response to changes in the wage rate. If the income effect is greater than the substitution effect, then work effort will fall in response to a higher wage rate, as in Figure A–12(a). If, on the other hand, the substitution effect predominates, then work effort will rise in response to an increase in wages, as in Figure A–12(b). If the two effects exactly offset each other, then work effort will be unchanged.

The response of labor supply to changes in wage rates is of particular interest to us in public finance because many taxes fall on labor income and consequently affect labor supply decisions.

INDEX